# ROBERT BURNS AND PASTORAL

# Robert Burns and Pastoral

*Poetry and Improvement in Late Eighteenth-Century Scotland*

NIGEL LEASK

OXFORD
UNIVERSITY PRESS

# OXFORD
### UNIVERSITY PRESS

Great Clarendon Street, Oxford, OX2 6DP,
United Kingdom

Oxford University Press is a department of the University of Oxford.
It furthers the University's objective of excellence in research, scholarship,
and education by publishing worldwide. Oxford is a registered trade mark of
Oxford University Press in the UK and in certain other countries

First published 2010
First published in paperback 2015

Published in the United States of America by Oxford University Press
198 Madison Avenue, New York, NY 10016, United States of America

British Library Cataloguing in Publication Data
Data available

Library of Congress Cataloging in Publication Data
Data available

ISBN 978–0–19–957261–8 (Hbk.)
ISBN 978–0–19–873242–6 (Pbk.)

In Memory of Joseph Macleod (1903–84), poet and broadcaster

# *Acknowledgements*

This book has been of long gestation. Early drafts of *Robert Burns and Pastoral* accompanied me on my return to Scotland from the English Faculty at Cambridge in the summer of 2004, when I was appointed to the Regius Chair in English at Glasgow University. Replanted in native soil, the project flourished in the congenial scholarly community of Glasgow University's School of English and Scottish Language and Literature, as well as with involvement in Scotland's various Burns networks. My research was facilitated by easy access to the unrivalled Burns collections held in Glasgow University Library, the Mitchell Library, and the National Library of Scotland. A full draft of the book was written during an AHRC-funded year's research leave in 2007–8: my thanks to the Council, and to Glasgow University for permitting me time out from a busy teaching and administrative schedule. It was completed in the summer of 2009.

The poet's 250th anniversary in 2009 provided opportunities to present work in progress at international Burns conferences in Glasgow, Edinburgh, Prague, and Vancouver: thanks to the organizers for inviting me to speak. I'm also grateful for invitations to lecture on Burns in Cambridge, Sheffield, Newcastle, London, Kolkata, Warsaw, Derry, Belfast, Dublin, Edinburgh, Dumfries, St Andrews, Perth, and Glasgow. This book wouldn't have been possible without the mighty labours of Burns editors and scholars past and present, particularly James Kinsley, whose monumental 1968 edition has been my point of reference throughout, and to J. De Lancey Fergusson and G. Ross Roy, for their fine edition of the poet's correspondence. Thomas Crawford's pioneering criticism from the 1960s, and newer perspectives on Burns from Carol McGuirk, Liam McIlvanney, Robert Crawford, and Gerry Carruthers, have informed every aspect of my research: my debts to them will be apparent in the chapters that follow. My critical approach was ultimately inspired by Raymond Williams's seminal *The Country and the City*, by John Barrell's work on John Clare and the politics of landscape, and by Annabel Patterson's *Pastoral and Ideology*.

Special thanks are due to Andrew McNeillie at Oxford University Press for encouraging me to write a 'big' book on Burns, and to Ian Duncan and Liam McIlvanney, readers for Oxford, for their positive and constructive comments on early drafts. A major personal debt is to Gerry Carruthers, who has been generous in sharing his knowledge of and enthusiasm for the poet, as well as his extensive experience of the often fractious world of Burns studies. Other Glasgow colleagues Colin Kidd, Kirsteen McCue, and Murray Pittock have read individual chapters and offered valuable advice and criticism: I am fortunate indeed to have had the benefit of their knowledge and friendship. (I look forward to further scholarly collaboration with Gerry, Murray, and Kirsteen as co-editors of

Oxford's recently commissioned *Collected Works of Robert Burns*, which will replace Kinsley as the standard scholarly edition for the twenty-first century.) My introduction also benefited from Dan Gunn's thorough overhaul of its style and argument. Shona Mackintosh provided assiduous editorial help in the final stages. All remaining shortcomings are my own. I'd also like to thank Neil Ascherson, John Barrell, Alex Benchimol, Chris Berry, Kirstie Blair, Valentina Bold, Iain Gordon Brown, Rhona Brown, Graham Caie, Jim Chandler, John Corbett, John Coyle, Richard Cronin, Bob Cummings, Leith Davis, Penny Fielding, Sarah Gibson, Douglas Gifford, Stuart Gillespie, Kevin Gilmartin, David Goldie, Dorian Grieve, Harriet Guest, Pauline Gray, Andrew Hook, Claire Lamont, Tom Leonard, Donald Mackenzie, Dorothy McMillan, Ralph McLean, Susan Manning, Hamish Mathison, Jon Mee, Michael Moss, Andrew Noble, Alan Riach, Daniel Sanjev Roberts, Simon Schaffer, David Shuttleton, David Simpson, Ken Simpson, Jeremy Smith, Martin Prochazka, and Nigel Wood. Thanks also to Jaqueline Baker, Ariane Pettit, Sylvie Jaffrey, and other members of Oxford's production team who saw the book through the press.

Earlier versions of Chs. 7 and 9 have been published in the *Burns Chronicle* (Winter 2006), 26–31, and *Romanticism's Debatable Lands*, edited by Claire Lamont and Michael Rossington (Basingstoke: Palgrave Macmillan, 2007), 64–79. Thanks to the Scottish National Portrait Gallery, Glasgow University Library, the Mitchell Library Glasgow, and Glasgow Culture and Sports, for permission to reproduce maps and images. Finally, my love and thanks to Evelyn, and our daughters Isabel and Flora, for their patience and support: 'Till a' the seas gang dry . . . And the rocks melt wi' the sun'.

# Contents

# Illustrations

*Picture Acknowledgements*: Plates 1, 2, 3, 7, and 8 courtesy of the Mitchell Library, Glasgow. Plates 4 and 5 courtesy of Glasgow University Library. Plate 6, courtesy of Kelvingrove Art Gallery, Glasgow Culture and Sport.

# List of Abbreviations

| | |
|---|---|
| Aiton | William Aiton, *General View of the County of Ayr: with Observations on the Means of its Improvement; drawn up for the Consideration of the Board of Agriculture* (Glasgow, 1811). |
| CG | *The Canongate Burns: The Complete Poems and Songs of Robert Burns*, intro. Andrew Noble, ed. Andrew Noble and Patrick Scott Hogg (Edinburgh: Canongate, 2001). |
| *CH* | *Robert Burns: The Critical Heritage*, ed. Donald A. Low (London: Routledge & Kegan Paul, 1974). |
| Chambers-Wallace | *The Life and Works of Robert Burns*, ed. Robert Chambers, rev. William Wallace, 4 vols. (Edinburgh: William Chambers, 1896). |
| CL | *The Letters of Robert Burns*, 2 vols., i. *1780–1789*; ii. *1790–1796*, ed. J. De Lancey Ferguson, 2nd edn. G. Ross Roy (Oxford: Clarendon, 1985). |
| *CPB* | *Robert Burns' Common Place Book*, ed. and intro. Raymond Lamont Brown (Wakefield: S.R. Publishers, 1969). |
| Crawford, *BPS* | Thomas Crawford, *Burns: A Study of the Poems and Songs* (1960) (repr. Edinburgh: Canongate Academic, 1994). |
| Currie | [James Currie] *The Works of Robert Burns; with an Account of his Life, and a Criticism of his Writings. To which are prefixed, Some Observations on the Character and Condition of the Scottish Peasantry*, 4 vols. (Liverpool, London, 1800). |
| Devine, *TRS* | T. M. Devine, *The Transformation of Rural Scotland: Social Change and the Agrarian Economy, 1660–1815* (Edinburgh: Edinburgh University Press, 1994). |
| Fullarton | Col. William Fullarton, *A General View of the Agriculture of the County of Ayr, with Observations on the Means of Improvement. Drawn up for the consideration of the Board of Agriculture and Internal Improvement* (Edinburgh: John Paterson, 1793). |
| Henley and Henderson | *The Poetry of Robert Burns*, ed. W. E. Henley and T. F. Henderson, 4 vols. (London: Blackwood, 1896). |
| Kil. | *Poems Chiefly in the Scottish Dialect by Robert Burns*, (Kilmarnock: John Wilson, 1786). |
| Kin. | *The Poems and Songs of Robert Burns*, ed. James Kinsley, 3 vols. (Oxford: Clarendon, 1968). [K 35] indicates the numeration of poems and songs in Kinsley's edition, and is provided at first citation wherever possible in the text, for ease |

# Introduction:
# The 'Heaven-Taught Ploughman'

*The uniform, constant, and uninterrupted effort of every man to better his condition . . . is frequently powerful enough to maintain the natural progress of things towards improvement, in spite both of the extravagance of government, and of the greatest errors of administration.*

(Adam Smith, *Wealth of Nations*, i. 443)

*Improvement makes strait roads, but the crooked roads without improvement are roads of Genius.*

(William Blake, *Marriage of Heaven and Hell*)

In this 250th anniversary of his birth, Robert Burns continues to be widely celebrated in Scotland and across the worldwide Scottish diaspora. That Burns is associated with humanitarian, democratic, and non-sectarian values is a cause for pride, as is the fact that a humbly born poet, rather than a politician, conqueror, or martyr, should be cherished by people of all social classes as a symbol of their national identity. Less positively, perhaps, the cult of Burns 'the Heaven-taught Ploughman' also promotes a pastoral view of the poet as elegist of a 'world we have lost', a Scotland of love, drink, and rural community destroyed by the forces of modern life. Pastoral nostalgia and the habits of consumption it promotes are extremely marketable: in 2007 *The Herald* newspaper announced that the 'Robert Burns brand' is currently estimated to be worth about £157 million a year to the Scottish economy.[1] Back in 1954 Hugh MacDiarmid fulminated against Burns nostalgia, and especially the Burns supper observed every 25 January, in a polemical book pointedly entitled *Burns Today and Tomorrow*: '[the Burns cult] knows nothing about him or his work—or the work that should be done in continuance of his—except the stupid and stereotyped sentiments it belches out annually'.[2] Of course MacDiarmid's fury didn't make an iota of difference, and the 'Immortal Memory' speeches continued unabated.

---

[1]  *The Herald* (Thurs. 25 Jan. 2007).
[2]  Hugh MacDiarmid, *Burns Today and Tomorrow* (Edinburgh: Castle Wynd, 1954).

If the public celebration of Burns goes from strength to strength, his reputation is today less secure in academic circles, especially in the field of eighteenth-century and Romantic studies, where the study of his poetry should naturally fall.[3] Over a century ago, his Victorian editors Henley and Henderson [i p. ix] described him as '*ultimus Scotorum*, the last expression of the old Scots world', a view sustained (albeit with qualifications attached) half a century later by David Daiches in his assessment of the poetry as 'a glorious Indian summer for native Scottish literature'.[4] Although such views are rare now amongst his academic interpreters, the idea that Burns's poetry is exclusively Scoto-centric, traditionary, and backward-looking, combined with a false perception of its linguistic unintelligibility to non-Scottish readers, has been largely responsible for its academic eclipse in university departments over the last fifty years.

Because Burns was arguably the most inventive poet writing in these islands between Pope and Blake, and creator of the first modern vernacular style in British poetry, such perceptions now stand in urgent need of revision.[5] For a start, the pith and energy of his Scots syntax and diction makes the recovery of meaning its own reward. (Not surprisingly, few Scots can now read the language as it was written in the eighteenth century without assistance, although many have the advantage of familiarity with Burns's better-known poems from their schooldays.) Moreover, when Burns wrote 'gie me ae spark o'Nature's fire, | That's a' the learning I desire', [K 57 ll. 73–4] he himself contributed to the myth of his 'Heaven-taught' genius; but he also knew that alert readers might notice submerged allusions to Pope and Sterne here. Christopher Ricks rightly insists that 'we sell Burns short if we begrudge him his skill with allusion'.[6] A major aim of the present study is to challenge the myth by attending to his artful and learned engagement with other writers (some of them quite unexpected), while at the same time appreciating the cultural work performed by the 'naive' ploughman persona.

Part of the problem is chronology. The 1780s, decade of Burns's major poetical creativity, was long consigned to the period of 'pre-romanticism', effectively obscuring its significance in relation to the poetry that preceded and followed it. Both his interest in popular song culture and his vernacular challenge to the classical literary canon signal his importance as a 'romantic precursor', but the fact that he died in 1796 (i.e. before the publication of *Lyrical Ballads*) meant

---

    [3] This case was made by Raymond Bentman in 'Robert Burn's Declining Fame', *Studies in Romanticism* 11/3 (1972), 206–24 and recently reiterated by Murray Pittock in 'Robert Burns and British Poetry', The Chatterton Lecture on Poetry, 2002, *Proceedings of the British Academy* 121 (2003), 191–211.

    [4] David Daiches, *Robert Burns* (London: G. Bell & Sons, 1952), 363.

    [5] Robert Crawford claims Burns as 'the most brilliantly distinguished eighteenth-century example of a British poet', *Devolving English Literature*, 2nd edn. (Edinburgh: Edinburgh University Press, 2000), 106.

    [6] Christopher Ricks, *Allusion to the Poets* (Oxford: Oxford University Press, 2002), 51.

that he was easily excluded from the romantic mainstream initiated by Words-worth, despite having influenced the latter's assault on 'poetic diction'.[7] Recent critical attention to the eighteenth-century culture of sensibility and the increas-ing critical acceptance of a 'long eighteenth century' have gone some way to relieve this problem: Carol McGuirk's important study of 1985, for example, locates Burns's poetry within the 'sentimental era', thereby also connecting it 'with the English and European literary mainstream.'[8]

A greater problem perhaps lies in the marginalization of Scottish literature and history relative to England, although this has now begun to be challenged effectively by a 'four nations' approach to British and Irish literature.[9] 'Scottish Romanticism' has been recently described (in relationship to an 'organic' English model) as 'an intermittent, shadowy anachronism, a temporal as well as a spatial border of Romanticism'. This holds also for its distinct chronology: (to continue the quotation) 'in Scotland, "Classical" and "Romantic" cultural forms occupy the same historical moment and institutional base, rather than defining succes-sive stages or periods'.[10] For instance, although the eighteenth-century Scottish literati espoused the neoclassical values of linguistic improvement and poetic decorum, they also had a keen appetite for the proto-romantic 'natural genius' and 'primitivism' promoted by Macpherson's *Ossian* (1760) and James Beattie's *The Minstrel* (1769–74). Although neither was written in Scots, their huge popularity makes the literati's largely affirmative response to Burns's Kilmarnock volume altogether more explicable.[11]

After all, Henry Mackenzie's famous description of Burns as a 'Heaven-taught ploughman' in *The Lounger* for 9 December 1786 [*CH* p. 70], itself alluded to *The Minstrel's* eponymous peasant-genius: 'let thy heaven-taught soul to heaven aspire, | To fancy, freedom, harmony, resign'd; | Ambition's groveling crew for ever left behind'.[12] Burns astutely played to the taste for poetic primitivism in the

---

[7] Pittock, 'Robert Burns and British Poetry', 192. For Romanticism's 'discovery of the people', see editors' introduction, Philip Connell and Nigel Leask (eds.), *Romanticism and Popular Culture in Britain and Ireland* (Cambridge: Cambridge University Press, 2009), 3–48.

[8] Carol McGuirk, *Robert Burns and the Sentimental Era* (Athens, Ga.: University of Georgia Press, 1985), p. xxvi.

[9] J. G. A. Pocock, *The Discovery of Islands: Essays in British History* (Cambridge: Cambridge University Press, 2005); John Kerrigan, *Archipelagic English: Literature, History, Politics, 1603–1707* (Oxford: Oxford University Press, 2008); Murray Pittock, *Scottish and Irish Romanticism* (Oxford: Oxford University Press, 2008).

[10] Editors' introduction to *Scotland and the Borders of Romanticism*, ed. Leith Davis, Ian Duncan, and Janet Sorensen (Cambridge: Cambridge University Press, 2004), 3.

[11] Liam McIlvanney, 'Hugh Blair, Robert Burns, and the Invention of Scottish Literature', *18th-Century Life*, 29/2 (Spring 2005), 25–46; Fiona Stafford, *The Sublime Savage: A Study of James Macpherson and the Poems of Ossian* (Edinburgh: Edinburgh University Press, 1988). On the question of periodization, see the editors' introduction to *Scotland and the Borders of Romanticism*, 3.

[12] James Beattie, *The Minstrel, in Two Books* (London, 1784), 4; Bk. 1 stanza vii.

epigraph to the Kilmarnock volume, tactically dropping Scots (despite the volume's title *Poems Chiefly in the Scottish Dialect*) for the fashionable idiom of sensibility, flaunting the pastoral virtues of simplicity and naturalism: 'The Simple Bard, unbroke by rules of Art, | He pours the wild effusions of the heart: | And if inspir'd,'tis Nature's pow'rs inspire; | Her's all the melting thrill, and her's the kindling fire'. [Kil., titlepage].

Detailed study of Burns's literary, social, and historical contexts in this book are intended to buttress my critique of the 'naive pastoral' and nostalgic inter-pretation of the 'Heaven-taught ploughman'. To this end, *Burns and Pastoral* offers fresh interpretations of all the major poems, and a narrower selection of his songs (the first to do so since Thomas Crawford's landmark study of 1960), although my main focus will be upon the poems first published in the Kilmar-nock and Edinburgh volumes of 1786 and 1787 during Burns's years as a working farmer, as well as other writings from the period leading up to his final abandonment of agriculture in 1792.

Central to the whole argument is the claim that the poetry owes its very existence, as well as its phenomenal success, to Burns's engagement with 'im-provement', the term by which the Scottish Enlightenment described its unprec-edented modernizing impetus. Although historians of the English countryside have tended to shy away from the old term 'agricultural revolution' to describe the pace of economic and social change taking place in the long eighteenth century, Scottish historians have recently recuperated the term 'revolution', arguing that 'nowhere else in western Europe was agrarian economy and society altered so quickly and so rapidly in the eighteenth century' as in Lowland Scotland [Devine, *TRS* p. 61]. Burns's predicament as a well educated but undercapitalized tenant farmer instigated a compensatory quest for poetic 'credit' as a means of transcending the social and economic impasse of his agricultural occupation, although this obliged him to master the practical and rhetorical imperatives of poetic patronage in his own inimitable fashion.

Mackenzie's view of Burns as 'Heaven-taught ploughman' was endorsed by many subsequent commentators, and is typified by Dr James Currie's belief that 'his poems, as well as his letters may be considered as . . . the transcripts of his own musings on the real incidents of his humble life' [*CH* p.132] (see Fig. 1). The notion that 'Burns is always autobiographical' has obstructed critical appre-ciation of the heteroglossic play of voices in his poetry, which is why for every critical analysis of the writing, there have been ten biographies. McGuirk describes the circular logic at work here: 'the man is his works, and they in their turn directly define the man' so the task of the critics is to analyse 'the various personality traits (or typically 'Scottish' qualities) in the poet's writ-ings'.[13] Although, *mutatis mutandis*, this is also true of Byron among the

---

[13] McGuirk, *Sentimental Era*, p. xviii.

FIG. 1. 'The Ploughman Poet'.

Romantic poets (indicating that an active libido may be a contributing factor), it's even more the case with Burns. Like his admirer Byron, Burns was a famous lover and a great love poet; but because love (that most pastoral of topics) is rather under-represented in the Kilmarnock and Edinburgh volumes, I have not dedicated a separate chapter to it here.[14] My only excuse is that Burns's love poetry (not to mention his love affairs) have had their dues elsewhere.

Burns's 'naive' persona was accurately disputed by John Logan as early as February 1787, in an unsigned article in the *English Review*, which insisted that 'Robert Burns, though he has been represented as an ordinary ploughman, was a farmer, or what they call a tenant in Scotland, and rented land which he cultivated with his own hands. He is better acquainted with the English poets than most English authors that have come under our review'[*CH* p. 76]. Logan shows no surprise here that a Scottish tenant farmer should have been an educated and literate man, and sceptically questioned Mackenzie's claims that he was either 'heaven-taught' or vocationally 'a ploughman'. (I shall tackle the complex issue of Burns's social class in the first chapter.) Mackenzie's view, later supported by Carlyle's version of the 'peasant hero', still prevails in the popular view of Burns, despite having being constantly challenged by scholars and biographers. Nevertheless, the clash of opinion between Mackenzie and Logan is instructive and will inform my approach in the chapters that follow. What kind of poetry did a struggling eighteenth-century Ayrshire farmer choose to write, if he chose to write poetry at all? As this book's title underlines, my approach is grounded upon an inquiry into the historical and ideological meanings of genre, especially georgic and pastoral, the classical forms for writing about rural life. Kurt Heinzelman and others have underlined the importance of georgic in the ideological work of improvement ('that massive cultural category that so dominated 18th century theory and practice'), to the extent that it was the 'most popular poetic genre of the time, one nominally about improvements in agronomy and one that carried the king's own name'.[15] But Burns apparently didn't read Virgil's *Georgics* until 1788, and notwithstanding the considerable influence on his own poetry of James Thomson's *Seasons* and other eighteenth-century works in the same genre, the vernacular voice of the 'ploughman poet' and his celebration of *carpe diem* are often at odds with the writerly decorum and didactic concerns of the georgic poet.

Nevertheless, Burns's poetry of the 1780s was in great measure connected to his occupational concern with the discourse of agricultural improvement, a body of literature which Heinzelman characterizes as 'prose georgics' (Chapter 8 makes a similar point concerning Burns's professional concerns as an Exciseman in the

[14] It is mainly confined to the small selection of songs published therein.
[15] Kurt Heinzelman, 'The Last Georgic: Wealth of Nations and the Scene of Writing', in Stephen Copley and Kathryn Sutherland (eds.), *Adam Smith's* Wealth of Nations: *New Interdisciplinary Essays* (Manchester: Manchester University Press, 1995), 171–94; 178–9.

years after 1788). In contrast with Wordsworth, and other romantic poets studied by Clifford Siskin and Thomas Pfau, poetry was never Burns's 'profession'.[16] Rather (as he put it, only slightly disingenuously, in the 1786 preface) his 'motive for courting the Muses' was 'to amuse himself with the little creations of his own fancy, amid the toil and fatigues of a laborious life'. [Kil. p. iv] As Burns expressed it in 'Epistle to James Smith', other poets might write for purposes of revenge, for 'needfu' cash' or self-promotion, but he 'rhyme[d] for *fun*' [K 79 ll. 25–30]. Although I'll qualify this claim somewhat in Chapter 3, it remains central to the image which Burns promoted of himself as a poet.

Although the Kilmarnock volume opens with a reference to 'The Simple Bard' and closes with 'A Bard's Epitaph', this book argues that Burns's poems and songs are impelled by a *pastoral* more than by a bardic voice.[17] William Empson proposed in 1935 that 'pastoral feeling' 'seems dogged by humbug, and has done for a long time', and at one level Burns (like other eighteenth-century poets and critics) shared this view.[18] Yet consider Boswell's account of James Macpherson's jejune distaste for Gray's pastoral *Elegy*, which burlesques Ossianic heroics: '"Hoot!" cried Fingal, "to write panegyrics upon a parcel of damned rascals that did nething [*sic*] but plough the land and saw corn". He considered that fighters only should be celebrated'.[19] Boswell made this observation in the early 1760s, but its irony may better have anticipated the public mood two decades later, in the aftermath of British defeat in America. The time was ripe for the ploughman poet, and for swords to be wrought into ploughshares, even if the pastoral moment of the 1780s would be rapidly overtaken by revolution and global war. I've already referred to the pastoral inclinations of the modern Burns cult, but an important task of the present study is to re-engage the genre with some of its more strenuous eighteenth-century meanings. To this end Chapter 2 explores the multiple ramifications of pastoral in its classical, as well as its eighteenth-century English and Scottish manifestations, alert to both banal and more dialectically challenging attributes of the genre in respect to Burns's poetic output, as well as its crossovers with related genres such as georgic, elegy, and satire.

The hallmark feature of Burns's reinvention of pastoral was his use of 'Scottish dialect', and his frequent eschewal of polite Augustan couplet verse in favour of sixteenth- and seventeenth-century Scots verse forms such as the 'Christ's Kirk', 'Cherry and Slae', and especially the 'standard habbie'. Many of his most famous

---

[16] Clifford Siskin, *The Work of Writing: Literature and Social Change in Britain, 1700–1830* (Baltimore: Johns Hopkins University Press, 1998); Thomas Pfau, *Wordsworth's Profession: Form, Class, and the Logic of Early Romantic Cultural Production* (Stanford, Calif.: Stanford University Press, 1997).

[17] See Katie Trumpener, *Bardic Nationalism: The Romantic Novel and the British Empire* (Princeton, NJ: Princeton University Press, 1997).

[18] William Empson, *Some Versions of Pastoral* (New York: New Directions, 1974), 9.

[19] James Boswell, *London Journal, 176–63*, ed. Frederick A. Pottle (London: Heinemann, 1950), 110.

poems (such as 'To a Mouse' and 'Holy Willie's Prayer') employ this hallmark 6-line stanza, three iambic tetrameters rhyming a a a, followed by a dimeter, rhyming b, another tetrameter rhyming a, and a concluding dimeter rhyming b. The habbie is indeed the heavy workhorse of Burns's poetry, although there's nothing 'heavy' about the aerial sound patterns and rhetorical ingenuity he achieves at his best, unmatched by any of his precursors.[20]

Although use of this stanza by earlier poets in the Scottish vernacular revival (including Sempill of Beltrees, after whose elegy on the piper 'Habbie Simson' the hallmark stanza is named[21]) focused on comedy and satire, we'll see Burns often deploying the form in a more sentimental and sententious manner. Gerry Carruthers notes that its subsequent naming as the 'Burns stanza' 'is typical of the amnesia that has been engendered with regard to Burns's forbears in the 18th century Scottish poetry tradition'.[22] But Burns's deployment of traditional verse forms like the habbie was far from conservative and backward-looking, especially in its engagement with the English Augustan poets and the idiom of sensibility. It breathed new life into the 'broken and mutilated' Scots vernacular tradition by engaging it with rural modernity and social change; as Thomas Campbell noted, 'Burns has given the *elixir vitae* to his dialect' [Lockhart, p. 227]. Unfortunately Burns's consummate success often seems to have deterred skilled followers, and poetry written in Scots was easily subsumed into the 'Kailyard', the purely nostalgic and parochial nineteenth-century version of Scottish pastoral.

Rather than viewing the Scots poet as restricted in linguistic range, Burns believed that he could access diverse registers (what he called the *copia verborum*) in a manner unavailable to the English poet. Far from writing exclusively in Scots, Burns deftly switched between Scots, Anglo-Scots, and English; many of his most celebrated poems (famously 'To a Mouse' and 'To a Mountain-Daisy') were couched in the idiom of sensibility, and many of the songs are written in English with only a 'sprinkling' of Scots diction. Carol McGuirk rightly complains that exclusive concentration on Burns as a Scots dialect poet simply 'encourages critics who are not themselves Scottish enthusiasts to presuppose a regional range for his achievements and [thus] to ignore Burns'.[23]

Indeed much confusion has been caused by the significance of his decision to write 'chiefly in the Scottish Dialect'. In his report on his parish of Mauchline for the *Statistical Account*, Burns's nemesis Revd William Auld noted that 'the Scots dialect is the language spoken, but it is gradually improving, and approaching nearer to the English' [*Statistical Account*, vi. 450]. Other ministers writing in the

---

[20] See Douglas Dunn, '"A Very Scottish Kind of Dash": Burns' Native Metric', in Robert Crawford (ed.), *Robert Burns and Cultural Authority* (Edinburgh: Polygon, 1999), 58–85.

[21] By Allan Ramsay, in 'Answer I' (Ramsay to Hamilton of Gilbertfield) 10 July 1719, who commends his correspondent's verse that 'hit the Spirit to a Tittle, | Of Standart *Habby*' (ll. 35–6) [Ramsay, i. 119].

[22] Gerard Carruthers, *Robert Burns* (Tavistock: Northcote House, 2006), 10.

[23] McGuirk, *Sentimental Era*, p. xvii.

*Account* also frequently 'associated [Gaelic and Scots] vernacular with old [rural] ways, and often with elements of the Scottish past from which they wish[ed] to disassociate themselves'.[24] Auld's linkage of 'improvement' with linguistic Anglicization was shared by many more progressive luminaries of the Scottish enlightenment, who often associated Scots with the old society and manners predating the 1707 Act of Union.[25] This widespread critique was later absorbed into a broader romantic analysis of an 'inauthentic' and fissured Scottish culture; Ian Duncan has recently argued that Burns's Romantic biographer John Gibson Lockhart was the first to characterize Scottish literature as split between a cosmopolitan rationalism, and an authentic, but unreflexive, 'true voice of feeling' articulated in the Scots language.[26] However, this does need some qualification: the success of Burns's poetry in its time shows that even the many linguistic 'improvers' among the Edinburgh literati were willing to countenance poetry (and especially song) in Scots when licensed by the aesthetics of 'native genius' and the generic allowances of pastoral.

In the very different climate of the twentieth-century Scottish Renaissance, largely in reaction to Hugh MacDiarmid's programme of 'synthetic Scots', the animus against Scots resurfaced in Edwin Muir's remark that 'the curse of Scottish literature is the lack of a whole language, which finally means the lack of a whole mind'.[27] Influenced by the notion of a self-divided 'Caledonian Antisyzygy', David Craig's widely read *Scottish Literature and the Scottish People* associated the 'reductive idiom' of eighteenth-century Scottish vernacular verse (as well as the 'poor man's defensive pose' which he discerned in the poetry of Allan Ramsay and Robert Burns) with 'the old constricting habits' of unimproved agriculture.[28] Following Muir, Craig found the verse forms and diction of Burns's poetry (compared, say, to the rural poetry of George Crabbe) to be

---

[24] Robert McColl Millar, '"Blind Attachment to Inverterate Custom": Language Use, Language Attitude and the Rhetoric of Improvement in the first *Statistical Account*', in Marina Dossena and Charles Jones (eds.), *Insights into Late Modern English* (Berne: Peter Lang, 2003), 311–30 at 328.

[25] See Janet Sorensen, *The Grammar of Empire in Eighteenth-Century British Writing* (Cambridge: Cambridge University Press, 2000), esp. 138–71.

[26] Lockhart drew on Schlegelian notions of cultural fragmentation, just as his twentieth-century followers drew on T. S. Eliot's idea of disassociated sensibility to analyse the fissure at the heart of Scottish writing. Ian Duncan, *Scott's Shadow* (Princeton: Princeton University Press, 2007), 60 See also Cairns Craig, *Out of History: Narrative Paradigms in Scottish and British Culture* (Edinburgh: Polygon, 1996), 82–118.

[27] Edwin Muir, *Scott and Scotland* (Edinburgh: Polygon 1982), 9. Alan Riach argues that Hugh MacDiarmid's early collections of Scots lyrics, *Sangshaw* (1925) and *Penny Wheep* (1926) torque Burns's agricultural world and idiom into 'a modernist or symbolist mode'. 'MacDiarmid's Burns' in Robert Crawford (ed.), *Robert Burns and Cultural Authority* (Edinburgh: Polygon, 1999), 201.

[28] David Craig, *Scottish Literature and the Scottish People, 1680–1830* (London: Chatto & Windus, 1961), 82. Lockhart had spoken in remarkably similar terms of Scots language poetry as 'written in the dialect of the lower classes . . . imply[ing] that they must be confined to a limited range of thought'. *Peter's Letters to his Kinsfolk*, 3rd edn., 3 vols. (Edinburgh 1819), iii. 329.

'incommensurate with the wholeness of experience', although he undermined his case by erroneously describing Burns as 'a crofter' and 'a primitive peasant tilling for subsistence crops'.[29]

The fact that Burns's poetry was influenced by the 'modern' politics of both the American and the French Revolutions is well attested.[30] Less often recognized is that it also responded to a revolutionary transformation nearer home, in the social and economic fabric of rural Scotland. In 1811 William Aiton wrote of Ayrshire during the lifetime of Robert Burns that 'never was so great a change effected in the condition of the people of any district, in so short a period' [Aiton, p. 89]. In England, William Cowper lamented that improvement was 'the idol of the age', while William Blake hymned the crooked roads of genius that it was forcing into straight turnpikes.[31] The Burns who wrote 'I have such an aversion to right line and method, that when I can't get over the hedges that bound the highway, I zig-zag across the road just to keep my hand in' [CL i. 131] can hardly be enlisted among the road-straighteners. This shows a whimsical Shandeyan pose, itself a bizarre kind of 'improvement' for an Ayrshire tenant farmer with mud on his boots.[32] No less than leading projectors and theorists like Sir John Sinclair, Adam Smith, and Adam Ferguson, Burns had serious doubts about many of the social and moral consequences of 'the straight road', and in this respect at least eighteenth-century Scottish culture may not have been quite as 'paradoxical' as proposed by David Daiches in 1964.[33]

The present book should remind us that the Scottish enlightenment wasn't confined to the learned institutions and polite drawing rooms of Edinburgh. Far from being an obscure provincial backwater, eighteenth-century Ayrshire was linked by the discourse and practice of improvement to the birth of the modern capitalist age.[34] Coterminous with the transformation of the agricultural economy, the decades of the 1760s, 1770s, and 1780s (the poet's formative years) saw the rise of manufactures, country banking, and the booms and busts of the new

---

[29] Craig, *Scottish Literature and the Scottish People, 1680–1830*, 79, 141, 95. On Crabbe, see p. 100.

[30] See e.g. Liam McIlvanney's *Burns the Radical: Poetry and Politics in Late Eighteenth-Century Scotland* (East Lothian: Tuckwell, 2002).

[31] *William Cowper, Verse and Letters*, selected by Brian Spiller (Cambridge, Mass., Harvard University Press, 1968), 462. Quoting *The Task*, Book 3. No line numbers.

[32] On Burns's debt to Sterne, see Kenneth Simpson *The Protean Scot: The Crisis of Identity in Eighteenth Century Scottish Literature* (Aberdeen: Aberdeen University Press, 1988), 219–45. See also McGuirk, *Sentimental Era*. Burns's 1787 letter to Ainslie here glosses lines 110–12 of his 'Epistle to James Smith' [K 79].

[33] David Daiches, *The Paradox of Scottish Culture: The Eighteenth Century Experience* (London: Oxford University Press, 1964).

[34] John Strawhorn, 'Ayrshire and the Enlightenment', in Graham Cruikshank (ed.), *A Sense of Place: Studies in Scottish Local History* (Edinburgh: Scotland's Cultural Heritage, 1988), 188–201 at 188 and *passim*; also Strawhorn (ed.), *Ayrshire at the Time of Burns* (Newmilns: Ayrshire Archaeological and Natural History Society, 1959).

credit economy, war, and empire, accompanied by religious and cultural enlightenment. Ayrshire was also highly 'globalized', to the extent that its landed elite benefited disproportionately from colonial expansion in the Caribbean and India, while rich and poor alike suffered palpably from the loss of the American colonies. Facing financial ruin and social ostracism in 1786, Robert Burns planned to seek employment in Jamaica as a 'Negro Driver' on one of the island's many Scottish-owned slave plantations.[35]

If at times Burns's poetry mounted a 'zigzag' criticism of improvement, elsewhere (especially in the Kirk poems, with their bitter satires on religious prejudice) it fully endorsed the rational spirit of enlightenment. After all, his formidable literacy was itself a product of Ayrshire's provincial enlightenment, distinguished by new civic institutions, turnpike roads, and postal service, facilitating the circulation of newspapers and letters. The fact that Burns never attended college doesn't mean that he was 'Heaven-taught'. Growing up near the flourishing market town of Ayr, with the encouragement of his father, he absorbed progressive theological views from the Moderate Presbyterian[36] ministers William McGill and William Dalrymple. He briefly attended school in Ayr, but was later educated by a personal tutor, John Murdoch, hired by his father, whose instruction included French and some Latin. In his formative years Burns seems to have had access to the Ayr Library Society, founded in 1762 with the names of McGill and Dalrymple heading its list of members.[37] William Boyd writes that 'it may have been this Library which led Burns...to realise the educational benefits of libraries for the people at large'.[38] Liam McIlvanney has examined the influence of Arthur Masson's *Collection of English Prose and Verse* on the young Burns, an anthology which 'would provide young Scots with a junior version of the Belles Lettres courses taught by Hugh Blair and others in the Scottish Universities'.[39] There is some warrant for Walter Scott's claim that Burns 'had an education not much worse that the sons of many gentlemen in Scotland' [*CH* p. 258].

[35] See Tom Devine, *Scotland's Empire 1600–1815* (London: Allen Lane, 2003), 320–45 at 334, and my essay 'Burns and the Poetics of Abolition', in Gerard Carruthers (ed.), *The Edinburgh Companion to Robert Burns* (Edinburgh: Edinburgh University Press, 2009), 47–60.

[36] 'Moderate' here refers to Church of Scotland Presbyterians touched by the spirit of Enlightenment (as opposed to 'Orthodox'), explained at greater length in Ch. 6.

[37] John Strawhorn has analysed the library holdings during Burns's lifetime, noting that its subscription income was sufficient to purchase two dozen new titles in good years, and build up to 700 books by 1804. These were supplied by the bookseller William Creech in Edinburgh (the poet's future publisher) and included the works of Adam Smith, Kames, Gibbon, Blair, Beattie, Sterne, and Boswell, as well as other works of travel, history, philosophy, and theology, the *Encyclopaedia Britannica* and the *Scots Magazine*. Strawhorn, 'Ayrshire and the Enlightenment', 195–6. This is picked up by Robert Crawford in *The Bard: Robert Burns, a Biography* (London: Jonathan Cape, 2009), 52.

[38] As affirmed in his 1791 letter to Sir John Sinclair [CL ii. 106–8]. William Boyd, *Education in Ayrshire through Seven Centuries* (London: University of London Press, 1961), 124.

[39] McIlvanney, *Burns the Radical*, 47.

Burns's education was later complemented by his membership of the 'Tarbolton Bachelors Club', a conversation club which he co-founded in 1780 with his brother Gilbert, encompassing (in Currie's words) 'five other young peasants', who sought to 'relax themselves after toil, to promote sociability and friendship, and to improve the mind' [Currie, i. 106].[40] The egalitarian ethic of Burns's verse epistles is captured in the Club's epigraph, probably penned by the poet himself: 'Of birth or blood we do not boast, | Nor gentry does our club afford; | But ploughmen and mechanics we, | In Nature's simple dress record' [Currie, i. 107]. Despite the serious intellectual issues debated by its members, the Club was also a matrix for the amorous exploits of 'Rob Mossgiel': the regulation book required members to flag a proactive heterosexuality, its permission to admire more than one woman nodding towards sexual licence, perhaps influenced by the example of Parson Yorick in Sterne's *Sentimental Journey*.[41] 'Practising enlightenment' in this libertarian sense entailed spirited resistance to the moral and sexual control of the Kirk Session, the 'houghmagandie pack'. Club sociability was the seedbed not only for the verse epistles but also for the 'Kirk Satires' (discussed in Chapters 3 and 6 respectively), widely circulated in manuscript around Tarbolton and Mauchline parishes to the fury of the orthodox faithful.

Burns's *published* poetry would not of course have been possible without John Wilson's small printing press in Kilmarnock, founded in 1782 (another symptomatic institution of the Ayrshire enlightenment), which published his *Poems, Chiefly in the Scottish Dialect* in the summer of 1786. Given that Wilson, and most of the subscribers to the Kilmarnock edition were enthusiastic Freemasons, the 'brotherhood of the mystic tye' also contributed in large part to the making of Burns the poet.[42] Burns was entered as a member of Lodge St David, Tarbolton, on 4 July 1781 (one of thirty or so Lodges established in late eighteenth-century Ayrshire), in the same room used for meetings of the Bachelor's Club.[43] When the St James Lodge seceded the following year, the poet followed, being elected to the important office of Depute Master in July 1784. Egalitarian participation

---

[40] Currie publishes the 'Bachelors' regulations and minute book in an appendix. Such conversation clubs were vehicles of enlightenment from Philadelphia to Calcutta. For a detailed account, see David D. McElroy, *Scotland's Age of Improvement: A Survey of Eighteenth-Century Literary Clubs and Societies* (Seattle: Washington State University Press, 1969) and 'Literary Clubs and Societies of Eighteenth-Century Scotland' (unpublished Ph.D. thesis, Edinburgh University, 1952), 265–9.

[41] The Rules and Regulations are published in Currie, i. 365–9. For Parson Yorick, see Corey Andrews, *Literary Nationalism in Eighteenth-Century Scottish Club Poetry* (Lampeter: Edwin Mellen, 2004), 249. The Bachelors were puritans compared to the small-town 'fornicators' celebrated in Burns's 'Court of Equity' [K 109], or the hard-toping libertines of Edinburgh's 'Crochallan Fencibles', for whom the bawdy 'Merry Muses of Caledonia' were collected and composed.

[42] More research needs to be done on this important topic. But see Andrews, *Literary Nationalism*, 268–97.

[43] For a full list see John Strawhorn, *Ayrshire at the Time of Burns*, 132.

in the 'mystic rites' of Masonry offered Burns a unique opportunity for social mobility, identification with a community of like-minded men opposed to the theological stranglehold of 'auld licht' Calvinism, as well as a safety net in the eventuality of financial ruin.[44] Many of the names of well-connected members of Burns's lodge will recur in Chapter 3's discussion of 'The Vision'.

If Burns's local celebrity as an Ayrshire 'bardie' was fostered by Masonic connections in Tarbolton, his fame at national level after the success of the Kilmarnock poems (including his coronation as 'Caledonia's Bard') was promoted by his major patron and fellow-mason the Earl of Glencairn, and other polite members of the Edinburgh lodges. Many Masons appear among the *c.*1,500 names on the subscription list of Burns's 1787 Edinburgh edition, published by William Creech, another 'brother of the *mystic tye*' [K 115 l. 2].[45] Corey Andrews notes however that Burns's Masonic poetry is largely concentrated in the years 1781–6, and falls off subsequent to that date; although Burns attended Masonic meetings during his Dumfries years, his enthusiasm seems to have waned after 1788, quite possibly as a result of encountering a more radical discourse of democratic fraternity in the writings of Tom Paine.[46] Whatever the truth about Burns's 'native genius', the 'Ayrshire enlightenment' was an essential precondition of the 'Burns phenomenon'.[47]

Adam Smith, who had few connections with Ayrshire, once quipped (heretically, for admirers of Burns) that 'it is the duty of a poet to write like a gentleman', and never actually met the Ayrshire poet, even although the latter called at Smith's house in Edinburgh with a letter of introduction.[48] Yet Burns quoted Smith's *Theory of Moral Sentiments* (first published in the year of his birth, 1759) in the Commonplace Book which served as the crucible for his Kilmarnock poems, and marvelled at the intellectual breadth and radical vision of *Wealth of Nations* when he read it in 1789: 'I would covet much to have his ideas respecting the present state of some quarters of the world that are or have been the scenes of considerable revolutions since his book was written' [CL i. 410]. Throughout this study I will develop a contrapuntal relationship between arguably the two most

[44] See John Brewer, 'Commercialisation and Politics', in Neil McKendrick, John Brewer, and J. H. Plumb, *The Birth of a Consumer Society* (London: Europa, 1982), 220 (quoted in Andrews, *Literary Nationalism*, 270.)

[45] Richard Sher, *Enlightenment and the Book*, 180–2.

[46] Andrews, *Literary Nationalism*, 354, 304. Masonic poems include: 'No Churchman am I' [K 27], 'The Farewell. To the Brethren of St James's Lodge, Tarbolton' [K 115], 'The Sons of old Killie' [K 128].

[47] John Strawhorn, 'Ayrshire and the Enlightenment', 195, 196.

[48] Smith's remarks on poetry quoted in *The Bee, or Literary Weekly Intelligencer*, 11 May 1791, republished in *Lectures on Rhetoric and Belles Lettres*, ed. J. C. Bryce, *Glasgow Edition of the Works and Correspondence of Adam Smith* (Indianapolis: Liberty Fund, 1985), 227–31 at 230. Smith subscribed to Burns's Edinburgh volume, and sought unsuccessfully to secure him patronage in the Salt Office.

influential Scottish writers of the eighteenth century, underlining their many points of convergence as well as divergence. The misappropriation of Smith as the father of modern neo-conservative economics has fostered a belief that Scotland's democratic bard can have had at best only a negative relationship to the glacial abstractions of the 'Scottish science of man', a belief that hasn't helped extricate Burns from the kailyard. By the same token, it has shorn Smith's philosophy of its sceptical and radical spirit, detaching it from its immediate context in the eighteenth-century Scottish discourse of improvement. It is too often forgotten that *Wealth of Nations* lambasted aristocracy, entails, rack-renting, monopolies, the apprenticeship system, state religion, British colonial policy in North America or Bengal, the slave trade, and any number of other pressing contemporary concerns which struck a chord with Burns. No less than Smith, Burns stood on the historical watershed, although his poetic 'zigzagging' was itself a portent of a Romantic self-consciousness that Smith could hardly have foreseen.

The first two chapters of *Burns and Pastoral* study, respectively, the poet's vocational involvement with the 'prose georgics' of agricultural improvement, and his related, but antithetical, engagement with the genre of Scots Pastoral, as inherited from Allan Ramsay and Robert Fergusson. The third focuses on Burns's poetic self-fashioning as an 'Ayrshire poet' as manifest in the Commonplace Book, the verse epistles, and especially 'The Vision', paying special attention to questions of sociability and patronage. Chapter 4 turns to the vexed question of Burns's politics in the cluster of poems that open the Kilmarnock volume, poems equally at home addressing social relations and popular politics in the rural Lowlands, or satirizing the 'high politics' of Westminster and the Court at St James. Chapter 5 studies the convergence of the farmer and the sentimentalist in Burns's animal poems, as well as their role in displacing and mediating problems of the human world. Chapter 6 turns to religion, finding in the Kirk satires and related poems manifestations of the poet's satirical genius at its closest rapprochement with the spirit of enlightenment. Chapter 7 returns to Burns at his most conventionally pastoral in representing the 'annals of the poor', studying the genesis and reception of 'The Cotter's Saturday Night', and 'Love and Liberty', which I read as a kind of inversion of the former poem, a 'Beggar's Saturday Night', although still beholden to pastoral. Chapter 8 surveys Burns's creative output during the Excise period, especially his 'making and mending' of Scottish songs; the second part of the chapter offers a reading of his narrative masterpiece 'Tam o' Shanter' in relation to his new vocational mobility, and the 'antiquarian' irony of his Dumfries circle. The final chapter follows Burns's life and poetry 'across the shadow line' into the realms of posthumous fame, as propelled by the biographical and editorial labours of Dr James Currie. The book concludes by reflecting upon the 'pastoral closure' posthumously imposed upon Burns's poetry, as well as briefly considering his still largely unacknowledged influence on Wordsworth and British Romanticism.

# 1

# Robert Burns and the 'New Husbandry'

*Farmin', and fencin', an' a';*
*Ploughin', and plantin', an' a';*
*Beha'd how our kintry's improvin',*
*An' poverty wearin' awa'.*
(Glasgow Chapbook, 1808)[1]

*the cheerless gloom of a hermit with the unceasing moil of a galley-slave . . .*
(Burns on farming at Mount Oliphant, Aug 1787)[2]

## ROBERT BURNS, TENANT FARMER

Scholars of the Scottish enlightenment have tended to undervalue the links between the philosophical spirit of the age and agricultural improvement, both of which fundamentally transformed man's relationship with nature in practical as well as in theoretical terms. Contemporaries agreed that this revolutionary pace of improvement began in the decades of the 1760s and 1770s, and despite major setbacks involving bad harvests and economic crises, gathered pace with the soaring price of agricultural products during the war decades after 1793. The virtual non-existence of peasant proprietorship of land in Scotland (in contrast to much of the rest of Europe) gave landowners a freer hand to implement change and eradicate customary rights, with only minimal legal challenges. The rapidity of change, historically unprecedented and possibly unique to eighteenth-century Scotland, helps to explain the dramatic contrast of temporalities which we encounter everywhere in Burns's poetry.

These 'revolutionary' decades correspond precisely with the life of Robert Burns, born in 1759, and coming of age as the son of an Ayrshire tenant farmer in the 1760s and 1770s. He continued as a farmer (with one interval) until his

---

[1] 'A New Song, sung at the Meeting of the Perthshire Florist and Vegetable Society, to the tune of "Woo'd and Marry'd an a"' (Glasgow: J. & M. Robertson, Saltmarket, 1808), in E. J. Cowan and Mike Paterson, *Folk in Print: Scotland's Chapbook Heritage 1750–1850* (Edinburgh: John Donald, 2007), 79.
[2] CL i. 137.

abandonment of Ellisland Farm in 1791, which saw his transition to urban life in Dumfries and full-time employment in the Excise, up to his early death in 1796. Although improvement was to a great extent 'a revolution from above', the Scottish landowners who instigated change were heavily dependent on the compliance and willingness of indigenous tenant farmers, men like the Burn[e]ses father and sons. The relationship between tenants and lairds is a crucial social threshold in Burns's poetry (represented in negative terms in 'The Twa Dogs', and more positively in 'A Vision'), but it also elicited much anxiety in the contemporary literature of improvement.

Lairds and their factors knew that the success of improvement depended on the practical ability of an educated and rational tenantry as much as the labourers who served them. In the words of John Barrell,

the determination of large landowners who had invested in enclosure . . . to see a quick return on the capital invested, helped to create a new order of tenant-farmers, literate, experimental, and business-men enough to survive the rack-renting system and establish themselves in rural society as men of some consequence, if not—they did not own the land they farmed—on a footing with the gentry.[3]

Nevertheless, tensions between tenants and the landowning class often obstructed the efficient implementation of improvement [Devine, *TRS*, p. 66]. Burn's occupational training as an improving tenant farmer, and his ambivalence regarding that role, was in large part responsible for the 'zig-zag', dialectical impulse of his poetry.

It is remarkable that no major study has yet addressed Burns's occupational involvement with the discourse and practice of agricultural improvement, perhaps the most immediate and practical concern of the Scottish Enlightenment. Burns 'came of age' in the years 1766–77 working on his father's 70-acre, unimproved farm of Mount Oliphant near Alloway. During the period of his major poetic creativity, he assisted his father as tenant of the 130-acre farm of Lochlie (1777–84) in the parish of Tarbolton. Subsequently, together with his brother Gilbert, he was himself tenant of the nearby 118-acre Mossgiel (1784–6), a farm on the Loudoun estates in the parish of Mauchline, sublet by Gavin Hamilton. In the years 1788–91, in the wake of his literary triumph in Edinburgh and before his disgruntled abandonment of farming for a career in the Excise, he farmed 170 acres at Ellisland, in the relatively unimproved countryside outside Dumfries, leased from the banker and entrepreneur Patrick Miller of Dalswinton. In Ayrshire 43 per cent of farmers worked possessions of less than 100 acres (which Devine describes as 'the 'improved' minimum threshold'), so in terms of acreage Lochlie and Mossgiel were relatively large farms, although their soil was poor and water-logged (see Fig. 2).

---

[3] John Barrell, *The Idea of Landscape and the Sense of Place: An Approach to the Poetry of John Clare* (Cambridge: Cambridge University Press, 1972), 71.

FIG. 2. 'Hairst Rig'. A coloured print of Ayrshire's landscape of improvement, looking west towards Arran. Note the hedges, mixture of grass and arable, and new farm buildings. In his ardour to foreground Burns's dalliance with Nelly Kilpatrick, the nineteenth-century artist has forgotten to show the rigs that still existed in the poet's lifetime. The old castle on the coast has been abandoned in favour of a new mansion house built inland, surrounded by plantations.

Burns's occupation as a tenant farmer, together with his pastoral title as 'Heaven-taught ploughman', have led to mighty confusions about his social class, and (not quite the same thing) class-*consciousness*. I'm heedful here of E. P. Thompson's caveat that 'if class was not available within people's own cognitive system, if they saw themselves and fought out their own historical battles in terms of "estate" or "ranks" or "orders", etc., then if we describe those struggles in class terms we must exert caution against any tendency to read back subsequent notions of class'.[4] Contrary to the ploughman myth, as tenant farmer

---

[4] 'Eighteenth-Century English Society: Class Struggle Without Class?' *Social History* 3 (1978), 148. Thompson's bipolar account of eighteenth-century society as divided between 'patricians and plebs' underestimates the emerging importance of the 'the middling sort'. For one of many critiques, see Tim Harris (ed.), *Popular Culture in England, c.1500–1850* (Basingstoke: Macmillan, 1995), 10. See also Dror Wahrman, *Imagining the Middle Class: The Political Representation of Class in Britain, c.1780–1840* (Cambridge: Cambridge University Press, 1995).

of Mossgiel Burns occupied the middle rung on the social hierarchy of the rural Lowlands, the most precarious lower edge of that rung, it is true, but still not too far below the group that Barrell calls the 'rural professional class', historically responsible for creating 'the landscape of parliamentary enclosure'.[5] Even a cursory reading of his biography and correspondence reveals that, as well as other farmers, Burns's social peers were 'lawyers, land agents . . . carters, carriers, and innkeepers: booksellers, printers, schoolteachers, entertainers, and clerks: drapers, grocers, druggists, stationers, ironmongers, shopkeepers of every sort'.[6]

This isn't to deny that Burns's social origins were humble, nor that although a tenant farmer, he might still be designated 'a peasant', to the extent that he worked physically on the land (in his 1791 letter to Sir John Sinclair, Burns signed himself off as 'A PEASANT',[7] although not without a touch of irony) [CL i. 108]. At a time when his radical political sympathies earned him the rebuke of his Excise superiors, in a letter of 13 April 1793 to John Erskine, Earl of Mar, Burns defensively described his entitlement, notwithstanding his 'humble station', to 'interest himself in 'the concerns of a People'. The letter goes on to cast an interesting light on his own perception of his social station: 'The uninformed mob may swell a Nation's bulk; & the titled, tinsel Courtly throng may be its feathered ornament, but the number of those who are elevated enough in life, to reason & reflect; & yet low enough to keep clear of the venal contagion of a Court; these are a Nation's strength' [CL ii. 209–10]. Despite his constant struggle for patronage (addressed in Chapter 3), consciousness of belonging to the 'middling sort' shores up the Whig rhetoric of 'independence' which saturates Burns's writing. In the political climate of the 1790s, it converged with a radical politics, the public expression of which incurred severe risks and reprimands.

Until he abandoned farming for a full-time career in the Excise in 1791, Burns was, then, a *labouring* poet, although maybe not a labouring *class* poet.[8] His father William Burnes had been driven by the high cost of agricultural wages to employ his teenage sons as labourers at the plough and the flail, and contemporary accounts of the poet's physique suggest that he may have been bodily

---

[5] Barrell, *Idea of Landscape*, 65.

[6] The list is John Brewer's, quoted by E. P. Thompson in *Customs in Common*, (London: Merlin, 1991), 88.

[7] According to the *OED*'s current definition, a 'peasant' is 'a person who lives in the country and works on the land, especially as a smallholder or labourer: (chiefly sociological); a member of an agricultural class dependent on subsistence farming'. The first part of this (but not the second) is applicable to Burns.

[8] See Tim Burke's nuanced essay on Burns in *Eighteenth-Century Labouring-Class Poets*, 3 vols. (London: Pickering & Chatto, 2002), iii. 103–15, expanded in his 'Labour, Education and Genius: Burns and the Plebeian Poetic Tradition', in Johnny Rodger and Gerard Carruthers (eds.), *The Fickle Man: Robert Burns in the 21st Century* (Dingwall: Sandstone, 2009), 13–24.

deformed by heavy labour carried out in his adolescence.[9] Although Burns later described himself as 'a dextrous Ploughman for my [teenage] years', life at Mt Oliphant was 'the chearless gloom of a hermit [combined] with the unceasing moil of a galley-slave' [CL i. 137]. As co-tenant with his brother Gilbert at Mossgiel and as sole tenant of Ellisland after 1788, he laboured alongside the men he employed. In his poem 'The Inventory' [K 86] he provided 'a faithfu' list, | O gudes an' gear, an' a' my graith' [ll. 2–3], in response to Pitt's 1786 taxes on horses, carriages, and servants. He described his three servants (a 'gaudsman' or ploughboy, a thresher, and a cowherd) with sardonic affection, describing how he 'rul[ed] them . . . discreetly' and 'labour[ed] them compleately'; 'For men, I've three mischievous boys, | Run de'ils for rantin' an' for noise; | A gaudsman ane, a thrasher t'other, | Wee Davock hauds the nowt in fother' (cattle in fodder) [ll. 34–7]. This is accurately reflected in Sir Walter Scott's recollection of his first meeting with Burns, in 1787 at the home of Adam Fergusson; 'I would have taken the poet, had I not known what he was, for a very sagacious country farmer of the old Scotch school—i.e. none of your modern agriculturalists, who keep labourers for their drudgery, but the *douce gudeman* who held his own plough' [*CH* p. 262]. (Note, however, Scott's qualification here, 'had I not known what he was'.)

In the wake of poetic fame, Burns ascended a rung on the ladder of agricultural status when he assumed the lease of Ellisland farm near Dumfries. William Clark, Burns's ploughman there, later recalled that the poet 'kept two men and two women servants; but he invariably, when at home, took his meals with his wife and family in the little parlour'. Heavily engaged with excise business during the winter malting season, 'he occasionally held the plough for an hour or so, and was a fair workman'. Clark also remembered him as 'a kind and indulgent master, [who] spoke familiarly to his servants, both in the house and out of it', although his temper could flare up in response to negligence. [Mackay, p. 442][10] These descriptions, together with Burns's own comments in the letter to the Earl of Mar, allow a clearer picture of his social station to emerge. He was certainly higher in rank than cotters and labourers, the 'rustic compeers' whose 'sentiments and manners' he wrote in 'his and their native language', and whose manual labour he hired. [Kil. p. iii] On the other hand, he ranked below freehold farmers (in Scotland dubbed 'bonnet lairds') and certainly below the landed gentry to whom he paid rent and from whom he sought patronage, men (and women) who

---

[9] It was customary in eighteenth-century Ayrshire for tacksmen, especially of smaller farms, to labour on the land with their wives and children [Aiton, p. 516].

[10] In his account of Burns's Ellisland years published in Lockhart's *Life of Burns*, Allan Cunningham (whose father was steward to the poet's landlord Patrick Millar) alleged that he 'neither ploughed, nor sowed, nor reaped, at least like a hard-working farmer', and that he over-indulged his servants. [Lockhart, p. 142] But the reliability of 'Honest Allan' Cunningham's account is questionable.

often appear in his poems as the objects of satirical resentment, but also of patriotic, and sometimes solicitous, eulogy.

As we'll see in subsequent chapters, Burns's poetry endowed the labourers' life with pride and dignity, cementing his subsequent reputation as the poet of the common man. Even after 1788 his relatively well-salaried professional career as Excise officer (of which he was less proud) demanded unremitting toil; it would be remarkable if his occupational labours hadn't left a profound mark on his poetry. But despite the myth of the 'Heaven-taught ploughman', he doesn't easily fit the category of eighteenth-century 'labouring class poet' in the mould of Stephen Duck or Mary Collier, nor did he see himself as such. Notoriously, he made uncharitable remarks about the mania for Scots poetry that his writing inspired: 'my success has encouraged such a shoal of ill-spawned monsters to crawl into public notice under the title of Scots Poets, that the very term, Scots Poetry, borders on the burlesque' [CL i. 382], and he was notably unsupportive to Janet Little, 'The Scotch Milkmaid'. But nonetheless Burns was consistently cited as a major inspiration for Scottish and Irish labouring-class poets such as James Hogg, Robert Tannahill, Samuel Thomson, and James Orr, not to mention English poets such as Robert Anderson, Robert Bloomfield, and John Clare.

Although John Barrell has little to say directly about Burns in *The Idea of Landscape and the Sense of Place: An Approach to the Poetry of John Clare*, his pioneering study provides a suggestive starting point for comparing the poetry of Burns the tenant farmer with that of Clare the landless labourer. Barrell's penetrating account of the influence of the unimproved English open-field system on Clare's spatial imagination appears to have no correspondence to the role of 'runrig' (the nearest Scottish equivalent of the open-field system) in the imaginative world of Burns: in fact, like other tenant farmers of his generation, he was practically involved in its eradication. As labouring denizens of rural life, both Burns and Clare engage critically with the eighteenth-century pastoral tradition, and share an intense awareness of locality, but their attitude to improvement is often at odds. For example, in one of many poems directly influenced by Burns, 'The Lamentation of Round-Oak Waters', Clare complains—in the voice of the 'injur'd brook' (l. 158)—about the effects of enclosure, especially tree-felling, on the Helpston landscape.[11] Ironically, Clare's poetic model here is Burns's 'Humble Petition of Bruar Water, to the Noble Duke of Athole' [K 172], where the personified river Bruar urges the noble landowner to fulfil his obligation to improve his estate by 'shading my banks wi' towering trees, | And bonie spreading bushes'(ll. 35–6).[12] For Clare the familiar rural landscape is in the process of being destroyed by enclosures; for Burns, on

---

[11] *John Clare*, ed. Eric Robinson and David Powell (Oxford: Oxford University Press, 1984), 18–23 at 22.

[12] Sounding like a contemporary improvement manual, the Bruar even specifies the nature of the plantation; 'lofty firs', 'ashes cool', 'fragrant birks', and 'close embowering thorns' (ll. 73–80).

the other hand, it is quite literally undergoing 'improvement', and although this can be destructive (as, famously, in 'To a Mouse'), it isn't necessarily or always so.

In contrast to Clare, writing on Burns's agricultural background has served mainly to supplement the flood of biographical information that has poured forth ever since the pioneering attempts of Robert Heron and Dr James Currie. Gavin Stott's little book *Robert Burns, Farmer* offers the general reader an excellent sketch of the poet's life and work against the background of eighteenth-century Scottish agriculture, but it isn't presented as a scholarly study.[13] Richard Fowler's chapter 'Ruinous Bargains' in his 1988 study *Robert Burns* goes into great detail regarding the soil chemistry of the Burns family farms, as well as collateral difficulties faced by Ayrshire farmers in the 1780s, in order to assess the poet's real success or failure as a farmer. Following in the tracks of Allan Cunningham, who opined that Burns 'had little of a farmer's prudence and economy' [Lockhart, p. 142], Fowler represents Burns as an incompetent agriculturalist, concluding that 'the Ellisland tenancy was more of a *bargain ruined* than *a ruinous bargain.*[14] This negative judgement (again following Cunningham and Lockhart) is balanced by a suggestion that it was Burns's failure as a farmer that engendered his success as a poet.

In 1787 Burns wrote to James Smith that 'Farming [is] the only thing of which I know any thing, and Heaven above knows, but little do I understand even of that, I cannot, I dare not, risk on farms as they are. If I do not fix, I will go for Jamaica' [CL i. 121]. At two crucial junctures in his career, Burns sought to abandon agriculture, the first time (to which he refers here) when, following Jean Armour's pregnancy in 1786, and pursued by the 'houghmagandie pack' of the Kirk Session, he planned to seek employment in Jamaica: the second, successfully, in the summer of 1791, when he finally abandoned Ellisland to work full time for the Excise. But Burns's ambivalence concerning farming was a result of acquired knowledge and experience rather than naivety. He harboured no illusions about the huge challenges facing undercapitalized farmers in the Ayrshire or Dumfriesshire agricultural climate of the 1780s.

Allan Cunningham described the typical Nithsdale farmer, at the time of Burns's arrival in the area, as being utterly hidebound; 'his hatred of innovation, made him entrench himself behind a breast-work of old maxims and rustic saws, which he interpreted as oracles delivered against *improvement'*. Cunningham doubted whether Burns's 'skill was equal to the task of improvement' under these conditions, especially as 'his trial was short and unfortunate' [Lockhart, p. 144]. Most problematically, Burns's farming career both in Ayrshire and Nithsdale coincided with a period when 'the new commercial ethos' created an 'unparalleled increase in rentals': on the Douglas estates in nearby Lanarkshire, for

[13] Gavin Sprott, *Robert Burns, Farmer* (Edinburgh: National Museums of Scotland, 1990).

[14] Richard Fowler, *Robert Burns* (London: Routledge, 1988), 155.

example, the rental rose from £1,426 in 1737 to £3,593 in 1774 and to £8,849 by 1815 [Devine, *TRS*, p. 46]. Added to this, in the years 1772–3 and 1783–4 bad weather conditions and appalling harvests in south-west Scotland caused rent arrears for many tenants, 'undermining the vital link between rising rentals, tenant income and landlord investment in further improvements'. Burns was no exception, finding himself dependent equally upon the caprices of the seasons and the whims of landlords, who frequently used adverse conditions as an excuse 'to weed out poor payers and inadequate farmers' [Devine, *TRS*, pp. 74, 47]. But the view of Burns as farmer *manqué* relies too heavily on a Romantic common-place expressed in William Blake's distinction between the straight roads of improvement and the crooked roads of genius. The Romantic association of natural genius, practical failure and early death was in part a product of the Burns myth, and it became a romantic orthodoxy that poetic genius and practical reason were spiritual enemies. As we'll see, it wasn't difficult for Burns's romantic admirers to set him on the crooked road, both as a necessary concomitant of creative genius, but also as part of a cautionary tale about the professional incapacities and moral flaws of great poets (especially those of humble background) whose life and works challenged the status quo.

Burns's fragmentary tour journals of 1787 show a keener eye for the state of Scottish agriculture than for picturesque landscape. Describing the climate and soil of Berwickshire and Roxburghshire as superior to Ayrshire in his Borders tour, he notes elliptically that 'turnip & sheep husbandry their great improvements', and marvelled at the 'magnificence of Farmers & farm houses'.[15] On his September tour of the Highlands he characterized the country near Cullen (in Banffshire) as 'sadly poor and unimproven, the houses, crops, horses, cattle, etc., all in unison', whereas at the town of Banff he noted 'improvements all over this part of the country—plenty turnips, wheat, house-hold kail, cabbage, &c'.[16] Despite this evidence to the contrary, John Gibson Lockhart insisted on constructing Burns as a proto-romantic enemy of improvement by doctoring portions of the *Highland Tour* and inserting them in his 1828 *Life of Burns*. Following Burns's observation that West Lothian was 'a fertile improved country', but that improvement had opened a social divide between 'elegant' gentlemen farmers and a 'rude' and 'stupid' peasantry, Lockhart inserted a long ruminative passage, purportedly written by Burns himself, which undercut the tone of the preceding;

I think that a man of romantic taste, a 'man of feeling', will be better pleased with the poverty, but intelligent minds, of the peasantry in Ayrshire (peasantry they are all, below

---

[15] *Robert Burns's Tour of the Borders*, ed. Raymond Lamont Brown (Ipswich: Boydell, 1972), 17.

[16] *Robert Burns's Tour of the Highlands and Stirlingshire*, ed. Raymond Lamont Brown (Ipswich: Boydell, 1973), 22. The editor (ibid.) notes that a further sentence on improvements at Duff House has been 'scored out by a steel nibbed pen, but not apparently by Burns'. It clearly wasn't permissible for a poet to discuss cabbages in two consecutive sentences!

the Justice of Peace), than the opulence of a club of Merse farmers, when he, at the same time, considers the Vandalism of their plough-folks etc. I carry this idea so far that an unenclosed, unimproved country is to me actually more agreeable as a prospect, than a country cultivated like a garden.   [Lockhart, p.114][17]

Lockhart commented 'it is hardly to be expected that Robert Burns should have estimated the wealth of nations entirely on the principles of a political economist' [Lockhart, p. 114]. Taking licence from Scott's description of Burns as a 'douce gudeman' (itself a contribution to Lockhart's biography), he represented Burns as an old-style farmer, albeit with a fashionable modern taste for picturesque landscape, in order to present him as a Romantic enemy to both improvement and political economy. But in thus 'Romanticizing' Burns, the Tory Lockhart was using Burns as a weapon against the Whig disciples of political economy in the ideological battle preceding the 1832 Reform Bill. And against his assumption that Burns's view was necessarily opposed to that of the political economists, I've commented above on Burns's declared admiration for Adam Smith's *The Wealth of Nations*. In the spirit of John Logan rather than Lockhart, then, I'm arguing that Burns's outlook and aspirations were shaped by his avocation as a Scottish tenant farmer, and with it the ideology of improvement that was so often attached to it in the 1770s and 1780s. Although a poetic precursor of Romanticism, Burns was also a creature of enlightenment, and his professional and intellectual relationship with agricultural improvement is of more than just biographical importance.

## AGRICULTURAL IMPROVEMENT IN EIGHTEENTH-CENTURY LOWLAND SCOTLAND

In today's post-agricultural, post-industrial Britain it's not easy to grasp the importance of what Burns dubbed 'the new husbandry' in the economic, moral, and even theological debates of the eighteenth century. In the aftermath of the 1707 Act of Union with England, the Scottish economy (after a difficult start) began to benefit from English and colonial markets. Black cattle sold at large profits south of the border, and the lucrative plantation trade in tobacco, sugar, and cotton created the accumulation of capital necessary for improved agriculture and manufactures, facilitated by the new banking system and the circulation of paper money. At the same time, enlightened philosophers such as Adam Ferguson and Adam Smith theorized the links between improved agriculture and the new commercial society as part of a broader inquiry into the transition from a pastoral and agricultural to a commercial society currently

---

[17] Compare the slightly different interpolated text in *Robert Burns's Tour of the Highlands and Stirlingshire*, 16–17. See also Mackay, p. 334.

underway in eighteenth-century Scotland. With the rise of industry and rapid urbanization, agriculture was exposed to market pressures as never before, perhaps the major factor distinguishing it from the old husbandry. But many commentators during the lifetime of Robert Burns, Adam Smith included, viewed improved agriculture, rather than industrial manufactures or mercantile trade with the colonies, as the principle vehicle of primitive accumulation necessary to establish the 'wealth of a nation'.[18]

Agricultural improvement wasn't entirely the product of the 1707 Act of Union with England, as the pre-Union Scottish Parliament had already got the ball rolling by passing an 'Act anent Lands lying Runrig' in 1695,[19] authorizing the abolition of the old system. Runrig (sometimes anglicized as 'runridge or mixed property') [Aiton, p. 69] was a system of communal land tenure practised over much of pre-improvement Scotland, whereby 'rigs' or arable strips of land were periodically reallocated to ensure an equitable distribution of land. Several families, co-habiting in the same 'ferm toun', shared the rent and allocated land by lots. This practice, and its Highland equivalent the *bailtean* [Whatley, p. 111] was dismissed by the agricultural improver Sir John Sinclair as 'Republican farming', at a time when the term was associated with the national enemy, revolutionary France.[20] Shared tenancies of this kind were on the decline in Burns's Ayrshire, but farmers still helped each other out with ploughing and harvesting. Labour on the Burns's farms was characteristic of south-west Scotland, insofar as the work was done by the sons and daughters of the farmer, as well as by a handful of unmarried labourers and servants, who formed a temporary part of the household. Cotters, who received their cot houses in lieu of a wage, were less numerous here than in the north-east, and were in the process of being rapidly cleared from the 'improved' rural landscape, as we'll see in Chapter 7's discussion of 'The Cotter's Saturday Night'.

Gavin Sprott writes of runrig,

the arable land was divided into the *croft* land which lay by the farmstead, and the *outfield*. The croft land was under almost constant crop, with a simple rotation of perhaps three seasons of oats, one of *bigg*, an old form of barley, and sometimes a crop of pease, and increasingly at this time, one year of fallow. The outfield was cropped with oats for three or four years in succession, until the return did not repay the labour, and the exhausted ground was left as grazing to recover for five or six years. The croft land got most of the

---

[18] See especially John Dwyer, 'Virtue and Improvement: The Civic World of Adam Smith', in Peter Jones and Andrew S. Skinner (eds.), *Adam Smith Reviewed* (Edinburgh: Edinburgh University Press, 1992), 190–216, and Eric Hobsbawm, 'Capitalisme et Agriculture: Les Reformateurs Ecossais au XVIIIe Siècle', *Annales* 33 (1978), 580–601.

[19] James Handley, *The Agricultural Revolution in Scotland* (Glasgow: Burns, 1973), 17.

[20] Rosalind Mitchison, *Agricultural Sir John: The Life of Sir John Sinclair of Ulbster, 1754–1835* (London: Geoffrey Bles, 1962), 149.

manure, the outfield very little. Beyond the outfield lay the permanent grazing, in Ayrshire just *the muir*, and generally known as *commonty*.[21]

'Commonties', moorlands, and other marginal lands were crucial for the survival of the cottars and others at the bottom of the rural hierarchy, who claimed customary grazing rights, as well as access to peat and turf for fuel, and stone, timber, heather, and bracken for building [Devine, *TRS*, p.142].

Even after the abolition of the mixed tenancy system, one of the major legacies of runrig around Burns's farms at Lochlie or Mossgiel was the laying out of unenclosed ploughed land in long strips or rigs which 'often snaked in shallow curves, up to thirty feet broad in the middle and tapering at the ends'.[22] Sometimes raised three feet above the *furrs* or furrows, rigs served as a primitive drainage system in a rainy environment, but made for difficult ploughing when four-horse team had to be driven at an oblique angle with the hooves of the outside animals mired in the muddy furrows. Clayey, unimproved soil rendered James Small's lighter two-horse ploughs unusable in eighteenth-century Ayrshire, despite the iconic image of Burns driving a Small's plough dressed in his Sunday best.[23] The shadows of the old rigs can still be seen on poor Scottish farmland or hillsides where extensive ploughing hasn't levelled them; memorials of an older rural landscape in which rectangular enclosed fields, stock-proof thorn hedges, dry-stane dykes, field ditches, and plantations were unknown.

Improvers frequently described the old farming in heavily pejorative language, evident in Burns's acquaintance Col. William Fullarton's *General View of the Agriculture of the County of Ayr* (1793); 'the farm houses were mere hovels, moated with clay . . . the dunghill at the door; the cattle starving and the people wretched. The land was over-run with weeds and rushes, gathered into very high, broad, serpentine ridges, interrupted with large baulks, such as still disgrace the agriculture of some English counties' [Fullarton, p. 9]. He resorted to a list of litotes to evoke this negation of rational farming; 'No fallows,—no green crops,—no sown grass,—no carts or wagons,—no stack yards; hardly a potato, or any other esculent root, and indeed no garden vegetables; unless a few Scotch Kail, which, with milk and oatmeal, formed the diet of the people' [ibid.].[24]

[21] Sprott, *Robert Burns, Farmer*, 10–11. For a discussion of cultural perceptions of the English open-field system, the nearest equivalent to runrig, in relation to parliamentary enclosures, see Barrell, *Idea of Landscape*, 98–109; Rachel Crawford, *Poetry, Enclosure and the Vernacular Landscape, 1700–1830* (Cambridge: Cambridge University Press, 2002), 45–64.

[22] Sprott, *Robert Burns, Farmer*, 13. In England, the equivalent to a 'rig' in the open-field system was a 'land'; 'a long piece of ground, ploughed into a ridge, running the whole length of a furlong—often about 200 yards—and anything between ten or twenty times longer than it was wide'. (The equivalent of a 'furlong' was the Scots 'ploughgang'.) Barrell, *Idea of Landscape*, 98.

[23] Sprott, *Robert Burns, Farmer*, 44–5.

[24] The potato was a relative newcomer to the Lowlands in the 1770s, although it is mentioned in both Burns's 'Holy Willie's Prayer' and 'The Brigs of Ayr': James Handley, *The Agricultural Revolution Revolution in Scotland* (Glasgow: John S. Burns & Sons, 1963), 29.

The removal of the seat of government from Edinburgh to London in 1707 had left the Scottish landed class leisure to 'cultivate their gardens' in the clubbable manner associated with enlightenment improvement, emulating the patriotic obsession of their social peers in Norfolk and other English counties. In 1723 Adam Cockburn of Ormiston and a group of landowners founded 'The Society of Improvers in the Knowledge of Agriculture in Scotland', the first agricultural society in Europe, which 'worked to make the new agriculture rational, damned custom as superstition and propagandized for [Jethro] Tull's system north of the border'.[25] The poet Allan Ramsay praised the Society in an unpublished poem of 1723 entitled 'The Pleasures of Improvement in Agriculture': 'continou Best of Clubs Long to Improve | your native Plains and ain your nations Love | Rowse evry Lazy Laird of each wide field | that unmanurd not half their Product yeild' [Ramsay, iii. 171–2 ll. 52–5]. In 1698 Cockburn had granted a longer lease than was usual to his tenant Robert Wight, and Wight became a sort of agricultural guinea pig, the first tenant in Scotland to enclose his farm with ditch and hedge and plant trees at his own expense. His son Alexander Wight continued the pioneering work and was recruited by the 10th Earl of Eglinton to initiate improvements on his estates in north Ayrshire in the 1740s and 1750s. Eglinton's 'Society for improving of Agriculture and Manufactures in the Shire of Ayr' failed to outlive its founder after he was murdered by a poacher in 1769. Nonetheless, improvement appears to have made slow progress in Ayrshire as in lowland Scotland generally, and the runrig system persevered well into the 1760s [Devine, *TRS*, p. 30].[26]

After the defeat of the 1745 Rebellion, legislation delivered the forfeited estates of the exiled landowners into the hands of the State, or the Board of Trustees, under the direction of Henry Home, Lord Kames (1696–1782), perhaps more than any other single individual the pivotal figure in the Scottish Enlightenment. The commissioners sought to assimilate the Gaels to lowland Scotland as an integrated part of 'North Britain', through communications, improved farming, military recruitment, and missionary activity by the Presbyterian Society for the Propagation of Christian Knowledge. Kames, a close associate of chemists and natural philosophers William Cullen, Joseph Black, and James Hutton, sponsored research and lecturing in soil chemistry and commissioned Andrew Wight (1719–92; son of Alexander) to tour the thirteen annexed estates and report on the progress of improvement.[27]

---

[25] Ibid. 73–4; Simon Schaffer, 'The Earth's Fertility as a Social Fact in Early Modern Britain', in Mikulas Teich, Roy Porter, and Bo Gustafsson (eds.), *Nature and Society in Historical Context* (Cambridge: Cambridge University Press, 1997), 124–47, 137; David D. McElroy, 'The Literary Clubs and Societies of Eighteenth-Century Scotland' (Ph.D. thesis, Edinburgh University, 1952), 19.

[26] See also Handley, *Agricultural Revolution*, 6, 8, 75.

[27] See Jean Jones, 'James Hutton's Agricultural Research and his Life as a Farmer', *Annals of Science* 42 (1985), 573–601, for the links between the practical concerns of the improving farmer and new research in the earth sciences.

The success of this survey resulted in a further ten surveys covering more than 4,000 miles and reporting on nearly the whole of Scotland, published between 1778 and 1784 under the title *Present State of Husbandry in Scotland*. In the preface to the 1778 volume, Wight (or possibly Kames himself) underlined the role of enlightened reason in transforming the rural economy: 'while the bulk of our farmers are creeping in the beaten path of miserable husbandry, without knowing better, or even wishing to know better, several men of genius, shaking off the fetters of custom, have traced out new paths for themselves, and have been successful, even beyond expectation', even if in the eyes of their 'slovenly neighbours' they were no more than 'giddy-headed projectors'.[28] Wight's encomia on the patriotic Ayrshire landowners who were struggling to bring their county out of agricultural backwardness is echoed in the county reports of Fullarton and his successor, William Aiton's of 1811, and resonates in the 'georgic eulogy' of Burns's poem 'The Vision'.

Given that one major bugbear of the landed improvers was over-cropping (exhausting the acid soil of south-west Scotland with annual plantings of oats, etc., dismissed by Aiton as 'scourge crops')[29] tenants were urged to sow grasses and practise more regular fallowing on newly enclosed land. As William Mackintosh of Borlum had put it as early as 1729 (at the time of writing he was a Jacobite political prisoner confined to Edinburgh Castle), '*Fallow* is the life of improvement: for however better and more beautiful *Inclosing* and *Planting* will render our Country, 'tis *Fallow* will readily make it fertile and rich'.[30] To promote such ends, landlords issued 'improving leases' that prescribed innovatory crop rotations and 'best practice'; a system of financial penalties was in force for tenants who failed to comply with the terms of the leases, although more enlightened lairds also offered financial subsidies for limning, manuring, and enclosing by way of encouragement. James Handley quotes a typical clause inserted in the tacks for some small farms on the estate of Capt. Cunningham of Thornton in the parish of Kilmaurs, near Kilmarnock, in February 1779 that illustrates the sort of pressure the leases placed on tenants:

It is agreed that until the Lands shall be Inclosed the Tenant shall plow and rest them so as not to Run them out. But after Inclosed as after-mentioned they must be Rested for six years after laid down to rest in Grass and no part to be plowed more than three successive crops, nor more than one third thereof shall be in Tillage at one time Excepting sixteen

[28] Andrew Wight, *Present State of Husbandry in Scotland, Extracted from Reports made to the Commissioners of the Annexed Estates and Published by their Authority*, 2 vols. (Edinburgh, 1778), i pp. vii, x.

[29] Aiton, p. 253.

[30] William Mackintosh of Borlum, *An Essay on the Ways and Means for Inclosing, Fallowing, Planting, etc. Scotland . . . By a Lover of his Country* (Edinburgh, 1729). Published by the Society of Improvers.

acres thereof to be managed as Croft Land which sixteen acres is to be laid off by itself and Inclosed by the Tenant at his own expense.[31]

Landowners and their factors were assiduous in enforcing such leases, threatening legal action and eviction in the case of non-compliance. In 1793 James Boswell wrote to his factor at Auchinleck that their terms 'must be followed without relaxation . . . no Estate can flourish where the tenants are not kept to steady order and regularity' [Whatley, p. 238]. Punitive as they could sound, improving leases (at least in theory) represented a contractual agreement between laird and tenant. William Burnes, struggling to improve poor farm land at Lochlie (not far from Thornton's Kilmaurs), had problems of a different nature arising from the fact that his landlord David McLure, an Ayr merchant, omitted to issue him with a written lease, a fact which contributed largely to the disastrous litigation that followed in the years 1782–4 [Mackay, p. 68].[32]

Farmers understandably objected that 'they are poor, and cannot forgo the want of a crop, and one crop cannot be expected to make up the loss of two'.[33] Improving land for farmers often meant exchanging the old cycle, however precarious, for present dearth and debt, with only the promise of better crops in future, a prospect more beguiling to their landlords than to tenants. In *Wealth of Nations*, which (unusually) took account of the conflicting interests of landowners and tenant farmers, Adam Smith criticized the former for charging rent on unimproved land which included the 'supposed interest or profit upon the expense of improvement', especially when the cost was born by the tenant rather than the landlord. High rents were adjusted to potential yield rather than current capacity in a harsh bid to 'incentivize' recalcitrant farmers. Smith also attacked rents set at a 'monopoly price' proportioned to the maximum sum that the tenant could afford to pay, rather than the improved or unimproved condition of the land, equivalent to 'rack-renting' [*Wealth of Nations*, i. 249]. Some landlords did recognize the difficulties facing tenant farmers, like Adam Fergusson of Kilkerran (Burns's 'aith-detesting, chaste *Kilkerran*') [K 81 l. 74] who noted that 'what I have said of the expense attending the improvement of land here, will shew how difficult it must be for many, without a great stock, to carry it very far'.[34] Inflexibility on the part of landlords proved the ruination (or near-ruination) of many tenants; in the case of William Burnes referred to above, the absence of a written lease resulted in McLure's denial (in claiming £500 worth of arrears in rent) that his tenant had actively laboured in improving the

---

[31] Quoted by Handley, *Agricultural Revolution*, 20. See also *TRS* Appendix 8 for full text of 'Improving Lease', Lockhart of Lee Estate, Lanarkshire, 1799, pp. 196–200.

[32] Fowler attributes this to the fact that McLure 'felt, or knew, that his title to the land was far from clear'. *Robert Burns*, 127.

[33] A quote from Mackintosh's *Treatise* which specifically addressed recalcitrant tenants on this matter. Quoted in James Fergusson, *Lowland Lairds* (London: Faber & Faber, 1959), 90.

[34] Reported in Wight, *Present State*, iii. 163.

boggy upland arable of Lochlie by carting soil worth more than the value of the half-yearly rental. McLure reneged on his original verbal agreement to pay for draining and liming, although in the end the law found against him [Mackay, p. 69].[35]

In 1776, the same year as the *Wealth of Nations*, Lord Kames had published his own influential book *The Gentleman Farmer*, one of the titles purchased by the Ayr Library Society in its year of publication.[36] Citing Pliny, Cato, and other classical authorities, Kames argued that 'agriculture justly claims to be the chief of arts: it enjoys besides the signal pre-eminence, of combining deep philosophy with useful practice'.[37] Although Kames's collaboration with Andrew Wight revealed that improvement was best practised in the spirit of collaboration between landowner and tenant, the book's title underlined Kames's concern with refashioning the moral and social identity of the landed gentry itself; 'how delightful the change, from the hunter to the farmer, from the destroyer of animals to the feeder of men!'[38] Active exertion on behalf of improvement offered the gentleman farmer health, happiness, social utility, and above all, an opportunity for patriotism: 'every gentleman farmer must of course be a patriot, for patriotism, like other virtues, is improved and fortified by exercise'. 'In fact', he added on a more disconsolate note, 'if there is any remaining patriotism in a nation, it is found among that class of men'.[39] As we'll see below, agrarian patriotism would become a dominant ideology in late eighteenth-century Britain.

Kames and his protégé Wight frequently represented 'rational' agriculture—abolition of the runrig system, enclosure and the planting of hedges and trees, crop rotation and fallowing, straightening and levelling of plough ridges, liming and manuring of soil, stock breeding, etc.—as a battle against custom and superstition, like James Thomson's 'Knight of Arts and Industry' banishing the 'Wizard of Sloth' in his 1732 poem *The Castle of Indolence*. In each county of Scotland Wight and his correspondents (he established a correspondence network to elicit information from landowners whom he had missed during his tours) eulogized a heroic band of enlightened landowners struggling against the 'torpor'—a frequently used term—of tenants adhering to old irrational practices, although occasionally a 'good tenant' was singled out for praise. The unimproved estate was described as 'being in a state of nature: no houses, no inclosures, no

---

[35] Burnes and his sons also procured lime from Cairnhill kilns to fertilize Lochlie's acidic fields (Mackay, p. 84).

[36] Strawhorn, 'Ayrshire and the Enlightenment', 196.

[37] Henry Home, Lord Kames, *The Gentleman Farmer. Being an attempt to Improve Agriculture, by subjecting it to the test of rational principles* (Edinburgh 1776), p. v. See Heinzelman, 'The Last Georgic: Wealth of Nations and the Scene of Writing', in Stephen Copley and Kathryn Sutherland (eds.), Adam Smith's *Wealth of Nations: New Interdisciplinary Essays* (Manchester: University of Manchester Press, 1995), 181.

[38] Home, *Gentleman Farmer*, p. xviii.

[39] Ibid. p. xvii.

wood, no lime or coal'.[40] Traditionally arable was gendered as female, and unimproved land often appeared in the discourse of Wight and his peers as an abject and tormented damsel, crying out to be rescued by chivalric improvers. Steele of Gadgirth, for example, wrote to Wight in a letter published in the *First Survey of Ayrshire*: 'as to the grounds which have been scratched and scourged by the tenants before I came to be in possession of it, they were such poor, hungry objects, and so cursed for the sake of their former persecutors, as made me despair of ever rousing them into a state of vigour and fertility; for even resting them did little or no good'.[41]

Despite Andrew Wight's frequent animadversions on Scotland's 'torpid' tenantry, at moments he recalled his own social background in a gesture of solidarity with the tenant class. For instance, while strongly recommending Kames's *Gentleman Farmer*, he proposed that if Kames had 'chose[n] to make his title page less formidable to poor country farmers, it would be more genuinely read, and I know of no book so proper to be consulted'.[42] Wight's concern to disseminate the spirit of improvement lower down the social scale was shared by the Aberdonian laird Sir Archibald Grant of Monymusk, who in 1757 published a homespun manual of improvement aimed at tenant farmers and entitled *The Farmer's New-Year Gift to his Countrymen, Heritors and Farmers* (it is discussed further in Chapter 5). Grant urged tenants and landowners 'to promote each other's advantage' in the business of improvement, so that while the former should avoid imposing high rents, the latter shouldn't refuse reasonable ones. Good husbandry permitted the wide social dissemination of civic virtue amongst the ranks of the unenfranchised small farmer: 'the most obscure person, and the most distant situations, can by his own practice and the influence which that may have upon others, be of real service to the community of which he is a member'.[43] The public ambitions of improvement extended beyond the usual limits of eighteenth-century civil society, an important consideration for understanding Burns's own relationship to the public sphere.

Elsewhere, however, Grant fulminated against backward tenants who 'will keep straightly to the old way...A great many of you are idle and trifle away a good deal of your time...As to your poor living I am sorry for it, but it is your own fault'.[44] It is hardly surprising that the estate papers of the Grants of Monymusk reveal frequent acts of sabotage committed under cover of darkness by those who appeared perfectly tractable in daylight; pilfering, breaking

---

[40] Observed of a Fife estate in 1782; quoted in Devine, *TRS*, p. 61.
[41] Andrew Wight, *Present State of Husbandry in Scotland* (Edinburgh, 1784), iii. 189.
[42] Ibid. 259.
[43] Archibald Grant, *The Farmer's New-Year Gift to his Countrymen, Heritors and Farmers* (Aberdeen, 1757), 33.
[44] Quoted in Fergusson, *Lowland Lairds*, 91.

enclosures, stealing peats and timber, damaging bridges, trespassing.[45] To be sure, this kind of sabotage was more likely to have been the work of cotters or landless labourers than Grant's tenants, but many of the latter also doubtless viewed the project of improvement as 'a ruinous bargain'.[46] William Fullarton regretted that in the early 1790s tenant farmers near manufacturing districts, influenced by Jacobin ideas, had formed radical 'associations' and pledged 'never to offer any marks of civility, to any person in the character of a gentleman'. He proposed the formation of loyalist counter-associations to counter this insubordination, and recommended a proactive use of improving leases to tame refractory tenants [Fullarton, pp. 69–70].[47] He blamed the rise of manufactures for the radicalization of the traditionally loyal tenant class: '[manufacture] is a dangerous instrument of improvement, while the plough and the spade have never threatened any peril to the country' [Fullarton, p. 88]. Agricultural improvement in late eighteenth-century Scotland may have been 'revolutionary' in a socio-economic, but certainly not in a political sense.

## 'PROSE GEORGICS': BURNS AND THE IDEOLOGY OF IMPROVEMENT

Soaring rents, exaggerated landlord expectations, and chronic lack of capital were only some of the problems which Robert and Gilbert Burns shared with other lowland tenants. While lairds employed both sticks and carrots, their tenants often complained about the landowners' blindness to practical conditions on the ground. Robert Burns exemplifies the predicament of the farmer at once stimulated by the ideological energy of improvement, and stymied by practical difficulties in implementing it. In his 1787 autobiographical letter to Dr John Moore he describes how (upon entering into the joint tenancy of Mossgiel farm with his brother Gilbert in 1784):

I read farming books; I calculated crops; I attended markets; and in short, in spite of 'The devil, the world and the flesh,' I believe I would have been a wise man; but the first year from unfortunately buying in bad seed, the second from a late harvest, we lost half of both our crops: this overset all my wisdom, and I returned 'Like the dog to his vomit . . .' [CL i. 143].[48]

---

[45] See H. Hamilton, *Selections from the Monymusk Papers, 1713–1755* (Edinburgh: Scottish History Society, 1945), 'Introduction'. Also Christopher Whatley, 'How Tame Were the Scottish Lowlanders during the Eighteenth Century?' in T. M. Devine (ed.), *Conflict and Stability in Scottish Society, 1700–1850* (Edinburgh: John Donald, 1990), 1–30 at 22.

[46] There seems to have been little organized resistance to improvement, however. See Devine *TRS* p. 66 and T. C. Smout, *A History of the Scottish People 1560–1830* (London: Fontana, 1998), 310.

[47] According to his New *DNB* entry, Fullarton had himself briefly joined the 'Friends of the People' in 1792, so this perhaps represented a bid to clear his name of imputed radicalism.

[48] Fowler points out that 'virtually all seed on the Scottish market for the 1784 sowing would have been bad seed, produced under the appalling weather conditions of 1782–3', *Robert Burns*, 132.

To make things even worse, Mossgiel was a high and wind-swept farm with 'a cold wet bottom', and the top-soil had been 'skinned' for building turf in the recent past, so its degraded soil presented a huge challenge to the Burns brothers.[49]

As we've seen, Burns grew up in an improving milieu. His father was by profession a gardener and horticulturalist who had helped landscape the Meadows in Edinburgh before moving west, where in 1750 he was employed by Ayrshire's pioneering improver Alexander Fairlie of Fairlie near Kilmarnock (subsequently factor to the Earl of Eglinton), and later Dr Fergusson of Doonholm, a retired London physician who was subsequently Provost of Ayr. In 'The Twa Dogs' Burns portrayed 'poor tenant bodies, scant of cash' having to 'thole a Factor's snash' [K 71 ll. 95–6] a description based on his own bitter memories of factorial bullying at Mount Oliphant. But in point of fact, he had close personal associations with Scotland's factorial class. His friend and agricultural adviser John Tennant of Glenconner (1725–1810) was factor to the Countess of Glencairn at Ochiltree.[50] Gavin Hamilton, dedicatee of the Burns's Kilmarnock volume, was factor to the Earl of Loudoun, while his close friends John Kennedy and John McMurdo were factors to, respectively, the Earl of Dumfries and the Duke of Queensberry at Drumlanrig Castle [see K 87, K 546]. In 1804 Burns's brother Gilbert became factor on the East Lothian estates of Lady Katherine Blantyre, where he moved with his mother, Burns's illegitimate daughter Bess, and their unmarried sisters [Mackay, p. 680].

Perhaps most notable of all, the father of Burns's friend Robert Ainslie (1734–94; he was also 'Robert') was factor to the Earl of Douglas and, as Tom Devine has shown in the chapter largely dedicated to Ainslie in *The Transformation of Rural Scotland*, one of the most notable agricultural improvers in eighteenth-century Scotland [Devine, *TRS*, pp. 82–92]. Burns visited Ainslie Senior at Berrywell, near Duns, on his Borders tour and, regarding his views on agriculture, wrote 'he is unexceptionably the clearest-headed, best-informed man I ever met with'.[51] The pastoral myth of the 'Heav'n taught ploughman' has occluded Burns's proximity to this branch of the 'rural professional class', effective executors of the social and economic transformation of late eighteenth-century rural Scotland.

---

[49] Sprott, *Robert Burns, Farmer*, 34.

[50] He was also father of James Tennant, addressee of Burns's 'Letter to James Tennant' [K 90], and of Charles Tennant, founder of Glasgow's St Rollox chemical works, and one of the biggest industrial dynasties of nineteenth-century Britain.

[51] *Robert Burns's Tour of the Borders*, 16. Ainslie's senior's home at Berrywell is alluded to in Burns's song 'Robin Shure in Hairst' in the reproachful voice of a young woman seduced by Ainslie junior: 'I gaed up to Dunse, | To warp a web o' plaiden; | At his Daddie's yett, | Wha met me but Robin' [K 251 ll. 1–4].

William Cobbett later wrote 'every farmer is more or less of a reader'.[52] That Burns was extremely well versed in the English and Scottish poets, essayists, and novelists is evident in the creative flowering of the mid-1780s, but its less often recognized that he was also learned in the 'prose georgics' of agricultural improvement. The 1787 letter to Moore mentions that during his teenage years he read Jethro Tull's *Horse-Hoeing Husbandry* (1731) and Adam Dickson's *Treatise of Agriculture* (1762).[53] He'd also read Thomas Hitt's *Treatise on Husbandry* (London, 1760), William Marshall's *Rural Economy of Yorkshire* (1788), and James Small's *Treatise on the Ploughs and Wheel Carriages* (1784), although he never employed Small's ploughs, for good practical reasons. This is probably only the tip of the iceberg, given the flood of publications on agricultural improvements pouring from the eighteenth-century press. Keith Tribe and Kurt Heinzelman have studied the links between literary georgic, eighteenth-century agricultural treatises, and the tradition of political economy retrospectively identified with the 1776 publication of Adam Smith's *Wealth of Nations*.[54] Smith commends the farming life over that of the merchant; 'the pleasures of a country life, the tranquillity of mind which it promises, and wherever the injustice of human law does not disturb it, the independency which it really affords, have charms that more or less attract every body' [*Wealth of Nations*, ii. 481]. As we'll see, the notion of agriculture 'independence' certainly had the strongest charms for Robert Burns, although personal experience may have led him to read the rest of this passage with considerable scepticism.

In addition to his practical experience of farming at Lochlie and his study of ploughing techniques, at the age of 17 Burns undertook a training course in 'Mensuration, Surveying, Dialling etc' in Kirkoswald (from which, he wrote, 'I returned home very considerably improved') [CL i. 140]: this clearly represents Burns's vocational aspirations, given that it was the kind of training undertaken by estate surveyors and would-be factors. In an attempt to repair the family's capital deficit and supplement the losses incurred in mainstream farming, he sought to establish a flax-dressing business in Irvine in 1781–2. Unfortunately the premises were destroyed by a Hogmanay fire, a disaster which put paid to the scheme, but in January of the following year (1783) he received the consolation of being awarded a £3 premium by the Commissioners and Trustees for Fisheries, Manufactures and Improvers in Scotland for 'lint[flax] seed saved for sowing'. Mackay describes flax as the 'wonder crop of the 1780s', and reminds us that Burns's apparently insignificant prize was equivalent to half a year's wage for the average farm labourer of the period. [Mackay, pp. 93–4].

---

[52] Quoted in Heinzelman, 'The Last Georgic', 171.

[53] Dickson's book is omitted from John Robotham's list of 'Burns's Reading' published in the *Bulletin of the New York Public Library*, 74 (Nov. 1970), 561–76.

[54] Keith Tribe, *Land, Labour and Economic Discourse* (London: RKP, 1978), 52–79; Heinzelman, 'The Last Georgic'.

Taking his cue from famous English stockbreeders such as Robert Bakewell of Leicester, Burns experimented with sheep breeding at Mossgiel (discussed in Chapter 5) and later introduced Ayrshire cattle to Nithsdale, as well as proposing a new method for dehorning young cattle to the agricultural improver William Fullarton, who personally commended Burns in his report to the Board of Agriculture [Fullarton, p. 58 n.]. Burns also demonstrated an expert knowledge of soil chemistry in describing his quest for limestone to manure the acidic soil of Ellisland in a 1790 letter to William Nicol (his friend, classics master at Edinburgh's High School, had purchased a farm in Dumfriesshire): 'we certainly found a species of stone all along the burn, sometimes in thick Strata & sometimes in loose pieces, which effervesced, & in several instances pretty strongly with the acid' [CL ii. 27]. Incidentally, this helps explain the mystery (raised by Fowler) concerning Burns's refusal to negotiate a liming contract with his landlord Patrick Miller when he took on the lease of Ellisland in 1788.[55] Burns preferred to spend Miller's £300 grant for improvements on a better farmhouse for his newly-wed wife Jean Armour and their young child, confident that there was a viable lime quarry on his land, and that he possessed the technical skill to locate and excavate it.

In 1788, Burns's patroness Mrs Francis Dunlop even thought highly enough of the poet's agricultural expertise to propose him for the new Chair of Agriculture at Edinburgh University, established by Sir William Pulteney with an endowment of £1,250. The job description specified one 'regularly bred to science, or at least interested in the studies of mechanics, chemistry, botany and natural history . . . acquainted with the maxims of observation and investigation in these sciences; active also to collect practical information; and of sound judgement, not to substitute abstract reasoning for practical rules on subjects so complicated in their actual circumstances and combinations'.[56] Burns, aware of his social disqualification, dismissed his candidacy for the Chair as 'an idle project' [CL i. 398]; sure enough, it went to Dr Andrew Coventry, an improving landowner from Kinross, whose innovative lectures were enthusiastically described by the young German historian Niebuhr, then a student at Edinburgh.[57] If Burns had ever been appointed to this unlikely professorial role, he'd doubtless have drawn upon personal experience to warn his students against a panglossian application of abstract theory to the practice of farming.

Like many modern farmers in the developing world, Burns was caught in limbo between the old and new agriculture, a hopeless, catch-22 predicament insightfully analysed by Adam Smith in the *Wealth of Nations*. Acknowledging the problem of 'ignorance and attachment to old customs' among some tenants (certainly not the tenant of Mossgiel) Smith wrote:

---

[55] Fowler, p. 147.
[56] Handley, *Agricultural Revolution*, 83.
[57] Ibid. 84.

the increase of stock and the improvement of land are two events which must go hand in hand, and of which the one can nowhere much out-run the other. Without some increase of stock there can be scarce any improvement of land, but there can be no considerable increase of stock but in consequence of a considerable improvement of land; because otherwise the land could not maintain it. These natural obstructions to the establishment of a better system cannot be removed but by a long course of frugality and industry; and half a century more, perhaps, must pass away before the old system ... can be completely abolished through all the different parts of the country. [*Wealth of Nations*, i. 327–8]

This impossible stand-off between available capital and improvement, I'll suggest in Chapter 3, was a formative pressure on Burns's turn to poetry as an alternative source of 'credit' in the crises years of 1784–5.

In June 1783, in the midst of the famine caused by successive bad harvests and the crisis of his father's litigation with McClure, Burns wrote to his cousin James Burnes, who, having abandoned farming, was prospering as a member of the urban bourgeoisie: he became a successful lawyer, and his son Provost of Montrose. Robert described the lamentable economic conditions that prevailed in Ayrshire, summing up many of the problems discussed in the preceding pages:

Farming is also at a very low ebb with us. Our lands, generally speaking, are mountainous & barren; and our Landholders, full of ideas of farming gathered from the English, and the Lothians and other rich soils in Scotland; make no allowance for the odds of the quality of land, and consequently stretch us much beyond what, in the event, we will be found able to pay. We are also much at a loss for want of proper methods in our improvements of farming: necessity compels us to leave our old schemes; & few of us have opportunities of being well informed in new ones'.   [CL i. 19].[58]

Quite apart from the vicious circle in which improving tenants were trapped, not to mention the disastrous weather conditions of 1782–5, farming, like manufacturing, was also a victim of the prevailing economic crisis: the disastrous debacle of the American war, the collapse of the Ayr Bank in 1772 (eighteenth-century Scotland's nearest equivalent to the Mississippi Company in France and the South Sea Bubble in England), and debts incurred by the over-ambitious building projects of the Ayrshire aristocracy. Rents and labour costs rocketed, and there was no equivalent increase to be had from a stubborn, undrained, and only partially enclosed farmland, its acidic soil still in the early stages of improvement, in which oats and barley were the only viable crops. The fact that the Burns family still raised the old black cattle for beef rather than milk reflects the poor grazing available on Lochlie farm, although they showed initiative in cultivating flax and wheat as well as the usual staples, in addition to implementing other improvements such as liming, ditching, and soil replacement.[59]

---

[58]  Note that Fullerton, himself an Ayrshire laird, made exactly the same point ten years later; 'the indiscriminate adoption of plans and systems, formed for other districts, soils and climates, was liable to infinite objections' [p. 17].

[59]  Sprott, *Robert Burns, Farmer*, 33–4.

I've referred above to the nightmare of William Burnes's litigation with his landlord, David McClure, which provides the background to the 1783 letter quoted above. McClure was himself in dire financial straits as a result of the Douglas Heron Bank crash, and, as we've seen, reneged on his (unwritten) promise to supplement the high rent of £130 per annum by providing lime for manuring, drainage, and other services. He issued a warrant of sequestration when the terminally ill William Burnes refused to pay the £500 back rent he demanded, on the grounds that the sum failed to take account of the improvements he had wrought since 1777. Although evidence that Burnes had been a diligent improver helped him win his case, thereby halving the rental backlog (which he duly paid), it transpired that McClure had been forced to mortgage his estate to another party, so the case ended up before Lord Braxfield at the Court of Session. William Burnes prevailed in the end, but anxiety caused by the threat of imprisonment, and (even after Braxfield's favourable judgement) steep legal costs, precipitated his death from tuberculosis on 13 February 1784. McLure was himself sequestrated in 1783, in debt to the tune of a staggering £45,383; it subsequently transpired that his legal claim to the land had been suspect all along [Mackay, pp. 109–17].

But the Burns brothers had already sprung to the initiative: as Gilbert later explained,

when my father's affairs grew near a crisis, Robert and I took the farm of Mossgiel . . . from Mr Gavin Hamilton, as an asylum for the family in case of the worst. It was stocked by the property and individual savings of the whole family, and was a joint concern among us. Every member of the family was allowed ordinary wages for the labour he performed on the farm. My brother's allowance and mine was £7 per annum each. [Mackay, p.125]

As a result of buying bad seed and a late harvest they lost half their crops in the first year alone. In a depressing repeat of the Lochlie experience, the landowner of Mossgiel, the 5th Earl of Loudoun (from whom Gavin Hamilton sublet) was himself heavily burdened with debt, and committed suicide in April 1786. His heirs were forced to auction off a substantial acreage of the Loudoun estates, including Mossgiel farm. As Fowler notes, with their credit rating low after the Lochlie litigation, 'the prospect of Robert and Gilbert raising a [bank]loan had now become very dim'.[60] It wasn't just the writ issued by James Armour against his daughters's seducer, and the unwelcome attentions of the 'houghmagandie pack', that determined Robert 'to publish and be damned' and flee to Jamaica. Farming as a livelihood seemed a practical impossibility, despite the stirring rhetoric of the improvers. As Burns memorably expressed the tenant's predicament, in the midst of that crisis; 'the best laid schemes o' *Mice* an' *Men*, | Gang

---

[60] Fowler, *Robert Burns*, 136.

aft agley, | An' lea'e us nought but grief an' pain, | For promis'd joy' [K 69 ll. 39–42].

Although Burns had seized the opportunity of educating himself in the theory and practice of improvement, like other farmers of his station he was stuck with limited capital resources, at a relatively early stage of 'primitive accumulation'. Poetry offered Burns the prospect of more than just a vent for his frustrations as a struggling farmer. Allan Cunningham and J. G. Lockhart initiated the romantic myth (the seeds of which were however laid by the poet himself) that Burns failed as a farmer precisely because of his whimsical poetic temperament; 'he was too wayward to attend to the stated duties of a husbandman, and too impatient to wait till the ground returned in gain the cultivation he bestowed upon it' [Lockhart, p. 143]. Despite the frequent 'boast of independence' that permeates much of his writing in this period and subsequently, Burns, like many other Lowland tenant farmers, was actually in a hopeless position of dependence as rents and prices soared.

From this perspective, ideologies of agrarian virtue and pastoral independence seemed to be cherished illusions. In a 1792 letter to Frances Dunlop, Burns highlighted social division in distinguishing between the ideal and the reality of agriculture:

'Tis, as a Farmer, paying dear, unconscionable rent, a *cursed life*!—As to a LAIRD farming his own property; sowing corn in hope, & reaping it, in spite of brittle weather, in gladness; knowing that none can say unto him, 'What dost thou!'—fattening his herds; shearing his flocks; rejoicing at Christmas; & begetting sons & daughters, until he be the venerated, grey-haired leader of a little Tribe—'tis a heavenly life!—but devil take the life of reaping the fruits that another must eat. [CL ii. 152]

In the chapters that follow, we'll see how Burns's predicament as a tenant farmer profoundly influenced the politics and social vision of the poems published in the Kilmarnock volume.

## 'AGRARIAN PATRIOTISM' AND SIR JOHN SINCLAIR'S *STATISTICAL ACCOUNT*

I will conclude this chapter by considering the wider ideological ramifications of improvement and its effects on Scottish (and British) society as a whole, in order to understand better the climate of opinion which afforded Burns's poetry such a favourable reception in 1787. Despite the dire human costs of the booms and busts of capital, the institutional pace of agricultural improvement in Scotland (as in England) greatly accelerated after the loss of Britain's 'first empire' in America in 1782. When the MP and agricultural improver Thomas Coke of Holkham went to inform King George III that Parliament had voted to end the American war, he hinted at the causes of British defeat by donning the plain russet clothes of a Norfolk yeoman (the colonial farmer militias were reputed to be 'clothed in homespun'). In the mid-1780s 'agrarian patriotism' represented a species of moral rearmament against the luxury and effeminacy that seemed responsible for the humiliating defeat of British forces by American farmers and backwoodsmen, inspirited by patriotic zeal and republican virtue.

Richard Drayton has argued that although earlier in the eighteenth century agricultural improvement had been associated with the 'country' party, who considered that 'liberty and sovereignty rose upwards from the landowners to the monarch . . . after 1783 . . . both George III and Pitt the Younger attempted to appropriate 'improvement' as a cause, respectively, of the Crown and of the Tories. They responded to those whom [C. A.] Bayly has styled 'agrarian patriots', who had come to see agriculture as the solution to 'the moral and material crises which a defeated Britain faced'.[61] Famously, George III was an enthusiastic improver, contributing articles to the *Annals of Agriculture* under the pseudonym 'Ralph Robinson', erecting a farmyard and farm offices adjacent to Richmond gardens, and earning the soubriquet of 'Farmer George'.[62] Drayton's study *Nature's Government* shows that the ideology of improvement was not only fundamental to the internal consolidation of the British State during the years of the revolutionary and Napoleonic wars, but also shaped the administrative and economic policies of the new overseas empire in India, South Africa, the Caribbean, and Canada.

It has never been appreciated that the rapturous reception given to Burns's Kilmarnock volume by the anglicizing Scottish literati in 1786 may have been partly motivated by their belief that the poetry of the 'Heaven-taught ploughman' was the literary equivalent of Coke of Holkham's russet dress. During his sojourn in Edinburgh Burns played up to this role, dressing in farmer's boots and jacket in the drawing rooms of the polite; one contemporary noted that he 'affected a rusticity or *landertness*' that was neither 'manly [n]or natural') [Chambers–Wallace, ii. 137]. But others relished the charisma of the 'farmer poet', as is evident from Alexander Nasmyth's canonical full-length portrait of Burns in agricultural dress, represented on the dustcover of this book. By the mid-1780s the civic virtue of agricultural improvement had become an ideological obsession with the British ruling classes, as well as the professional classes and 'middling sort'.

The immediate context of the Burns phenomenon may have been Scotland's leading role in inaugurating British 'agrarian patriotism', signalled by the foundation in 1783 of the 'Highland and Agricultural Society', with branches in London and Edinburgh.[63] The Society was formed by landowning gentry from

[61] Richard Drayton, *Nature's Government: Science, Imperial Britain, and the 'Improvement' of the World* (New Haven: Yale University Press, 2000), 88.

[62] Ibid.

[63] Handley, *Agricultural Revolution*, 73; Mitchison (*Agricultural Sir John*, 88) gives an earlier date of 1778.

the north and west of Scotland, in the wake of the bad harvests and ensuing famine of 1782–3. It is often remembered for its patriotic endeavours in bringing about the repeal of the post-Culloden ban on Highland dress, promoting Ossianic researches and employing a piper and Gaelic professor: but for all its official espousal of tartanry, the Society materially benefited from moneys raised by restoring the forfeited estates to the heirs of the exiled Jacobite gentry.[64]

Its title notwithstanding, the Highland Society's remit extended to the whole of Scotland, and it spawned numerous local agricultural societies such as (in Burns country alone) the Kilmarnock Farmer's Club, the Carrick Farmer's Club, and the Symington Society and County Association.[65] In the first century of its existence the parent body dispensed the sum of £130,000 in premiums for essays on the practicalities of developing the Highlands, cattle breeding, or crop research. Given the currency of physiocratic beliefs that only a populous nation could sustain a flourishing agriculture as well as providing the military manpower for defence against foreign threats, the gentlemen of the Society (in contrast to their Highland landlord successors in the 1820s and 1830s) actively opposed the emigration of their hard-pressed Gaelic tenantry to North America. This was the occasion for Burns's bitter satire of 1786 against Lord Breadalbane and the London Highland Society in 'The Address of Beelzebub' [K 108], although it's significant that the poem was never published during his lifetime.

By far the most significant 'agricultural patriot' in late eighteenth-century Scotland, as well as in Britain at large, was the Caithness landowner and parliamentarian Sir John Sinclair of Ulbster. A man of indefatigable energy and tireless (although often tiresome) application, Sinclair put his personal experience as an improving Highland landlord to the service of the nation, establishing the British Fisheries Society (1786), the Society for the Improvement of British Wool (1790), and, after relentlessly lobbying the Prime Minister William Pitt, the institution of the Board of Agriculture in 1793. (The agricultural reports on the County of Ayrshire by Fullarton and Aiton, cited throughout this book, were written for submission to the Board in London.) The secretary of 'The Board of Agriculture and Internal Improvement' (its full title) was Arthur Young, author of *Rural Oeconomy* (1770) and editor of *Annals of Agriculture*, who had only recently pinned his colours to the government mast.[66] As we've seen, Sinclair dismissed unimproved multiple tenancies and runrig cultivation as 'republican farming', pushing for the consolidation of small farms and the enclosure of common land. C. A. Bayly writes of Sinclair's Board of Agriculture that it 'inherited the themes and attitudes of agrarian patriots and agricultural

[64] Mitchison, *Agricultural Sir John*, 89.

[65] Handley, *Agricultural Revolution*, 76. Burns felt uncomfortable in the company of the Kelso farmers, 'all gentlemen, talking of high matters', and keeping fox hunting horses 'from 30 to 50£ value'. Burns, *Tour of the Borders*, 21, 22, 25.

[66] Mitchison, *Agricultural Sir John*, 149. See also Heinzelman, 'The Last Georgic', 183–5.

societies of the eighteenth century. Its members transformed them into a scientific and statistical method for the integration of state and empire.'[67] Institutionalized at national level by such men as Sinclair, Pitt, and Henry Dundas, the Scottish Enlightenment's ideology of improvement thus played a disproportionate role in establishing the governing ideologies of Britain's 'new imperial age'.

In many respects, however, Sinclair's most enduring achievement was in planning, orchestrating, and successfully completing *The Statistical Account of Scotland*, an enormous database covering all aspects of Scottish social, economic, and cultural life, and the first modern survey of its kind, published between 1791 and 1798. Although Sinclair's Prospero-like presence permeates all twenty-one volumes, the *Statistical Account* is a huge multi-authored text composed from responses to questionnaires sent out to the ministers of 950 Church of Scotland parishes in May 1790: this was Lord Kames's, or Andrew Wight's, survey in spades. The Earl of Buchan (about whom we'll hear more in Chapter 8) had attempted a similar scheme under the auspices of the Scottish Society of Antiquaries in the 1780s, but had failed to mobilize the necessary networks for collecting data.[68]

Sinclair was upfront about his motive in resisting the shock waves from revolutionary Paris: a responsible state, solicitous for the 'real happiness' of its subjects, should exercise transparency by making facts available to them to facilitate amelioration, and in order to pre-empt the sort of 'visionary theory' that had brought down the French *ancien régime*.[69] James Handley aptly describes the *Account*'s 'cinemascopic picture' of Scotland on the cusp of the modern age: 'Agricultural Scotland from the Rhinns of Galloway to John O'Groats is captured in bold relief: soil, crops and grasses, cattle, sheep, swine, oxen and horses, size of farms, rents, leases, implements, inclosing and planting, manures, fuel, wages, prices, population, food and housing for all grades of the community, times of sowing and harvesting, methods of work, rotations, roads, vehicles, customs, superstitions, traditions, ancient monuments.'[70] The *Statistical Report* is a crucial intertext for Burns's pastoral 'manners-painting strain', casting an often-critical light on a whole society in the grip of a massive transformation into modernity.

Alexander Broadie has suggested that the characteristic disposition for improvement amongst the Scottish literati eschewed utopian idealism in favour of

[67] C. A. Bayly, *Imperial Meridian: The British Empire and the World, 1780–1830* (Harlow: Longman, 1989), 123.

[68] Rosemary Sweet, *Antiquaries: The Discovery of the Past in Eighteenth-Century Britain* (London: Hambledon & London, 2004), 90–1. Sinclair succeeded largely because he'd secured a grant of £2,000 from the King to fund a Society for the Benefit of the Sons of the Clergy, which clearly prompted the ministers of the General Assembly into action.

[69] Sir John Sinclair, *Specimens of Statistical Reports, Exhibiting the Progress of Political Society from the Pastoral State, to that of Luxury and Refinement* (London, 1793), pp. vii, ix.

[70] Handley, *Agricultural Revolution*, 99–100.

'a guarded or qualified optimism'.[71] This captures well the flavour of Sinclair's assessment of the gains and losses attendant upon improvement in his synoptic *Specimens of Statistical Reports exhibiting the Progress of Political Society from the Pastoral State, to that of Luxury and Refinement*, published in 1793 as part of an unsuccessful campaign to institute a Statistical Account of England.[72] *Specimens* illustrates the much-discussed Scottish Enlightenment's 'Four Stages' model of social development in action, making it clear that the theory applied as much to the uneven development of contemporary Scotland as to the genesis of world history.[73] In both cases development was geographically uneven, depending on a concatenation of social, economic, and ecological factors, and the reverend contributors to the survey were as quick to condemn as to praise the social and moral consequences of improvement.

Standing out rather incongruously from the proliferation of ministerial reports was an anonymous letter to Sinclair describing the role that the correspondent had played in assisting Robert Riddell of Glenriddell in establishing the 'Monk-lands Friendly Society Library', Dumfries; the letter was published as an appendix to volume iii of the *Statistical Account*. The author turns out to be none other than Robert Burns: ironically, amongst the ministers who contributing to the *Account* was his old enemy Revd 'Daddy' Auld, reporter for the parish of 'Machlin' [*Statistical Account*, vi. 445–52]. Burns's letter captures the broader social agenda of the spirit of improvement and popular enlightenment, addressing 'every country gentleman, who thinks the improvement of that part of his own species, whom chance has thrown into the humble walks of the peasant and the artisan, a matter worthy of his attention' [CL ii. 107]. After a rather patronizing snipe at some of the 'trash' ordered by the plebeian subscribers to Riddell's circulating library, Burns lists a sample of works purchased, including books by the luminaries of the Scottish Enlightenment Blair, Robertson, Hume, and Mackenzie. He concludes with the thought that 'a peasant who can read, and enjoy such books is certainly a much superior being to his neighbour, who, perhaps, stalks beside his team, very little removed, except in shape, from the brutes he drives'. Wishing success to Sinclair's 'patriotic exertions', 'THE PEASANT'

---

[71] Alexander Broadie, *The Scottish Enlightenment: The Historical Age of the Historical Nation* (Edinburgh: Birlinn, 2007), 38.

[72] It was blocked by the Anglican bishops who feared to divulge tithe income in the volatile political climate of the early 1790s.

[73] For the classic study of the 'Four Stages' Model, see Ronald Meek, *Social Science and the Ignoble Savage* (Cambridge: Cambridge University Press, 1976); for a more recent overview, Murray Pittock 'Historiography', in *The Cambridge Companion to the Scottish Enlightenment*, ed. Alexander Broadie (Cambridge: Cambridge University Press, 2003), 258–79. See also Robert McColl Millar, 'Blind Attachment to Inverterate Custom': Language Use, Language Attitude and the Rhetoric of Improvement in the first *Statistical Account*, in Marina Dossena and Charles Jones (eds.), *Insights into Late Modern English* (Berne: Peter Lang, 2003), 311–30.

signed off with characteristic panache [CL ii. 108]. It is not as a contributor to the *Statistical Account,* nor indeed as an improving farmer, that Robert Burns is remembered by posterity. Yet the connection narrows the gap between the Olympian prospect of enlightened Edinburgh, and the localized perspective of Burns the Ayrshire 'bardie', the subject of the chapters that follow.

# 2

## Scots Pastoral

Melebèus:
Huyl wè fre nâti' fèlds an' dèrest hèm
Are fors't to flè, in forran klyms to rèm;
Thù raxt at èz, aniou the shâdan bûs
O that brâd bèch, meist wù the silvan mûs
An' tèch the wu'uds, responses to thy leis
To echo bak fâr Amarillis' preis. '

(Alexander Geddes, 'The First Eklog of Virgil,
Tránslâtit into Skottis vers.')[1]

These simple bards, by simple prudence taught,
To this wise town by simple patrons brought,
In simple manner utter simple lays,
And take, with simple pensions, simple praise.

(Charles Churchill, 'The Prophecy of Famine: A Scots
Pastoral Inscribed to John Wilkes', ll. 135–8).[2]

### BURNS AND PASTORAL

Beyond its immediate appeal to the sentimental cult of 'natural genius', the image of 'Heaven-taught ploughman' was essentially a pastoral one, and as such was quite susceptible of being 'smoked' by a sceptical observer such as John Logan, as I argued in the Introduction. Although contemporaries didn't rush to identify Burns's poems as 'versions of pastoral' (any more than they recognized Wordsworth's *Lyrical Ballads* as pastoral verse)[3] this chapter proposes that the

---

[1] 'Three Scottish Poems, with a Previous Dissertation on the Scoto-Saxon Dialect', in *Transactions of the Society of the Antiquaries of Scotland*, i (Edinburgh, 1792). Geddes is here demonstrating his distinctive Scots orthography. Also included here is his translation of the *First Idyllium* of Theocritus. See note 120.

[2] *Poetical Works of Charles Churchill, with memoir, critical dissertation, and explanatory notes*, by Revd. George Gilfillan (Edinburgh: James Nichol, 1855), 66.

[3] Stuart Curran points out that although the critical attack on *Lyrical Ballads* 'never explicitly relat[ed] Wordsworth's attempt to a generic reformation . . . the terms of reproach and the standard critical vocabulary for treating pastoral—especially of Theocritus—are the same'. *Poetic Form and British Romanticism* (Oxford: Oxford University Press, 1986), 101, 100. My use of the Empsonian term 'versions' here acknowledges, in the words of Annabel Patterson, that 'defining pastoral has

Kilmarnock and Edinburgh poems represented a powerful transformation of the eighteenth-century tradition of Scots and English pastoral, imbued with a new quality of poetic realism and vernacular energy. In the pages that follow I'll explore some of the consequences of this claim, in the hope of casting new light on the meaning of Burns's poetry, as well as its subsequent critical reception.

Burns scholarship has given a wide berth to what's commonly regarded as the moribund neoclassical genre of pastoral, one which nevertheless saturated the literary marketplace in the shape of pastoral songs, dramas, elegies, romances, satires, political allegories, and (especially) love eclogues. When 'pastoral' is used in connection with Robert Burns, it is usually in the negative sense of a genre dedicated to projecting an artificial upper-class view of rural life radically alien to the natural genius of the 'heaven-taught ploughman'. The Romantic apotheosis of Burns as Scotland's national poet located him more centrally within the Ossianic tradition named by Katie Trumpener as 'Bardic Nationalism' (he appears at his most 'bardic' in the 1787 Edinburgh edition's 'Dedication to the Caledonian Hunt'); or else, in a more discriminating account preferred by modern critics, sporting with the role of 'Ayrshire bardie' in what Jeff Skoblow describes as a 'takeoff on the rhetoric of the Poet Genius industry'.[4]

In selecting the 'armorial bearings' of his art in 1794, Burns chose not the bardic harp, but a crossed 'Shepherd's pipe & crook', with the mottoes 'Wood Notes Wild' and 'Better a wee bush than nae bield'.[5] Tellingly, he specified 'I do not mean the nonsense of Painters of Arcadia; but a Stock-&-horn, & a Club, such as you see at the head of Allan Ramsay, in Allan's quarto Edition of the Gentle Shepherd' [CL ii. 285].[6] This isn't to deny the bardic features of Burns's poetry, for there is no firm dichotomy there between pastoral pipe and bardic harp, any more than between pipe and georgic plough, a generic cross-over I'll discuss below. I'm cognizant of Ralph Cohen's warning that 'a genre does not exist independently; it arises to compete or to contrast with other genres . . . so that its aims and purposes at a particular time are defined by its interrelationship

---

been a lost case as early as the 16th century'. Annabel Patterson, *Pastoral and Ideology: Virgil to Valery* (Oxford: Clarendon, 1988), 7. I share Patterson's view that Empson's is 'the most important and the least helpful' approach to the problem of definition.

    [4] Jeffrey Skoblow, *Dooble Tongue: Scots, Burns, Contradiction* (Newark: University of Delaware Press; London: Associated University Presses, 2001), 141; see also Robert Crawford, *Devolving English Literature*, 2nd edn. (Edinburgh: Edinburgh University Press, 2000), 94–5.

    [5] 'Wood notes wild' quotes line 134 of Milton's *L'Allegro*, where it refers to Shakespeare.

    [6] Burns refers to the portrait of Ramsay by David Allan in the Foulis edition of *The Gentle Shepherd* (Glasgow 1788). The 'stock and horn' is imitated in the frontispiece to the second volume of Burns's Glenriddell Manuscripts. Largely absent from Burns's poetry and song is the Celtic harp (so beloved of Ossian, Walter Scott, James Hogg, and Tom Moore ) although 'Bardie' Lapraik does possess a '*moorlan harp*'. [K 58 l. 45]. 'Ode on General Washington's Birthday' alludes to the 'Columbian' and 'Hibernian' harp, but not a 'Caledonian' harp.

with and differentiation from others'.[7] After all, as William Blake established in his nearly contemporaneous *Songs*, 'pastoral' Innocence and 'bardic' Experience are mutually engaged, so that the pastoral idyll of 'Spring' is already ironically compromised by the 'Little Boy Lost' and 'On Another's Sorrow'.

Given a critical reluctance to recognize 'pastoral Burns', it's heartening to encounter Annabel Patterson, in her magisterial 1988 study *Pastoral and Ideology*, dedicating a chapter to Burns's song 'The Fête Champêtre' [K 224] as an instance of the ironic dismantling of neoclassical pastoral, even if her reading in the end supports the normal view of Burns's largely negative understanding of the genre. Like other manifestations of polite pastoral, William Cuninghame of Annbank's lavish 'Fête Champêtre' for the Ayrshire gentry (the occasion of Burns's 1788 song) turns out to have been far from politically unmotivated, despite the allegorical expulsion of politics from the arcadian scene by 'Love' and 'Beauty': I quote from the fourth and seventh verses;

> When Love and Beauty heard the news,
> The gay green-woods amang, man,
> Where gathering flowers and busking bowers
> They heard the blackbird's sang, man;
> A vow they seal'd it with a kiss
> Sir Politicks to fetter,
> As their's alone, the Patent-bliss,
> To hold a Fête Champetre.—
>
> When Politics cam there, to mix
> And make his ether-stane [magical amulet], man,
> He circl'd round the magic ground,
> But entrance found he nane, man:
> He blush'd for shame, he quat his name,
> Forswore it every letter,
> Wi' humble prayer to join and share
> This festive Fête Champetre.—    (ll.17–24; 49–56)

Burns here adopts the distinctive 'Killicrankie' stanza used to great effect in his earlier political song 'When *Guilford* Gude' [K 38], and it's marked by a 'sprinkling' of Scots diction, both features which distinguished it from the enamelled language of those fashionable English pastoral songs that Burns complained 'gravel me to death' [CL ii. 318]. The 'Sir Politics' debarred from Annbank's picnic has of course little to do with radical politics as they would be understood after 1789, so much as the highly managed and corrupt politics of eighteenth-century Scottish county electioneering. (The gatecrasher's very title 'Sir Politics' suggests as much.)[8]

---

[7] Ralph Cohen, 'History and Genre', *New Literary History* 17/2 (1986), 207.

[8] His approach, as the Canongate editors note, alludes to Satan's attempt to penetrate Eden in *Paradise Lost* (CG, p. 692).

Annabel Patterson reads Burns's song as

neatly allegoris[ing] the double message of this Scottish gentleman's pastoral, the magic circle of idyllic manners and aesthetic pleasure that were supposed to exclude political experience while implicitly supporting a conservative ideology. It would be putting it too strongly to call this version or theory of pastoral, and the reading of Virgil's *Eclogues* that it demanded, a cultural conspiracy.[9]

She nevertheless proceeds to examine how late eighteenth-century poets such as Burns performed the task of unmasking the 'cultural conspiracy' of neoclassicism which had suppressed the critical and potentially destabilizing charge of 'Virgilian dialectic' (I will return to this below.) Patterson reads the 'Fête Champetre' as exemplifying the form of neoclassical pastoral theorized by Rapin and Fontenelle, and imported to Britain in the work of Pope and his followers, suggesting that (like Annbank's party) 'the presence of ideology in [this form of eighteenth-century pastoral] is more inferred and intimated than spoken'.[10] Disappointingly, however, she has nothing to say about other versions of Burnsian pastoral, turning her attention instead to the ideological inflections (among the English and Irish poets studied) of Charles Churchill's parodic 'Prophecy of Famine', Oliver Goldsmith's 'Deserted Village', George Crabbe's 'anti-pastoral', and William Wordsworth's 'hard pastoral'.

Burns's awareness of the concealed agenda of the 'enamelled' pastoral idiom that saturated the late eighteenth-century poetry scene is evident in the ironic undertow of 'The Fête Champetre'. Yet in his more chameleon-like moments, he sometimes showed complicity with fashionable pastoral, particularly when seeking patronage (or more personal favours) from the various upper-class women who attracted him; witness his adoption of the pastoral soubriquet 'Sylvander' to Nancy McLehose's 'Clarinda' in the couple's torrid correspondence of 1787–8 ('I like the idea of Arcadian names in a commerce of this kind', he jested) [CL i. 189]. Rarely, and usually when obliged to compose mediocre lyrics to scaffold a traditional Scottish melody, Burns lapsed into what he called 'Namby Pamby', as in his song 'Phillis the Fair', addressed to Phillis McMurdo, daughter of the Earl of Queensberry's factor [K 418]. More often, anticipating Wordsworth's rejection of 'poetic diction', he made no secret of his impatience with 'the whining cant of love . . . Darts, flames, cupids, loves, graces, and all that farrago, are just a Mauchline [sacrament] a senseless rabble' [CL i. 165].[11]

---

[9] Annabel Patterson, *Pastoral and Ideology*, 193–4.

[10] Ibid. 199. Patterson disputes J. E. Congleton's influential view in *Theories of Pastoral Poetry in England, 1684–1798* (Gainesville: University of Florida Press, 1968) that discerns two rival traditions of pastoral, a 'Golden Age' theory emanating from Rapin, and a 'rationalist' strain developing the ideas of Fontenelle, dismissing it as a storm in a critical tea-cup. She argues that both schools alike betrayed the potential for political and social critique implicit in classical pastoral.

[11] The reference here is to a 'Holy Fair', discussed in Ch. 6.

Burns vented his frustration with pastoral enamel in the bawdy brilliance of his mock-pastoral 'Ode to Spring' sent to George Thomson in January 1795 [K 481]. He explained that, looking over 'a Magazine Ode to Spring' with a friend (maybe a poem of the same title by Anna Barbauld, or possibly Janet Little) he'd been challenged to produce a pastoral ode 'on an original plan', including 'verdant fields', 'budding flowers', 'chrystal streams', '& a love story into the bargain' [CL ii. 336];

> When maukin bucks, at early fucks,
> In dewy glens are seen, Sir;
> And birds, on boughs, take off their mowes,
> Amang the leaves sae green, Sir;
> Latona's sun looks liquorish on
> Dame Nature's grand impètus,
> Till his pego rise, then westward flies
> To roger Madame Thetis.    (ll. 1–8)

This was certainly 'original' in its hymning of the fecundity of nature, and its pastoral intimacy with 'the birds and the bees': although it was hardly the sort of thing that Thomson was likely to publish. No less than 'The Fête Champêtre', 'Ode to Spring' reveals Burns's sophisticated awareness of, and critique, of the debasement of pastoral in the 'magazine poetry' of the eighteenth-century neoclassical tradition.

Burns's 'Ode to Spring' isn't merely a personal revolt against an exploded taste, however. On the contrary, it is in line with Dr Johnson's high-profile attacks on pastoral in *The Rambler*,[12] and especially with Hugh Blair's influential criticism of 'our common Pastoral-mongers' in the 39th *Lecture on Rhetoric and Belles Lettres*: 'to the frequent repetition of common-place topics [the shepherd mourning for his unfaithful lover, or the shepherd's singing contest] which have been thrummed over by all Eclogue Writers since the days of Theocritus and Virgil, is owing much of that insipidity which prevails in Pastoral Compositions'.[13] Blair has had a bad press from Burns scholars, sometimes for good reasons, but there's no reason to doubt that the poet would have concurred with Blair's demand; 'why may not Pastoral Poetry take a wider range? Human nature, and human passions, are much the same in every rank of life; and wherever these passions operate on objects that are within the rural sphere, there may be a proper subject for pastoral'.[14]

Blair's recognition that Burns had achieved just such a 'wider range' might help to explain his championship of the poet, despite his serious reservations

---

[12] Samuel Johnson, *The Rambler* 36 and 37, 21 and 24 July, 1750.

[13] Hugh Blair, *Lectures on Rhetoric and Belles Lettres*, 3 vols. (Dublin, 1783), iii. 143.

[14] Ibid. 144.

about passages of 'indecency' and 'licentiousness' [*CH* pp. 81–2].[15] William Wordsworth certainly had no scruples in recognizing in Burns the qualities of a great pastoral poet. Writing to Coleridge in February 1799, he paid tribute to the enduring power of Theocritan pastoral over the urban comedies of Aristophanes or Congreve ('read Theocritus in Ayrshire or Merionethshire and you will find perpetual occasion to recollect what you see daily in Ayrshire or Merionethshire') [*CG*, p. 131]; and he went on to hail Burns as the modern avatar of the Greek poet. Like the author of the *Idylls*, Burns described 'manners connected with the permanent objects of nature and partaking of the simplicity of those objects ... the communications that proceed from Burns come to the mind with the life and charm of recognitions' [*CH* p. 131].[16]

I follow Wordsworth in making the case here, and more expansively in the chapters that follow, that Burns's engagement with pastoral was considerably more capacious than his ironic parody of the 'aristocratic' version exposed in 'The Fête Champetre'. Annbank's picnic certainly supports Roger Sales's point that eighteenth-century pastoral 'provided sheep's clothing for aristocratic wolves, or indeed for anybody who was on the side of the victors in the civil war which was fought for control of rural society'.[17] More recently, however, Michael McKeon has argued, against this view, that 'by the end of the 18th century [pastoral] serves as a cultural screen against which material change itself acquires not only its meaning but its ongoing intelligibility'.[18]

The fact that pastoral could serve simultaneously as a 'screen' and a tool for critique is explained by Patterson's account of 'Virgilian dialectic', and the tradition of political exegesis going back to Servius, that located Virgil's *Eclogues* squarely within the historical and political context of the 'last phases of the civil war between Brutus and Cassius, representing the old republic, and Antony and Octavian, agents and heirs of Caesarian centrism'.[19] In the first *Eclogue* (which along with the ninth is most concerned with the theme of exile and dispossession) the pastoralist Meliboeus, evicted from his farm to give place to Octavian's veterans, compares his bitter fate with that of the 'contented' shepherd Tityrus, who having made his peace with the 'liberty' of the new Roman regime and its ruler, Augustus Caesar, is free to enjoy pastoral leisure:

---

[15] See Liam McIlvanney in 'Hugh Blair, Robert Burns, and the Invention of Scottish Literature', *18th-Century Life* 29/2 (Spring 2005). The perception of a 'pastoral Burns' may have reconciled Blair's conflicting taste for 'primitive' genius and modern literary 'correctness', without the risks earlier incurred by his championship of *Ossian*.

[16] See also Russel Noyes, 'Wordsworth and Burns', *PMLA* 59 (1944), 813–32.

[17] Roger Sales, *English Literature in History 1780–1830* (London: Hutchinson, 1983), 17.

[18] Michael McKeon, 'The Pastoral Revolution', in Kevin Sharpe and Steven Zwicker (eds.), *Refiguring Revolutions: Aesthetics and Politics from the English Revolution to the Romantic Revolution* (Berkeley and Los Angeles: University of California Press, 1998), 267–90 at 267.

[19] Patterson, *Pastoral and Ideology*, 3.

Where the broad beeche an ample shade displays,
Your slender reed resounds the sylvan lays,
O happy TITYRUS! While we, forlorn,
Driven from our lands, to distant climes are born,
Stretch'd careless in the peaceful shade you sing,
And all the groves with AMARYLLIS ring.[20]

Patterson underlines the grammatical split between 'tu' and 'nos' in the Latin text, 'a plural that immediately confronts the reader with a choice of identification'.[21] If Tityrus represents the triumph of pastoral content as a blend of *otium, eros*, and successful patronage of the kind that would be found so serviceable to the landowning ideology of Neoclassicism, Meliboeus foreshadows the voice of the dispossessed farmer/intellectual, and the fate of the republican *vis activa* in an epoch of political tyranny. Despite a traditional identification of Virgil with the figure of Tityrus, Patterson suggests that the identification of the poet's own voice is actually uncertain, showing (across the ten *Eclogues*) 'how a writer can protect himself by dismemberment, how he can best assert his ownership of the text by a widely shifting authorial presence'.[22] I'll return at the end of this chapter to the bearing of Patterson's 'Virgilian dialectic' on Burns's own poetry, as well as his own crisis of threatened dispossession and exile, around the time of his publication of the Kilmarnock volume.

Neoclassical theory discerned the absolute standard of pastoral in Theocritus and Virgil, or at least in a selective interpretation of that body of Greek and Roman 'idyllic' or 'bucolic' poetry, as it was commonly designated. While Theocritus excelled in 'nature and simplicity', his imitator Virgil had 'refined upon his original',[23] therefore providing the most apt model for modern imitations in the genre. Like Wordsworth in the passage quoted above, Burns follows Allan Ramsay (and others) in reversing the priority, although the influence of Theocritan naturalism is matched by the continuing importance of Virgil at the level of ideology.

Robert Burn's only direct statement on the eighteenth-century pastoral debate is expressed in his 'Sketch, or, A Poem on Pastoral Poetry' [K 82] which Kinsley speculates was written during the Mossgiel period around 1785–6. The poem

---

[20] This is the same passage quoted in Geddes's Scots orthography in the epigraph to the present chapter. I quote here from James Beattie's 1760s translation of Virgil's *Eclogues* in *Original Poems and Translations* (London, 1760), 89–90; less current than the translations of Dryden or Joseph Warton, Beattie's version has nevertheless greater cultural contiguity to Burns (James Beattie, *Poetical Works*, with a new intro. by Roger J. Robinson (London: Routledge/Thoemmes, 1996)). In the ninth Eclogue the shepherd Moeris complains that his 'antient lands' have been 'usurped' by a 'rapacious lord' and he has been driven into exile, despite the best efforts of the poet Menalcas to save the land amidst the 'dreadful clang' of civil war (pp. 171–3).

[21] Patterson, *Pastoral and Ideology*, 2.

[22] Ibid. 4.

[23] Alexander Pope, 'A Discourse on Pastoral Poetry', in *Pope: Poetical Works*, ed. Herbert Davis, intro. Pat Rogers (Oxford: Oxford University Press, 1978), 11.

(unusually for Burns) calls for a renaissance of classical, and especially Theocritan, pastoral, which it identifies with the 'Shepherd-sangs' of the eighteenth-century revival of Scottish vernacular poetry.[24]

> But thee, Theocritus, wha matches?
> They're no herd's ballats[25], Maro's catches;
> Squire Pope but busks his skinklin patches
>            O' Heathen tatters:
> I pass by hunders, nameless wretches,
>            That ape their betters.
>
> In this braw age o' wit an' lear,
> Will nane the Shepherd's whistle mair
> Blaw sweetly in his native air
>            And rural grace;
> And wi' the far-fam'd Grecian share
>            A rival place?     (ll. 19–30)

In the following stanzas it emerges that neither 'Maro' [Virgil] nor Pope and his school, but Allan Ramsay (whose Scots diction and trademark 'habbie' stanza the poem adopts) was the very man to inherit Theocritus's mantle in 'paint[ing] auld Nature to the nines'. The distinctive Scottish topography of Ramsay's *Gentle Shepherd* replaces Popes's neoclassical Arcadia; 'Nae gowden streams thro' myrtles twines, | Where Philomel...Her griefs will tell!'; 'In gowany glens thy burnie strays, | Where bonie lasses bleach their claes; | Or trots by hazelly shaws and braes | Wi' hawthorns gray' (ll. 39–42, 49–52). The poem's reference to the classical pastoralists reverses the neoclassical preference for Virgil over Theocritus on the grounds of the latter's superior realism (i.e. 'Maro's catches aren't "herd's ballats" or shepherd songs in any believable sense, any more than Pope's'), alluding to the English pastoral debate between (*inter alias*) Pope and Ambrose Philips in the 1710s discussed below. Allan Ramsay is praised as Theocritus's true heir and identified (via Ramsay) with a realistic Scottish poetic idiom and setting, against the Arcadian version exemplified by Pope's 'skinklin [showy] patches'.

As is clear from the final stanza of Burns's 'A Sketch', pastoral realism didn't preclude an idyllic view of nature, although in the course of the eighteenth century Scottish, like English, rural poetry increasingly incorporated the

---

[24] The poem is well within Burns's range, although doubts have been cast on the attribution on account of its literary allusiveness. See Kin. iii. 1145–6.

[25] Kinsley and other modern editors misleadingly capitalize 'herd' here, thereby introducing an allusion to David Herd, editor of *Ancient and Modern Scottish Songs* (1776). Quite apart from the fact that Burns nowhere else refers to Herd (whose anonymously published volume he designates 'Wotherspoon' after its Edinburgh publisher) this destroys the sense of the line, which is correctly glossed as 'Virgil's "catches" aren't real "shepherds songs"'.

georgic, 'hard pastoral' described by Raymond Williams, John Barrell, Annabel Patterson, and Michael McKeon.[26] 'Hard' pastoral (in which category I include 'counter- or anti-pastoral') tends to a more political engagement with other genres such as georgic in its 'realist' representation of rural labour, whereas 'soft' pastoral celebrates the privileged *otium* of Tityrus, ornamental, eroticized, and 'apolitical', as the poet 'sports with Amaryllis in the shade'. 'A Sketch' sets out to make exceptionalist claims for the poetry of Scottish common life, and the realist pathos of the Scots idiom and rural landscape, against the Arcadian pastoral model. But unlike many of Burns's poems studied in the chapters that follow (most typically, 'The Cotter's Saturday Night', discussed in Chapter 7), the pastoral idiom of Burns's 'A Sketch' is 'soft' rather than 'hard', placing it closer to such pastoral songs as 'Ca' the Yowes' [K 185] than the poems in the Kilmarnock volume.

The enormous subsequent success of Burns's verse (not to mention the literal force of his occupational identity as a farmer poet) had the effect of naturalizing 'Scots pastoral' to the point that its generic affiliations became almost invisible, personifying a genre within the folds of the poet's biography as 'Ayrshire ploughman'. As I suggested in the introduction, the rise of the Burns cult in the urbanised nineteenth century, and the ongoing 'celebration' of Burns in some of the more nostalgic manifestations of Scottish culture, has ironically drawn him back into the orbit of a new version of 'soft' pastoral, albeit one that reflects a sentimentalized apotheosis of the 'common man', rather than a leisured aristocracy enjoying a 'fête champêtre'.

## GENERIC CROSSOVERS: LOVE AND LABOUR

Pastoral poetry had a long history in Scotland before the era of Burns: as R. D. S. Jack notes in *The Italian Influence on Scottish Literature*, seventeenth-century Scottish poets, such as Sir Robert Ayton, Drummond [of Hawthornden], and Sir William Alexander, fostered 'a cult of pastoral' largely inspired by the Italian poets Tasso and Guarini.[27] But the genre had been shaken up by the neoclassical debate around the turn of the eighteenth century, more visible to poets of Burns's generation than was the courtly heritage of their seventeenth-century Scottish precursors. As we've seen, neoclassical pastoral held little appeal for the

---

[26] Barrell argues that late eighteenth-century pastoral suffered attenuation 'except insofar as it could be brought into various kinds of relation with Georgic' (*Poetry, Language, Politics* [Manchester University Press, 1988], 115). For Barrell's more recent reflections on political pastoral, see his essay 'Rus in Urbe', in Philip Connell and Nigel Leask (eds.), *Romanticism and Popular Culture* (Cambridge: Cambridge University Press, 2009), 109–27.

[27] R. D. S. Jack, *The Italian Influence on Scottish Literature* (Edinburgh: Edinburgh University Press, 1972), 156. Jack shows this influence continuing into the eighteenth century, especially in the poetry of William Hamilton of Bangour and Dr Alexander Pennecuik, attested to by quality editions of Tasso's *Aminta* and Guarini's *Pastor Fido* published by the Foulis Press in Glasgow (p. 152).

'ploughman poet', to the extent that it promoted aristocratic *otium* and an idyllic picture of rural life. After all, Rapin explicitly excluded from Arcadia 'Fishers, Plow-men, Reapers, Hunters', and Fontenelle 'Ploughmen, Reapers, Vine-dressers, or Huntsmen', to the extent that the life of such agricultural workers was too harsh to harmonize with the ideas of 'tranquillity and innocence' essential to the genre.[28] In his juvenile *Discourse on Pastoral Poetry* (1709), Pope described pastoral as 'an image of what they call the golden age', and its matter the 'imitation of the action of a shepherd', the latter not based on contemporary reality, so much as an Arcadian age when 'the best of men followed the employment'.[29] This clearly rules out an Ayrshire poet inspired by his 'hamely muse' while 'drudg[ing] thro dub' an' mire | At pleugh or cart'.

The appropriate classical genre for describing rural *labour* was of course georgic, which, as Anthony Lowe has argued, experienced a 'revolution' in the seventeenth century, emerging from its almost total eclipse by pastoral, as the spirit of social reform and 'the New Husbandry inspired such poets as Herrick, Marvell, and Milton to write new forms of georgic'.[30] Whatever its Roman origins or its radical seventeenth-century credentials, eighteenth-century georgic was a genre that promoted the practical concerns and improving social vision of the landed classes: there's after all only a small slippage between 'Georgian' and 'Georgic'.[31] Moreover, as Alfred Lutz notes, 'by stressing a preordained harmony between providence and progress, [georgic] maintained a link between them, so that temporality—economic change and progress—appeared as an aspect of a providential design'.[32] This isn't the whole picture, of course: Donna Landry proposes that the tradition of labouring-class women's poetry that she studies in *The Muses of Resistance* represents 'a georgic mode written from inside the experience of rural labour instead of from without, as in the Virgilian manner'.[33] Landry's claim is partly born out by the poetry of the 'Heaven-taught plough-man', whatever the problems (addressed in the previous chapter) of describing Burns as a labouring-class poet. But generic boundaries are enforced by the difficulties of writing georgic in Scots. For as Joseph Addison wrote of the politics of address in his 'Essay on Georgic', prefaced to Dryden's popular

---

[28] Congleton, *Theories of Pastoral Poetry*, 59, 68.

[29] *Pope: Poetical Works*, 9–10.

[30] Anthony Low, *The Georgic Revolution* (Princeton: Princeton University Press, 1985), 354.

[31] Although Books 1–3 of the *Georgics* address the smallholder, the poem as a whole is addressed to Virgil's wealthy and well-connected patron Maecenas, and through him to Caesar (Virgil, *The Eclogues and The Georgics*, trans. C. Day Lewis, intro. and notes R. O. A. M. Lyne [Oxford: Oxford University Press, 1983], pp. xxiv–xxv).

[32] Alfred Lutz, '"The Deserted Village" and the Politics of Genre', *Modern Language Quarterly* 55/2 (June 1994), 149–69, 4 of 13. See also Kevis Goodman, *Georgic Modernity and British Romanticism: Poetry and the Mediation of History* (Cambridge: Cambridge University Press, 2004).

[33] Donna Landry, *The Muses of Resistance: Labouring-Class Women's Poetry in Britain, 1739–1796* (Cambridge: Cambridge University Press, 1990), 22.

translation of Virgil (1697), 'tho' the scene of both [pastoral and georgic] lies in the same place, the speakers in them are of a quite different character, since the precepts of husbandry are not to be delivered with the simplicity of a ploughman, but with the address of a poet'.[34]

In the previous chapter I discussed the development of Burns's literacy in relation to the 'prose georgics' of the eighteenth-century discourse of agricultural improvement, where the Virgilian 'address of a poet' had been generalized into the 'work of writing', especially (as Kurt Heinzelman argues) in the case of 'the last georgic', Adam Smith's *Wealth of Nations*. Beyond promulgating a 'larger georgic application of labour as a societal bonding agent' in that work, Smith was also promoting 'a new and precisely *English*-language version of the georgic' in his university *Lectures on Rhetoric and Belles Lettres*; 'he taught [his students] writing, how to effect improvement through writing. He taught them . . . to write clear, serviceable prose that could bestow and command exchange-value.'[35] At this point, georgic intersects with the fraught domain of language politics, the backdrop to many of the problems (and some of the achievements) of eighteenth-century Scottish writing, not least Burns's poetry.[36] Scottish linguistic 'improvement' inevitably fostered a 'cultural cringe', evident in Smith's observation that 'we in this country are most of us very sensible that the perfection of language is very different from that we commonly speak in . . . the farther one's stile is removed from the common manner [the] it is so much the nearer to purity'.[37] For all the literary-critical achievements of the Scottish enlightenment, linguistic 'improvement' rendered comic writing difficult, creating the often-remarked 'disembodiment' of eighteenth-century Scottish prose. Commenting on the prose style of the historian William Robertson, Edmund Burke complained that 'he writes like a man who composes in a dead language, which he understands but cannot speak'.[38] In complete contrast was Burns's triumphal assertion of the comic and satirical potential of the demotic language in his poetry 'chiefly in the Scottish dialect'.

Unlike georgic, pastoral poetry had evolved from its Theocritan origin as a body of poetry voiced (or rather sung) by shepherds, ploughman, threshers, and

---

[34] Included in *Works of Virgil*, trans. John Dryden, 2 vols. (Glasgow 1769), i, p. xxvii.

[35] Kurt Heinzelman, 'The Last Georgic', 171–94 at 191, 193. See also Clifford Siskin, *The Work of Writing* (Baltimore: Johns Hopkins University Press), 118–29.

[36] Crawford, *Devolving English Literature*, 16–44, and (ed.), *The Scottish Invention of English Literature* (Cambridge: Cambridge University Press, 1998); Janet Sorensen, *The Grammar of Empire in Eighteenth-Century British Writing* (Cambridge: Cambridge University Press, 2000); Charles Jones, *A Language Suppressed: The Pronunciation of Scots in the Eighteenth Century* (Edinburgh: John Donald, 1995).

[37] Adam Smith, *Lectures on Rhetoric and Belles Lettres*, ed. J. C. Bryce, *Glasgow Edition of the Works and Correspondence of Adam Smith* (Indianapolis: Liberty Fund, 1985), 42.

[38] Quoted by John Butt in 'The Revival of Vernacular Scottish Poetry', in Frederick W. Hilles and Harold Bloom (eds.), *From Sensibility to Romanticism: Essays Presented to Frederick A. Pottle* (Oxford: Oxford University Press, 1965), 220.

other rural labourers, via the Virgilian dialectic, to the seventeenth-century court in which 'many a poet had dispensed with the sheep, the sheep-hook, and the pipes in pursuit of more rarefied interests'.[39] Michael McKeon proposes that despite the obvious differences between Virgil's *Eclogues* and *Georgics* (including the differences between 'vigorous land cultivation and tranquil animal herding'),[40] the two poems 'also operate within the same basic scheme of oppositions', and by means of a complementary 'reversal of values'.[41] Thus if Virgil's second *Georgic* begins with practical instructions to the industrious husbandman, it ends with the spectre of war and urban corruption, hymning 'a *locus amoenus* of uncultivated plenty that Virgil compares to life in the Saturnalian Golden Age'. Conversely, the contest between Alexis and Corydon in the fourth *Eclogue* reminds us that 'a species of ambition and *negotium* is inseparable from pastoral values and that the *Eclogues* are insistent in their thematization of the normative 'artistry' of emulation, competition, and craftsmanship'.[42]

Virgil's georgic idea that *labor omnia vincit* ('labour conquers all') directly echoes the *Eclogues* assertion that *amor omnia vincit* ('love conquers all'), as the *rota Vergilii* turns from pastoral, via georgic, to epic.[43] No reader of Burns would question his statement in the Kilmarnock Preface that the values of pastoral *otium* ('the little creations of his own fancy, amid the toil and fatigues of a laborious life'), [Kil. p. iv] rather than georgic *negotium*, represent the dominant spirit of his poetry and song. It was undoubtedly the pastoral and vernacular 'simplicity of a ploughman' rather than the georgic 'address of a poet' that impelled the enormous success of Burns's 1786 Kilmarnock volume.[44]

At the same time, we need to keep generic reversals in mind to make sense of Burns's poems in the pastoral tradition, poems as deeply engaged with questions of politics and religion, class tension, poverty, and social change as they are with wine, women, and song. Raymond Willliams's description of Crabbe's project in 'The Village' and other poems as 'counter-pastoral' ('to paint the Cot, | As Truth will paint it, and as Bards will not') has somewhat overshadowed a sense of pastoral's internal dialectic, as well as its absorption of 'hard' georgic values in the second half of the century.[45] Starting with *Five Pastoral Eclogues* in 1745

---

[39]  Anthony Low, *Georgic Revolution*, 7.

[40]  McKeon, 'Pastoral Revolution', 268.

[41]  Ibid. For Patterson on the generic cross-over between georgic and pastoral see *Pastoral and Ideology*, 134.

[42]  McKeon, 'Pastoral Revolution', 269.

[43]  See Heinzelman, 'The Last Georgic', 189. 'Amor omnia vincit' was one of Burns's favourite Latin tags. See Robert Crawford, *The Bard*, 272.

[44]  In some respects this accords with Siskin's argument that 'the work that [the eighteenth century] georgically initiated became the full-time lyrical work of the period we call Romanticism', (*Work of Writing*, 126). However, as I argued in the introduction, 'ploughman' Burns hardly fits Siskin's model of the 'professionalized' writer.

[45]  Raymond Williams, *The Country and the City* (London: Hogarth, 1993), 90–5.

(wrongly attributed to Thomas Warton) whose shepherds are transported to war-torn contemporary Germany, through Chatterton's *African Eclogues* (1770), Edward Rushton's abolitionist *West-Indian Eclogues* (1787), Southey's *Botany Bay Eclogues* (1795), and even Coleridge's *Fire, Famine and Slaughter: A War Eclogue* (1796), the genre increasingly shook off the Arcadian idyll as it approached the revolutionary decade. Political pastoralists now identified more with the plight of exiled Meliboeus in war-torn Mantua, rather than being satisfied to hymn Tityrus's 'pastoral content'.[46]

## PASTORAL THEORY AND THE VERNACULAR

As I've suggested in my reading of Burns's 'A Sketch', the roots of Scots pastoral lie deep in the neoclassical debate. Pope's *Discourse on Pastoral* distastefully alluded to a rival tradition of indigenous, or Spenserian, pastoral. Overwhelmed by enthusiasm for the primitive energy of Theocritus, Spenser had emulated the Greek's use of the rustic Doric dialect; but, Pope cautions, while the latter maybe had 'its beauty and propriety in the time of Theocritus . . . the old English and country phrases of Spenser were either entirely obsolete, or spoken only by people of the lowest condition', a criticism parroted in late eighteenth-century criticisms of Burns's employment of Scots.[47]

Spenser's example had, however, inspired Ambrose Philips and his court Whig associates Addison, Steele, Tickell, and Dennis, who engaged in a protracted quarrel with Pope and the neoclassical school, including Gay, Swift, Congreve, Walsh, and Arbuthnot. Rekindled in 1713–14 in the pages of the *Guardian* (nos. 22, 23, 28, 30, 32, and 40) in a controversy between Tickell and Pope, the debate focused on the English pastoral realism of Ambrose Philips. Tickell attacked Pope by endorsing Philip's 'Spenserian' employment of an English rural setting, rustic proverbial idioms, and native superstitions ('hobthrushes, fairies, goblins, and witches') as opposed to the Parnassian 'machinery' of classical deities, set in an idealized and delocalized Arcadia.[48] Already visible here is the link between vernacular pastoral and the poetic representations of 'popular superstition' evident in Burns's' 'Address to the Deil', 'Halloween', and 'Tam o' Shanter' (his engagement with popular antiquarianism is further discussed in Chapter 8).

Disguising his allegiance to the 'golden age theory' of the 'ancients', Pope's *Guardian* 40 essay adopted a *reductio ad absurdum* in provincializing Arcadia;

---

[46] See Curran, *Poetic Form*, 95–9. Curran makes a powerful case for the enduring importance of pastoral in mainstream Romanticism.

[47] *Pope: Poetical Works*, 12.

[48] For an account of the ideological underpinnings of the debate, see Patterson, *Pastoral and Ideology*, 206–14; and for its relation to Scottish poetry, Thomas Crawford, *Society and the Lyric* (Edinburgh: Scottish Academic Press, 1979), 72–8.

'I should think it proper for the several writers of pastoral, to confine themselves to their several counties.' To this end, he quoted an antique 'pastoral ballad' in the 'Somersetshire dialect' in which 'the words Nymph, Dryad, Naiad, Fawn, Cupid, or Satyr, are not once mentioned throughout the whole work', but which was nevertheless redolent with 'that spirit of Religion, and that Innocence of the Golden Age, so necessary to be observed by all writers of Pastoral'. 'Cicily. *Rager, go vetch tha kee, or else tha zun | Will quite be go, bevore c'have half a don. |* Roger. *Thou shouldst not ax ma tweece, but I've a bee | To dreave our bull to bull the parson's knee.*'[49] For all its satirical intentions, this provided an opening for vernacular pastoral.

Pope's burlesque was the cue for John Gay's more extended parody (albeit with a lesser commitment to 'realist' representation of rural speech) in *The Shepherd's Week* (1714), the 'Proeme' of which claimed to attempt 'the right simple Eclogue after the true ancient guise of Theocritus...my Love to my native Country *Britain* much pricketh me forward, to describe aright the Manners of our own honest and laborious Ploughmen, in no wise sure more unworthy a *British* Poet's imitation, than those of *Sicily* or *Arcadie*'.[50] Margaret Anne Doody writes that 'the mock-mock-mock levels of [Gay's] "Proeme" guide us inescapably to the view that pastorals are all imitations, and imitations of an unreality. The genre is an absurdity, and the only way to manage it is to get out of it, to mix up its manners and question its conventions'.[51] Arguably Gay implemented this artful generic 'mixture' even more successfully in his 'Newgate Pastoral' *The Beggar's Opera* than in *The Shepherd's Week*. If the influence of the latter is everywhere in Burns's poetry, at least as mediated by Ramsay and Fergusson, then that of the former is strongly evident in his 'Beggar's pastoral' 'Love and Liberty', albeit largely shorn of its political allegory.

## ALLAN RAMSAY AND SCOTS PASTORAL

Surprisingly enough, the burlesque intentions of Gay's *Shepherd's Calendar* appear to have passed unnoticed in many quarters: for all its self-conscious artifice, one strain of eighteenth-century pastoral had a tendency to veer towards literal realism, a tendency that reached its climax in Burns.[52] It was only a short step from Gay's mélange of archaisms and dialect words (plucked from various English counties), via Thomas Purney's *Pastorals in the Simple Manner of Theocritus* (1716), to Allan Ramsay's ingenious employment of Scots 'Doric' as a 'realist' pastoral idiom. In part Ramsay took the hint from Scottish pastoral

---

[49] *Pope: Poetical Works*, 599; see also T. Crawford, *Society and Lyric*, 75–6.

[50] Quoted in Margaret Anne Doody, *The Daring Muse: Augustan Poetry Reconsidered* (Cambridge: Cambridge University Press), 100.

[51] Ibid., 101.

[52] See Curran, *Poetic Form and British Romanticism*, 92.

songs that had already proved a hit on the London stage, inspiring earlier collections like Thomas D'Urfey's *Pills to Purge Melancholy* (1699) and its successors. Ramsay's equation of Scots with Theocritan 'Doric' gave a new cultural dignity to the attenuated Scottish poetry tradition that he sought to revive in *The Evergreen* (1724) and in his own poetic works, however much he was also dependent upon earlier patriotic collections such as James Watson's *Choice Collection of Comic and Serious Scots Poems* (1706–13), as well as demotic broadside literature.[53] Murray Pittock has suggested that Watson's miscellaneous inclusion of popular broadside poetry alongside earlier poems in Scots such as 'Christis Kirk' and Montgomerie's 'The Cherrie and the Slae', as well as seventeenth-century Scots poems in English by Aytoun, Drummond, and Montrose, implied 'a parity of literary forms', paving the way for Ramsay's more ambitious project of 'claiming high cultural forms for vernacular use'. As such earlier critics as W. J. Courthope, J. W. Mackail, and J. E. Congleton proposed, this situates Ramsay as an important Romantic precursor, although more recently the claim has fallen on deaf ears.[54]

Despite its popularity, pastoral ranked low in the Augustan hierarchy of poetical genres, which meant that poetry written in the Scots 'Doric' idiom was conventionally limited to pastoral eclogues and elegies (often burlesques, like Ramsay's own 'Elegy on Maggie Johnston', written in the 'standard habbie' stanza), epistles, songs and ballads, and the 'peasant brawl' genre of the Christ's Kirk tradition; but odes, epics, and tragedies, as well as poetry in the newly fashionable georgic mode, were ruled out of court. Nevertheless, Ramsay's grafting of neoclassicism onto the indigenous Scottish vernacular tradition proved immensely formative for the poets of the Scottish poetry revival, not least Fergusson and Burns.

Stuart Curran's argument that even at its most idyllic, '18th century pastoral had been more or less tinged with politics' was especially true of Scottish pastoral.[55] Jacobite politics underpinned the pastorals of Ramsay as well as the more courtly Italianate idiom of Hamilton of Bangour, often mining the Virgilian themes of dispossession and exile. Perhaps more frequently, bucolic or idyllic verse was taken to indicate the peace and prosperity that lowland Scotland had allegedly enjoyed following union with the old enemy England. Given the Scotophobic climate of the 1760s, however, this was hardly a quietist

---

[53] See Harriet Harvey Wood, 'Burns and Watson's *Choice Collection*', in *Studies in Scottish Literature* 30 (1998), 19–30. Wood's doubts as to 'whether Burns ever saw the Choice Collection' (p. 28) are unwarranted given Burns's reference to the *Collection* in his 'Strictures on Scottish Songs and Ballads', where he describes it as 'the first of its nature . . . published in our own native Scottish dialect'. R. H. Cromek, *Reliques of Robert Burns* (London, 1808), 223.

[54] Murray Pittock, *Scottish and Irish Romanticism* (Oxford: Oxford University Press, 2008), 47, 32.

[55] Curran, *Poetic Form*, 96

or apolitical position in a decade when few could afford the complacency of what Colin Kidd calls 'banal unionism'.[56] In a 1792 essay in *The Bee*, Ramsay of Ochtertyre explained that the Scottish Borders had become the *locus classicus* of pastoral song only after the cessation of Anglo-Scottish conflict at the regal union of 1603; 'amidst these Arcadian vales, one or more original geniuses might arise . . . who were determined to give a new turn to the taste of their country-men . . . Love, which had formerly held a divided sway with glory and ambition, became now the master passion of the soul.'[57] According to this view, the 'shepherd's sang', as well as its sister-genre the georgic (consummated in the Border poet James Thomson's hugely popular *The Seasons*), celebrated the peace and concord accompanying the Union, in contrast to the Bardic strain of *Ossian* and the elegiac poems of a lost national integrity that it inspired.[58]

Ramsay's Jacobite sympathies didn't interfere with his attempt to construct a more representative 'British' poetic in the wake of the 1707 Union, promoting the interests of Scottish language, literature, and culture. In the preface to *The Evergreen* he criticized the *Northern Poet* who set his pastorals in Arcadia, for 'the *Morning* rises (in the Poet's Description) as she does in the *Scottish* Horizon. We are not carried to *Greece* or *Italy* for a Shade, a Stream, or a Breeze . . .' [Ramsay, iv. 236]. In the preface to his 1721 *Poems*, this was buttressed by a strong claim for the diglossic range available to the educated Scots speaker, whose 'Scotti-cisms', Ramsay insisted, stood in the same relation to standard English as Theocritus's Doric dialect to literary Attic:

good Poetry may be in any Language . . . These are no Defects in our's, the Pronunciation is liquid and sonorous, and much fuller than the *English* of which we are Masters, by being taught it in our Schools, and daily reading it; which being added to all our own native Words, of eminent Significancy, makes our Tongue by far the completest: For Instance, I can say; *an empty House, a toom Barrel, a boss Head*, and *a hollow Heart* . . . The *Scotticisms*, which perhaps may offend some over-nice Ear, give new Life and Grace to the Poetry, and become their Place as well as the *Doric* Dialect of *Theocritus*, so much admired by the best Judges   [Ramsay, i. p. xix].

Although Pittock rightly observes of this passage that Ramsay's exemplary images here (*an empty House, a toom Barrel, a boss Head, and a hollow Heart*) are

[56] Colin Kidd, *Union and Unionism: Political Thought in Scotland, 1500–2000* (Cambridge: Cambridge University Press, 2008), 23–31. Kidd's claim that 1707 Union and the defeat of Jacobitism in 1746 'largely settled the question of Scotland's relation with England' (p. 24) perhaps underestimates ongoing tensions in the 1760s, and throughout the period with which this study is concerned.

[57] [Ramsay of Ochtertyre] 'On Scottish Songs', *The Bee* (Wed. 13 April 1791), 201–10 at 203. Ramsay's essay may have suggested the argument of Hector MacNeill's long poem *The Pastoral, or Lyric Muse of Scotland* (Edinburgh, 1808), which attributed a civilizing influence to the pastoral songs of the Borders, in contrast to the martial themes of the old ballads.

[58] Rachel Crawford, *Poetry, Enclosure, and the Vernacular Landscape, 1700–1830* (Cambridge: Cambridge University Press, 2002), 94; Katie Trumpener, *Bardic Nationalism* (Princeton, NJ: Princeton University Press, 1997), 3–34.

'depressing and anticlimactic', reflecting the suppressed culture of post-1707 Scotland, Ramsay's ingenious neoclassical defence of Scots nevertheless proved immensely enabling in legitimizing the poetic idiom of his successors Fergusson and Burns, and in establishing Scots as the dominant non-standard literary language of the Anglophone world.[59]

Another important linguistic resource for Ramsay's followers was his *Collection of Scots Proverbs* (1737), prefaced with a dedicatory essay to 'The Tenantry of Scotland, Farmers of the Dales, and Storemasters of the Hills', Ramsay's only sustained attempt at Scots prose. Ramsay hailed the tenantry (with an implied rebuke to the landowning class) as 'the Bees that make the Honey, that mony a Drone licks mair of than ye do . . . How toom wad the Landlord's Coffers be, if he didna rug his Rent frae the Plough-gang and the green Sward?' [Ramsay, v. 62].[60] Beyond their role as guardians of national prosperity and virtue, the tenantry were also the custodians of the Scots language and its rich mine of proverbial lore, represented by the 2,522 proverbs (complete with glossary) collected here. Ramsay's dedication and proverbs represent the antithesis of Hume's, Sinclair's, or Beattie's proscriptive lists of Scotticisms to the extent that they are actively engaged in promoting common usage rather than 'embalming' a dying language. He exhorted his readers to 'gar your Bairns get [the proverbs] by Heart; let them have a Place amang your Family-Books; and may never a Window Sole through the Country be without them' [Ramsay, v. 61]. The *Collection* enjoyed a success within Scotland comparable to *The Gentle Shepherd* itself, circulating in chapbooks as well as in successive quality editions, ensuring the survival of many proverbs that would otherwise have dropped out of circulation in a rapidly changing society. Thanks to Ramsay, the proverb became a staple of the Scots poetry revival, inspiring the vernacular commonplaces that distinguish the voice of so much of Burns's best-known poetry.

The nuclei of Ramsay's most successful work, the pastoral drama *The Gentle Shepherd* (1725), were the two eclogues 'Patie and Roger' and 'Jenny and Meggy' (printed earlier in 1720 and 1723 respectively) [Ramsay, i. 138–48] that stemmed directly from the 'realist pastoral' of Gay, Phillips, and Purney, as well as a selection of the Scots songs which he had been collecting for some years, and which had appeared in the first volume of the *Tea-Table Miscellany* (1723). There's been a tendency in Scottish studies to overplay Ramsay's provincial and folkloristic roots, rather than acknowledging his poetry as part of a cosmopolitan project of European extent, marked for example by his close patronage relationship with the erudite statesman and poet Sir John Clerk of Penicuik. As Alexander Fraser Tytler noted in 1800, Ramsay successfully domesticated and vernacularized sixteenth-century Italian pastoral dramas such as Tasso's *Aminta*

---

[59] Pittock, *Scottish and Irish Romanticism*, 46.

[60] For a brief discussion of Ramsay's text, see David Craig, *Scottish Literature and the Scottish People, 1680–1830* (London: Chatto & Windus, 1961), 24–5.

and Guarini's *Pastor Fido*, idealized romances set in an Arcadian golden age for the delectation of a courtly audience. Tytler admired the degree to which (to a greater extent than the Italians) 'the persons of the Scotish pastoral are the actual inhabitants of the country where the scene is laid; their manners are drawn from nature with a faithful pencil'. Despite his worries (shared by Hugh Blair, James Beattie, and other Scottish critics) that Ramsay's use of the 'obsolete' Scottish dialect limited the poetic range and audience of his pastoral drama, he proceeded to a detailed comparison of Ramsay with Tasso and Guarini, largely in favour of the former.[61]

Much commentary on *The Gentle Shepherd* has focused on Ramsay's 'Theo-critan' employment of Scots/Doric and his enhanced pastoral realism; what is often overlooked, despite its deeply conventional romance plot, is the extent to which the pastoral drama engages and reactivates the Virgilian dialect discussed by Patterson, transposed into the Scottish ideological context. Ramsay's hero Patrick, ('Patie', the eponymous 'gentle shepherd'), although at one level a Tityrus figure, is in fact the heir of the 'sequestrated' Royalist landowner Sir William Worthy, so the well-developed sense of 'pastoral content' revealed in his conversations with fellow shepherd Roger and his lover Meg is ideologically compromised by its historical context. It is also notable that the (limited) leisure time afforded Patie by his pastoral labours is spent in a rigorous course of self-improvement, a far cry from the *otium* of Pope's shepherds. If Ramsay's conventional solution to the generic problem of mixing high and low is expressed in his oxymoronic title (Patie is both 'gentle' by blood and a 'shepherd' by upbringing) his 'restoration' to the landed class is mediated by a programme of 'embourgo-isement' under the sign of intellectual 'improvement'.

Unlike 'Laird Kytie's son', to the manor born, who 'gangs about sornan frae Place to Place, | As scrimp of Manners, as of Sense and Grace' (*The Gentle Shepherd*, III. iv 39–40), Patie has been well educated by his guardian Symon; 'he delites in Books:—He reads, and speaks | With Fowks that ken them, *Latin* words and *Greeks*' (III. iv. 65–6).[62] It is perhaps no surprise that Allan Ramsay, bookseller and proprietor of Britain's first circulating library, should give so much emphasis to Patie's books in both the English and Scottish literary canon. Symon mentions that when Patie 'drives our sheep to Edinburgh port, | He buys some books of history, sangs, or sport', going on to mention Shakespeare, Ben Jonson, Drummond of Hawthornden, William Alexander, and Abraham Cowley (III. iv. 69–76). Here, despite the conventional pastoral trope of Patie's gentle blood, lies the origin of the image of the erudite peasant so important to the Scottish vernacular tradition, and Burns in particular, notwithstanding the

---

[61] *Poems of Allan Ramsay, a new edition, to which are prefixed a life of the author [by George Chalmers] and remarks on his poems [by Alexander Tytler, Lord Woodhouselee]*, 2 vols. (London: Cadell & Davies, 1800), i, pp. cxxiv, cxxxviii–cxlviii.

[62] For text of *The Gentle Shepherd*, see Ramsay, ii. 205–77; for quotations, pp. 249–50.

competing myth of the 'Heaven-taught ploughman'. As Sir William puts it, 'Reading such Books can raise a Peasant's Mind | Above a Lord's that is not thus inclined' (III. iv. 84–5).[63] In contrast to Ramsay's *gentle* shepherd', however, Peter Zenzinger is correct to argue that 'in Burns, the nobleman and the simple man have evolved not only into two distinct persons, but into opposing forces'; the 'honest man, though e'er sae poor' is now elevated to the rank of 'king o' men', while the 'birkie ca'd a lord' is ridiculed as a 'coof'.[64]

It is perhaps not so much the extended 'restoration' plot as the Scots idiom and dialectical possibilities of the individual eclogues that compose it which made *The Gentle Shepherd* such a usable resource for subsequent Scottish poets. Ramsay's shepherds modernize a traditional pastoral theme by attacking the profit motive, anticipating Burns's attack on 'luxury's contagion'. In the opening eclogue, Patie and Roger debate the uses of wealth, as Patie attributes Roger's unhappiness to a heartless and mercenary fixation with profit or 'o'ercome'; 'Were your bein Rooms as thinly stock'd as mine, | Less you wad lose, and less you wad repine. | He that has just enough, can soundly sleep; | The O'ercome only fashes Fowk to keep' (I. i. 45–8) [Ramsay, ii. 214].

Murray Pittock has commented in some detail on Jacobite allusions in *The Gentle Shepherd*, as Sir William Worthy returns to take possession of his estates confiscated during the Cromwellian Protectorate.[65] The emphatic (although politically quiescent) Jacobitism that permeated the poetry of Ramsay and his circle in the 1720s and beyond kept open the dialectical possibilities of Virgilian pastoral against the foreclosure wrought by the ideological stasis of neoclassical 'golden ageism'. To this extent it successfully 'repossessed the pastoral for Scottish literature . . . just as Macpherson was to do with the epic thirty-five years later'.[66] *The Gentle Shepherd's* chronotopic specificity, itself signalling Ramsay's 'new' pastoral realism, revived the traditional theme of exile and dispossession central to Virgil's *Eclogues*, and which, as Patterson shows, had been mined by Royalist poets during the interregnum.[67] But Ramsay's vision isn't merely a backward-looking nostalgia for 'the old agriculture': true, the shepherds Glaud and Symon associate the Commonwealth period with rapacious and rack-renting absentee landlords (II. i. 39–45) but the restoration of the

---

[63] Compare Burns's letter to Sir John Sinclair discussed in the previous chapter [CL ii. 106–7].

[64] Peter Zenzinger, 'Low Life, Primitivism and Honest Poverty in Ramsay and Burns', *Studies in Scottish Literature* 30 (1998), 56–7.

[65] Pittock, *Scottish and Irish Romanticism*, 53–7.

[66] Ibid. 57.

[67] Namely, the Royalist poet John Ogilbie's rendering of Meliboeus's contrast between his own exile and Tityruus's good fortune in the *First Eclogue*, in his 1654 translation of Virgil; 'I envie not, but wonder thou'rt so blessed, | Since all with Sequestration are opprest'. The word 'sequestration' here is used in the technical sense employed in the Long Parliament, referring to the confiscated estates of the Royalist aristocracy (Patterson, *Pastoral and Ideology*, 171). Burns's father was the victim of another kind of 'sequestration' in 1783–4.

'Meliboean' Sir William guarantees responsible estate management premised equally on both agricultural improvement and social trusteeship. Pastoral critique of a disharmonious 'world turned upside down' dovetails into the drama's georgic resolution, as Sir William rewards the trusty Symon and Glaud with 'endless feu', pledging that; 'I never from these Fields again will stray: | Masons and Wrights shall soon my House repair, | And bussy Gardners shall new Planting rear; | My Father's hearty Table you soon shall see | Restor'd, and my best Friends rejoyce with me (V. iii. 163–7). At one level this is clearly a model for Scottish cultural and economic renewal, premised on a 'future anterior' ideal of Stuart rule accommodated to the new Whig political regime, corresponding with Ramsay's own vision of Scottish history.[68] But political nostalgia is only half the story here; in the words of Thomas Crawford, 'the magical agent of fairy-tale, the Warlock, is identified with the social class and the ethic of sober reason which will dominate the next hundred years, and therefore with the historic process itself'.[69]

Matthew McDiarmid observes that for all its limitations, the romantic comedy of *The Gentle Shepherd* 'was the freest treatment of the country theme that serious poetry could then have permitted, and it was in its pastoral form that the Scots language found its first ambitious use. It made Fergusson, and therefore Burns, possible' [McD i. 157].[70] Scots pastoral emerged as an identifiable and culturally autonomous sub-genre in the wake of Ramsay, actively promoting Scottish cultural interests within the union, often under the banner of patriotic antiquarianism. In 1761, Thomas Percy wrote to a Welsh correspondent that

the Scotch . . . are everywhere recommending the antiquities of their country to public notice, vindicating its history, setting off its poetry, and by constant attention to their grand national concern have prevailed so far as to have the [broken jargon] Dialect they speak to be considered as the most proper language for our pastoral poetry. Our most polite Ladies [affect to lisp out] warble Scottish Airs, and in the Senate itself whatever relates to the Scottish Nation is always mentioned with respect . . . Far from blaming this attention to the Scotch, I think it does them much credit.[71]

It is clear that by the 1760s Scots pastoral had emerged as a rival to the neoclassical and Parnassian variety that continued to permeate English poetry and song culture high and low. Not all English commentators were as admiring

---

[68] Steve Newman, 'The Scots Songs of Allan Ramsay: "Lyrick" Transformation, Popular Culture, and the Boundaries of the Scottish Enlightenment', *Modern Language Quarterly* 63/3 (Sept. 2002), 277–314 at 291.

[69] T. Crawford, *Society and the Lyric*, 93.

[70] Ramsay's formal influence on his followers's use of the traditional 'habbie' and 'Christ's Kirk' stanzas flowed through other channels, as neither is employed in *The Gentle Shepherd*.

[71] Percy to Evan Evans, 1761, quoted by James Kinsley, 'The Music of the Heart' in Donald A. Low (ed.), *Critical Essays on Robert Burns* (London: Routledge & Kegan Paul, 1975), 133. See also Philip Connell, 'British Identities and the Politics of Ancient Poetry in Later Eighteenth-Century England', *Historical Journal* 49/1 (2006), 189.

as Percy, however, as is evident in Charles Churchill's Scotophobic satire of 1760 *The Prophecy of Famine: A Scots Pastoral Inscribed to John Wilkes*. As the title suggests, Churchill viewed pastoral as the Scottish genre par excellence, the cultural sign under which the Bute administration sought to smuggle the values of Jacobite absolutism and self-seeking Scottish adventurism into the government of mid-eighteenth-century Britain. Scottish poets and artists such as Allan Ramsay father and son, John Home, James Macpherson (author of the 'old, new, epic pastoral, Fingal'), and David Mallett (or Malloch, co-author with James Thomson of 'Rule Britannia') had poured like hungry wolves over England's lush pastures, revelling in the virtuous claims of pastoral 'simplicity', much vaunted by the new theorists of primitivism Hugh Blair and Joseph Warton: 'Thence simple bards, by simple prudence taught . . . take, with simple pensions, simple praise' (ll. 135–8).].[72] Even more to the point, Churchill brought his satirical target into sharp focus by embedding a pastoral dialogue in Scots between two starving Scottish shepherds, Jockey and Sawney, and their visit to the Cave of Famine, whose grim personification foresees for them rich pickings south of the border, and a better future for hungry Scotsmen in London. The shepherds lament the hardship of a pastoral life in barren and unyielding Caledonian climes, and echo Virgil's first and ninth *Eclogues* by complaining of the war and bloodshed unleashed on their land during the 1745 Rebellion; 'Ah silly swains! to follow war's alarms; | Ah! what hath shepherds' lives to do with arms?' (ll. 393–4). Fortunately, however, with the accession of a Scottish prime minister in the shape of the Earl of Bute, the tide has changed, and 'times of happier note are now at hand, | And the full promise of a better land' (ll. 445-6). (All aboard the gravy train!).[73]

The cultural work of Scots pastoral described by Percy and attacked by Churchill in the 1760s was still visible to William Roscoe a few decades later, enhanced now by the poetry of Burns. Roscoe's magisterial *Life of Lorenzo de Medici* (1796) compared the patrician Lorenzo's employment of the Tuscan *lingua contadinesca* (peasant dialect) for pastoral poetry with the achievements of Ramsay and 'the Ayrshire ploughman' in the Scottish vernacular; 'neither in Italy, nor in any other country, has this species of poetry been cultivated with greater success'.[74] For Roscoe, the triumph of 'Scots pastoral' in naturalizing a classical and foreign tradition seemed to be largely *sui generis*, bearing in mind that it was considered to be the humblest of literary genres. As is clear from Roscoe's account, however, by 1796 its consummation seemed attributable to the poetry of Robert Burns. Burns's success had largely eclipsed the achievements

---

[72] 'The Prophecy of Famine', 62–80.

[73] Churchill was countered by the English poet John Langhorne's *Genius and Virtue: A Scotch Pastoral* (London, 1763).

[74] William Roscoe, *The Life of Lorenzo De' Medici, Called The Magnificent*, 2nd edn., 2 vols. (London: Cadell & Davis, 1796), i. 196. As we'll see in the final chapter, Roscoe, a friend of Dr Currie, was originally invited to collaborate in the writing of Burns's biography for the posthumous edition.

of other Scots language poets, like Alexander Ross (whose *Helenore, or the Fortunate Shepherdess*, first published in 1768, was an intelligent response to Ramsay's *Gentle Shepherd*),[75] or the poems of Robert Fergusson discussed in the next section. And by now the generic label of 'pastoral' was itself disappearing from the scene, itself a sign of an emergent Romantic naturalism challenging the self-consciousness of genre.

## ROBERT FERGUSSON'S 'HAME CONTENT'

Burns memorably described Robert Fergusson as 'my elder brother in Misfortune, | By far my elder Brother in the muse' [K 143 ll. 3–4]. Robert Crawford comments that 'with no other poet in the Scottish tradition did Burns identify so closely. He was not so much preceded by Fergusson as haunted by him.'[76] Because of the fame of his Edinburgh poems, Fergusson's role as a pastoral poet has been easily overlooked. Nevertheless, as his editor Matthew McDiarmid pointed out in 1954, 'it was as a pastoralist in the school of Shenstone and Cunningham that Fergusson made his first appearance as a poet' [McD i. 158].

In a recent reassessment of Fergusson's reviled English-language pastorals 'Morning, Noon and Night' (first published in the *Edinburgh Magazine* in 1771), Susan Manning underlines the traditional association of pastoral with poetic noviciate (Virgil's *Eclogues*, Spenser's *Shepheardes Calendar*, Pope's *Pastorals*). She argues that despite the Popean enamel of these poems, 'ideological blandness was not an option for Fergusson . . . evoking national feeling in conventional pastoral diction, Fergusson was neither naïve, nor cringingly deferential to 'English' models'.[77] Taking issue with the view of him as an artless poet of the demotic, Manning argues that Fergusson's diglossic command of both Scots and English is 'dictated by the demands of poetic diction', indicating the extent to which his 'anglo-latinic macaronics' (inspired by Drummond, Swift, and Thomson) would profoundly influence Burns.[78] John Pinkerton's view of

---

[75] Ross's poem was the occasion for James Beattie's sole venture into Scots language poetry in the verse epistle 'To Mr Alexander Ross at Lochlee' (1768), mentioned in Ch. 3. Space prohibits consideration of *Helenore* here; although long and sometimes diffuse, its surprising narrative resolution and its descriptive energy earned it the admiration of Burns, Wordsworth, and Sir Walter Scott.

[76] 'Robert Fergusson's Robert Burns', in Robert Crawford (ed.), *Robert Burns and Cultural Authority* (Edinburgh: Polygon, 1999), 8.

[77] Susan Manning, 'Robert Fergusson and Eighteenth Century Poetry', in Robert Crawford (ed.), *'Heaven-Taught Fergusson': Robert Burns's Favourite Scottish Poet* (Phantassie: Tuckwell, 2003), 87–112 at 97–8.

[78] Ibid. 100–1. For example, the rhymes 'Anacreontic' and 'Pontic' in Fergusson's 'Caller Water' inspire Burns's 'fracas' and 'Bacchus' in 'Scotch Drink'. Carole McGuirk, 'The Rhyming Trade': Fergusson, Burns, and the Marketplace', in Crawford (ed.), *'Heaven-Taught Fergusson'*, 135–59 at 136.

Fergusson as an artless vernacularist ignorant of Scottish poetic tradition (like more recent designations of him as a 'folk poet')[79] ignores his bid to complete Gavin Douglas's project (i.e. the Scots *Aeneid*) with a Scots translation of Virgil's *Eclogues* and *Georgics*, although he died at the age of 24 before making any progress with this ambitious plan.[80]

Welcome as is Manning's critical reassessment of Fergusson's English poetry, her locating him on Pope's (rather than Philips's and Ramsay's) side in the neoclassical pastoral debate in 'endorsing an anti-naturalist aesthetic', risks underestimating Fergusson's debts to the Ramsayan tradition of Scots Pastoral discussed above.[81] Fergusson's serious ambitions as a pastoral poet are graphically illustrated by the vignette of a shepherd with his crook sitting in a Scottish pastoral landscape, featured on the title page of his first (1773) volume of poems. As Manning herself admits, Ramsay's Scots eclogue 'Richy and Sandy' (as well as those from *The Gentle Shepherd* discussed in the previous section), were among the inspiration for Fergusson's first exercise in Scots pastoral, 'An Eclogue, to the Memory of Dr William Wilkie, late Professor of Natural Philosophy in the University of St Andrews', published in the *Edinburgh Magazine* in October 1772, and again in the 1773 volume.[82]

The death of Wilkie (lamented by the shepherds Geordie and Davie in Ramsayan couplets) reminds us that Fergusson, unlike Ramsay and Burns, was a university graduate who had received a classical education at St Andrews University under the special mentorship of Wilkie. A distinguished natural philosopher as well as the author of a flatulent epic entitled *The Epigoniad* (1757–9) that won the praise of David Hume, Wilkie was also a noted agricultural improver, a fact that isn't lost on 'Geordie'; 'You saw yourself how weel his *mailin* thrave, | Ay better faugh'd an' snodit than the lave' [McD ii. 84 ll. 65–6]. This georgic infusion praises Wilkie (very much in the language of agricultural improvement) for straightening his rigs, enclosing his fields, and purging his crops of weeds and thistles. It necessarily qualifies Fred Freeman's view of Fergusson as a 'Tory Traditionalist' and anti-improver, however much his most significant exercise in Scots pastoral 'The Farmer's Ingle' (discussed in Chapter 7 in relation to Burns's 'Cotter's Saturday Night') idealizes 'the wholly outmoded *gudeman* system of farming', albeit in the distinct idiom of 'hard' pastoral incorporating a strong georgic element.[83]

---

[79] John Pinkerton, *Antient Scotish Poetry*, I p. cxl; cf. Jack, *Italian Influence*, 154.

[80] Butt, 'Vernacular Scottish Poetry', 232.

[81] Ibid. 97. Ramsay's mock elegies ('Maggie Johnson', 'Lucky Wood', 'John Cooper', and 'Lucky Spence's Last Advice') were Edinburgh poems that doubtless influenced Fergusson's urban muse, far from 'bucolic rusticity and the kailyard'.

[82] Manning, 'Fergusson and Eighteenth Century Poetry', 98.

[83] F. W. Freeman, 'Robert Fergusson: Pastoral and Politics at Mid-Century', in Andrew Hook (ed.), *The History of Scottish Literature*, ii. *1660–1800* (Aberdeen: Aberdeen University Press, 1987), 141–55 at 143.

The fact that Fergusson's Scots poetry began to appear in Ruddiman's *Edinburgh Magazine* in 1772, just a decade after Churchill's scotophobic *Prophecy of Famine*, perhaps explains the note of defiant nativism that's quite foreign to the poetry of Ramsay. It is well illustrated in Fergusson's nationalistic 'Elegy on the Death of Scots Music', first published in the *Edinburgh Magazine* in March 1772. Returning the mock elegy in the 'Habbie Simpson' tradition to more serious purposes, the occasion for Fergusson's poem was the death of the violinist and composer William MacGibbon, who (ironically), despite his important contribution to Scottish tradition, also 'played the music of Corelli, Germiniani, and Handel, with great execution and judgement' [McD i. 257]. Going beyond Ramsay's recipe for the 'domestication' of pastoral and praise for the 'saft music' [l. 2] and 'hameil lays' [l. 29] of Scottish song, Fergusson assumes a combative cultural xenophobia which would influence Burns:

> Now foreign sonnets bear the gree,
> And crabbit queer variety
> Of sounds fresh sprung frae *Italy*,
>     A bastard breed!
> Unlike that saft-tongu'd melody
>     Which now lies dead.
>
> Could *lav'rocks* at the dawning day,
> Could *linties* chirming frae the spray,
> Or toddling *burns* that smoothly play
>     O'er gowden bed,
> Compare wi' *Birks of Indermay?*
>     But now they're dead.   [McD ii. 39 ll. 49–60]

The poem's final stanza becomes quite literally a *crie de guerre* ('fight till MUSIC be restor'd, | Which now lies dead', ll. 65–6), although Fergusson's exemplar of Scots music, the pacific pastoral song *Birks of Indermay* (or 'Invermay') seems a strange rallying call for what Murray Pittock calls a 'literature of combat'.[84] The 'foreign sonnets' and Italianate operas criticized by Fergusson are of course cognate versions of 'soft' pastoral in the Arcadian or Parnassian mode; but his specific targets here are presumably the 'pretentious settings, overloaded with trills and other prettifications' by Edinburgh-based Italian composers such as Domenico Corri, Pietro Urbani, and Guisto Tenducci, which, according to David Daiches, 'were destroying the native vigour and simplicity of Scots song'.[85] Ironies abound

---

[84] See Pittock, *Scottish and Irish Romanticism*, 27, and 125–6 for a different reading of Fergusson's 'Elegy'. The English words for the beautiful song 'Birks of Indermay' were written by David Mallett. Appearing in the third volume of the *Tea-Table Miscellany*, an extended version was published by David Herd in *Ancient and Modern Scottish Songs and Ballads* in 1776.

[85] *Paradox of Scottish Culture*, 31, 33. This is clearly a matter of taste, but Daiches overlooks Francesco Barsanti's fine setting of Ramsay's 'Corn Riggs are Bonny', or Francesco Geminiani's 'Lass of Paty's Mill', not to mention the virtuoso Italianate variations of McGibbon's setting of

in the fact that Fergusson himself composed English lyrics for the Italian tenor Tenducci for Thomas Arnes's opera *Artaxerxes* (1769), albeit set to traditional Scottish airs such as 'Braes of Balandene' and 'Lochaber No More' [McD ii. 3–4]. Fergusson's allusions to Mallett's 'Birks of Endermay' and the example of McGibbon's musical achievements actually suggest that 'Scots Music' may have been enriched rather than 'killed off' by the influence of Italian composers such as Corelli and Geminiani, just as eighteenth-century Scots pastoral poetry had benefited from the examples of Theocritus and Virgil, or the English pastorals of Pope and Shenstone. Once again we need to grasp the hybrid interfusion of high culture with the demotic Scots tradition; at stake here is the non-deferential juxtaposition of Scots vernacular with literary English and Latin, the 'crabbit variety' of the concert hall mingled with the 'saft music' of street and byre, Burns's great poetic inheritance.

It is perhaps ironic that Fergusson's most impressive achievement concerns pastoral's urban dialectic, one that certainly wasn't matched by Burns, whose 'Address to Edinburgh' [K 135] is one of his weakest performances. After all, Fergusson eked out his short working life as a clerk in Edinburgh's Commissary Record Office copying legal documents at a penny a page, an existence enlivened by enthusiastic involvement in the city's dining and drinking clubs, most notably the Cape Club. The urban orientation of Fergusson's pastoral, including 'The Farmer's Ingle', is already visible in the conventional pastoral values of 'Hame Content. A Satire', first published in the *Edinburgh Magazine* in July 1773. The poem's subtitle makes explicit McKeon's argument that 'pastoral is . . . an ancient form of satirical or 'political' poetry, because the praise of one term [the country] always carries a reciprocal . . . critique of the latter [the town]'.[86] Leaving the city and its obsessive pursuit of 'wardly gear', the city poet seeks refuge from summer heat under 'the caller shady trees' of the countryside. Yet this isn't merely *beatus ille qui procul negotiis*; 'hame content' is a populated Nature whose pastoral values are social rather than solipsistic, based on the economics of sufficiency rather than 'o'ercome' or profit, and the superfluous desire for 'eistacks' or luxuries.[87] Fergusson's refugee from the city breathes the fresh air as he watches the country people labouring in the fields;

'Bonnocks of Beer Meal', published in *Collection of Scots Tunes* (1746). Concerto Caledonia's fine performances of both songs are available on the CD *Mungrel Stuff: Francesco Barsanti (1690–1772) and Others* (Linn Records, 2001); McGibbon's 'Bonnocks of Bear Meal' is performed by David Greenberg on the CD *Kinloch's Fancy: A Curious Collection of Scottish Sonatas and Reels* (Marquis Classics, Toronto, 1997).

[86] McKeon, 'Pastoral Revolution', 268.

[87] See Matthew Simpson, '"Hame Content": Globalization and a Scottish Poet of the Eighteenth Century', *Eighteenth-Century Life* 27/1 (2003), 107–29. Simpson convincingly relates 'Hame Content' to the anti-luxury arguments of Sir George Mackenzie's *Moral History of Frugality, with its Opposite Vices* (1691), while ignoring the generic pressures of the 'Virgilian dialectic'.

> 'Mang herds, an' honest cottar fock,
> That till the farm and feed the flock;
> Careless o' mair, wha never fash
> To lade their KIST wi' useless CASH,
> But thank the GODS for what they've sent
> O health enough, and blyth content.   [McD ii. 157 ll. 25–30]

Patie's pastoral politics as articulated in Act IV, scene ii of *The Gentle Shepherd* are reiterated here both in the poem's critique of upper class *otium* and foreign travel, in favour of 'Hame content'. The urban surplus economy and its health-destroying addiction to luxuries are bad enough; but even worse is the remedy proposed, the Grand Tour to 'Italy, or Well o' Spaw, | Or to Montpelier's safter air; | For far aff FOWLS hae FEATHERS fair' (ll. 66–8).[88] In a passage echoed by Burns in 'The Twa Dogs', Fergusson castigates the bored gentry who, distracted by the allure of the foreign, never set foot on their own estates. In the lines that follow, the poem returns to the Ramsayan *querelle* between Arcadia and the 'simple, saft' Scots pastoral; 'On Leader haughs an' Yarrow braes, | ARCADIAN herds wad tyne their lays, | To hear the mair melodious sounds | That live on our POETIC grounds' [McD ii. 157 ll. 89–92].

If the conventional pastoral politics of 'Hame Content' depend on a summer *villagatura* from city to the country, Fergusson's 'The Daft Days' signals a reverse, winter migration to the city. The summery pastoral landscape of *The Gentle Shepherd* now appears in the negative garb of litote: 'From naked groves nae birdie sings, | To shepherd's pipe nae hillock rings' (McD ii. 33 ll. 7–8). By contrast, the winter city of Edinburgh ('Daft Days' was the derogatory Presbyterian term for the interval between Christmas and Hogmanay) is warm and hospitable, 'A beild for mony caldrife soul' (l. 20), where 'reaming ale' (l. 34) and the 'canty Highland reel'(l. 50) 'invest the dawning of the year' (l. 56). On the one hand this is addressed to Scotland's landowning gentry who 'wintered' in their Edinburgh town houses to pursue legal business in the Court of Session, supervise the education of their sons and marry off their daughters, or participate in the capital's club culture. At the same time, the urban migration sounds a warning note, gesturing to a more popular audience: behind the poem's celebration of urban conviviality there lurks the threat of violence and disorder, invoked in the 'great god of *Aqua Vitae*' (l. 61) who 'sways the empire of this city', attracting the unwanted attention of the dreaded City Guard. As Ian Duncan points out, just as Fergusson's rural pastorals incorporate a georgic 'reversal of values', the urban poems of popular festivity represent 'a capacious kind of excitement, with room for bouts of moral and political sermonizing'.[89]

Fergusson's unfinished masterpiece 'Auld Reikie: A Poem' (1773) was clearly inspired by the 'urban georgics' of Swift and Gay. Yet the poem's bracing Scots verse, its 'manners-painting strain' and the trope of *rus in urbe* (see especially

---

[88] Fergusson quotes from Ramsay's *Collection of Scots Proverbs*, ch. 11 no. 16, 'Faraway fowls have fair feathers' [McD ii. 291].

[89] Ian Duncan, 'Fergusson's Edinburgh', in Crawford, *'Heaven-Taught Fergusson'*, 65–84 at 71.

ll. 195–218) keep it closer to the pastoral than the georgic tradition. The poet begins with an apology to Edinburgh that 'o'er lang frae thee the Muse has been | Sae frisky on the SIMMER's Green' [McD ii. 109 ll. 7–8] before revisiting the anti-pastoral trope of wintry nature already employed in 'The Daft Days'. Urban life represents modernity cut loose from nature's cycle ('Thou canst charm | Un-fleggit by the year's Alarm', ll. 17–18). But in 'Auld Reikie' the traditional pastoral opposition between rural virtue and city corruption underpinning 'Hame Content' is complicated by the fact that an artificial urban life now appears as the portal to a more intense experience of nature herself. It is as if Fergusson, in exposing the pastoral myth of pristine nature, is glossing Hugh Blair's remark that 'it was not until men had begun to assemble in great cities, after the distinction of ranks and station were formed, and the bustle of Courts and large societies were known, that Pastoral Poetry assumed its present form'.[90] It is a measure of Fergusson's literary sophistication that the pastoral-primitivist vision, soon to be so powerfully literalized in the poetry of 'the Heaven-taught ploughman', is here exposed as a fiction of modernity.

This is nowhere more apparent than in the poem's treatment of 'Edina's Roses', the city's reputation for stink and ordure that are central to 'Auld Reikie'. Prostitutes, 'hungry writers', and shit-bespattered macaronis exemplify the effects of urban luxury, vice, and corruption. Duncan connects Fergusson's scatological references with an Augustan rhetoric of antithetical substitution ('Stink, *instead of* Perfumes') and oxymoron ('*clarty* odours *fragrant* flow').[91] (Later Fergusson advises the reader that 'GILLESPIE's snuff should prime the Nose | Of her that to the Market goes' (ll. 219–20); the stench may be preternatural, but modern 'improvements' can offer an antidote.) Lines 43–50 had already proposed a more complex irony in which the city's foul stink itself provides a form of aesthetic education unavailable to the country-dweller;

> But without Souring nocht is sweet;
> The Morning smells that hail our Street,
> Prepare, and gently lead the Way
> To Simmer canty, braw and gay:
> Edina's Sons mair eithly share,
> Her Spices and her Dainties rare,
> Then he that's never yet been call'd
> Aff frae his Plaidie or his Fauld.   (ll. 43–50)

The paradox of modernity lies in the fact that the 'souring' of city life makes (to quote Duncan one last time) 'Edinburgh citizens more fit to inhabit [the pastoral season of summer]—to savour its spices and dainties—than the traditional denizen of pastoral, the shepherd . . . the migration from country to town is a type of effectual *calling*, marked by an accession of taste'.[92] Despite the darker

---

[90] Hugh Blair, *Lectures on Rhetoric and Belles Lettres*, iii. 336.
[91] Duncan, 'Fergusson's Edinburgh', 73.
[92] Ibid. 74.

undercurrents and the melancholy that pervades some of Fergusson's poetry, this is ultimately a redemptive vision of urban modernity. At one level, 'Auld Reikie's' patriot politics lament Scotland's post-1707 predicament symbolized by the ruined condition of Holyrood Palace (ll. 281–4). On the other, at lines 313–28, the poem lavishes praise on Edinburgh's Lord Provost George Drummond (1687–1766), promoter of civic improvement in the shape of the Infirmary, the Exchange, the North Bridge, New Town, etc. [McD ii. 280], even if subsequent Provosts have failed to sustain his achievements. For all its ambivalence concerning the effects of improvement, 'Auld Reikie' clearly represents one terminus of the rural tradition of Scottish pastoral, signalling the emergence of a new poetry of urban modernity.

At the same time, Fergusson's generic 'migration' remains deeply beholden to the values of the 'Scots pastoral' tradition that it seeks to transcend, and which, as we'll now see, inspired Burns ('meeting with Fergusson's Scotch Poems, I strung anew my wildly-sounding rustic lyre with emulating vigour') [CL i. 143].[93] Burns purchased his own copy of Fergusson's 1782 edition in early 1786 when he was preparing the Kilmarnock volume—he may even have worked with an open copy beside him—and as we'll see in subsequent chapters, the debt was immense.[94] Fergusson's early death at the age of 23 contracted his most creative period to a mere two years; but nevertheless, one can only speculate upon the reasons for his failure to achieve anything like Burns's poetic fame among his contemporaries. (Mackenzie's famous *Lounger* review of Burns claims, for example, that 'the provincial dialect which Ramsay and [Burns] have used, is now read with a difficulty which greatly damps the pleasure', as if Fergusson's Scots poetry had never been published [*CH* p. 69].) Of course, it may be that Fergusson was simply ahead of his time, out of synchrony with the agrarian patriotism that gripped Scotland in the mid-1780s, and which discovered in Burns its national voice.

## BURNS'S KILMARNOCK POEMS
## AND THE *COPIA VERBORUM*

On 31 July 1786, John Wilson of Kilmarnock completed a run of 612 copies of a handsome 240-page octavo volume entitled *Poems Chiefly in the Scottish Dialect, by Robert Burns*, selling for the modest price of three shillings. The volume

---

[93] But if Gilbert Burns is correct in recalling that the Burns family possessed copies of the *Edinburgh Magazine* for 1772, while they were still farming at Mount Oliphant (which included some of Fergusson's most important Scots poems) then he may have been familiar with the poetry at a much earlier date. Currie, *Life and Works of Robert Burns*, i. 67. The *Edinburgh Magazine* for 1772 contained 'The Daft Days', 'Elegy on the Death of Scots Music', 'King's Birthday in Edinburgh', 'Caller Oysters', 'Braid Cloth', 'Eclogue to the Memory of Dr Wilkie', 'Hallow-Fair', and 'The Tron-Kirk Bell'.

[94] 'McGuirk, 'The Rhyming Trade', in Crawford (ed.), *Heaven-Taught Fergusson*, 135, 154.

contained forty-four poems, including four songs, as well as a short preface and a glossary by the poet: unconventionally, the dedication, to the poet's friend Gavin Hamilton, was buried more than halfway through the volume, and (as I'll suggest in Chapter 3) burlesqued the normal conventions of dedication and patronage. Although he was assiduous in seeing his book through the press, Burns could afford to be cavalier because he published by subscription, building on his existing local reputation as the author of 'Kirk satires' and verse epistles that had already circulated widely around Ayrshire in manuscript form.

Richard Sher characterizes Kilmarnock as a 'distribution subscription edition' (modelled on the blind Dr Blacklock's *Poems on Several Occasions*) whereby 'friends and well-wishers bought up large quantities for local sale by word of mouth'; this model of subscription only worked, however, if the price was low enough for copies to be resold to purchasers of modest means.[95] Although he later downplayed the number of subscribers to the Kilmarnock edition, Wilson's records show that more than 400 copies were ordered through advance subscriptions, by seven individuals alone.[96] Such were the egalitarian credentials of Kilmarnock, in contrast to the Edinburgh edition of the following year, with its fulsome dedication to the aristocratic members of the Caledonian Hunt and its copious subscription list, comprising the names of over 1,500 of Scotland's great and good, pledged to receive a total of 2,876 copies at five shillings apiece. The Edinburgh volume was, moreover, published by William Creech, the leading publisher of the Scottish Enlightenment.[97]

Despite its modest origins, the Kilmarnock volume was a runaway success, being avidly sought after by readers from all social backgrounds, from Edinburgh as well as Ayrshire and the south-west of Scotland; a month after publication only thirteen copies remained unsold. The story of the subsequent turn of events has loomed large in 'Burnslore', as the poet abandoned his immediate plans to emigrate to Jamaica and, in November 1786, headed for Edinburgh at the behest of Dr Blacklock, in order to publish a second edition of his poems. Less often remarked is the manner in which Burns's Preface and poems skilfully constructed the persona of the 'Simple Bard, unbroke by rules of Art', together with a partially submerged biographical narrative to match, loosely based on the contemporary crisis afflicting his own life, but disclaiming any literary influences other than the poetry of Ramsay and Fergusson. In this final section I'll scrutinize Burns's prefatory disclaimer in relation to some of the conventions of 'Scots pastoral' explored in the rest of the chapter.

[95] Richard Sher, *The Enlightenment and the Book* (Chicago: University of Chicago Press, 2006), 230.

[96] Robert Aiken (145), Robert Muir (72), Gilbert Burns (70), James Smith (41), Gavin Hamilton (40), Logan of Laight (20), and David McWhinnie (20). Sher, ibid.

[97] Ibid. 232. See Hamish Mathison, 'Gude Black Prent': How the Edinburgh Book Trade Dealt with Burns's Poems', *Bibliotheck* 20 (1995), 70–87.

John Wilson's Kilmarnock printing press had been established just a few years earlier in 1782, and although his work was mainly confined to bills, tradesman's cards, and letterheads, in 1785 he'd brought out an edition of Milton's *Paradise Lost* [Mackay, 232–6].[98] Surviving copies of Burns's flier circulated to subscribers reveal that he'd originally intended to publish poems *exclusively*, rather than 'chiefly', in the 'Scottish Dialect', but in the event the book contained a mixed bag, from the full Scots of 'Halloween' and 'The Auld Farmer's New-Year Morning Salutation' to the neo-Augustan 'graveyard' style of English poems such as 'Despondency, an Ode' and 'To Ruin'. Edinburgh critics naturally associated Burns's Ayrshire 'dialect' poetry with the volume's provincial publication, but in fact Wilson had never before published a volume of Scots poetry, and because 'at the time there was no fashion for vernacular poetry . . . to embark on such a course was quite daring and original' [Mackay, p. 332].

The appearance of a volume of poems 'Chiefly in the Scottish Dialect' in Kilmarnock in 1786 was thus a completely unheralded star in the poetic firmament, even if its success would inspire a flood of imitations from Wilson's press (and others like it) over the following decades. Not surprisingly, Burns's poetic employment of 'the Scottish Dialect' announced in the book's title has been the main focus of critical debate since the first reviews of the Kilmarnock volume, a debate largely polarized between what I'll term 'naïve' and 'sceptical' views. For there's an extraordinary lack of consensus amongst early reviewers about Burns's language, and the debate often echoes the earlier language of the Pope/Ambrose Philips dispute. Henry Mackenzie (principle champion of the 'naïve' view of Burns) regretted that the poems' 'provincial dialect' rendered them difficult of understanding, which shows him accepting the Preface's 'realist' claim that the poet 'sings the sentiments and manners, he felt and saw in himself and his rustic compeers around him, *in his and their native language*' [Kil. p. iii, my italics]. (It is a paradox of course that the Preface needed to make this claim in standard English.) Although Burns's statement had a profound influence on romantic vernacular theorists, especially Wordsworth, those who accepted the 'naïve' view that Burns 'wrote as he spoke' ran the risk of confounding the self-conscious poet with his various literary personae, especially the voice of the 'Heaven-taught ploughman'.[99] This ultimately supported David Craig's damaging judgement that the Scots poetry of Burns and his peers suffered from a 'reductive idiom' and 'limitation of range', reflecting the realities of a 'disintegrating' culture'.[100] A clever, postmodernist version of the naïve thesis is

[98] Wilson later moved his business to Ayr where in 1803 he launched the *Ayr Advertiser*; here, in 1811, he printed William Aiton's *Treatise on Moss-Earth* and included other works of agricultural improvement amongst his variegated list.

[99] A view held by R. L. Stevenson, Matthew Arnold, and Burns's editor W. E. Henley. See Raymond Bentman, 'Robert Burns's Use of Scottish Diction', in Hilles and Bloom (eds.), *From Sensibility to Romanticism*, 239–58 at 240.

[100] Craig, *Scottish Literature*, 13, 74, 82.

resurrected (to sophisticated effect) in Jeff Skoblow's recent study of Burns *Dooble Tongue*.[101]

The naive interpretation may have had negative repercussions for Burns criticism, but the sceptical view has led to problems of its own. Echoing Pope's criticism of Spenserian pastoral, James Anderson (writing, like Mackenzie, in 1786), attributed the difficulty of the poems to the fact that they were 'faithfully copied from . . . the ancient Scottish bards', and recommending that in future Burns employed a 'measure less antiquated' [*CH* p. 74]. This view was later reiterated by John Logan, who complained (in letter to Mackenzie, 28 February 1787) of 'a kind of Imposture not infrequent among poets of conveying Modern ideas in a dialect of Antiquity' [*CH*, p. 79]. Later, Robert Southey denied that Burns's diction had any relation to spoken Scots, and designated it (referring to the antiquarian forgeries of Chatterton) as 'a kind of Rowleyism, composed of all the Scotch words they can collect' [*CH* p. 169]. An element of this view survives in Raymond Bentman's modern judgement that 'the "Scottish" poems are written in a literary language, which was mostly, although not entirely, English, in grammar and syntax, and, in varying proportions, both Scottish and English in vocabulary'.[102]

True as this may be in one sense, Bentman's view is potentially misleading to the extent that, in the absence of any written Scots standard, Burns could hardly have written in 'pure vernacular Scottish', although the Kilmarnock poems were probably the nearest to such a thing that many of his eighteenth-century readers had ever experienced on the page.[103] Their excitement was evoked by Robert Heron, in his otherwise unreliable 1797 *Memoir*, who remembered how 'plough-boys and maid servants' spent their hard-earned wages on Burns's poems, because they 'were written in a phraseology, of which all the powers were universally felt; and which being at once, *antique, familiar,* and now *rarely written,* was hence fitted for all the dignified and picturesque uses of poetry, without being disagreeably obscure' [*CH* p.122]. Heron captures the wide social range of Burns's poetry (we might recall Burns's insistence that his 'strongest wish' was 'to please my Compeers, the rustic Inmates of the Hamlet' [CL i. 70]) as well as the problematic relationship between the 'varieties' of spoken Scots, contemporary popular culture, and Burns's literary language.

Murray Pittock rightly challenges the naive view on the grounds that 'because Burns is a sophisticated writer, writing in Scots is always a poetic option for him,

---

[101] Skoblow, *Dooble Tongue*, 183, privileges a performative and oral Scots 'vulgate' as a kind of 'troth-speech', which always transcends the appropriative schemes of standard English.

[102] Bentman, 'Robert Burns's Use of Scottish Diction', 239.

[103] Although attempts were made in the late eighteenth century to construct a 'polite' standard Scots, the most important by James Adams and Alexander Geddes. See Jones, *A Language Suppressed*, 14–21.

not an educational necessity.'[104] I've already explored Burns's literacy at some length, and like many educated Scots of the eighteenth century, Burns also possessed extensive capacity in spoken standard English; his acquaintance Dugald Stewart commented on 'the fluency, and precision, and originality of his language, when he spoke in company; more particularly as he aimed at purity in his turn of expression, and avoided more successfully than most Scotsmen, the peculiarities of Scottish phraseology' [Kin. iii. 1543]. By the same token, when Burns sought to underline (rather than *avoid*) these 'peculiarities' for poetic effect, he could do so with great literary skill, a point which Stewart fails to mention.

The best key to understanding Burns's poetic language is the poet's own notion of the *copia verborum*, doubtless influenced by Allan Ramsay's account (in the preface to his 1721 poems) of the diglossic range available to the educated Scots poet, discussed earlier in this chapter. After Burns's death, the Edinburgh literatus Dr Robert Anderson recalled a conversation with Burns in Edinburgh in 1787 in which the poet reviewed his linguistic tool-kit with extraordinary technical fluency:

It was, I know, part of the machinery, as he called it, of his poetical character to pass for an illiterate ploughman who wrote from pure inspiration. When I pointed out some evident traces of poetical inspiration in his verses, privately, he readily acknowledged his obligations and even admitted the advantages he enjoyed in poetical composition from the *copia verborum*, the command of phraseology, which the knowledge and use of the English and Scottish dialects afforded him; but in company he did not suffer his pretensions to pure inspiration to be challenged, and it was seldom done where he might be supposed to affect the success of the subscription for his Poems.   [Kin. iii. 1537–8]

Here Burns allows the pastoral mask to slip for a moment, although not without expressing some concerns for the damage such candour might do to his subscription list. He underlines the fact that, rather than struggling with an 'impoverished' or 'restricted' idiom, the Scots poet who commands both 'the English and Scottish dialects' in fact enjoys a peculiar advantage over others limited to standard English poetic diction alone (such a consideration might have determined Burns's final decision to publish 'chiefly' rather than 'exclusively' in 'Scots dialect'). As Jeremy Smith argues, Burns's *copia verborum* ('abundance of words') signifies a language that 'contains sufficient vocabulary for all registers (i.e. elevated, plain, demotic)': and his particular skill was 'to shift from one register of language to another in accordance with the social situation of his language'.[105]

As many critics have pointed out, the poetic diction of the Kilmarnock poems is drawn from a wide range of sources; English-language poets such as Pope, Thomson, Gray, Goldsmith, and Shenstone, as well as Scottish precursors, from

---

[104] Pittock, *Scottish and Irish Romanticism*, 147.
[105] Jeremy Smith, '*Copia Verborum*: Linguistic Choices in Robert Burns', *Review of English Studies* NS 58/233 (2007), 76, 84. See also Currie, i. 331.

Montgomerie and Sempill to Ramsay and Fergusson; it also ranged over an extensive linguistic gamut, from Anglo-Latinic macaronics and the rhetoric of sensibility, to the homely Scots proverbs of Ramsay's collection.[106] At the same time the Preface's claim that the poems imitated the 'native language' of the poet's 'rustic compeers' demands serious consideration as a function of the volume's overall plan. The collection played to its cultural location by flaunting a rural Ayrshire dialect (evoked in 'Epistle to Davie' as 'hamely, *westlin* jingle' [K 51 l. 6]), highlighted by the poet's own word-list in the glossary to the poems. As we'll see in the next chapter, Burns's geographical location as an 'Ayrshire bardie' was an important theme of such poems as 'The Vision' and the 'Epistle to Willie Simson', and several of the poems deliberately employ a strong rural dialect. Although there are problems with distinguishing any such thing as 'eighteenth-century Ayrshire dialect' (because, as David Murison writes, 'almost nothing in Ayrshire dialect had been recorded [before] 1786 when the Kilmarnock edition appeared'), Burns's verse-epistle correspondent Willie Simson later insisted that 'the Glossary to Burns's poems gives a good idea of the Provincial Terms in Ayrshire'.[107] As Murison points out, Burns's Scots vocabulary (employing over 2,000 words) is highly eclectic, drawing from a wide number of Scottish dialects; but his rural poems do feature a number of words from the poet's native Kyle, words such as *crunt, daimen, gloamin shot, ha bible, icker, jauk, kiaugh, messan, pyle, raucle, rockin, roon, shangan, thummert, wiel, winze, wintle.*[108] If Kilmarnock's glossary sought to render local terms intelligible to Edinburgh readers, the expanded 1787 glossary included general Scots terms, indicating Burns's ambitions for the Edinburgh volume south of the border, and in the colonies.

William Simson's essay 'Provincial Terms and Glossary', appended to Aiton's *General View of the Agriculture of Ayr* (1811), is arguably more concerned with the orthoepy of Ayrshire speech than with its lexicography, especially in the marked difference of its vowels from standard English.[109] But one remarkable feature of Simson's essay (dismissed by Murison as 'irrelevant' and 'misguided')

---

[106] For an argument that Burns valued English poetry more highly than the verse of Ramsay and Fergusson, see John C. Weston, 'Burns's Use of the Scots Verse-Epistle Form', *Philological Quarterly* 49/2 (April 1970), 188–210 at 208.

[107] David Murison, 'The Speech of Ayrshire in the Time of Burns', in John Strawhorn (ed.), *Ayrshire at the Time of Burns* (Kilmarnock: Ayrshire Archaeological and Natural History Society, 1959), 222–31 at 222, 226. 'Ayrshire belongs to the large dialect area called mid-Scots which covers all Lowland Scotland except Roxburgh-, Selkirk- and East Dumfries-shire, as far north as the middle of Angus' (p. 226).

[108] David Murison, 'The Language of Burns', in Donald Low (ed.), *Critical Essays on Robert Burns* (London: RKP, 1975), 54–69 at 63.

[109] This interest was to some extent shared by Burns: although his glossary to the Kilmarnock edition mentions only grammatical variations, his remarks added to the much extended Edinburgh glossary dilate upon the correct Scots pronunciation of the fricative and diphthong, stressing the affinity of Scots with French and Latin, rather than English.

is his argument that Ayrshire dialect, like other dialectal variants from standard English customarily dismissed as 'Scotticisms or vulgarisms', is 'consonant to the Greek classics, in the purest state of that language'. This, Simson argues, should be a matter of pride to Scots speakers, and the envy of their English neighbours. Admitting that Burns's Kyle dialect differed little from other Lowland dialects, Simson proposed that, in relation to standard English, it 'bore a striking likeness to some of the Greek dialects when compared to the true Greek language', especially 'the DORIC, which was first used among the Lacedemonians, and the inhabitants of Argos . . . and which appears exemplified in the writings of Archimedes, Theocritus, and Pindar . . . [it] seems to have a predilection for the sound of A, in preference to that of E, I, O, U, EA, and AI'.[110]

Re-emerging here is the old argument, familiar to us from Ramsay's preface, that sought to legitimise Scots as a 'Doric' dialect, as well as its literary suitability for 'Theocritan' pastoral poetry. The connection was certainly visible to Burns's patron, the Earl of Buchan, however half-hearted his praise, in a letter to the poet, for the beauty of 'these little doric pieces of yours in our provincial dialect'. (This from the man who sought to naturalise nightingales on the 'arcadian' banks of his estate at Dryburgh on the chilly banks of the Tweed!) But notwithstanding his intense patriotism, Buchan felt that Burns should move beyond Scots pastoral to 'attempt works of greater magnitude, variety, and importance', in the Augustan English of his beloved James Thomson [Chambers-Wallace, ii. 46].[111]

## DISPOSSESSION AND THE 'VIRGILIAN DIALECTIC'

In comparison with James Hogg's candour in entitling his first published volume of 1801 *Scottish Pastorals*, Burns's Kilmarnock volume explicitly disavows its generic affiliations, while at the same time smuggling in a sophisticated reassessment of the scope of pastoral itself.[112] While acknowledging a poetic debt to 'the genius of a Ramsay' and 'the glorious dawnings of the poor, unfortunate, Ferguson' [Kil. p. v] the Preface artfully disavows any relationship with classical pastoral:

The following trifles are not the production of the Poet, who, with all the advantages of learned art, and perhaps amid the elegancies and idlenesses of upper life, looks down for a rural theme, with an eye to Theocrites [*sic*] or Virgil. To the Author of this, these and other celebrated names their countrymen are, in their original language, 'A fountain shut

---

[110]  William Simson, 'Provincial Terms and Glossary', in Aiton, pp. 681–93 at 681–3.

[111]  Alexander Geddes was more encouraging, advising Burns; 'Nor cast thine aiten reed aside: | Bot trim, an' blaw it mair an mair'. 'Epistle to . . . the Scottish Society of Antiquaries', in *Three Scottish Poems, with a Previous Dissertation on the Scoto-Saxon Dialect* (Edinburgh, 1792), i. 453.

[112]  James Hogg, *Scottish Pastorals: Poems, Songs, &c. Mostly Written in the Dialect of the South*, ed. Elaine Petrie (Stirling: Stirling University Press, 1998). Although acknowledging the example of Burns, Hogg's real debt here is to Allan Ramsay.

up, and a book sealed'. Unacquainted with the necessary requisites for commencing Poet by rule, he sings the sentiments and manners, he felt and saw in himself and his rustic compeers around him, in his and their native language'   [Kil. p. iii].

The claim here to be 'unacquainted' with 'Theocrites and Virgil' underpins the ploughman persona of many of the poems that follow, especially the 'Epistle to Lapraik's' attack on those who 'think to climb Parnassus | By dint o' Greek!' [K 57 ll. 71–2]; his literary *ignorance* authenticates the poet's portrayal of the world of his 'rustic compeers' in 'his and their native language'. But Douglas Dunn rightly warns that the Preface's claims are wrapped in 'the seven veils of irony'.[113] Like the footnoted quotation from Shenstone that follows,[114] Burns's allusion ('a fountain shut up, and a book sealed') as a metaphoric statement of his ignorance of Theocritus or Virgil, already questions his naive claims to be a *literal* (rather than a *literary*) pastoralist. For his text here is a loose rendition, or else a misquotation, of The Song of Solomon 4: 12, 'A garden inclosed is my sister, my spouse; a spring shut up, a fountain sealed.' Moreover, knowledge of the biblical context undermines the obvious sense of the quotation, to the extent that the original verse actually gestures towards the Hebrew poet's erotic *enjoyment* of his lover.[115] As Burns memorably expressed it elsewhere, 'The wisest Man the warl' saw | He dearly lov'd the Lasses, O' [K 45 ll. 15–16].[116]

Given the currency of Virgil in the eighteenth-century educational curriculum, and the extent of Burns's literacy as discussed in the previous chapter, it would have been strange if Burns hadn't encountered the *Eclogues*, one of the most widely translated and imitated classical texts of the eighteenth century.[117] This suspicion is heightened by close attention to the Preface's statement of ignorance concerning the classical poets 'in their original languages',[118] but not (by implication) in any one of the many English translations that proliferated throughout the eighteenth century.[119] (Geddes's translations of Theocritus and

---

[113] Douglas Dunn, 'Burns's Native Metric', 61.

[114] McGuirk writes that 'what Burns admired in Shenstone, especially his elegies, was his effort at an unadorned "middle" English style and his echo of the Horatian values with which Burns was also familiar from the work of Allan Ramsay' [McGuirk, *BSP* p. 209].

[115] Joseph Warton claimed that The Song of Solomon ('the most exquisite Pastoral now extant') was a powerful influence on Theocritus' *Idylls*. See 'A Dissertation Upon Pastoral Poetry' in The Works of Virgil, in *English Verse, The Aeneid translated by the Rev. Christopher Pitt, the Eclogues and Georgics, with notes on the whole, by the Rev. Joseph Warton*, 4 vols. (London: Dodsley, 1763), 46.

[116] 'Green Grow the Rashes. A Fragment'.

[117] See Steven R. McKenna, 'Burns and Virgil', in Gerard Carruthers (ed.), *The Edinburgh Companion to Robert Burns* (Edinburgh: Edinburgh University Press, 2009), 137–49.

[118] Noted by Jeffrey Skoblow in *Dooble Tongue*, 116. But Burns's qualification somewhat counters Skoblow's confidence that 'Glossary or no, Scottish dialect and rural experience will not be spoken of or comprehended in terms alien to itself', ibid.

[119] In addition to Dryden's influential translation of the *Eclogues*, Burns might have been familiar with James Hamilton's *Virgil's Pastorals translated into English Prose; as also his Georgicks*

Virgil into 'Skottis vers', quoted at the head of this chapter, post-dated the Kilmarnock volume).[120] Like the Keats of 'On First Looking into Chapman's Homer', Burns isn't so much denying that he'd read classical pastoral, but unapologetically hinting that he's read it in *translation*, a plea for the entitlement of the democratic intellect. As we saw above, his familiarity with both Theocritus' 'shepherd sangs' and 'Maro's catches' is clearly stated in 'A Sketch', probably written in 1785–6. It would have been hard for the 'ploughman poet' to dodge comparisons with Virgil: as Dr John Moore wrote to him May 1787, 'Virgil before you proved to the world that there is nothing in the business of husbandry inimical to Poetry'.[121] Burns stated his ignorance of the *Georgics* (which he thought superior to the *Aeneid*) before 1788, when he thanked Frances Dunlop for her gift of 'Dryden's Virgil': 'When I read the Georgics, and then survey my own powers, 'tis the idea of a Shetland Pony drawn up by the side of a thorough bred Hunter, to start for the Plate' [CL i. 278–9]. In so far as he acknowledged Virgil at all (and it was part of his pastoral role to disavow such literary influences), it should now be clear why his poetic aspirations followed the *Eclogues* rather than the *Georgics*, a case he made strategically in 'The Vision', as argued in the next chapter.

Exposing the submerged pastoral allusion in Burns's 'Preface' has the effect of opening up his poetry to the play of generic self-consciousness that Annabel Patterson calls the 'Virgilian dialectic'. I've argued in this chapter that the legacy of the 'Scots pastoral' of Ramsay and Fergusson helped localize Burns's poetry in cultural and linguistic terms. I'll close with the suggestion that, at the very point of denying a privileged 'pastoral' view of rural life in the Preface to Kilmarnock, Burns returned to the problematic of Virgil's *Eclogues* in the very act of naturalizing the genre.

In one of the few readings attentive to Burns's sequencing of the poems, Jeffrey Skoblow argues that 'the story told by the structural arrangement of the Kilmarnock volume is a story about audience . . . the arrangement of these pieces constitutes a further performance—a kind of structural narrative (even a biographical

---

(Edinburgh 1742) (which included an appendix on agricultural improvement in Scotland); Christopher Pitt's *Works of Virgil* (see n. 115); and Beattie's 'Pastorals of Virgil' published in *Original Poems and Translation* (London, 1760). Regarding Theocritus, he might have read Creech's (1684) or Fawkes's (1767) translations, or Josiah Relph's translation of the 19th *Idyll* into Cumberland dialect in 1747. See Penny Wilson, 'Classical Greek and Latin Literature', in Stuart Gillespie and Peter France (eds.), *Oxford History of Literary Translation in English* (Oxford: Oxford University Press, 2005), iii. 184. Thanks to Stuart Gillespie for information.

[120]   It is interesting that Geddes saw fit to translate Virgil's first Eclogue into 'Edinburgh dialect', whereas Theocritus' First *Idillion* is rendered in 'the Buchan dialect (which may be called the Scottish Doric)' ('Three Scottish Poems', 462).

[121]   MS letter reproduced in Peter J. Westwood (ed.), *Definitive Illustrated Companion to Robert Burns*, 7 vols. (Irvine: Distributed National Burns Collections Project, 2004–6), iii. 2241.

narrative, ending with the Bard's own epitaph)'.[122] In addition to his authorial 'disememberment' in assuming a variety of different poetic voices throughout the collection, Burns's arrangement of his poems in the Kilmarnock and Edinburgh volumes builds up an accumulative framework of internal reference, so that the meaning of each poem is to some extent influenced by the reader's sense of what has come before, and what lies ahead. In contrast to Blake's ironic parallelism in ordering the *Songs of Innocence and Experience*, Burns introduces a subliminal but nonetheless all-pervading personal narrative of failure, dispossession, and exile that shapes the whole, a narrative subtext entirely lost in James Kinsley's chronological presentation of the poems. In the chapters that follow, although my discussion of individual poems is thematic rather than sequential, I'll keep an eye on the significance of the placement of individual poems within the running order of the Kilmarnock and Edinburgh editions.

Kilmarnock's pastoral politics are stated at the outset in an eclogue between two dogs (*not* two shepherds) favourably comparing the hard life of the poor to the *otium* of the rich, a theme sustained in the 'hard pastoral' of 'Cotter's Saturday Night', although this is immediately qualified in the latter case by 'To a Mouse's' harsh meditation on dispossession and homelessness. The superstitions of the rural poor are the subject of 'The Holy Fair' and 'Halloween', although the headnote to the latter poem undermines the 'heaven-taught' persona of the Preface in promising 'entertainment to a philosophic mind . . . among the more unenlightened in our own' age [K 73]. 'The Vision', a pitch for patronage among 'the pride of Coila's plain', is deliberately held back to tenth place: its 'polite' georgic tone is perhaps intended to mitigate the raucous vernacular satire on George III in 'A Dream' that immediately precedes it.

A cluster of largely Scots pastoral poems on whisky, Calvinism, and farming (especially the relationship between man and beast) fill up much of the first half of the book, a prelude to its 'dark centre', dominated by English lyrics in the fashionable 'graveyard manner' concerned with unrequited love, despondency, and ruin. At this point, 'On a Scotch Bard gone to the West Indies', 'From thee Eliza I must go', and 'The Farewell' pick up the submerged biographical narrative to identify the poet as a type of Virgil's vagrant shepherd Meliboeus, unjustly forced to leave his farm and travel into exile. Financial failure and the compensatory pleasures of friendship and poetry are common themes of the group of vernacular epistles that dominate the latter section of Kilmarnock. Taking up the rear is 'A Bard's Epitaph', in which a 'posthumous' Burns runs

---

[122] Skoblow, *Dooble Tongue*, 174. See also Paul Magnusson's argument that 'reading the writing around a poem, reading the location, requires reading a particular version of a poem in the unique details of its publication, the material specificity of its utterance. The more precise one is about that particular utterance, the clearer the connections between text and context become'. *Reading Public Romanticism* (Princeton, NJ: Princeton University Press, 1998), 6.

over his personal failings, concluding with the unconvincing moral: 'know, prudent, cautious, *self-controul* | Is Wisdom's root'.

Consideration of the 'Virgilian dialectic' permits a reading of Burns's pastoral as *unheimlicht*, dispossessed, for all its subsequent influence on the sentimental construction of a 'grounded' Scottish identity. Fergussonian 'Hame Content' is already only a cherished memory in a globalized world of agricultural improvement, the booms and busts of capital, rapid social change, colonialism, and slavery. Burns assumed a distinctively Meliboean voice in describing his motives for publication in his 1787 letter to Moore ('the story of Myself'), that crucial supplement to the submerged poetic autobiography of Kilmarnock; 'Before leaving my native country for ever, I resolved to publish my Poems . . . I thought they had merit; and 'twas a delicious idea that I would be called a clever fellow, even though it should never reach my ears a poor Negro-driver, or perhaps a victim to that inhospitable clime gone to the world of Spirits' [CL i. 144].

# 3

# The Making of a Poet

*No 'pre-established harmony' existed between the clay soil of Mossgiel and the empyrean soul of Robert Burns; it was not wonderful that the adjustment between them should have been long postponed.*

(Thomas Carlyle, 1828)[1]

*There must be, in the heart of every bard of Nature's making, a certain modest sensibility, mixed with a kind of pride, that will ever keep him out of the way of those windfalls of fortune, which frequently light on hardy impudence and foot-licking servility.*

(Burns to Sir John Whiteford, 1 Dec. 1786 [CL i. 68])

## THE FIRST COMMONPLACE BOOK

The early genesis of Burns's poetic self-fashioning is nowhere better illustrated than in the Commonplace Book which he began in April 1783, at the very nadir of his family's fortunes. His father William Burnes was deeply mired in litigation over Lochlie, and the farm was beset with problems caused by bad weather, crop failure, and high prices caused by the disastrous American war. It simply wasn't the case (as the letter to Whiteford went on to boast) that, early or late, the poet enjoyed 'an independent fortune at the plough-tail' [CL i. 68]. According to Gilbert Burns, the Commonplace Book was originally intended to record 'farming memorandums' [Lockhart, p. 35]; it ended up as a repository for literary quotations, song and poem drafts, confessions, meditations, and *sententiae* characteristic of a budding poet in the sentimental vein. Crucially, it served as the literary vehicle for Burns's passage from 'soil' to 'soul', in Carlyle's pun.

The aspiring poet announces both his financial incapacity and his goodness of heart to man and beast alike in the *Book's* titular heading; 'Observations, Hints, Songs, Scraps of Poetry, &c. by Robt. Burness; a man who had little art in making money, and still less in keeping it; but was, however, a man of some sense, a great deal of honesty, and unbounded goodwill to every creature—rational or irrational' [*CPB* p. 1]. This established the 'hair-brained, sentimental' persona

---

[1] *CH* p. 374.

with considerable panache, a persona that we'll see developed in the vernacular epistles: harping on the theme of financial incapacity seems somehow to license a young farmer to embark on the socially pretentious project of keeping a Commonplace Book in the first place.[2]

Yet as it turns out, the Commonplace Book is addressed to a polite reader and *not* one of the 'rustic compeers' hailed in the preface to Kilmarnock.[3] 'It may be some entertainment to a curious observer of human-nature', Burns wrote, 'to see how a ploughman thinks and feels under the pressure of Love, Ambition, Anxiety, Grief, etc.' [*CPB* p. 1]. Burns's 'curious observer' here acknowledges Adam Smith's theory of the 'internal spectator' as formulated in the *Theory of Moral Sentiments* (a work later quoted in the Commonplace Book), an idea that would inspire the closing stanza of 'To a Louse'. In his transcriptions from the Commonplace Book later made in the Glenriddell Manuscripts, Burns recalled that his original intentions in keeping the book had been '*to write myself out* [my italics]; as I was placed by Fortune among a class of men to whom my ideas would have been nonsense'. He had cherished 'the fond hope that, some time or other, even after I was no more, my thoughts would fall into the hands of somebody capable of appreciating their value'.[4] This was aimed at Robert Riddell, which maybe explains why Burns now drops the 'internal spectator' in favour of the friendly patron. But evident here is the emergence of a *posthumous* literary self quite at odds with the pastoral persona of the Kilmarnock preface, which aspires to *write itself into* a sympathetic community distinct from that of his 'rustic compeers'.

In her fine study *Robert Burns and the Sentimental Era*, Carol McGuirk discusses Burns's 'pursuit of intense responsiveness that always created some pathology of feeling in a text'.[5] Burnesian sentimentalism (gleaned, as he frequently informed his correspondents, from the writings of Sterne, Mackenzie, Shenstone, and Macpherson [CL i. 17]) is both a symptom of improvement at the level of the subject and a refusal of the goal of material prosperity that is one of its leading aspirations. Rather than simply representing a 'pre-capitalist' critique of getting and spending, however, sentimentalism offers a *surplus* response to people, things, and events in the world whose form mirrors, just as its

---

[2] For a brief but suggestive discussion of the eighteenth-century Commonplace Book, see John Guillory, *Cultural Capital: The Problem of Literary Canon Formation* (Chicago: University of Chicago Press, 1993), 87–9.

[3] This questions John C. Weston's claim that Burns discovered in the genre of the Scots epistle the perfect vehicle for dramatically projecting his self-portrait as painted in the Commonplace Book, 'Robert Burns's Use of the Scots Verse-Epistle Form', *Philological Quarterly* 49/2 (April 1970), 188–210 at 199.

[4] *The Glenriddell Manuscripts*, a facsimile with intro. and notes by Desmond Donaldson (Wakefield: EP Publishing, 1973), ii. 31.

[5] Carol McGuirk, *Robert Burns and the Sentimental Era* (Athens, Ga.: University of Georgia Press, 1985), p. xxv.

content critiques, the laws of the new capitalist economy. Sentimental surplus is about improving the heart, rather than the land (or one's bank balance), internalizing the surplus value that the tenant farmer was enjoined to extract by the prescriptive terms of his 'improving lease'. Burns here replaces the motor of social emulation (so central to the ideology of improvement) with a sublime aspiration associated with 'natural genius', entailing a complex relationship between a georgic investment in futurity, and a pastoral impulse of *carpe diem*. As we'll see below, preferring the 'hair-brained' impulse of poetry to the quest for immediate material rewards both cements Burns's sympathetic bond with the horizontal community of fellow bardies, and lodges an appeal, on the vertical level, to an audience of polite patrons of the kind that few eighteenth-century poets could do without. This is a relationship which it has proved much harder for Burns criticism to recognize in its understandable haste to celebrate the poet's 'democratic' values.

John Guillory speculates that the eighteenth-century Commonplace Book 'had to be discarded as a matrix of composition in order for the Romantic loco-descriptive lyric to set itself against the rhetorical commonplace, or to resist the compositional methods of $18^{th}$ century poetry'.[6] Just such a localizing move is laid bare in Burns's Commonplace Book entry for August 1785 to the effect that, despite his admiration for the patriotic poetry of Allan Ramsay and Robert Fergusson, he was 'hurt to see other places of Scotland, their towns, rivers, woods, haughs, &c., immortalized', while

my dear native country, the ancient Bailieries of Carrick, Kyle, and Cunningham . . . a country, the birthplace of many famous Philosophers, Soldiers, and Statesmen, and the scene of a great many important events recorded in Scottish History . . . [is forgotten] . . . we have never had one Scotch Poet of any eminence, to make the fertile banks of Irvine, the romantic woodlands and sequestered scenes on Aire, and the heathy mountainous source, and winding sweep of Doon, emulate Tay, Forth, Ettrick, Tweed, &c.  [*CPB* pp. 46–7][7]

Burns's aspires to snatch the laurels from the poets of Edinburgh and the Borders and sing the beauties of Ayrshire, especially his native bailierie of Kyle. His success in so doing is demonstrated in songs praising his local Ayrshire rivers Doon, Lugar, Afton, as well as other Scottish rivers such as the Devon, Bruar, and Nith; as his biographer James Currie later wrote, all were consequently immortalized as 'classic streams . . . their borders . . . trod with new and superior emotions' [Currie, i. 150].

---

[6] Guillory, *Cultural Capital*, 88.

[7] Burns may be alluding specifically to Fergusson's 'Hame Content', with its favourable comparison of Tweed, 'Fortha', and Tay's charms to Arno and Tibur [McD ii. 159 ll. 75–82], or his English pastoral ode 'The Rivers of Scotland'; '*Thames, Humber, Severn*, all must yield the bay | To the pure streams of Forth, of Tweed, and Tay' [McD ii. 45 ll. 126–7].

Burns's desire to 'write himself out' was thus complemented by an impulse to poeticize his own locality, closely linked to the linguistic aims of 'Poems Chiefly in the Scottish Dialect' discussed in the previous chapter. In both the verse epistles (especially 'To Willie Simson' [K 59]) and the pastoral/georgic address of 'The Vision' [K 62] he identifies the sympathetic community of fellow bardies and upper-class patrons with his (and their) native Ayrshire. As Penny Fielding has recently argued, Burns's 'growing status as an icon of locality drew attention to the place of Scotland in the national cultural geography of Britain and to places within Scotland as forms of the local'.[8] Despite the sentimentalized image of worldly incapacity, Burns's poetic self-fashioning depended on identification with the social networks of his native county, as well as the new opportunities afforded him by eighteenth-century Ayrshire's provincial enlightenment.

## VERSE EPISTLES IN THE KILMARNOCK VOLUME

As I argued in Ch. 2, the 'pastoral paradox' of the Kilmarnock preface lies in its 'naturalistic' disavowal of literary artifice, combined with a surreptitious display of learning. The fact that the verse epistles were originally circulated in manuscript and were indeed not 'composed with a view to the press' [Kil. p. iv] can easily mislead the critic into believing that 'they are resistant to the processes of literary criticism . . . inadmissible as evidence, they do not offer themselves for our appraisal'.[9] While there's no denying that their homespun rustic idiom and conversational vitality do qualify them for the title of Burns's 'most characteristic poems', or that they played a pivotal role in defining his public identity as man and poet,[10] there's a danger that an over-candid reading will miss a trick in ignoring the rhetorical and generic expectations attached to these poems. After all, according to Gilbert Burns, it was his brother's recital of 'Epistle to Davie' in the summer of 1784 that first suggested the idea of his 'becoming an author . . . I was of the opinion it would bear being printed, and that it would be well received by people of taste' [Mackay, pp. 159–60]. David Fairer writes of the popular eighteenth-century genre of verse epistle that 'no poetic form is more obviously "between manuscript and print" in the ways it entangles private and public, allowing a glimpse of the handwritten letter through the formalities of a printed page'.[11] This

[8] Penny Fielding, *Scotland and the Fictions of Geography: North Britain, 1760–1830* (Cambridge: Cambridge University Press, 2008), 40.

[9] Liam McIlvanney, *Burns the Radical: Poetry and Politics in Late Eighteenth-Century Scotland* (Phantassie: Tuckwell, 2002), 101.

[10] Ibid.

[11] David Fairer, *English Poetry of the Eighteenth Century, 1700–1789* (Harlow: Pearson Education, 2003), 60. For a detailed recent study of the genre, see Bill Overton, *The Eighteenth-Century Verse Epistle* (Basingstoke: Palgrave Macmillan, 2007), esp. 1–31, 66–105.

doubtless explains why the genre was especially popular with 'women of various social ranks, [and] men from the artisan and labouring classes': his Scots epistles were amongst the most widely imitated of all Burns's poetry.[12]

The verse epistles represent Burns's consummate skill in deploying the traditional forms of the habbie or 'Cherry and Slae' stanzas while creating a sense of informal epistolary 'conversation' in Scots. His major poetic model (as acknowledged at lines 13–18 of 'Epistle to Willie Simson' [K 59]) was the published epistolary exchange of 1719 between Allan Ramsay and Lt. William Hamilton of Gilbertfield.[13] Although both men were 'dedicated workers in the vineyard of the vernacular revival',[14] both Ramsay and Hamilton sought to capture the spirit of Horace in translation, analogous to the influence of Theocritan and Virgilian pastoral upon eighteenth-century Scots poets discussed previously.[15] Horace's critical perspective on a corrupt Rome as viewed from 'retirement' on his Sabine farm added to his attractions for oppositional Scottish poets, writing at a distance from the new metropolis of post-1707 Britain. Eschewing Popean couplets and Augustan diction, Ramsay and Hamilton preferred the habbie stanza and broad Scots in order to catch something of the racy colloquialism and conversational ease of the Latin original.[16] Margaret Doody asks of Horace's *sermones*, 'did any poet before Horace ever write so much about writing itself, about styles and genres and the difficulty or ease of writing?'[17] Recurrent features of the genre common to both Ramsay and Burns are an opening poetic compliment, in which the poet 'rooses' (praises) his correspondent's superior skill, bravura attempts at 'crambo-jingle' or feats of rhyming (often deploying sustained hypermetric stresses at line endings), as well as a self-conscious spirit of experimentation using Scots idiom. The male correspondents frequently 'sign off' with a future assignation, usually in a tavern.

---

[12] Overton, ibid. 50.

[13] Hamilton was a retired army officer and Lanarkshire landowner best known for his 'Last Dying Words of Bonnie Heck' (1706) and his 'translation' of Blind Harry's epic poem *William Wallace* (1722). John Weston, 'Burns's Use of Scots Verse-Epistle Form', *Philological Quarterly* 49/2 (April 1970), discovers at least eight 'convincing verbal correspondences' between Burns's and Ramsay and Hamilton's epistles (p. 206). Fergusson is a lesser model, given that he only engaged in two epistolary exchanges; see MaDiarmid ii. 69–74; 151–4, 243.

[14] Weston, 'Verse-Epistle Form', 190.

[15] Like Burns as discussed in Ch. 2, Ramsay's more limited education meant that he had 'feasted on [Horace's] beautiful thoughts dress'd in British'. Quoted by John Corbett, *Written in the Language of the Scottish Nation: A History of Literary Translation into Scots* (Clevedon: Multilingual Matters, 1999), 102.

[16] Ramsay's epistles perhaps convey the spirit of Horace more accurately than his direct 'imitations', which 'are often crude, concrete and obvious when his source is sophisticated, intellectual and light' (Corbett, ibid. 103). Weston disagrees ('Verse-Epistle Form', 192–3).

[17] Margaret Doody, *The Daring Muse: Augustan Poetry Reconsidered* (Cambridge: Cambridge University Press, 1985), 93–4.

Because the verse epistle was by definition a 'distant conversation'[18] it emphasized the local affiliations of its interlocutors; Ramsay, for example, is identified with the Pentlands outside Edinburgh, Hamilton with his Lanarkshire estate at Gilbertfield. The finest of the sequence, Ramsay's third and final epistle of 2 September 1719 praises Hamilton, the 'well-bred' soldier-farmer, living in virtuous Horatian retirement on his small estate near Cambuslang: had Caesar followed the same course, Ramsay suggests, he'd have avoided 'the Senate's Durks and Faction loud' [Ramsay, i. 131–4 l. 23]. It turns out, however, that the life of an improving Lowland laird is far from idle: paraphrasing Horace's *Odes* ('Thus to *Leuconoe* sang sweet *Flaccus*', l. 11. 43), Ramsay urges his correspondent to take a break from the toil of farming, in a passage that must have pleased Burns in its advocacy of *carpe diem*; 'Yet sometimes leave the Riggs and Bog, | Your Howms, and Braes, and shady Scrog, | And helm-a-lee the Claret cog, | To clear your Wit: | Be blyth, and let the Warld e'en shog, | As it thinks fit' (ll. 25–30). In this cavalier spirit of epicurean enjoyment, the epistles digress to attack critics and their learned pretensions, lauding the superior pleasure of poetry over worldly pursuits (especially money-making), and celebrating the pleasures of drink and tavern sociability.

In addition to imitating the literary models of Ramsay and Hamilton (as well as later attempts by James Beattie and Fergusson),[19] Burns's epistles served to promote his emergent fame as an 'Ayrshire bardie'. Although he did address epistles to his social superiors (Gavin Hamilton, Andrew Aiken, Robert Graham, Hugh Parker), those published in the Kilmarnock volume specifically address men of his own class, friends from the Tarbolton Bachelor's Club and the Court of Equity, 'the hairum-scairum, ram-stam boys' [K 79 l. 165] at loggerheads with the Mauchline Kirk Session, fellow bardies such as James Smith, William Simson, Davie Sillar, John Lapraik, and John Rankine. Struggling tenant farmers, linen-drapers, grocers, school-teachers, post-masters, these men were the nascent *petit bourgeoisie* of rural Ayrshire, educated in the aspirational ideology of improvement but, like Burns father and sons, victims of the booms and busts of the new capitalist economy, particularly the long repercussions of the Ayr Bank failure of 1772, as well as the terrible weather and worse harvests of the early 1780s. They were indeed in this sense (like their precursor Robert Fergusson) his 'brothers in misfortune'.[20]

Robert Crawford notes that 'bardie' is a Scots pun, the word serving both as a diminutive of 'bard'—in the grandiose Ossianic sense—but also 'a Scots

---

[18] Overton quoting John Newbery (*Eighteenth-Century Verse Epistle*, 7).

[19] In 1768 Beattie published a virtuoso Scots verse epistle 'To Mr Alexander Ross of Lochlee, author of *The Fortunate Shepherdess*' in *The Aberdeen Journal*, under the telling pseudonym of 'Oliver Oldstile', the sole poetic offering in Scots by a celebrated linguistic anglicizer. Burns quoted a stanza in a letter to Mrs Dunlop in March 1788 [CL i. 256].

[20] See McIlvanney, *Burns the Radical*, 103–7.

adjective meaning "bold, impudent of speech . . . forward, quarrelsome" . . . being bardie meant being bolshie; in the months after his father's death [in 1784],
that was what Burns wanted to be'.[21] The Ayrshire bardies sought a vent for their
frustrated aspirations in a swaggering poetical rejection of social emulation in a
class-bound society, and (in quieter moments) a more introspective desire for
sentimental 'self-improvement'. Inspired by Ramsay and Fergusson, as well as by
English poets such as Shenstone, Goldsmith, and Gray, they circulated their
verse epistles in manuscript, taking advantage of Ayrshire's new roads and postal
service (Lapraik was himself postmaster in Muirskirk).[22]

One of Sillar's poetic correspondents identified the phenomenon as being
particularly associated with Ayrshire; 'I did never ken | Sic plenty o' *Ramsaic*
men: | In ilka house, baith butt an' ben, | In Allan's line, | There's twenty now,
for every ten, | Sin I hae mins.'[23] (It's notable that the writer, an outsider
temporarily resident in Irvine, regretted that much of this 'Ramsaic' verse
satirically lashed 'auld licht' ministers, identifying it with progressive Moderate
views.) Whatever the political and theological opinion aired in the epistles, the
Canongate editors rightly note that the genre's requirement of 'a degree of
creative, technical parity between the correspondents' was unfortunately denied
to Burns, although 'his desire for the comforts of a poetic coterie was so strong that
he often seriously overemphasized the talents of his correspondents' [CG, p. 54].

With the exception of the poems addressed to James Smith and Davie Sillar,
Burns's Kilmarnock epistles all respond to prior correspondents; Lapraik's song
'When I Upon thy Bosom lean', a verse epistle from Simson praising Burns's
anti-clerical satire 'The Holy Tulzie', or one of John Rankine's satirical 'Dreams'
(Burns's note states that 'a certain humorous dream of his was then making a
noise in the world') [K 47, l.4].[24] 'Epistle to James S[mith]' [K 79], the first of
the epistles published in the 1786 volume, was unique in addressing a non-poet,
which is maybe why Burns asks his busy linen-draper friend, at line 23, 'Hae ye a
leisure-moment's time | To hear what's comin?' Unlike more pretentious breth-
ren who rhyme for fame or revenge, or even 'needfu' cash', Burns's sole aim,
which 'I never fash', is to 'rhyme for *fun*' [ll. 29–30]. Nevertheless, the poet's

---

[21] Robert Crawford, *The Bard: Robert Burns, a Biography* (London: Jonathan Cape, 2009), 155.

[22] Until the road improvements following the two Turnpike Acts of 1766 and 1774, 'the
circulation of persons and goods was severely limited' and depended on horses and other pack
animals. In Loudoun parish in 1750 there were no carts, but there were 250 by 1791. John Loudon
McAdam (inventor of 'tarmac') returned from America in 1783 'to become a member of the
Ayrshire Turnpike Trustees for 13 years before going south to eventual fame', John Strawhorn (ed.),
*Ayrshire in the Time of Burns* (Ayrshire Archaeological and Nat. Hist. Soc., 1959), 152, 250.

[23] 'Epistle to the Author, by J. H*******N', in David Sillar, *Poems* (Kilmarnock: John Wilson,
1789), 88.

[24] Although Rankine's 'Dreams' are all lost, they were probably anti-clerical and/or political
satires; I'll argue in the next chapter that Burns borrowed the title for his own 'A Dream' [K 113],
satirizing George III.

embarrassment at the extent of his poetic ambition is revealed in the seventh stanza;

> This while my notion's taen a sklent,
> To try my fate in guid, black *prent*;
> But still the mair I'm that way bent,
>          Something cries, 'Hoolie!'
> 'I red you, honest man, tak tent!
>          Ye'll shaw your folly.   (ll. 37–42)

Heeding the warning (in what turns out to be an instance of false modesty), Burns resolves to forgo publication in favour of pastoral content ('[I'll] teach the lanely heights an' howes | My rustic sang', ll. 53–4): echoing Grey's *Elegy*, he'll be content to 'lay me with th' *inglorious dead* | Forgot and gone!' (ll. 59–60). This leads on to a bucolic celebration of *carpe diem* and 'life's . . . enchanted fairy-land' (l. 68), never, however, quite free from an underlying anxiety about future prospects.[25] The epistle ends with a defiant glance at 'ye, douce folk, that live by rule', and an oath of friendship sworn to Smith as one of the 'ram-stam boys, | The rattling squad'(ll. 165–6).

The two 'Epistles to J. L[apraik], An Old Scotch Bard' [K 57, 58] the first of which is dated April Fool's Day 1785, stand in a closer relation to the Ramsay/ Hamilton correspondence than any of the others, especially regarding their informal meditations on the art of poetry.[26] The first compliments Lapraik, identified with the Ayrshire town of Muirkirk (l. 24), on his song, praising his unparalleled 'ingine' (genius) and 'hamely' muse by comparing it with the Scots poems of Ramsay and Fergusson (ll. 79–83). Following the Ramsay model, Burns disingenuously identifies himself as 'nae *Poet*, in a sense, | But just a *Rhymer* like by chance' (ll. 49–50). He criticizes the pride of 'your Critic-folk' (l. 55) and the 'jargon o' [their] Schools' (l. 61) before making his famous appeal, 'Gie me ae spark o'Nature's fire, | That's a' the learning I desire' (ll. 73–4). (As with the Preface's disavowal of literary learning, this profession of 'untaught' genius alludes to Sterne and Pope [Kin iii. 1059]).

Burns's Shenstonian disdain for 'the ducat's dirty sphere'[27] adds a more urgent critical tone to the epistle; 'Awa ye selfish, warly race, | Wha think that havins, sense an' grace | Ev'n love an' friendship should give place | To *catch-the-plack*! | I dinna like to see your face, | Nor hear your crack' (ll. 115–20). I'll comment in subsequent chapters on Burns's complicated attitude to charity and welfare; here,

---

[25] As well as the quote from Thomas Gray's *Elegy* here, there's also an allusion at lines 85–90 to the 'Eton College Ode'.

[26] Burns copied both into his Commonplace Book in June 1785 [*CPB* pp. 34–42].

[27] Shenstone, *Elegies*, ix l. 44. See 'Lines written on a Bank-Note' [K 106] a poetic 'overwriting' that literally cancelled the monetary value of a Bank of Scotland guinea note; the closing couplet ('For lake o' thee I leave this much-lov'd shore, | Never perhaps to greet old Scotland more!') dates the poem to 1786.

rather unusually, an offer of material assistance underwrites the assertion of sympathetic community: 'Each aid the others', | Come to my bowl, Come to my arms, | My friends, my brothers!' (ll. 124–6). The offer was particularly appropriate given that Lapraik, formerly a freehold farmer at Dalfram (note the densely agricultural idiom of the two opening stanzas of the second 'Epistle') had been ruined in the Ayr Bank crash and forced to sell his land; but he was briefly imprisoned for debt in this same year of 1785, where he composed many of the poems published by Wilson in 1788 [Kin. iii.1057].[28]

The point is reiterated even more insistently in the 'Second Epistle to L[apraik]' [K 58] in which 'the social, friendly, honest man' (l. 87) is preferred to the '*city gent*. . . purse-proud, big wi' cent per cent' or 'paughty, feudal *Thane*', (ll. 61, 63, 67) even, or especially, because he has been the butt of misfortune. Poets choose '*wit* and *sense*' rather than material prosperity; this one would prefer to be turned adrift to beg rather than having to 'shift' with the proud and prosperous, a theme further discussed below (ll. 75–8). Stanzas 14 and 15 underline the epistle's investment in what McGuirk terms 'sentimental election': 'not only the legitimacy of being poor, but the ultimate salvation of "none but" the "social, friendly, honest, man" is emphasized. Burns combines Calvinist predestination with his own notion of "Nature's plan" . . . the result is the dogmatic defence of secular spontaneity which is so characteristic of Burns's early poetry'.[29]

The 'Epistle to Davie [Sillar], a Brother Poet' [K 51] gives this notion of 'sentimental election' its fullest articulation. (Preceding the two 'Epistles to Lapraik' in Kilmarnock, it's concern with the theme of indigence may have determined its placement immediately after 'To a Mouse'.)[30] Composed in the difficult 'Cherry and Slae' stanza, the poem opens with one of Burns's finest evocations of a Scottish winter landscape as the setting for a complaint about social injustice; the view of Ben Lomond (visible from Ayrshire) underlines the poem's 'western' topography, also associated with its 'westlin jingle':

> While winds frae off BEN-LOMOND blaw,
> And bar the doors wi' driving snaw,
>     And hing us owre the ingle,
> I set me down, to pass the time,
> And spin a verse or twa o' rhyme,
>     In hamely, *westlin* jingle:

---

[28] Lapraik (despite Burns's compliments, a lesser poetic talent than Sillar) included here some doggerel verse entitled 'Observations on the Douglas and Heron Bank'. His eulogy on the Earl of Dundonald blamed the crash for Ayrshire's ruination ('That woful Bank, that plague of plagues; | Had fairly kicked her off her legs') that is, until the improving Earl established a Tar-Works at Muirkirk. *Poems on Several Occasions* (Kilmarnock: John Wilson, 1788), 97.

[29] McGuirk, *Sentimental Era*, 29. See also McIlvanney, *Burns the Radical*, 116–17.

[30] It was probably drafted earlier in autumn of 1784, and only later reworked as an epistle to Sillar [K iii. 1039].

> While frosty winds blaw in the drift,
>       Ben to the chimla lug,
> I grudge a wee the *Great-folk's* gift,
>       That live sae bien an' snug:
>       I tent less, and want less
>             Their roomy fire-side;
>       But hanker, and canker,
>             To see their cursed pride.   (ll. 1–14)

Douglas Dunn has commented on the way in which the poem's baroque verse form seems strangely at odds with its argument in favour of simple folk. Yet, as he points out, 'in each set of the last four lines, there is a change of tempo and rhythm to which the probable response is a metrical shock in the form of a disconcerting uplift . . . the disyllabic rhymes unsettle the iambic cadence of the first ten lines . . . and introduce a jolt to the sonic system which has been established in the preceding lines'.[31] The chiming disyllables of the 'wheel' concluding each stanza aptly convey the sense of anxiety that permeates the poem, not so much born of social envy, but rather the poor man's 'hankering and cankering' at the arrogant pride of the rich.[32] This is not far from the outspoken social critique of 'Man was Made to Mourn' discussed in the next chapter [K 64 ll. 19–20].

In the stanzas that follow, the poet finds consolation for his resentment, and fear of poverty, in praising the resilience of the 'honest heart' [l. 35] to the buffets of fortune. Central to the egalitarian ethic of the epistles is the Augustan belief, derived from Pope, Gay, and Shenstone (as well as Ramsay and Hamilton), and circulating freely amongst these Ayrshire 'brethren in misfortune', that 'honest poverty' is a nobler path to improvement than the chimeras of worldly wealth and fame. The word 'honesty', with its earlier Popean and Jacobite associations, had a more contemporary resonance in Tom Paine's *Common Sense* (1776): 'Of more worth is one honest man to society, and in the sight of God, than all the crowned ruffians that ever lived.'[33] As with so many of Burns's other poems (especially 'To a Louse' [K 83]), 'Epistle to Davie' rejects the notion of social emulation as the basis of the distinction of ranks, theorized by Adam Smith as the cement of commercial society: 'the pleasures of wealth and greatness . . . strike the imagination as something grand and beautiful and noble, of which the attainment is well worth all the toil and anxiety which we are so apt to bestow

---

[31] Douglas Dunn, 'A Very Scottish Kind of Dash', 67.

[32] McIlvanney, *Burns the Radical*, 108, also underlines the poem's 'shifting moods' and 'brooding, anxious tone'.

[33] *The Tom Paine Reader*, ed. Michael Foot and Isaac Kramnick (London: Penguin, 1987), 79 Robert Crawford points out the echo here of the American Declaration of Independence, dedicated to 'Life, Liberty, and the Pursuit of Happiness', a formulation which must have made a deep impression on the 17-year-old poet: 'Burns and the Heart of Europe', paper given at the Glasgow Burns Conference, 17 Jan. 2009.

upon it'.[34] (As I'll argue in Chapter 6, Burns was aware that Smith himself qualified this view.)

Defying the system of social deference, the speaker of 'Epistle to Davie' would prefer 'to lye in kilns and barns at e'en' (l. 29) than struggle to emulate the rich, given that 'the last o't, the warst o't, | Is only but to beg' (ll. 27–8) Burns's sentimentalized image of the 'independence' of the beggar's life here is rather unconvincing, as if such 'Commoners of air' (l. 43) could really benefit from '*Nature's* charms', even if they were indeed 'free alike to all' and somehow beyond the cash nexus. McIlvanney rightly indicates that 'the real condition of being "But either house or hal" (l. 45) is one of miserable indigence, not liberty, as Burns acknowledges in the tenderly empathetic address "To a Mouse"'.[35] As I'll argue in discussing 'Love and Liberty' [K 84], this is the rhetoric of 'beggar pastoral', a view lying one notch below Burns's defiant (and untruthful) assertion of his 'independence at the plough' as a symbol of freedom from emulation, patronage, and the pursuit of worldly wealth. Celeste Langan identifies vagrancy as 'the framing issue of Romantic form and content', proposing that the abstraction of the vagrant's mobility and expressivity (i.e. entreaty or begging) 'crucially elevate[s] the vagrant to the status of the poet's double', which certainly connects with the Meliboean subtext of Burns's Kilmarnock poems.[36]

In Burns's case, the argument goes that happiness and the 'good heart' rather than worldly ambition (his disavowal of literary 'lear' in these lines belongs to the mask, not the man) are sufficient for true fraternity:

> It's no in titles nor in rank;
> It's no in wealth like *Lon'on Bank*,
>   To purchase peace and rest;
> It's no in makin muckle, *mair*:
> It's no in books; it's no in Lear,
> To make us truly blest:
> If Happiness hae not her seat
>   And center in the breast,
> We may be *wise*, or *rich*, or *great*,
>   But never can be *blest*:
> Nae treasures nor pleasures

---

[34] Adam Smith, *Theory of Moral Sentiments*, ed. Knud Haakonssen (Cambridge: Cambridge University Press, 2002), 214. That the poets may have had Smith in their sights here is suggested by Lapraik's limp poem entitled 'On Emulation': 'The man who has a fortune got, | And riches in great store, | Ought not, for that, to be preferr'd | To virtuous men, though poor' (*Poems*, 137).

[35] McIlvanney, *Burns the Radical*, 110.

[36] Celeste Langan, *Romantic Vagrancy: Wordsworth and the Simulation of Freedom* (Cambridge: Cambridge University Press, 1995), 14, 17. Langan's thesis, however, is based on the Wordsworthian encounter between poet and beggar, '*the transcendental surplus and the empirical deficit*', rather than a Burnsian fear of slippage into the latter condition. However 'pastoralized', the Burnsian beggar is always at one level a spectre of personal ruin as well as a figure of capable imagination.

> Could make us happy lang:
> The *heart* ay's the part ay,
> That makes us right or wrang.    (ll. 57–70)

Praise of the 'good heart' is of course an eighteenth-century commonplace, propagated everywhere from the ethics of Shaftesbury and Hutcheson, through Fielding's *Tom Jones* to Shenstone's *Elegies* and Mackenzie's *Man of Feeling*. But considering that Sillar had farmed at Spittalside, near Tarbolton, before trying his luck, unsuccessfully, as a teacher, grocer, and poet, and that the poem is therefore a conversation between two failing tenant farmers, it's maybe significant that 'good heart' had a specialized meaning in the contemporary discourse of agricultural improvement. The practice of keeping poor land in fallow to improve its fertility was described in some detail by Virgil in *Georgics*, 1. 106–17, and Dryden's translation employed this very idiom. 'But those unhappy Soils the Swain forbears, | And keeps a Sabbath of alternate Years: | That *the spent Earth may gather heart again*; | And, better'd by Cessation, bear the Grain.| . . . But sweet Vicissitudes of Rest and Toil | Make easy labour, and renew the soil.'[37] 'Good heart' was also employed in this sense closer to home, by Sir Adam Fergusson of Kilkerran in Ayrshire, in a letter published in Andrew Wight's 1785 survey *The Present State of Husbandry in Scotland*; 'instead of running out their lands, by ploughing them up as soon as they are fit to produce a poor crop of corn, as was the practice formerly, [my tenants] are now sensible of the importance of having them in *good heart*'.[38] Of course 'keeping a Sabbath of alternate years' obliged the tenant farmer to forgo the regular and assured financial returns of an annual crop, however small, in exchange for the nebulous prospect of enhanced future harvests. But as a major strategy of agricultural capitalism, the rationale of fallowing casts an interesting light on the epistles' advocacy of *carpe diem* and their poetic defence of the 'good heart' over 'catch the plack'.[39]

The poor man's supposedly 'improvident' enjoyment of the present moment was the target of Coleridge's criticism in a 1795 lecture that also employs the metaphor of capitalist acquisitiveness; 'possessing no stock of happiness [the poor] eagerly seize the gratifications of the moment, and snatch the froth from the wave as it passes by them'.[40] Burns's impatience with moralizing of this sort is patent, and doubtless constitutes the political message of the epistles, but writing

---

[37] *Virgils' Works, Containing his Pastorals, Georgics and Aeneis*, trans. John Dryden, 3 vols. (London, 1763), i. 216. Italics mine.

[38] Andrew Wight, *Present State of Husbandry* (1784), iii. 164. Italics mine. See also *OED* 'Heart' (21a) which lists other contemporary usages.

[39] As Burns jauntily expressed the matter in an early song; 'The past was bad, and the future hid; its good or ill untried; O | But the present hour was in my pow'r, and so I would enjoy it, O' [K 21 ll. 16–17: 'My Father was a Farmer'].

[40] Quoted in *Coleridge's Writing on Politics and Society*, ed. John Morrow (Princeton: Princeton University Press, 1991), i. 33.

(and later publishing) poetry on the *carpe diem* theme does nonetheless itself represent a strategy for translating immediate enjoyment into a 'stock of happiness'. Burns as frustrated farmer/poet here grasps the dialectical tension between sentimental surplus and the reality of material failure, the contradiction between theory and practice lying at the heart of the ideology of improvement. In one sense of course this defiant rejection of worldly wealth makes a virtue of necessity; but beyond that, the poetic celebration of the 'good heart' foreshadows romantic aesthetics in acknowledging the role of symbolic capital in the construction of literary genius. As Pierre Bourdieu argues, this functions 'like a generalized game of "loser wins" . . . a systematic inversion of the fundamental principles of all ordinary economies', in the pursuit of aesthetic 'autonomy'.[41]

Burns's epistle 'To W[illie] S[imso]n, Ochiltree, May 1785' [K 59] is the most self-conscious of the epistles in literary terms, acknowledging that the dominie of Ochiltree was a Glasgow University graduate, as well as a talented antiquarian and amateur orthoepist, whose theory of the Doric aspects of Ayrshire dialect I discussed in the previous chapter. Burns opened by thanking Simson for his own flattering epistle praising his satire on the 'auld lichts' 'The Holy Tulzie';[42] the poet continues by modestly disavowing any intention (in 'kittling up my *rustic reed*', l. 29) of competing 'Wi' *Allan*, or wi' *Gilbertfield . . .* or *Ferguson*, the writer-chiel, | A deathless name' (ll. 15–18). This is perhaps disingenuous, however, to the extent that (reflecting his remarks in the Commonplace Book discussed above), Burns resolves his 'anxiety of influence' by clearing a distinct regional space for himself, and the other Ayrshire bardies who sing in praise of the local muse Coila:

> Nae *Poet* thought her worth his while,
> To set her name in measur'd style;
> She lay like some unkend-of isle
> Beside *New Holland*,
> Or whare wild-meeting oceans boil
> Besouth *Magellan*.
>
> *Ramsay* an' famous *Ferguson*
> Gied *Forth* an' *Tay* a lift aboon;
> *Yarrow* an' *Tweed*, to monie a tune,
> Owre Scotland rings,
> When *Irwin, Lugar, Aire* an' *Doon*,
> Naebody sings.   (ll. 37–48)

Burns and Simson's singing of 'auld COILA's plains an' fells' (l. 55) puts Ayrshire, hitherto a *terra incognita* like the 'unkend isles' of the southern Pacific, on the

<hr/>

[41] See Pierre Bourdieu, 'The Field of Cultural Production: or: the Economic World Reversed', in *The Field of Cultural Production*, ed. and introd. Randal Johnson (Cambridge: Polity, 1993), 29–73 at 39.
[42] Otherwise known as 'The Twa Herds' [K 52].

poetic map of Scotland, alongside the rivers praised by Ramsay and Fergusson. These stanzas draw on a topical metaphor from the new geographical discourse of eighteenth-century Britain, especially the obsession with Cook's discoveries in the South Seas.[43] They underline the paradoxical *cosmopolitanism* of Burns's poetic self-identification with his native region; as Penny Fielding writes, 'locality cannot be experienced at first hand but only as a literary structure . . . the pre-existence of Coila's territory can only be understood in the geographical discourses of 18th century exploration'.[44] 'Epistle to Willie Simson' reminds us not only that the 'spontaneous' sympathetic community of the verse epistles is modelled on the literary correspondence between Ramsay and Hamilton, but is itself also a 'distant conversation' dedicated to the construction of Scottish national identity through an accretion of local filiations, allusions, and dialect words. After discussing the theme of patronage in relation to Burns's poetic self-fashioning in the next section, the remainder of the chapter will explore the idea of locality as it is developed in 'The Vision'.

## BURNS AND THE PROBLEM OF PATRONAGE

Despite the importance of an ideal of 'horizontal sociability' in the epistles, Burns's rank as a tenant farmer inserted him into the hierarchical social structure and patronage networks of eighteenth-century Scotland, a society founded on systematic inequality. His strenuous rhetoric of 'independence' disguises the reality of structural *dependence*, the corollary of which, his need for patronage, marks all the poetry written in the period until 1788, when his Excise commission (however much of a mixed blessing in other respects) at least ensured a regular, pensionable salary. Patronage in early-modern Scotland has been graphically described by Rosalind Mitchison as a 'filament' which 'went through all levels of society like the mycelium of dry rot through old woodwork'.[45] Although this was true elsewhere in eighteenth-century Britain, it was particularly pervasive north of the border, given that Scotland 'had the most concentrated pattern of landownership in Europe' [Whatley, p. 145]. The role of patronage in the appointment of Kirk ministers was a major source of contention in Burns's Scotland (further discussed in Ch. 6), but the related question of *literary* patronage was also a moot issue.

Despite a longstanding critical view that Dr Johnson's famous 'Letter to Lord Chesterfield' signalled the end of the old system, recent scholarship suggests that

---

[43] See Jonathan Lamb, *Preserving the Self in the South Seas, 1680–1840* (Chicago: Chicago University Press, 2001).

[44] Penny Fielding, *Scotland and the Fictions of Geography*, 44–5.

[45] Quoted by Whatley, p.177. See also R. M. Sunter, *Patronage and Politics in Scotland, 1707–1832* (Edinburgh: Donald, 1986), and Michael Fry, *The Dundas Despotism* (Edinburgh: Edinburgh University Press, 1992).

matters weren't so cut and dried, especially in Scotland.[46] Ian Duncan writes that 'patronage frames the professional culture of polite letters in the Scottish Enlightenment and post-Enlightenment, differentiating it from the more thoroughly market-based professional culture that would emerge later in 19th century Britain'.[47] It is easy to be taken in by Burns's disdain for literary patronage, a dismissive view which was by the 1780s in any case a rhetorical norm for many ambitious poets. (It also suggests another motive for his increasing drift to radicalism in the years after 1791: E. P.Thompson argues that 'the profound resentments generated by client status, with its attendant humiliations and its impediments to the career open to talents, fuelled much of the intellectual radicalism of the early 1790s'.)[48]

Burns's attitude to patronage is sentimentalized in the Kilmarnock Preface's address to 'Learned and Polite' readers, aptly described by Jeffrey Skoblow as 'baited schmalz': 'Not the mercenary bow over a counter, but the heart-throbbing gratitude of the Bard, conscious how much he is indebted to Benevolence and Friendship, for gratifying him, if he deserves it, in that dearest wish of every poetic bosom—to be distinguished' [Kil. p. v].[49] Dedicating his Edinburgh volume to the patrician Caledonian Hunt the following year, Burns proclaimed that 'though much indebted to your goodness, I do not approach you, my Lords and Gentlemen, in the usual stile of dedication . . . that path is so hackneyed by prostituted Learning, that honest Rusticity is ashamed of it.—Nor do I present this Address with the venal soul of a servile Author, looking for a continuation of those favours: I was bred to the Plough, and am independent' [Henley and Henderson, i. 5].[50]

If in the Kilmarnock dedication Burns ducks the role of servility (specified here as the 'mercenary' relationship of a shopkeeper to his bourgeois client) by recourse to the language of sentiment, in the Edinburgh text he prefers the patrician discourse of civic humanism and Scottish patriotism: 'I come to claim the common Scottish name with you, my illustrious Countrymen' [Henley and Henderson, i. 5]. Burns's skill with this kind of dedicatory address has increasingly come under critical scrutiny, linking him to the wider discourse of eighteenth-century patronage. Robert Folkenflik describes it as a 'neat trick', placing Burns within the tradition of Pope who 'set the tone for the rejection of

---

[46] Especially Dustin Griffin, *Literary Patronage in England, 1650–1800* (Cambridge: Cambridge University Press, 1996).

[47] Ian Duncan, *Scott's Shadow*, 25.

[48] E. P.Thompson, *Customs in Common* (London: Merlin, 1991), 33.

[49] Skoblow, *Dooble Tongue*, 119.

[50] See Sher, *Enlightenment and the Book* (Chicago: University of Chicago Press, 141–4 for dedicatory conventions in Scottish enlightenment publishing. The *Edinburgh Advertiser* of 28 November 1788 praised the poet's decision to 'resume his flail' by signing the lease for Ellisland farm, comparing him favourably to 'Stephen Duck, the Poetical Thresher' who was encouraged to take holy orders by 'his ill-advised patrons': 'the poor man, hurried out of his proper element, found himself quite unhappy; became insane; and with his own hands, it is said, ended his life' [Mackay, p. 436].

the patronage system in theory (if not always in fact) which became a norm for ambitious poets in later years'.[51] But Dustin Griffin and Robert Korshin remind us that in the 1780s patronage was still a necessary precondition of publication: patrons weren't merely patrician cash cows, but often assumed the function of literary agents or referees in the modern publication system.[52] As Peter Murphy puts it, 'the world that the patronage poetry delineates is the world that Burns had to live in, as a writer', even if only a portion of Burns's poems have eulogistic intentions.[53]

We saw in Ch. 2 that the subscribers to the Kilmarnock volume were either members of the poet's local social network, or of Ayrshire's professional bourgeoisie, men such as Robert Aiken, John Ballantine, and Gavin Hamilton.[54] In contrast to the Edinburgh volume's conventionally placed dedication to the Caledonian Hunt, Kilmarnock resituated the customary dedication with a preface, capriciously inserting its 'Dedication to G. H. Esq' [K 103] (Gavin Hamilton) over halfway through the volume.[55] Jeff Scoblow wittily proposes that this is carefully calculated: 'placed at the start of the volume, such a text might appear as if Burns were to have farted upon entering the room (instead, we get the mellifluities of the Preface)'.[56] Dedication is represented not as a flattering plea for financial support, but rather (as in the other verse epistles) the expression of sentimental fraternity. Burns works hard to purge the spectre of flattery before he can get down to the actual work of dedication. Despite sharing a surname with the Duke of Hamilton, he cheekily hints, his dedicatee (a Mauchline 'writer' or solicitor) is only a commoner. (ll. 1–10). Title is normally the prerequisite for a dedicatee, but the 'laigh'-ness (lowness) of this 'ploughman poet' is such that he doesn't *need* a titled patron; and in any case, if he fails as a poet, he has other recourses: 'For me! So laigh I need na bow, | For LORD be thanket, *I can plough*; | And when I downa yoke a naig, | Then, LORD be thanket, *I can beg*; | Sae I shall say, an' that's nae flatt'rin, | It's jist *sic Poet* an' *sic Patron* [Kin. i. 243 ll. 13–18]. This rehearses the familiar Burnsian equation of 'independence at the plough' and a stated willingness to beg if that fails, absolving him from mercenary considerations.

Having cleared the hurdle of flattery, the 'Dedication' artfully proceeds to list Hamilton's mundane virtues 'As Master, Landlord, Husband, Father. | He does

---

[51] Robert Folkenflik, 'Patronage and the Poet Hero', *Huntingdon Library Quarterly* 48/4 (Autumn, 1985), 363–79, 367.

[52] Griffin, *Literary Patronage*; Robert Korshin, 'Types of Eighteenth-Century Literary Patronage', *Eighteenth-Century Studies* 7/4 (Summer 1974), 453–73.

[53] Peter Murphy, *Poetry as an Occupation and an Art in Britain, 1760–1830* (Cambridge: Cambridge University Press, 1993), 58.

[54] On subscription publication, see Sher, *Enlightenment and the Book*, 224–35, and William Christmas, *The Lab'ring Muses: Work, Writing, and the Social Order in English Plebeian Poetry, 1730–1830* (Newark: Associated University Presses, 2001), 28.

[55] Like the addressees of the other epistles, only initials identified Gavin Hamilton in the 1786 and 1787 editions.

[56] Skoblow, *Dooble Tongue*, 188.

na fail his part in either' (ll. 35–6), before reminding the reader at lines 45–6 that his dedicatee *does* in fact possess all the qualities that fawning poets praise in their patrons: 'he's the poor man's friend in need, | The GENTLEMAN in word and deed' (ll. 45–6).[57] After digressing to attack the 'lang, wry faces' of the hypocritical Kirk elders who have harassed the theologically Moderate lawyer (l. 62), Burns's 'Dedication' ends conventionally by wishing prosperity to Hamilton and his family. (ll. 96–112). In a characteristic 'pastoral' move, however, Burns concludes by imagining Hamilton as 'downwardly mobile', levelled down to his own social station, a fate, he suggests, which might be a consequence of the financial misfortune that has ruined Lapraik or Sillar and threatens the poet himself. For in this eventuality the vertical patronage relation would be dissolved and replaced by horizontal fraternity: Hamilton could reap some consolation from the fact that he might count Burns not as 'your much indebted, humble servant' but that the two men could then shake hands as 'FRIEND(s) and BROTHER(s)!' (ll. 118, 134). Burns was fond of this 'downwardly mobile' gesture when addressing his social superiors, repeating it in the final stanza of his 'Extempore to Gavin Hamilton. Stanzas on Naething' [K 99] and, in more conventionally pastoral fashion, his patron Robert Aiken in the opening stanza of 'The Cotter's Saturday Night' [K 72].[58] Taking licence from pastoral convention, he inverts the energy of his own poetic aspirations in the mirror of his patron's downward mobility, thereby cancelling the difficult posture of deference, and replacing vertical with horizontal sociability.

The 'Dedication' is a masterpiece of Burns's 'asklent' (sideways) wit, deconstructing eighteenth-century conventions of deference in the interest of sentimental sincerity. But the fact that Gavin Hamilton had urged Burns to publish his poems in 1786 (and generously subscribed to the Kilmarnock volume), shouldn't blind us to the fact that he was also the landlord of Mossgiel Farm, to whom the Burns brothers were struggling to pay the rent. In the event, Robert donated £180 from the profits of the Edinburgh volume to his brother Gilbert, a capital sum that enabled him to struggle on as tenant farmer until 1797. In 1788, however, Burns fell out with Gavin Hamilton, who wanted him to stand surety for Gilbert's 'cash account'. Burns refused on the plausible grounds that his brother had already had his money, but Hamilton never forgave him for his truculence [Mackay, p. 405]. The sentimentalized image of fraternity developed here shouldn't blind us to the material realities of eighteenth-century power and patronage.

Burns's attitude to patronage fluctuated wildly between blank refusal, through the sort of witty disavowal represented by the 'Dedication to Gavin Hamilton', to the bare-faced grovelling of 'To Robert Graham of Fintry Esq., with a request for an Excise Division' [K 230]. Interesting in this light are his remarks to the

---

[57] These lines are repeated verbatim in Burns's epistle 'To the Rev. John M'math, Inclosing a Copy of Holy Willie's Prayer' [K 68] at ll. 31–2.

[58] See also his address to Miss Wilhelmina Alexander in the two final stanzas of 'The Bonie Lass o'Ballochmyle', verses to which she seems to have taken exception [K 89].

upper-class Mrs Frances Dunlop (who claimed descent from William Wallace) in a letter of 15 January 1787; 'Your patronising me, and interesting yourself in my fame and character as a poet, I rejoice in; it exalts me in my own idea; and whether you can or cannot aid me in my subscription, is a trifle. Has a paltry subscription-bill any charms to the heart of a bard, compared to the patronage of the descendant of the immortal Wallace?' [CL i. 86]. What more effective tactic could a poet employ to solicit subscriptions? As Dustin Griffin notes, 'while [Burns] refuses to grovel, he finds it perfectly appropriate for the poet to ask forthrightly for benevolence from "the great", and for the patron to bestow it'.[59]

## 'THE VISION': LABOUR, POETRY, CREDIT

'The Vision' [K 62] has only recently begun to recover from the hostility of many earlier critics. In their view, the poem's shift from full Scots in the first eight habbie stanzas to Augustan poetic diction distinguishing both the description of the Muse Coila's mantle (stanzas 12–22) and Coila's speech (taking up nearly the whole second part or 'Duan') illustrated the split personality of the 'Caledonian antisyzygy'. As David Daiches expressed it in his influential 1950 reading of 'The Vision', the poem suffered from an uneasy 'mixture of neo-classic conventions with Scots realism', which he attributed to Burns's misplaced attempt to 'gesture . . . for a genteel audience'. 'The Vision' revealed how badly Burns could get it wrong when 'he had his eye on the wrong audience'.[60] By contrast, a decade later Thomas Crawford describes 'The Vision' as 'one of Burns's highest achievements . . . the very summit of [his] work as a national poet' [Crawford, *BPS* 191–2].

Crawford is surely correct, and 'The Vision's' ambitious scope is not least evident in its deft handling of genre. Importantly, the local muse Coila conse-crates Burns's pastoral identity as a 'rustic bard', doubting that he can 'paint with *Thomson's* landscape-glow' (l. 248). Sustained use of the habbie stanza, even after the shift into English diction, preserves the poem's link with the Ramsayan 'Scots pastoral' tradition. McGuirk rightly notes the personal and vocational, rather than eulogistic, emphasis of the 1786 Kilmarnock version of 'The Vision', some fifty lines shorter than the text published in the Edinburgh edition of Burns's poems, which I'll discuss below [McGuirk, *BSP* 208]. Nevertheless, even in the version of 1786, 'The Vision' is in fact the most 'georgic' of all the poems published in the Kilmarnock volume, just as 'The Cotter's Saturday Night' is the most conventionally 'pastoral', according to the generic expectations discussed in Chapter 2. Burns's description of Ayrshire and its gentry in *The Vision* (especially the Edinburgh version) successfully emulates the georgic praise of 'retired'

---

[59] Griffin, *Literary Patronage*, 262–3. As I'll argue in Ch. 6, this accords with Burns's views of ecclesiastical patronage.

[60] Daiches, *Robert Burns*, 147–8.

opposition statesmen and patriotic landowners in James Thomson's *The Seasons* (1726–46).[61] Under the mask of pastoral modesty, Burns displays his poetic accomplishments, revealing his mastery of what he calls the 'digressive' genre of georgic and topographic verse description, as a local, and potentially national, bard in search of patronage.

Some of Burns's best critics assume that Coila's speech in the second Duan 'does not belong to Burns. It is a manifesto for the kind of poet Burns knows his genteel public would wish him to be'.[62] McIlvanney finds Coila the Muse's metamorphosis into a 'tapetless, ramfeezl'd hizzie' in the second 'Epistle to Lapraik' [K 58], a 'more typical' representation of the Burnsian muse. Her productivity is that of the female artisan, like the cottage spinner with her 'rock and wee pickle tow' (distaff and reel) hard pressed to spin rhymes: 'So dinna ye affront your trade, | But rhyme it right'(ll. 23–4), the poet commands.[63] True as this is in many respects, it risks abstracting an 'authentic' Burns from the historical and material contingencies of his poetic career, as if it were possible to abstract the meaning of any poem from its social inflections or its ambitions for a reading audience. To approach Coila as a figure for patronage as discussed in the previous section raises a question that has too often been shunned by Burns scholarship.[64]

The autobiographical elements and descriptive realism of the poem's opening stanzas set the stage for Coila's sudden visionary apparition, according to the narrative conventions of medieval dream poetry. While other country folk have been enjoying the 'roaring play' of the curling stones (suggesting that this may be another 'Saturday night' poem, like 'The Cotter'), while scavenging 'maukins' (hares) have satisfied their hunger by raiding 'the kail-yard green', the poet has been condemned to hard physical labour. He's worked all day at 'The Thresher's weary *flingin-tree*', separating the grain from the *caff* or straw, the most physically exacting task of the farming year (l. 7).[65] Not for Burns the new threshing machines extolled by Fullarton in his *County Report*.[66]

---

[61] See Gerard Carruthers, 'James Thomson and Eighteenth-Century Scottish Literary Identity', in Richard Terry (ed.), *James Thomson: Essays for the Tercentenary* (Liverpool: Liverpool University Press, 2000), 165–90 at 182–4.

[62] McIlvanney, *Burns the Radical*, 72. McGuirk, *Sentimental Era*, 40, argues that 'Burns [for once] allows himself to be the object of condescension . . . [His] persona is depressed from the outset as well as passive during the narrative.'

[63] McIlvanney, *Burns the* Radical, 73–4.

[64] See Robert Crawford, *The Bard*, 193.

[65] Quite possibly the choice of threshing here connects Burns with the counter-pastoral of Stephen Duck, author of 'The Thresher's Labour' (1730). Duck also published a poem entitled 'A Vision', dedicated to his patron Queen Caroline.

[66] Burns's 'flinging tree' refers to a hand-held 'swingle of the flail'. Fullarton described the new horse-driven threshing machines to abridge labour available in the 1780s and 1790s at the steep cost of £30 or £40 [Fullarton, pp. 29–30].

Physical labour alongside his men was one of Burns's many attempts at economy, but his mind wasn't evidently on the job. John Blane, the 'gaudsman' (ploughdriver) at Mossgiel, and one of three labourers employed by the Burns brothers, later recalled how 'in the laborious employment of husbandry, the Peculiarities of Burns's mind were easily discernible—While engaged in Thrashing, it was evident that his mind was particularly occupied, from the varied alternations from slow to quick which rendered it dangerous & even impossible for another to Keep time with him but in an hour or two he was quite exhausted & gave in altogether' [Mackay, p. 142]. The pleasure of 'southing' poetry in Burns's mind cut across the rhythm of threshing, even to the point of putting his fellow workers at risk, as well as exhausting the bard himself. It is a bit like Damon losing time with the birds on account of his overheated passion in Burns's bawdy 'Ode to Spring' [K 481].

Despite inhabiting an 'auld clay biggin', with 'rattons squeaking about the riggin',[67] Burns evokes a situation which can afford the poet some privacy ('lanely, by the ingle-cheek') and the physical space available for retreat ('Ben i' the *Spence*, right pensivelie, | I gaed to rest') (ll. 11–12). As Gavin Sprott comments, 'although the best room in Mossgiel was still called *the Spence*, it was not the *ben* room of the older Ayrshire houses, but part of a modern house built only a few years before by Gavin Hamilton who had sublet the farm' to the Burns brothers (see Fig. 3).[68] Despite the rats in the rafters, the 'spence' in Mossgiel was a theatre for reflection, a site for cultivating poetic inwardness which, in the language of the 1786 Preface, offered 'some kind of counterpoise to the struggles of a world, always an alien scene, a task uncouth to the poetical mind' [Kil. p. iv]. But it's this very space of inwardness, symptomized by the poet's propensity for rhyme, which is blamed for his failure as an 'improving' tenant farmer:

> All in this mottie, misty clime,
> I backward mused on wasted time,
> How I had spent my *youthfu' prime*,
>     An' done nae-thing,
> But stringing blethers up in rhyme
>     For fools to sing.
>
> Had I to guid advice but harket,
> I might, by this, hae led a market,
> Or strutted in a Bank and clarket
>     My *Cash-Account*;
> While here, half-mad, half-fed, half-sarket,
>     Is a' th' amount.   (ll. 19–30)

---

[67] Sounding more like the old farm at Lochlie rather than the relatively modern dwelling of Mossgiel.

[68] Gavin Sprott, *Robert Burns, Farmer* (Edinburgh: National Museums of Scotland, 1990), 23.

Fig. 3. 'Mossgiel'. A coloured print showing Burns's farmhouse and detached steading, in the new style. Note the four-horse plough team.

Commentators have tended to assume that Burns refers here to something like a modern current account, but in eighteenth-century Scotland the term had a specialized meaning. In his discussion of the contemporary banking system in *Wealth of Nations*, Adam Smith (*Wealth of Nations*, i. 395) explains that Bankers 'granted what they called cash accounts, that is by giving credit to the extent of a certain sum . . . to any individual who could procure two persons of undoubted credit and good landed estate to become surety for him'. Smith blamed easy credit for the collapse of the Douglas Heron Bank in Ayr in 1772, given that the Bank 'was more liberal than any other had ever been, both in granting cash accounts, and in discounting bills of exchange'. However, the purpose of this easy credit, and the flood of paper money issued by the bank, was the patriotic motive of advancing 'the whole capital which was to be employed in those improvements of which the returns are the most slow and distant, such as the improvement of land' (ibid. 412).

Writing in the mid-1780s, when the repercussions of the Ayr bank crash were still being felt in south-west Scotland, it's unlikely that Burns would have been

able to 'strut into a Bank and clark his Cash Account', even if he possessed
better credit than would have been available to the son of William Burnes, the
ruined tenant of Lochlie. Tenants simply shouldered the debts incurred by
the landowning class; David McClure, landlord of Lochlie, was himself bank-
rupted as an indirect result of the Ayr Bank crash, and even the 5th Earl of
Loudoun, from whom Gavin Hamilton rented Mossgiel Farm (which he
sublet to Robert and Gilbert Burns) was driven by his debts to commit suicide
in April 1786.

Given his reiterated attack on 'ye selfish, warly race', it's unlikely that Burns's
turn to 'guid black *prent*' with the Kilmarnock volume was primarily intended as
a money-making venture, although he did expect to raise the nine guineas
required to pay his shipboard to Jamaica, in order to avoid the necessity of
indenturing himself to his future employer [Mackay, p. 160]. In view of the low
financial returns for poetry in the late eighteenth century such a scheme would
have been quixotic, although one unintended outcome of the Kilmarnock (and
even more so of the Edinburgh) volumes was in fact to raise considerable sums of
money. Burns may have made £54 profit from Kilmarnock, and as much as £700
from the Edinburgh edition, the copyright of which he sold to Creech for another
100 guineas [Mackay, p. 236].[69] In January 1787 he wrote to Patrick Miller, 'now,
when by the appearances of my second edition of my book, I may reckon on a
middling farming capital, there is nothing I wish for more than to resume the
Plough' [CL i. 86–7].

I suggested above that the verse epistles vindicated the exchange of 'crambo-
jingle' as a sort of alternative 'gift-economy', affirming the values of 'horizontal'
social solidarity and 'good-heartedness' in defiance of worldly failure. But if, in
the sentimental tradition, the epistles reject money-grubbing, worldly ambition
and flattery, they quite openly admitted to their *poetic* ambitions. The rationale
for this seems to lie in complicated eighteenth-century meaning of the word
'credit', which despite its financial connotations, also approximated to Bourdieu's notion of symbolic or cultural capital to which I've alluded above, *inverting* the laws of financial profit.[70] As the opening stanzas of 'The Vision' make
clear, Burns blamed his poverty on his passion for poetry, not the contingencies
of bad harvests, high rents, or Bank collapses. In proleptically Romantic mood,
poetry becomes a figure for the failure of his credit, at least until his Muse Coila
assures him otherwise.

---

[69] Sher, *Enlightenment and the Book*, 234, 232.

[70] Burns's understanding of the term 'credit' is comically illustrated in 'Poor Mailie''s dying
advice to her *yowie*—like herself an 'improved' Fairlie sheep, rather than a 'blastet, Moorland toop':
'but ay keep mind to moop an' mell, | Wi' sheep o' credit like thysel'! ('Death and Dying Words', [K
24] ll. 54–6).

## MAPPING COILA'S MANTLE

The poet's 'infant aith, half-form'd, was crusht' (l. 44) by the unannounced entrance of Coila, at once supernatural apparition and 'tight, outlandish *Hizzie*', whose shapely legs are only matched by the poet's 'BESS' (or, comically, 'bonie JEAN' in later versions) (ll. 62–3). Clad in tartan silks and crowned with holly, the poet instantly recognizes her for 'some SCOTTISH MUSE', but her 'hare-brain'd sentimental trace' (l. 55) places her in the convivial company of flesh and blood associated with the epistles.[71] Although the reader has to wait until the second Duan for Coila's speech, when she does speak there's no ambiguity concerning her purpose; 'All hail *my own* inspired Bard! | In me thy native Muse regard! | Nor longer mourn thy fate is hard, | Thus poorly low! | I come to give thee such *reward*, | As *we* bestow' (ll. 139–44). Borrowing the 'machinery' of 'the light aerial band' from Pope's *Rape of the Lock* [Kin. iii. 1073], Burns has Coila unfold a hierarchy of supernatural muses, the higher echelons of which supervise soldiers, statesmen, and poets. But although she has been dispatched by the (male) '*Genius* of the Land', (l. 145) and despite her initial identification as 'some SCOTTISH MUSE', Coila introduces herself as a lesser, local spirit 'bounded to a district-space . . . Where once the *Campbells*, chiefs of fame, | Held ruling pow'r', alluding to the Earls of Loudoun, upon whose Kyle estates Burns's farm of Mossgiel was situated (ll. 193, 201–2). Coila's lowly place in the hierarchy of the 'aerial band' determines her role as the guardian of 'the humbler ranks of Human-kind, | The rustic Bard, the lab'ring Hind, | The Artisan' (ll. 175–8).[72] By means of Coila, Burns carefully figures his poetic consecration in deferential terms, emphasizing that it's a local, before it's a national, event.

Returning to the first Duan, the description of Coila's mantle that takes up its remaining stanzas qualifies Allan Ramsay's critical strictures on the Scottish nobility in his 1724 poem 'The Vision' (published in *The Evergreen*), to which Burns's title responds [Ramsay, iii. 81–94]. Ramsay's Jacobite vision of Scotland dwyning under incorporated union with England is challenged, both in the Kilmarnock text of 'The Vision', and especially in the seven stanzas added to the Edinburgh edition, by the georgic prospect of cultural and economic renaissance portrayed on Coila's mantle. But in contrast to Adam Smith, for whom improvement was a direct consequence of Union, Coila represents it as a

---

[71] This quotes l. 157 of Burns's 'Epistle to Smith', which according to the careful arrangement of the Kilmarnock volume is placed two poems anterior to 'The Vision'.

[72] In a 1788 letter to Frances Dunlop, Burns claimed that Coila was inspired by Beattie's praise for the muse 'Scota' in Alexander Ross's *Helenore, or The Fortunate Shepherdess*, in his verse epistle to the same [CL i. 256]. But Coila's English address evidently owes little to 'Scota', who had exhorted *her* poet to express himself in full Doric; 'Speak my ain leed, 'tis gueed auld Scots I mean, | Your soudland gnaps I count not worth a prine' (*Helenore, or the Fortunate Shepherdess*, ed. John Longmuir [Edinburgh: William Nimmo, 1866], 137).

patriotic Scottish activity, localizing civic virtue by allusion to Ayrshire's 'lordly domes' (l. 78) and great estates. Notably (in the Edinburgh text) she trumpets the pacific rebirth of Scotland's heroic national past, initially represented by William Wallace, 'His COUNTRY's SAVIOUR' (l. 103) who had repelled 'their Suthron foes' (l. 102).[73] If Ramsay's 'Vision' is one intertext for Burns's poem (echoed in his title), then, as the Canongate editors note, his use of the term 'Duan' to signal the poem's divisions alludes to another, James Macpherson's *Ossian*, but to the end of inverting that poem's meaning. In contrast to 'Ossian's melancholy wandering in a ghostly landscape littered with the Celtic warrior dead, a culture irretrievably lost', 'The Vision' represents 'a virile poet celebrating an Ayrshire landscape energised by the power and beauty of its rivers and its organic, living connection with its heroic dead' [CG, p. 70].

Coila's account of 'the growth of a poet's mind' in lines 205–40 draws upon Beattie's account in *The Minstrel*, combined with a virtuoso condensation of Thomson's description of Winter, Spring, Summer, and Autumn in *The Seasons*. Her remarks propose another kind of sentimental election by casting an indulgent eye upon the poet's straying on 'Pleasure's devious way', excused on the grounds that 'the *light* that led astray, | Was *light* from Heaven' (ll. 239–40). As crowned by Coila's holly crown at the conclusion of the second Duan, Burns gains new credit as Ayrshire's local poet. It is precisely his *pastoral* genius, Coila informs him, that establishes this claims to patronage:

> I taught thy manners-painting strains,
> The *loves*, the *ways*, of simple swains,
> Till now, o'er all my wide domains,
>         Thy fame extends;
> And some, the pride of *Coila's* plains,
>         Become thy friends.    (ll. 241–6)

This reference to 'the pride of *Coila's* plains' indicates that Burns was already playing for higher stakes in the patronage game than could be won by paying 'asklent' compliments to his landlord Gavin Hamilton, or to 'bourgeois' patrons such as Robert Aiken or John Ballantine. Importantly, however, as in the 'Dedication to the Caledonian Hunt', the poem justifies its bid for credit in terms of local patriotism as opposed to flattery, always anathema to the democratically minded Burns. There's little doubt of the sincerity of 'The Vision's' panegyric on the improving Ayrshire gentry, and nor does it necessarily conflict with the 'The Twa Dogs'' indictment of a corrupt ruling class who have reneged on their social trusteeship, as we'll see in the next chapter. Chris Whatley rightly emphasizes that in eighteenth-century Scotland 'respect for landed authority was

---

[73] This would please Mrs Dunlop when she read 'The Vision', proud of her descent from Wallace.

conditional and not granted as a matter of course', despite the disproportionate power of a quasi-feudal elite [Whatley, p. 153].

The poet's coronation relieves him from the vocational self-doubts he's suffered in his rural shades, although this is premised on his assumption of a polite (and humble) pastoral role. Burns the 'rustic bard' allows himself to be overshadowed by such canonical poets as Thomson, Shenstone, or Gray, like a 'lowly Daisy' to the 'unrivall'd Rose', or a 'juicy Hawthorn' to the oak tree's 'army shade' (ll. 253–58).[74] Something is stirring in the undergrowth, although I don't agree with McIlvanney that the 'juicy Hawthorn' prefigures the Liberty Tree.[75] Quite the reverse in fact, given the poem's manifest concern with praising 'the pride of Coila's plains' and their 'lordly domes'. Even here, the trope of pastoral modesty easily disguises the moral and political inversion of 'pastoral politics', as Coila urges her poet: 'never murmur nor repine; | Strive in thy *humble sphere* to shine; | And trust me, not *Potosi's mine*, | Nor *King's regard*, | Can give a bliss o'ermatching thine, | A rustic Bard' (ll. 259–64). Peter Murphy observes that 'pastoral figures ambition as non-ambition, but this fiction must lapse in the face of the physical world'.[76] As we all know, Burns did discover the means to criticize a corrupt aristocracy in the Paineite language of 'honest poverty'. But not in 'The Vision', where Coila is a figure for the poet's prospective credit with the Ayrshire gentry, holding out a more productive relationship of patronage than the hopeless dependence of the tenant farmer.

Coila's greenish '*Mantle* large' (l. 67) depicts an image of the '*well-known* Land' (l. 72) of Ayrshire which draws the poet's 'gazing wonder':

> Here, rivers in the sea were lost;
> There, mountains to the skies were tost:
> Here, tumbling billows mark'd the coast,
>          With surging foam;
> There, distant shone, *Art's* lofty boast,
>          The lordly dome.
>
> Here, DOON pour'd down his far-fetch'd floods;
> There, well-fed IRWINE stately thuds:
> Auld, hermit AIRE staw thro' his woods,
>          On to the shore;
> And many a lesser torrent scuds,
>          With seeming roar.
>
> Low, in a sandy valley spread,
> An ancient BOROUGH rear'd her head;

---

[74] McGuirk (*Sentimental Era*, 43) notes that here 'Burns is obviously trying hard to be an oak (a Thomson, a Gray) at the same time that he is assuring his readers that he is happy enough as a hawthorn'.

[75] McIlvanney, *Burns the Radical*, 73.

[76] Peter Murphy, *Poetry as an Occupation and an Art*, 74.

> Still, as in *Scottish Story* read,
>         She boasts a *Race*,
> To ev'ry nobler virtue bred,
>         And polish'd grace.    (ll. 69–90)

This long ekphrastic description of Coila's mantle that closes the first Duan in the Kilmarnock text puzzled David Daiches, who described it as a sort of 'aerial photograph' of the districts presided over by Coila.[77] In contrast to the solitary, private ruminations of the poet in his humble spence (which he periodically refers to, using a Thomsonian turn of phrase, as 'my native shade of life', CL i. 281]), Coila's mantle exhibits a public prospect appropriate to the local gentry eulogized in the Edinburgh text of the poem. At one level the mantle represents what John Barrell describes as the 'equal wide survey' of the eighteenth-century landowning classes—Pope's Bolingbroke, Thomson's Lyttleton—who (it was alleged) could see the harmonious landscape 'prospect' by dint of their leisurely exemption from labour or 'mechanical' occupation.[78] We've seen how Burns's Commonplace Book entry, and the 'Epistle to Willie Simson' sought to legitimize his self-election as 'Ayrshire's Bard', in the localizing spirit of Ramsay and Ferugusson. The device of Coila's mantle embodies Burns's claims as a 'rustic poet' to both inhabit and transcend his 'humble sphere', via his regional self-identification as a poet of Ayrshire first, and of Scotland second. Regional as well as national solidarity here overcomes class difference: in this respect Burns contributes to a characteristic eighteenth- century construction of post-Union Scottish identity.

In criticizing Burns's lack of ambition in merely 'circulat[ing] his poems among the inhabitants of the county in which he was born' (once again he got the wrong end of the stick), Henry Mackenzie's *Lounger* review of December 1786 aimed 'to place [Burns] in a higher point of view, to call for a verdict of his country on the merit of his works' [*CH* p. 68]. This appeal by Scotland's leading literary figure certainly contributed to the *national* poetic fame which generated Burns's Edinburgh edition, concrete embodiment of his passage from 'county' to 'country'. Appropriately, the version of 'The Vision' published in 1787 showcased the Ayrshire worthies who, as we'll see below, had been relatively downplayed in the Kilmarnock text.[79] The poem's cumulative growth confirms Charles Withers's claim that eighteenth-century 'Scotland as a national space

---

[77] Daiches, *Robert Burns*, 146.

[78] John Barrell, *English Literature and History, 1730–80: An Equal, Wide Survey* (London: Hutchinson, 1983), 17–50.

[79] Burns may also have been responding to an attack on the Ayrshire gentry in the *Edinburgh Evening Courant* on 13 Nov. 1786 by a native of Dumbartonshire, who grumbled that Ayrshire's failure to patronize Burns 'is a reflection on the county and a disgrace to humanity' [*CH* p. 65].

was, in some respects, only understood at all in consequence of the inductive integration of local knowledge to form a picture of the nation'.[80]

Scottish geographical and antiquarian writing in this period was, like georgic poetry, preoccupied with the gentlemanly prospect; 'through the surveying of estates close to home as useful local knowledge, the genealogies of local families of note, and the description of local and remarkable natural features in human production'.[81] Despite its sublime vistas of Ayrshire landscape ('Here, rivers in the sea were lost; | There, mountains to the skies were tost', ll. 73–4), Coila's mantle is a cartographic rather than an iconic representation of the county, a map rather than a landscape view. Although Burns had no training in polite picturesque sketching or painting, he was well versed in the artisanal practices of surveying and mapping; after all, drawing field and estate plans was part of the education of an ambitious eighteenth-century Scottish tenant farmer. At the age of 17 his father had sent him to Kirkoswald to 'learn Mensuration, Surveying, Dialling, &c. in which I made a pretty good progress' [CL i. 140]. His continued interest in cartography is evident in a letter of April 1789 to Edinburgh bookseller Peter Hill in which he requested that a copy of 'Ainslie's map of Scotland' be sent to him at Ellisland [CL i. 392].

D. G. Moir has shown how the Scottish county map in the eighteenth century developed from the estate map, devised for the purposes of improvement such as enclosures, drainage, plantation, etc.[82] The process began in the 1730s with Richard Cooper's maps of the Lothians, continuing with William Edgar's maps of Tweeddale and Peebles, John Laurie's maps of Midlothian, and Matthew Stobie's of Roxburghshire. In 1747–55 William Roy was commissioned by the Duke of Cumberland in the aftermath of Culloden to produce a military survey of Scotland, precursor of the modern Ordinance Survey, although as a manuscript map it wasn't publicly available. Although there's a wealth of local detail of what became known as 'Burns country' represented on Roy's map, late eighteenth-century Ayrshire hadn't fared much better in the cartographic construction of Scotland than in poetic encomium, compared to the more 'improved' Lothians and Borders.

---

[80] Charles W. J. Withers, 'How Scotland Came to Know Itself: Geography, National Identity and the Making of a Nation, 1680–1790', *Journal of Historical Geography* 21/4 (Oct. 1995), 371–98 at 373.

[81] Ibid. 375.

[82] D. G. Moir, *Early Maps of Scotland to 1850*, 2 vols. (Edinburgh: Royal Scottish Geographical Society, 1973), i. 117. See also I. H. Adams, *The Mapping of a Scottish Estate* (Edinburgh: Dept. of Education Studies, 1971), and for military mapping, Yolande O'Donoghue, *William Roy 1726–1790: Pioneer of the Ordnance Survey* (London: British Museum Publications, 1977). Dependence of county upon estate maps explains the fact that cartographical representations of farms and settlements situated on great estates was far superior. Thus, for example, the Armstrongs' map (discussed below) represents the Burns farms at Mount Oliphant and Mossgiel (both situated on the large estates of Provost Fergusson and the Earl of Loudoun) but *not* Lochlie, owned by the Ayr merchant David McLure. John Strawhorn, 'An Introduction to Armstrong's Maps', in id. (ed.), *Ayrshire at the Time of Burns* (Newmilns: Ayrshire Archaeological and Natural History Society, 1959), 232–55 at 245, 247.

Nevertheless, in 1775, the English mapmaker Captain Andrew Armstrong (assisted by his son Mostyn) published his *New Map of Ayrshire, Comprehending Kyle, Cunningham, & Carrick*, on a scale of 1 inch to 1 mile. (At the time Burns was a 16-year-old working on his father's farm at Mount Oliphant.) Although the map was criticized by contemporaries, John Strawhorn has convincingly demonstrated on the basis of a careful scrutiny, that its outline is 'carefully drawn, and remarkably accurate in detail'.[83] With its curious baroque title plate, and its picturesque view of a 'papingo shoot' at Kilwinning Abbey (see Fig. 4),[84] the Armstrongs' map is in many respects a graphic analogue of Burns's 'The Vision', a suggestion I'll develop in the closing section. The parallel is also evident in the map's dedication, 'To the Nobility, Gentry, and all the Subscribers for the County of Ayr', its intense focus on the landed estates of its patrons, its concern with local antiquities and ruins, and its combination of county survey with relief landscape representation.[85]

## GEORGIC EULOGY IN THE 'ADDITIONAL STANZAS'

The Stair manuscript of *The Vision*, dispatched by Burns to his patron Mrs Stewart of Stair in September 1786, added nineteen stanzas to the first Duan as published in 1786, following line 90, 'describing the estates and lairds of Kyle'; seven of these stanzas were retained in the Edinburgh edition published the following year (ll. 91–132) [Kinsley iii. 1069].[86] But these weren't just tagged on as an afterthought to curry favour with wealthy would-be patrons. In a letter of Jan. 1787 to Mrs Frances Dunlop, the poet wrote; 'when I composed my *Vision* long ago, I had attempted a description of Koyle [*sic*], of which the additional stanzas are a part, as it originally stood' [CL i. 85]. As this makes clear, the

---

[83] Strawhorn, 'Introduction to Armstrongs' Maps', 245. D. G. Moir (*Early Maps*, i. 118) reiterates contemporary criticisms of the Armstrongs' map. In 1789 the Earl of Eglinton commissioned John Ainslie, the outstanding Scottish surveyor of his time, to survey and map his estates in Ayrshire, as well as the Baronies of Kilwinning and Eglinton, producing a superior map to that of the Armstrongs (ibid. 121).

[84] Doubtless a Masonic allusion, given the importance of the Abbey as the alleged birthplace of Scottish Masonry.

[85] Moir, *Early* Maps, i. 246. According to the conventions of eighteenth-century cartography, hills and mountains were represented in perspective, shaded to suggest a light from the north-west.

[86] See also John McVie, *Burns and Stair* (Kilmarnock: 'Standard' Press, 1927), 79–87. In addition to the landed worthies praised in the 1786 text and the Edinburgh stanzas, the Stair manuscript eulogizes the following: John Hamilton of Sundrum and his daughters (ll. 6–12), John Dalrymple, 2nd Earl of Stair, and the new incumbent of Stair House, Major-General Alexander Stewart and his wife (ll. 14–18), Capt James Montgomerie of Coilsfield, Lord Auchinleck and his son James Boswell (ll. 1–5), Sir John Whiteford of Ballochmyle, Claude Alexander and his sister Wilhelmina (ll. 6–24), the Countess of Dumfries (ll. 1–5), Mr Farquar Gray of Strathblane (ll. 6–12), Sir William Cunninghame of Auchenskeith (ll. 13–18), and James Dalrymple of Orangefield (ll. 25, 30).

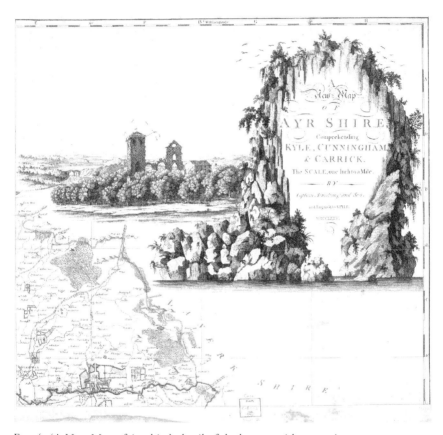

Fig. 4. 'A New Map of Ayrshire': detail of the baroque title engraving.

panegyric on the Ayrshire gentry, and the related theme of patronage, were integral to the poem's original conception when it was composed, probably in 1785.[87]

More interesting is why Burns decided to *remove* the nineteen additional 'eulogic' stanzas from the poem as published in the Kilmarnock edition in the summer of 1786. 'The Vision's' placement as tenth out of the forty-four or so poems and songs included in Kilmarnock suggests that he may actually have wished to *de-emphasize* Coila's georgic vision of Ayrshire, and the poet's deferential relationship to his social and cultural landscape, in accordance with the 'pastoral' and egalitarian aims of the volume. In fact, the only worthies mentioned in the Kilmarnock text of 'The Vision' are Col. William Fullarton, George Dempster of Dunnichen, and James Beattie, as well as (in passing) 'the *Campbell's,* chiefs of fame'. (Dempster and Beattie have no local connections, but this is perfectly appropriate, because Coila is here describing the charges of a higher order of muses dedicated to 'SCOTIA's Race', her 'sodgers', 'patriots', and 'bards', rather than her own Ayrshire wards.)[88] Added to the list in the 1787 Edinburgh volume are the Montgomeries of Coilsfield (ll. 109–14), the Lord Justice Clerk Sir Thomas Miller of Barskimming (ll. 115–20), and Professors Matthew and Dugald Stewart of Catrine (ll. 121–5) upon whom I'll comment below.

These additional stanzas are often (and quite rightly, in one sense) seen as detrimental to the poetical quality and unity of the poem: Henley and Henderson describe them as 'strikingly inferior to those published in the original edition' (i. 350) In concluding this long chapter, I'll comment on the 'lairds of Kyle' with reference to the visual analogue of Armstrong's county map of 1775 (see Fig. 5). Scrutinizing the topography of Burns's Ayrshire on Armstrong's map, we get a clearer sense of the social geography that the poem is negotiating, in which sense Burns's poem appears to be a rather literal description of 'facts on the ground'. The map graphically epitomizes Henry Cockburn's (litote-ridden) description of Scotland before the Reform Act, as being 'not unlike a village at a great man's door...no popular representation, no emancipated burghs, no effective rival of the Establishment Church, no independent press, no free public meetings, and no...trial by jury; patronage was 'really all the government that the country then admitted of'.[89]

Remarkable to the modern eye is the dominance of the 'lordly domes' surrounding Mauchline in the 1770s, especially striking when compared to the sparse pre-improvement landscape represented on the Roy map just twenty years earlier.[90]

---

[87] Henley and Henderson [i. 350] suggest that 'the published stanzas were revised for the Kilmarnock volume, the others remained untouched. Burns...states that the stanzas added to the '87 Edition formed part of the poem as "it originally stood" but the probability is that they were almost entirely recast' while, presumably, the "Stair" stanzas were not'.

[88] In stanza 6 of the second Duan, as published in 1786 [Kil. p. 93].

[89] Henry Cockburn, *Life of Lord Jeffrey,* 1:74, quoted by Duncan, *Scott's Shadow,* 24.

[90] In 1793 Fullarton [p. 14] described Ayrshire in 1750 as resembling 'the dark and gloomy periods of the lower ages when...the North of Europe, under barbarous landlords, with serfs and bondsmen or their cultivators, exhibited...scenes of ignorance and indigence'.

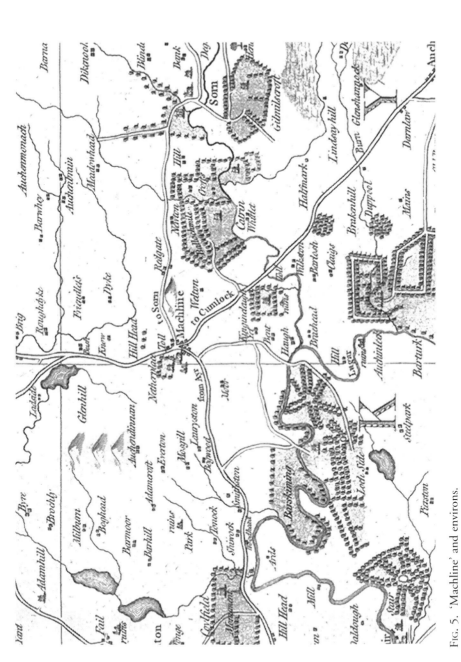

FIG. 5. 'Machline' and environs.

As Strawhorn notes, 'the confident and emphatic representation of the great estates, and the progressive character of the changes they were working on the landscape is revealed. Mansion houses are shown, sometimes beside deserted ruins of abandoned castles, parklands are stippled in, and the countryside is being clothed with new and extensive woodlands'. The prominence afforded to 'areas of park and plantation' is of course explicable by the fact that 'these were the homes of the Subscribers for whom the Armstrongs were catering...and one suspects that a certain tactful embellishment would possibly be awarded to those seats whose owners were on the list of subscribers'.[91] A similar principle (however prospective) may have determined Burns's criterion of inclusion in 'The Vision''s additional stanzas.

Eighteenth-century Ayrshire had eight Earls—Eglinton, Cassilis, Glencairn, Stair, Loudoun, Dumfries, Glasgow, and Dundonald—and even as late as the Return of Owners of Land and Heritages in 1872, fourteen great landowners still owned a staggering more than half the entire county.[92] But the inclusion of prominent Edinburgh lawyers (Barskimming, Auchinleck) and university professors (Beattie, Matthew, and Dugald Stewart) in 'The Vision''s list of worthies reminds us of the intimate links between institutional power and the landed interest in enlightenment Scotland.[93] The lairds (both noblemen and commoners) exercised huge social power beyond their own estates, often consolidated by Masonic networks of the kind discussed in the Introduction: as sheriffs and justices of the peace, commissioners of supply (assessing and gathering land tax), heritors and patrons of local kirks with the (often contested) right of presenting ministers, responsible for overseeing poor relief, schooling, roads and turnpikes, and after 1793 raising militias.[94]

Each of the plantations surrounding a castellated icon on the Armstrongs' map marks the seat of a powerful landowner: Ballochmyle, Auchinleck, Barskimming, Stair, Coilsfield, Sorn Castle, Enterkine, etc. etc. Between these great piles with their ornamental parks and plantations is an expansive white hinterland composed of still largely unenclosed rigs and scattered clachans, although the number of cot houses is notably reduced in comparison with the Roy map. Apart from coal-pits marked at Stevenston, Newton-upon-Ayr, and Dailly, and quarries and early industrial sites at Muirkirk and Cumnock, there's as yet little evidence in 1775 of the development of textile and other manufacturing, or of the coal-mining industry that would transform Ayrshire in the century to come. Although some new roads are marked,

---

[91] Strawhorn, 'Introduction to Armstrongs' Maps', 246–7. He suggests that subscription was a key factor when the Armstrongs couldn't decide 'whether to represent a bonnet-laird as occupying a farmhouse or a more exalted residence' (ibid.).

[92] John Strawhorn, *Ayrshire: The Story of a County* (Newmilns: Ayrshire Archaeological and Natural History Society, 1975), 148.

[93] Between 1752 and 1811, 88% of entrants to the Faculty of Advocates came from landed families. See John Clive, 'The Social Background of the Scottish Renaissance', in N. T. Phillipson and Rosalind Mitchison (eds.), *Scotland in the Age of Improvement* (Edinburgh: Edinburgh University Press, 1970; repr.1996), 228.

[94] Strawhorn, *Ayrshire*, 144–5.

neither is there much evidence here (apart from the numerous plantations) of farm enclosure and consolidation, or the construction of planned villages.

Consider 'the pride of Coila's plains' (alluded to in the extended text of 'The Vision'), as they are graphically represented on the Armstrongs' map. I'll orientate their properties in relation to Burns's farm at Mossgiel, to convey a sense of the intense local focus of his prospective patronage network.[95] To the south-west at Stair House dwelt Major-General Alexander Stewart, veteran of the American war ('who far in Western climates fought') and his wife Catherine, to whom Burns sent the 'Stair Manuscript' (Stair, p. 106 ll. 16–17).[96] Due west, Coilsfield House was the home of the 'martial Race' of Hugh Montgomerie, later 12th Earl of Eglinton ('sojer Hugh' of 'The Author's Earnest Cry and Prayer', ll. 109–14). The Montgomeries of Eglinton were the most powerful family in Ayrshire, and their prominence in 'The Vision' suggests that Burns was keen to attract their attention. Unfortunately he failed, and in the event had to make do instead with the patronage of the relatively powerless and encumbered Earl of Glencairn when he arrived in Edinburgh in 1787.[97]

To the south-west, Barskimming House was the estate of the 'aged judge' Sir Thomas Miller of Barskimming (later Lord Glenlee), Lord Justice Clerk, and elder brother of Burns's future landlord at Ellisland, Patrick Miller of Dalswinton, banker, improver, and pioneer of steam navigation (ll. 115–20). (This was, in the event, a more successful patronage connection than his appeal to the Eglintons.) Due south, Auchinleck was owned by the Boswells, father and son; interestingly, Coila awards them the 'classic bays' (in contrast to Burns's rustic holly) for their literary labours (Stair, p. 107 ll. 1–6).[98] A mile or so due east, Ballochmyle was the home of Sir John Whitefoord, Master of the St James Lodge, Tarbolton, ruined in the Heron bank crash (ibid. ll. 7–18).[99] The distinguished father and son, Professors Matthew and Dugald Stewart, owned Catrine Bank House, due south-east: Dugald, the leading British philosopher of the late enlightenment

[95] Robert Crawford suggests that the poem's topography 'is in part a walking poem retracing earlier riverbank rambles' along the rivers Ayr and Lugar, but adds that this 'was not just a stroll in nature. It also marked the direction of his literary ambitions', *The Bard*, 92.

[96] All references here are to the additional stanzas as published in Kinsley's edition of 'The Vision' [K 62] i. 103–13. 'Stair' indicates the additional stanzas published at the foot of the page with separate numeration from the Edinburgh version upon which his text is based.

[97] See William Donaldson, 'The Glencairn Connection: Robert Burns and Scottish Politics, 1786–96', *Studies in Scottish Literature* 16 (1981), 61–79 at 69. The fact that the Glencairn family was in a state of decline may explain why they're omitted from 'The Vision'.

[98] Burns's attempt to solicit patronage from this quarter was notoriously unsuccessful (see his letter to James Boswell's factor Bruce Campbell of 13 Nov. 1788 [CL i. 335–6]), although Boswell's son Alexander subsequently played a prominent role in raising money for the Burns monument at Alloway.

[99] Ballochmyle was purchased by the rich nabob Claude Alexander in 1786; his sister Wilhelmina, praised here (Stair p. 108 ll. 19–24) was the unreceptive subject of Burns's song 'The Bonie Lass of Ballochmyle' [K 89].

and romantic period, was Burns's most significant personal contact with the literati of the Scottish Enlightenment (ibid. ll. 121–6).

Neither the Cunningham estates of Col. William Fullarton at Dundonald (ibid. p. 108 ll. 19–24) nor of James Dalrymple of Orangefield (ibid. ll. 25–30) are represented on this section of the Armstrong map, but both are important members of Coila's cast of worthies. Dalrymple ('a heart too warm, a pulse too hot') is important because he introduced Burns to his future patron the Earl of Glencairn (married to Dalrymple's sister), as well as presenting the poet to the Canongate Kilwinning Lodge in Edinburgh in December 1786. Also unrepresented on this section of the map is Loudoun Castle, seat of Mossgiel farm's proprietors the Earls of Loudon, 'the *Campbells*, chiefs of fame' (l. 201) (to the east of Kilmarnock): the suicidal 5th Earl left as his only heiress his young daughter Flora Mure Campbell, who in 1804 married the English aristocrat Francis Rawdon, 1st Earl (and later Marquis) of Hastings and 2nd Lord Moira; by marriage he became (as if he needed another title) 6th Earl of Loudoun. Hastings (no relation of Warren) achieved fame as Governor General of India 1812–23, and later of Malta, dying at Naples in 1826. It was through the Hastings patronage that Jean Armour Burns and the poet's trustees secured the successful careers of his two sons, Col. William Nichol Burns (1791–1872) and Lt. Col. James Glencairn Burns (1794–1865), in the East India Company Army. Once again, with uncanny prescience, 'The Vision' conjured up future patrons and guardians of the poet and his progeny.

In this respect at least, 'The Vision' speaks for itself. Coila as a figure for local consecration has the power to transform the poet's credit from the horizontal 'subscription' network of the Kilmarnock volume to a vertical relationship with 'the pride of Coila's plains', beyond that successfully aspiring to the Scottish elite represented by the Caledonian Hunt, dedicatees of the Edinburgh volume. This potential patronage network, so important to the making of Burns the poet, is practically invisible in the Kilmarnock text, although the prior existence of the 'additional stanzas' enabled him to add it in subsequent manuscript versions for distribution (e.g. the Stair Manuscript), or published texts (the Edinburgh edition) of the poem. What's remarkable is that in 1786 this was still a *virtual* vision of patronage, although one that helped to secure the poet's subsequent fame, embodying a set of *real* social relations, the credit of which was worth, literally, a lot more than could otherwise be hoped for by a virtually bankrupt tenant farmer of Burns's standing. Many, of course, would argue that it was the ultimate *success* of Burns's quest for patronage, avidly pursued during the Edinburgh sojourn and realized in the Excise commission, which muted the poet in the man.

# 4

# Pastoral Politics

*Of more worth is one honest man to society, and in the sight of God, than all the crowned ruffians that ever lived.*

(Tom Paine, *Common Sense*, 1776)[1]

*Burns's politics always smell of the smithy.*

(Hugh Blair)

## BURNS AND POLITICS

Although all critics agree that Burns is a manifestly political poet, no aspect of his life and writing has engendered more controversy than the nature of his politics. Robert Crawford's recent biography *The Bard* justifiably makes much of Revd James MacDonald's account of dining with Burns in Dumfries in the summer of 1796, where the terminally ill poet is described unequivocally as 'a staunch republican'. But, MacDonald continued, 'Burns repeated an ode he composed on the Pretender's birth day, replete with grand imagery & brilliant expression'.[2] Ideologically, this is a characteristic Burnsian non sequitur in its lurch from Jacobin to Jacobite partisanship, although as Crawford comments, there's nothing really untoward about it, given that 'heresies in politics and religion that set [Burns] on the side of 'staunch republicans' and against the 'unco guid' were vital to his life and poetry'.[3]

Beyond a whimsical poet's sympathy for the underdog, whether the defeated Stuart dynasty, the rebellious American colonists, or the persecuted British radicals of 1792–4,[4] the poet was proud that he had 'a few first principles in

---

[1] *The Tom Paine Reader*, ed. Michael Foot and Isaac Kramnick (London: Penguin, 1987), 79.

[2] Robert Crawford, *The Bard: Robert Burns, a Biography* (London: Jonathan Cape, 2009), 395.

[3] Ibid. 397. Bob Harris asks pertinently whether, in calling Burns a republican, MacDonald meant 'an opponent of monarchy and the balanced Constitution . . . [or simply] a reformer and opponent of war against revolutionary France' *The Scottish People and the French Revolution* (London: Pickering & Chatto, 2008), 11.

[4] Colin Kidd underlines the importance of Burns's 'politics of sentiment', in 'Burns and Politics', Gerard Carruthers (ed.), *The Edinburgh Companion to Robert Burns* (Edinburgh: Edinburgh University Press, 2009), 61–73 at 70–1.

Religion and Politics which, I believe, I would not easily part with' [CL i. 77]. But despite an understandable inclination (in some cases backed up by good evidence) to embrace a 'radical Burns', we shouldn't always expect programmatic 'first principles' from an impecunious and unenfranchised poet, chafing at the bit of patronage.[5] They are certainly not very visible in those most 'overtly' political poems, the 'Election Ballads' written for the Dumfries Burgh elections in 1790, and the Kirkcudbright County election of 1795.[6] Even when assessing Burns's radical sympathies in the more ideologically polarized climate of the revolutionary decade, we need to recall that as an oath-sworn Exciseman, Burns was, in his own words 'a *Placeman* . . . so as to gag me from joining in the cry' [CL ii. 166] and was severely reprimanded in late 1792 when he did so.

Attempts to find a correlation between Burns's political views and his patronage networks are frustrated by the fact that (as William Donaldson points out), under the patronage of the Foxite Whigs Glencairn and Henry Erskine in the late 1780s Burns often played the Jacobite card, and supported the Tory candidate Johnstone of Westerhall in the Dumfries election of 1790; while under the patronage of the Dundasite Tory Robert Graham of Fintry during the early 1790s, his politics moved in the direction of the Foxites and beyond, to the 'staunch republicanism' that at least covertly sympathized with French revolutionaries and British radical reformers.[7] Colin Kidd sceptically refutes any expectation of ideological consistency in the factional world of late eighteenth-century British (and Scottish) politics, arguing that 'undoubtedly, Burns's political loyalties were difficult and cross-grained; but so, it transpires, were the party-politics of his time'.[8] Rather than trying to achieve a global schematization of Burns's elusive 'first principles' by piecing together fugitive comments in the correspondence, anecdotes of radical affiliation, or 'lost poems', then, the present chapter will study some of Burns's social and political attitudes as expressed in the poetry itself.

In the wake of the 1707 Act of Union (with the dramatic exception of the two Jacobite rebellions) Scottish politics were largely confined to the ambit of the parish-pump. Power had been removed to London, the franchise was miniscule even by eighteenth-century standards (around 0.2 per cent of the Scottish population had the right to vote, less than the total electorate of Dublin),[9] and

---

[5] The *Canongate* editors insist with some justice that Burns's radicalism has been systematically denied and distorted, but attempt to remedy this by recovering 'lost' radical poems that have often turned out to be falsely attributed. See CG, pp. ix–xcix, and for a critique, Gerard Carruthers, 'Alexander Geddes and the Burns "Lost Poems" Controversy', *Studies in Scottish Literature* 31 (1999), 81–5, and 'The New Bardolatry', *Burns Chronicle* (Winter 2002), 9–15.

[6] See Kidd, 'Burns and Politics', 67–9.

[7] William Donaldson, 'The Glencairn Connection: Robert Burns and Scottish Politics, 1786–1796', *Studies in Scottish Literature* 16 (1981), 61–79 at 68.

[8] Kidd, 'Burns and Politics', 63.

[9] T. M. Devine, *The Scottish Nation, 1700–2000* (London: Penguin, 2000), 196.

the representative system was corrupt: micro-management at local level was in the hands of kirk ministers, justices of the peace, and lairds. But largely due to the rapid pace of improvement, by the 1780s this had begun to change, so that, as Thomas Crawford writes, 'the American Revolution and the Enlightenment, agrarian crisis and class conflict, were very much in sight from the horizon of Mauchline in 1786' [Crawford, *BPS* 237]. I've already discussed some of the social frustrations experienced by Burns's tenant class in the rural Lowlands, a class endowed with the progressive mandates of improvement but stymied by high rents and undercapitalization. Liam MacIlvanney has convincingly shown that Burns's sympathy for the plight of 'honest poverty', especially that experienced by the cotter and labouring classes (like his identification with the rebellious American colonists abroad), was shaped by the 'contractarian principles of Presbyterian thought', and the eighteenth-century 'Real Whig' or Commonwealth tradition.[10]

It is often forgotten that the American, and not the French revolution, was the really significant 'world-historical' event for Burns's poetry, the great body of which was written before 1789.[11] Many ordinary people in the years spanning both revolutions first encountered radical politics via the writings of Thomas Paine: Burns may have been one of them. If there's a common resonance between Burns's line 'The cottage leaves the palace far behind' and Paine's 'the palaces of kings are built on the ruins of the bowers of paradise', it's because both writers are mining the radical potential of eighteenth-century pastoral.[12] Paine's *Common Sense* (from which this is quoted) was published anonymously in 1776 and enjoyed massive circulation in America, as well as on this side of the Atlantic. A damaging attack on the British monarchy which promoted the virtues of republican government (as well as 'the manly principles of Independence'), it was crucial in disseminating revolutionary politics in America and anticipated many of the themes of *Rights of Man*.[13]

The style (if not the political content) of Burns's bold treatment of British high politics 'chiefly in the Scottish dialect' has much in common with Paine's 'intellectual vernacular prose', which, as Olivia Smith indicates, was, previous to Paine, 'a language that was alleged not to exist'.[14] But unfortunately Burns,

---

[10] Liam MacIlvanney, *Burns the Radical: Poetry and Politics in Late Eighteenth-Century Scotland* (Phantassie: Tuckwell), 7.

[11] Ibid. 3–5.

[12] Thomas Paine, *Common Sense*, in *The Thomas Paine Reader*, ed. Foot and Kramnick, 67.

[13] Ibid. 103. An Edinburgh edition was reprinted with the purported aim 'to shew the real spirits and view of the Colonies, or rather of their leaders in rebellion; which cannot fail to rouse the indignation of every Briton'. [Anon.] *Common Sense: Addressed to the Inhabitants of America* (Edinburgh and Stirling, 1776), titlepage. Was this genuine loyalism or a clever feint? But Bob Harris (I, 79) argues that 'Paine's influence in Scotland prior to the second half of 1792 seems to have been strictly limited'.

[14] Olivia Smith, *The Politics of Language, 1791–1819* (Oxford: Clarendon, 1984), 36.

unlike Blake, Wordsworth, or Coleridge, nowhere mentions Paine in his writings; although it's almost certain that he had read *Common Sense* and *Rights of Man* Parts 1 and 2 (1791–2), the evidence is only anecdotal.[15] That his silence was tactical is suggested by Mrs Dunlop's remark in a letter to the poet written in the summer of 1791, commenting that *Rights of Man* 'is indeed much calculated to sow the seeds of discontent, if not revolution, in Britain next . . . . . . You see I take it for granted you read whatever is meant in support of the equal and independent rights of man.'[16] If Burns ever replied to her, the letter has been lost or destroyed.

This chapter discusses three main areas of Burns's politics, focusing on the group of poems that open the Kilmarnock volume. My first section examines the critique of class society, and attitudes to the poor, in 'Twa Dogs' and 'Man was Made to Mourn'. The second addresses the politics of 'John Barleycorn' in the 'Scotch Drink' poems, issues arising from the production and consumption of alcohol in Burns's own agricultural world, but also touching upon attitudes to Scotland's political representation and national identity. In addition to protesting about the Scottish tax regime, these poems make their political pitch by mobilizing a customary discourse of the 'moral economy of provision', perhaps the nearest thing to a genuinely 'popular politics' in eighteenth-century Scotland. Despite the growing influence of laissez-faire arguments, the 'moral economy' still determined official policy in Scotland at the end of the century.[17] My concluding section studies Burns's spirited, demotic treatment of 'high politics' in Westminster and the Court in poems concerned with the American War and King George III's birthday.

## THE DIVISION OF RANKS: 'TWA DOGS' AND 'MAN WAS MADE TO MOURN'

Burns' readers might have been excused for taking 'The Twa Dogs' [K 71] (the poem that opens the Kilmarnock volume) as a kind of pastoral eclogue. It is a strange kind of eclogue to be sure, given that the poem's interlocutors are talking dogs rather than shepherds, but it's squarely within the Scots pastoral tradition both in its employment of 'braid Scots', and its indictment of aristocratic manners. The affectionate conversation between the dogs (it's *not* a flyting

---

[15]  In the wake of Thomas Muir's trial in August 1793, Burns allegedly 'called upon his sometime neighbour, George Haugh, the blacksmith, and handing him copies of Paine's Common Sense and Rights of Man, desired him to keep these books for him, as, if they were found in his own house, he would be a ruined man' (Chambers-Wallace, iv. 55–6.) I agree with Kinsley that 'On Tom Paine's Death' [K 685] is not Burns's work, unless he had been converted to the government cause.

[16]  William Wallace (ed.), *Robert Burns and Mrs Dunlop* (London, 1898), 327–8.

[17]  See Harris, 'Bread, Dearth and Politics, 1795–1801', in *The Scottish People*, 185–222.

dialogue like Fergusson's 'Causey and Plainstanes'), and their critical yet forbearing view of human vanities, owes much to the sentimental congeniality of Burns's verse epistles. Yet Burns's Scots diction and pastoral setting characteristically disguise his literary antecedents; Pope's 'Bounce to Flop: An Heroick Epistle from a Dog at Twickenham to a Dog at Court',[18] and perhaps more pertinently Cervantes's 'exemplary novel' *El coloquio de los perros* (1613), translated as *A Dialogue between Scipio and Bergansa, Two Dogs belonging to the City of Toledo Giving an Account of their Lives and Adventures, with their Reflections on the Lives, Humours, and Employments of the Masters they lived with*, available in several early and mid-eighteenth-century English translations.[19]

Like the epistles, 'The Twa Dogs' is a critical meditation on the contemporary social order, albeit from an animal rather than a human perspective. Localized in Burns's native Kyle, the dialogue between the Laird's pet, a Newfoundland called Caesar, and Luath, 'a *ploughman's* collie, | A rhyming, ranting, raving billie' (ll. 23–4) (named after Cuchullin's hound in Ossian, but also Burns's own farm dog, maliciously killed on the eve of his father's death), expatiates on '*the lords o' the creation*' (l. 46), namely their human masters, from cotters to kings. James Currie perceptively comments that 'the dogs of Burns, excepting in their talent for moralizing, are downright dogs; and not like the Horses of Swift, or the *Hind and the Panther* of Dryden, men in the shape of brutes' [Currie, i. 297]. This 'downright dogginess' is well exemplified in Burns's inspired description of Luath: 'His *breast* was white, his towzie *back*, | Weel clad wi' coat o' glossy black; | His gawsie tail, wi' upward curl, | Hung owre his hurdies wi' a swirl' (ll. 33–6). Although Caesar's inscribed brass collar shows him to be 'the *gentleman* an' *scholar*',[20] in contrast to his human master he is one of nature's gentlemen, enjoying complete social mobility: 'But tho' he was o' high degree, | The fient a pride na pride had he, | But wad hae spent an hour caressan, | Ev'n wi' a Tinklergipsey's *messan*' (ll. 15–18).[21] Burns resists any easy class stand-off between his patrician and plebeian dogs; both possess a curiosity about the other's world that transcends, even reverses, a partisan viewpoint. To this extent the dogs possess a

---

[18] Like 'Twa Dogs', written in tetrameter couplets and employing stanzas of varying lengths.

[19] For 'Bounce and Flop', see Richard Fowler, *Robert Burns* (London: Routledge, 1988), 245–7. Burns eschews Pope's moral dualism, identifying his dogs in relation to a dynamics of social class (i.e. patrician Caesar and plebeian Luath) rather than Pope's country/court dichotomy. Regarding Cervantes's novalla, I cite part of the title of an anonymous 1766 London translation, dedicated to the Marquis of Rockingham. Crawford [*BPS* 169] notes that the link between 'The Twa Dogs' and Cervantes's novella was first made by the German scholar Ritter.

[20] In addition to its obvious historical associations, 'Caesar's' name may also be inspired by Thomas Day's large Newfoundland dog of the same name in *Sandford and Merton* (1783–9). See Christine Kenyon-Jones, *Kindred Brutes: Animals in Romantic-Period Writing* (Aldershot: Ashgate, 2001), 49.

[21] Line 16 is echoed in Burns's 'Extempore Verses on Dining with Lord Daer' [K 127], l. 40.

truly philosophical view of society that many members of the ruling classes (as we learn in ll. 150–70) are deficient in.

Adam Smith had asserted in *Wealth of Nations* (i. 118) that 'nobody ever saw a dog make a fair and deliberate exchange of one bone for another with another dog; nobody ever saw one animal by its gestures and natural cries signify to another, this is mine, that yours; I am willing to give you this for that'. Lacking the disposition to truck and barter, Smith wrote, *fawning* was a dog's only recourse for getting what he wanted: 'man sometimes uses the same arts with his brethren, and when he has no other means of engaging them to act according to his intentions, endeavours by every servile and fawning attention to gain their good will' (ibid.). In theory at least, commerce distinguished humanity from the speechless dependency of the animal condition, articulating a set of interlocking exchange relations that liberate society from the vertical shackles of feudal dependence. But Burns's point here is rather different from Smith's in representing dogs who do talk (and in Scots at that); also, like the poet, they possess a moral detachment from the 'catch-the-plack' mentality of *homo economicus*. In contrast to Smith's dogs, Burns's don't 'fawn', any more than the 'rustic bard' will flatter his dedicatee or patrons.[22]

This is immediately evident in the fact that Caesar, for all his pet status, is a devastating critic of his aristocratic master. A social parasite, the antithesis of the improving gentry praised in 'The Vision', the latter lives on racked rents and conspicuous over-consumption; 'sauce, ragouts, an' sic like trashtrie, | That's little short of downright wastrie' (ll. 63–4). What he can't consume is shovelled up by the numerous retinue who feast upon his leavings. Even his huntsman or '*Whipper-in*', a 'wee, blastiet wonner', eats better than 'ony *Tenant-man*' (ll. 65–7]). Caesar's portrait recalls Smith's account of the role played by conspicuous consumption in the downfall of the old feudal aristocracy (*Wealth of Nations*, ii. 512). 'All for themselves, and nothing for the people' indeed: yet in lines 71–86 Luath responds to Caesar with a graphic portrait of the hardships endured by the cotter class, while stressing that on the whole they're 'maistly wonderfu' contented' (l. 84). The contrast is heightened by Caesar's account of upper-class disdain for social inferiors, '*delvers, ditchers* an' sic cattle': 'They gang as saucy by poor folk, | As I wad by a stinkan brock' (ll. 91–2). In Swiftian mood, Burns here satirizes social snobbery as an animal loathing, a leap across the species boundary rendered all the more disturbing by a talking dog's generic description of rural labourers as 'cattle'.

---

[22]  A more disturbing thought, given Caesar's slave name and the collars, is the dogs' resemblance to African slaves, especially given the late composition of 'Twa Dogs' after Burns's decision to seek work as a 'Negro Driver' [K iii. 1104]. For a penetrating reflection on the analogy see Srinivas Aravamudan's chapter 'Petting Oroonoko', in *Tropicopolitans: Colonialism and Agency, 1688–1804* (Durham, NC: Duke University Press, 1999), 29–70.

Moving up the hierarchy of rural labour to tenant farmers, Caesar portrays the poet's own social class in lines later evoked by Burns in his letter to Dr Moore, describing his father's humiliation by the factor of Mount Oliphant farm [CL i. 136]: 'poor *tenant-bodies*, scant o' cash, | How they maun thole a *factor's* snash; | He'll stamp an' threaten, curse an' swear | He'll *apprehend* them, *poind* their gear.' (ll. 95–8). Notwithstanding this severe provocation, the poem refuses to represent the poor as animated by social resentment; moreover, as Luath rejoins, they're 'no sae wretched's ane wad think' because they're accustomed to living on the brink (l. 103). Exploited and unenfranchised, they nevertheless possess a civic consciousness, their political passions directed to the affairs of the 'Kirk and State' (in that order): 'They'll talk o' *patronage* and *priests*, | Wi' kindling fury i' their breasts | Or tell what new taxation's comin, | An ferlie at the folk in LON'ON' (ll. 119–22). Yet despite that 'kindling fury', domestic contentment of the kind idealized in 'The Cotter's Saturday Night', and the ritual folk customs of the farming year, Halloween, the Harvest Kirn, and Hogmanay, create an atmosphere of 'social Mirth' that has Luath barking with empathetic joy (l. 138). Their good nature apart, the collie concedes that the poor are too often mere pawns in a game of political self-advancement played by their lairds;

> There's monie a creditable *stock*
> O' decent, honest, fawsont folk,
> Are riven out baith root an' branch,
> Some rascal's pridefu' greed to quench,
> Wha thinks to knit himsel the faster
> In favor wi' some *gentle Master*,
> Wha, aiblins, thrang a *parliamentin*,
> For *Britain's guid* his saul indentin'.   ([ll. 141–8)

If there's a hint of irony in this final statement, it's lost on Caesar, who interrupts Luath's speech lamenting this default of civic virtue; '*For Britain's guid!* guid faith! I doubt it. | Say rather, gaun as PREMIERS lead him: | An' saying *aye* or *no's* they bid him' (ll. 150–2). This vindicates the poem's 'dogginess', as by a clever ironic reversal Caesar's so-called 'independent' Laird is himself obliged to fawn to his parliamentary managers and ministers, deprived of any real virtue or self-determination. It is not just that the ruling class lack the 'wonderfu' contentment' of the poor (or indeed even their willingness to 'lay aside their private cares, | To mind the Kirk an' State affairs', ll. 116–18), but rather that they're obliged to practise a fawning subservience more dog-like than the 'independence' of 'honest poverty'.

Caesar's critique of upper-class lifestyle in the poem's final sections opens with a magnificent satire on the Grand Tour, a familiar target for eighteenth-century poets, specifically echoing Fergusson's satirical 'Hame Content' [McD ii. 159 ll. 73–4]. 'There, at VIENNA or VERSAILLES, | He rives his father's auld entails; | Or by MADRID he takes the rout, | To thrum *guittarres* an' fecht wi' *nowt*' (ll. 159–62).

Once again, rather than being '*For Britain's guid*!' this is 'For her destruction! |
Wi' dissipation, feud an' faction! ([ll. 169–70). The naive Luath now understands why 'they waste sae mony a braw estate' (l. 172) but still he refuses to
succumb to class hatred, cherishing a positive view of improving lairds dedicated
to the best interests of their dependants: 'O would they stay aback frae courts, |
An' please themselves wi' countra sports, | It wad for ev'ry ane be better, | The
*Laird*, the *Tenant*, an' the *Cotter*!' (ll. 175–8).

In lines 179–84 Luath portrays the gentry in more complimentary terms than
Caesar ('The ne'er-a-bit they're ill to poor folk', l. 184), although possibly, given
the ironic framework of Burns's dialogue, this is because of his naivety. Caesar
scornfully warns Luath not to waste his 'envy' on the rich (Caesar's term at l. 190,
not Luath's), listing the torments of idleness, hypochondria, social vanity,
debauchery, drink and whoring, female scandal-mongering, and gambling at
cards. The poor man has his quota of hard graft: but 'his *acre* till'd, he's right
enough' (l. 202).[23] In contrast, life for the idle rich is nothing but neurotic
frustration: 'They loiter, lounging, lank an' lazy; | Tho' deil-haet ails them, yet
uneasy; | Their days, insipid, dull an' tasteless; | Their nights, unquiet, lang an'
restless' (ll. 207–10).[24]

With the odd exception, Caesar concedes (nodding to Luath's picture of the
'hame contented' Laird at lines 175–9), 'this is Gentry's life in common' (l. 230).
As a picture of the 'lairds o' human kind' it's pretty devastating; as dark falls, the
dogs rather lamely part, agreeing to meet some other day, rejoicing 'they were na
*men* but *dogs*' (l. 236). Caesar's account of a servile, irresponsible, and corrupt
landed class in the opening poem of Kilmarnock sets the tone for the rest of
the volume, particularly in view of the image of 'Great Folks' developed in 'The
Author's Earnest Cry and Prayer' and 'A Dream'. By the time the reader arrives
at 'The Vision', Coila's eulogy on the civic virtue of the Ayrshire landed elite can
only offer a slight note of redemption. Despite their pastoral view of a contented
labouring class, Burns's dogs certainly can't be accused of fawning.

A more fatalistic picture of social injustice emerges from Burns's 'Dirge', 'Man
was Made to Mourn' [K 64] set to the tune of 'Peggy Bawn'. Like 'The Twa
Dogs' it's a poem of encounter, although there's nothing dialogic about the
hoary old sage's melancholy discourse on 'the miseries of Man' (l. 16) addressed
to the listening 'young stranger', set against the winter landscape of 'the banks of
Aire'. Based on a traditional seventeenth-century ballad entitled 'The Age and
Life of Man' that Burns recalled his mother singing to an elderly uncle, the poem
(written in English, with fashionable echoes of Shenstone, and the 'graveyard

---

[23] This perspective on what Goldsmith called the peasant's 'light labour' is Caesar's rather than
Luath's, and possibly ironically qualified.

[24] The pastoral contrast alludes to Patie's speech in Ramsay's *Gentle Shepherd*, IV. ii. 81–4: 'The
spleen, tint Honour, and affronted Pride, | Stang like the sharpest Goads in Gentry's Side' [Ramsay,
ii. 259].

poets' Blair and Young) actually touches on some surprisingly contemporary themes [Kin. iii. 1088]. Beyond its conventional lament for the harshness and brevity of human life, it focuses specifically on the 'hundreds [who] labour to support | A haughty lordling's pride' (in an earlier draft, l. 20 is more specific in naming 'The Lordly Cassilis' pride').[25] While the Sage reiterates the 'pastoral' lesson underlined in 'The Twa Dogs' (ll. 41–8, 'the Rich and Great' aren't quite as happy as they seem), this poem is unable to offer any prospect of 'pastoral content' to the labouring poor. Although he can support himself in his 'youthful Prime', the Sage complains that superannuation is a bitter prospect, when 'Age and Want, Oh! Ill-matched pair! | Show Man was made to mourn' (ll. 39–40).

The politics of 'Man was Made to Mourn' emerge more directly in the poem's assertion of the 'right to work'. Gilbert Burns recalled its genesis in the fact that his brother 'could not well conceive a more mortifying picture of human life, than a man seeking work' [Kin. ii. 1087]. It is a sentiment elaborated in the eighth stanza:

> See, yonder poor, o'erlabour'd wight,
> So abject, mean and vile,
> Who begs a brother of the earth
> To give him leave to toil;
> And see his lordly *fellow-worm,*
> The poor petition spurn,
> Unmindful, tho' a weeping wife,
> And helpless offspring mourn.   (ll. 56–64)

The capitalization of agriculture has replaced the relatively self-sufficient cotter with a landless rural proletariat too numerous to find employment. The principles of the 'new husbandry' may be to blame, but Burns's animus here is directed against the 'lordly *fellow worm*' who refuses to give the able-bodied worker 'leave to toil', despite his knowledge of the ruinous domestic consequences of unemployment. Significantly, the poem is silent concerning the availability of parish relief, or any other form of welfare in mitigation of this dire situation.

'Man was Made to Mourn' touches obliquely on a grey area of the eighteenth-century Scottish Poor Law, concerning the right of the able-bodied unemployed to parish relief. In the first 'Epistle to Lapraik' [K 57] Burns wrote to his needy correspondent; ' "Each aid the others" ', | Come to my bowl, Come to my arms, | My friends, my brothers!' (ll. 124–6). The faith in mutual assistance expressed in these lines is strongly held, and notably neither the 'deserving poor' of 'The Cotter's Saturday Night', nor the 'undeserving' beggars of 'Love and Liberty' make any claims on welfare, whether voluntary or assessed. (In fact Burns's thoughts on charity are best developed in poems about animals, as we'll see in

---

[25] It is appropriate that, according to Andrew Wight, the Earl of Cassilis's factor was a certain 'Mr Bulley' (*Present State of Husbandry in Scotland, Extracted from Reports made to the Commissioners of the Annexed Estates and Published by their Authority,* 4 vols. [Edinburgh, 1784], iii. 168).

the next chapter.) The poet's reticence on the subject of parish relief may have contributed to James Currie's ideologically motivated claim, in his Burns edition of 1800, that Scotland had no Poor Law [Currie, i. 10–11].

This widely held view was based on a half-truth. In contrast to the English 'Speenhamland' system that acknowledged a statutory right to welfare support, Scottish poor relief was largely in the hands of the Kirk Session, who carefully scrutinized the moral circumstances of each case before granting any allowance, the funds for which were drawn largely from voluntary donations such as church collections, fines, mortcloth fees, etc. (No wonder the poor considered being 'on the parish' as deeply degrading.)[26] The original statute had defined those eligible for relief as the 'poor, aged and impotent', but contained no orders concerning the provision of work for the unemployed; although in the event, the new social and economic upheaval of the late eighteenth century resulted in a situation where the majority of parishes did stretch their limited provision to assist the 'able-bodied' unemployed.[27]

Increasing pauperism caused by the social dislocations of improvement soon put excessive pressure on parish funds, however, leading to the introduction of 'assessment' (either legal or voluntary), whereby parishes were forced to 'demand a rate from landowners [who] could then pass half the burden to their tenantry'. This 'tax on property for the relief of poverty' was greatly resented by most of those concerned [Currie, i. 10].[28] The heritors of Burns's Mauchline had agreed to an assessment or 'stent' in 1771 'in order to prevent begging in the parish', half paid by themselves, and half by their tenantry; the tenants of Mossgiel Farm would have been required to shoulder some of the burden. Burns's friend and landlord Gavin Hamilton was responsible for collecting the 'stent' of £19. 10s. 2d. per annum, but his failure to do so—whether deliberately or by default— resulted in his being legally summoned by the Kirk Session in 1784. This lay at the root of his dispute with Revd Auld referred to in 'Holy Willie's Prayer' [Mackay, pp.126–7]. Reluctance on the part of the heritors in the face of the ever-mounting number of paupers meant that by the early 1790s the Parish funds were hopelessly overstretched, leading the minister to complain that 'the burden of maintaining the poor is most unevenly divided . . . it is the poor in Scotland who maintain the poor' [*Statistical Account*, vi. 448].

---

[26] R. A. Cage, *The Scottish Poor Law, 1745–1845* (Edinburgh: Scottish Academic Press, 1981), 42, 28. Friendly Societies were just beginning to supplement Parish Relief, as in Mauchline; see *Statistical Account*, vi. 449. Rosalind Mitchison argues that although the Scottish Poor Law provided basic relief to the needy, in contrast to England it had never established 'a clear right in a claimant to relief, or even a clearly defined standard of living which it could protect' 'The Poor Law', in T. M. Devine and Rosalind Mitchison (eds.), *People and Society in Scotland*, i. *1760–1830* (Edinburgh: John Donald, 1988), 252–67 at 252, 254. But Cage argues that legal assessments were introduced in the Acts of 1574, 1625, and 1663 (*Scottish Poor Law*, 7–8.)

[27] Mitchison, 'The Poor Law', 254–5.

[28] Ibid. 252. See esp. Aiton, p. 641.

When Burns wrote 'Man was Made to Mourn' he couldn't have known that just a few years later, the Second Part of Paine's *Rights of Man* would sketch the principles of a national welfare system, or that in 1792 the French Legislative Assembly would replace private charity with state sponsored *bienfaisance*, declaring that 'every man has the right to subsistence through work, if he is able-bodied, and to free assistance if he is unable to work'.[29] (The Thermidorean regime quickly re-privatized charitable assistance.) Although Burns would have had no truck with welfare dependence, he clearly believed in the basic human rights to labour and to provision; the author of 'To a Mouse' (himself on the verge of becoming an economic emigrant) can't have been oblivious to the fact that the social upheaval created by improvement had established a newly mobile labour force, demanding new welfare solutions.

But 'Man was made to Mourn' of course doesn't anticipate any such revolutionary proposals as those of Paine or the French Assembly, simply lamenting the injustice of unemployment as the unacceptable face of social change and class inequality. At the same time, more radically, the poem unequivocally rejects the notion (cherished by Malthus and the evangelicals in the next decade) that poverty is part of nature's plan: 'If I'm design'd yon lordling's slave, | By Nature's law design'd, | Why was an independent wish | E'er planted in my mind?' (ll. 65–8). For Burns's pre-revolutionary Sage, however, only death is the true leveller, and only in death will the poor man find relief.

## JOHN BARLEYCORN

In Virgil's sixth *Eclogue*, the drunken Silenus, captured by two shepherds and a nymph, enchants his listeners as he sings of the beginning of the world, and of poetry. It is an incident alluded to in the opening habbie stanza of Burns's poem 'Scotch Drink' [K 77], which follows 'The Twa Dogs' in the running order of Kilmarnock: 'Let other Poets raise a fracas | 'Bout vines, an' wines, an' druken *Bacchus*' (ll. 1–2). Burns's comic use of rhyming macaronics ('fracas/Bacchus') evokes Fergusson, as does the ironic allusion to lines 19–30 of the latter's poem 'Caller Water'; Burns 'sings the juice *Scotch bear* can mak us, in glass or jug' (l. 5) (that's to say *both* whisky and beer), in contrast to Fergusson's watery anacreontic.[30]

---

[29] Gareth Stedman Jones, *An End to Poverty? A Historical Debate* (London: Profile Books, 2004), 113–14 at 118.

[30] McGuirk, *BSP* p. 232–3, assumes that the poem refers to whisky only. 'Nappy', or strong ale, isn't mentioned here, but elsewhere is a favourite Burnesian epithet, partly on account of its all-purpose rhyming potential (in the eighth stanza of 'Epistle to John Goldie' [K 63], it rhymes with 'happy', 'sappy', and 'drappie'). In 'Tam o'Shanter' [K 321] Burns names both 'tippeny' (a 'thin, yeasty beverage, made of malt; not quite so strong as the table-beer of England') and 'usquabae' (whisky) as common offspring of 'inspiring bold *John Barleycorn*!': 'Wi' tippenny, we fear nae evil; | Wi' usquabae, we'll face the Devil!' (ll. 105–8).

Importantly, both this poem and its companion, 'The Author's Earnest Cry and Prayer' [K 81] hymn the power of Scotch Drink to anaesthetize those 'prest wi grief an' care . . . | Till he forgets his *loves* or *debts*, | An' minds his griefs no more', as expressed in Burns's Scots paraphrase of Proverbs 31: 6–7 that serves as an epigraph to the poem. But 'Scotch Drink' also addresses symbolic power at a political level; in both these poems, Burns appropriates the patriotic celebration of English agricultural produce in georgic poems such as John Philips's *Cyder* (1708) and John Dyer's *The Fleece* (1757) for the uses of 'Scots pastoral'. Both 'Scotch Drink' and its companion are concerned that Scottish national identity, embodied in whisky, is now threatened by fiscal intervention from London, in breach of the articles of the 1707 Treaty of Union which had granted substantial tax concessions to Scottish brewers and distillers.

In eighteenth-century Scotland and England 'beer and ale, along with bread, were the most important commodities in a family's budget, with the average family spending more on these goods than any other item'.[31] Adapting E. P. Thomson's emphasis on the importance of the eighteenth-century 'bread nexus', we might speak of a 'meal and barley nexus' mediating social conflict in Scotland: for controlling the fluctuating prices of oatmeal and barley (rather than wheat, the English staple) was one of the principle factors in preserving the rule of law.[32] When meal and barley were short, the much-vaunted stability of eighteenth-century Scotland simply broke down, one of the factors that leads Christopher Whatley to question what he calls 'the orthodoxy of passivity' amongst many historians of eighteenth-century Scotland. [Whatley, pp. 149–83].[33]

In the rush to interpret 'Scotch Drink' as a symptomatic celebration of Scots inebriety, it's easily to forget that barley/bere, grown primarily for the production of ale, beer, and whisky, was also an important staple for Scottish farmers, and that 'Rab Mossgiel' was no exception. Political threats to the Scottish distillers were also threats to the livelihood of tenant farmers; in 1795, the freeholders of Linlithgow petitioned their MP against restrictions on whisky distilling on the grounds that it lowered the price of barley 'the principal article from which the farmers and tenants are enabled to pay their rents'.[34] At an era when wheaten bread was beginning to replace the traditional Scots preference for oatmeal and barley,[35] Burns's 'Scotch Drink' champions the homespun culinary virtues of

---

[31] James Handley, *The Agricultural Revolution in Scotland* (Glasgow, 1963), 124.

[32] E. P. Thompson, 'The Moral Economy of the Crowd', in *Customs in Common* (London: Merlin, 1991), 189.

[33] See also Whatley's essay 'How Tame Were the Scottish Lowlanders during the Eighteenth Century?', in T. Devine (ed.), *Conflict and Stability in Scottish Society, 1700–1850* (Edinburgh: John Donald, 1990), 1–30.

[34] Quoted by Henry Hamilton in *An Economic History of Scotland in the Eighteenth Century* (Oxford: Clarendon, 1963), 109. See also Handley, *The Agricultural Revolution in Scotland*, 124.

[35] Dr Johnson's *Dictionary* notoriously defined 'Oats' as 'a grain which in England is generally given to horses, but in Scotland supports the ordinary people'.

barley bannocks and Scotch broth, second in importance only to barley's distilled 'juice': 'Let husky Wheat the haughs adorn, | An' Aits set up their awnie horn, | An' Pease an' Beans, at een or morn, | Perfume the plain: | Leeze me on thee *John Barleycorn*, | Thou king o'grain!' (ll. 13–19). Burns' figurative evocation here alludes to his own ballad 'John Barleycorn' [K 23], possibly written in the early 1780s, but first published in the Edinburgh edition in 1787.[36] His masterful reworking of traditional material allegorizes the ploughing and harvesting of barley, followed by the process of steeping, malting, mashing, fermenting, washing, and distillation to produce whisky (the term 'heart's blood' here specifically implies whisky rather than beer) as the ritual sacrifice and rebirth of its eponymous hero:

> They wasted, o'er a scorching flame
> The marrow of his bones;
> But a Miller us'd him worst of all,
> For he crush'd him between two stones.
>
> And they hae taen his very heart's blood,
> And drank it round and round;
> And still the more and more they drank,
> Their joy did more abound.   (ll.41–8)

'John Barleycorn' narrates an agricultural (and distinctly *Scottish*) Eucharistic feast, replacing wheaten bread with barley, and wine with whisky, symbols of redemptive flesh and blood, and transforming the three Eastern kings of the first stanza from the epiphanic heralds of Christ's nativity into Barleycorn's assassins.[37] 'Scotch Drink' likewise represents alcohol consumption as a profane Eucharist consecrating the whole social body; beer and whisky (as opposed to the more expensive wine) are identified as the favoured consolations of the poor and downtrodden: '. . . oil'd by thee, | The wheels o' life gae down-hill, scrievin, | Wi' rattlin' glee' (ll. 29–30). Given the manifold ways in which alcohol fuels 'the life o' public haunts', excessive taxation quite literally threatens the life of the whole social body.

In the poem's concluding section, Burns turns from the social benefits to the contemporary politics of 'Scotch Drink', anticipating its sequel 'The Author's Earnest Cry'. An important influence here is another Fergusson poem, 'Drink

---

[36] Partly based on chapbook standards such as *The Whole Trial and Indictment of Sir John Barleycorn, Knight* [Kin. iii. 1017]. Although Burns's 'John Barleycorn' was first published, like 'To a Haggis', in the Edinburgh volume of 1787, common knowledge of the chapbook among his readers may explain 'Scotch Drink''s allusion to an as-yet unpublished song.

[37] In 1716 John Willison's *Sacramental Directory* described the sacrificial symbolism of the Eucharist in terms which anticipate Burns's ballad: 'Christ was crushed in the wine-press of his father's wrath, till the blessed juices of his body, his precious blood, did gush out in abundance for the redemption of our souls.' *A Sacramental Directory, Or a Treatise Concerning the Sanctification of a Communion Sabbath* (Edinburgh, 1716; Aberdeen, 1846), 231. Rachel Crawford, *Poetry, Enclosure, and the Vernacular Landscape* (Cambridge: Cambridge University Press, 2002), 125, notes a similar theme in John Philips's English georgic, *Cyder*.

Eclogue. Landlady, Whisky, Brandy',[38] a flyting dialogue that associates imported foreign Brandy with rapacious landlordism [McD ii. 212 ll. 62–8].
Burns's fourteenth stanza condenses Fergusson's criticism of Brandy, the consumption of which is accounted a form of unpatriotic 'treason': 'Wae worth that
*Brandy*, burnan trash! | Fell source o' monie a pain an' brash! | Twins mony a
poor, doylt, druken hash, | O' half his days; | And sends, beside, auld *Scotland's*
cash | To her warst faes' (ll. 85–90). Burns's reference to Scotland's cash being
squandered on 'her worst faes' (i.e. Brandy's French producers) suggests that he
refers to smuggled liquor here, for the high taxes imposed on legally imported
brandy naturally benefited the British Revenue.[39] An example of the government's misguided attempts to impose heavier tax on 'home-made liquor' referred
to in lines 109–14 of 'Scotch Drink' is the case of Ferintosh whisky, whose
distiller, Duncan Forbes of Culloden, had been exempted from tax in compensation for the destruction of his 'ancient brewery of Aqua Vitis' by Jacobite forces
in 1688. This privilege was ended in 1784 with a hefty lump sum payment of
£21,000 from the Treasury; as Graham Smith sardonically notes, 'not bad
compensation'.[40] Given the political rationale for the exemption, there's surely
a note of irony in Burns's reference to 'loyal *Forbes's Charter'd boast*' (l. 113).

The politics of 'Scotch Drink' and 'The Author's Earnest Cry' are unintelligible without some grasp of the historical background to eighteenth-century taxes
on Malt and Distilling, and the prevalence of 'smuggling' (in Scotland the term
meant illicit whisky distilling as well as illegal importation).[41] This was of
primary importance to the Georgian state: William Ashworth writes that 'a
powerful argument can be made that the [eighteenth-century] foundation of
the English/British fiscal state was built upon the public's addiction to alcohol',
and Scotland was certainly no exception.[42] Resentment at the imposition of
various malt and brewing taxes in the decades after the union led to widespread
rioting and civil disturbances throughout Scotland under the cry of 'No Union,
no Malt Tax'.[43] Increased duties of course led to widespread smuggling or 'free
trade', heartily supported by the populace; the criminality of smuggling was lent
a political lustre to the extent that it was often associated with Jacobite resistance

---

[38] Although Fergusson employs decasyllabic couplets rather than the habbie stanza.

[39] Ironically, Revd William Auld similarly complained, in his entry for Mauchline in the
*Statistical Account*, that, whereas half a century before 'good two-penny, strong-ale, and home-
spirits were in vogue: but now even people in the middling and lower stations of life, deal much in
foreign spirits, rum-punch, and wine'. 'Patriotic resolutions', he complained, 'had been frustrated by
heavy taxes and smuggling. [*Statistical Account*, vi. 449–50].

[40] Graham Smith, *Robert Burns and the Excise* (Ayr: Alloway Publications, 1989), 19.

[41] Ibid. 17. See pp. 11–20 for a concise account of British government attempts to impose a
uniform excise regime on Scotland.

[42] William Ashworth, *Customs and Excise: Trade, Production and Consumption in England,
1640–1845* (Oxford: Oxford University Press, 2003), 210.

[43] Smith, *Burns and the Excise*, 15–16.

to the post-1707 tax regime, an association exploited by Walter Scott in his portrayal of the Porteous Riots in *Heart of Midlothian*.

Official discouragement of spirit drinking was half-hearted, considering the benefits to the exchequer, given that excise taxes on the distillation of spirits rose more times during the eighteenth century than on any other goods, from contributing 3 per cent of the total of revenue income in 1723, to 10 per cent in 1820.[44] In many impoverished areas of Scotland, illicit whisky distillation provided 'almost the only means of converting [farmers'] victual into cash for the payment of rent and servants; and whisky may, in fact, be called our staple commodity'.[45] The fact that 'the distillery in Scotland is in a thousand hands'[46] injured not only the revenue but also more strictly controlled English distillers, who pressurized parliament to impose a tighter regime on their northern neighbour. The drive to clamp down on illicit stills during the dearth of 1783–4 underpins Burns's reference in the penultimate stanza, which, given his future profession, also resounds with unintended irony; 'Thae curst horse leeches o' th' Excise, | Wha mak the *Whisky stills* their prize! | ... bake them up in brunstane pies | For poor damn'd *Drinkers*.' (ll. 115–20).

Pressure from the English distillers resulted in the Wash Act of 1784, which increased duties on Scottish whisky on both sides of the border, inspiring Burns's poem (to give it its full title) 'The Author's Earnest Cry and Prayer, to the Right Honorable and Honorable, the Scotch Representatives in the House of Commons' [K 81].[47] Despite the pompous, Solomonic title, Burns introduces himself as 'a simple Bardie' (l. 5), signing off 'Your humble Bardie sings an prays, | While *Rab* his name is' (ll. 143–4)).[48] As in 'A Dream' (discussed below), the poem's comic effect and critical tension derives from this rustic persona admonishing 'ye chosen FIVE AND FORTY' (l. 133), the Scottish representatives at Westminster, some of whom are named at lines 73–84 in a roll-call reminiscent of the additional stanzas of 'The Vision': '*Dempster*, a true blue Scot I'se warran; | Thee, aith-detesting, chaste *Kilkerran*; | An' that glib-gabbet Highlan Baron, | The Laird o' *Graham*; | An' ane, a chap that's damn auldfarran, | *Dundass* his name' (ll. 73–8).[49]

[44] Ashworth, *Customs and Excise*, 223.

[45] Hamilton, *Economic History of Scotland*, 108. Quoted from the report on Ross-shire in the *Statistical Account*.

[46] In the words of John Stein, giving evidence to the Committee on Distilleries, ibid.

[47] McIlvanney (*Burns the Radical*, 80) notes the title's reference to the 'cry and prayer' in 2 Chronicles 6:19 in which Solomon exhorts God to deal justly with the people of Israel, as well as the echo of Shakespeare's *Julius Caesar* ('and Brutus is an honourable man').

[48] Burns's note to l. 117 identifies the speaker as a 'village politician' of the kind identified in 'The Twa Dogs', a regular at 'Nanse Tinnock's' tavern in Mauchline, 'where he sometimes studies Politics over a glass of guid auld *Scotch Drink*'.

[49] Burns cancelled a stanza alluding to Hugh Montgomerie, 12th Earl of Eglinton, Member of Parliament for Ayrshire 1784–9 (hence 'my watchman stented, | If e'er bardies are represented', ll. 85–6). This was probably on account of its allusion to the Earl's speech defect, limiting his powers

The Scots MPs are well able to 'to mak harangues' (l. 70) in parliament; the problem isn't that they can't speak out, rather that they won't. As McIlvanney notes, throughout the poem 'almost every word that the metre stresses is pregnant with irony, is overlaid with the accents of mockery'.[50] Burns's irony casts a huge question mark over Scotland's whole system of political representation, if 'representation' it can be called. In contrast to the civic energy of Ayrshire's gentry praised by Coila in 'The Vision', the 'FIVE AND FORTY' seem bound in a conspiracy of silence, unwilling to air Scotland's grievances.[51]

The suggestion is of course that they're more concerned with '*posts* and *pensions*' than 'speaking out' in their country's interests, echoing Caesar's condemnation of parliamentary corruption at lines 150–1 of 'The Twa Dogs'. The poem insinuates a litany of political grievances affecting Scotland, from the address to 'Irish lords' in the first line (given the anomaly that the sons of Scottish, but not Irish, peers remained ineligible to hold Scottish seats); through the reference to 'her *lost Militia*' at line 92 (a reference to the governments refusal to allow Scottish militias in the aftermath of the '45, inflaming opinion and leading to the formation of the 'Poker Club'); and finally to the fact that 'the chosen FIVE AND FORTY' (l. 133) underline the grave under-representation of Scottish interests at Westminster, and the ease with which her MPs could be manipulated by larger coalitions.

Burns solicits ironic pathos from the sad picture of his 'roupet *Muse*' 'sittan on her arse | Low i' the dust' (ll. 7–8), hoarse in the throat from lack of drink: in stanza 7, she merges with the portrait of a feminized 'Scotland', 'greetan owre her thrissle' (l. 37), doubly abused by Excisemen ('Seizan a *Stell*, | Triumphant, crushan't like a mussel, | Or laimpet shell', ll.40–2) and smugglers in league with French vintners (ll. 47–8). Although this, like previous stanzas, appeals to a sense of comic pathos in portraying Scotland's 'drouthy' condition, the poem develops a more menacing tone after line 85. If the 'representatives' won't take up the matter to help 'auld Scotland [get] back her *kettle*' (i.e. whisky distilleries, l. 86), then the mob will. The worm will turn, Burns hints, as a much-abused Scotland 'rin[s] red-wud | About her *Whisky*' (ll. 95–6):

> An' L—d! If ance they pit her till't,
> Her tartan petticoat she'll kilt,
> An' durk an' pistol at her belt,
>     She'll tak the streets,
> An' rin her whittle to the hilt,
>     I' the first she meets!

---

of oratory in Westminster Hall, but as I've argued in Ch. 3, Burns may have wished not to offend the most powerful magnate in Ayrshire whose family is praised in 'The Vision'.

[50] McIlvanney, *Burns the Radical*, 80.

[51] The satirical power of the poem is somewhat weakened by Burns's note to the title; 'This was written before the Act anent the Scotch Distilleries, of session 1786; for which Scotland and the Author returns their most grateful thanks' [see Kin. iii. 1140].

> For G–d-sake, Sirs! then speak her fair,
> An' straik her cannie wi' the hair,
> An' to the *muckle house* repair,
>     Wi' instant speed,
> An' strive, wi' a' your Wit an' Lear,
>     To get remead.   (ll. 97–108)

Rather than representing the metamorphosis of 'a feeble old woman' into 'a revolutionary amazon' (as Liam McIlvanney proposes),[52] I prefer to read 'red-wud' Scotland brandishing her 'whittle' as the symbol of an older expression of popular politics widely practised in eighteenth-century Scotland. Even 'Scotland's' gender is appropriate here, given the fact that plebeian women were often active in mob assaults on granaries, warehouses, and customs officers in eighteenth-century Scotland: in 1711, at least four mob attacks on warehouses by largely female crowds were recorded, some numbering one or two hundred. Chris Whatley notes that 'it was not unusual for men to wear women's clothes, and thereby disguise themselves and take part in what was a universal rite of provocation of the forces of law and order'.[53] The role of women in such riots, as in the rest of Europe, indicated the gendered associations of nurture and bodily provision; transvestite men played on this symbolism at the same time as they assumed an effective disguise.[54]

The fact that Scotia 'kilts up' her 'tartan petticoat' and metamorphoses into a wild Highlander represents transvestism in the other direction, in a particularly effective use of the image, and as we'll see below with further ramifications for Burns's cultural politics. The underlying threat of mob violence here is set off in stark relief by the final stanzas, where the 'humble bardie' gets into some serious political bargaining with the prime minister. If Pitt can engineer some 'commutation' (l. 121) of the Wash Act by taxing 'tea an winnocks' (windows, l. 119) instead, 'Rab' will be much obliged. Flexibility on Pitt's part will, he promises, ensure the support of the Scottish populace against 'yon mixtie-maxtie, queer hotch-potch, | The [Fox–North] *Coalition*' (ll. 125–6). Neither will she renege on her promise: 'Auld Scotland has a raucle tongue; | She's just a devil wi' a rung; [knife] | An' if she promise auld or young | To tak their part, | Tho' by the neck she should be strung, | She'll no desert' (ll. 127–32). By the end of the poem, then, the feeble representatives have been effectively bypassed, as the 'humble bardie''s 'earnest cry and prayer' (or rather, the threats of his 'raucle tongue') pressurize the British Prime Minister to recall his paternalistic obligations towards his Scottish subjects—or else!

---

[52] McIlvanney, *Burns the Radical*, 84.

[53] Whatley, 'How Tame Were the Scottish Lowlanders?', 13.

[54] Scott's smuggler Robertson dressed as a woman during the storming of the Edinburgh Tolbooth in the early chapters of *Heart of Midlothian*. For an Italian analogy see Peter Burke, 'The Virgin of the Carmine and the Revolt of Masaniello', *Past and Present* 99 (1983), 3–21.

Although it's easy to see such threats as comic posturing on the part of a humble poet, E. P. Thompson and others have underlined the role of the eighteenth-century crowd in enforcing paternalistic attitudes to provision and the 'moral economy' of provision, at least until the triumph of free market ideology in the early nineteenth century. Thompson writes, with only an ounce of exaggeration, that 'the crowd defined, in the largest sense, what was politically possible'.[55] Given the absence of a Scottish militia, burgh councils and landed proprietors were under special pressure to regulate markets and buy in cheap grain and meal during scarcity, for fear of social unrest. A decade later, in January 1796, Burns acknowledged the dynamics of the 'moral economy' when he wrote to Mrs Dunlop from Dumfries 'we have actual famine, & that too in the midst of plenty', adding ominously 'How long the *Swinish Multitude* will be quiet, I cannot tell: they threaten daily' [CL ii. 375]. As Whatley proposes, 'it was the fear of the potential *flammability* of the Scottish mob which goes a long way towards explaining the comparative absence of food-rioting in Scotland' after 1750.[56] As Burns's head note rather complacently records, Pitt did in fact remedy the terms of the Wash Act, although the problem recurred in 1789, the occasion for the poet's open letter to Pitt published in the *Edinburgh Evening Courant* on 9 February, and signed pseudonymously 'John Barleycorn'.[57] [CL i. 371–5].

It is extremely hard to judge the tone of the 'Postscript' of 'The Author's Earnest Cry and Prayer', with its chauvinistic panegyric on a whisky-soaked Scots militarism. McIlvanney reads it as 'an ironic salute to the martial virtue of the Scots, its speaker no longer the "simple Bardie" but "an unnamed ignoramus" who celebrates "the hireling thug of the state", in other words the standing army which was the *bête noir* of the classical republican tradition'.[58] This certainly gets Burns off the hook of loyalism, but it perhaps wishfully attributes more radicalism to the passage that it warrants. If we read it more literally as an appeal (albeit a rather threatening one) to Pitt's paternalism, it connects more closely with the tone of the main body of the poem. Burns offers up his valiant, whisky-inspired Scottish soldier to buttress British power in wars against 'effeminate' wine-bibbing Frenchmen and Spaniards: 'Let half-starv'd slaves in warmer skies, | See future wines, rich-clust'ring, rise; | Their lot auld Scotland ne'er envies, | But, blyth and frisky, | She eyes her freeborn, martial boys, | Tak aff their Whisky' (ll. 145–50).

[55] 'Patrician Society, Plebeian Culture', *Journal of Social History* 7 (1974), 382–405.

[56] 'How Tame Were the Scottish Lowlanders?', 17. Bob Harris writes that 'schemes of relief were often reactive, a direct response to disturbance or threatened disturbance; to this extent they were less paternalistic than pragmatic' (*Scottish People and the French Revolution*, 214).

[57] Burns believed that Pitt was about to fall from power over the Regency Bill, and likened his abandoned condition to that of the Scottish Distillers, as well as the farming interest 'the most numerous and most useful part of the Community' who depended on the Distilling industry [CL i. 374].

[58] McIlvanney, *Burns the Radical*, 84–5.

Not only does this accord with 'Scotch Drink's' disdain for French wine and brandy, it also chimes with a familiar trope of culinary chauvinism in the tradition of Scots pastoral. A more famous example is of course Burns's 'To a Haggis' [K 136], in which the anaemic eater of 'ragouts', 'olios', and 'fricassees' compares so unfavourably to the '*haggis fed*' Scottish rustic: 'clap in his walie nieve a blade, | He'll mak it whissle; | An' legs, an' arms, an' heads will sned, | Like taps o' thrissle' (ll. 36–42). For all the comedy, the militaristic overtones of these lines chime with the portrait of Scottish valour in the postscript to 'The Author's Earnest Cry and Prayer': 'Nae cauld, faint-hearted doubtings tease him; | Death comes, with fearless eye he sees him' (ll. 169–70). Here's the deal, Billy Pitt, the poem is saying: give us back our cheap whisky, and in return you'll get a plentiful supply of brave Scottish soldiers to fight your wars; but just try reneging on your promises, enshrined in the terms of the 1707 Union, and an equivalent violence will be unleashed on the Excise officers of the British state.

The poem ends on a bathetic note, with a picture of happy old Scotland, soaked in affordable whisky as she 'moistifys' her 'leather' (pisses herself), revelling in the fact that her drunken 'blether' (i.e. the poem) has compensated for the tongue-tied silence of her feckless parliamentarians. Even this squalid image illustrates how in the imperfect world of post-Union Scotland, 'FREEDOM and WHISKY gang thegither, | Tak aff your whitter' (ll. 185–6). Burns's poem plays on the coercive power of the popular will and the demotic word, in a corrupt and pre-democratic political culture. Eighteenth-century bardies may be unrepresented in Westminster, like the ordinary people themselves; but, as Percy Shelley (as it happens both a teetotaller and a pacifist) later expressed it, they may still be 'the unacknowledged legislators of mankind'.

The two poems on 'Scotch Drink' so prominently placed near the beginning of the Kilmarnock volume are crucial to Burns's construction of Scottish identity. However in the regulative and evangelical climate of the 1790s, they were immediately recognized as problems within his corpus. In 1795, Hector Mac-Neill's anti-Jacobin ballad *Scotland's Skaith; or the History of Will and Jean* diagnosed the nation's 'skaith' (affliction) as precisely the dangerous Burnsian conjunction of dram drinking and popular politics, especially his association of 'Freedom and whisky'.[59] *Scotland's Skaith* was the inspiration for Sir David Wilkie's painting *Village Politicians*, which caused a sensation at the Royal Academy in 1806; Wilkie returns to the earlier pastoral image of the rustic boor as a comic figure, an image which both Fergusson and Burns were anxious to reject. Of course it's a huge irony that the author of 'Scotch Drink' and 'The Author's Earnest Cry and Prayer' ended up as an excise officer. Both poems also doubtless contributed to the widespread belief, encouraged by Burns's early

[59] After the works of Burns, *Scotland's Skaith* was probably the bestselling poem in Scots of the decade, going through fourteen editions in twelve months after its publication in 1795, and circulating widely in chapbook form until the 1830s.

biographers Robert Heron and Dr James Currie, that Burns's genius was destroyed by constant alcoholic 'overstimulation', a view which I'll discuss in the final chapter.

## AMERICA LOST

In a 1788 letter to Frances Dunlop Burns subversively compared the triumphant rebellion of the American colonists to the Glorious Revolution of 1688, slipping in a note of sympathy for the Stuart cause to boot: 'in this very reign of heavenly Hanoverianism, & almost in this very year [i.e. 1788], an empire beyond the Atlantic has had its REVOLUTION too, & for the very same maladministration & legislative misdemeanors [*sic*] in the illustrious and sapientipotent Family of H[anover] as was complained of in the "tyrannical and bloody house of STUART"' [CL i. 337]. It is instructive to compare Burns's outspoken private views here with his 1784 ballad 'A Fragment' ('When Guilford good') [K38] that already reveals an impressive grasp of the American war and the ensuing political crisis, while also linking up with the political pitch of 'The Author's Earnest Cry'. Burns had been advised not to publish 'A Fragment' in the Kilmarnock edition on the grounds that it might alienate potential Foxite patrons, but after being approved by Glencairn and Henry Erskine, it appeared in the Edinburgh edition of 1787.[60] Set to the stirring Jacobite air 'Killiecrankie',[61] 'A Fragment' is a virtuoso compression into 'braid Scots' ballad stanzas of the complex political events of the previous decade 1773–83. In the opening lines, 'Guilford's' (the prime minister Lord North) 'goodness' is questioned by his unreliable steering of the ship of state (he 'did our hellim [rudder] thraw, man' (l. 2); 'thraw' is glossed by Burns as 'to sprain, to twist, to contradict').[62] These stanzas satirize the bumbling ineptitude of the British aristocrats who effectively lost the American war:

> B[urgoyne] gaed up, like spur an' whip,
>     Till *Fraser* brave did fa', man;
> Then lost his way, ae misty day,
>     In *Saratoga* shaw, man.
> C[ornwallis] fought as lang's he dought,
>     An' did the Buckskins claw, man;
> But [*Clinton's*] glaive frae rust to save,
>     He hung it to the wa', man.   (ll. 25–32)

---

[60] See his letter to Erskine in Dec. 1786 when he writes, 'I suspect my political tenets, such as they are, may be rather heretical in the opinion of some of my best Friends' [CL i. 77].

[61] Named for the 1689 battle in which Claverhouse's Jacobite army triumphed over McKay's government forces, albeit at the loss of their leader's life.

[62] *Poems Chiefly in the Scottish Dialect* (Edinburgh, 1787), 365.

This refers to General Burgoyne's defeat at Saratoga in 1777 by the Continental army, and the death of Brigadier Simon Fraser (son of the Jacobite Lord Lovat executed in 1747); and General Clinton setting off from New York in October 1781 with reinforcements for Cornwallis, who was blockaded by a Franco-American army at Yorktown. Clinton turned back pusillanimously and hung his 'glaive' (sword) on the wall when he heard that Cornwallis had surrendered. The Generals' failure to coordinate operations proved the decisive blow to British hopes, attracting the mutual recrimination of both parties. Burns's poem bluntly addresses the highly sensitive question of the British high command's fitness for purpose.[63] It was maybe this aspect of the poem (rather than its treatment of British foreign policy in a 'braid Scots' ballad) that drew Hugh Blair's remark, upon reading it, that 'Burns's politics always smell of the smithy' [Kin. iii. 1026].

Kinsley dismisses the poem as 'a squib: a humorous account of events that others besides Burns had found tragic-comic' [Kin. iii. 1026]. However, the remainder of the poem suggests that its political analysis is rather more serious than this assumes, given that the fifth to ninth stanzas are concerned with the political chaos that ensued in Britain in the wake of defeat in America. Burns knew that there had been little sympathy for the American cause in Scotland. Unlike the Ulster Scots and Irish, the Scottish, and especially Highland, settlers in the American colonies had sided with the King and were disliked by the rebellious colonists.[64] Despite the dire consequence of Britain losing her American colonies, one positive outcome for the British government was that Scottish loyalism (regarded as unreliable in the wake of the 1745 Rebellion) had been tried and tested. As a result, Colley suggests, the overall consequence of the loss of America was a strengthening, rather than weakening, of the Union; 'one important periphery . . . had been lost. But another, Scotland, had become linked to the centre to a greater degree than ever before, fastened tight by cords of mutual self-interest.'[65]

But 'A Fragment' diverts attention away from what Burns regarded as Scotland's unpalatable role in supporting this disastrous war, to her instrumentality in winning the peace. Above all, the poem stakes a claim for Scotland's agency in

[63] Kin. iii. 1028. See also Roger J. Fechner, 'Burns and American Liberty' in Kenneth Simpson (ed.), *Love and Liberty*, (East Linton: Tuckwell, 1997), 274–88 at 280, which suggests correspondences between Burns's account of the American war and reports published in the *Scots Magazine* and newspapers such as *The Edinburgh Evening Courant* (pp. 281–2).

[64] See Andrew Hook, *Scotland and America* (London: Blackie, 1975), 47–72, and Susan Manning, *Fragments of Union: Making Connections in Scottish and American Writing* (Basingstoke: Palgrave, 2002). This raises a question-mark over Burns's narrative, in 'Address of Beelzebub' [K 108] of the would-be emigrant Glengary Highlanders being converted to the republican cause: given that they aimed to settle in 'the wilds of CANADA' rather than in the republican USA, such a 'conversion' would have been unlikely.

[65] Linda Colley, *Britons: Forging the Nation, 1707–1837* (London: Pimlico, 1994), 144.

defeating the unpopular Fox–North coalition, and its replacement (with George III's strong support) by Pitt the Younger's 'Mince Pie administration' in December 1783, so called because it wasn't expected to survive beyond Christmas, although in point of fact it lasted until 1801. As in 'The Author's Earnest Cry', Burns supported Pitt because, like his father Lord Chatham 'the Great Commoner', he was a reformer who had strongly opposed the war with America (Burns would develop a less positive opinion of 'Billy Pitt' in the revolutionary decade): 'The Saxon lads, wi' loud placads, | On *Chatham's Boy* did ca', man; | An' Scotland drew her pipe and' blew: | 'Up, Willie, waur them a' man!' (ll. 53–6).[66]

At line 59, 'Slee' Henry D[undas's] role in canvassing Scottish support for Pitt undergirds a sense of Scotland's new agency within British post-war politics, expressed in terms of Highland military prowess, Burns's positive extrapolation of what he regarded as her (regrettable) loyalism during the American crisis. As I've argued above, this was a pragmatic *quid pro quo*, because Scottish loyalty to the Union was always conditional, and demanded its reward. This complex message is perhaps clearest in the final stanza, with its anticipation of the Postscript to 'The Author's Earnest Cry and Prayer' as a militarized 'Caledon' (Scotland) discards her bagpipe and reaches for her dirk to support William Pitt and the new ministry:

> But, word an' blow, *N[orth], F[ox] and Co.*
>     Gowff'd *Willie* like a ba', man,
> Till *Suthron* raise, an' coost their claise
>     Behind him in a raw, man:
> An' *Caledon* threw by the drone,
>     An' did her whittle draw, man;
> An' swoor fu' rude, thro' dirt an' blood,
>     To mak it guid in law, man.    [ll. 65–72]

To the radical antiquary Joseph Ritson, writing in 1794, the 'merit in some of the satirical stanzas' of 'A Fragment' (i.e. Burns's commendable support for the American colonists, and his mockery of the British officer class) was compromised by the poem's support for Pitt's ministry: 'the character of his favourite minister seems to have operated like the touch of a torpedo; and after vainly attempting something like a panegyric, he seems under the necessity of relinquishing the task'. Ritson was writing at a time when Pitt's reformist promise was a faded memory, so his criticism of Burns is perhaps unduly harsh. But he still thought well enough of his 'political ballad' to include it in his anthology *Scotish Songs*.[67]

---

[66] Like the air to 'A Fragment', 'Up, Willie, waur them a' man' is a Jacobite song, this time concerning the indecisive battle of Sherriffmuir (1715).

[67] Joseph Ritson, 'An Historical Essay on Scotish Song', in *Scotish Songs, in two volumes* (London: Joseph Johnson, 1794), I, lxxv, and II, 123.

## THE KING'S BIRTHDAY

As the Kilmarnock edition was about to go to press in the summer of 1786, Burns read the poet laureate Thomas Warton's 'Ode for His Majesty's Birth-Day, June 4th 1786' 'in the public papers' and was immediately prompted to reply by writing his own Birthday Ode to George III entitled 'A Dream' [K 113].[68] With the collapse of the Fox–North coalition, and popular support for the new ministry led by Pitt in 1783, the situation was improving for the unpopular 48-year-old monarch, who favoured Pitt and loathed Fox. Just a decade earlier, John Wesley had warned that 'the bulk of the people in every city, town, and village . . . do not so much aim at the ministry . . . but at the king himself . . . They heartily despise his Majesty, and hate him with a perfect hatred': the loss of the American colonies had hardly improved matters.[69]

As in Burns's ballad, however, Lord North rather than George III was now identified as national scapegoat for the loss of America, and the king who had so recently prepared an abdication speech began an impressive exercise in damage limitation. Warton's 'Birthday Ode' for 4 June 1786 played its modest part in the wake of this process: it's significant that in 'the mood of defensive introspection' following the American debacle,[70] the laureate needed to represent George as custodian of liberty, rather than a tyrant who had oppressed his American subjects with disastrous consequences. In comparing British to Greek liberties, Warton assiduously played down suspicions that he was simply flattering his royal patron.[71] His ode modelled itself on the work of the Greek poets Alcaeus, Pindar, and Theocritus, 'stern arbiters of glory's bright awards' and scourges of tyranny; as such, appropriate models for a laureate ode to a British king 'who rules a people like their own, | In arms, in polish'd arts supreme; | Who bids his Britain vie with Greece'.[72]

Burns's 'A Dream' represents a more ambiguous response to Warton's poem than has usually been assumed, given that the latter was not merely a 'sycophantic work' in the usual sense of the term [CG, p. 60].[73] Frances Dunlop's account of

---

[68] The poem's title derives from the humorous anti-Kirk satires circulated by Burns's friend John Rankine 'then making a noise in the world' [K 47].

[69] Quoted in Colley, *Britons*, 208.

[70] Ibid.

[71] Thomas Warton, 'Ode for His Majesty's Birth-Day, June 4th 1786', *Poems on Various Subjects* (London 1791), 233.

[72] p. 236. In the 'Birthday Ode for June 4th 1787' composed the following year, Warton chided Dryden for his 'promiscuous praise' of Charles II; had George III been his subject, he artfully concluded, 'The tuneful Dryden had not flatter'd here, | His lyre had blameless been, his tribute all sincere!' (p. 244). See my remarks on changing conventions of dedicatory flattery in Ch. 3.

[73] Robert Folkenflik rightly places 'A Dream' within the context of eighteenth-century laureate satire in 'Patronage and the Poetic Hero', *Huntingdon Library Quarterly* 48/4 (Autumn 1985), 363–79, 371–3.

'A Dream''s reception in London has understandably informed critical discussion of Burns's poem ever since; 'numbers at London are learning Scots to read your book, but they don't like your Address to the King, and say it will hurt the sale of the rest' [Kin. iii. 1191]. She suggested that Burns might 'spill the ink-glass' over one of the verses, almost certainly the third with its veiled Jacobitical assertion; 'There's monie *waur* been o' the Race, | And aiblins *ane* been better | Than You this day (ll. 25–7) (George might be better than most of the royal 'Race', but a Stuart king would have been better still, Burns hints.)

The poem's headnote serves to wrap its satire in a protective envelope, like the device of employing animals to criticize the landed class in 'The Twa Dogs'. Nevertheless, the epigraph sounds a defensive note: '*Thoughts, words, and deeds, the Statue blames with reason: | But surely* Dreams *were ne'er indicted Treason*' [Kin. i. 265]. After reading Warton's soporific 'Ode', Burns's preamble tells us, 'the Author was no sooner dropt asleep, than he imagined himself transported to the Birth-day Levee; and, in his dreaming fancy, made the following Address'. Moreover, like Warton's Greek bards of liberty, the poet claims that he is only tearing 'the tinsel gift of flattery' from the royal brow in order to hold up to him the mirror of truth; but unlike the pensioned laureate, he doesn't owe the king any debt of obligation.[74] Whatever Burns's real feelings towards George III, 'A Dream' bears out Colley's observation on the related field of graphic satire of the monarch in the 1780s that it 'usually sought to provoke ridicule not hatred. [Satirists] were more likely now to represent the king as a figure of fun than as a corrupt or over-powerful monarch.'[75]

As with 'The Author's Earnest Cry', the stanzas which follow make much of the poet's rude and rustic persona; he is an 'uncouth sight' (l. 7), a 'simple Poet' (l. 76) whose use of a 'braid Scots' diction laced with pawky proverbial wisdom makes no concessions to the courtly ambience of the king's levee. Christopher Whatley writes that 'the King's birthday was a rare quasi-institutionalised occasion in the Scottish calendar when it was considered legitimate (for those in power there was little choice) for the lower orders to castigate and even engage in ritual assaults on their superiors'.[76] In acknowledgement of the Saturnalian ritual of the King's Birthday, Burns employs the 'Christ's Kirk' stanza (also employed in 'The Holy Fair') with its association of the peasant brawl: the specific model is Fergusson's use of the same verse form in 'Hallow Fair' and 'Leith Races'.[77]

---

[74] John Wolcot's ('Peter Pindar') *Instructions to a Celebrated Laureate: alias the Progress of Curiosity; alias a Birth-Day Ode...* (published the following year, in 1787) followed Burns's 'A Dream' in satirizing the king by parodying the 'thund'ring stanza' of Warton's Pindaric 'Birthday Ode' for 1787. Wolcot surpassed Burns in ridiculing Warton's portrait of the king's virtues, insisting upon George III's gross inferiority to the great Plantagenet and Tudor kings of the past.

[75] Colley, *Britons*, 210.

[76] Whatley, 'Burns: Work, Kirk and Community', in Kenneth Simpson (ed.), *Burns Now* (Edinburgh: Canongate Academic, 1994), 110. Whatley refers to Fergusson's poem 'The King's Birthday in Edinburgh' (1771) and other contemporary works.

[77] But eschewing the habbie stanza of Fergusson's 'King's Birthday in Edinburgh'.

The poem's speaker identifies himself as a Scots tenant farmer struggling to keep his head above water in the tough post-war tax regime:

> And now Ye've gien auld *Britain* peace,
> Her broken shins to plaister;
> Your sair taxation does her fleece,
> Till she has scarce a tester:
> For me, thank God, my life's a *lease*,
> Nae *bargain* wearin faster,
> Or faith! I fear, that, wi' the geese,
> I shortly boost to pasture
>              I' the craft some day.   (ll. 46–54)

Striking an autobiographical note here, the bardie complains that his lease is proving such a 'ruinous bargain' that he'll soon be joining his geese in foraging for sustenance in the 'craft' (or infield) surrounding his farmhouse.[78]

Chapter 1 proposed that the pastoral idiom of the Kilmarnock volume caught the national mood of 'agrarian patriotism' as a response to the post-1783 crisis.[79] 'A Dream' certainly plays up its agricultural persona to make its satirical point, although the poem's comic rusticity barely conceals the serious political criticism that it delivers. The bardie's vernacular address is all the more powerful compared to Warton's flatulent pastoral, evoking the letter rather than the spirit of Theocritus to convey (for once) a 'principled' laureate ode to the King. Burns exploits the generic licence of the Kilmarnock volume to give a new edge to the blunt political conscience of 'soft' pastoral. After all, *this* bardie is 'unacquainted with the necessary requisites for commencing Poet by rule', unlike the King's laureates; 'the *Poets* too, a venal gang, | Wi' rhymes weel-turn'd an' ready, | Wad gar you trow ye ne'er do wrang, | But ay unerring steady, | On sic a day' (ll. 14–18). To this extent, 'A Dream' represents a slyly opportunistic vehicle for criticizing the King, appropriating and literalizing Warton's profession of sincerity and his evocation of pastoral virtue.

The fourth stanza of 'A Dream' metaphorically touches on the loss of the American colonies under George's kingship, a plain 'fact' which only a flatterer would forbear mentioning ('*facts* are cheels that winna ding', l. 30): 'Your *royal nest*, beneath *Your* wing, | Is e'en right reft and clouted, | And now the third part o' the string, | An' less, will gang about it | Than did ae day' (ll. 32–6). The next stanza criticizes George's poor choice of ministers who must bear the

<hr/>

[78] In the 1787 glossary, Burns defines 'craft' as 'a field near a house, *in old husbandry*' (p. 350). This suggests that the speaker may be an old-fashioned farmer who hasn't yet dispensed with the old infield/outfield division.

[79] Crawford, *Poetry, Enclosure and the Vernacular Landscape*, 107, claims, however, that the myth of 'Farmer George' was largely a construct of the 1790s, and the posthumous mythmaking of John Galt's *George the Third, His Court, and Family*, 2 vols. (London, 1824). This is born out by the fact that Burns makes no allusion to the king's own agricultural pursuits in 'The Dream'.

responsibility for the 'refting and clouting' of Britain's first empire; the allusion to the king's misplaced trust in 'chaps, wha in a *barn* or *byre* | Wad better fit their station | Than courts yon day' (ll. 43–4) is specifically aimed at Charles Fox, one half of the Fox–North Coalition, a man detested by the King.[80]

Just a few years later in 1789, Burns's sympathy for the recently insane George in the 'Ode to the Departed Regency Bill' [K 258] was still largely a pretext for his attack on Fox, the Prince of Wales, and the Portland Whigs, whose hopes of forming a Regency had been dashed by the king's sudden recovery. (If the king read the poem he might have half-forgiven Burns for 'A Dream'.) The 'Ode''s strained sub-Miltonic apostrophes continue the earlier attack on the Foxites in what must qualify as Burns's *least* radical poem: 'No Babel-structure would *I* build | Where, Order exiled from his native sway, | Confusion may the REGENT-sceptre wield, | While all would rule and none obey', ll. 41–4). Only Burns's Blakean sympathies for Milton's Lucifer and the Fallen Angels (to whom the Foxites are compared at lines 59–74) hints at his increasing rapprochement with the opposition over the next few years.[81] By 1792, when Burns's adaptation of the Jacobite song, 'Here's a Health to them that's awa' [K 391], was published (anonymously) in the radical *Edinburgh Gazetteer*, he'd completely changed his tune, to the extent of proposing 'a health to Charlie, the chief o' the clan' (l. 11). 'Charlie' Fox (as opposed to Stuart) now took his place with Erskine, Lauderdale, MacLeod, and the other pro-revolutionary Scots Whigs of 'the Buff and Blue'.

In the second half of 'A Dream', Burns's bardie turns his attention to George's wife, Queen Charlotte, and the couple's 'bonie Bairntime' or extensive family, evidence of their energetic sex life. (In a later bawdy song 'Why should na poor folk mowe' [K 395], Burns concluded his comical rendering of the democratic 'right to mowe' (fuck) with a loyal toast to the British monarchs: 'Here's George our gude king and Charlotte his queen, | And lang may they tak a gude mowe!', ll. 27–8).[82] The eleventh stanza damns the Prince of Wales with the faintest of praise, deploying a magnificent pearl of agricultural wisdom in the spirit of Allan Ramsay's *Scots Proverbs*; 'Yet aft a ragged *Cowte's* been known, | To mak a noble *Aiver*' (ll. 91–2, 'the wildest colt may make the noblest horse'). The bardie hopes

[80]  The heavy jowled, unshaven Fox was also denounced by Burns as 'yon ill-tongu'd tinkler' in 'The Author's Earnest Cry', and 'When Guilford Gude' refers to Fox's 'tinkler jaw' (l, l. 40). See Kidd, 'Burns and Politics', 65–6.

[81]  Donaldson ('The Glencairn Connection', 64–5), locates Burns's 'conversion' to later in the year 1789. Remarkably, the text of Burns's 'Ode' published in the London *Star* on 17 April 1789 under the pseudonym 'Agricola', was doctored by the editor Peter Stuart (himself a pensioner of the Portland Whigs) to make it read like a satire on Pitt's government, rather than on the disappointed Foxite opposition. See Lucylle Werkmeister, 'Robert Burns and the London Newspapers', *Bulletin of the New York Public Library* 65/8 (Oct. 1961), 483–504.

[82]  The fact that Burns send a copy of this 'tippling ballad' to his Tory patron Graham of Fintry in the same letter of 5 January 1793 in which he sought to exculpate himself from charges of harbouring radical sympathies hardly suggests that he viewed it as politically subversive [CL ii. 174].

that, despite his profligate habits, the Prince will turn out to resemble his distinguished historical namesake Henry V ('Him at *Agincourt* wha shone', l. 95).[83] The poem then moves on to laugh at the Dukes of York and Clarence, while the penultimate stanza lectures George's six daughters not sneer at '*British-boys*' who (the bardie cheekily implies) are better hung than 'German-Gentles' (l. 124). Signing off with a 'God bless you a'!' (l. 127) the final stanza concludes by hoping that things will get better for the Royals, since they can hardly get worse. The full Scots diction of the poem's closing statement is splendidly opaque in its pawky, proverbial gesture of well-wishing, hinting that this incompetent king and his dysfunctional family will end up getting their just desserts, whatever those may be: 'An I hae seen their *coggie* fou, | That yet hae tarrow't at it; | But or the *day* was done, I trow, | The laggen they hae clautet | Fu' clean than day' (ll. 131–5).

This is at once befittingly irreverent, a spectacular instance of *lèse-majesté*, but also, despite the comic satire, plainly spoken and sincere in accordance with Burns's pastoral agenda. In 'A Dream', the King is taken to task in an irreverent agricultural idiom particularly suited to the emergent myth of 'Farmer George'. Burns was taking advantage of an opportune historical moment to demonstrate his gifts of rustic independence, at a moment when even the poet laureate needed to disavow flattery in praising the royal virtues. The rustic (or canine) address of Burns's political pastorals artfully 'bespatter' kings and 'Great folks' from below, while at the same time maintaining a tone of couthy (but also deeply *conditional*) loyalism; this is maybe what Burns meant by saying 'I have avoided taking a Side in Politics' [CL i. 465].

In striking contrast is Burns's related 'Ode for General Washington's Birthday' [K 451], composed in 1794 but not published for nearly a century. (Washington's birthday was on 22 February 1732.) In early February 1794 John Syme mentioned in a letter to Alexander Cunningham that '[Burns] is halfway in a grand elevated & sublime Pindaric ode to Liberty—not of the Gallic species tho'.[84] The poet may have been swayed by Tom Paine's dedication of Part I of *Rights of Man* to Washington, and his comment in Part II: 'I cannot help remarking, that the character and services of this gentleman are sufficient to put all those men called kings to shame'.[85] Commentators have missed the important point that, more radically than 'A Dream', Burns's 'Ode for Washington's Birthday' responds to Thomas Warton's 'Birthday Odes' to George III of 1786 and 1787.[86]

[83] The Prince's intimacy with 'tinkler' Charlie Fox is of course reminiscent of Hal's friendship with 'funny, queer, *Sir John*' Falstaff (ll. 95–9).
[84] MS in Peter J. Westwood, *Definitive Illustrated Companion to Robert Burns*, 8 vols. (Irvine: Distributed National Burns Collections Project, 2004–6), v. 2915. An earlier fragmentary draft of the opening of Burns's Washington Ode entitled 'Ode for Hibernia's Sons' lauded the endeavours of the Irish reformers. (See CG, pp. 819–20. The manuscript is now lost.)
[85] *The Tom Paine Reader*, ed. Foot and Kramnick, 290. Paine later changed his mind, violently attacking America's first president in his *Letter to George Washington* (ibid. 490–502).
[86] McIlvanney, *Burns the Radical*, 184, hints at the connection, but without elaborating.

Burns's 'Ode' is actually a *more* direct response (although a less successful poem) to the extent that it imitates the Pindaric stanza and 'sublime' idiom of the originals. Warton's 1786 Grecian trio of Alcaeus, Pindar, and Theocritus are negated in the 'Ode''s opening lines: 'No Spartan tube, no Attic shell, | No lyre Eolian I awake; | 'Tis Liberty's bold note I swell, | Thy harp, Columbia, let me take' (ll. 1–4). Later, at ll. 31–3, Burns rebuffs Warton's evocation (in the 1787 'Ode') of 'Albion's bards' Chaucer, Spenser, and Dryden: 'The Bards that erst have struck the patriot lyre, | And rous'd the freeborn Briton's soul of fire, | No more thy England own' (ll. 31–3). In the dark days of Pitt's Terror, 'England in thunders calls—'The Tyrant's cause is mine!' (l. 39). Things are no better in the 'wild heaths' of 'Caledonia', where the 'soul of freedom' represented by William Wallace lies 'immingled with the might Dead!' (ll. 47–8). Burns's appropriation of the language of Warton's 'Birthday Odes' to celebrate Washington's birthday (like a latter-day Cincinnatus, he had returned to the plough after overthrowing tyranny), is particularly effective here given the Laureate's damage limitation in attempting to salvage George III's reputation after the American debacle.

Burns's 'Ode for Washington's Birthday' offers a private glimpse of Burns's 'staunch republicanism' during the heightened political tension of the revolutionary decade. Gareth Stedman Jones has recently proposed that the convergence between the enlightenment social thought of Adam Smith, Condorcet, Paine (and others) with the republican and democratic revolutions in America and France marked 'a historical turning point' by initiating a distinctly modern radicalism that proposed 'an end to poverty'. This epoch-making goal would be achieved by democratizing (rather than abolishing) commercial society, rejecting both the unmitigated greed of Mandevillean *laissez-faire* and the austere classical republicanism favoured by many radicals that ruled out both commercial modernity and the idea of historical progress.[87] Stedman Jones writes of 'Paine's radical reshaping of Smith's account of commercial society and his dramatic proposal to end poverty through a programme of social insurance and redistributory taxation' in the second part of *Rights of Man* (1792).[88]

Tom Paine's views of cheap government and low taxes must have been extremely attractive to the author of 'Is there, for Honest Poverty' [K 482]; as an Exciseman (like Paine) and after 1788 a tax collector by profession, Burns was well placed to grasp the radical potential of his proposals for public education, unemployment benefit, and state pensions, to be achieved by progressive taxation rather than private charity. Coming of age as a poet in the 'sentimental era', Burns had inherited a sympathetic attitude to the poor and outcast from such writers as Sterne and Mackenzie. Yet increasingly in the course of the 1790s,

---

[87]  Gareth Stedman Jones, *An End to Poverty? A Historical Debate* (London: Profile Books, 2004), 9–10.

[88]  Ibid. 57. See also Emma Rothschild, *Economic Sentiments: Adam Smith, Condorcet, and the Enlightenment* (Cambridge, Mass.: Harvard University Press, 2001).

Burns follows Paine in dignifying the poor and the unenfranchised with 'the rights of man', as immortalized in the 1795 song: 'For a' that, and a' that, | Their tinsel show, and a' that; | The honest man, though e'er sae poor, | Is king o' men for a' that' (ll. 13–16). For both Paine and Burns the triumph of the 'independent mind' (l. 23) entails the abolition of aristocratic distinction, followed by the triumph of universal fraternity; 'For a' that, and a' that, | Its comin yet for a' that, | That Man to Man the warld o'er, | Shall brothers be for a' that' (ll. 37–40). As Marilyn Butler notes, this is 'probably the closest rendering in English of the letter and spirit of the notorious Jacobin "Ca ira"'.[89]

Unfortunately, as I argued at the beginning of this chapter, the same spirit of political reaction that consigned Paine and Condorcet's notion of an 'end to poverty' to oblivion in the 1790s destroyed any direct evidence of Burns's reading of Paine. While Paine's republicanism was already current in the 1780s, his most far-reaching social ideas weren't published until 1792, after much of Burns's poetry was written; nevertheless, Paine's views serve as a useful yardstick for assessing Burns's attitudes to poverty and social injustice. As we'll see in Chapter 7, in the decades after Burns's death, the emergence of an evangelical interpretation of poverty as part of God's plan meshed with a depoliticized *laissez-faire* economics that preferred private charity to the 'right' to poor relief. In Scotland this was largely associated with the charismatic Revd Thomas Chalmers, who declared 'the poor shall be with us always . . . it is vain to look for the extinction of poverty from the world'.[90] Ironically, this argument found ideological leverage in the notion of 'independence' as a function of 'self-help', contributing in large part to the bourgeois apotheosis of Burns in the Victorian era.

---

[89] Marilyn Butler, 'Burns and Politics', in Robert Crawford (ed.), *Burns and Cultural Authority* (Edinburgh: Polygon, 1999), 86–112 at 102. Thomas Crawford [*BPS* p. 365] notes that Burns's final line echoes Paine's prediction in *Rights of Man*, 'For what we can foresee, all Europe may form but one great Republic, and man be free of the whole.' His suggestion that it 'represents the transformation of the Masonic idea of Brotherhood into the French revolutionary ideal of Fraternity' goes some way to explaining its androcentrism.

[90] Quoted in Cage, *Scottish Poor Law*, 90.

# 5

## Beasties

*The division of life into vegetal and relational, organic and animal, animal and human ... passes first of all as a mobile border within living man, and without this intimate caesura the very decision of what is human and what is not would probably not be possible.*

(Giorgio Agamben, *The Open*)[1]

*I'm truly sorry Man's dominion*
*Has broken Nature's social union*
(Burns, 'To a Mouse', ll. 7–8)

### MAN AND BEAST

Inquiry into the 'intimate caesura' between human and animal existence was an important concern of the eighteenth-century Scottish 'science of man'. Descartes's notion of animals as organic machines had been questioned by John Locke, who believed that 'Brutes have Ideas, and that they reason, tho' they are not capable of comparing and comprehending these ideas.'[2] David Hume insisted, sceptically, that reasoning by the association of ideas was common to both species, and that any explanation of human passions was also applicable to animals, thereby questioning claims for man's sovereignty over creation. Nevertheless, Lord Monboddo's proto-Darwinian derivation of mankind from the orang-utan earned him widespread ridicule, while John Gregory proposed (more modestly) that instinct linked man and beast, even as reason divided them. Adam Smith considered that animals had a claim to be 'objects of gratitude and resentment', but his teacher Francis Hutcheson had gone further in suggesting that they possessed rights, perhaps the first philosopher to formalize such a claim.[3] In

---

[1] *The Open: Man and Animal*, trans. Kevin Attell (Stanford, Calif.; Stanford University Press, 2004), 15.

[2] *Essay Concerning Human Understanding*, ed. P. H. Nidditch (Oxford: Clarendon, 1975), 159–60.

[3] On Hume, see David Perkins, *Romanticism and Animal Rights* (Cambridge: Cambridge University Press, 2003), 23–4 and Aaron Garrett, 'Anthropology: the "Original" of Human Nature', in Alexander Broadie (ed.), *Cambridge Companion to the Scottish Enlightenment* (Cambridge: Cambridge University Press, 2003), 79–93, 83–9. On Monboddo, see Keith Thomas,

*Man and the Natural World* Keith Thomas places the Scottish philosophical inquiry within the wider context of what he calls 'the narrowing gap' between the human and animal worlds in the early modern period. He traces the change in attitudes to a variety of influences; the gradual replacement of animal by machine power; a demographic decline in the number of people practising animal husbandry; an increase in pet-keeping in a rapidly urbanizing society; developments in physiology and natural history; and not least, the rise of sensibility, emblematized by Uncle Toby's mawkish sympathy for the fly in *Tristram Shandy*.[4]

As a boy Robert Burns would have been familiar with the 'intimate caesura' from his father's 'Manual of Religious Belief, in a Dialogue between a Father and his Son'. Burnes senior warned, in conventional terms, against 'placing the animal part [of the soul] before the rational, and thereby putting ourselves on a level with the brute beasts', but he qualified this by specifying that the point of this '[was] not to the utter destruction of the animal part, but to the real and true enjoyment of them, by placing Nature in the order that its Creator designed it' [Chambers-Wallace, i. 455–9 at 458]. Burnes's emphasis on the 'pleasure' and 'enjoyment' associated with the (regulated) animal soul was a departure from Calvinist orthodoxy, as we'll see in the next chapter, and an important influence on his son's understanding of human sensibility.

As a working farmer Robert Burns lived closer to the animal world than most eighteenth-century writers, depending on beasts for agricultural labour, transport, nourishment, and clothing, as well as companionship. Perhaps we'll look in vain in his poetry for animal epiphanies like those of Rilke's 'Eighth Elegy' ('the open that lies so deep in an animal's face'), or MacDiarmid's gnomic 'the inward gates of a bird are always open'.[5] Unlike the other eighteenth-century and Romantic poets discussed by David Perkins and Christine Kenyon-Jones, Burns's relationship to the animal world was both instrumental and sentimental: stockbreeding and the rationalization of the animal economy were essential elements of agricultural improvement, yet poet Burns knew that animals were living creatures and not just commodities, and as such demanded care and compassion.

---

*Man and the Natural World: Changing Attitudes in England, 1500–1800* (Harmondsworth: Penguin, 1983), 130–2; John Gregory, *A Comparative View of the State and Faculties of Man with those of the Animal World* (1765), 6th edn. (Edinburgh, 1774), 20; Frances Hutcheson, *A System of Moral Philosophy*, 2 vols. (London, 1755), i. 316; Adam Smith, *Theory of Moral Sentiments*, ed. Knut Haakonssen (Cambridge: Cambridge University Press, 2002), 111.

[4] See Perkins, *Romanticism and Animal Rights, passim,* and Christine Kenyon-Jones, *Kindred Brutes: Animals in Romantic-Period Writing* (Aldershot: Ashgate, 2001), esp. 1–9.

[5] Rainer Maria Rilke, *Duino Elegies,* trans. David Young (New York: Norton, 1978), 'Eighth Elegy', 71; Hugh MacDiarmid, 'On a Raised Beach', *Selected Poems*, ed. Alan Riach and Michael Grieve (Harmondsworth: Penguin, 1994), 178 l. 36.

It is not surprising therefore that beasts have such a central place in his poetry, although the extent to which the animal poems reflect the social, political, and philosophical themes of 'Scots pastoral' outstrips expectations. Burns's 'To a Mouse' is, justifiably, the most famous 'theriophilic' poem of the eighteenth century, and as we'll see, engages many of the concerns shared by a working farmer and the Scottish literati.[6] But the success of this one poem (and, in a different animal register, of 'To a Louse') has perhaps detracted attention from the other 'beastie' poems of the Kilmarnock volume, even if they represent slighter achievements in the same genre.

## SHEEP AND POETRY

The 'Death and Dying Words of Poor Mailie, the Author's Only Pet Yowe, an Unco Mournfu' Tale' [K 24] was Burns's first poem (as opposed to song) written in Scots, composed in 1782 during the Lochlie period, and transcribed in the first Commonplace Book. Critics have noted that the poem (as well as, more obviously, its title) echoes William Hamilton of Gilbertfield's 'The Last Dying Words of Bonnie Heck: A Famous Greyhound in the Shire of Fife', first published in James Watson's *Choice Collection of Comic and Serious Scots Poems* (1706). ('Poor Mailie's' tetrameter couplets depart from Hamilton's use of the habbie stanza, however.) Although Burns's 'The Twa Dogs', studied in the previous chapter, is an excellent example of his theriophilic satire, it's strange that neither Caesar nor Luath owes as much to 'Bonnie Heck' as does the ovine 'Poor Mailie'.

Murray Pittock notes that the tragic-heroic genre of 'Last Words' was a frequent feature of broadside literature, satirized by eighteenth-century Scots poets such as Hamilton, Ramsay, and Burns by being placed in the mouth of greyhounds, ewes, or elderly bawds. This comic hybridization of high and low, which Burns inherited from Ramsay, also performed a more serious cultural role; 'the threnody on the departed perpetually alludes to the end not of a human [or animal] life merely, but of a way of life and a society as a whole'.[7] The *Canongate* editors note that Heck's rhetorical death speech parodies the fifteenth-century Scottish epic *Blind Harry's Wallace*, which Hamilton of Gilbertfield published in a revised and modernized version in 1722 [CG, p. 46]. In that case, then 'Poor Mailie' is a parody of a parody, to the extent that a sheep's death by rope parodies

---

[6] Kenyon-Jones, *Kindred Brutes*, 12, defines the theriophilic tradition as 'a philosophical stance which satirizes human pretensions by reminding us of our kinship with animals'.

[7] Murray Pittock, *Scottish and Irish Romanticism* (Oxford: Oxford University Press, 2008), 37–8. Another more remote influence (given its English idiom) is Robert Fergusson's anti-sentimentalist parody 'The Sow of Feeling', although it's uncertain whether Burns had read Fergusson's poem as early as 1782. See McD ii.130, i. 179.

a greyhound's death by hanging, which in turn parodies the brutal execution of the Scottish patriot William Wallace at Smithfield Market in London. In 1785–6 Burns composed 'Poor Mailie's Elegy' [K 25] as a pendant to 'The Death and Dying Words', clearly now with a view to publication; this poem's habbie stanzas show a clear debt to Fergusson's 'Elegy on the Death of Mr David Gregory'. I'll note the different emphasis of the later poem below, as Burns's exploration of animal identity shifted from the mock-heroic Scottish vernacular register of 'Bonnie Heck' to the distinctively sentimental idiom of 'To a Mouse'. The Two 'Poor Mailie' poems take sixth and seventh place respectively in the running order of Kilmarnock.

Part of the comic effect of Hamilton's 'Bonnie Heck' lies in its bathetic relationship to the sort of epic bombast represented by *Blind Harry's Wallace*, but at the same time the poem also has a serious point to make about animal ethics; namely Heck's (and evidently Hamilton's) outrage at the practice of hanging old hunting dogs;

> 'Alas, alas,' quo' bonnie Heck,
> 'On former days when I reflect!
> I was a dog much in respect
>       For doughty deed;
> But now I must hing by the neck
>       Without remeed.
>
> 'Oh fy, sire, for black, burning shame,
> Ye'll bring a blunder on your name!
> Pray tell me wherein I'm to blame?
>       Is't in effect
> Because I'm cripple, auld, and lame?'
>       Quo' bonnie Heck.   (ll. 1–12)[8]

Keith Thomas comments that in the seventeenth century working dogs were 'regarded unsentimentally; and they were generally hanged or drowned when they had outlived their usefulness. 'My old dog Quon was killed', wrote one Dorset farmer in 1698, 'and baked for his grease, of which he yielded 11lbs.' It was not these necessary animals, but the unnecessary ones, hounds and lapdogs in particular, which received the real affection and the highest status.[9] In the light of this, Heck is maybe protesting against a category mistake for which he'll pay the ultimate penalty; as a superannuated hound rather than a sheepdog he surely deserves better treatment than hanging (or worse still, stoning to death, as is suggested at l. 53). For all the comedy of the poem, Hamilton makes a serious

[8] 'The Last Dying Words of Bonnie Heck', in *Before Burns: Eighteenth-Century Scottish Poetry*, ed. and intro. Christopher MacLachlan (Edinburgh: Canongate, 2002), 15–17.

[9] Thomas, *Man and the Natural World*, 102.

appeal to the reader's pity and kindles outrage at the cruel practice of destroying dogs in their dotage after a lifetime of faithful service.

Gilbert Burns later described the incident at Lochlie farm upon which 'The Death and Dying Words of Poor Mailie' (and of course 'Poor Mailie's Elegy') were allegedly based:

> [Burns] had, partly by way of frolic, bought a ewe and two lambs from a neighbour, and she was tethered in a field adjoining the house at Lochlie. He and I were going out with our teams, and our two younger brothers to drive for us, at mid-day, when Hugh Wilson, a curious looking awkward boy, clad in plaiding, came to us with much anxiety in his face, with the information that the ewe had entangled herself in the tether, and was lying in the ditch. Robert was much tickled with Hughoc's appearance and postures. Poor Mailie was set to rights, and when we returned from the plough in the evening, he repeated to me her *Death and Dying Words* pretty much in the way they now stand. [Currie, iii. 380]

Gilbert seems concerned to recollect his brother's amusement at Hughoc's horrified reaction to Mailie's accident than the sufferings of the ewe herself, which he perhaps considered a little below the dignity of poetic genius. Hughoc's reaction certainly accounts for lines 7–16 of Burns's poem, in which the boy is cast as the intermediary between dying ewe and negligent master; but it's Mailie's dying admonishment to the latter, and last advice to her son and daughter (colloquially, her 'toop-lamb' and 'yowie') which occupy the main text of the published poem. Gilbert's information that Mailie's death by strangulation was actually averted heightens the comedy, underlining the parodic pathos attached to the dying speech of a sheep.

In his *History of the Earth*, Oliver Goldsmith baldly asserted that 'the sheep, in its servile state, seems to be divested of all inclinations of its own; and of all animals it appears the most stupid'.[10] Burns's poem completely refutes this moralizing condemnation of sheep; crucial to its comic effect is the anthropomorphic nature of Mailie's refined personality as a 'sheep o' credit' [l. 56]. Internal evidence from the two poems reveals that she is no mere 'blastet, moorlan' sheep of the type indigenous to lowland Scotland [l. 54] but a scion of improved stock, and moreover, as the title informs us, the farmer's 'pet'. (The term 'pet' has a rather specialized Scots sense here as 'a hand-reared lamb or sheep'.)[11] An earlier draft of 'Poor Mailie's Elegy' complete in six stanzas provides specific detail of Mailie's pedigree, while making it clear that Burns's motive for keeping pet sheep, albeit on a small scale, was more than merely 'a frolic':

---

[10]   Oliver Goldsmith, *History of the Earth*, 2nd edn., 8 vols. (London, 1779), iii. 40.

[11]   *Concise Scots Dictionary*, ed.-in-chief Mairi Robinson (Aberdeen: Aberdeen University Press, 1985), s.v. pet. David Perkins overlooks this specialized sense of the word, as well as Mailie's economic importance as valuable breeding stock, in an otherwise excellent discussion of the poem in *Romanticism and Animal Rights*, 49–52.

She was nae get o' runted rams
Wi' woo' like gaits, an' legs like trams;
She was the flow'r o' Fairlie lambs
    A famous breed!
Now Robin greetan chows the hams
    O' Mailie dead!

O Fortune, how thou does us mock!
He thought in her he saw a stock:
Would heave him up, Wi' hyvie folk
    To cock his head;
Now a' his hopes are gane like smoke
    For Mailie's dead!    [Kin. i. 35 ll. 13–24]

In this early version, Mailie is born of 'famous breed' of Fairlie lambs, produced by the stockbreeder and agricultural improver Alexander Fairlie of Fairlie, factor of the Earl of Eglinton, and she had clearly cost Burns a hefty sum of money.[12] Lines 19–24 explain that Mailie, more than just the poet's 'pet', was also a financial investment. Along with flax dressing and other agricultural projects, she represented Burns's aspirations to be a stockbreeder, who 'thought in her he saw a stock: | Would heave him up, with hyvie folk | To cock his head'. Distinguished from local Ayrshire breeds with their straggling, goat-like wool and legs like 'trams' (in Scots the upright posts of the gallows), Mailie's descent from improved Fairlie stock quite literally embodies the poet's own aspirations to social and economic improvement.[13] Line 20 plays on the double sense of the word 'stock' (meaning both 'pedigree' and 'financial assets'), proposing that success in breeding a race of improved sheep would have quite literally enhanced the poet's own 'stock', enabling him to hold his head up in the company of 'hyvie' (prosperous) folk.

In *The Animal Estate*, Harriet Ritvo characterizes the early nineteenth-century display of prize animals at agricultural shows as a 'ceremonial re-enactment of the traditional rural order . . . remind[ing] ordinary farmers that the men who could afford to raise prize animals were their natural leaders, at the same time that the opulence of the display underlined the exclusiveness of high stock breeding'.[14] Clearly Burns's Fairlie ewe is a considerably downscaled version of the Durham

---

[12] Writing in 1793, William Fullarton stated that in twenty years Fairlie had 'established a reformation so complete [on Eglinton's estates] that it is universally adopted . . . almost on every estate in Ayrshire' [*General Description*, 21]. As well as being James Boswell's 'respectable neighbour', Fairlie had employed the poet's father William Burnes when he first came to Ayrshire in 1750 [Kin. iii., 1020]. See also Gavin Sprott, *Robert Burns, Farmer* (Edinburgh: National Museums of Scotland), 28–9.

[13] Burns would have made a better investment with a breeding ram rather than a Fairlie ewe, but doubtless lacked the ready capital to make such an expensive purchase.

[14] Harriet Ritvo, *The Animal Estate* (Cambridge, Mass.: Harvard University Press, 1987), 52.

ox that weighed in at 3,000 lbs, sold for £150, and toured England and Scotland in 1801 in a specially designed carriage.[15] Nonetheless, a homespun product of the same ideology of improvement, she boasts a gentle pedigree, and in relative terms her offspring could have been extremely lucrative for a struggling tenant farmer such as Burns. The poem's mockery of the indigenous species of 'runt'd rams' is also characteristic of what Ritvo calls 'the denigration of most old-fashioned strains' compared to those being developed by new techniques of stockbreeding in the period.[16] But in the end Burns's comic genuflection to the Earl of Eglinton's factor is sardonically self-directed: Mailie has died of strangulation, once again dashing all the poet's hopes of improvement, thereby striking Burns's familiar note; 'the best laid schemes o' *Mice* an' *Men*, | Gang aft agley'.

In the eight-stanza version of 'Poor Mailie's Elegy' published in Kilmarnock, Burns erased his reference to Fairlie's 'famous breed' as well as the stanza in which he'd hoped to 'heave himself up, with hyvie folk'. Stanza 6 offers an alternative genealogy for his only pet 'yowe': 'She was nae get o' moorlan tips, | Wi' tauted ket, an' hairy hips; | For her forbears were brought in ships, | Frae 'yont the TWEED: | A bonier *fleesh* ne'er crossed the clips | Than *Mailie's* dead' (ll. 31–6). Mailie now has an English pedigree, like the fashionable Cheviots, crosses of Borders sheep with Robert Bakewell's new Leicestershire breeds; together with the more hardy Blackface, these cross-breeds were revolutionizing Scottish sheep husbandry in this period. But Burns's decision to omit the 'aspirational' stanza here is well-advised, given his attack on social emulation in the verse epistles and other poems in the Kilmarnock volume. And more to the point, Burns's road to improvement is now beginning to follow the 'zigzag' vocation of poetry rather than the straight turnpike of agriculture.

These circumstantial remarks on the significance of Mailie's pedigree help to illuminate the real comic significance of 'The Death and Dying Words'. At lines 17–24 Mailie delivers an admonishment to her master via the distraught Hughoc;

> 'Tell him, if e'er again he keep
> As muckle gear as buy a *sheep*,
> O, bid him never tye them mair,
> Wi' wicked strings o' hemp or hair!
> But ca' them out to park or hill,
> An' let them wander at their will:
> So, may his flocks increase an' grow
> To *scores* o'lambs, and *packs* o' woo'!'     [(ll. 17–24)

[15] Ibid. 45.     [16] Ibid. 64.

In chiding her feckless master for his bad husbandry, Mailie reminds him of the weighty financial investment involved in stockbreeding, doubting whether he will ever again possess 'as muckle gear as buy a sheep'. The practice of tethering, which has been her own undoing, is fatal to any hopes the farmer might have of receiving a return on his investment; let the sheep graze freely, and the woolly flock will multiply, she advises him. Mailie's speech paraphrases the advice contained in many of the manuals of agricultural improvement which Burns was reading in these years; its comedy lies in the ironic reversal whereby it's the 'improved' beast who now lectures the *un*improved husbandman on the errors of his ways.

The practice of tethering was one of the *bêtes noirs* (if the term is pardonable here!) of eighteenth-century improvers; like runrig and overcropping, it was redolent of the bad old husbandry. Col. Fullarton complained of pre-improvement Ayrshire: 'as there were no inclosures, the horses and cattle are either *tethered*, during the Summer months, or trusted to the direction of a herd and cur-dog, by whom the poor starving animals were kept in constant agitation. [Fullarton, p.11]. Responsible enclosure with dykes or stockproof thorn hedges enable the free grazing of livestock, which could therefore 'wander at their will' on 'park or hill'. Mailie hopes that her motherless lambs will be nourished with cow's milk and fed with 'taets o' *hay* an' ripps o' *corn*': 'An' may they never learn the gaets, | Of ither vile, wanrestfu' *Pets*!— | To slink thro' slaps, an' reave an' steal, | At stacks o' pease, or stocks o' kail' (ll. 35–8). Carefully placed enclosures will ensure that sheep are excluded from arable and kailyards while they can enjoy free grazing.

Although Burns alludes to 'Bonnie Heck's' hopes for his puppies in the final stanza of Hamilton's poem, the homiletic tone of Mailie's speech to her son and daughter refers more directly to Ramsay's poem 'Lucky Spence's Last Advice' [Ramsay, i. 22–6] spoken by a dying bawd to her brothel girls 'black-Eyed *Bess* and mim Mou'd *Meg*' (l. 13). Lucky Spence is replete with sound (criminal) advice; 'CLEEK a' ye can be Hook or Crook, | Ryp ilky Poutch frae Nook to Nook' (ll. 31–2). Burns compounds the comic intertextuality here by having his 'sheep of credit' sound more like a respectable matron than an old bawd, as she warns her daughter against sexual skulduggery: 'O, may thou ne'er forgather up, | Wi' onie blastet, moorland *toop*; | But ay keep mind to moop an' mell, | Wi' sheep o' credit like thysel' (ll. 53–6). Mailie ends with a magnanimous promise to bequeath Hughoc her 'blather' (bladder), an instance of the traditional Scots 'mock-testimony' employed in Dunbar's *Testament of Mr Andro Kennedy* and surviving in old ballads such as *Lord Randal* and *Edward* [Kin. iii. 1018]. On condition, of course, that he faithfully transmits to his master her dying wish that the offending tether be instantly burnt. Exhausted by her homiletic energy, poor Mailie turns her head to the wall and expires with a last dying bleat.

The comic emphasis of Burns's pendent 'Poor Mailie's Elegy' has shifted from sententious sheep to grieving poet. It is interesting that in this later poem Burns characterizes himself as a 'bardie' rather than 'master' (his denomination in

'Death and Dying Words'; in the earlier, six-stanza draft of 'Poor Mailie's Elegy', he's 'Robin', an epithet which survives at line 46 of the published poem). As Robert Crawford notes, this is the first time that Burns described himself as a bardie, which 'allows him to remain at one with his local audience'.[17] As mentioned above, the pendent is composed in the habbie stanza of Fergusson's 'Elegy on the Death of Mr David Gregory'. Fergusson's opening lines 'Now mourn, ye college masters a'! | And frae your ein a tear let fa'[18] is brilliantly reworked (and largely Anglicized) by Burns as 'Lament in rhyme, lament in prose, | Wi' saut tears trickling down your nose' (ll. 1–2). But Burn's 'Elegy' now adopts a mock pathos quite distinct from the 'Bonnie Heck' model of 'The Death and Dying Words', with its anthropomorphic characterization of animal monologue. Mailie passes from being a refined matron (rather than a mendacious bawd) in sheep's clothing to a 'metonymical human', in Claude Lévi-Strauss's sense of the term.[19] In this new sentimental economy, Burns foregrounds Mailie's status as a 'pet' (in the usual modern, rather than the traditional Scots sense referred to above) rather than a potentially valuable commodity, just as his own identity has passed from being that of patriarchal 'master' to a 'bardie'. Burns takes pains to stress that he's mourning a companion rather than an item of farm stock:

> It's no the loss o' warl's gear,
> That could sae bitter draw the tear,
> Or mak our *Bardie*, dowie, wear
>     The mourning weed:
> He's lost a friend and neebor dear
>     In *Mailie* dead.
>
> Thro' a' the toun she trotted by him;
> A lang half-mile she could descry him;
> Wi' kindly bleat, when she did spy him,
>     She ran wi' speed:
> A friend mair faithfu' ne'er cam nigh him,
>     Than *Mailie* dead.    (ll. 7–18)

Beyond the mock bathos, there's a note of genuine affection in the second stanza, as the poet describes Mailie's fidelity and pleasure (that 'kindly bleat') in his presence. The sentimental note is developed in lines 25–30 as the melancholy bardie mentions the 'briny pearls' which spring from his eyes when he sees Mailie's 'livin image' in her ewe (ll. 25–30).

Like Christopher Smart's cat 'Jeoffrey', Shenstone's 'Lucy', Gilbert White's tortoise 'Timothy', Southey's spaniel 'Phillis', or Byron's Newfoundland 'Pilot',

---

[17] Robert Crawford, *Devolving English Literature*, 2nd edn. (Edinburgh: Edinburgh University Press, 2000), 93.

[18] McD ii. 1. ll. 1–2.

[19] Thomas, *Man and the Natural World*, 113.

Mailie's death results in her apotheosis as pet, her economic value now translated into affective nostalgia by an aspiring bardie who writes her elegy.[20] Unlike most other poetic pet-keepers of the long eighteenth century, as a farmer Burns's proximity to the animal world was by its nature economic and instrumental. Mailie's untimely death has taught him a severe lesson in improved animal husbandry: pedigree sheep should be allowed to graze free, not tethered to a post. But more important than enforcing any such stern moral, Mailie's untimely death clinches the affective relationship between man and beast, given that her economic potential as breeding stock is defunct, and now devolves entirely upon her 'toop' and 'yowe'. Burns the farmer is lost in the poet, who now aspires to the sentimental credit of a fashionable bereavement.

Keith Thomas notes that 'when cherished pets died, the bereaved owners might be deeply upset...in the eighteenth [and nineteenth] centur[ies] the remains of pets might be covered with an obelisk or sculptured tomb', like Byron's monument to his dog Pilot at Newstead.[21] The poet who in 'Epistle to J[ames] S[mith]' contemplates 'lay[ing]' himself with Thomas Gray's 'inglorious dead' (l. 59) now erects a durable, if homely, poetic monument to his strangled sheep, which incidentally serves as the first of a series of poems 'chiefly written in the Scottish dialect', and therefore a foundation for his sentimental consecration as a local and national poet. As Gerry Carruthers notes, the 'Poor Mailie' poems 'set out a terrain that becomes pronounced in Burns's poetic oeuvre, that of questioning the boundary between the spheres of nature and of humanity'.[22] And for all their 'slightness', these poems also reflect the progress of Burns's vocational self-fashioning from improving farmer to aspiring poet discussed in Chapter 3.

## THE RIGHTS OF MAGGIE

The boundary between man and beast further narrows in the next 'beastie' poem published in the Kilmarnock volume, 'The Auld Farmer's New-Year-morning Salutation to his Auld Mare, Maggie, on giving her the accustomed ripp of corn to hansel in the New-year' [K 75] (I'll refer to the poem as 'Auld Mare Maggie'). In many respects this eighteen-stanza poem is the most moving of Burns's animal sketches, a poem that (as Perkins points out) 'Robert Frost might have envied for its raciness and voice'.[23] There's hardly a trace of the mock pathos and literary sentimentalism of the 'Poor Mailie' poems and 'To a Mouse'. Unlike Burns's

---

[20] Ibid. 114. See also Kenyon-Jones, *Kindred Brutes*, 11–38. Gilbert Burns recalled that 'The Twa Dogs' originated in a memorial poem for Burns's beloved collie Luath entitled 'Stanzas to the Memory of a Quadruped Friend' [K iii. 1104].

[21] Thomas, *Man and the Natural World*, 118.

[22] Gerard Carruthers, *Robert Burns* (Tavistock: Northcote House, 2006), 10.

[23] Perkins, *Romanticism and Animal Rights*, 52.

sheep, dogs, mice, and lice, Maggie is neither a 'pet' nor a 'pest', but a working animal whose relationship with her human employer transcends species boundaries.

In its relative artlessness, 'Auld Mare Maggie' illuminates a more caring relationship between master and beast than the situation anatomized in 'Bonnie Heck', or indeed Burns's song 'The Auld Man's Mare's Dead' [K 585]. Here the auld mare dies sick and hungry because she's been cruelly exploited by her master. Burns often associated horses with rural demotic Scots, as in this case, with its tongue-twisting inventory of the defunct mare's ailments; 'She was cut-luggit, painch-lippit, | Steel-waimit, staincher-fittit, | Chanler-chaftit, lang-neckit, | Yet the brute did die' (ll. 1–4).[24] William Aiton jested that working horses, like the Scots people themselves, who lacked a standard, were 'much hurt' by 'the want of a FIXED LANGUAGE'; each of their masters employed a different 'lingo', so 'the poor animal would need a *glossary* before it can understand the orders it receives' [Aiton, p. 500]. Kilmarnock's placement of 'Auld Mare Maggie' immediately after 'Halloween' brings together the two poems in Kilmarnock that employ the densest rural Scots idiom, heightening the contrast with the mixed linguistic register that immediately follows in 'The Cotter's Saturday Night'.

Again employing the habbie stanza, 'Auld Mare Maggie' takes the familiar Burnsian form of an address by the 'Auld Farmer' to his 'Auld Mare' (the titular parallelism between man and horse develops gracefully throughout the poem), in whose working life he finds the measure for his own. Maggie, like her master, was once robust and energetic, a characteristic of the workhorses of the regions.[25] Carole McGuirk suggests that Maggie's height and strength mark her out as one of the new Clydesdale breed, but in this case (in contrast to 'Poor Mailie') it may be more significant that she's not an 'improved' breed at all, any more than that the 'auld Farmer' is a practitioner of the 'New Husbandry' [McGuirk, *BSP* p. 230].[26]

Gone here is the literary self-consciousness of the talking animals of 'Twa Dogs' and 'Death and Dying Words', replaced by the Farmer's deeply felt address to his superannuated fellow-labourer:

> Tho' now thou's dowie, stiff, an' crazy,
> An' thy auld hide as white's a daisie,

---

[24] Another instance of Burns's 'equestrian Scots' is his famous 1 June 1787 letter to William Nicol from Carlisle, written in full Scots, with its famous description of 'Jenny Geddes', his 'auld, ga'd Gleyde o' a meere': 'When ance here ringbanes and spavies, her crucks and cramps, are fairly soupl'd, she beets to, beets to, and ay the hindmost hour the tightest' [CL i. 120].

[25] Fullarton, p. 53, claims that 'the valuable, hardy breed of strong work horses, so remarkable, in [Ayrshire], and the adjoining county of Lanark, had been chiefly owing to some Flanders or Holstein stallions, brought over last century by one of the Dukes of Hamilton'.

[26] Sprott, *Robert Burns, Farmer*, 43, suggests that 'Burns's time in Ayrshire was just before the general spread of the big Clydesdale horse from Lanarkshire'.

> I've seen thee dappl't, sleek an' glaizie,
> A bonie gray:
> He should been tight that daur't to *raize* thee,
> Ance in a day.   (ll. 7–12)

The old farmer recalls how twenty-nine years before, the young filly Maggie, a dowry gift from his father-in-law, had proudly borne home his young bride from her wedding. He recalls Maggie's spirit and vigour, her jubilant skill at outstripping the gentry's 'droop-rumpl't' (short-rumped) hunters over a course of 'sax Scotch miles':

> When thou was corn't, an' I was mellow,
> We took the road ay like a Swallow:
> At *Brooses* thou had ne'er a fellow,[27]
> For pith an' speed;
> But ev'ry tail thou pay't them hollow,
> Whare'er thou gaed.   (ll. 49–54)

We might recall Burns's evocation of his limping muse as 'spavet Pegasus' who gathers speed and energy in 'Epistle to Davie' [K 51] lines 147–54, or the fantastical cosmic canter of the homesick 'Jenny Geddes' in 'Epistle to Hugh Parker', [K 222], lines 28–36: 'I'd heeze thee up a constellation, | To canter with the Sagitarre, | Or loup the ecliptic like a bar; | Or turn the pole like any arrow' (ll. 28–31).[28] The speed, strength, and regularity of the horse's hoof-beats, bonded into a single centaurian unity with her rider, aptly symbolized the poet's skilful fusion of language, rhythm, and metre.

But Maggie's greatest service to the 'auld Farmer' has been at the plough. Serving as the 'fittie-lan' or back left-hand horse in the four-animal plough-team still commonly employed in 1780s Ayrshire, she and her master could plough 'sax rood' (l. 65; an acre and a half) during one eight-hour working day in clear March weather. Burns's evocation of her 'pith an' pow'r' (l. 70) in pulling the heavy plough over 'sprittie knowes' acknowledges the hardship of working the high rigs and sloping, muddy, half-improved fields of Lochlie or Mossgiel. The old mare has been a prolific breeder, for as the Farmer proudly acknowledges, 'My Pleugh is now thy *bairn-time* a'; | Four gallant brutes, as e'er did draw' ('my plough team is now composed of your brood, four gallant horses . . .', ll. 85–6),[29] not to mention her other six foals sold for 'thretteen pund an' twa' each (£13. 2*d.*) (ll. 87–90), a hefty sum indeed when we recall that Robert's and Gilbert's annual allowance at Mossgiel was a mere £7.

---

[27] According to Burns's gloss to the 1787 volume, 'broose' is 'a race at a country wedding who shall first reach the bridegroom's house on returning from the church' (*Poems* [Edinburgh, 1787], 348).

[28] The source for ll. 422–6 in Byron's great equestrian poem, *Mazeppa*.

[29] For a detailed poetic description of Burns's own four-horse plough team at Mossgiel in Feb. 1786, see 'The Inventory' [K 86, ll. 5–27].

Although herself a dowry-gift, Maggie has brought financial rewards. But this poem isn't primarily concerned with the instrumental value of farm animals, any more than was 'Poor Mailie'. Existential rather than economic identification between man and beast wins out here over the profit margin: 'Monie a sair daurk we twa hae wrought, | An' wi' the weary warl' fought! | An' monie an *anxious day* I thought | We wad be beat! |Yet here to *crazy Age* we're brought, | Wi' something yet' (ll. 91–6). 'Wi something yet': the poem concludes with a reflection on the plight of superannuation in men and beasts alike. At one level this responds to the predicament of Hamilton of Gilbertfield's 'Bonnie Heck', an elderly hound condemned to death by a heartless master, the very moment that age has limited his utility. Here Burns underlines the theme of charity in the poem's titular 'hansel-gift' of a 'ripp of corn' (the farmer's customary hand-out bonus to his workers to welcome in the new year); it's sustained in the reference (at l. 75) to his giving 'thy *cog* a wee bit heap | Aboon the timmer' (filling the feed-bag above the rim) in times of winter hardship; and concludes, inspirationally, with a reflection on the entitlement of age to a share of provision:

> An' think na, my auld trusty *Servan*',
> That now perhaps thou's less deservin,
> An' thy *auld days* may end in starvin;
>          For my last fow,
> A heapet *Stimpart*, I'll reserve ane
>          Laid by for you.    (ll. 97–102)[30]

The 'rights of Maggie' as they emerge from Burns's poem are evidently quite distinct from the 'auld mare's' present ability to 'purchase' protection by dint of her continuing usefulness to man.[31] Anthropomorphized as an 'auld trusty *Servan*'', the Farmer's promise to provide for her in the final stanzas is impelled by a sense of her creaturely *entitlement* to charity. Adam Smith was willing to allow that 'those animals … that have been remarkably serviceable to their masters, become the object of a very lively gratitude'. Nonetheless, he still harboured some doubts on the grounds of species difference; 'they are still far from being perfect and complete objects, either of gratitude or resentment; and those passions still feel, that there is something wanting to their entire gratification'.[32] William Aiton, glossing Smith's view of charity as a form of sympathetic exchange, wrote conventionally that 'when a person, from a sense of duty,

---

[30]  As Kinsley indicates, in the glossary to the 1787 edition Burns defined 'fow'—or firlot—as a bushel, and 'stimpart' as 'the eighth part of a Westminster bushel'. The correct measure is actually 'the quarter of a peck, which was a quarter-firlot', but the point is that the Farmer sets aside a carefully regulated portion of his own limited provision to feed his old mare [Kin. iii. 1128]. Burns also uses 'stimpart' to measure horse fodder in the letter to Nichol [CL i. 120].

[31]  The gist of Frances Hutcheson's argument for animal rights. See *A System of Moral Philosophy*, 2 vols. (London, 1755), i. 314.

[32]  Smith, *Theory of Moral Sentiments*, 111–12.

contributes voluntarily to the relief of such as he knows to be really necessitous, and receives in return their warmest thanks, the minds of the giver and receiver are equally improved' [Aiton, p. 642]. As a dumb beast (albeit one who elicits strong demotic Scots from her master) Maggie remains silent, so we can never know whether or not she participates in this exchange: but, *contra* Smith (and Aiton), the old farmer's charity expresses an unconditional benevolence that doesn't look for any acknowledgement: although we might recall that his life with Maggie had begun with her status as a dowry gift.

It is significant that Burns seems more willing to countenance charity to dumb animals such as Maggie, where the only return is an unreciprocated or 'imperfect gratification', than *conditional* charity to humans on Smithian terms. This is a view shared by Wordsworth, in such poems as 'The Old Cumberland Beggar' and 'Simon Lee': in the former, Wordsworth's beggar shows not an ounce of gratitude to his benefactors (which, the poem makes clear, strengthens rather than weakens the charitable resolve of the villagers); and reacting to 'Simon Lee''s tearful thanks, the speaker of the latter poem exclaims, 'Alas! The gratitude of men | Has oftener left me mourning' (ll. 103–4).[33] As I've indicated in the previous chapter, the Sage in Burns's 'Man was made to Mourn' [K 64] seems oblivious to the claims of charity or welfare when he laments (once he has lost his 'usefulness to his kind', l. 36) that 'Age and Want, Oh! Il-matched pair! | Show man was made to mourn' (ll. 39–40). But the question is eclipsed by the poem's anger at the spectacle of a 'lordly fellow-worm' refusing an able-bodied man the right to work.

Poverty and the threat of ruin were or course palpable experiences for Burns, and as I've argued in Chapter 2, provide a linking thread in the 'Meliboean' subtext of Kilmarnock. The reluctance of 'honest Poverty' to accept welfare may have been linked to Burns's resentment of the fact that Scottish Poor Relief was controlled by the 'parish state', although this needn't imply that he was opposed in principle to private charity, however much he might have disliked the Smithian 'condition of gratitude'.[34] As with his 'independent' attitude to patronage, this reticence concerning welfare became a major theme in the ideology

---

[33] See David Simpson's discussion in *Wordsworth, Commodification and Social Concern: The Poetics of Modernity* (Cambridge: Cambridge University Press, 2008), pp. 17–53.

[34] This latter suggestion is borne out by Burns's Shandeyan 'execration of Poverty' in a 17 Jan. 1791 letter to Peter Hill: 'By thee, the venerable Ancient, though in thy invidious obscurity, grown hoary in the practice of every virtue under Heaven, now laden with years & wretchedness, implores from a stony-hearted son of Mammon whose sun of prosperity never knew a cloud, a little, little, aid to support his very existence, and is by him denied & insulted' [CL ii. 65]. The continuation of the passage has clear personal application. The *Canongate* editors note that this passage was published anonymously in *The Glasgow Advertiser* on 29 April–2 May 1791, associating it with a poem entitled 'Remember the Poor' (which they suggest is by Burns) published in the same paper on 27 January 1794, as part of a charitable appeal for the victims of the winter famine of 1793–4. To my eye, neither the poem's style, nor the direct appeal for charity at lines 35–42, seem characteristic of Burns [CG, pp. 483–7].

of the poet's posthumous reputation. Thomas Carlyle wrote admiringly in 1828, '[Burns] preferred self-help, on the humblest scale, to dependence and inaction, though with hope of far more splendid possibility' [*CH* p. 380]. As we'll see in discussing 'To a Mouse', it's ironic that Burns is closer to anticipating modern ideas of welfare entitlement in his animal poems than his attitudes to human poverty.

One final observation is due concerning 'the rights of Maggie'. No critic seems to have noticed that Burns's long title 'The Auld Farmer's New-Year-morning Salutation to his Auld Mare, Maggie, on giving her the accustomed ripp of corn to hansel in the New-year' alludes to the title of Sir Archibald Grant of Monymusk's *The Farmer's New-Year Gift to his Countrymen, Heritors, and Farmers, for the Year 1757*. Published in Aberdeen two years before Burns's birth, Grant's book was a pioneering (if homespun) manual of agricultural improvement, the celebrity of which was presumably sufficient for Burns to expect many of his readers to pick up the titular allusion.[35] Although the title doesn't appear in references to Burns's reading, it's possible that the book formed part of his father's small library, especially likely given William Burnes's north-eastern provenance and 'improving' disposition.

Despite Monymusk's supercilious assurance that a farmer's poverty revealed him to be 'ignorant or negligent, except in special cases of uncommon calamities',[36] the book takes special care to promote a spirit of cooperation between lairds and their tenants, underlined in the title. 'It is reciprocally to the interest of heritor and tenant', Grant wrote, 'to promote each other's advantage, and thereby cultivate the proper friendships, which should be betwixt such connections; therefore oppressive rents or services should not be imposed, nor reasonable ones refused; and all prudent encouragement should be given and taken for all reasonable improvement'.[37] This to some extent reflects an ideal, paternalistic discourse of improvement, defining relations between landowners and tenants in terms of reciprocal rights and duties. But as we saw in Chapter 1, it's a far cry from the reality of rack-renting and incipient financial ruin in Burns's Ayrshire. To read 'The Auld Farmer's Salutation' with reference to Grant's 'Farmer's New Year Gift' is to glimpse a huge irony underlying Burns's poem. The 'Auld Farmer's' promise to his 'Auld Mare' portrays a practice of benevolent paternalism between man and beast that in the human world is more honoured in the breach than in the observance. Grant speaks of 'friendship' between proprietor and tenant, the promotion of mutual advantage rather than a relationship of instrumental exploitation. Burns's poem relocates that social ideal in a paternalistic past (as McGuirk notes, 'The Auld Farmer' may be canvassing a notion of the

---

[35]  See James Handley, *The Agricultural Revolution in Scotland* (Glasgow, 1963), 14.

[36]  Sir Archibald Grant of Monymusk, *The Farmer's New-Year Gift to his Countrymen, Heritors, and Farmers, for the Year 1757* (Aberdeen, 1757), 2.

[37]  Ibid. 2.

*paternal* as well as the patriarchal) [McGuirk, *BSP* 230],[38] and in a cross-species relationship, rather than in the human present of the agrarian capitalist nexus.


## OF MICE AND MEN

'To a Mouse, On turning her up in her Nest, with the Plough, November, 1785' [K 69] is justly hailed as Burns's greatest animal poem, possibly his greatest poem in the lyric mode. Alongside its companion poem, 'To a Mountain Daisy, On turning one down, with the Plough, in April 1786' [K 92] it did much to create the iconic image of the ploughman poet, an image consolidated by Gilbert's recollections in a 1798 letter to Dr Currie: 'The verses to the "Mouse and Mountain Daisy" were composed on the occasions mentioned, and while the author was holding the plough: I could point out the particular spot where each was composed. Holding the plough was a favourite situation for Robert for poetic compositions, and some of his best verses were produced while he was at that exercise' [Currie, iii. 383–4]. Such was the power of Gilbert's contribution to the Burns cult that visitors to Mossgiel are still shown the field where the 'Heaven-taught ploughman' turned up the mouse's nest.

In their use of what McGuirk terms 'the sentimental structure of benevolent condescension',[39] both 'To a Mouse' and 'Mountain Daisy' differ from other animal poems in the Kilmarnock volume, like 'The Death and Dying Words of . . . Poor Mailie' and 'Auld Mare Maggie'. 'To a Mouse', as we'll see, expresses a sincerely felt, because potentially shared, sympathy with the victims of 'man's dominion', whether they be mice or men. In 'To a Mountain Daisy' the sympathy is more strained because its object is, conventionally, a wild flower, so that Burns is driven to a rather contrived employment of the pathetic fallacy.

Gilbert Burns's comments about the composition of the two poems obscures the fact that both are very 'literary' poems; whereas 'To a Mouse' successfully absorbs its sources, 'To a Mountain Daisy' sinks under the burden of literary self-consciousness. So much has been written in the last twenty years about male Romantic poets appropriating the work of female precursors that it's odd that so little has been said about 'To a Mouse''s major source, Anna Barbauld's well-known lyric 'The Mouse's Petition to Dr Priestley Found in the Trap where he had been Confined all Night' (although David Perkins has made a useful start in his study *Romanticism and Animal Rights*.)[40] Although Burns nowhere mentions

---

[38] McGuirk here suggests that it 'may be the most successful of the poet's attempts in the years following William Burnes's death to capture something of his upright father's voice and values'.

[39] *Robert Burns and the Sentimental Era* (Athens, Ga.: University of Georgia Press), 7.

[40] *Romanticism and Animal Rights*, 7–13. Perkins makes no claims for a direct influence. Crawford briefly mentions the resemblance between ll. 41–2 and ll. 45–6 of Barbauld's 'Mouse's Petition' in a footnote [*BPS* 167].

'The Mouse's Petition', he elsewhere pays a tribute to Barbauld's 'sweet song', dubbing her the modern 'Sappho' in his 'Sketch' or 'Poem on Pastoral Poetry', discussed in Chapter 2 [K 82]. The volume of Barbauld's *Poems* in which 'The Mouse's Petition' was published appeared in 1773, and its popularity can be gauged by the fact that a fifth edition had been published by 1777.[41] It seems to have been one of the most popular magazine poems of the 1770s, appearing (for example) in the issue of Ruddiman's *Edinburgh Weekly Magazine* for February 1773 alongside Robert Fergusson's 'A Tavern Elegy'.[42]

Some obvious formal differences between the two poems may have thrown critics off the scent. 'The Mouse's Petition', written in common ballad form (with four-line stanzas of alternating iambic tetrameter and trimeter) ventriloquizes the mouse's plea to Dr Priestley; it's a gently facetious dramatic monologue, and, given the animal speaker, closer to Burns's 'Death and Dying Words of Poor Mailie' than the sentimental address of 'To a Mouse'. Like Burns's mouse poem, though, Barbauld's expresses sympathy with an animal victim of human oppression; in the tradition of Yorick's famous apostrophe to the starling in Sterne's *Sentimental Journey*, it miniaturizes the plight of the human captive. Barbauld's mouse (evidently better endowed with the power of foresight than Burns's) 'tremble[s] at th' approaching morn, | Which brings impending fate' (ll. 7–8) and urges, against the human 'tyrant': 'Let not thy strong oppressive force | A free-born mouse detain' (ll. 11–12).[43]

Given that the mouse has been trapped 'for the sake of making experiments with different kinds of air' (as the poem's revised title in the 1792 edition informs us) its trepidation is understandable: Barbauld alludes to her friend Dr Priestley's celebrated experiments which resulted in his discovery of oxygen, as described in *Experiments and Observations on Different Kinds of Air* (1774–86). Priestley believed that his experiments with the air pump would 'extirpate all terror and prejudice' and, writing as a Rational Dissenter, that 'the English hierarchy (if there be anything unsound in its constitution) . . . has equal reason to tremble even at an air pump, or an electrical machine'.[44] But it's not only the English hierarchy who tremble, Barbauld suggests; Priestley's zealous faith in improvement and the 'rapid progress of knowledge' look rather less edifying from the perspective of the mouse, who is about to be sacrificed to science in his air pump.

Burns translates Barbauld's captive mouse and the impending Priestleyian air-pump experiment into a pastoral idiom, as the farmer's ploughshare cuts through

---

[41] In addition to the thematic connections discussed below, ll. 43–8 of Burns's 'Epistle to Davie' paraphrase ll. 23–4 of Barbauld's poem, where her mouse begs his captor 'Let nature's commoners enjoy | The common gifts of heaven.'

[42] *Edinburgh Magazine*, 18 Feb. 1773, p. 241.

[43] I cite the 1773 text published in Roger Londsale, *Eighteenth-Century Women Poets* (Oxford: Oxford University Press, 1990), 302–3.

[44] Quoted in Jenny Uglow, *The Lunar Men* (London: Faber & Faber, 2003), 76–7.

the mouse's 'wee-bit housie', leaving it homeless and hungry in the winter landscape. In both cases however the creature is victim of 'improvement': it's often forgotten that despite Burns's sympathy for the mouse, his plough is the agent of its ruination, a fact underlined by the poem's title. Thomas Crawford perceptively argued that 'To a Mouse' is 'linked by subtle and tenuous threads to the preoccupations of the first epistles, and to such poems as "Man was made to Mourn", as well as to the hatred of economic exploitation which fills the "Address of Beelzebub"; it too, can only be fully understood in the context of the Scottish Agrarian Revolution' [Crawford, *BPS* 164]. Although the fate of Burns's 'cleared' mouse is rather more open-ended than Barbauld's (the latter being in the unhappy situation of a condemned criminal on the eve of execution), the violence of its fate is deftly realized in the lines 'Till crash! The cruel *coulter* past | Out thro' thy cell' (ll. 29–30). As well as being the *agent* of improvement, however, Burns is also, potentially, its victim. At the time of publishing (if not of writing) this poem, his 'Meliboean' fate appeared to be forced emigration to Jamaica, a result of mounting debts and bad harvests, as well as the Jean Armour debacle.

A major contrast between Barbauld's and Burns's poems lies in register and address: employing a tender and solicitous Scots diction, exploiting the homiletic potential of the habbie stanza to the full, 'To a Mouse' is rich in naturalistic observation, its diction softened by sibilance and diminutives. It both responds to and reassures the terrified petitioner of Barbauld's poem in its switch from colloquial Scots to Augustan English in the first two stanzas:

> Wee, sleeket, cowran, tim'rous *beastie*,[45]
> O, what a panic's in thy breastie!
> Thou need na start awa sae hasty,
>> Wi' bickering brattle!
> I wad be laith to rin an' chase thee,
>> Wi' murd'ring *pattle*!
>
> I'm truly sorry Man's dominion
> Has broken Nature's social union,
> An' justifies that ill opinion,
>> Which makes thee startle,
> At me, thy poor, earth-born companion,
>> An' *fellow mortal*!   (ll. 1–11)

Burns's source for 'Man's dominion' and 'Nature's Social Union' is the third epistle of Pope's *Essay on Man*, descriptive of the state of Nature when 'Man walk'd with beast, joint tenant of the shade; | The same his table, and the same

---

[45] Ritter traced the structure of this famous line to Matthew Prior's rendering of Hadrian's 'animula, vagula, blandula', namely, 'Poor little, pretty, fluttering thing', adapted by Green, Fielding, and Oldys. 'Thus the English neo-classic tradition has made its own peculiar contribution to one of the best-known lines in Scottish vernacular poetry' [Crawford, *BPS* 165].

his bed; | No murder clothed him, and no murder fed'.[46] In this ecological golden age before the rise of man's 'Conquest, Superstition and Tyranny', 'When Love was Liberty, and Nature Law',[47] rational man imitated the instinctual harmony of the animal kingdom, including 'all [its] forms of social union'.[48] Burns's narrator apologizes to the mouse for the fall from grace embodied in the progress of civilization (notably in this case the agricultural economy) but reassures the 'tim'rous beastie' that *this* farmer at least is willing to spare the life of a 'fellow mortal', even if most would have destroyed it with 'murdr'ing *pattle*' (l. 6). It is a tribute to Burns's mastery of register that his apology retains a colloquial lightness of touch, and doesn't sink under the freight of its Popean allusion.

Although as a tenant farmer Burns was disqualified from field sports by the draconian eighteenth-century Game Laws (he seems only to have possessed a gun when he joined the Excise Office), he abstained from poaching, and was consistently opposed to shooting animals, especially out of season.[49] His views are clearly stated in his poem 'On Seeing a Wounded Hare limp by me, which a Fellow had just shot at' [K 259] written during his Ellisland period. In a letter enclosing this poem sent to Patrick Miller in June 1789, Burns described the incident which gave rise to his poem, the wounding of a parent hare during the leveret-raising season, as 'not only a sin against the letter of the law, but likewise a deep crime against the *morality of the heart.* We are all equally creatures of some Great Creator'. He fulminated against the flagrant 'power which one creature of us has to amuse himself by and at the expense of another's misery, torture & death' [CL i. 418].[50] Yet Burns had no scruples in employing a poaching metaphor to describe his seduction of Elizabeth Paton in the 'Epistle to J[ohn] R[ankine]' [K 47].[51] Opposition to blood sports was an aspect of the fashionable culture of sensibility, as well as an ethical stick with which to beat the sporting gentry, but despite these lapses the poet seems to have held a genuine aversion to killing animals for pleasure.

Burns's notion of the 'morality of the heart' binding humans to the animal world raises questions of charity and 'the moral economy of provision' that I've

---

[46] 'Essay on Man', iii. 4 ll. 152–4 in *Pope's Poetical Works*, ed. Herbert Davis, with intro. by Pat Rogers (Oxford: Oxford University Press, 1978), 263.

[47] Ibid. iii. 4. 208.

[48] Ibid. iii. 4. 179.

[49] See his beautiful song, 'Now Westlin Winds, and Slaught'ring Guns' [K 2], first published near the end of the Kilmarnock volume, with its debt both to Pope's *Windsor Forest* (especially Pope's line 'with slaught'ring Guns th'unweary'd Fowler roves'), and Thomson's *Autumn*. In the version published by George Thomson in *Select Scottish Airs* in 1799, the opening line was changed from the Popean 'slaught'ring guns' to 'sportsman's guns' to avoid offence [*CG*, p. 154].

[50] On contemporary attitudes to hunting see Perkins, *Romanticism and Animal Rights*, 64–88.

[51] ''Twas ae night lately, in my fun, | I gaed a rovin wi' the gun, | An' brought a *Paitrick* to the *grun*, | A bonie *hen*' (ll. 37–40). In 'Tam Samson's Elegy' [K 117], added to the Edinburgh edition of *Poems* in 1787, Burns poked affectionate fun at the 'worthy old Sportsman' who was also a fellow Mason.

already broached. He returns to this theme in the often overlooked third stanza of 'To a Mouse', which, incidentally, draws directly on the language of Barbauld's 'Mouse's Petition'. Unlike the other beasties so far considered, mice were vermin, pests rather than pets, and accordingly fair game for the farmer, especially considering the fact that they were prolific breeders and prodigious consumers of grain. In his *History of the Earth* (1779), Oliver Goldsmith noted that, 'fearful by nature, but familiar by necessity [the mouse] attends upon mankind, and comes an unbidden guest to his most delicate entertainments. Fear and necessity seem to regulate all its motions.' He described the 'long-tailed field-mouse' as 'extremely voracious, and hurtful in gardens and young nurseries, where they are killed in great numbers. However, their fecundity quickly repairs the destruction.' Goldsmith was rather more generous in describing its cousin the *short*-tailed field-mouse (presumably the species addressed in Burns's poem): 'this, as well as the former [species], are remarkable for laying up provision against winter; and Mr Buffon assures us they sometimes have a store of above a bushel at a time'.[52] The mouse's proximity to, and dependence upon man as a source of provision, as well as its almost human power of hoarding winter stores, are important issues in both poems under scrutiny here.

Here are the sixth to eighth stanzas of Barbauld's 'The Mouse's Petition':

> Thy scattered gleanings of a feast
> My scanty meals supply;
> But if thine unrelenting heart
> That slender boon deny,
>
> The cheerful light, the vital air,
> Are blessings widely given;
> Let nature's commoners enjoy
> The common gifts of heaven.
>
> The well-taught philosophic mind
> To all compassion gives;
> Casts round the world an equal eye,
> And feels for all that lives.   (ll. 17–28)

Barbauld's mouse pleads the 'slender boon' of entitlement to glean crumbs from Priestley's table. If that's denied by the philosopher's 'unrelenting heart', then at least the creature deserves liberty as one of 'nature's commoners'.[53] Moving to a more persuasive argument (the mouse is after all thieving vermin, more clearly stated in Burns's poem than in Barbauld's, for reasons of address), this well-informed rodent petitioner appeals to Priestley's pantheistic doctrine of

---

[52] Oliver Goldsmith, *History of the Earth, and Animated Nature.* 2nd edn., 8 vols. (London, 1779), iv. 74–5.

[53] See note 41 above.

animated matter, in order to exhort compassion for 'all that lives', and (at line 33, alluding to the doctrine of metempsychosis) admonishing him, 'Beware, lest in the worm you crush | A brother's soul you find'.[54] (This might have inspired Blake's adage 'the cut worm forgives the plough' in *The Marriage of Heaven and Hell.*) The mouse concludes with a blessing on Priestley's 'hospitable board' and, in the final stanza, points the moral of 'do as you would be done by': 'So, when unseen destruction lurks, | Which mice like men may share, | May some kind angel clear thy path, | And break the hidden snare' (ll. 45–8).

Although Barbauld's poem is itself a tour de force of sentimental mock-seriousness, it's eclipsed by the pithy, vernacular brilliance of Burns's 'To a Mouse'. Take Burns's development of Barbauld's reference to the 'scattered gleanings of a feast' in the third stanza, responding to the strictures of eighteenth-century naturalists such as Goldsmith (as well as time-honoured practices of agricultural pest control) in acknowledging the claims of the mouse's 'bare life' against the statutory crime of theft:

> I doubt na, whyles, but thou may *thieve*;
> What then? poor beastie, thou maun live!
> A *daimen-icker* in a *thrave*
>     'S a sma' request:
> I'll get a blessin wi' the lave,
>     An' never miss't! (ll. 13–18)

'*Daimen-icker* in a *thrave*' refers to the portion of the farmer's corn here 're-quested' by the mouse as a form of charitable gleaning, resembling the 'stimpart' measure allocated by the farmer to 'Auld Maggie'. Contrasting with Buffon's account of prodigious hoarding cited above, Burns glosses this densely colloquial and agricultural idiom as 'an ear of corn now and then'.[55] Whether or not one believes that the mouse possesses natural rights like a human, Burns describes it as a 'poor, earth-born companion, | An' *fellow mortal!*' (ll. 11–12). As Perkins points out, 'etymologically, the mouse is a companion (*com-panis*) in that it eats the speaker's bread—or grain. It is a companion because it lives in the same place and undergoes similar experiences.'[56] The 'right of commons' here cuts across species boundaries and includes the permission to glean, participation in a moral rather than an exchange economy.

---

[54] Perkins, 11, points out that ll. 37–8 of Barbauld's poem questions whether animals possess immortal souls.

[55] *Poems*, 350. 'Daimen' means 'rare, occasional'; 'icker' is an ear of corn, derived from Old English 'ear'; 'thrave' is 'a measure of cut grain'. Kinsley quotes Sir John Sinclair's later 1812 usage; 'a threave of wheat, consisting of 28 sheaves, each sheaf measuring 30 inches round.' [Kin. iii. 1093]. ''S a sma' request' indeed! See Pittock, *Scottish and Irish Romanticism*, 154, for further discussion of the linguistic connotations.

[56] Perkins, *Romanticism and Animal Rights*, 10.

The third stanza's final lines, 'I'll get a blessing wi' the lave, | An never miss it!' acknowledge that the fractional share of corn gifted to the mouse will consecrate or 'bless' the remainder of the farmer's harvest. Burns's lines allude implicitly to the text of Deuteronomy 24: 19, 'When thou cuttest down thine harvest in thy field, and hast forgot a sheaf in the field, thou shalt not go again to fetch it: it shall be for the stranger, for the fatherless, and for the widow: that the LORD thy God may bless thee in all the work of thine hands.' In the Old Testament this prefigures Boaz's allowance to the widowed Moabite Ruth who has been forced to leave her native land by famine: 'she gleaned in the field until even, and beat out that she had gleaned: and it was almost an ephah of barley' (Ruth 2: 17). Boaz's permission to Ruth (soon to be his wife) leads to a very considerable future 'blessing' in the birth of Obed, ancestor of King David, and of course, the line of Jesus Christ.[57]

Burns the farmer takes poetic licence in rejecting a commonsense view of pest control, but not just in order to make a sentimental point about compassion for animals. The poem also takes a leaf from Virgil's book in comparing small things to great ('si parva licet componere magnis': *Georgics*, 4. 176.) In so doing it turns against the current thinking of agricultural improvers, for whom gleaning represented the superstitious prejudices of the bad old husbandry (perhaps also underlining Burns's employment of the archaic Ayrshire idiom of 'daimen-icker'). Col. William Fullarton's view is symptomatic in approving current harvesting practice in Ayrshire: 'the stubble is cut extremely short, and no corn is left to encourage gleaners and other pilferers' [Fullarton, p. 29]. Wordsworth's poem 'Goody Blake and Harry Gill' addressed the same question in another context, respecting Goody's (thwarted) sense of entitlement to winter fuel; Burns's 'blessing' is experienced by the avaricious Harry Gill in Wordsworth's poem as a curse. Attitudes to gleaning were also changing fast in late eighteenth-century England, as poor relief was increasingly institutionalized along the work-house system attacked by Wordsworth in 'The Cumberland Beggar'.[58] In Scotland, as we've seen, charity was still largely controlled by the Kirk, although increasingly assessment rendered welfare statutory in line with the English model.

Like many of Burns's best poems, 'To a Mouse' has a winter setting; and although the episode to which its title alludes occurs in November, 'bleak *December's winds* ensuin', | Baith snell an' keen! (ll. 23–4). This is the winter ploughing, and the harvest has long since been taken in. Despite the benevolent

---

[57] Note here the parallel discourse of measurement, signifying the careful allocation of the moral economy, Burns's 'daimen icker in a thrave' to Ruth's 'ephah of barley'.

[58] The *Monthly Reviewer* departed from the spirit of poetical charity by recommending that Goody 'should have been relieved out of the two millions annually allowed by the state to the poor of this country, not by the plunder of an individual'. See 'Goody Blake and Harry Gill', in William Wordsworth and Samuel Taylor Coleridge, *Lyrical Ballads*, ed. R. L. Brett and A. R. Jones, 2nd edn. (London: Routledge, 1991), 54, 325.

farmer's permission to the mouse to glean an occasional ear of corn in a stook, gleaning is of course a seasonal entitlement, and now it's simply too late in the year. The pathos of the mouse's predicament is that its winter shelter and its grain store have been dispersed by the plough, and without 'foggage green' amongst the dry stubble there's no hope of reconstruction or replacement. This introduces a darker mood into the poem, exposing the farmer's offer of charity as being really an empty gesture (even if a farmer's charity to a mouse could be considered a serious proposition). The sole recourse for the farmer is to nurture pity, or maybe, as we'll see in the final stanza, sympathetic self-pity.

In a far more subtle manner than 'To a Mountain Daisy', the reflexive turn taken at the end of 'To a Mouse' incrementally transforms the mouse's sudden de-housing into a story about human eviction, although as McGuirk indicates (and in contrast to its sister poem), 'Burns establishes his mouse as a normal mouse before turning it to sentimental purposes'.[59] More precisely, before the poet discovers an image of his own fate in the mouse's ruin, its animal predicament is very gently anthropomorphized and translated into the contemporary context of agricultural clearance. The mouse which 'cozie here, beneath the blast . . . thought to dwell' is 'now . . . turn'd out, for a' thy trouble, | But house or hald, | To thole the Winter's *sleety dribble*, | An' *cranreuch* cauld!' (ll. 31–6). (The gaelic loan-word 'cranreuch' here adds a powerful touch of locality to the poem.)

In his penultimate stanza, Burns deftly reworks Barbauld's homiletic, 'So, when unseen destruction lurks, | Which mice like men may share', into the now proverbial lines, 'The best-laid schemes o' *Mice* an' *Men*, | Gang aft agley, | An' lea'e us nought but grief an' pain, | For promis'd joy!' (ll. 41–2). The poet's identification with the Mouse's homelessness is a triumph of compression, compared with the rather laborious metamorphosis of the crushed daisy into (by turns) an 'artless Maid' and suffering 'Bard', over several stanzas of the latter poem. The idiomatic compression of 'To a Mouse' results from its skilful use of full Scots diction, whereas 'To a Mountain Daisy' applies a sprinkling of Scots words to a framework of neo-Augustan English ('Alas! Its no thy neebor sweet, | The bonie *Lark*, companion meet!', ll. 7–8). This doubtless explains why the latter poem held such an appeal to the Edinburgh critics; Henry Mackenzie singled out these of 'Mountain Daisy' as 'truly pastoral . . . mark[ing] the pencil of the poet, which delineates Nature with the precision of intimacy, yet with the delicate colouring of beauty and taste' [*CH* p. 69].

The final stanza of 'To a Mouse' suddenly exposes the poet in the nakedness of his self-pity, like the homeless mouse shivering in the cleared stubble, although it's done with a light touch. Burns concludes 'To a Mouse':

[59] *Sentimental Era*, 9.

Still, art thou blest, compared Wi' *me*!
The *present* only toucheth thee:
But Och! I *backward* cast my e'e,
    On prospects drear!
An' *forward*, tho' I canna see,
    I *guess* an' *fear*!    (ll. 43–8)

As McGuirk points out, this is rather spoilt by the contradiction between the mouse's vain 'foresight' or 'best-laid schemes' (as stated at ll. 39 and 41) and the claim that she's touched by the 'present' alone.[60] The return to 'blest' (or 'blessing') in the first line of the final stanza casts a bleak retrospective light on the farmer's 'blessing wi' the lave' at line 17. Not only is too late in the season for the mouse's plight to be relieved by a '*daimen-icker* in a *thrave*', it's also too late for the ploughman either to give, or (by extension) receive, charity. The mouse's blessing is now strictly relative to the speaker's, which is to say that it isn't really a blessing at all.

Although this last stanza risks defusing the poem's effect by moving from compassion to self-pity, it's artistically important for Burns to break the analogy between mice and men at the end.[61] After all, it's a post-lapsarian poem in which 'Man's dominion | Has broken Nature's social union', and therefore line 12's celebration of a compassion based on shared creaturely existence can only be momentary. Death has entered Arcadia, the old Scottish agricultural order with its moral economy of provision has felt the 'coulter crash' of improvement. The neatly elliptical evocation of future ruination ('I *guess* an' *fear'*) conjures the poet's troubled consciousness in lonely separation from both animal and human worlds, now lacking even the compensatory companionship of a 'brother in misfortune' like Davie Sillar in Burns's epistle. It also foreshadows the prospect of ruin for Burns the tenant farmer, at the end of the poem exposed as the 'spoiler spoiled', for as we've seen, no claim on human charity is ever lodged in Burns's poetic universe. But the last stanza still compares well with the heavy, enfolding allegory of 'To a Mountain Daisy', which (with its allusion to Young's *Night Thoughts*) [K iii. 1174] has 'Stern Ruin's *plough-share*' turning over the clod and burying the poet in an earthy furrow-grave. (l. 51). This mood picks up the stilted English graveyard idiom of the group of poems ('To Ruin', 'Winter, A Dirge', and 'A Prayer, in the Prospect of Death') composed during Burns's melancholy flax-dressing sojourn in Irvine in 1781–2, poems that appear in a

---

[60] *Sentimental Era*, 9. Kinsley notes an echo of Johnson's *Rasselas* here [K iii. 1093], but there's also an allusion to Smith's *Theory of Moral Sentiments*, pt. 1 ch. 1 l. 12, 6th edn., ed. Knut Haakonssen (Cambridge: Cambridge University Press, 2002), 15–16.

[61] Perkins, *Romanticism and Animal Rights*, 12–13, 'wish[es] that Burns had not written the stanza. In it the superior claims to be worse off than the inferior,' thereby converting a socio-political analysis of the relationship between humans and animals (as well as between the rich and poor) into a tragic vision of existence.

dark cluster halfway through the Kilmarnock volume. Yet here, in the act of contemplating his own fate in that of the creature he has dispossessed, the ploughman rehearses the sentimental surplus that foreshadows his alternative vocation as poet.


## 'TO A LOUSE' AND UPWARD MOBILITY

Despite being described by Kinsley as 'a minor triumph of whimsy' [Kin. iii. 1147] 'To a Louse, On seeing one on a Lady's Bonnet at Church' [K 83] is only 'minor' to the extent that its louse/object represents a minuscule point on Burns's diminishing scale of animal life. It is both an ambitious poem and a poem about ambition, ascending from its minor register to cast a deeply satirical eye over the social totality, as expressed in its closing, Smithian appeal to an 'internal spectator': 'O wad some Pow'r the giftie gie us | *To see oursels as others see us*!' (ll. 43–4). By contrast to the pets, pests, and 'metonymic humans' surveyed so far in this chapter, the louse is a nightmare beastie, universally loathed, the object of proverbial disdain.[62] Although Burns once again employs the trusty habbie stanza, the staccato interrogative of his opening lines ('HA! Whare ye gaun, ye crowlan ferlie! | Your impudence protects you sairly') announces a shift away from the condescending trochees of 'Wee, sleeket, cowran, tim'rous *beastie*, | O what a panic's in thy breastie!'

According to Goldsmith's *History of the Earth*, the louse outdid even the toad, serpent, spider, or beetle as an object of human revulsion: 'while all wonder at the strangeness of each other's aversions, they all seem to unite in their dislike to the Louse, and regard it as their natural and most nauseous enemy'.[63] Goldsmith's microscopic description of the 'hermaphroditic' louse still has the power to turn the stomach, with its oblong head, hard, transparent skin, antennae covered with bristly hair, ruddy claws, and cloven tail, 'the whole resembling clear parchment, and, when roughly pressed, cracking with a noise'.[64] If the mouse is a bold hoarder and timid feeder, the louse simply gluts itself on the blood of its host: 'When the louse feeds, the blood is seen to rush, like a torrent, into the stomach; and its greediness is so great, that the excrements contained in the intestines are ejected at the same time, to make room for this new supply.'[65] It is a parasitic machine for feeding and excreting, even taking both its colour and its shape from the blood with which it gorges itself, yet 'it most frequently suffers from its gluttony, since it gorges to such a degree, that it is crushed to pieces by the slightest impression.'[66] At the risk of forgetting the comical and satirical frame of

---

[62] As in 'Address to the Deil', where the witch's 'caintrip wit' makes the 'gudeman' impotent, rendering his *warklum* ('tool')'no worth a louse' [K 76 ll. 64–5].

[63] *History of the Earth*, vii. 270.

[64] Ibid. 271.          [65] Ibid.          [66] Ibid. 273.

Burns's poem, the louse exemplifies Julia Kristeva's notion of 'the not-self' or 'abject' in *The Powers of Horror*, as a consumer of blood and distributor of excrement, the creature is 'what is permanently thrust aside in order to live'.[67] Its loathsome traits gloss Burns's flyting Scots diction in lines 7–8 'Ye ugly, creepan, blastet wonner, | Detested, shunn'd, by saunt an' sinner.' There's also something *spectacular* about the repugnant louse, captured by Burns's epithets 'crowlan ferlie' (l. 1; a 'ferlie' is a curiosity, a marvel) and 'blastet wonner' (l. 7) ('wonder'), and it's consequently the louse's spectacular ascent of Jenny's expensive 'Lunardi' bonnet which provides the poem's central drama.

Like other eighteenth-century poets Burns was fascinated by miniature Lilliputian worlds, exemplified in Stephen Duck's poem 'On Mites. To a Lady', published in *Poems on Several Occasions* (1738): 'The little Things, elate with Pride, | Strut to and fro, from Side to Side: | In tiny Pomp, and pertly vain, | Lords of their pleasing Orb, they reign.'[68] Margaret Anne Doody reads Duck's poem as an instance of an 'animal or insect charivari, the creatures monstrously acting so very humanly'.[69] Like the courtiers of Lilliputia, Duck's mites enact at microscopic level the follies and vanities of the Court of St James, pompously oblivious of their lowly position in the chain of being, and their parasitic dependence on rotten cheese.[70] There's clearly something of this in Burns's 'To a Louse', although the mites' petty vanity in Duck's poem belongs as much to the hair-tossing 'Jenny' as the louse itself.

Another source closer to home is Robert Fergusson's 'The Bugs' (1773), a poem which also hails the horrors of the microscopic insect world [McD ii. 146 ll.17–20]. Fergusson's poem describes an ecological disaster afflicting Edinburgh during the reign of James IV, whereby deforestation caused an infestation of the city by a hoard of dispossessed bugs. The bugs have little respect for class distinctions, although the poem implies that the wind is more likely to blow them into the 'domes and palaces' of the rich than the cottages of the poor. [McD ii. 147 ll. 46–58]. The poem perversely eroticizes infestation by imagining male lovers envying the bug's free access to their beloved's intimate places, the 'deep carnation' bite 'midst the lilies of fair CHLOE's breast' (ll. 80–1). In a witty closing

---

[67] Julia Kristeva, *The Powers of Horror: An Essay on Abjection*, trans. Leon S. Roudiez (New York: Columbia University Press, 1982), 3.

[68] Quoted in Margaret Anne Doody, *The Daring Muse: Augustan Poetry Reconsidered* (Cambridge: Cambridge University Press), 129. See also Susan Stewart, *On Longing: Narratives of the Miniature, the Gigantic, the Souvenir, the Collection* (Durham, NC: Duke University Press, 1993), 37–69.

[69] Doody, *Daring Muse*, 129. She defines the Augustan poetic *topos* of 'charivari' as 'a mixture of the celebratory and the violent, enacted by a crowd', often a sort of 'communal corrective or mockery'.

[70] There's no evidence that Burns knew Duck's poem, but the fact that he addresses his insect charivari 'to a Lady' (implying that she of all creatures might benefit from a lesson in *vanitas*) accords well with the Louse's affront to Jenny's lady-like pride. Although 'strutting' is a common indicator of pomposity, there's possibly a verbal echo of Duck's mites, 'Strut[ing] to and fro, from Side to Side', in Burns's 'I canna say but ye strunt rarely | Owre *gawze* and *lace*' (ll. 3–4).

passage, Fergusson parodies the pastoral trope of *beata illis*, the 'Happy Man': 'Happy the Bug, whose unambitious views | To gilded pomp ne'er tempt him to aspire' (ll. 139–40). Securely embedded in the hovels of the poor, the unambitious bug avoids the fate of the 'Bug of State', brushed away by Chambermaids or fatally dosed with 'Oliphant's' insecticide powders (l. 147).

Whereas Fergusson's bugs promiscuously infest rich and poor alike, Burns's upwardly mobile parasite is concerned exclusively with seeking richer pastures. This leading idea of the louse's social presumption may have been inspired by another, exactly contemporaneous, louse poem. As far as I'm aware, no commentator on Burns's poems has connected it with Peter Pindar (nom de plume of John Wolcot), 'The Lousiad: an Heroi-Comic Poem', a bold exercise in *lèse-majesté* which would doubtless have appealed to Burns. The first canto of this four-canto poem was published in 1785 and proved so popular that it was in a sixth edition by 1786, and sold tens of thousands of copies. Wolcot produced three more cantos over the next few years while making substantial changes to the first. Given that 'To a Louse' was probably composed at the end of 1785, it's quite possible that Burns was familiar with at least 'The Lousiad''s first canto, which narrates the poem's principal episode, elaborated in subsequent cantos.[71]

In his 'Address to the Reader', Wolcot jokes about 'The Lousiad''s superiority to other famous poems in the mock-heroic genre: Homer's *Batrachomyomachia*, Boileau's *Lutrin*, Garth's *Dispensary*, and Pope's *Rape of the Lock*.[72] Canto I describes how, to his horror and indignation, George III discovers a louse sprawling on his plate during dinner. Automatically assuming that it had fallen from the hair of his kitchen staff (of course ruling out the royal family) the king resolves to 'snip from cooks the honours of each pate; | The *humble scullions*, with their tails of pig, | Shall lose their coxcomb locks, and wear a wig.'[73] This edict foments a palace revolution as the kitchen staff join ranks, and the 'Cook-Major' resolves that to 'no KING on earth shall crop my locks'.[74] The anti-monarchical satire is only mitigated at the end, when the cooks prepare to draw up 'a *sensible* PETITION' in the hope that the king's 'gracious heart may melt away like butter'.[75]

Wolcot's poem probably provided Burns with no more than the germ of the idea for 'To a Louse'. In contrast to 'A Dream' (which I've also linked with Wolcot's satire), Burns here burlesques the upwardly-mobile, bourgeoise Jenny rather than the King. Mauchline Kirk, rather than the court, is the exemplary site for social spectatorship, with its medley of rich and poor, a small-town theatre for

---

[71] Thanks to Jon Mee for introducing me to 'The Lousiad' on the wintry slopes of Stob Ghabhar. 'Peter Pindar' contributed to Thomson's *Select Scottish Airs*; in 1796 Burns described him as 'a delightful fellow, & a first favourite of mine' [CL ii. 375].

[72] 'Peter Pindar', *The Lousiad: An Heroi-Comic Poem* (London, 1785). 'To the Reader', n.p.

[73] *The Lousiad*, 15.

[74] Ibid. 18.

[75] Ibid. 22.

both devotional hypocrisy and fashionable display.[76] Burns's dramatic mono-
logue identifies its speaker as an old-fashioned farmer, not unlike the voice of
'The Author's Earnest Cry and Prayer' or 'Scotch Drink', but lacking (except in
the concluding stanza) the sentimental pathos of 'To a Mouse' and 'To a
Mountain Daisy'.

As a farmer of the middling sort, the speaker is removed both from the *demi-
monde* of the poor (the louse's natural habitat in his view) and from the small-
town orbit of Jenny's upward mobility. Punctilious and proper in his bluff
manner, he reacts with chivalric outrage to the louse's ambition, and it's through
his eyes that we see the build-up of Jenny's impending crisis of humiliation,
although that crisis is left hanging as the final stanza turns to moralizing
reflection. We saw that in 'The Bugs' Fergusson alluded to the lover's jealousy
aroused by the 'deep carnation' on 'fair Chloe's breast', although this is somewhat downplayed by Burns.[77] (Although there's a hint of sexual admiration in
his 'O *Jenny* dinna toss your head, | An' set your beauties a' abread!', ll. 37–8).
The speaker's concentration is indeed fixed (but with growing outrage, rather
than sexual envy) on the louse lodged 'snug an tight' under Jenny's 'fatt'rels'
(l. 20) rather than on the minister and his sermon, until, driven by ambition, it
emerges into public view. William Aiton complained that Ayrshire Sunday service
was indeed a theatre of distraction, 'the people gazing around them at the audience,
or making signs and gestures to their friends . . . no attention is paid to that most
solemn part of the sermon' [Aiton, p. 166]. Given the speaker's reflection in the final
stanza ('What airs in dress an' gait wad lea'e us, | An' ev'n Devotion!'), Burns might
be suggesting that he derives greater spiritual benefit from reflecting on Jenny's
*vanitas* than he would have done attended to the minister's fire and brimstone.

In the opening stanza, the speaker censures the 'impudence' which gives the
louse free reign to 'strunt rarely Owre *gawze* and *lace*', even if (at ll. 5–6) he
doubts that the lady's fragrant person will offer much in the way of a dinner to
the hungry parasite.[78] Burns's control of ironic register is impressive here: a

---

[76] Burns was himself a consummate actor in this respect. Sillar later recalled that he 'wore the
only tied hair in the parish; and in the church, his plaid, which was of a particular colour, I think
*fillemot*, he wrapped in a particular manner round his shoulders'. As Mackay points out, men of the
peasant class cut their hair short, while the middling and upper classes wore powder or wigs; 'by
wearing his hair long and gathered in a beribboned queue at the back, Robert was clearly showing
that he regarded himself as a cut above his fellows'. Jenny wasn't alone in her sartorial affectation
[Mackay, p. 76].

[77] For a different reading, see Murray Pittock, 'Nibbling at Adam Smith', in Johnny Rodger and
Gerard Carruthers (eds.), *Fickle Man: Robert Burns in the 21st Century* (Dingwall: Sandstone, 2009),
118–31 at 123. Pittock sees the speaker's sexual interest in Jenny undermining the Smithian pose of
disinterested spectator.

[78] In 'The Lousiad', the monarch sees the louse 'in solemn state, | Grave as a Spaniard, march
across the plate!' (p. 6). Burns's speaker rather misses the point, given that lice feed on blood rather
than dirt.

slightly mocking chivalric regard for the lady is matched by disdain for the poor;
'How daur ye set your fit upon her— | Sae fine a *Lady*! | Gae somewhere else and
seek your dinner | On some poor body' (ll. 9–11; hardly a charitable attitude to
the poor). The louse is guilty of huge presumption: he represents the impurity
which Mary Douglas calls 'matter out of place'.[79] In the third stanza the speaker
seeks to restore propriety by imagining the louse (now, for the only instance in
the poem, collectivized) back in its customary habitat:

> Swith, in some beggar's haffet squattle;
> There ye may creep, and sprawl, and sprattle,
> Wi' ither kindred, jumping cattle,
> > In shoals and nations;
> Whare *horn* nor *bane* ne'er daur unsettle,
> > Your thick plantations.   (ll. 13–18)

Burns's insistent, sibilant, verbal detail evokes the chaotic *charivari* of the insect
world (the 'jumping cattle' presumably represent *fleas* who've here joined their
'kindred' lice), inhabiting the unwashed hair of beggars where they'll be unmo-
lested by horn or bone combs, or other engines of polite disinfestation.[80] In the
1780s this conceit possessed a specific geographical connotation, namely the
North American 'plantations', originally populated by the outcasts of Britain and
Ireland, but recently transformed into an independent republic.[81]

Burns's ambitious louse spurns such its usual pastures among the unwashed
poor: 'Na faith ye yet! ye'll no be right, | Till ye've got on it, | The vera tapmost,
towrin height | O' *Miss's bonnet* (ll. 21–4).[82] In contrast to the tone of charitable
condescension that dominates 'To a Mouse', the speaker here has no scruples
about pest-control, in threatening the louse with a fatal dose of mercury rosin or
insect powder: 'My sooth! right bauld ye set your nose out, | As plump an' grey as
onie grozet: | O for some rank, mercurial rozet, | Or fell, red smeddum, | I'd gie
ye sic a hearty dose o't, | Wad dress your droddum!' (ll. 25–30). The comic effect
of Burns's Scots here burlesques the speaker's chivalric indignation (especially the
absurd feminine rhymes grozet/rozet and smeddum/droddum), as well as the
inspired Hogarthian description of the louse's 'nose' as a swollen, rotund 'grozet'
(gooseberry). In Goldsmith's minute description, the louse's proboscis is 'a

---

[79] Mary Douglas, *Purity and Danger: An Analysis of the Concepts of Pollution and Taboo* (London: Routledge, 1991).

[80] Pittock, 'Nibbling at Adam Smith', 123, points out that in eighteenth-century Scotland, being 'put to the horn' meant being proclaimed an outlaw or bankrupt.

[81] See Burns's 'Address of Beelzebub' [K 108] where the Highland gentry conspired to prevent their dispossessed tenantry from emigrating to Canada, preferring them to 'creep and sprawl and sprattle' in the dives and brothels of the metropolis.

[82] This clearly inspired Robert Tannahill's poem 'The Ambitious Mite: A Fable', in which the heroic insect ascends a six-inch horse hair, only to be shaken into the gutter. *Works of Robert Tannahill, with a Life of the Author*, ed. Philip A. Ramsay (London: Fullarton, n.d.), 130–2.

pointed hollow sucker', so it's more likely (if we dare assume that Burns was familiar with insect anatomy) that the 'nose' is in fact the parasite's distended, blood-swollen belly 'lodged partly in its breast and back', 'either a faint red, or a full or bright brown' as it fills up with blood.[83] The higher the louse climbs, the greater his presumption as he 'sets out his nose', increasingly plumped full of Jenny's blood, before the horrified observer. (This goes some way towards satisfying the claims of realism, because the tiny louse would be barely visible until swollen up to 'grozet' size with blood.) Burns's louse is evidently unmindful of the pastoral outlook of Fergusson's 'Happy Bug', who preferred 'honest poverty' to the ambitions of the 'Bug of state', willing to run the risk of state execution (a dusting with 'Oliphant's' insecticide!) for overreaching.

In his essay in Gordon Brown's *Red Paper on Scotland* (1975), David Craig reads 'To a Louse' as a clear statement of Burns's revolutionary sympathies: 'already the louse has come to stand for all the dispossessed and propertyless who one day will come and squat in the big houses when the upper class nightmare of a *jacquerie* comes to pass'.[84] Craig's 'already' suggests that this might be more true of a poem written a decade later than 1785, when the term *jacquerie* had entered the political vocabulary, but it oversimplifies the poem's politics in having the louse 'stand for' the revolutionary masses and 'Jenny' the 'upper classes'. Even if this were an accurate gauge of the poem's comic tone, it would be hardly flattering for 'poor folk' to be represented by a blood-sucking, excrement-voiding parasite. The louse doesn't 'stand for' the dispossessed, he colonizes and feeds off their unwashed, famished bodies, and (as Burns makes quite clear) is consequently reviled by both poor and rich, 'saunt an' sinner'.

By the same token, Jenny is hardly a personification of the *ancien régime*. The italicization of 'sae fine a *Lady!*' at line 10 offers a loophole for Burns's irony, insinuating the fact of Jenny's social pretensions early in the poem. James Mackay notes the tradition that identifies the poem's 'Jenny' with Jean Markland (one of the 'Mauchline Belles' [K 42]), a shopkeeper's daughter who later married James Findlay, Burns's future Excise instructor, and therefore 'sae fine a Lady' by aspiration rather than by birth [Mackay, p. 150].[85] Jenny's finery, and particularly her fashionable 'Lunardi' bonnet, typifies the growing sartorial luxury of Mauchline parish in the 1780s. Revd William Auld commented in the *Statistical Account* [iv. 450]: 'as to dress, about fifty years ago there were few

---

[83] Goldsmith, *History of the Earth*, vii. 272.

[84] David Craig, 'The Radical Literary Tradition', in Gordon Brown (ed.), *The Red Paper on Scotland* (Edinburgh: EUSPB, 1975), 289–303 at 293.

[85] See Harriet Guest, 'These Neuter Somethings: Gender Difference and Commercial Culture in Mid-18th Century England', for contemporary satire on aspiring shopkeepers' daughters. Kevin Sharpe and Steven N. Zwicker, '*Refiguring Revolutions: Aesthetics and Politics from the English Revolution to the Romantic Revolution* (Berkeley and Los Angeles: University of California Press, 1998), 173–96 at 175–9.

females who wore scarlet or silks. But now, nothing is more common, than silk caps and silk cloaks; and women, in a middling station, are as fine as ladies of quality were formerly'.[86] Jenny is a Mauchline bourgeoise aspiring to 'fine ladyship', *not* (as Craig supposes) a member of Ayrshire's landed class. Her fashionable bonnet, imported from Glasgow or England, conveys the fact that as successful shopkeeper's daughter she is herself prosperous enough to be 'upwardly mobile'. Both her social aspirations and the fact of her 'conspicuous consumption' are grotesquely literalized by the ascendant louse, who gluts himself on her blood, impelled by a seemingly blind instinct towards the 'vera tapmost, towrin height | O *Miss's bonnet*'.

It is not so much her bonnet as the 'crowlan ferlie' strutting upon it which draws the unwanted attention, not just of the speaker, but also now of other distracted members of the congregation ('Thae *winks* an' *finger-ends*, I dread, | Are notice takin!', ll. 41–2). The comic effect lies in the fact that Jenny mistakes the winks and finger- pointing for admiration, preening herself accordingly: 'O *Jenny*, dinna toss your head, | An' set your beauties a' abread!' (ll. 37–8). Because she's oblivious to the miniature succubus crawling up her bonnet, Jenny vainly misjudges the reason why she's the centre of attention. Even her hair-tossing makes the louse all the more horribly visible; soon she's the only member of the congregation blind to the parasite's encroachment upon her finely turned-out person.

The final stanza deflates the tension of Jenny's imminent humiliation by a turn to moral reflection:

> O wad some Pow'r the giftie gie us
> *To see oursels as others see us*!
> It wad frae monie a blunder free us,
>     An' foolish notion:
> What airs in dress an' gait wad lea'e us,
>     And ev'n Devotion!   (ll. 43–8)

As Daiches finely puts it, this shows Burns's 'ability to direct an apparently casual, "occasional" poem to a didactic conclusion... expressed with all the simple gnomic quality of a country proverb'.[87] As frequently noted, the lines 'O wad some Pow'r the giftie gie us | *To see oursels as others see us!* (ll. 43–4) closely follows the wording of Adam Smith's account of vanity in *Theory of Moral Sentiments*: 'this self-deceit, this fatal weakness of mankind, is the source of half

---

[86] 'To a Louse' is fascinated by costume: as well as the 'Lunardi' we have the 'auld wife''s 'flainen toy' (l. 32) (an unfashionable close-fitting cap worn by tenant's wives), the 'bit duddy boy's *wylecoat*' (l. 34) or undervest. Jenny's affectation is quite different from the spiritual ostentation of the 'high, exalted, virtuous Dames, | Ty'd up in godly laces' pilloried by Burns in 'Address to the Unco Guid' [K 39].

[87] Daiches, *Robert Burns*, 193.

the disorders of human life. *If we saw ourselves in the light in which others see us, or in which they would see us if they knew all, a reformation would be unavoidable. We could not otherwise endure the sight* (my italics).[88] 'To a Louse' thus endorses Smith's notion of the internal spectator, to the extent that the poem explores the consequences of vanity, the failure to adjust the partiality of one's self-perception in respect of the disinterested perception of others.[89] If Jenny had possessed the 'giftie' of *'seeing herself as others see her'* ('others' here meaning the speaker, other members of the congregation, even the reader as *hypocrite lecteur*) then, quite simply, she'd have avoided what's coming to her, although I think the final stanza's conditional voice leaves the inevitability of Smith's 'unavoidable reformation' deeply uncertain.

Because in *Theory of Moral Sentiments* Smith diagnosed social emulation (rather than historical necessity) as the driving force of modern commercial society, it's often been assumed that he *endorsed* vanity as a regulative principle of social cohesion, and that the 'internal spectator' therefore served as a mechanism to adjust the individual subject to passive conformity with the hierarchical community of sympathy.[90] This would of course set Burns's 'To a Louse' completely at odds with Smith's theory, given that the poem turns the principle of social emulation on its head. But in point of fact, when read closely, Smith's argument reveals a stoical undercurrent which is morally critical of vanity and emulation. This was actually strengthened in Smith's revisions to the 6th edition of 1790, which stated that the 'disposition to admire, and almost to worship, the rich and the powerful, and to despise, or, at least, to neglect persons of poor and mean condition, though necessary both to establish and to maintain the distinction of ranks and the order of society, is . . . the great and most universal cause of the corruption of our moral sentiments'.[91]

By contrast, the 'giftie' of 'see[ing] oursels as others see us' derives from a stoic indifference to self, the very opposite of the self-regard underlying social vanity. Smith (to a greater extent than Burns in 'To a Louse') argues that the judgement

---

[88] *Theory of Moral Sentiments*, pt. III ch. 2, 5th edn. (London, 1781), 222 (henceforth *TMS*). Burns's own signed copy in Glasgow University Library is the 6th edn. of 1790, extensively revised by Smith [Kin. iii. 1021] but the poet must refer to an earlier edition, probably the 5th. For this passage in the 6th edn., in which the wording is largely unchanged, see *Theory of Moral Sentiments*, ed. Haakonssen, 184. See also Broadie, *The Scottish Enlightenment*, 285.

[89] For a reflection on the misogyny of satires on female *vanitas* and the capitalist market, see Michael McKeon, 'The Pastoral Revolution', in Sharpe and Zwicker, *Refiguring Revolutions*, 283.

[90] See *TMS* 84–5: 'Of the origins of ambition and of the distinction of ranks'; 'From whence, then, arises that emulation which runs through all the different ranks of men, and what are the advantages which we propose to that great purpose of human life which we call bettering our condition? To be observed, to be attended to, to be taken notice of with sympathy, complacency, and approbation, are all the advantages which we can propose to derive from it. It is the vanity, not the ease or the pleasure, which interests us.'

[91] *Theory of Modern Sentiments*, ed. Haakonssen, 72.

of the 'internal spectator', 'this inmate of the breast, this abstract man, the representative of mankind, and substitute for the Deity', is quite distinct from 'what the world approves or disapproves of'.[92] Only stoical self-knowledge can arm us against the slings and arrows of the world, including the prospect (constantly underlined in the Kilmarnock poems) of material ruin. The final stanza of 'To a Louse' reveals that Burns (who probably hadn't yet read Smith's account of the 'self-interested' mechanism of commercial society theorized in *Wealth of Nations*) had recognized, and clearly endorsed, the philosopher's moral critique of the subjective and group psychology of commercial society.

I want in conclusion to return to Jenny's fashionable bonnet, with its unusually topical designation. The bonnet was named after the dashing young Vincenzo Lunardi (1759–1806), secretary to the Neapolitan Embassy in London, who in September 1784 flew a hydrogen balloon from London to Hertfordshire. Arriving in Scotland, in 1785 Lunardi made a spectacular flight from Edinburgh to Cupar, Fife, across the Firth of Forth followed by a further four flights. As the 'Yuri Gargarin' of the eighteenth century, he modestly described himself as 'Your *Highness*' and 'King of the Air', earning the praise of the *Scots Magazine* for 'the cool, intrepid manner in which [he] conducted himself'. Like Burns a year or so later, his celebrity was such that Hon. Henry Erskine introduced him to the Crochallan Fencibles Club, where he entertained the company with an account of his experiences at the notorious 'Beggar's Benison' at Anstruther in Fife.[93] London fashion had been quick to capitalize on the fame of 'Lunardi whom all the ladies love', following the example of the Montgolfier craze in Paris; the 'Lunardi bonnet' was 'appropriately constructed of gauze, or thin muslin, extended on a wire, the upper part expanding into the dimensions of a miniature balloon'.[94] On 23 October 1784 the *Morning Post* reported that 'the *Lunardi bonnet*, and the *Lunardi garters* are presently to be followed by the *Lunardi chemise* &c &c. Thus say the female fashion mongers west of Temple Bar!' The fashionable beauty 'Miss Bailey', it continued, was the 'first that sported the Lunardi bonnet, which is now worn by all the *high-fliers* in town'.[95] Burns's 'To a Louse' was probably written in late 1785, suggesting that the Scottish fashion system was responding to Lunardi's more recent 1785 flight across the Forth. Burns, whom we know from the 'Postscript' to 'Epistle to S[imson]' [K 59] was

---

[92] *TMS* p. 208.

[93] Alexander Fergusson, *The Rt Hon. Henry Erskine, Lord Advocate of Scotland* (Edinburgh: Blackwood, 1882), 266–7. For the balloon mania in mid-1780s France and Britain, see Robert Darnton, *Mesmerisim and the End of Enlightenment in France* (Cambridge, Mass.: Harvard University Press, 1968), 18–45, and Uglow, *The Lunar Men*, 370–4. For a contemporary chapbook account of Lunardi's flight in verse, see Edward J. Cowan and Michael Paterson, *Folk in Print: Scotland's Chapbook Heritage 1750–1850* (Edinburgh: John Donald, 2007), 69–72.

[94] Fergusson, *Rt.Hon. Henry Erskine*, 268.

[95] *Morning Post*, 23 Oct. 1784. Thanks to Harriet Guest for this reference. 'High-flier' of course had a different connotation in Scotland, where it referred to a member of the Evangelical party of the Kirk. 'To a Louse' perhaps satirizes *both* sartorial and evangelical affectation.

interested in ballooning,[96] borrowed some of Lunardi's sangfroid to characterize his louse's intrepidity. Like 'his Highness' Lunardi, the mock-heroic louse aspires to the 'vera tapmost, tow'rin height' of Miss's bonnet [McGuirk, *BSP* 224].

There's a traditional mock-heroic quality to the louse's upward mobility: according to the old maxim, pride comes before a fall. As a receptive reader of Pope, Burns was familiar with *The Dunciad*'s bathetic inversion of sublime ascent in the 'art of sinking'; and we might recall that the poem's 'empire of dullness' is based on the social miscibility of the new credit economy which brings 'the Smithfield Muse to the ears of Kings'.[97] The higher the Dunces ascend, the deeper they'll plunge into the stinking effluvium of the Fleet-ditch. Jenny's 'high-flying' balloon bonnet and its tiny insect aeronaut miniaturize Pope's mock-epical satire on commercial society, offering a potent metaphor for the sublime frisson of social ascent, but also its precariousness when supported by nothing more than hot air and stretched silk.

At one level then Jenny's balloon bonnet symbolizes 'improvement' as sublime inflation, paper credit as the vehicle of economic 'take-off'. Even Adam Smith, critic as well as prophet of the new order, warned that 'the commerce and industry of the country . . . cannot be altogether so secure when they are . . . suspended upon the Daedalian wings of paper money as when they travel about upon the solid ground of gold and silver' [*Wealth of Nations*, i. 420]. Smith's classical trope of Daedalian wings is updated by Burns's allusion to the Lunardi bonnet, a silken replica (twice removed) of the floating bubble which, since the South Sea crisis of the early 1720s, had figured both the rapid inflation of share prices and their sudden collapse, when 'the bubble burst'.[98] Although this was a familiar conceit of eighteenth-century poetry, Burns might have been familiar with Allan Ramsay's 1720 poem 'The Rise and Fall of the Stocks' with its admonition, 'Sae Britain brought on a' her Troubles | By running daftly after Bubbles.'[99] Both in Ramsay's poem, and the visual emblematic tradition underlying Chardin's 1734 painting 'Soap Bubbles *or* Young Man Blowing Bubbles',[100] the bubble also represented a 'bagatelle', not a bad emblem for a poem that—in the tradition of 'The Lousiad'—is after all a heroic apostrophe to an insect.[101]

---

[96] The poet was later acquainted with James 'Balloon' Tytler, pioneer Scottish balloonist, author of much of the 2nd edn. of *Encyclopaedia Britannica*, and political radical, forced to flee to America in 1792.

[97] See *The Dunciad*, Bk.1 l. 2.

[98] Charles Mackay's account of 'Bubblemania' in his *Extraordinary Popular Delusions, and the Madness of Crowds* (London, 1841) is still unrivalled.

[99] *Poems of Allan Ramsay*, 4th edn. (Edinburgh, 1727), 263.

[100] *Chardin* (London: Royal Academy of Arts; New York: Metropolitan Museum of Art, 2000), 208.

[101] All these associations are present in the closing lines of Anna Barbauld's later poem 'Washing Day' (1797): 'Earth, air, and sky, and ocean, hath its bubbles, | And verse is one of them—this most of all.' Lonsdale, *Eighteenth Century Women Poets*, 310, ll. 79–86.

The shift from balloon to bubble is important for the crescendo of Burns's 'To a Louse', as Jenny's bubble-like pride inflates towards a moment of crisis, albeit one never reached within the poem itself. The same is true of the louse, which (returning to Goldsmith's description) hideously distended by its feast of blood, 'most frequently suffers from its gluttony, since it gorges to such a degree, that it is crushed to pieces by the slightest impression'.[102] The louse has become a kind of insect balloon or taut bubble of blood, stretched to bursting point, rendering it victim to its own gluttony. To this extent both Jenny and her parasitic nemesis share with Burns's 'Mouse' and 'Mountain Daisy' the fate of impending 'ruin'. For all its comic tone, the poem plays out a major pastoral theme of the Kilmarnock volume, evoking the fragility of human aspirations, the grim Meliboean spectre of dispossession. If the lady's bonnet miniaturizes the vanity of human wishes, then the louse embodies a diminutive, comic version of its attendant 'Ruin', as in the *prosopopeia* of Burns's poem of the same title: 'And thou grim Pow'r, by Life abhorr'd, | While Life a *pleasure* can afford, | Oh! Hear a wretch's prayer!' [K 12 ll. 15–17]. Moving beyond the animal topos, 'To a Louse''s fashionable allusion attaches it to one particular moment of the *comedie humaine*, the 'scene of improvement' in 1780s Ayrshire, just as its conclusion seeks to universalize that moment in an act of moral reflection that is hardly a prayer, despite its ecclesiastical setting.

---

[102] *History of the Earth*, vii. 273.

# 6

## Hellfire and Common Sense

*Prejudice stood as another insurmountable bar to all improvements. The ambition of the people, at that time, was not to improve the soil, but to reform the church; —not to destroy weeds and brambles; but to root out heresy; —not to break up the stubborn soil, but to tread down the whore of Babylon.*

(William Aiton, *General View of the Agriculture of the County of Ayr*, 75)

*The desires, rectified by the Word of God, must give clearness of judgement, soundness of mind, regular affections, whence will flow peace of conscience, good hope, through grace, that all our interests are under the care of our Heavenly Father. This gives a relish to animal life itself . . .*

(*William Burnes*, 'A Manual of Religious Belief, in a Dialogue between Father and Son')[1]

### AULD LICHTS, NEW LICHTS

'To a Louse''s Kirk setting, with its concluding meditation on Adam Smith's 'internal spectator', is an appropriate point of departure for the present chapter. In the pages that follow, I'll argue that Burns's Kirk satires, and related poems on religious matters, bring him closer to a mainstream 'enlightenment' position, and voice a harsher criticism of popular attitudes, than many of his other writings. This is well illustrated in the 1786 verse 'Letter to James Tennant, Glenconner' [K 90] where Burns speaks of lending his friend (the miller of Ochiltree) his copies of Smith's *Theory of Moral Sentiments* and Thomas Reid's *Inquiry into the Human Mind on the Principles of Common Sense*; he requests, however that he 'peruse them an' return them quickly'. For the lender fears that, deprived of any reading but the devotional works of 'Bunyan, Brown and Boston', he'll start to 'grunt a real Gospel groan' (ll. 18–22). It is a reaction that aptly represents the impact of enlightenment reading on the religious sensibilities of many of Ayrshire's 'middling sort' in the later decades of the eighteenth century. That's not to say that Burns was an enlightenment freethinker of the 'Rameau's Nephew' stamp. Nor (like Blake, Coleridge, Hazlitt, and many of the English

---

[1] Text in Chambers-Wallace, i. 455–9 at 459.

Romantics) was he a Dissenter or Nonconformist, but remained throughout his life a practising member of the established Church of Scotland. Burns was more forthright about satirizing beliefs and practices that he abhorred than in making doctrinaire statements reflecting his 'improved' religious sensibility. He none-theless subscribed to the principles of an enlightened Calvinism associated with the Moderate party in the Church of Scotland, colloquially known as the 'new licht': correspondingly, the main target of his satire was the 'Popular' party or orthodox mainstream, known as the 'auld licht'.

Although Christianity might seem far removed from the pagan origins and occupational concerns of the pastoral tradition, in fact the genre was historically permeated with Christian theology, typology, and satire. Eighteenth-century pastoral poets took their lead from Milton's equation of shepherd and pastor in *Lycidas*, as well as Adam and Eve's expulsion from the Edenic *hortus conclusus* in *Paradise Lost*. In his 'Messiah: A Sacred Eclogue', Pope transformed Virgil's 4th *Eclogue* ('Pollio') into a sublime prophecy of Christ's birth.[2] Although Burns's 'Cotter's Saturday Night' aspires to the Christian 'pastoral sublime' of Milton and Pope, as we'll see in the next chapter, his best religious poetry was written in the satirical vein. Indeed, his involvement in the controversies racking the Kirk in his native Ayrshire, at a time of huge theological as well as socio-economic change, provides a crucial dimension for understanding his transition from farmer to poet, as discussed in Chapter 3. As with his other poems, Burns's Kirk satires often assume a rustic Scots persona and address in their engagement with the relationship between tradition and improvement, although generally in a less sympathetic spirit than in the 'Scotch Drink' or animal poems.

In the 'Postscript' to his epistle 'To W[illie] S[imson], Ochiltree' [K 59] Burns cast the theological controversy raging in late eighteenth-century Ayrshire in an absurd light. Joking about the provenance of the nicknames 'auld' and 'new licht' for the Orthodox and Moderate parties in the Kirk, he offered his correspondent a Swiftian parable to explain the whole 'tulzie' or polemic. Young and old shepherds fall out over whether the new Moon is a complete replacement for the old that has been worn out 'like a sark, or pair o' shoon' (l. 122), or whether it was in fact just 'the *auld moon* turn'd a newk | An' out o' sight' (ll. 135–6). The latter 'scientific' view is preferred by 'beardless laddies' whose improved literacy makes them consider themselves better informed than their 'auld dadies' (ll. 142–4). The quarrel turns violent and rages in many lands (showing that Burns was aware that Ayrshire disputes were only part of a global conflict between enlightenment and religious orthodoxy) until 'the *Lairds*' intervene 'by strict commands' (l. 155) to put an end to the bloodletting, presumably by institutionalizing articles of belief in ecclesiastical 'confessions', and enforcing subscription to them.

---

[2]  On Christian pastoral, see Stuart Curran, *Poetic Form and British Romanticism* (Oxford: Oxford University Press, 1986), 89–92.

Although this parable seems to betoken a defeat for the 'new lichts', in fact, Burns insists, the latter continue to profess their heretical views in the most 'barefac'd' way. (ll. 159–62). Accordingly, the frustrated 'auld lichts' plan to take a balloon ride into space in order to spend a month observing the moon's waning, and return to earth bearing its 'hindmost *shaird*' as conclusive empirical proof of their theory (ll. 169–80). Although this is obscure, Burns seems to be satirizing the orthodox belief in the literal interpretation of Scripture as irrefutable evidence of the theological doctrines of the Westminster Confession of Faith as approved by the Church of Scotland in 1647, which also promoted Calvin's doctrines of Original Sin and of Predestination. Of course the larger joke—on the 'auld lichts'—is that both old and new light radiate from a common source, namely the moon as it orbits the earth, reflecting the light of the sun. And beyond that, as Burns warns his fellow bardie Simson, poets should in any case know better than to become embroiled in 'polemical divinity':'Sae, ye observe that a' this clatter | Is naething but a 'moonshine matter' . . . | I hope we, *Bardies*, ken some better | Than mind sic brulzie' (ll. 181–6).

For the modern reader Burns's Kirk Satires are practically unintelligible without some grasp of the political and theological issues at stake.[3] Politically, the 'new licht' or Moderate party supported the Patronage Act of 1712 in which lay patrons (i.e. local gentry and heritors), rather than the elders or congregation, were given the power to present Ministers to vacant parishes. Many took the 1712 Act to contravene the Security Act passed in 1707 (as part of the Treaty of Union) guaranteeing popular election as a fundamental principle of Presbyterianism, but later regarded by the leading lights of the Scottish enlightenment as a primitive throwback to the early days of the Reformation. Adam Smith, for instance, argued that 'the clergy, in order to preserve their influence in those popular elections, became, or affected to become . . . fanatics themselves, encourag[ing] fanaticism among the people . . . so small a matter as the appointment of a parish priest occasioned almost always a violent contest, not only in one parish, but in all the neighbouring parishes, who seldom failed to take part in the quarrel'. Like many of the enlightenment literati, Smith regarded the popular elections of ministers as the principle cause of 'keeping up the old fanatical spirit' in Scotland [*Wealth of Nations*, ii. 398–9]. Smith's point is endorsed by modern historians who represent disputed presentations as amongst 'the most persistent

---

[3] Burns seems to have been largely unconcerned with the Presbyterian Seceders or Dissenters, who by 1800 constituted a staggering quarter of all Lowland Scots. See Callum G. Brown, 'Protest in the Pews: Interpreting Presbyterianism and Society in Fracture during the Scottish Economic Revolution', in T. M. Devine (ed.), *Conflict and Stability in Scottish Society, 1700–1850* (Edinburgh: John Donald, 1990), 84. For an account of similarities as well as differences between the 'auld' and 'new lichts', see Freidhelm Voges, 'Moderate and Evangelical Thinking in the Later Eighteenth Century: Differences and Shared Attitudes', *Records of the Church History Society* 22 (1986), 141–57.

and geographically widespread cause of popular unrest in Scotland between 1730 and 1843'.[4]

*Pace* Adam Smith, many Scots regarded the Patronage Act, like the Malt taxes discussed in Chapter 4, as a violation of the terms of Union, an anglicizing and 'Erastian' incursion on the hallowed Presbyterian doctrine of the 'Two Kingdoms'.[5] This problem rankled throughout the whole period, culminating in the 'Disruption' of 1843 when the evangelical opponents of patronage walked out of the General Assembly to found the 'Free Church'. Richard Sher's study of the Moderate literati of Edinburgh portrays the triumph of the institutionally well-rooted but minority Moderate cause in eighteenth-century Scotland over the Calvinist orthodoxy of the Popular party, which he identifies as a major factor in enabling the extraordinary intellectual efflorescence in the decades immediately preceding, and contemporaneous with, the life of Robert Burns.[6]

As well as the political difference surrounding the question of patronage, the two main parties harboured some major theological disagreements. Although (in contrast to liberal and dissenting Protestants in Geneva, England, and Ulster) the Moderates continued to subscribe to the articles of the Westminster Confession, they rejected the orthodox emphasis on the doctrines of original sin, election, and predestination, especially the Calvinist notion of justification by faith rather than works, and of salvation by grace alone.[7] Major theological influences were the writings of Professors Francis Hutcheson and his successor William Leechman at Glasgow University, as well as the 'Common Sense' philosophers James Beattie, Thomas Reid, and Dugald Stewart.

Burns's views were at a more local level influenced by John Goldie (1717–1809), a lay theologian, mathematician, and wine merchant from Kilmarnock who published *Essays on Various Important Subjects Moral and Divine* in 1779. In his 'Epistle to John Goldie' [K 63], Burns hailed Goldie ('terror o' the whigs', l. 1)[8] for having routed 'Bigotry', 'Superstition', 'Enthusiasm', and 'Orthodoxy'; mimicking the voice of a violent and drink-soaked member of the Popular party, the satire pillories the religious bigotry that Goldie's book had

---

[4] Brown, 'Protest in the Pews', 99. Whatley questions this claim regarding the period up to 1750, but concedes that it may have been true during Burns lifetime (*Scottish Society*, 182 n. 144).

[5] For a succinct explanation, see Colin Kidd, *Union and Unionisms: Political Thought in Scotland, 1500–2000* (Cambridge: Cambridge University Press, 2008), 215–19.

[6] Richard Sher, *Church and University in the Scottish Enlightenment: The Moderate Literati of Edinburgh* (Edinburgh: Edinburgh University Press, 1985). See also Colin Kidd, *Subverting Scotland's Past* (Cambridge: Cambridge University Press, 1993), 185–204.

[7] Colin Kidd, 'Scotland's Invisible Enlightenment: Subscription and Heterodoxy in the Eighteenth-Century Kirk', *Records of the Scottish Church History Society* 30 (2000), 28–59, 57–8. Kidd argues that fear of encouraging secession may have prompted many Moderate ministers to continue subscribing, even when they harboured private scruples.

[8] In the Scottish religious context 'whig' refers to orthodox Calvinists rather than members of the British political party of that name.

forced into a bitterly defensive position. Goldie shares this distinction (l. 25) with the English Presbyterian polemicist Dr John Taylor of Norwich (1694–1761) who had taught Divinity at Warrington Dissenting Academy, and was the author of *The Scripture Doctrine of Original Sin* (1741), a book that did much to drive a wedge between English Presbyterian Dissent and orthodox Calvinism.[9] Taylor (like his follower Goldie) attacked a literalist reading of the Bible and an excessive dependence on the articles of the Westminster Confession: in fact Goldie quoted Athanasius as his authority in describing literalist readings of the Bible as 'blasphemy'.[10]

Another important influence on Burns was the Moderate Ayr minister Revd William McGill's *Practical Essay on the Death of Jesus Christ* (1786), the alleged Arianism or Socinianism of which stirred up a storm of protest, leading to a charge of heresy before the Synod of Glasgow and Ayr in 1789. In defending himself against one of his assailants (Revd William Peebles), McGill argued that he, not the orthodox, was the true Protestant: for orthodox ministers were setting up the authority of the Westminster Confession of Faith over the Scriptures, and thereby denying 'the right of private judgement, and the great principles of protestant liberty, as distinguished from the infallibility, implicit faith, and slavery of the church of Rome'. Commenting on this passage, Liam McIlvanney points out that Burns followed McGill in 'habitually describ[ing] his Old Light adversaries in the stigmatizing terminology of Roman Catholicism'.[11]

It is perhaps misleading to label the theology of the 'new lichts' 'Arminian' or 'Socinian' as did many of their Calvinist opponents; more important was the liberal temper and rational Christianity they promoted.[12] Neither is it helpful simply to identify the theologically 'enlightened' Moderate clergy with socially progressive views, and the Evangelicals with conservatism, although as Aiton's remark in the epigraph to the present chapter suggests, Calvinist popular opinion was often set against 'improvement'. But some Evangelical as well as Moderate ministers were assiduous agricultural improvers: Andrew Wight complimented the Ayrshire clergymen of all persuasions for their temporal as well as spiritual leadership in this matter. In fact Wight believed that ministers were the best instruments for instructing tenant farmers in the principles of improvement 'as they have a more immediate commerce with the country people than the gentlemen of estates'.[13] The contribution of many Evangelical ministers (such as Revd

---

[9] Dr Taylor was awarded an Honorary DD by the University of Glasgow in 1756, and strongly supported by Professors William Leechman and Adam Smith.

[10] Walter McGinty, *Robert Burns and Religion* (Aldershot: Ashgate, 2003), 33.

[11] Liam McIlvanney, *Burns the Radical* (East Linton: Tuckwell, 2002), 135.

[12] Robert Heron explicitly accused the Moderate ministers of Ayrshire, Renfrew, and Dumbarton of going beyond Leechman's Arminian heresies to embrace Priestley's Unitarianism. *Observations made in a Journey through the Western Counties of Scotland, in the Autumn of 1792*, 2nd edn., 2 vols. (Perth, 1799), ii. 351.

[13] Andrew Wight, *Present State of Husbandry in Scotland*, 2 vols. (Edinburgh, 1778), i. 185.

William Auld of Mauchline, who had been educated at Edinburgh, Glasgow, and Leyden universities) to Sinclair's *Statistical Account* supports this claim, and should question the stereotype, supported by much of Burns's satire, that the Evangelicals were blinkered reactionaries in social as well as theological matters.[14]

In the light of Burns's flamboyant rebellion against the sexual mores of the Mauchline Kirk Session (expressed most trenchantly in poems such as 'The Fornicator' [K 61] ), it's surprising to discover that something of the intellectual base of his rebellion may have been inherited from his stern father.[15] With the assistance of John Murdoch, Burnes senior had composed *A Manual of Religious Belief in A Dialogue between Father and Son* for the spiritual instruction of his children. This catechism expresses an Arminian theology emphasizing the role of (well-regulated) 'pleasure', 'desire', and 'the animal soul' in the Christian life, anathema to orthodox Calvinism. The passage quoted in the epigraph to this chapter probably influenced his son's lines in 'The Vision' which, in mitigating the waywardness of 'Pleasure', insisted that 'the *light* that led astray, | Was *light* from Heaven' [K 62 ll. 239–40]. (Wordsworth took particular issue with this line in his poem 'To the Sons of Burns'.)[16] It finds an echo, however, in Burns's later claim that 'almost all my Religious tenets originate from my heart' [CL ii. 73].

As a boy at Mount Oliphant farm near his 'native ground' of enlightened Ayr, Burns came under the sway of the New Light ministers Dalrymple and McGill, part of the 'candid lib'ral band . . . Of public teachers' praised in 'To the Rev. John M'Math' [K 68 ll. 79–80]. In his 1787 letter to Moore, Burns described his boyhood involvement in the 'polemical divinity' which 'was putting the country half-mad' and how, 'ambitious of shining in conversation parties on sundays between sermons' he set to 'puzzle Calvinism with so much heat and indiscretion that I raised a hue and cry of heresy against me which has not ceased to this hour' [CL i. 136] His exposure to liberal Presbyterianism continued in Tarbolton parish under the tutelage of Patrick Wodrow and John McMath, although this changed when he moved, aged 25, to the parish of Mauchline, within the spiritual jurisdiction of the conservative Revd William Auld. Religious polemic was the seedbed of Burns the poet; and the Kirk satires were its first fruit.

The fame of Burns's brilliant satire on the Calvinist mindset in 'Holy Willie's Prayer' and other poems has encouraged many of his admirers to see the poet as contributing to the deliverance of the Scottish common people from the repressive spirit of the reformation, reinstating the rich and often bawdy medieval folk traditions suppressed by John Knox and the Reformers, and sustained in the eighteenth century by orthodox Calvinists such as Willie Fisher and the 'Daddie' Auld. In this view, Burns's enlightened attack on Calvinism is the auxiliary of his

---

[14]  On Auld, see John Strawhorn, 'Ayrshire in the Enlightenment', 192.

[15]  See CL i. 139 for Burns's contretemps with his father.

[16]  Wordsworth misquotes from 'The Vision' at ll. 41–2: see *Wordsworth: The Poems*, ed. John O. Hayden, 3 vols. (Harmondsworth: Penguin, 1977), i. 659.

political radicalism, championing a more authentic (and attractive) Scottish identity—richly vernacular, democratic, and sexually liberated. It is a very appealing formula, but unfortunately it doesn't conform to the facts.

The 'auld licht' or orthodox majority were called the 'Popular Party' for a good reason, and despite their entrenched attachment to the old theology, the radical spirit of the Covenanters often led them to sympathize with rebellious American colonists or French revolutionaries. It is a fact that the sympathies of many left-leaning Scottish 'friends of the people' (including Burns's patron, the Whig lawyer the Hon. Henry Erskine, or the radical martyr Thomas Muir of Hunters-hill) were closer to the Popular party in the Kirk than to the Moderates. Under the intellectual leadership of Principal William Robertson and the political leadership of Henry Dundas, the Moderates did show a liberal spirit in promoting Catholic Relief (the unpopularity of which led to riots in Glasgow and Edinburgh) and the abolition of the Slave Trade, but their notion of 'enlightenment' stopped short of supporting challenges to the status quo in Philadelphia or Paris. There's no simple equation here between theological and political liberalism, or between repressive Calvinist theology and political tyranny, although Burns's support for both the American and French revolutionaries make it clear that his allegiance to the political values of the Moderates was limited.

It is often forgotten that in his 1786 'Heaven-taught ploughman' review, Henry Mackenzie took considerable pains to parry charges of Burns's 'irreligion', as well as underlining the ideological serviceability of the poet's satires on Ayrshire extremism to the Edinburgh Moderates: 'if we consider the ignorance and fanaticism of the lower class of people in the country where these poems were written' wrote Mackenzie, 'fanaticism of that pernicious sort which sets *faith* in opposition to *good works*, the fallacy and danger of which, a mind so enlightened as our Poet's could not but perceive; we shall look upon his lighter Muse, not as the enemy of religion, (of which in several places he expresses the justest sentiments), but as the champion of morality, and the friend of virtue' [*CH* p. 70]. This suggests another important reason for the success of Burns's Kilmarnock volume among the anglicizing literati of Edinburgh.

Mackenzie's point was later picked up by John Nichol in his lively 1882 study of Burns. 'No wonder the liberals, whose weakness lay in lack of demagogic art', he wrote playfully, 'clapped their hands and drank their claret with added relish "upon that day"! Here was a man of the people, speaking for the people, and making the people hear him, fighting their battles in a manner hitherto unknown among their ranks.'[17] But Nichol (himself no friend to orthodoxy) judged that Burns's religious satire would have been much more effective, more to the

---

[17]  John Nichol, *Robert Burns: A Summary of his Career and Genius* (Edinburgh, 1882), 23. See also Carlyle's description of Burns as 'the fighting man of the New-Light Priesthood' [*CH* p. 377]. Burns's attack on orthodoxy in popular Scots verse was far more potent than the 'cauld harangues' of such 'New Licht' ministers as Revd George Smith, satirized in 'The Holy Fair'.

advantage of 'religious freedom in Scotland', had it not been for the fact that 'he was in part, at least, fighting for his own hand'. He referred, of course, to the poet's sexual peccadilloes and his thirst for revenge after the public humiliation he had suffered at the hands of the Kirk's 'houghmagandie squad'.[18] Nichol is certainly right to suggest that the poet's attack on the 'Holy Willies' and their ilk was hardly disinterested, but as I've already argued, it's only fair to acknowledge that Burns's sexual rebellion was in part a deliberate act of defiance against Scotland's 'parish state', and not solely an exercise in private hedonism.

## KIRK SATIRE IN THE RESERVED CANON: 'THE HOLY TULZIE' AND 'HOLY WILLIE'S PRAYER'

Nichol's interpretation of Burns as the demagogic voice of the Moderates is born out by the 'burlesque lamentation' of 'The Holy Tulzie' [K 52] (sometimes known as 'The Twa Herds'),[19] whose speaker caricatures the bigotry underpinning popular hostility to patronage. Although it circulated widely in manuscript, it was never published during Burns's lifetime and thus remained (like the more famous 'Holy Willie') as part of the 'reserved canon'.[20] But this 'first of my poetic offspring that saw the light' [CL i. 144] is worthy of consideration here partly because of Burns's use of pastoral allegory to satirize the 'tulzie' or falling out (on account of parish boundaries rather than doctrine) between two 'auld licht' ministers, Alexander Moodie of Riccarton and John Russell of Kilmarnock, the 'twa herds' of the alternative title.[21] Horrified by the schism the 'holy tulzie' has created in orthodox ranks, the poem's protagonist represents the 'auld licht' on the defensive. Troublingly, he refers to the congregation (who, rather than upper-class patrons, have elected both ministers) as 'Brutes', although the bestial metaphor is to some extent licensed by the poem's title and its pastoral frame: 'You wha was ne'er by Lairds respeckit, | To wear the Plaid; | But by the vera Brutes eleckit | To be their Guide' [ll. 21–4]. Walter McGinty asks of this 'is Burns really mocking the ability of ordinary members of a congregation to choose their minister, or has he carried the anti-patronage argument *ad absurdum* to raise doubts about it?'[22] The poem continues the attack on patronage in

---

[18] Nichol, *Robert Burns: A Summary*, 24. 'With rueful face and signs of grace | I pay'd the buttock-hire . . . before the Congregation wide') 'The Fornicator' [K 61], ll. 17–18, l. 9.

[19] The poem was first printed in 1796 by Stewart and Meikle as a pamphlet entitled 'The Twa Herds: An Unco Mournfu' Tale'.

[20] As employed by Gerald Carruthers, *Robert Burns* (Tavistock: Northcote House, 2006), 3.

[21] The fifth stanza of 'The Ordination' [K 85] also picks up the pastoral allegory exemplified here (incidentally one further developed in the short satirical squib entitled 'The Calf' [K 125] that followed 'The Ordination' in the Edinburgh volume).

[22] McGinty, *Burns and Religion*, 47.

stanza 15, where the speaker exhorts his followers 'Come join your counsels and your skills | To cowe the Lairds, And get the Brutes the power themsels | To chuse their Herds' (ll. 87–90). Although the 'auld licht' makes his complaint in 'plain, braid Lallans' (associated with the popular party in the 'Postscript' of 'To Willie Simson, Ochiltree' [K 59 l. 119]) the Scots idiom of this poem, like that of 'The Ordination', is a vehicle for coarse and violent prejudice.

The poem's ecclesiastical satire (echoing, as the Canongate editors indicate, the pastoral allusions of Milton's *Lycidas* [CG, p. 557]) allegorizes the Moderate predators of the orthodox flock as 'the Fulmart, Wil-cat, Brock an' Tod' (pine martin, wild cat, badger, and fox, l. 31), all of whom, the speaker fears, will take advantage of the 'Holy Tulzie' to break into the sheepfold and prey upon the faithful. In the seventh and eighth stanzas the stentorian pulpiteer 'Black Jock' Russell is cast as an adept in sheep husbandry (ll. 47–8 inject a note of typically Burnsian comic bathos by representing Hell—'the burning dub'—as a sheep dip!):

> And wha like Russell tell'd his tale;
> His voice was heard o'er moor and dale:
> He kend the L—d's sheep ilka tail,
>     O'er a' the height;
> An' tell'd gin they were sick or hale
>     At the first sight.—
>
> He fine a maingie sheep could scrub,
> And nobly swing the Gospel-club;
> Or New-Light Herds could nicely drub
>     And pay their skin;
> Or hing them o'er the burning dub,
>     Or shute them in.—    (ll. 37–48)

Liam McIlvanney suggests that Burns's support 'for the *Ayrshire* New Light, fighting authoritarian Calvinism in its heartland' is distinct from any broader affiliation with Moderatism as 'the party of politeness or the party of patronage'.[23] But attention to the complex ironies of 'The Holy Tulzie' renders this claim problematic, to the extent to which the poem indirectly endorses the principles of *both* politeness and patronage in its attack on 'authoritarian Calvinism'. Witness the bigoted speaker's criticism of (i.e. Burns's *inverted praise for*) the Ayrshire 'new licht' ministers (or 'auld licht' waverers) Dalrymple, McGill, William McQuhae, David and Andrew Shaw, and Patrick Wodrow, the predators (l. 31) who, it is feared, will take advantage of the 'tulzie' to ravage the sheepfold. The speaker sincerely hopes that Russell and Moodie will bury their differences, and that the 'auld lichts' will rally in order to banish 'that curst cur ca'd Common Sense...o'er the seas to France' (ll. 93–5). Burns's Kirk satires

<hr/>

[23] McIlvanney, *Burns, the Radical*, 133.

persistently equate the 'new licht' with 'Common Sense', which of course associates it with the 'Learning' (l. 92) and politeness of Common Sense philosophers such as Reid, Beattie, and Stewart.[24] Polite learning or 'common sense' is also the hallmark of the enlightened ministers castigated in 'The Holy Tulzie''s final stanza, namely, the speaker's disdain for their 'eloquence', 'nervous excellence' (l. 98), 'pathetic manly sense' (l. 99), and power to penetrate the heart (l. 101), which concludes Burns's inverted panegyric on the Ayrshire liberals.

The speaker's bigoted support for the Act of Security here, as well as his demagogic, coarsely expressed, appeal to 'the Brutes', must question Burns's stance in this instance as a 'poet of the people'. In 1819, Revd Hamilton Paul, 'new licht' minister of Broughton, Glenholm, and Kilbuchie, distorted Burns's attack on the popular party to suggest that the poet was an opponent of democracy. 'No curse can befall a nation with regard to the civil administration of its affairs more pregnant with calamity than universal suffrage; and, consequently, if that mode of election be pernicious in politics, it must be terribly fatal in matters of religion. It is a kind of anomaly in ecclesiastical economy, that the most ignorant of mankind should sit in judgement on the qualifications of those who are to be their teachers. This practice is thus reprobated by Burns with singular felicity— "To get the brutes the pow'r themselves | To choose their herds".'[25]

Writing during a later period of ideological conflict, Revd Paul enlists Burns's Moderatism in the service of his own Toryism, however ill it fits with the democratic sympathies abundantly evident elsewhere in Burns. (Paul's attribution to Burns of the term 'the brutes' for the people ignores the poem's ironic framework.) As suggested in Chapter 3, there are significant crossovers between literary and Kirk patronage, and I've shown how Burns was well able to solicit patronage from upper-class sponsors while at the same time insisting on his 'independence'. As McGinty points out, 'Burns associated more with New Light Ministers who supported Patronage than with Auld Lights who opposed it, while he himself at a later stage in his life, worked the then system of Patronage quite unashamedly when seeking to further his career in the Excise'.[26] Rather than remaining securely tamped down in the local controversies of late eighteenth-century Presbyterianism, the question of patronage re-emerges here to worry the claim that Burns's poetic self-fashioning, as well as his radical politics, were 'radical-democratic' in any consistent

---

[24] Burns's understanding of 'Common Sense' is clearly expressed in his 1789 satire on the McGill affair entitled 'The Kirk's Alarm' [K 264]: 'A heretic blast has been blawn i' the West— | That what is not Sense must be Nonsense, Orthodox | That what is not sense must be Nonsense' (ll. 3–5). On the association between Moderates and Common Sense philosophy, see Voges, 'Moderate and Evangelical Thinking', 144.

[25] Revd Hamilton Paul, *Poems and Songs of Robert Burns, with a Life of the Author* (Ayr: Wilson, M'Cormick, & Carnie, 1819), p. xxxviii.

[26] McGinty, *Burns and Religion*, 190.

modern sense, reminding us of the importance of understanding his poetry in its historical, theological, and ideological context.

'Holy Willie's Prayer'[K 53] is justly praised as the greatest of Burns's religious satires; like many of the other poems in this group, its ironic (or in Burns's language 'asklent') use of dramatic monologue, itself undercuts the literalist method of textual exegesis promoted by the orthodox. Willie's unctuous self-righteousness of course depends on the orthodox Calvinist belief in predestina-tion; the God he addresses 'Sends ane to heaven an' ten to hell, | A' for thy glory' (ll. 3–4). Burns succinctly mocks the belief in original sin, and a vengeful God who can send the new-born baby straight to hell 'to gnash [his] gooms, and weep, and wail' (l. 21). Because he is a 'chosen sample' Willie need not fear damnation, so when his 'fleshy thorn' forces him to drink and fornication, it's interpreted as God's way of prompting humility in his Elect, a view which exposes Willie's enormous presumption.

As Kinsley indicates, the poem is steeped in biblical allusion revealing the extent of Burns's scriptural knowledge, and as 'a prayer' it follows the traditional scheme of invocation: praise, confession, and penitence, intercession and petition [Kin. iii. 1049]. Despite Willie's smug faith, the final stanzas, which refer to the Moderate Presbytery of Ayr's overturning of the Mauchline Kirk Session's process against Burns's patron Gavin Hamilton in January 1785, again show the 'auld lichts' on the defensive. The poem was clearly too libellous for Burns to consider printing, but as he later noted, its circulation in manuscript 'alarmed the kirk-session so much that they held three several meetings to look over their holy artillery, if any of it was pointed against profane Rhymers.—Unluckily for me, my idle wanderings led me, on another side, point blank within the reach of their heaviest metal' [CL i. 144] (Burns here referred to Jean Armour's pregnancy). Like 'The Holy Tulzie', although widely circulated in manuscript by Burns, it was first published in a pirated pamphlet by the Glasgow broadside publisher Stewart & Meikle after the poet's death. In the light of my remarks on the politics of the Kirk satires, it's significant that when Burns was soliciting the patronage of the Earl of Glencairn to procure him a post in the Excise in 1788, he enclosed a copy of 'Holy Willie', clearly the most effective way he could conceive of winning the Earl's admiration [CL i. 224].

## THE POPULAR SUPERNATURAL: 'THE HOLY FAIR', 'ADDRESS TO THE DEIL', AND 'HALLOWEEN'

I turn now to those Kirk satires actually published in the Kilmarnock volume, as opposed to the poems of the 'reserved canon'. It needs to be emphasized that, despite the fact that Burns's poetic fame in Ayrshire rested largely upon the success of his manuscript Kirk satires, he deliberately downplayed them in his first published volume. The only poems in Kilmarnock that explicitly satirize the 'auld lichts' are 'The Holy Fair' [K 70] and 'Address to the Deil' [K 76]. Passing criticisms also occur in 'A Dedication to G[avin] H[amilton], Esq.' [K 103], the 'Postscript' of 'To W[illie] S[imson], Ochiltree' (as we've seen above), and 'Epistle to J[ohn] R[ankine]' [K 47]. Religion is addressed in a number of Kilmarnock's other poems in a non-satirical mode, most prominently 'The Cotter's Saturday Night' (discussed in the next chapter), the gloomy song 'Winter, a Dirge' [K10], and 'A Prayer, in the Prospect of Death' [K 13] written during the Irvine sojourn of 1781. But Susan Manning rightly argues that in poems such as the 'Epistle to a Young Friend' [K 105] 'the poetry is . . . at its weakest when it adopts the tones of sentiment without edge; its idiom slackens in the equivocating logic of the middle ground . . . it's hard to be a passionate Moderate'.[27]

Burns clearly played down religious satire in the Kilmarnock edition for fear of the 'holy artillery' of the Kirk session in the Ayrshire bastion of orthodoxy. Throwing caution to the winds as he prepared the Edinburgh edition the following year, he added 'The Ordination' [K 85], 'The Calf' [K 125], and 'Address to the Unco Guid' [K 39], giving a much stronger flavour of religious satire to the volume as a whole. Edinburgh was of course the bastion of the Moderates, and we've seen how attacks on Ayrshire bigotry played well with the literati and the wider circle of Burns's polite patrons. In the remainder of this chapter, I'll survey these published poems, concluding with a reading of the related 'Brigs of Ayr' [K 120], which casts the theological schism of the Church of Scotland in a broader social and cultural light.

'The Holy Fair' [K 70] is written in Burns's 'manners painting strain' and as such, is linked to other 'genre' poems illustrative of lowland rural life, such as 'Halloween' or (in a different vein) 'The Cotter's Saturday Night'. The poem may have been partly inspired by Allan Ramsay's 'The Marrow Ballad' (subtitled 'on seeing a strolling congregation going to a field meeting, May 9th, 1738') which satirized the antinomian extremism and anti-patronage stance of Ebenezer Erskine and Thomas Mair, acolytes of Edward Fisher's *The Marrow of Modern Divinity* (1738) [Ramsay, iii. 244–5]. Like Burns, Ramsay represented the effects of overheated Calvinist enthusiasm as 'houghmagandie' in the bushes, although the earlier poet's 'strolling congregation' are antinomian seceders from the established Kirk rather than upholders of Presbyterian orthodoxy.

'The Holy Fair' exemplifies one of the most remarkable rituals of eighteenth-century popular Presbyterianism, when the congregations of several parishes gathered annually to celebrate communion, the climax of several days of field preaching by different ministers. In the wake of the Reformation, the festal Eucharist of the 'Holy Fair' (probably originating at an evangelical meeting at

---

[27] Susan Manning, 'Burns and God', in Robert Crawford (ed.), *Robert Burns and Cultural Authority* (Edinburgh: Polygon, 1999), 125–6.

the Kirk of Shotts near Glasgow in 1630) evolved to replace Catholic Mass in the Reformed Calendar, as noted by Robert Heron in 1797: 'the annual celebration . . . in the rural parishes of Scotland, has much in it of the old *Popish* festivals, in which superstition, traffic, and amusement, used to be strangely intermingled'.[28] Critical commentary of this kind was voiced by both Episcopalian and Moderate Presbyterian commentators throughout the eighteenth century, most notably in the anonymous 'Letter from a Blacksmith to the Ministers and Elders of the Church of Scotland' (1759).

Burns's 'Holy Fair' was based on the poet's personal experience of the annual Communion held in Mauchline on the second Sunday of August 1785, when more than 1,200 people crammed into tents and booths in the Kirk yard before taking Communion, sampling the spiritual wares of different preachers, as well as the more carnal fare of victuallers and 'brewster-wives' who catered for their bodily appetites. But despite its folkloric subject matter, it's also a profoundly 'literary' poem, and in technical terms develops the difficult, nine-line medieval Scots 'Christ's Kirk' stanza that both satirized and celebrated the 'peasant brawl', in order to capture the demotic energies of popular worship.[29] It is worth heeding that slightly detached but sympathetic generic expectation in assessing Burns's attitude to the phenomenon he describes.

Burns's poem opens with the narrator encountering three allegorical '*hizzies*' who represent respectively 'Hypocrisy', 'Superstition', and 'Fun', the opposed yet intermingled qualities that constitute the experience of the Holy Fair. 'Fun' quickly claims the poet as her own and invites him to join her: as all commentators have noted, she's based on Fergusson's allegorical 'Mirth' in 'Leith Races', but both the religious occasion and the religious satire of Burns's poem (quite alien to Fergusson's more light-hearted purpose), demand the presence of her other two, more serious, sisters. 'Hypocrisy' presides over the 'Chosen swatch' (l. 86) and the 'auld licht' preachers satirized in lines 100–53, whereas 'Superstition' embodies the popular religious disposition of the crowd as they mix heavy drinking with prayer.[30] 'Fun' on the other hand represents the crowd's promiscuous mixture of bucolic and erotic enjoyment with religious worship, as well as the poet's delight in the exuberance of the common people in festive mood.

---

[28] 'Heron's Memoir of Burns', in Hans Hecht, *Robert Burns: The Man and his Work* (1936) (Ayr: Alloway Publishing, 1981), 264.

[29] Allan H. MacLaine writes 'the scene is described from the point of view of an amused spectator who takes no part in the action and is presumably on a higher social and intellectual level than the merrymakers. The tone of the satire, however, is usually genial and good-natured.' *Scots Poems of Festivity: The Christis Kirk Tradition* (Glasgow: ASLS, 1996), pp. v–vi. The genre had been modernized by Robert Fergusson in 'Hallow Fair' and 'Leith Races' (1773), the latter being Burns's most immediate source. See also Murray Pittock, *Scottish and Irish Romanticism* (Oxford: Oxford University Press, 2008), 51.

[30] McGinty, *Robert Burns and Religion*, 211, fails to discern the presence of 'Superstition' anywhere in the poem, but this may be a case of not seeing the wood for the trees.

The satirical qualities of 'Holy Willie or 'The Ordination' are certainly evident here, but they're combined with a more light-hearted attitude to popular religion than in such poems as 'The Twa Herds' or 'The Ordination'. The 'Holy Fair''s central concern is to celebrate a carnivalesque intermingling of the sacred and profane, the spiritual and the carnal, the high and the low. As readers of Swift well know, critics of Calvinist enthusiasm had long conflated spiritual enthusiasm with sexual arousal, exemplified in the case of Burns by his description (in a letter of August 1784) of a chiliastic cult called the 'Buchanites' that had seceded from the Presbytery Relief Sect in Irvine, and lived in neighbouring barns and woods sharing all things in common and practising free love. Their founder, Elspat Buchan, 'pretends to give them the Holy Ghost by breathing on them, which she does with postures & practices that are scandalously indecent' [CL i. 22]. It is odd to hear such a disapproving note from the author of 'The Fornicator', evidently alert to devotional heavy breathing either within or without the body of the Kirk.[31]

'The Holy Fair''s intermingling of spirituality and carnality is achieved through an inventive use of poetic form: Burns's dense Scots diction and his mastery of the heavily stressed 'Christ's Kirk' stanza, with its interlinking *ababcdcd* rhymes and its repetitive refrain or 'bob-wheel'. The spiritual/carnal doublet is promoted by abundant use of the rhetorical technique of syllepsis, or zeugma; 'Here, some are thinkan on their sins, | An' some upo' their claes' (ll. 82–3). In a familiar trope, the fire and brimstone preaching of 'auld licht' Revd Alexander Moodie is described as sufficient to frighten the devil himself (ll. 100–8) whereas clerical hypocrisy is embodied in the persona of Revd Alexander Miller:

> Wee [Miller] niest, the Guard relieves,
>       An' Orthodoxy raibles,
> Tho' in his heart he weel believes,
>       An' thinks it auld wives' fables:
> But faith! the birkie wants a *Manse*,
>       So, cannilie he hums them;
> Altho' his *carnal* Wit an' Sense
>       Like hafflins-wise o'ercomes him
>            At times that day.    (ll. 145–53)

Miller may privately regard Orthodox doctrines as 'auld wives's fables' but, needful of a parish, he's careful to pander to the popular creed. Seen in the light of Burns's account of patronage in 'The Twa Herds', this exposes popular election as a licence for clerical hypocrisy, not to mention demagoguery. (Ironically, Miller was subsequently presented to the parish of Kilmaurs by

---

[31] For wider discussion of this theme, see Raymond Bentman, 'Robert Burns's Declining Fame', *Studies in Romanticism* 11/3 (1972), 215–19.

the Earl of Eglinton in the face of violent opposition from the congregation [Kin. iii. 1102].)

Having stirred up the tempo with a panegyric on alcohol in lines 163–71 ('Leeze me on Drink! it gies us mair | Than either School or Colledge'), Burns really cuts to the chase with his marvellous satire on the preaching of 'Black Jock' Russell whom we encountered as one of the 'Twa Herds'. Moodie's preaching has entwined spiritual enthusiasm with sensuality, likened at line 116 to 'cantharidian [aphrodisiac] plaisters', but Russell further arouses the alcohol-fired 'kittled notions' of his congregation by harrowing their souls. However, the day is getting late, and some are beginning to nod off, which permits Burns to insert a deft touch of bathos. One somnolent listener awakes in terror convinced that he can hear the roaring of hellfire, only to discover that ''twas but some neebor *snoran* | Asleep that day' (ll. 197–8).

As Kinsley points out, 'The Holy Fair' translates the peasant brawl of the 'Christ's Kirk' tradition into 'a battle of doctrine, words, and histrionics' fought out between the Mauchline preachers [Kin. iii. 1099]. Despite his ironic reduction of Russell's hellfire eloquence, Burns awards the preacherly palms to the 'auld licht' ministers. The fact that the orthodox have all the best tunes is evident in lines 127–35, where Burns criticizes the bland anglicized eloquence of the Moderate Revd George Smith:

> What signifies his barren shine,
>     Of *moral pow'rs* and *reason*;
> His English style, an' gesture fine,
>     Are a' clean out o' season.
> Like SOCRATES or ANTONINE,
>     Or some auld pagan heathen,
> The *moral man* he does define,
>     But ne'er a word o' *faith* in
>         That's right that day.   (ll. 127–35)

Smith's 'cauld harangues' may avoid the 'hypocrisy' and 'superstition' of the 'auld licht', but they're entirely lacking in spiritual power or popular appeal. His abstract rhetoric is decorporealized, hence 'the godly''s need to get a compensatory 'lift' from their 'jars and barrels'. As we've seen in other poems, there's often a knife-edge tension between an 'improved' and a populist Burns, and in the Kirk satires or the poems of the 'reserved canon' we've charted the triumph of the former over the latter. It is not so much that Burns here mimics the perspective of the orthodox, as Thomas Crawford suggests [*BPS* 72], it's rather that the poem's blazing celebration of demotic energy (as in 'Scotch Drink' or 'The Author's Earnest Cry and Prayer') here makes the 'new licht' flame burn with a dim light. Smith's 'English style and gestures fine' speedily send a congregation of the faithful off to the beer tent, while his rationalist insistence on justification by good works, rather than faith, lacks the power to grip the superstitious imaginations of an 'unimproved' and inebriated congregation.

Given Burns's stated sympathy with the tenets of Moderate theology, his criticism of Smith's sermon is far-sighted, reflecting a critical analysis of the hegemonic weaknesses, as well as the intellectual strengths, of enlightenment. In rural Ayrshire 'the people' prefers their religion unimproved, although this is hardly a vindication of the fanaticism, and hypocrisy, of their spiritual leaders. The poem ends appropriately with an orgiastic celebration of drink and sex (the zeugma underlines the fact that this is a kind of mock sacrament, like the conclusion of 'Love and Liberty') for which the assembled congregation have been warmed up, rather than warned off, by the days' preaching:

> There's some are fou o' *love divine*;
> There's some are fou o' *brandy*;
> An' monie jobs that day begin,
> May end in *Houghmagandie*
> Some ither day.   (ll. 239–43)

Although there's considerable historical evidence for both sexual dalliance and heavy drinking at eighteenth-century Holy Fairs, it's instructive to note what the poem omits, as well as what it satirically highlights. In his study *Holy Fairs: Scotland and the Making of American Revivalism*, Leigh Schmidt observes that 'there is no reference to the communion sacrament itself, the "central solemnity" of the Holy Fair, at a time when 'the communion at Mauchline drew between 1240 and 1400 people annually to the Lord's table. Given such numbers, the successive table servings and solemn sacramental meditations would have gone on all day. Burns, in neglecting these activities in his poem, revealed the selective vision of a disengaged, sardonic spectator.'[32] On the other hand, Callum Brown's claim that only 20 per cent of parishioners actually received the sacrament on such occasions may vindicate Burns's precision as a social observer: many of the celebrants were, quite literally, only there for the beer.[33]

'The Holy Fair' dismantles modern stereotypes of the solemn austerity of Presbyterian devotion, a view of popular evangelical enthusiasm that stands in antithetical relationship to the image of pious family worship painted in 'The Cotter's Saturday Night'. Nevertheless, Burns's attitude to this carnivalesque manifestation of popular religion puzzled contemporary commentators. In his *Animadversions on Some Poets and Poetasters of the Present Age* (1788), the labouring-class Paisley poet James Maxwell castigated Burns's liberal theology

---

[32] Leigh Eric Schmidt, *Holy Fairs: Scotland and the Making of American Revivalism* (Princeton, NJ: Princeton University Press, 1989), 175.

[33] Callum G. Brown, *Religion and Society in Scotland since 1707* (Edinburgh: Edinburgh University Press, 1997), 73. Brown also notes that, given the resulting absenteeism from work, landowner pressure dictated that Holy Fairs were only held once a year in early August.

from a conservative (although not, it seems, an orthodox) position, especially 'Address to the Deil'. But Maxwell also had a lot to say about 'The Holy Fair', discovering blasphemy in the poem's very title 'The most solemn ordinance Christ hath ordain'd, | Which hath in his church, since his passion, remain'd [i.e. the Sacrament of Communion], | This infidel scoffer calls that but a Fair, | To which rakes and harlots together repair'.[34] Conceding that the festal sacrament was indeed 'grossly abused' by many celebrants, Maxwell identified Burns with the 'rakes and harlots' described in his poem, calling down the wrath of an avenging God to punish him.[35] For all his doggerel, at least Maxwell's belief in the possibility of redemption, more liberal than Willie Fisher's, allowed 'Satan inspir'd' Burns' some chance of avoiding hellfire. In a contrasting reading of the poem, Burns's polite ministerial apologist Revd Hamilton Paul confidently identified 'The Holy Fair's' indebtedness to the 'Christ's Kirk' tradition with a regulative form of 'Hudibrastic humour', entirely missing Burns's enjoyment of the carnivalesque excesses of the day. 'There is hardly any part of our form of public worship less edifying than field or tent preaching', wrote Paul, 'and the incoherent harangues uttered by one who combines the gesticulations of a mountebank with those of an auctioneer, are calculated to amuse the populace, but not to instruct them.'[36] Paul reads Burns's poem as part of a systematic and orchestrated attack on 'auld licht' Calvinism, as if Burns were a religious reformer rather than a poet. 'Choosing forms of worship from poetic tales': as William Blake well knew, when a poet tackles religion it's often his fate to be enlisted in the ranks of the doctrinaire, and Burns was no exception.

Paul seems dedicated to extracting 'Fun' (as well, of course, as 'Superstition') from Presbyterian worship; of the original 'three hizzies' encountered on Galston Muir, perhaps only 'Hypocrisy' remains intact in this account. 'Burns', he continued approvingly, 'has contributed his share towards accomplishing the abolition of tent preaching and stools of repentance—proving the disastrous consequences of popular elections, and leading the liberal mind to a rational view of the nature of prayer . . . checking that flood of fanaticism with which the land is in danger of being deluged, by those who darken counsel by words without knowledge.'[37] A similar view of the poem from a source closer to Burns is expressed in a marginal note by his Dumfriesshire neighbour Robert Riddell in his copy of Thomas Pennant's *A Tour in Scotland* (1769). Pennant had regretted the 'fighting and other indecencies' which mar the annual Communion sacrament in many Scottish parishes; Riddell's marginal comment reads 'Vide Burns's

[34] James Maxwell, *Animadversions on Some Poets and Poetasters of the Present Age* (Paisley, 1788), 7. Actually the term 'Fair' has been used critically to describe the festal sacrament by Thomas Rhind in 1712, so it wasn't Burns's coinage (Schmidt, *Holy Fairs*, 170).

[35] Maxwell, *Animadversions*, 7.

[36] Revd Hamilton Paul, *Poems and Songs of Robert Burns*, p. xxxix.

[37] Ibid. pp. xlii–xliii.

Holy Fair—a poem that lashes this shameful abuse. RR.'[38] Such responses reveal that Burns's contemporaries more commonly read the poem as a critique, rather than a celebration, of popular religion and carnival festivity.

To some extent Schmidt's modern assessment supports these contemporary views in proposing that Burns's poem was largely instrumental in bringing about the demise of the old 'Holy Fairs' in nineteenth-century Scotland, Ulster, and North America. The premodern notion of the sacrament as a communal feast in which the celebrants sat together around a table was 'improved' into the hierarchical space of family pews, with an orderly queue at the Communion table, while the communal cup was replaced by individual glasses to prevent contamination. 'To Burns's Victorian interpreters, the "sanctimonious sensuality" of the festal communions paled before "the sacrament of domestic reunion". Worship within the "Paradise of Home" put to shame such great religious meetings as the "motley gatherings" for the eucharist.'[39] We'll see in the next chapter that the family piety of 'The Cotter's Saturday Night' did indeed have huge resonance for nineteenth-century readers, albeit at the cost of a very selective reading of Burns's poem.

The most influential reinterpretation of Burns's poem however was John Gibson Lockhart's penultimate Letter LXXVI in *Peter's Letters to his Kinsfolk* (1819), which fixed on Burns's account of the Holy Fair (retitled here, more augustly, 'the Country Sacrament') as a crucial indicator of the spiritual condition of Scotland. Lockhart's narrator, a Welsh visitor named 'Peter Morris', marginalized Burnesian 'houghmagandie' ('a solemn devotion was imprinted on every downcast eyelid and trembling lip around me'),[40] in order to resituate the festal Eucharist firmly at the centre of the occasion. Bypassing the partisan squabbling of 'auld' and 'new lichts', Lockhart aestheticized Scottish popular religion, finding in 'rustic assemblies like these' the 'true characteristics of every race of men', 'natural germs of that, which, under the influence of culture, assumes a prouder character, and blossoms into the animating soul of a national literature'.[41] (The implication is that Burns's poem needs 'correction' if it is to serve as a synecdoche of the nation's literature.) Ian Duncan rightly discerns 'something unwholesome' about Lockhart's attempt to squeeze popular religion into the service of a reinvented Scottish culture, as his 'purple prose metamorphoses the erotic vitality of Burn's Holy Fair into a hectic, vampiric illusion'.[42]

---

[38]   Thomas Pennant, *A Tour in Scotland; MDCCLXIX*, 4th edn. (London, 1776), marginal note at p. 101. This copy, heavily annotated by Robert Riddell, is in the Murray Collection in Glasgow University Library (Mu6-d.9).

[39]   Schmidt, *Holy Fairs*, 200.

[40]   J. G. Lockhart, *Peter's Letters to his Kinsfolk*, 3rd edn., 3 vols. (Edinburgh: W. Blackwood, 1819), iii. 324.

[41]   Ibid. 326.

[42]   Duncan, *In Scott's Shadow: The Novel in Romantic Edinburgh* (Princeton: Princeton University Press, 2007), 64.

Enlightenment thinkers perceived a generic notion of 'superstition' as the main obstacle to improvement, a concept of the popular supernatural that covered a multitude of errors obstructing spiritual as well as social progress. 'Superstition' might be based on an irrational fear of ghosts or a Calvinistic terror of hellfire; it might entail reverence for traditional agricultural practices such as runrig cultivation, or a refusal to accept the new labour-abridging winnowing machines on the ground that they were the '*Deil's wind*' [Aiton, p. 77]; it might take the form (in Smith's *Wealth of Nations*) of popular hatred of grain merchants as 'engrossers' or 'forestallers', and a justified suspicion of market forces. All over Europe the enlightened savants followed Bayle and Voltaire in applying the scalpel of reason to such popular prejudices, which many believed were fomented by the cunning connivances of priestcraft.

At his most 'enlightened', Burns can sound a Humean note: 'away with old-wife prejudices and tales! Every age and every nation has had a different set of stories; and as the many are always weak, of consequence they have often, perhaps always been deceived' [CL i. 258].[43] Yet there is another side to this, for the author of 'Tam o' Shanter' and 'Halloween' was not only an enthusiast for popular superstitions, as well as being a powerful storyteller in the popular idiom. He was also, in Ted Cowan's formulation, a 'superstitious sceptic' who 'knew that the phantoms would soon conspire to destroy the enchantment, sensing that where the Reformation had failed, the agrarian transformations, which so bedevilled his own agricultural enterprises, would succeed in combination with such powerful allies as philosophy'.[44]

This is nowhere better illustrated than in Burns's 'Address to the Deil' [K 76], published at fifth place in the Kilmarnock edition immediately follow-ing 'The Holy Fair'. It is a masterpiece of sceptical burlesque, largely achieved (once again) through the poem's full Scots idiom and popular, proverbial register. The poem begins with a learned back-slapping apostrophe to the dark sublime of Miltonic 'Prince . . . of many throned pow'rs' (quoted as the poem's epigraph), immediately ridiculed in the opening lines by the familiar address of 'Auld Hornie, Satan, Nick, or Clootie' (l. 2). Yet, as Cowan notes, there's a nervousness to the poem's laughter, maybe because, as Burns wrote in 1787 (in complete contradiction to his above-quoted scepticism) 'I am natural-ly of a superstitious cast' [CL i. 93].[45]

The Devil is of course a time-honoured habitué of Scottish writing from William Dunbar's 'Dance of the Sevin Deidly Sins' through James Hogg's *Confessions of a Justified Sinner* and James Robertson's contemporary *Testimony of Gideon Mack*. In 'Address to the Deil' he's the folk trickster and mischief-

[43] See Edward J. Cowan, 'Burns and Superstition', in Kenneth Simpson (ed.), *Love and Liberty: Robert Burns, A Bicentenary Celebration* (Phantassie: Tuckwell, 1997), 229–38 at 236.
[44] Ibid. 237.
[45] Ibid. 234.

maker of popular tradition, rather than the malevolent genius of 'Address of Beelzebub' [K 108]. As an apparition, he is either, quite literally, the embodiment of an old wives' tale ('I've heard my rev'rend *Graunie* say, | In lanely glens ye like to stray', ll. 25–6) or, when experienced first-hand, a delusion of the senses. The comic relief from superstition experienced in stanzas 7 and 8 resembles the 'hellfire snoring' interrupting Black Jock Russell's preaching in 'The Holy Fair', but it also shows Burns's powers as a storyteller to raise goose-pimples:

> Ae dreary, windy, winter night,
> The stars shot down wi' sklentan light,
> Wi' you, *mysel*, I gat a fright:
>          Ayont the lough;
> Ye, like a *rash-buss*, stood in sight,
>          Wi' waving sugh:
>
> The cudgel in my nieve did shake,
> Each bristl'd hair stood like a stake,
> When wi' an eldritch, stoor, *quaick, quaick*,
>          Amang the springs,
> Awa ye squatter'd like a *drake*,
>          On whistling wings.    (ll. 37–48)

For all its comic energy, this is a higher-critical apologetic for superstitious terror rather than a Voltairean sneer, at once exposing it to sceptical reason, but also expressing its power over the imagination. The devil may turn out to be only a duck, but this hardly diffuses the power of the apparition. As Burns wrote in his letter to Dr Moore, 'to this hour, in my nocturnal rambles, I sometimes keep a sharp look-out in suspicious places; and though nobody can be more sceptical in these matters than I, yet it often takes an effort of Philosophy to shake off these idle terrors' [CL i. 135]. The devil takes the blame for a multitude of evils, from minor mishaps such as curdling milk, or rendering the 'young Guidman' impotent, to darker mischiefs such as drowning the traveller in the frozen ford. Demonic interference is also blamed for economic failure, a sort of jinx in the productive system. At lines 79–84 Burns knowingly mocks popular attitudes to Freemasonic *diablerie* in which 'some cock, or cat' must be sacrificed to appease the devil raised by 'MASON's mystic *word* an' *grip*', before proceeding to a masterly poetic paraphrase of the Fall, and the Devil's persecution of Job: 'Then you, ye auld, snick-drawing dog! | Ye cam to Paradise incog, | An' play'd on a man a cursed brogue | (Black be your fa'!) | An' gied the infant warld a shog, | 'Maist ruin'd a' (ll. 91–6).

Allusion to the Arminian rejection of Calvin's doctrine of repudiation here, with a concomitant stress on redemption ('*Maist* [almost] ruin'd a') is followed in the final stanzas by the 'Bardie''s comically expressed hopes for his own salvation: the Deil may believe that he's bound for the 'black pit', 'But faith! he'll turn a corner jinkan, | An cheat you yet' (ll. 119–20). Francis Jeffrey perceptively described this as an instance of Burns's 'relenting nature':[46] the poem's grand climactic flourish proposes that, if there's hope of redemption for the 'rantin drinkin *Bardie*', then there may also be hope for the Deil himself:

> But fare you weel, auld *Nickie-ben*!
> O wad ye tak a thought an' men!
> Ye aiblins might—I dinna ken—
>          Still hae a *stake*:
> I'm wae to think upo' yon den,
>          Ev'n for your sake.   (ll. 121–6)

In his correspondence Burns often struck an attitude by identifying himself with the Devil's 'dauntless magnanimity' ('Give me a spirit like my favourite hero, Milton's Satan' [CL i. 95]), but here the situation is reversed; the Devil is advised to identify himself with the 'Bardie''s saving grace, his 'relenting nature', if he wishes to mend. The suggestion itself, so offensive to the orthodox mindset, was already an article of the sentimental world-view, as in *Tristram Shandy*, 'I declare, quoth my uncle Toby, my heart would not let me curse the devil himself . . . But he is cursed and damned already, to all eternity, replied Dr Slop. I am sorry for it, quoth my uncle Toby.'[47]

Although Revd Hugh Blair objected to the 'indecency' of lines 61–6 (describing the Devil's power to prevent ejaculation during sexual intercourse), it's unlikely that the poem's theology did Burns any harm among the Moderate Edinburgh literati. By contrast, in Ayrshire, 'Address to the Deil' did have the power to offend almost as much as 'The Twa Herds' and 'Holy Willie'. It goaded James Maxwell into a doggerel refutation, the stilted English diction and metrical ineptitude of which (especially compared with Burns's fluid Scots habbie stanzas) completely hamstrung its criticism: 'To Satan this Infidel writes without dread, | Because in rebellion they're jointly agreed. | Against all the laws in the scriptures forth held, | He strives to the utmost to have them expell'd.'[48] The 'auld lichts' didn't *always* have the best tunes.

Although 'Halloween' [K 73] isn't about religion, it shares 'Address to the Deil''s fascination with popular superstition, describing some of the ways in which 'some merry, friendly, countra folks' apply for supernatural assistance in divining their future spouses. At 252 lines, Burns's longest poem (excluding the cantata sequence of 'Love and Liberty'), 'Halloween''s lack of narrative development may account for the fact that it's never been one of Burns's best-loved poems, although it probably influenced Keats's treatment of the same theme in 'St Agnes Eve'. The poem is divided into discrete sections, each of which describes a different spell for divining the future, together with anecdotes of

---

[46] Review of Cromek's *Reliques, Edinburgh Review* 26 (Jan. 1809), 249–76 at 263.
[47] *Tristram Shandy* III. xi. The parallel is noted by Kin. iii. 1132–2.
[48] Maxwell, *Animadversions*, 6.

the mishaps that can befall the participant when the spell backfires.[49] In most cases the desired outcome is an apparition of the future spouse, but there's always a risk that the spell will raise 'the *foul Thief*' (l. 120) instead. As in 'Address to the Deil', Burns invokes the figure of the 'rev'rend Graunie' as sub-narrator (ll. 117–80), again underlining the fact that popular superstitions are literally 'old wives' tales'.

As a celebration of popular festivity 'Halloween' does resemble 'The Holy Fair', and like that poem employs the 'Christ's Kirk' stanza (and full Scots diction) in which 'spritely rustic follies [are] seen by a superior and amused spectator'.[50] In contrast, however, are its antiquarian headnote and footnotes, glossing the vernacular account of folk customs, their detached tone starkly contrasting with the authorial persona established by the Kilmarnock preface: 'The passion of prying into Futurity makes a striking part of the history of Human-nature, in its rude state, in all ages and nations; and it may be some entertainment to a philosophic mind, if any such should honor the Author with a perusal, to see the remains of it, among the more unenlightened in our own' [Kin. i. 152]. The rationalizing paratexts work in ironic counterpoint to the verse, enforcing the poem's affectionate scepticism concerning popular belief. One example will suffice here, the sixth stanza's description of pulling corn stalks for divinatory purposes:

> The lasses staw frae'mang them a',
>     To pou their *stalks o' corn*;*
> But *Rab* slips out, an' jinks about,
>     Behint the muckle thorn:
> He grippet *Nelly* hard an' fast;
>     Loud skirl'd a' the lasses;
> But her *tap-pickle* maist was lost,
>     When kiutlan in the *Fause-house*
>                 Wi' him that night.   (ll. 46–54)

Burns's footnote to line 47 explains 'they go to the barn-yard, and pull each, at three several times, a stalk of Oats. If the third stalk wants the *top-pickle*, that is, the grain at the top of the stalk, the party in question will come to the marriage-bed any thing but a Maid' [Kin. i. 154]. Nelly loses her virginity to Rab as predicted by the missing 'top-pickle', but the reason is hardly occult; in a rapid metaphoric substitution, the lost 'tap-pickle' *is* her virginity, forfeited while 'kiutlan' ('cuddling') with

---

[49] These are, in sequence; pulling out a stock of kail (ll. 28–45), 'interpreting' a stalk of oats (ll. 46–54), burning nuts in the fire (each one representing a lad or lass) to see whether they burn together or jump apart (ll. 55–90), throwing a 'clew' of blue yarn into the kiln (ll. 91–108), eating an apple in the mirror by candlelight (ll. 109–25), repeating the 'hemp-seed' spell (ll. 127–80), winnowing with an empty 'wecht' (winnowing hoop) (ll. 181–207), 'fathoming the stack' (ll. 199–207), 'sleeve wetting' in a burn at the confluence of three farms (ll. 208–34), and dipping the hands of a blindfolded person into 'three luggies' or water dishes.

[50] MacLaine, *Scots Poems of Festivity*, 112.

her partner during the Halloween festivities. In a similarly sceptical vein, demonic apparitions (like those at ll. 165–71 or 201–6) turn out to be nothing more than a stray 'Grumphie' (pig), or an 'auld moss-oak' looming out of the darkness. As in 'Address to the Deil', the supernatural is mocked as the antithesis of enlightenment, notwithstanding its undeniable power over the human affections.[51]

## 'A CANDID, LIB'RAL BAND': RELIGION AND IMPROVEMENT IN THE EDINBURGH POEMS

I'll close this chapter by considering two very different poems added to the Edinburgh volume, 'The Ordination' [K 85] and 'The Brigs of Ayr' [K 120]. In a certain sense the former represents a return to the carnivalesque idiom and 'Christ's Kirk' stanza of 'The Holy Fair', but with the detached enjoyment of the narrator of the earlier poem now replaced by a course, bigoted voice, more like that of the speaker of 'The Holy Tulzie'. If 'Address to the Unco Guid' [K 39] (another religious satire added to the Edinburgh volume) is concerned with spiritual 'Hypocrisy', its companion poem 'The Ordination' is concerned rather with her vulgar twin 'Superstition', in some of her more repellent sectarian manifestations.

'The Ordination' returns to the issue of patronage discussed above in relation to 'The Holy Tulzie'. Its occasion was the presentation of the 'Auld Licht' minister Revd James Mackinlay to the Laigh Kirk in Kilmarnock in August 1785. Previously, the Moderates William Lindsay and John Mutrie had held the charge, although Lindsay's presentation had been severely obstructed by mob violence. What seems to have particularly incensed Moderate opinion was the fact that Mackinlay's presentation was a result of the patronage of the Whig Earl of Glencairn, who had in this instance evidently succumbed to popular pressure, or at least reacted to fear of popular disturbance. (By an ironic twist, and presumably no thanks to this particular poem, he would become Burns's own major patron.[52]) The paradox is expressed in the now-familiar voice of 'auld licht' prejudice:

> Lang, *Patronage*, wi' rod o' airn,
>   Has shor'd the Kirk's undoin;
> As lately [Fenwick], sair forfairn,
>   Has proven to its ruin:

---

[51] Crawford criticized 'Halloween''s 'elements of superciliousness, of conscious superiority, and even of thinly disguised cruelty' [*BPS* p.124]. His perceptive reading of the poem's episodic structure and lack of narrative development echoes the criticism of antiquarian discourse discussed in Ch. 8, in its fixation with the particular, and its fragmentary and associative parataxis.

[52] See William Donaldson, 'The Glencairn Connection: Robert Burns and Scottish Politics, 1786–96', *Studies in Scottish Literature* 16 (1981), 68–72.

> Our Patron, honest Man! [Glencairn],
>     He saw mischief was brewin;
> An' like a godly, elect bairn,
>     He's wal'd us out a true ane,
>         And sound this day.   (ll. 64–72)

The speaker's customary condemnation of patronage is opportunistically suspended, in praise of Glencairn's inspired choice of an 'auld licht' clergyman, a suspension that allows Burns to expose hypocrisy (as well as superstition) in the orthodox ranks. 'The Ordination' was the strongest satires on the 'auld lichts' yet published by Burns when it appeared in the Edinburgh volume in 1787, although it had of course, like the others, already circulated locally in *samizdat*: as with the published text of 'The Holy Fair' in Kilmarnock, the names of the ministers were asterisked to avoid charges of libel, although here they were initialized to facilitate identification.

The opening stanza echoes the demotic energy of 'The Holy Fair' as Kilmarnock's weavers and artisans flock to the Laigh Kirk, and thence to Begbie's tavern, to 'pour divine libations | For joy this day' (ll. 8–9). But the language of joy soon turns to figurative cruelty, as the mob turn on the hated target of 'Common Sense' whose persecution is now guaranteed by Mackinlay's ordination, and who, at lines 98–9, is driven back to '*Jamie Beattie*' to 'mak . . . her plaint'. Burns here exerts the graphic physicality of Scots idiom to represent the violent passions of his orthodox speaker; Mackinlay will 'blaud' (thrash) 'Common Sense' with his flail (l. 15), 'clap a *shangan*' (fasten a can or a cleft stick) on her tail, and set the children to pelt her with dirt (ll. 16–19). 'Heresy' will be 'whanged' (whipped) (l. 26), just as later in the poem, 'Orthodoxy' flogs her foes 'Learning', 'Common Sense', and 'Morality' through Kilmarnock with a 'cat o' nine tails' (l. 93). In a disturbing Swiftian touch, the speaker exults at the sight of Morality being flayed, her skin peeling off like an onion (l. 105).

As the voice of prejudice works itself up into a passion of fanatical hatred, Burns grotesquely literalizes the term 'new licht' as a scene of immolation, as the mob 'light a spunk' (match) and roast their victims in the flames (ll. 124–7). The footnote to line 120 defines 'New-light' as 'a cant phrase, in the West of Scotland, for those religious opinions which Dr Taylor of Norwich has defended so strenuously'. The footnote exposes the target of hatred as remarkably innocuous, ironically undercutting the fanatical views expressed in the verse. Burns replays the kind of mob violence threatened in 'The Author's Earnest Cry and Prayer', but here revealed in an altogether unsympathetic light. It underlines Callum Brown's claim that that disputed patronage, to a greater extent than malt riots, may have been 'the most persistent and geographically widespread cause of popular unrest in Scotland' during Burns's lifetime.[53]

---

[53] Brown, 'Protest in the Pews', 99.

The speaker's idea of worship is characterized by the same benighted crudeness. Lines 19–22 mock the 'holy clangor' of cacophonous and dissonant psalm singing, reminding us of the 'auld licht' insistence that the precentor 'read the line' of each psalm so that the illiterate, or those without a copy of the text, could join in.[54] The selection of a 'proper text' for the lesson is drawn from the most unenlightened and violent passages in the Old Testament:

> How graceless *Ham* leugh at his Dad,
>   Which made *Canaan* a niger;
> Or *Phineas* drove the murdering blade
>   Wi' whore-abhorring rigour;
> Or *Zipporah*, the scauldin jad,
>   Was like a bluidy tiger
> I' th' inn that day.   (ll. 30–6)[55]

McGinty points out that all three texts are concerned with taboos 'relating to the self-righteous and judgemental elements of those religious peoples who think of themselves as the 'elect'.[56] The censure isn't of course aimed specifically at the Jews of the Old Testament, who simply behaved like other 'primitive' peoples, but rather at Burns's contemporaries, the eighteenth-century orthodox. Their sense of 'election' is exposed as a form of violent sectarianism, justifying their conduct by a literalist interpretation of the morally redundant values of such carefully chosen Old Testament texts.[57]

At lines 73–6 of 'The Ordination', the triumphant repossession of Kilmarnock by the 'auld lichts' prompts the speaker to recommend that the Moderate remnant cut their losses and retreat to 'the wicked town of [Ayr]' (l. 75). And with them, they hope that their ally 'Auld Hornie' (the Devil) must 'detach | Wi' a' his brimstone squadrons' (l. 88–9). The 'wicked town' is the setting of 'The Brigs of Ayr', one of Burns's few urban poems, discussion of which will close this chapter, broadening out the antagonism between 'auld and new lichts' from polemical divinity to a wider exploration of the dialectical relationship between custom and 'improvement'.

---

[54] The cessation of this practice apparently caused many parishioners to turn their backs on the Kirk and join Seceder congregations (ibid. 96).

[55] There's a subtle theological rationale to Burns's (footnoted) selection of Genesis 9: 22, Numbers 25: 8, and Exodus 4: 25. The first two lend themselves to racial hatred, not just the 'negrification' of Ham's descendants, but also Phineas's zealous slaughter of an Israelite man sleeping with a Midianite woman; the third text alludes to Moses' wife Zipporah brutally circumcising her young son with a sharp stone.

[56] McGinty, *Robert Burns and Religion*, 221.

[57] In the *Manual of Religious Belief*, William Burnes had written that the laws of the Jewish Commonwealth 'can be neither binding on us, who are not of that commonwealth, nor on the Jews, because their commonwealth is at an end' (Chambers-Wallace, i. 457).

Religion wasn't the only battleground between 'improvement' and tradition in the town of Ayr in the mid-1780s.[58] Although its economic growth had been set back by the failure of the Douglas Heron Bank in 1772, Robert Heron noted (at the end of the following decade) that 'the city of Ayr may now look back on every former period of its history, as less splendid than its present condition'.[59] With a rapidly expanding population of around 4,000, Ayr exported coal to Ireland and imported timber and iron from the Baltic; most of the surrounding land was enclosed and improved, and although manufacturing was still inconsiderable, the textile and weaving industries were growing, and collieries had been established at nearby St Quivox and Newton-upon-Ayr.[60] Sixty new houses had been built in the town alone in the decade of the 1780s, mainly in the New Town on the north side of the river, and a new five-arch bridge (the focus of Burns's poem) was erected in 1786–8, to increase the volume of traffic, which the old fifteenth-century bridge could no longer accommodate [*Statistical Account*, vi. 38–9].

Robert Heron found that conspicuous consumption of the Ayr bourgeoisie resembled that of the burghers of Dumfries and Edinburgh, rather than the more 'douce' inhabitants of Perth or Glasgow; 'It is the character of the shewy gentleman, not that of the luxurious although *ostensibly* frugal and simple citizen, which predominates here.'[61] It wasn't just the fashionably Arminian tinge of its theology that in the eyes of some landward contemporaries justified the soubriquet of 'the wicked town of Ayr'. At the other end of the social scale, the *Statistical Account* noted wealth and improvement had come at a cost; the numbers of the poor had rocketed, with paupers flocking in from neighbouring parishes to claim the 'poor stent', including a proliferation of 'unfortunate women' whose illegitimate children had been fathered by roving soldiers and sailors.[62]

Burns dedicated 'The Brigs of Ayr' (written shortly after the publication of the Kilmarnock edition in the autumn of 1786) to his patron John Ballantine, Esq., banker, merchant, and proprietor of Castlehill estate near Kilmarnock, elected Provost of Ayr in 1787. As in his 'half-way' dedication of the Kilmarnock poems to Gavin Hamilton, Burns here stressed his personal 'independence' (l. 8), skilfully disavowing any intention to 'labour hard the panegyric close, | With all the venal soul of dedicating Prose'(ll. 13–14). Ballantine was Dean of the Guild of Stone Masons and an enthusiast for the new bridge, designed by the leading London-Scots architect Robert Adam. To a greater extent than 'The

[58] Appropriately enough, the entries on Ayr in the *Statistical Account* were provided by 'the Rev. Drs McGill and Dalrymple'.

[59] Robert Heron, *Observations made in a Journey through the Western Counties of Scotland, in the Autumn of 1792*, 2 vols. (Perth, 1799), ii. 339.

[60] *Statistical Account*, vi. 18–44 at 41–3; Heron, *Observations*, ii. 340. See also John Strawhorn, 'Ayrshire in the Enlightenment', in Graham Cruikshank (ed.), *A Sense of Place History: Studies in Scottish Local History* (Edinburgh: Scotland's Cultural Heritage, 1988), 188–201.

[61] Heron, *Observations*, ii. 340–1.

[62] Ibid. 44.

Vision' (a poem whose ambitions it shares in many respects), 'The Brigs of Ayr' seeks to address the 'tradition/modernity' debate in terms of verse form and diction as well as content. Kinsley succinctly describes its formal divisions, 'consist[ing] of a dedication (ll. 1–24) in Augustan English; a narrative introduction (ll. 25–90), at first diffuse and only lightly touched with Scots diction, but moving into a firmer and more natural style, with a heavier Scots element, as the poet reaches his main theme; a dialogue between the Brigs (ll. 91–191); and an epilogue in which Burns returns to the "high" manner of the English Augustans' [Kin. iii. 1200].

Although its hybrid mixing of the styles of Thomson and Fergusson is less successful than in 'The Vision', it seems pointless to reiterate Daiches's blaming of the poet for resorting to 'the English tradition' in which he was unable to 'distinguish frigidity from liveliness or competent verifying from living poetry'. ('The Edinburgh literati must have liked it,' he adds waspishly.[63]) In fact the irregular heroic couplets of 'The Brigs' derive as much from Burns's main source, Fergusson's 'Mutual Complaint of Plainstanes and Causey, in their Mother Tongue' as 'English neoclassicism'.[64] The poem forsakes Fergusson's shorter, octosyllabic line for a more ambitious amalgam of decasyllabic couplets, with the odd alexandrine and triplet thrown in; the effect, together with a rather monotonous placement of the caesura, has led critics to condemn the metrical effect (like the mixed diction) as 'awkward, rough and ragged'.[65] But Burns struggles to integrate 'improvement' at a formal level whilst keeping the poem in touch with Scots poetic tradition, an ambition fully in keeping with the poem's central argument.

The narrative introduction at lines 25–90 echoes the autumnal shift from country to city, from pastoral to urban eclogue, in the opening lines of Fergusson's 'Daft Days' and 'Auld Reekie'. Burns's 'simple Bard' (l. 47) leaves the country to wander through the nocturnal streets of 'the ancient brugh of *Ayr*', described here in some topographical detail. He overhears a dialogue (he's now characterized as 'our warlock Rhymer', l. 71) between the two spirits 'that owre the *Brigs of Ayr* preside' (l. 72). As in 'The Vision', Burns's explanation for the supernatural apparitions is tinged with irony, befitting (in Crawford's expression) the role of 'the Bard in a Rational Society' [Crawford, *BPS* 196]. Breaking with the sceptical detachment of 'Halloween''s paratext, Burns playfully introduces a 'supernatural' dialogue between the two 'Brig- spirits' by insisting that 'Bards are second-sighted' and 'ken the lingo of the sp'ritual folk; | Fays, Spunkies, Kelpies, a'' (ll. 73–5).

The flyting that follows comes with a wealth of descriptive detail well beyond the simpler dialogic exchange of Fergusson's 'Plainstanes and Causey'. Auld Brig

[63] Daiches, *Robert Burns*, 248.
[64] And beyond Fergusson to a venerable tradition of Scots couplet verse detailed by Henley and Henderson (i. 394).
[65] Ibid.

appears as 'of ancient Pictish race', complete with 'Gothic' wrinkles (ll. 77–8)[66] and later in the poem he is associated with 'plain, braid Scots' and the ancient virtues it symbolizes (l. 167). Yet despite the poem's Anglicized introduction and epilogue, it's noteworthy that enlightened 'New Brig' argues his corner in Scots rather than 'improved' English. This has the effect of questioning any simple binary opposition between English/modernity and Scots/tradition, revealing that, as with Burns's poetic project in general, it is quite possible to articulate a modern perspective in Scots.

Far from basking in any complacent pride in his venerable antiquity, 'Auld Brig' is consumed with anger tinged with jealousy, as he views the half-built 'New Brig' (striking a chord here with the 'angry' voice of 'The Ordination'): 'It chanc'd his new-come neebor took his e'e, | And e'en a vex'd and angry heart had he! | Wi' thieveless sneer to see his modish mien, | He, down the water, gies him this guid-een' (ll. 87–90). Lines 81–4 succinctly personify 'New Brig', with a demand, at line 84, that 'head' be rhymed with 'bead', in the Scots manner: '*New Brig* was buskit in a braw, new coat, | That he, at *Lon'on*, frae ane *Adams* got; | In's hand five taper staves as smooth's a bead, | Wi' virls an' whiligigums at the head' (ll. 81–4). Compared to 'Auld brig's' sombre Gothic architecture, Adams's design includes five piers ornamented with bands of metal ('virls') and fantastical baroque wreaths ('whirligigums' is glossed by Burns as 'useless ornaments, trifling appendages'). Kinsley notes that this referred to the fact that 'the piers of the old bridge have simple buttresses; those of the new bridge are circular, with open balusters above' [Kin. iii. 1204]. The introduction thus provides a rich architectural and antiquarian context for the brigs's flyting dialogue that follows.

'Auld Brig' opens by challenging his neighbour's vanity, suggesting that although crooked with age, he'll still be standing long after the 'New Brig' has been reduced to 'a shapeless cairn' (l. 110). (In the event, this was prophetic: flood damage in 1877 required that the New Brig had to be practically rebuilt at a cost of £15,000) [Henley and Henderson, i. 394]. 'New Brig' plays on the eighteenth-century sense of the word 'Gothic' meaning 'shapeless' in asking how Auld Brig's 'ruin'd, formless bulk o' stane an' lime, | Compare wi' bonie *Brigs* o' modern time?' (ll. 101–2). 'Men of taste' (l. 103), he insists, prefer a soaking in the 'Ducat-stream' ford rather than offend their aesthetic sensibilities by crossing such 'an ugly, Gothic hulk as you' (l.106). In retaliation, 'Auld Brig' suggests that modern architecture just isn't capable of building a structure able to withstand the combined waters of the tributary streams of the river Ayr, Lugar, Greenock, and Garpal, when in spate.

'New Brig' further condemns 'Gothic' architecture by alluding to the fashionable discourse of the picturesque: 'Gaunt, ghastly, ghaist-alluring edifices, |

---

[66] This alludes to the antiquarian John Pinkerton's thesis that the Picts, aboriginal inhabitants of Scotland, originated in Scandinavia, and were therefore older cousins of the 'Gothic' Anglo-Saxons who later settled in England [Kin. iii. 1204].

Hanging o'er with threat'ning jut like precipices' (ll. 130–2).[67] He associates this style with pre-reformation Catholic idolatry ('a doited Monkish race', l. 144), hardly distinguishable from the fanaticism of the early Protestant Reformers and Covenanters who have dominated seventeenth-century Ayrshire, and who held that 'sullen gloom was sterling true devotion' (l. 147). Neither species of fanaticism, he argues at lines 148–9, is welcome in modern, enlightened Ayr, echoing Burns's praise of Ayr's Moderates McGill and Dalrymple in 'To John M'math'.[68]

This is the cue for 'Auld Brigs's most effective sally: in a spirited defence of his 'wounded feelings' (l. 151) he favourably compares the 'worthy' Provosts, 'douce *Conveeners*', and '*godly Writers*' of the past, with their corrupt modern equivalents (l. 159). (This is ironically qualified, however, by the fact that the poem's dedicatee, the 'Writer' or solicitor John Ballantine, was considered by the orthodox to be distinctly 'ungodly'.) 'Auld Brig' decries modernity as a 'melancholy alteration' (l. 163) complaining that the town of Ayr is now inhabited by a 'base, degen'rate race' (l. 165).

> Nae langer Rev'rend Men, their country's glory,
> In plain, braid Scots hold forth a plain, braid story:
> Nae langer thrifty Citizens, an' douce,
> Meet owre a pint, or in the Council-house;
> But staumrel, corky-headed, graceless Gentry,
> The herryment and ruin of the country;
> Men, three-parts made by Taylors and by Barbers,
> Wha waste your weel-hain'd gear on damn'd *new Brigs* And *Harbours*!    (ll. 166–73)

At one level this picks up on the critique of a luxurious and effete gentry in 'The Twa Dogs', and (especially given Heron's remarks quoted above) Burns had some warrant for criticizing the ostentation of the gentry and wealthy burgers of Ayr. Yet the closing alexandrine, for all its metrical awkwardness, again qualifies 'Auld Brig's' criticism. The 'improving' project of building new bridges and harbours hardly seems a 'waste' of 'weel hain'd' investments, but rather money spent in the public's best interest. And given the fact that Burns's dedicatee John Ballantine was the major promoter of the new bridge scheme, there are clearly limits to the poet's sympathy with the point of view expressed in these lines.

Although the poem's 'flyting' dialogue distinguishes this exchange of views from the more eirenic conversation of 'The Twa Dogs', the form does allow for the emergence of a dialectical perspective, a point that has been noted by most commentators. For although 'New Brig' is allowed to have the last word at lines

---

[67] Ironically, in 1786 the value of the Gothic was of course in the process of being rediscovered, its irregular 'sublime' aesthetic recuperated against the neoclassical baroque and rococo.

[68] Given that, according to the *Statistical Account*, there wasn't a single Roman Catholic resident in Ayr in this period, New Brig's satire here is clearly aimed at orthodox Calvinists [*Statistical Account*, vi. 38].

174–91, his triumph isn't total. True, coming as it did between 'The Holy Fair'
and 'The Ordination' in the 1787 volume, 'New Brig''s attack on the orthodox
clergy might be allowed to carry some weight in unambiguously echoing the
views of 'priest-skelping' Burns.[69] Once again picking up on an allusion in the
Kirk satires, line 190 invokes 'Common Sense', but here employed in a more
general secular sense to oppose the 'plain dull stupidity' of the old burgesses.[70]
But when 'New Brig' turns on 'Auld Brig' for abusing Magistrates, and then
boasts that 'In *Ayr*, Wag-wits nae mair can have a handle | To mouth "A Citizen,"
a term o' scandal' (ll. 182–3) he's on less solid ground. Neither feudal law nor
religious superstition hold sway in 'improved' modern Ayr, and hereditary power
must give way to new wealth. Yet the attentive readers might recall Burns's
censure, in the 'Second Epistle to Lapraik' [K 58] of the 'purse-proud' 'city-gent'
(l. 61) or 'cit' (l. 77) with whom he 'wadna shift'.

Thomas Crawford notes that after his sudden and rather arbitrary support for
the forces of social progress, Burns 'seems to tire of the poem' [Crawford, *BPS* 197].
Maybe it would be more accurate to say, that in the spirit of Enlightenment, he
tires of the 'clishmaclavers' and 'bloody wars' (l. 192) that incarnadine Scotland's
history. Like Hume, Robertson, and Smith, Burns here turns his back on the
irresolvable factional conflicts between the forces of progress and of tradition,
'new lichts' and 'auld lichts', cavaliers and convenanters, whigs and tories,
antagonisms that for several bloody centuries have absorbed all the energies of
Scottish society. If Fergusson's 'Plainstanes' and 'Causey' conclude their 'flyting'
by threatening litigation, in the end they settle out of court, hoping that fines
levied on pedestrians who 'walk not in the proper track' will be used to support
the poor. Although there's no such reconciliation between the two Brigs, Burns's
epilogue, adopting the georgic tones and Augustan diction of Thomson's *Seasons*,
ushers in a 'fairy train' (l.195) dancing on the frozen river to harmonious music
provided by 'arts of Minstrelsy' and 'soul-ennobling Bards' (ll. 200–1). This
certainly seems a bizarre way to conclude the poem, but in fact it represents a
fitting paean to the nobler spirit of improvement, and not just in terms that
award the palms of victory to the 'New Brig'. The music of a new enlightened
'republic of taste' drowned out the ill-spirited polemic of the two brigs, indicating a
brighter, more harmonious future for Ayr, and for Scotland. Burns takes pains to
underline the fact that the music is distinctly Scottish, evoking the spirit of the
Highland fiddler James McLauchlan to whose '*Strathspeys*' (l. 204) and 'melting
airs' (l. 205) the fairies dance, perhaps looking forward to the creative impetus of
his own song-gathering in the years to come.

The final section returns to the georgic register of the additional stanzas of
'The Vision', with its panegyric on Ayrshire's improving gentry and their estates

---

[69] 'The Kirk's Alarm' [K 264 l. 70].
[70] Although this latter reference also conjures up l. 167, where 'Auld Brig''s 'Rev'rend Men . . . in
plain, braid Scots hold forth a plain, braid story'.

depicted on Coila's mantle. In a rather abrupt abandonment of the poem's winter setting, the 'Genius of the Stream' leads an allegorical procession of the four seasons clad in pastoral array; Spring followed by Rural Joy, crowned with 'flow'ry hay', Summer leading 'yellow Autumn wreath'd with nodding corn' (l. 222), Winter led by 'Hospitality with cloudless brow' (l 224), etc. It is a Thomsonian tableau of pastoral plenty which is a far cry from Burns's own experiences of bad harvests and soaring rents.[71] The closing couplets sound the *leitmotif* of the Scottish enlightenment, in their allusion to the text of Isaiah 2: 4; 'they shall beat their swords into plowshares, and their spears into pruninghooks'. In conclusion, Burns hails the spirit of agricultural improvement triumphing over 'tulzies', both holy and profane: 'Last, white-rob'd Peace, crown'd with a hazle wreath, | To Rustic Agriculture did bequeath | The broken, iron instruments of Death, | At sight of whom our Sprites forgat their kindling wrath' (ll. 231–4).

---

[71] Following in the allegorical train are some of the same local worthies praised in 'The Vision' (which, in its expanded version, was published eight poems later in the sequence of Burns's 1787 Edinburgh volume): 'Courage with his martial stride' (l. 225) is Hugh Montgomerie of Coilsfield; 'Benevolence, with mild, benignant air' (l. 227) is Mrs Stewart of Stair, and 'Learning and Worth' (l. 229) Professor Dugald Stewart of Catrine Bank.

# 7

# The Annals of the Poor

*In the villager's cottage such constancy springs,*
*That peasants with pity may look down on kings.*

[(John Cunningham, 'Damon and Phillis:
A Pastoral Dialogue', 1766)[1]

*Is there, for honest Poverty*
*That hings his head, and a' that;*
*The coward-slave, we pass him by,*
*We dare be poor for a' that!*

[K 482 ll 1–4][2]

## 'A TABERNACLE OF CLAY'

In 1800 Burns's boyhood tutor John Murdoch wrote of the poet's birthplace in Alloway: 'it was, with the exception of a little straw, literally a tabernacle of clay. In this mean cottage . . . I really believe, there dwelt a larger portion of content than in any palace in Europe. [Burns's poem] *The Cotter's Saturday Night* will give some idea of the temper and manners that prevailed there' [Currie, i. 88]. By the time of John Keats's pilgrimage to Alloway in 1819, the 'tabernacle of clay' was already an established shrine for literary tourists; despite serving as an ale-house, it quickly assumed a role equivalent to the manger in Bethlehem, as Burns's reputation grew to almost Christlike proportions in Victorian Scotland.[3] Material testimony to the poet's own 'honest poverty', the cottage and the content-ed family life which it symbolized allayed bourgeois fears about the iniquities of poverty, as if the 'tabernacle of clay' could somehow erase the spectacle of the crowded tenements and choleric slums that disgraced modern Scottish cities. For an urban, industrialized, and increasingly provincialized Scottish nation, both the

---

[1] John Cunningham, *Poems, Chiefly Pastoral* (Dublin, 1766), 87.
[2] For these lines' problematic allusion to slavery here see my essay 'Burns and the Poetics of Abolition', in Carruthers (ed.), *Edinburgh Companion to Robert Burns* (Edinburgh: Edinburgh University Press, 2009), 47–60.
[3] See Nicholas Roe, 'Authenticating Robert Burns', in Crawford (ed.), *Robert Burns and Cultural Authority*, 159–79 at 167–70.

birthplace cottage and its poetic epitome, 'The Cotter's Saturday Night' [K 72], more than any other of Burns's poems, underwrote his claims to 'national bardship'.[4]

Despite its radical edge, Burns's vision of 'honest poverty' doubtless contributed to the 'soft' pastoral ethic of the 'Kailyard' that underpinned nineteenth-century Scotland's attempt to tackle the problems of mass urban society. Symptomatic of this was Revd Thomas Chalmers's success in 1819 in persuading Glasgow Council to 'create a new parish in the mushrooming industrial east end of the city in which he sought to re-create a rural parish in the urban setting'. Removing this new parish of 'St John's' from the city's statutory system of poor relief, the Council permitted Chalmers to replace it with voluntary support in the old rural style, 'backed up with intensive Sunday-school and evangelistic endeavour to encourage family self-reliance'.[5] Although evangelical 'popular enlighteners' such as Chalmers preferred natural history and political economy to poetry in inculcating the urban working class with the values of the new capitalist society, their intense focus on pious domesticity drew inspiration from Burns's powerful image of the self-reliant cotter family.

Like 'The Twa Dogs', 'Halloween', and 'The Holy Fair', 'The Cotter' rehearsed (to quote its epigraph from Gray's 'Elegy') 'the short and simple annals of the Poor'. But this chapter will argue that its nineteenth-century popularity depended upon a selective reading that highlighted the poem's account of the freedom and piety of the poorest ranks of the Scottish peasantry; and as Richard Finlay argues, that 'freedom was more to do with middle-class individualism and anti-aristocratic sentiment than Jacobinism'.[6] To this end I will excavate some of the cultural detritus heaped upon 'The Cotter's Saturday Night' in order to explore the image of the cottage in relation to pastoral politics in the decades of the 1780s and 1790s, focusing on some of Burns's attitudes to poverty already touched upon in Chapters 4 and 5.

Allan Cunningham seems to have been the first commentator to have described Burns's 'Love and Liberty: A Cantata' [K 84] (the longest, and most significant work in Burns's reserved canon) as 'a sort of Beggar's Saturday-night' [*CH* p. 407]. In the second part of the chapter I'll examine the function of this

---

[4]  See Richard Findlay, 'The Burns Cult and Scottish Identity in the Nineteenth and Twentieth Centuries', in Kenneth Simpson (ed.), *Love and Liberty. Robert Burns: A Bicentenary Celebration* (East Lothian: Tuckwell, 1997), 69–78 at 72. See also Smith's warnings about the 'torpor' induced by divided labour in *Wealth of Nations*, ii. 368.

[5]  Callum G. Brown, *Religion and Society in Scotland since 1707* (Edinburgh: Edinburgh University Press, 1997), 97. See also R. A. Cage, *The Scottish Poor Law, 1745–1845* (Edinburgh: Scottish Academic Press, 11981), 90–110, and J. V. Smith, 'Manners, Morals and Mentalities: Reflections on the Popular Enlightenment of Early Nineteenth-Century Scotland', in Walter Humes and Hamish Paterson (eds.), *Scottish Culture and Scottish Education, 1800–1980* (Edinburgh: John Donald, 1983), 25–54 at 31.

[6]  Findlay, 'The Burns Cult', 71.

'beggar pastoral' as an antithetical version of 'the annals of the poor' that reveals Burns's ideological distance from evangelicals and bourgeois philanthropists. Carol McGuirk has insightfully argued that 'The Cotter' and 'Love and Liberty', written about the same time in the autumn of 1785, both 'describe characters at the bottom of the economic and class system. The deserving poor (the cotter's family) choose pious submission—hard work, sobriety, thrift. The beggars—the undeserving poor and proud to say so—choose rebellion: vagrancy, thievery, drunkenness, extravagance' [McGuirk, *BSP* p. 220]. In contrast to 'The Cotter', 'Love and Liberty' was simply not recuperable by the 'unco guid', as underlined in its final song 'Let them cant about DECORUM, | Who have character to lose' (ll. 272–3).

For all their differences, however, the two poems have more in common than their shared pastoral idiom, contemporaneous composition, and 'Saturday night' settings. Both are also vehicles for Burns's poetic ambition to the extent that they represent exercises in formal experimentation, the first employing Spenserian stanzas unique to his œuvre, the second developing a 'Scots Cantata' form that frames its dramatic songs with narrative *recitativos*. I'll go on to compare the reception of both poems in order to illuminate the distinction between Burn's 'official' and 'reserved' canon in the Romantic period. Comparing the politics of the two yields some surprises, as the more conventional and pious pastoral of 'The Cotter' turns out to harbour a radical subtext, while the rebellious antino-mianism of 'Love and Liberty' discloses a darker and more critical view of the social bond uniting its marginalized tavern hedonists, as well as a surprising history of Tory appropriation.


## COTTAGE POLITICS


Shifting to a broader British context, Anne Bermingham has recently suggested that Thomas Gainsborough's 'Cottage Door' paintings, dating from the mid- and late 1770s, are the first significant treatment of cottage life in British art, as such 'harbingers of a new and emerging discourse of nationhood and private life, and as indices of the contradictory ideas and desires this discourse harboured'.[7] By contrast, the cottage scene was already a well-established genre in eighteenth-century pastoral poetry. Scholars have traced numerous antecedents for Burns's cottage scene in Thomson's *Seasons*, Gray's 'Elegy in a Country Churchyard' and Goldsmith's *Deserted Village*, but especially in the Scottish tradition of Allan Ramsay's *Gentle Shepherd* and Robert Fergusson's 'The Farmer's Ingle' (1773).

---

[7] See esp. *The Cottage Door* (1777), and *Cottage Door with Children Playing* (1778). Ann Bermingham, 'The Simple Life: Cottages and Gainsborough's Cottage Doors' in Peter de Bolla, Nigel Leask and David Simpson (eds.), *Land, Nation and Culture: Thinking the Republic of Taste* (Basingstoke: Palgrave Macmillan, 2005), 37–62 at 38.

Formally, the Spenserian stanzas of 'The Cotter' are indebted to Shenstone's 'Village Schoolmistress' (1742) and Beattie's *Minstrel* (1771) rather than to Spenser himself, whom Burns probably hadn't read in 1785.[8] As Kinsley notes, it was primarily through Shenstone and Beattie 'that the Spenserian stanza—adorned in varying degree with antique diction—came to be associated with rustic manners' [Kin. iii. 111].

As I argued in Chapter 2, the moral claim that 'the *Cottage* leaves the *Palace* far behind' (l. 168) lies at the heart of eighteenth-century 'pastoral politics', a claim made emphatically by Pope, Goldsmith, Shenstone, and Gray, as well as by Ramsay, Fergusson, and Burns. Yet the political ends to which this poetic argument was adapted were highly equivocal. John Barrell has discussed the rejection, by the 1770s, of the 'soft' pastoral figure of the carefree shepherd exemplified in John Gay's *Shepherd's Week*, in favour of a georgic image of hard and productive rural labour: only the fact that the poor worked so hard made it permissible for poets to represent their pastoral repose as they recovered from their labours. Barrell describes this qualified permissiveness,

prescrib[ing] the terms on which [the poor] may relax—in the evening, after a hard day's work; after the harvest, on their way to the ritual feast; during the harvest, at meal-breaks, but never far from the hooks and scythes which indicate that they are resting only for a moment; never in the alehouse, if they are not to attract the disapprobation that [the painter George Morland's] labourers attracted, who change from 'hinds' to 'boors' as soon as they reach for a drink.[9]

Above all, Barrell argues, this 'hard' pastoral is 'essentially domestic: it celebrates no longer the imagined vitality of the rural community, but the imagined peace of a properly conducted family life'.[10] Although the values of 'hard' pastoral aren't inevitably associated with property and power, they were easily appropriated as a conservative argument, especially in the revolutionary decade. The most famous instance is William Paley's *Reasons for contentment; addressed to the labouring part of the British public* (1792), in which the poor are 'reminded' of the benefits of their condition and the ills attendant upon luxury and leisure: 'being without work is one thing; reposing from work is another. The one is as tiresome and insipid, as the other is sweet and soothing. The one in general is the fate of the rich man, the other is the fortune of the poor.' Paley illustrates his point with a vignette lifted straight from Gainsborough (it might almost be from Burns's 'The Cotter', except for its summery outdoors setting): 'I have heard it

---

[8] See Kin. iii. 1111–18, and David Hill Radcliffe, 'Imitation, Popular Literacy, and "The Cotter's Saturday Night"', in Carol McGuirk (ed.), *Critical Essays on Robert Burns* (New York: G. K. Hall, 1998), 251–62, for detailed studies of Burns's sources.

[9] John Barrell, *The Dark Side of the Landscape: the Rural Poor in English Painting, 1730–1840* (Cambridge: Cambridge University Press, 1980), 21.

[10] Ibid. 69–70.

said that if the face of happiness can anywhere be seen, it is in the summer evening of a country village. Where, after the labours of the day, each man, at the door, with his children, amongst his neighbours, feels his frame and his heart at rest, everything about him is pleased and pleasing, and a delight and complacency in his sensations far beyond what either luxury or diversion can afford. The rich want this; and they want what they must never have.'[11]

In comparing Gainsborough's 'Cottage Doors' with Paley's diatribe in a recent essay, Barrell comments that 'it seems unlikely that Paley's tract could persuade many of the rural poor that they were happy; it was probably more successful in persuading the rich that the poor ought to be happy . . . and that there was no justification, therefore, for popular disaffection, 'grumbling', and radicalism'.[12] This kind of persuasion of course lies squarely within the courtly pastoral tradition, and it's one heavily underlined in the much-derided dedicatory first stanza of Burns's 'The Cotter's Saturday Night, Inscribed to R. A[iken], Esq' (to give the poem its full title). Robert Aiken was a prosperous Ayr lawyer, referred to by Burns as his 'first kind patron', who collected the names of 145 subscribers for the Kilmarnock edition, almost a quarter of the total.[13] The opening 'inscription' to Aiken follows the epigraph from Gray in warning 'Ambition' and 'Grandeur' not to disdain 'the short and simple annals of the Poor'. The poet is characteristically anxious to disavow 'mercenary' patronage in favour of sentimentalized friendship, although the rhetorical address suggest that he is not himself one of 'the lowly train' he sings:

> My lov'd, my honor'd, much respected friend,
> No mercenary Bard his homage pays;
> With honest pride, I scorn each selfish end,
> My dearest meed, a friend's esteem and praise:
> To you I sing, in simple Scottish lays,
> The *lowly train* in life's sequester'd scene;
> The native feelings strong, the guileless ways,
> What A[iken] in a *Cottage* would have been;
> Ah! tho' his worth unknown, far happier there I ween!    (ll. 1–9)

---

[11] William Paley, *Reasons for Contentment; Addressed to the Labouring Part of the British Public* (Carlisle, 1792), 16–17.

[12] John Barrell, 'Cottage Politics', in his *The Spirit of Despotism: Invasions of Privacy in the 1790s* (Oxford: Oxford University Press, 2006), 225. This doesn't equate pastoral *generically* with conservative argument; for an account of pastoral poetry written by urban radicals in the 1790s, see Barrell's essay 'Rus in Urbe' in Philip Connell and Nigel Leask (eds.), *Romanticism and Popular Culture* (Cambridge: Cambridge University Press, 2009), 109–27.

[13] Aiken had successfully defended his friend Gavin Hamilton before the Presbytery of Ayr in 1785, an episode alluded to in 'Holy Willie's Prayer'.

The closing sentiment is one which neither Aiken, nor (especially) the poem's many plebeian readers, would be likely to credit, although it proceeds to present such an idealized vision of contented poverty that many doubtless wished they could. Once again Burn's dedicatory rhetoric reveals itself as 'baited schmaltz':[14] if in 'Dedication to G[avin] H[amilton], Esq.' [K 103] he imagines the landlord of Mossgiel levelled to social 'brotherhood' with the humble poet, here he imagines a 'pastoralized' Aiken as 'downwardly mobile', relegated to 'the lowly train' of cotter, not equal to but *beneath* him in the rural hierarchy.

While faulting this stanza as 'preposterous sentimentalism', Daiches points out that Burns's dedication to 'Aiken in a *Cottage*' 'indicates his desire to keep an eye on a city audience'.[15] This is well taken, although it's hardly intended as a compliment, and it's supported by the *Edinburgh Magazine's* judgement in 1802 that 'there can be no stronger proof of city prejudices and ignorance on the subject, than to suppose that truth and elegance are inconsistent, in describing the real manners of peasants. "The Cotter's Saturday Night" of Burns, who was himself a peasant, is most faithfully exact, both in language and costume, and is at the same time so far from exhibiting any thing low or course, that in sublimity and tenderness, it bids defiance to the most delicate taste.'[16]

As this judgement makes clear, for all its lowly position in the hierarchy of genres, eighteenth-century pastoral's claim to represent humble manners in decorous language made it one of the most technically demanding for the poet. Burns is praised here for achieving the difficult balancing act between a rural realism drawing heavily on Scots idiom (assisted by the biographical reassurance that he 'was himself a peasant', ignoring the poem's first stanza), and a quality of aesthetic 'delicacy' that, from the perspective of a city audience, seemed so difficult to attain. Its success in achieving this criterion makes 'The Cotter' the most conventionally 'pastoral' of all Burns's poems, although it is an ambition hard for modern readers to sympathize with.

## 'PEACE TO THE HUSBANDMAN': PASTORAL IDEALISM AND THE COTTER CLEARANCES

In a letter of April 1790 Burns described Oliver Goldsmith as 'my favourite poet', misquoting lines 425–6 from *The Deserted Village* (1770): '—States of

---

[14] Jeffrey Skoblow, *Dooble Tongue: Scots, Burns, Contradiction* (Newark: University of Delaware Press, 2001), 119.

[15] David Daiches, *Robert Burns* (London: G. Bell & Sons, 1952), 154.

[16] 'Observations on the *Gentle Shepherd* and Strictures on Pastoral Poetry', *Edinburgh Magazine*, NS (June 1802), 417.

native liberty possest, | Tho' very poor, may yet be very blest',[17] to underline his resentment that the 1707 Union had all but annihilated Scotland's 'Independence, & even her very Name!' [CL ii. 23–4]. In characterizing this 'blessedness', Goldsmith's poem projected a 'soft' pastoral image of the peasant as exempted from the yoke of hard labour: 'A time there was, ere England's griefs began, | When every rood of ground maintained its man; | For him light labour spread her wholesome store, | Just gave what life required, but gave no more' (ll. 57–60).[18] In line with an older pastoral image deriving from Gay and (and to a lesser extent) Ramsay, Goldsmith's leisured peasantry flirted with coy maidens and quaffed nut-brown ale in the tavern, while innocuously chatting about politics with other 'village statesman' (ll. 222–6).

Unlike Burns's 'The Cotter' and its major source, Robert Fergusson's 'The Farmer's Ingle', however, Goldsmith's idealized view of 'Sweet Auburn' is emphatically pitched in the past tense: 'A time there *was*, ere England's grief's began'. Goldsmith's 'Meliboeian' pastoral laments the fate of a peasantry which has been driven from the land by the 'accumulation of wealth', enclosures and agricultural improvement: 'Princes and lords may flourish or may fade; | A breath can make them, as a breath has made; | But a bold peasantry, their country's pride, | When once destroyed, can never be supplied' (ll. 54–6). As we'll see, Goldsmith's famous lines resonate in the final stanzas of Burns's 'The Cotter', but oddly enough without any acknowledgement that the cotter class celebrated in the poem was 'already history'.

Burns's 'The Cotter' is more strongly influenced by Fergusson's 'hard' pastoral realism than Goldsmith's leisurely account of rural life, although both poets share the latter's ideological critique of luxury and commerce. In conformity to the rules of the 'new pastoral', Fergusson's 'gudeman' farmer returns to the bosom of his family at the end of a hard day's work. As the epigraph from Virgil's 5th *Eclogue* spells out, the poem portrays an image of economic sufficiency (although certainly not prosperity) which is the fruit of relentless labour, and which provides a haven from bleak winter cold. The 'Farmer's Ingle' itself, the warm place by the hearth, 'bangs fu' leal the e'enings coming cauld, | And gars snaw-tapit winter freeze in vain; | Gars dowie mortals look baith blyth and bauld, | Nor fley'd wi' a' the poortith o' the plain' (ll. 5–8) [McD ii. 136]. Unlike the alcohol-free interior of the Cotter's household, the 'gudeman' (or tenant farmer) is welcomed home from the fields with a 'refreshing synd | O nappy liquor' (ll. 20–1) and the 'couthy cracks' (l. 46) of the family and servants gathered around the ingle includes racy gossip about Jock and Jenny's wooing, and Marion's stint on the 'cutty-stool' for bearing a bastard wean. The fact that

---

[17] The original lines read 'states of native strength possessed, | Though very poor, may still be very blest'.

[18] Roger Lonsdale (ed.), *New Oxford Book of Eighteenth Century Verse* (Oxford: Oxford University Press, 1984), 523–33. Barrell, *Dark Side*, 77–8.

this isn't the Sabbath eve, and that the farm is presumably located in the more laid-back Lothians (rather than Burns's Calvinistic Ayrshire) may also account for these differences. Yet Fergusson takes pains to underline the orderliness of the gudemen's dwelling; 'a' his housie looks sae cosh and clean; | For cleanly house looes he, tho' e'er sae mean' (ll. 17–18). Despite the poem's relative permissiveness, the gudeman's physical fatigue after hard labour is aptly symbolized by the 'cruizy' or oil lamp which, as the night draws on, 'can only blink and bleer' (l. 104): 'Tacksman and cottar eke to bed maun steer, | Upo' the cod to clear their drumly pow, | Till wauken'd by the dawning's ruddy glow' (ll. 106–9). It's up in the morning early and back to work for farmers and servants alike.

Fergusson's group (compared to Burns's) isn't so much what today we'd call a 'nuclear family' as an extended household composed of tenants, cottars, and servants. As we saw in discussing Burns's own social rank, the 'gudeman' or tenant farmer represented a relatively privileged rung on the social ladder of eighteenth-century rural Scottish labour. In the eleventh stanza the goodwife 'her hireling damsels bids' and the family's own (plural) 'hawkies bound' (ll. 95–6; 'hawkie' means milk cow) contrast with the 'The Cotter's italicized *only Hawkie* (l. 93) whose milk produces the 'weel-hain'd kebbuck' and the Cotter's 'soupe' in Burns's poem. T. C. Smout describes the pre-improvement Lothian gudeman's 'but and ben' as the hub of rural community, incorporating, besides the gudeman's family, two young menservants who ploughed, threshed, and herded the cows, and a couple of maids besides who lived permanently in the household. 'The gudewife's table in the but was laid for master and man alike; the staple of life was porridge, for breakfast and supper: dinner was out of the kail-pot, consisting of barley broth with greens and bannocks of barley or pease-meal ... All the food was produced on the farm: only the salt was extraneous to the domestic economy.'[19]

At the time Fergusson's poem was written in the early 1770s, however, especially in the progressive Lothians, the gudeman was just beginning to metamorphose into the capitalist farmer, 'a man of middle-class affluence and expectations, who built his tall stone house to stress his self-identification with the "landed interest" and to separate himself sharply from the labourers whose work he controlled'.[20] (In this respect, Ayrshire was behind the Eastern lowlands and borders; Burns later noted that the habitués of the Kelso Farmers' Club, in contrast to those of Ayrshire, were 'all gentlemen, talking of high matters'.[21]) Hence despite the realism of description and the sustained use of Scots, both the present tense of Fergusson's poem (in stark contrast, as I've already pointed out, to the past tense of Goldsmith's *Deserted Village*) and the *sententia* of the final stanza are marked by a certain pastoral *idealism*. Daiches describes 'The Farmer's Ingle' as a 'more successful though a less ambitious poem' than 'The Cotter' to

---

[19] T. C. Smout, *A History of the Scottish People, 1560–1830* (London: Fontana, 1998), 284.
[20] Ibid. 288.
[21] *Robert Burns's Tour of the Borders*, ed. R. Lamont Brown (Ipswich: Boydell, 1972), 21.

the extent that it avoids the 'self-conscious moralising' of the latter, as well as adhering to full Scots diction throughout, in contrast to Burns's frequent switches of register.[22] True, there is no embarrassing intrusion of an Aiken-like patron in 'The Farmer's Ingle', but nevertheless Fergusson's plural pronoun in the poem's final lines ('our wants') refers to the urban-dwelling polite reader, in a conventional pastoral trope that goes back to Virgil:

> Peace to the husbandman and a' his tribe,
> Whase care fells a' our wants frae year to year;
> Lang may his sock and couter turn the gleyb,
> And bauks o' corn bend down wi' laded ear.
> May SCOTIA's simmers ay look gay and green,
> Her yellow har'sts frae scowry blasts decreed;
> May a' her tenants sit fu' snug and bien,
> Frae the hard grip of ails and poortith freed,
> And lang lasting trains o' peaceful hours succeed.    (ll. 109–17)

It might be an exaggeration to say with Fred Freeman that the 'gudeman' system of farming was 'wholly outmoded' at the time Fergusson wrote, a judgement which seems more appropriate to the rural world of Burns's cotters.[23] As Freeman goes on to admit, the poem employs the term 'industry' in several places throughout to underline 'an exact balance of rest and industry which yields maximum productivity'.[24] Fergusson's physiocratic account of the dependence of urban life on the labours of the husbandman ('Whase care fells a' our wants frae year to year') was no longer self-evident in a mercantilist economy increasingly founded upon colonial luxuries, one of the foundations of Britain's new economic prosperity, although as we've seen it was an important claim of eighteenth-century 'agrarian patriotism'. A more realistic picture of a dying pastoral world is presented in *An Eclogue*, whose herd 'Sandie' grumbles that his wife has been seduced by a craving for tea, and other imported luxury goods, to squander his small property and neglect her domestic duties [McD ii. 88 ll. 81–4]. This is the self-sufficient, organic world of Ramsay's *Gentle Shepherd* (or indeed of 'The Farmer's Ingle') thrown into crisis and disharmony.

As I mentioned above, both 'The Cotter''s admirers and detractors have shared a tendency to read the poem autobiographically, the latter assuming that its considerable literary artifice is damaging to the truthfulness of its subject matter.[25]

---

[22] Daiches, *Robert Burns*, 151, 158.

[23] Fred Freeman, 'Robert Fergusson: Pastoral and Politics at Mid Century', in Andrew Hook (ed.), *History of Scottish Literature*, ii. *1660–1800* (Aberdeen: Aberdeen University Press, 1987), 141–56 at 143.

[24] Ibid. 144. Freeman also notes Fergusson's positive comments about agricultural improvement in his 'Eclogue to the Memory of William Wilkie', discussed in Ch. 2 above (ibid. 146).

[25] For a recent instance, see Walter McGinty, *Robert Burns and Religion* (Aldershot: Ashgate, 2003), 218.

An outcome of the biographical reading has been a persistent blindness to the obvious fact, underlined in its title, that it portrays a cotter household, rather than Burns's own tenant farming class.[26] This despite the fact that, as we saw above, the narrator's voice quite patently stands at an equal distance from the polite perspective of his dedicatee Robert Aiken, and from 'the lowly train' of cotters who are his subject, the 'them' whose pastoral virtues he idealizes. Even in a poem as faithful to pastoral convention as 'The Cotter', it's unlikely that Burns would have overlooked the nuances of social differences to which he was elsewhere so sensitive; as, for example, with his careful differentiation of the 'gentry', 'ha'folk' (servants), 'tenant man', and 'Cot-folk' in lines 60–70 of 'The Twa Dogs', discussed in Chapter 4.

For all the poverty and hardship that he'd suffered at Mount Oliphant and Lochlie, the domestic scene portrayed in 'The Cotter' is not Burns's own world. Granted, his birthplace was an 'auld clay biggin' in Alloway, but the myth begins to unravel when we realize that the Burnes's cottage had little in common with the traditional cottar's dwelling, described by Gavin Sprott as 'a basic house and byre with no developed throwe-gang, but a simple hallan or partition dividing the people from perhaps a single cow or calf'.[27] By contrast, the cottage built by William Burnes in the 1750s (rather badly, because one of the gables collapsed when Robert was a baby) was 'in the fashion of the new Midlothian dwellings, built of modern clay mortar rather than turf and timber, the roof supported on modern wall-head couples and with a fire set into a solid stone gable hearth with a flue in the thickness of the masonry, suitable for burning coal' rather than the traditional peat.[28] Burnes senior was at this stage neither cotter nor tenant, but owned (rather than rented) the Alloway cottage, leasing it out when he embarked on his career as a tenant farmer at Mount Oliphant. Adjacent to it was a five-acre smallholding where the poet's mother Agnes kept poultry and *four* cows (compare 'The Cotter''s 'only Hawkie') for milk and cheese.

William Burnes may have provided a model for the old cotter's Presbyterian piety, even if, as we saw in the previous chapter, he had imbibed a progressive theology unacceptable to many in orthodox Ayrshire. Head gardener to Provost Fergusson of Ayr before taking the lease of Mount Oliphant, his responsibilities had included laying out the grounds (walls and shrubberies and an avenue of elms), in the latter's handsome mansion house of Doonholm, all in the most fashionable modern taste [Mackay, p. 30]. Burns's farmhouses at Mount Oliphant, Lochlie, Mossgeil, and Ellisland had little in common with the dwelling described in 'The Cotter'. In Sprott's words, although Burns 'was familiar with the old houses of the Ayrshire countryside, he did not live in them'.[29]

---

[26] Although McGuirk notes [*BSP* 229] 'The poem is not completely autobiographical, however: Burns describes a family several degrees poorer than his own.'

[27] Gavin Sprott, *Robert Burns, Farmer* (Edinburgh: National Museums of Scotland, 1990), 17.

[28] Ibid. 25.

[29] Ibid. Lockhart described Mossgiel as the 'auld clay biggan', but the description more properly belongs to Burns mythology rather than biography [Lockhart, p. 108].

If the biographical myth of 'cotter Burns' has been largely foisted upon the poem by posterity, its role in perpetuating a historical myth of the endurance of the cotter class ('Long may thy hardy sons of *rustic toil* | Be blest with health and peace and sweet content!', ll. 174–5) is, by contrast, self-induced. In 1690, cottars had composed up to one-third of Scotland's rural population, receiving land, lodgings, and some provisions from tenant farmers in return for seasonal labour. But their precarious condition a decade or so before Burns was writing was noted by Adam Smith in Book I of *The Wealth of Nations*: 'there still subsists in many parts of Scotland a set of people called Cotters or Cottagers, though they were more frequent some years ago that they are now . . . In ancient times they seem to have been common all over Europe. In countries ill cultivated and worse inhabited, the greater part of landlords and farmers could not otherwise provide themselves with the extraordinary number of hands which country labour requires at certain seasons' [*Wealth of Nations*, i. 220].

As Smith well understood, the cotters belonged to the old 'unimproved' economy of the rural lowlands, but were rapidly disappearing in the decades of the 1770s and 1780s. Tom Devine has criticized a tendency amongst social historians to ignore the virtual elimination of the cotter class mainly as a result of the 'rationalization' of labour (crop rotations made farmers prefer to hire full-time rather than seasonal labourers) and the consolidation of farm holdings in this period [*TRS* pp. 144, 136–64].[30] He identifies a process of Lowland clearances every bit as drastic as the better-known Highland clearances, although the existence of plentiful alternative employment south of the Highland line preserved many of the cotters from the hardships suffered by their Highland cousins. They were especially vulnerable to clearance because (unlike most sub-tenants and tenants) they didn't possess formal leases, so could be evicted at will, which partly explains both the rapidity of their clearance from the land, and the fact that it is poorly documented in estate records.[31] The fact that cotters (who usually, as in Burns' poem, hired out their children as farm servants to supplement their income)[32] had the privilege of cultivating small plots of land adjacent to their cots provided them with a degree of self-sufficiency, in stark contrast to full-time agricultural labourers who were directly subject to the discipline of their masters and the fluctuations of food prices.

The effects of the 'cotter clearances' on Scottish rural society appear to have been every bit as dramatic as the transformation evoked by Goldsmith in

[30] Rental inflation in the later decades of the eighteenth century also meant that cotter holdings were less economical to farmers than maximizing their grazing land.

[31] Of sixty Ayrshire parish records in the *Statistical Account*, only twenty-four contained information on cotters, obscuring the fact of their existence and their rapid eviction from the agricultural landscape (*TRS* p. 140). This may explain why the phenomenon has passed under the radar of Burns scholarship.

[32] Like other tenants, the Burns family employed servants from the cotter class, like Elizabeth Paton (see below).

*The Deserted Village*: 'Sunk are thy bowers in shapeless ruin all, | And the long grass o'ertops the mouldering wall; | And trembling, shrinking from the spoiler's hand, | Far, far away, thy children leave the land (ll. 47–50).[33] Despite the tendency of the reporters of the *Statistical Account* to underestimate the phenomenon, Devine cites the minister of Kilmany in Fife referring to 'the annihilation of the little cottagers', and the reporter from Marrikie in Angus described how 'many of the little cottages are exterminated'. Nearer Burns country, the reporter for Kilwinning wrote that 'the cottages are now, in great measure, demolished'. At Colmonell in Ayrshire, whereas in the 1760s 'there was hardly a tenant who had not one or more cottagers on his farm', there were 'very few' in the entire parish by 1790 [*TRS* pp. 140–1]. A note of regret is evident in some of the reports: the correspondent for Carnwath in Lanarkshire wrote 'some of the intelligent farmers are now sensible of their mistake, in allowing their cott-houses to fall into ruins; for although the rent of these houses was not an object of importance, yet they were the nursery of the servants both male and female that were wanted in the country' [*Statistical Account*, vii. 193]. Other observers noted that cotter dwellings were systematically dismantled so that they couldn't be occupied by vagrants, and their stones used to construct dykes and walls for the new farm enclosures [*TRS* p. 140].

Clearance seems to have elicited little resistance from the victims of such massive social engineering by the landowning class. Unlike the Highland cotters whose planned emigration for Canada was resisted by their lairds, the subject of Burns's vituperative satire 'The Address of Beelzebub' [K 108], it appears that many of the lowland cotters didn't actually 'leave the land' on the 'Goldsmithian' pattern, but relocated to the towns or new planned villages springing up all over Scotland in the same decades, where they worked either in mills or factories, or in the diverse occupations that sprang up ancillary to the newly capitalized rural economy [*TRS* p. 150]. By contrast, it was Robert Burns the ruined tenant farmer who was forced in 1786 to contemplate fleeing to the colonies.

William Aiton, writing in the decade after Burns's death, was critical of the failure of paternalistic intervention to prevent the drastic migration of cotters from the Ayrshire landscape. At the same time, as a good disciple of *Wealth of Nations*, he attributed it to competitive wage rates: 'the strong hardy race, who inhabited these homely buildings, not meeting with due encouragement in the country, and tempted with higher wages from the cotton or other manufactories, have deserted their rural habitations, and frugal and virtuous habits, and have taken up their abodes in towns, where . . . their health has been impaired, and

---

[33] Raymond Williams points out that Goldsmith's poem makes a 'negative identification' between the writer whose hopes of settling in Sweet Auburn have been thwarted by clearance, and the fate of the village itself. In point of fact, he argues, 'the creation of a desert landscape is an imaginative rather than a social process; it is what the new order does to the poet, not to the land'. *The Country and the City* (London: Hogarth, 1993), 78–9.

their morals contaminated'. He viewed this as both an economic and a moral disaster, complaining that the departure of the cotters had created a labour shortage, so that farmers were obliged to hire 'indolent Highlanders, or vagrant Irishmen'. To remedy the situation he proposed a 'cottage plan' in which a new cottage would be constructed on every farm of over 100 acres and settled with 'this useful class of society' who constituted (and Aiton quoted from Goldsmith and Burns to reinforce the point) the moral backbone of the nation. [Aiton, pp. 521–7]. Of course he was whistling to the wind.

## 'THE COTTER'S SATURDAY NIGHT'

Despite the realism of the poem's 'manners-painting strain', these seismic shifts in Lowland rural society pass apparently unnoticed in 'The Cotter'. Burns's lines 'The toil-worn COTTER frae his labour goes. . . . . | And weary, o'er the muir, his course does hameward bend' (ll. 14,18) lightly Scoticizes the familiar pentameters of Gray's 'Elegy': 'The lowing herd wind slowly o'er the lea, | The ploughman homeward plods his weary way' (ll. 2–3).[34] Burns's cotter is evidently a practitioner of the old 'runrig' cultivation, who's been labouring with his plough-team on the outfield 'o'er the moor' rather than in the consolidated field system of the 'improved' farm. As his cot comes into view he anticipates Sabbath repose in the bosom of his family: more probably it would have been part of a clachan or 'cot-toun', but Burns chooses to emphasize his dwelling as a 'sequester'd scene' for aesthetic reasons (l. 6). The domestic scene licenses a stronger use of Scots diction:

> At length his lonely *Cot* appears in view,
> Beneath the shelter of an aged tree;
> Th' expectant wee-things, toddlan, stacher thro'
> To meet their *Dad*, wi' flichterin noise and glee.
> His wee-bit ingle, blinkan bonilie,
> His clean hearth-stane, his thrifty *Wifie's* smile,
> The *lisping infant*, prattling on his knee,
> Does a' his weary kiaugh and care beguile,
> And makes him quite forget his labor and his toil.    (ll. 18–27)

The long Spenserian stanza and the pentameter line permit the descriptive depth and extension requisite for such domestic scene-painting: it's a pastoral vision of the clean and orderly peasant household. As Beattie wrote of the 'Gothick structure' of the Spenserian stanza in his introduction to *The Minstrel*, 'it allows the sententiousness of the couplet, as well as the more complex modulation of

---

[34] Roger Lonsdale, *New Oxford Book of Eighteenth Century Verse* (Oxford: Oxford University Press, 19894), 354.

blank verse', while admitting both 'simplicity and magnificence of sound and language'.[35] Burns carefully modulates his Scots and English diction, as in 'stacher', 'flichterin', 'wee-bit ingle', 'blinkan', and the distinctively Ayrshire dialectal term 'kiaugh', alongside '*lisping infant*' and the English cadence of 'quite forget his labour and his toil'. Lines 20–1 and 25 convert the litotes of 'The Elegy''s much-quoted line, 'No children run to lisp their sire's return, | Or climb his knees the envied kiss to share'[36] into descriptive affirmation, and despite the different verse forms, Burns also pays tribute to Gray in the decorous iambs of the final alexandrine line. 'The Cotter' thus marries the rural setting and diction of Fergusson's 'Farmer Ingle' to its English model, as well as altering his *ababbcdcdd* rhyme scheme, restoring Beattie's fidelity to the closing alexandrine of the Spenserian original.

The family circle is completed when the old cotter's sons and eldest daughter Jenny return from work as servants on the neighbouring farms. Compared to the relaxation enjoyed by Goldsmith's peasants, or the 'couthy crack' of Fergusson's group, Burns's family reunion is presided over by the watchful parents, and the children are subject to paternal 'admonition due' (l. 45) and pious exhortations. In contrast to the defiant anti-aristocratic sentiments of the poem's final stanzas, the cotter exhorts his children to obey their tenant-employers: 'Their Master's and their Mistress's command | The *youngkers* a' are warned to obey' (ll. 46–7). Jenny's 'sair-won penny-fee' is dedicated to 'help her *Parents* dear, if they in hardship be' (l. 36), although given their frugality and ceaseless industry (the mother all the time works with her 'needle and her shears'), there's no indication that this will be necessary.

Burns is reminding his polite readers that this cotter family, proud in their self-sufficiency, needn't be the objects of either parish or voluntary charity. This is an important detail, given that some contemporaries justified the elimination of the cotters (and the razing of their dwellings) on the grounds that they 'placed a burden on the Poor Law . . . Cothouses had long been seen as repositories of the poor, aged and infirm, and of migrants from other parishes' [*TRS* p. 144]. As we'll see in Chapter 9, James Currie and later commentators seized upon the poem's portrayal of the domestic affections and economic self-sufficiency of the Scottish peasantry as a support for their polemic against the Poor Law, although this isn't an important concern of Burns's poem. 'Honest poverty' is here (as elsewhere in Burns) too proud to beg. The family's 'Cheerfu' Supper' of porridge, washed down with milk from their '*only Hawkie*', and a slice of 'weel-hain'd kebbuck' (well-matured cheese) in honour of Jenny's suitor, enforce the image of frugal but healthy sufficiency. Although, unlike Fergusson, Burns abstains from patriotic moralizing on Scottish food at this point (perhaps reserving the subject for his celebrated debunking of foreign 'fricassees', 'olios',

---

[35] James Beattie, Preface to *The Minstrel, in Two Books* (London, 1784), p. xii.
[36] 'Elegy', ll. 23–4.

and 'ragouts' in 'To a Haggis' [K 136]), the supper passage is very much in the 'Scots pastoral' tradition of 'The Farmer's Ingle'.

The arrival of Jenny's 'blate and laithfu' (l. 69) young man initiates the 'amorous' stanzas 7–10 which have posed something of a problem for modern critics. Although Jenny is a picture of sentimental innocence, her mother with her 'woman's wiles' (l. 70) spies the 'the *conscious flame* | Sparkle in *Jenny's* e'e, and flush her cheek', and is therefore relieved to discover that her man is 'nae wild, worthless *Rake*. (ll. 59–60, 63). The innocent love of the happy couple, deriving straight from Ramsay's Patie and Peg, is squarely within the polite pastoral tradition, in which (as Tom Crawford somewhere quips) the only creatures to get pregnant are the livestock. In the ninth stanza, as in the dedicatory stanza to Aiken signalling his distance from the cotter's social level, Burns assumes the knowing voice and Anglicized diction of the philosophical observer ('I've paced much this weary, *mortal round*, | And sage EXPERIENCE bids me this declare—', ll. 75–6) before offering up a voyeuristic picture of 'a youthful, loving, *modest* Pair' (l. 79) embracing under a flowering hawthorn, self-consciously enforcing his moral emphasis on their innocence. But the sentimental pathos is undercut by the exclamatory rhetoric of the stanza that follows: 'Is there, in human form, that bears a heart— | A wretch! A villain! lost to love and truth! | That can, with studied, sly, ensnaring art, | Betray sweet *Jenny's* unsuspecting youth? | Curse on his perjur'd arts! dissembling, smoothe!' (ll. 82–6).

This is pretty fresh coming from the man who had recently seduced his mother's servant Elizabeth Paton, justifying John Logan's description of Burns as 'a Country Libertine' [*CH* p. 79]. The poet even burlesqued his own rakish reputation as 'Rob Mossgiel' in the contemporaneous song 'O leave novels' [K 43]: 'Beware a tongue that's smoothly hung; | A heart that warmly seems to feel; | That feelin heart but acks a part, | 'Tis rakish art in Rob Mossgiel' (ll. 9–12). His warning of the seductive potential of false sensibility 'that warmly *seems* to feel', and line 9's echo of 'The Cotter''s 'dissembling, smoothe!' make it easy to sympathize with Tom Crawford's description of 'The Cotter''s ninth stanza as 'one of the most nauseating ever published by a reputable poet' [Crawford, *BPS* 179]. (Fortunately for Jenny, it's not the novels of Richardson and Fielding but the Authorised Version which make up her Saturday night reading.) I'm less alarmed than Crawford because behind the apparent hypocrisy something rather more interesting seems to be going on in Burns's lubricious imagining of 'the ruined Maid' and her distracted parents.

In part, Burns's rather forced outrage at the possibility of Jenny's seduction registers his impatience with sentimentalized pastoral courtship, more squarely, and obscenely, expressed in the burlesque song; 'When maukin bucks, at early fucks' [K 481]. But the image he raises (and the poem seeks to alert and to allay our anxieties in equal measures) evokes the well-worn sentimental trope of the ruined maid, exemplified by Goldsmith in lines 327–32 of *The Deserted Village*. Goldsmith personifies the ruination of 'Sweet Auburn' in his vignette of a 'poor, houseless, shivering female' city prostitute lamenting the day 'she left her wheel and robes of country brown':

> She once, perhaps, in village plenty blest,
> Has wept at tales of innocence distressed;
> Her modest looks the cottage might adorn,
> Sweet as the primrose peeps beneath the thorn;
> Now lost to all; her friends, her virtue fled,
> Near her betrayer's door she lays her head.

If Burns challenges his polite reader to contemplate Jenny's innocence in detachment from a prurient image of her seduction, stanza 9 seems to acknowledge the failure of any such possibility. His contrary handling of the scene introduces a discordant note to the cottage idyll, hinting at the duplicity of pastoral itself, the idealization of a timeless and pristine innocence no longer manifest in the manners of contemporary society. In this respect Burns's cotters have joined the ranks of other Arcadians, including even Fergusson's tenants, who have come to exist purely as a literary or moral ideal of innocence rather than a contemporary social fact, however much the poem's conclusion strongly disavows the fact. *The English Review* remarked of 'The Cotter' in 1787 that '[the poem] draws a domestic picture of rustic simplicity, natural tenderness, and innocent passion that must please every reader whose feelings are not perverted' [*CH* p. 77]. But in a fallen world of urban sophistication and self-conscious sensibility, this seems to imply, whose feelings are not 'perverted'?

Even if I'm right to read 'The Cotter''s 'amorous stanzas' as a reflection on the limits of conventional pastoral, it's still a very oblique manner of referring to the ruination of the cotter class. I've argued in Chapter 5 that Burns gets closest to addressing some of the dire human consequences of improvement in 'To a Mouse', where the 'cleared' cotter is represented as a small rodent, and where the poet's plough is itself the engine of destruction: 'Thy wee-bit *housie*, too, in ruin! | Its silly wa's the win's are strewin! | An' naething, now, to big a new ane, | O' foggage green! (ll. 19–22). There is none of that in 'The Cotter', although Burns's moralizing is certainly evident (far too evident for many of the poem's modern critics) in the stanzas which follow describing the old patriarch's Bible reading and the family prayers.

In many respects Burns' poem conforms up to this point with the polite image of the rural poor underpinning Gainsborough's *Cottage Doors*, or Paley's *Reasons for Contentment*. The cotter is shown, exhausted from his incessant toils, resting in the bosom of his family, in a household which is clean, frugal, and sober to boot.[37] Nothing at all remains of the idle, flirtatious clowns who people the

---

[37] Peter Zenziger writes that 'a real cotter would have drawn quite a different picture of his situation from the one we find here', 'Low Life, Primitivism, and Honest Poverty in Ramsay and Burns', *Studies in Scottish Literature* 30: 43–58, 52.

pastorals of Pope, Gay, or (with some qualification) Ramsay, and the cottage is a far cry from the anarchy of Poosie-Nansie's tavern in 'Love and Liberty', discussed in the second half of this chapter. Crawford accurately describes stanzas 12–16 as 'the real centre of the poem: the description of family worship from which everything else radiates . . . with its noble Scots diction, it is worthy to be the kernel of the poem' [Crawford, *BPS* 179–80].

The fact that Burns's cotters are pious to a fault seemed anomalous to some critics in the light of his satirical portraits of Presbyterian hypocrisy in 'Holy Willie's Prayer'. In his dreary moralizing study of Burns for Morley's *English Men of Letters* (!) series in 1887, John Campbell Shairp speculated that 'the religion described . . . in 'The Cotter's Saturday Night' is, it should be remembered, his father's faith, not his own'. Based on the equation between the old cotter and William Burnes initiated by Murdoch, this justified Shairp in reading the shade of Burns a fatherly lecture on the evils propagated by his Kirk satires: '[Burns] connect [ed] in the minds of the people so many coarse and even profane thoughts with objects which they had regarded till then with reverence.'[38] Shairp slyly imputes blame for the betrayal of Jenny and her social class on Rab Mossgiel, wayward son, seducer, and destroyer (rather than elegiast) of traditional rural concord.

The Covenanting zeal of the old cotter's call to worship *'And let us worship* GOD!' (l. 108, which, Burns told Gilbert, was the poem's original inspiration [Kin. iii. 1111]), and the 'artless singing' of the psalm tunes 'Dundee, Martyrs, Elgin', represent primitive Presbyterian family worship in a very different light from that of the Kilmarnock 'auld lichts' in 'The Ordination', with its implicit criticism of ragged 'read the line' psalmody. Burns accurately describes the Scottish convention of following the psalm-singing with readings from 'the big ha'-bible'(from the New and Old Testaments respectively) in stanzas 13 and 14, and finally, in stanza 15, family prayers led by the father.

As in 'The Ordination', the texts chosen by 'the priest-like Father' from 'the sacred page' reflect the poem's themes. The cotter is identified with the Jewish Patriarchs: Abraham 'the Friend of God'; Moses, waging his war of extermination on the wicked Amalekites' (Exodus 17: 8–16); King David 'groaning beneath the stroke of Heaven's avenging ire' (l. 123), a reference to the death of his son Absalom, God's revenge for David's adulterous seduction of Bathsheba (2 Samuel 18: 33); the lament of Job; and the prophet Isaiah's 'wild, seraphic fire'. The readings from the New Testament focus on Christ's atonement, his poverty and homelessness, and the vision of St John of Patmos, rising to a Miltonic sublimity in its prophecy of the apocalyptic destruction of Babylon:[39]

---

[38]  John Campbell Shairp, *Robert Burns* (London: Macmillan, 1887), 189, 20.

[39]  Burns may have had theological qualms about some of these texts, like other 'rational' Presbyterians: for instance, Moses's genocidal extermination of the Amekelites, or (in the New Testament), Christ's atonement, clearly spelt out at l. 128: 'How guiltless blood for guilty man was shed'. The allusion to David's seduction of Bathsheba possibly refers back to the 'amorous stanza' 10, and Burns's 'remorse' for his own seduction of Betsey Paton.

How He, who bore in heaven the second name,
Had not on Earth whereon to lay His head:
How His first *followers* and *servants* sped;
The *Precepts sage* they wrote to many a land:
How *he*, who lone in *Patmos*, banished,
Saw in the sun a mighty angel stand;
And heard great *Bab'lon's* doom pronounced by Heaven's command.   (ll. 134–5)

In stanza 16, family prayers are led by 'The *Saint*, the *Father*, and the *Husband*' (l. 137) but Burns chooses a curious quotation from Pope's *Windsor-Forest* to express their spiritual transport: 'Hope "springs exulting on triumphant wing"' (l. 138). Pope's lines 111–14 read: 'See! from the brake the whirring pheasant springs, | And mounts exulting on triumphant wings: | Short is his joy; he feels the fiery wound, | Flutters in blood, and panting beats the ground'.[40] It is hard to account for this qualification of the allusion by its immediate context, unless once again Burns is hinting that the cotter world, like Pope's exultant pheasant, is on the very brink of destruction.

James Currie praised 'The Cotter''s power in rising 'at length [from the tender and moral] into a strain of grandeur and sublimity, which modern poetry has not surpassed . . . In no age or country have the pastoral muses breathed such elevated accents, if the *Messiah* of Pope be excepted, which is indeed a pastoral in form only' [Currie, i. 315]. Currie here grasps the Virgilian range of Burnsian pastoral in comparing 'The Cotter' to Pope's 'Messiah', itself an imitation of the 4th *Eclogue*, which sings 'paulo maiora canamus'—'a somewhat grander song'. But Currie forbears mentioning the *political* theology underlining 'The Cotter's sublimity. For the approved limits of pastoral are here transcended by a note of spiritual radicalism emerging from Burns's apotheosis of cottage-virtue that draws on the Covenanting traditions of seventeenth-century Ayrshire:

Compar'd with this, how poor Religion's pride,
In all the pomp of *method*, and of *art*,
When men display to congregations wide
Devotion's every grace, except the *heart*!
The POWER, incens'd, the Pageant will desert,
The pompous strain, the sacerdotal stole;
But haply, in some *Cottage* far apart,
May hear, well-pleas'd, the language of the Soul,
And in His *Book of Life* the Inmates poor enroll.   (ll. 145–53)

Burns's celebration of the 'religion of the heart' here, opposing simple family prayers to the pomp and ceremony of Episcopalian and Catholic worship, had huge appeal for his nineteenth-century admirers; it was the poem's piety, rather than its pastoral nostalgia, which made it the favourite in the Burns canon. As

---

[40] *Pope: Poetical Works*, 41.

Leigh Schmidt writes, 'to [Burns's] heirs, not only had he managed to expose all that was wrong with religious festivity in "The Holy Fair", but in . . . "The Cotter's Saturday Night", he had succeeded in capturing the admirable abode of true religion, the home . . . true religion consisted in such simple acts of family devotion, not in festivity, pageantry and pomp'.[41]

Commenting on the most famous of the poem's many painterly interpretations, Sir David Wilkie's iconic *Cottar's Saturday Night* (1835), Duncan Macmillan argues that the inspiration for Wilkie's painting was the Veto Act of 1835 which granted Presbyterian congregations the right to veto a patron's nominee to a parish, though not themselves to elect them (see Fig. 6). It was massive popular resentment following the overturning of the Veto Act in 1843—a triumph of the Tory landowning interest—which led directly to the Disruption and the establishment of the Free Church, the significance of which as an instance of the 'spilt radicalism' of Victorian Scotland is perhaps hard for us to understand today.[42] It is highly ironic of course, in the light of Chapter 6's study of Burns's disdain for popular patronage, and his devastating satire of Calvinist orthodoxy, that 'The Cotter' should have indirectly stoked the fires of a resurgent nineteenth-century evangelical Presbyterianism.

In 'The Cotter''s final stanzas Burns shifts from a spiritual to a more temporal radicalism by evoking a 'patriotic sublime' that moves the ideological focus of the poem from the Covenanting era to more contemporary struggles for liberty:

> From Scenes like these, old SCOTIA's grandeur springs,
> That makes her lov'd at home, rever'd abroad:
> Princes and lords are but the breath of kings,
> 'An honest man's the noble work of GOD':
> And *certes*, in fair Virtue's heavenly road,
> The *Cottage* leaves the *Palace* far behind;
> What is a lordling's pomp?—a cumbrous load,
> Disguising oft the *wretch* of human kind,
> Studied in arts of Hell, in wickedness refin'd!    (ll. 163–71)

Just as the earlier praise of Jenny's sexual innocence issued in a nervous denunciation of the cynical rake who might undo her, so Burns' panegyric on

---

[41] Leigh Schmidt, *Holy Fairs: Scotland and the Making of American Revivalism* (Princeton, NJ: Princeton University Press), 200. 'Pompous strain' and 'sacerdotal stole' seem to rule out Presbyterian worship, often characterized by ragged psalm-singing led by a precentor, and presided over by a minister in his 'Geneva Cloak' and bands (J. G. Lockhart, *Peter's Letters to his Kinsfolk*, 3rd edn., 3 vols. [Edinurgh: W. Blackwood, 1819], iii. 314). Partly on the evidence of l. 17, where the weary cotter hopes 'the *morn* in ease and rest to spend', Claire Lamont speculates that the cotters are Seceders, and have no plans to attend the Kirk on Sunday morning. 'Burns's Saturday Night: Work and Time in Agricultural Poems of his Era', paper read at Robert Burns 1759–2009 Conference, University of Glasgow, 16 Jan. 2009.

[42] Duncan Macmillan, *Painting in Scotland: The Golden Age* (Oxford: Phaidon, 1986), 181. See Andrew Drummond and James Bulloch, *The Scottish Church, 1688–1843* (Edinburgh: St Andrew's Press, 1973), 244–66.

Fig. 6. *The Cotter's Saturday Night*, oil, by Sir David Wilkie (1835). Note how Wilkie has romanticized the scene by representing the Cotter family in antique costume.

the domestic virtues of the cotters here modulates into a scathing attack on the aristocratic 'lordling', particularly over-determined in that final line, 'Studied in arts of Hell, in wickedness refined!' It is as if Jenny's diabolical seducer (wittily travestied by Daiches as a 'villain in a black cloak and curled black mousta-chios')[43] has returned in the guise of a 'wicked lordling'. This stanza wreaks havoc with the kind of pastoral argument shortly to be associated with Paleyan Loyalism, a 'reason for contentment' ostensibly aimed at the labouring classes, but more likely seeking to reassure the men of property. Kinsley's note to lines 165–6 ('Princes and lords are but the breath of kings | 'An honest man's the noble work of GOD') underlines the fact that Burns is quoting Pope's *Essay on Man*, as well as echoing Goldsmith; but this seems less remarkable than the anticipation of his 1794 song, 'Is there, for honest Poverty' [K 482]: 'A prince can mak a belted knight, | A marquis, duke, an a' that; | But an honest man's aboon his might, | Gude faith he mauna fa' that!'

Early commentators on 'The Cotter' seem to have passed over Burns's attack on luxury and aristocratic privilege (to some extent licensed by conventions of

---

[43] Daiches, *Robert Burns*, 158.

'pastoral politics') in order to praise its portrait of a dignified and pious Scots peasantry. Even the Tory Robert Heron, writing in 1793, seemed oblivious to the Painite attack on the 'lordling's pomp', citing the poem as proof that 'the manners of our rustics can afford subjects for pastoral poetry more elevated and more amiable than those which are exhibited in Gay's *Shepherd's Week*' [*CH* p. 97]. But by 1808 Francis Jeffrey, while full of praise for 'The Cotter''s 'tenderness and truth', was complaining more generally of Burns's 'too fierce... tone of defiance... indicat[ing] rather the pride of a sturdy peasant, than the calm and natural elevation of a generous mind' [*CH* 184]. As we'll see below, 'The Cotter' was the most widely imitated of all Burns's poems in the decades after 1790, but seldom by politically (as opposed to theologically) radical poets.

The final two stanzas mark the real transition from the register of polite pastoral ('what A[iken] in a *Cottage* would have been') to the political sublime of 'the *Patriot* and the *Patriot bard*' (l. 188). Fergusson and Goldsmith meet in the following benediction:

> O SCOTIA! my dear, my native soil!
> For whom my warmest wish to Heaven is sent!
> Long may thy hardy sons of *rustic toil*
> Be blest with health, and peace, and sweet content!
> And O may Heaven their simple lives prevent
> From *Luxury's* contagion, weak and vile!
> Then, howe'er *crowns* and *coronets* be rent,
> A *virtuous Populace* may rise the while,
> And stand a wall of fire, around their much-lov'd ISLE'    (ll. 172–80)

In the final stanza, Wallace represents the Scottish patriot tradition, more famously evoked in Burns's rousing anthem, 'Scots, wha hae wi' Wallace bled' [K 425].[44] Stanza 20's vision of the virtuous peasantry rising up and standing like a 'wall of fire' in the face of threatened invasion to defend their 'ISLE' (alluding, interestingly, to Britain as a whole rather than just Scotland) maybe refers to the bitter campaign for a Scottish militia which radicalized even the most politically cautious figures of the Edinburgh Enlightenment.[45] Physiocratic principles equated the wealth with the populousness of a nation, particularly its peasantry: Burns follows Goldsmith here in his implicit opposition to the prospect of cotter emigration, however understated. Although inconsistent with his *sympathy* for Highland emigration in 'Address of Beelzebub', Burns's lines certainly seemed radical enough to Irish republican leader Wolfe Tone when he quoted them to

---

[44] Burns allegedly recited 'The Cotter''s patriotic stanzas upon leaving Scottish soil for the first time in his life at Coldstream, during the Borders tour of 1787 [Mackay p. 306].

[45] See John Robertson, *The Scottish Enlightenment and the Militia Issue* (Edinburgh: John Donald, 1985).

inspire the 'United Irishmen' militia which tried to seize control of Ireland from British rule in the following decade.[46]

The 'honest poverty' of agrarian republicanism (set against urban and upper-class corruption and luxury) was a familiar strain in eighteenth-century Country Party and Whig opposition discourse, and would become radicalized after 1790.[47] The 'Heaven-taught Ploughman' sometimes played up this political version of pastoral for his Whig patrons, as in his letter to the Earl of Mar in April 1793, when he thundered: 'BURNS was a poor man, from birth; and an Exciseman, by necessity: but—I will say it!—the sterling of his honest worth, no poverty could debase; & his independent British mind, Oppression might bend, but could not subdue!—Have not I, to me, a more precious stake in my Country's welfare, than the richest Dukedom in it?' [CL ii. 209]. Although the closing stanzas of 'The Cotter' are denounced as mere bombast by Daiches and other modern critics,[48] a reading alert to the political language of the 1780s reveals something rather different, as Burns's conclusion breathes radical energy into the quiescent genre of cottage pastoral.

## 'THE COTTER': RECEPTION, IMITATION, INFLUENCE

Dozens of imitations of 'The Cotter' appeared over the next few decades, usually picking up the 'loyalist pastoral' strain of Burns's poem, while excluding the radicalism of the final stanzas. The most interesting in this respect is an English 'translation' and abridgement entitled *The Cottagers' Saturday Night: A Poem Containing a very pleasing and affecting Description of a Cottager and his Family*. First produced under the auspices of Hannah More in 1794, and published by J. Evans in London for *Cheap Repository Tracts, The Cottager's Saturday Night* was still circulating in the 1820s: the National Library of Scotland possesses a handsome copy of the Evans penny broadsheet (with cut), as well as another chapbook text of the same poem, published by W. MacNie, Stirling, in 1828.[49] The Evans text cuts Burns's twenty-one stanzas down to fourteen, but given that so much of Burns's original employs English diction, the work of cultural and

---

[46] In an unpublished essay of 1790. See Thomas Bartlett (ed.), *Life of Theobald Wolfe Tone, compiled and arranged by William Wolfe Tone* (1826), expanded edn., 2 vols. (Dublin, 1998), ii. 1778.

[47] See Liam McIlvanney, *Burns the Radical: Poetry and Politics in Late Eighteenth-Century Scotland* (East Linton: Tuckwell, 2002), 24–37.

[48] Daiches, *Robert Burns*, 160, 161, dismisses the final stanzas as 'exhibitionist moralizing', 'overdoing the patriot note'.

[49] *The Cottagers' Saturday Night: A Poem Containing a very pleasing and affecting Description of a Cottager and his Family* (London: Printed by A. Applegarth, Stamford St: J. Davis, J. Nisbet, J. and C. Evans, n.d.), NLS AP.5.206.01. *Prophecies of Thomas the Rhymer... An Account of the Battle of Bannockburn... 'The Cottagers' Saturday Night'* (Stirling: W. Macnie, Bookseller, 1828), NLS L.C.2876 (15).

ideological translation is actually more demanding than the 'Englishing' of Burns's verse.

The exclusions necessary to render 'The Cotter' fit for the polemical purposes of *Cheap Repository Tracts* offer a kind of photographic negative of its radical subtext. Predictably the poem loses its Scottish 'costume' (the old cotter's 'bonnet' becomes a 'hat'), its lightly erotic account of Jenny's innocence, and its anti-aristocratic animus; the tone of piety is amplified to bring it into line with the evangelical theology promoted by Hannah More and her associates, so for example Burns's 'Creator' (at l. 142) becomes a 'Redeemer'. The 'literary' epigraph from Gray and 'The Cotter''s 'embarrassing' dedicatory stanza to Aiken are omitted, as is the much admired stanza 9 with its picture of 'happy love', probably in order to enhance its popular appeal. The description of 'Scotia's food' in stanza 11 is cut—evangelicals may have preferred to pray on an empty stomach[50]—and the poem's pious 'kernel' gets underway with Burns's stanza 12. Burns's description of psalm-singing in stanza 13 is both anglicized and evangelized, with Isaac Watts's hymnody replacing the Scottish Psalter: 'In Psalms and Hymns their ardent praises rise, | Compos'd by various men of worthy name. | And chiefly *Watts* assists the heaven-ward flame, | With verse sublime, fitted for holy lays: | Compar'd with these, Italian airs are tame' (stanza 10). Stanza 17's praise of family worship over 'the pomp of method and of art' is of course retained, but stanzas 19 and 21, the former with its pastoral reversal 'the *cottage* leaves the *palace* far behind', and the latter with its patriotic eulogy of William Wallace 'stem[ming] tyrannic pride', are predictably lost.

The poem concludes with a Loyalist revision of Burns's patriotic stanza 20 in which 'SCOTIA' becomes 'Britain': 'O Britain! my most dear, my native soil! | For whom my warmest wish to Heav'n is sent!' (stanza 14). The evangelical version still sets itself against 'Luxury's contagion', but gone is the radical strain of Burns's final lines in this stanza: 'And from each Cot, may prayer and praise be sent, | To God's high throne, that He may deign to smile, | And like a wall of fire surround our much-lov'd Isle'. In this significant revision, 'God' rather than a peasant militia provides Britain's defensive firewall. It says a lot for 'The Cotter''s contemporary popularity, and its Loyalist potential, that it was deemed suitable for 'translation', abridgement, and distribution (for the price of a penny) to an English popular readership as a *Cheap Repository Tract*. In the absence of any detailed contemporary analysis of the politics of Burns's original, Evans's 'Cottagers' Saturday Night' provides a fascinating indicator of the popular appeal of

---

[50] The Macnie chapbook text, in attempting to market the English translation to a Scottish popular readership, many of whom would know the original, needed to 're-insert' the Scots supper stanza (12), although the 'hawkie' who 'yont the hallan snugly chews her food' now becomes 'their only cow . . . that in the orchard peaceful chews the cud' (pp. 22, 23)!

Burns's pastoral poem in the revolutionary decade, but also of the problems of employing it as a vehicle of Tory ideology.[51]

David Hill Radcliffe has shown how the pious and domesticated cottage interior of Burns's 'Cotter' was further sentimentalized in the Scottish 'Kailyard' literature of the early nineteenth century: 'imitations of the Cotter had become a recognised genre by 1824... as Burns's piety and patriotism evolved into the reconstituted Tory politics espoused by *Blackwoods* and the Lake Poets'.[52] It is telling that the emphasis tends to shift from Saturday night to Sunday morning in the titles of many of the imitations, often the work of Dissenting or Seceding ministers. Examples are John Struther's *The Poor Man's Sabbath* (1804), James Hyslop's *The Scottish Sacramental Sabbath, in imitation of 'The Cotter's Saturday Night'* (1820), and John Gilmour's *The Sabbath Sacrament* (*c*.1828). Although we shouldn't discount the evangelical radicalism that energizes some of these performances, many are soaked in a crude pastoral nostalgia for a lost rural world, content simply to prop up dominant ideologies and religious pieties, albeit frequently of a nonconformist persuasion. The imitators weren't exclusively Scottish: there's a return to English Spenserians in an otherwise close but politically anodyne imitation, 'The Peasant's Sabbath' by 'M' (probably the work of an English Dissenting minister) published in the *Poetical Magazine* in 1810, and a number of English labouring class poets, most notably John Clare, reworked 'The Cotter' in diverse local contexts.[53]

The suggestion that Burns's original was never an entirely comfortable model for conservative writers is borne out by John Wilson's prose essay 'The Radical's Saturday Night', published in *Blackwood's Magazine* in December 1819. Pastoral idealization of the rural poor is reinvented here as class paranoia which tacitly acknowledges the radical Burnesian subtext that I've been exploring: the poem's critique of the forms of orthodox worship are now construed as atheism. Challenging the ahistoricity of the original, Wilson seeks to update Burns's rosy vision of 'honest poverty' in the light of current political concerns. Guest of a family of cotters who seem to have walked straight out of the pages of the Kilmarnock volume, the narrator has a terrible nightmare (perhaps he's had too much 'weel-hain'd kebbuck' before retiring to bed) in which it turns out that the cottage family are all atheists, radicals, and sensualists:

The old man, speaking to me as if to a well-known neighbour... said, 'alas! Is this the Cotter's Saturday Night?' 'I have been at the kirk tonight with the committee of reform',

---

[51] See Kevin Gilmartin, *Writing Against Revolution: Literary Conservatism, 1790–1832* (Cambridge: Cambridge University Press, 2006).

[52] David Hill Radcliffe, 'Imitation, Popular Literacy, and "The Cotter's Saturday Night"', in Carol McGuirk (ed.), *Critical Essays on Robert Burns* (New York: G. K. Hall, 1998), 264.

[53] At least two poems in Clare's 1821 *Village Minstrel*, 'The Woodman' and 'Sunday' loosely imitated 'The Cotter''s Spenserian stanzas and the idealized domestic setting, although they lack the evangelical piety of the Scottish imitations. In a later poem entitled 'The Cottager', Clare's version of Burns's cotter is old-fashioned, stolidly Tory, and Anglican.

cried [his son] with an oath, 'and a merry meeting we had of it.' The old man mildly asked what had been done; and the ruffian answered, 'we have levelled the old crazy building with the ground—the pews, and lofts, and rafters—the pulpit too . . . by the bones of Thomas Paine they made a glorious bonfire! and turned all the church-yard as bright as day—the manse itself looked red in the blaze. Had the ghosts leapt from their graves, they might have fancied it hell-fire.' And here, methought, the drunken Atheist laughed convulsively, as if to suppress the terror that his impiety forced into his own coward heart.[54]

The cotter's granddaughter (the 'Jenny' figure) has become a prostitute at the age of 15, and the cottage is a scene of hunger, filth, and disorder. Wilson's nightmare vision is something of a Burnsian *capriccio*, drawing heavily on 'Tam o' Shanter''s description of a 'bleezing' Kirkalloway with its infernal occupants to convey his vision of Scotland as an atheist republic. But when the narrator wakes up and pinches himself, he is relieved to discover that it was only a dream, and joins the real family at church for Sunday worship.

Wilson's vision of the 'disorderly cottage' may have been swayed by Elizabeth Hamilton's 1808 novel *The Cottagers of Glenburnie: A Tale for the Farmer's Ingle-Nook*, the first Scottish novel to be published in Edinburgh.[55] Here the Fergussonian or Burnsian cottage is recast as a squalid hut full or dirt, disorder, and idleness, crying out for reform and regulation. As Ian Duncan comments, picking up the links between improvement and the cotter clearance suppressed in Burns's 'The Cotter', *Glenburnie's* definition of 'culture' 'required the abolition of original conditions under the slogan of their reformation'.[56] Hamilton's novel is in turn evoked in what may be the most significant Scottish literary response to Burns's 'The Cotter' (albeit seldom recognized as such), Walter Scott's 1818 *The Heart of Midlothian*. Scott's novel can be seen as a massive and elaborate articulation of the 'submerged' plot of Burns's poem: it consciously plunders his account in the characterization of the pious 'Davie Deans', whose daughter Effie is betrayed and seduced by the smooth, dissembling Robertson. The fate of seduction is only *imagined* for the cotter's 'Jeanie', but it becomes the hinge upon which Scott's whole protracted narrative turns.[57]

The moral disorder which leads Effie to the brink (infanticide, imprisonment, threatened execution) is redeemed by Jeanie's pilgrimage to London to obtain her sister's pardon from the Queen via the Duke of Argyll. As a reward for her unswerving virtue Jeanie is employed as a dairymaid and housed in a model cottage on the Duke's estate at Roseneath on the Clyde, the sort of orderly

---

[54] [John Wilson], 'The Radical's Saturday Night', *Blackwood's Magazine* 6 (Dec. 1819), 257–62.

[55] Ian Duncan, *Scott's Shadow: The Novel in Romantic Edinburgh* (Princeton, NJ: Princeton Unversity Press, 2007), 70.

[56] Ibid. 72.

[57] Scott cites Hamilton's *Glenburnie* (not Burns's 'The Cotter'!) in noting the over-indulgent treatment of their children by the Scots peasantry, which is one root of Effie's disobedience. Sir Walter Scott, *The Heart of Midlothian*, ed. and intro. Tony Inglis (London: Penguin, 1994), 99.

planned cottage in which improving estate owners were being urged to house their tenants by philanthropists and architects such as Sir Thomas Bernard, William Atkinson, and John Wood.[58] Scott's novel brilliantly rescues Burns's 'The Cotter' from its pastoral cul-de-sac by reinscribing it within a narrative of historical progress and social hierarchy. At the same time, the central plot of Jeanie's redemptive journey sustains the poem's moral focus on the exemplary virtue of the Scottish cotter class.

Although Burn's 'The Cotter' is a towering influence on nineteenth-century Scottish literature, its pastoral affirmation of the evergreen virtues of the cotter class is given a more tragic inflection by Wordsworth, whose cottage poems perhaps owe more to the explicitly radical poetry of rural complaint.[59] However, 'Michael' (1800), one of a series of poems described by Wordsworth as 'Cumberland Pastorals', does engage directly with Burns's 'The Cotter' in its account of Michael's piety, thrift, and sobriety, and the 'hard' pastoral depiction of the Lakeland cottage economy.[60] In contrast to Burns's bare acknowledgement of social change in 'The Cotter', the ruined sheepfold which frames the narrative of the old patriarch Michael, his thrifty wife Isabel, and his son Luke, like Wordsworth's view of pastoral poetry itself, is a symbol for the rapid attenuation of the traditional rural life-world.[61] Luke's vulnerability when removed from the virtuous cottage economy may at one level evoke Burns's lubricious anxiety about Jenny's seduction, although Wordsworth has purged any hint of eros or courtship from Michael's cottage, focusing on a wayward son rather than daughter. Luke goes to the bad as soon as he moves to the city, and is eventually forced to emigrate to the colonies in disgrace. (Was the poet thinking of Burns's Jamaica plan at this point, fresh in his mind from reading Currie's biography?)[62]

In his February 1799 letter to Coleridge quoted in Chapter 2, Wordsworth praised the power of Burnsian pastoral in depicting 'not transitory manners reflecting the wearisome unintelligible obliquities of city-life, but manners connected with the permanent objects of nature and partaking of the simplicity

[58] Ann Bermingham, 'The Simple Life', 42–7. See also William Aiton's 'cottage plan' discussed above.

[59] This is especially true of the 1797–8 'The Ruined Cottage', later revised to become the first book of *The Excursion*, published in 1814.

[60] See 'Michael', ll. 95–7, in Jonathan Wordsworth (ed. with critical intro.), *The Ruined Cottage, The Brothers, Michael* (Cambridge: Cambridge University Press, 1985), 70.

[61] The homely fare prepared by Michael's wife Isabel ('Each with a mess of pottage and skimmed milk, | Sate round their basket piled with oaten cakes, | And their plain home-made cheese', ll. 101–3) is clearly inspired by Burns's 'halesome *Porritch*, chief o' *SCOTIA'S* food', and the 'weel-hained kebbuck' prepared by the Cottar's 'frugal wife' (ll .92–9).

[62] See my essay, 'Burns, Wordsworth, and the Politics of Vernacular Poetry', in Peter de Bolla, Nigel Leask, and David Simpson (eds.), *Land, Nation and Culture, 1740–1840* (Basingstoke: Palgrave Macmillan, 2005), 217.

of those objects. Such pictures most interest when the original must cease to exist'
[*CH* p. 131]. This latter statement is only apparently paradoxical; what Wordsworth means—very much against the manifest drift of Burns's 'The Cotter'—is
that the human 'permanence' represented by pastoral is *more* richly endowed
with poetic affect when the original rural world which it portrays has ceased to
exist. But maybe Wordsworth here puts his finger on the particular—and to
modern critics often elusive—pathos of 'The Cotter's Saturday Night'.

## 'THE BEGGAR'S SATURDAY NIGHT'

As mentioned above, Burns's 'Love and Liberty: A Cantata' [K 84] was written
contemporaneously with 'The Cotter's Saturday Night' in the autumn of 1785.
But by contrast to the latter, which took pride of place in the Kilmarnock volume, it
was first published in 1799 as an unauthorized chapbook entitled 'The Jolly
Beggars', and was therefore largely invisible to readers during Burns's lifetime.[63]
Its rather haphazard emergence on the critical horizon in the romantic period and
beyond, however, saw it assume central place in Burns's canon, a position it
maintains today: Thomas Crawford describes it as 'the masterpiece of Burns's
early Ayrshire period . . . the highest single achievement of the popular song culture
of the 18th century'.[64] Like 'To a Mouse' and many of Burns's other poems, 'Love
and Liberty' is 'authenticated' by a biographical anecdote which records the poet,
with his friends John Richmond and James Smith, visiting 'Poosie-Nansie''s tavern
in Mauchline late one night, where they witnessed 'much jollity amongst a company
who by day appeared abroad as miserable beggars' [Chambers-Wallace, i. 244].

   As is so often the case with Burns, this apparently spontaneous creation turns
out to have a considerable literary hinterland in both the 'great' and 'little'
traditions of eighteenth-century British literature, to cite Peter Burke's useful
distinction.[65] From the former, the Cantata draws on a tradition of 'beggar
pastoral' with its roots in Fletcher's *Beggar's Bush* (?1622) and Richard Brome's
popular *Joviall Crew, or the Merry Beggars* (1641), converted into a comic opera
in 1760 with musical arrangements by William Bates. The huge success of Gay's
*Beggar's Opera* doubtless inspired this *rifacciamento*, and as Crawford surmises,
Gay's 'Newgate pastoral' also 'helped to organise the social commentary in

---

   [63] Burns's manuscript circulated around friends and family, and in 1787, during or after his
Edinburgh visit, he made a revised copy for Lady Don, sister of his patron Glencairn, now known
as the 'Don MS' [Kin. iii.1151]. First publication was *The Jolly Beggars; or, Tatterdemallions.
A Cantata* (Glasgow: Stewart and Meikle, 1799).
   [64] Thomas Crawford, *Society and the Lyric: A Study of the Song Culture of Eighteenth-Century
Scotland* (Edinburgh: Scottish Academic Press, 1979), 187, 210. For a study of the poem's sources,
see Crawford, BPS, pp.130–46; *Society and the Lyric*, 185–212; Kin. iii. 1148–62; John C. Weston,
*Robert Burns. The Jolly Beggars: A Cantata* (Northampton, Mass.: Gehenna, 1963).
   [65] Peter Burke, *Popular Culture in Early Modern Europe* (repr. Aldershot: Scolar Press, 1994), 28.

Burns's cantata', even if it eschews Gay's political allegory.[66] Regarding Scottish sources, as far as I'm aware no critic has noted the strong influence of Alexander Pennecuik's 'Marriage between Scrape, Monarch of the Maunders, and Bobber-lips, Queen of the Gypsies', published in his 1720 collection *Streams from Helicon*. As in 'Love and Liberty', Pennecuik's narrative is interspersed with songs both Scots and English (one being 'Old Sir Simon', employed by Burns for 'The Merry-Andrew's Song'); moreover the poem's beggars make much of their 'Liberty' in defiance of 'King GEORGE' and the law.[67]

From the 'little tradition' of popular song, as Crawford has painstakingly demonstrated, Burns would have known (amongst others) 'The Gaberlunzie Man' and 'The Jolly Beggar'; he seems however to have derived his title from 'A Scots Cantata' in Ramsay's *Tea-Table Miscellany*, and drawn largely on two other songs from that collection, 'The Happy Beggars' and 'The Merry Beg-gars'.[68] Another suggestive analogy unremarked by critics (this time from con-temporary visual culture), is William Dent's graphic satire dated August 1786 entitled *The Jovial Crew or Merry Beggars. A comic opera as performed at Brighton by the Carleton Company*. Alluding to Brome's comic opera, Dent satirizes the Prince of Wales, his 'wife' Mrs Fitzherbert, and the Whig politicians Fox, Sheridan, Burke, et al. as a band of 'merry beggars' who include a rake, a doxy, a 'gut-scraper', a mutilated soldier, and a 'fanatical Preacher'. The date of this London print make it an unlikely source for Burns's Cantata, however, unless an earlier variant was in circulation.[69] As with Gay's *Beggar's Opera*, the topic had great potential for political satire; but Burns (despite his penchant for the form, as we've seen in 'A Dream') resisted the temptation here. Only in 'The Merry-Andrew's Song' does he indulge in satirizing 'a Tumbler ca'd the Premier', and the song was dropped from later manuscripts, probably in the interests of aesthetic unity, as I'll argue below [K iii. 1151–2].

The Cantata's very full scene setting (and rudimentary plot) is carried by the *recitativo*, the Scots idiom of which contrasts with the lyrical content of English and Anglo-Scots songs, set to a combination of Scottish and English melodies, performed by the dramatis personae in turn. In this respect, like 'The Cotter''s Spenserians, 'Love and Liberty' represents a young poet's *bravura*, showcasing his mastery of diverse Scots verse forms in the *recitativo*: the 'Cherry and Slae' in

---

[66] *Society and the Lyric*, 200. For a detailed account of the genesis of beggar pastoral see Henley and Henderson, ii. 291–304.

[67] Alexander Pennecuik, *Streams from Helicon; or, poems on various subjects. In three parts*. 2nd edn. (London, 1720). The Edinburgh imprint of the same year is lacking this poem, which perhaps explains why it has been missed by scholars. It is possible that Burns alludes to this source in line 218–19 of 'Love and Liberty' where the 'Bard of no regard' sings 'But there it streams an' richly reams, | My HELICON I ca' that'.

[68] *Society and the Lyric*, 198–201.

[69] British Museum Satires 6980.

lines 1–28 and 236–49; common ballad measure in lines 49–56; 'Christ's Kirk' in lines 49–56; and the familiar habbie in lines 117–28.

Although 'Love and Liberty' is centrally concerned with hedonistic pleasure, it also picks up on the theme of ruination elaborated in 'Epistle to Davie' [K 51], 'the last o't, the warst o't, | Is only but to beg' (ll. 27–8). I suggested in Ch. 3 that Burns's idealized view of the beggar's life lacks the power to convince, as if 'Commoners of air' (l. 43) with their 'craz'd banes' and 'thin bluid', could really derive much solace and warmth from '*Nature*'s charms', 'free alike to all' (ll. 45, 48). The sentimentalized beggar features here, as elsewhere in Burns, as an imaginary figure for the poet himself, dedicated to the values of *carpe diem* in the face of financial ruin and exile. The antithesis between the beggar's life and that of the 'warldly race' (still more the 'unco gude') is after all a pastoral antithesis: simplicity versus sophistication, innocence versus corruption, content-ment versus ambition, communal affiliation versus individual aggression; in short 'the abstract opposition between nature and artifice'.[70]

The Cantata's social critique derives directly from the pastoral politics of Ramsay's 'The Merry Beggars': 'Whoe'er would be merry and free, | Let him list, and from it he may learn; | In Palaces who shall you see, | Half so happy as we in a Barn!'[71] This of course resonates with 'The Cotter''s pastoral ethic, 'The *Cottage* leaves the *Palace* far behind', with the proviso that the site of Liberty is now the Barn (or tavern), and *not* the orderly and industrious cottage. Although sympathy with the piety and thrift of the 'deserving poor' is replaced here by the beggars' instinctual pursuit of illicit pleasures, at one level the poet admires the heroism of both groups in refusing to be bowed down by poverty and social disadvantage.

Perhaps for this reason, we're given almost no 'external' perspective on the beggars, along the lines of the opening stanza of 'The Cotter', or the 'enlight-ened' head- and footnotes to 'Halloween'.[72] McGuirk notes the poet's evident admiration for both the cotters' domestic piety and the beggars' love of pleasure, to the extent that both groups embody the cardinal Burnesian virtue of 'inde-pendence'. But she also rightly underlines the fact that he nevertheless distances himself from both cotters and beggars by (respectively) sentimentalizing, or ironizing, their poverty, unable to identify with their 'unthinking acceptance of their lot' [McGuirk, *BSP* 220]. Acute as this is, we shouldn't lose sight of Burns's notion of poetry as itself an alternative vocation, a 'counterpoise to the struggles of [the] world', an idea reflected and satirized in the final section of 'Love and Liberty'. Unlike Wordsworth in 'The Old Cumberland Beggar' and related

---

[70] See Michael McKeon, 'The Pastoral Revolution', in Kevin Sharpe and Steven Zwicker (eds.), *Refiguring Revolutions: Aesthetics and Politics from the English Revolution to the Romantic Revolution* (Berkeley and Los Angeles: University of California Press, 1998), 268.

[71] Allan Ramsay, *The Tea-Table Miscellany*, 18th edn. (Glasgow, 1782), 365.

[72] The only exception is the footnote to l. 9 describing Poosie-Nansie's as 'a noted Caravansary in M[auchline], well known to and much frequented by the lowest order of Travellers and Pilgrims'.

poems, Burns has no interest here in reflecting on the ethics of charity, more concerned to sympathize poetically with the beggars' brief and defiant Saturday-night hedonism, than to reflect upon the cold Sabbath of hunger to which they'll awake. (The charitable impulse is burlesqued in the opening description of the soldier's doxy soliciting a kiss from her lover, her mouth likened to a begging bowl: 'she held up her greedy gab, | Just like an aumous dish', ll. 23–4). Moreover, despite the antinomianism of the closing song, its social critique is largely pre-political: this is certainly not a poetry that puts its hand in its breeches pockets, to adapt Keats's remark. Like Fergusson's city pastorals discussed in Ch. 2, the opening *recitativo* of Burns's beggar pastoral turns indoors, away from the winter storm howling outside to the warm uproar of present enjoyment. Rather than seeking consolation from Nature, the 'merry core | O' randie, gangel bodies' (ll. 7–8) in Poosie-Nansie's pursue more tangible fleshly pleasures that always threaten to undo the fragile bond of sympathy that unites them, temporarily, in hedonistic glee.

Burns's original manuscript title 'Love and Liberty' is usually linked to the account of extramarital love in lines 91–4 of Pope's 'Eloisa and Abelard', but a more appropriate source is Pope's description of 'pre-political' social bonds in Epistle 3 of the *Essay on Man*: 'Converse and Love mankind might strongly draw, | When Love was Liberty, and Nature Law. | Thus States were form'd; the name of King unknown, | 'Till common int'rest plac'd the sway in one.'[73] Pope here sketches a conjectural history of social progress in which society is initially based on pleasurable instinct and economic equality, 'Nature rising slow to Art' (l. 169), a situation all too soon replaced by private property, law, and kingship. Pope's Arcadian reign of Love and Liberty is severely tested when applied to the denizens of Poosie-Nansie's, but for all its comedy Burns's poem is a serious bid to understand the original meaning of social contract and the rule of law. In an exercise in poetic primitivism which is far from sentimentalizing its subjects, 'Love and Liberty' deliberately conflates the social underclass of late eighteenth-century Ayrshire with Pope's instinctual progenitors of society, contrasted with the current upholders of the law who timidly prefer 'negative freedom' to human community based on the 'Liberty' of pure desire. As the 'Bard of no regard' sings at line 222, 'But lordly WILL, I hold it still, | A Mortal sin to thraw that.'

The beggars all have diverse origins, and all share the common fate of having 'fallen out' from various 'walks of life' into a condition of vagrancy and criminality. (The fact that they're not native to the parish further underwrites their illegality, according to the terms of the Scottish Poor Law.)[74] Eight 'swaggering'

---

[73] 'Eloisa to Abelard', ll. 91–4; *Essay on Man*, Epistle 3, ll. 207–10, *Pope: Poetical Works*, ed. Herbert Davis (Oxford: Oxford University Press, 1978), 112–13, 264.

[74] See Cage, *The Scottish Poor Law*, 9–15. Its basis was the revealingly titled 1574 'Act Anent the Punishment of Strong and Idle Beggars and Provision for Sustentation of the Poor and Impotent' (p. 2).

songs are performed by the dramatis personae (in order of precedence) the 'Son of Mars', the 'Martial Chuck', the 'Merry Andrew', the 'Highlandman's widow', the 'Pigmy Scraper', and the 'Sturdy Caird' (Tinker), the whole concluding with two songs by the 'Bard of no regard'. According to Burns's friend Richmond, an early draft contained 'three scenes more which are now totally lost, viz. a Sailor, a Sootyman, and Racer Jess' (the simpleton daughter of the tavern keeper 'Pussy' Gibson) [Kin. iii. 1148]. Like Blake's Canterbury Pilgrims, the group represents diverse Platonic types, a diversity rather unfortunately homogenized in Thomas Stewart's alternative title 'The Jolly Beggars'. All possess a modicum of virtue amongst their vices, except possibly the bullying 'Caird', the only member of the group who can boast a legitimate trade in 'clouting cauldrons'.

In the songs Burns shows off a precocious skill in matching newly minted lyrics to traditional Scottish and English melodies. This is well exemplified in the first song, 'I am a Son of Mars' set to the reel tune 'Soldier's Joy', where internal rhymes (e.g. 'wench' and 'trench' at l. 31) mark the musical phrases of the dance tune, exemplifying what Burns called in the Commonplace Book the 'redundancy of syllable' that 'glides in, most melodiously with the respective tunes to which they are set'.[75] Although the mutilated war veteran has been abandoned by the country he has so loyally served, he is nonetheless 'as happy with my wallet, my bottle and my Callet, | As when I us'd in scarlet to follow a drum' (ll. 43–4). He contrasts with the maimed and disbanded soldiers who populate the poetry of Southey and Wordsworth in the 1790s; not only is the 'son of Mars' blissfully happy, he's also willing (fortified with a bottle) to 'meet a troop of HELL at the sound of a drum' (l. 48). If Burns intended social criticism of the fiscal-military state at this point, it's certainly very muted.

The 'Martial Chuck''s song, set to the lively air 'Sodger Laddie' in six–eight time, is also a highly successful fusion of lyric and melody; it's a song which, as Daiches points out, not so much flouts as *ignores* social convention.[76] The 'Chuck''s mistake has been to prefer the 'respectable' regimental chaplain to her 'sodger laddie' (another opportunity for 'priest-skelping Burns' to grind his axe), and on the rebound she has become common sexual property; 'Full soon I grew sick of my sanctified *Sot*, | The Regiment AT LARGE for a HUSBAND I got; | From the gilded SPONTOON to the FIFE I was ready; | I asked no more but a SODGER LADDIE' (ll. 69–72). Despite her time as 'camp whore', in the end she's been reunited in tipsy bliss with her 'old boy'; to this extent her fidelity makes her (in McGuirk's words) 'pass as the ingénue' of the poem' [McGuirk, *BSP* 223].[77]

---

[75] *CPB*, 48.

[76] Daiches, *Robert Burns*, 220.

[77] Cedric Thorpe Davie regards this as the best song in 'Love and Liberty', and one of the two or three finest songs by Burns. 'Robert Burns, Writer of Songs', in Donald Low (ed.), *Critical Essays on Robert Burns* (London: Routledge Kegan Paul, 1975), 168.

The contrast with the innocent sexuality of 'The Cotter''s 'Jenny' couldn't be more marked. Less successful is the awkwardly placed 'Merry-Andrew's Song' set to the 'feeble' English air 'Auld Sir Symon', referred to above.[78] Absent in Burns's later drafts and in Stewart's 'The Jolly Beggars', it's also omitted by some modern editors on the grounds that it interferes with the poem's dramatic unity, 'the central triangle of tinker-carlin-fiddler' [McGuirk, *BSP* p. 220].

The 'Highland Widow's song' marks the shift from the 'overture' to the main 'action' of 'Love and Liberty', as the 'raucle Carlin' laments the hanging of her 'gallant, braw, JOHN HIGHLANDMAN' (l. 92 and refrain). Like the soldier and his 'chuck', the Carlin has warm memories of her lover who though 'The lalland laws he held in scorn ... still was faithfu' to his clan' (ll. 90–1); he's a type of the Highland hero/outlaw in the ballad tradition of 'Gilderoy' or 'Macpherson's Lament'. Despite her moving fidelity, the Carlin is soon the object of amorous competition between the 'Pigmy Scraper' and the 'Sturdy Caird' (whose songs are set, respectively, to the Scots airs 'Whistle o'er the Lave o't' and 'Clout the Caudron', two favourites in Burns's repertoire). When the unpleasant Caird wins the 'raucle carlin' by bullying and main force, she has no hesitation in accepting his protection: 'The Caird prevail'd—th' unblushing fair | In his embraces sunk; | Partly wi' LOVE o'ercome sae sair, | An' partly she was drunk' (ll. 181–4). The Popean syllepsis here underpins Burns's irony in the *recitativo*, undoing the lyrical pathos of her song and the absurdity of her professions, in a world motivated by drink and the urgent appetites of the moment.

McGuirk is one of the few critics who notes that Burns's view of both 'love' and 'liberty' here is 'darker than is usually acknowledged ... the gap between the songs' conventional lyric statements and the beggars' actual conduct is emphasized throughout' [McGuirk, *BSP* 221]. The thwarted 'Sir VIOLINO' drinks a toast to the happy couple but promptly slakes his frustrated desire with another man's (the Bard's) woman; again the *recitativo* unmasks conventional pastoral idiom as a mere periphrasis for sexual appetite: 'But hurchin Cupid shot a shaft, | That play'd a DAME a shavie— | The Fiddler RAK'D her, FORE and AFT, | Behint the Chicken cavie' (ll. 190–3). 'The wee Apollo' turns out to have Dionysian propensities after all.[79] Despite the conviviality, this is a world of 'dog eats dog'; but given that the cuckolded 'Bard' has two remaining 'Deborahs', and therefore 'WIFE ENEUGH for a' that' (l. 215), and that he in any case subscribes to a primitive version of Nietzsche's will to power, he's content to give his blessing to her defection. Moreover (like Burn's persona in 'Epistle to Davie'), it's part of his poetic nature to

[78] A favourite song, nevertheless, of Fielding's Squire Western [Kin. iii. 1323] and as we've seen, employed by Pennecuik in 'Marriage between Scrape ... and Bobberlips'.
[79] See John Purser, ' "The Wee Apollo" ' Burns and Oswald', in Kenneth Simpson (ed.), *Love and Liberty: Robert Burns, A Bicentenary Celebration* (East Lothian: Tuckwell, 1997), 326–33. Purser argues that Burns's fiddler is based on the Scottish musician James Oswald, editor/author of the *Caledonian Pocket Companion*.

cut his losses: 'Tho Fortune sair upon him laid, | His heart, she ever miss'd it. | He had no WISH but—to be glad, | Nor WANT but—when he thristed' (ll. 201–4).

The 'Bard of no regard', described more honorifically as 'a wight of HOMER's craft' (l. 194) concludes 'Love and Liberty' with two songs that encapsulate the beggars' philosophy, and (by way of a finale) restores a momentary poetic harmony to a world dominated by 'Nature's Law'. The pastoral pursuit of *carpe diem* is never far from the Hobbesian war of each against all in a perpetual struggle for (limited) resources. Set to the air 'For a' that', associated with the Jacobite song 'Though Geordie reigns in Jamie's Stead', and later employed by Burns for the radical anthem 'Is there for Honest Poverty' [K 482], the 'Bard of no regard' celebrates the triumph of ephemeral pleasure divorced from the demands of poetic justice; 'In raptures sweet this hour we meet, | Wi' mutual love an a' that; | But for how lang the FLIE MAY STANG, | Let INCLINATION law that' (ll. 224–7). As Daiches points out, 'the entire Petrarchan tradition of love poetry is implicitly dismissed' by these lines.[80]

The Bard is to some extent putting a brave face on things; there's a particular irony in the fact that of all the characters in Poosie-Nansie's it's the poet who comes out worst in material terms. Perhaps for this very reason, he emerges triumphantly as 'the losers' loser', his song greeted with 'a thunder of applause'— well beyond those of his rivals. Doubly defeated in the material stakes, in the end he wins the laurels for his song. And although cuckolded by the 'pigmy scraper', he's still able to hymn the triumph of 'inclination', holding no grudge against the female sex that has betrayed him. His magnanimity is, of course, shored up by the 'TWA DEBORAHS' 'rejoicing' at his side; perhaps he has little reason, after all, for feeling hard done by. At one level the 'Bard of no regard' is a figure for Burns the bardie; his enjoyment of playing a beggar role is revealed in his 1791 letter to Charles Sharpe, in which the pseudonymous 'Johnie Faa' describes himself as an itinerant fiddler and ballad-seller, whose mother was 'spouse to a marching regiment . . . the Muses baptized me in Castalian streams, but the thoughtless gypseys forgot to give me A NAME' [CL ii. 86–7]. 'Johnie Faa' is of course a darker antithesis of the 'Heaven-taught Ploughman', a relationship analogous to that between 'Love and Liberty' and 'The Cotter's Saturday Night'.

Just as the father of poetry, Homer, is identified in Burns's footnote to line 194 as 'the eldest Ballad singer on record', so the epic tradition is conflated in the finale with its lowest incarnation in the travelling balladeer; appropriately enough, then, the antinomian creed of the Bard's closing song represents a distillation of the true and primitive poetic philosophy. As Thomas Crawford points out, 'the final chorus, as well as being sung around the anacreontic bowl, also parodies a religious rite, with common cup, creed and grace'.[81] Sounding a

---

[80] Daiches, *Robert Burns*, 228.
[81] *Society and the Lyric*, 208.

note of Blakean antinomianism, it's an appropriate climax to 'The Beggar's Saturday Night', just as the old Cotter's Bible reading strikes a sublime note in 'Love and Liberty''s saintly companion poem. 'A fig for those by law protected! | LIBERTY's a glorious feast! | Courts for Cowards were erected, | Churches built to please the PRIEST (ll. 254–7). *Carpe diem* is an abiding theme in Burns's poetry and song, and there's no doubt that the Cantata's 'glorious feast' powerfully transformed the eighteenth-century genre of 'beggar pastoral' that it had inherited from both the literary and popular traditions. As we'll see in the next chapter, the 'love and liberty' of Poosie-Nansie's reappears, albeit briefly, in Tam's 'unco sight' through the window of Kirkalloway, but perhaps with a stronger warning attached.

'Love and Liberty' was, of course, relegated to the 'reserved canon' of Burns's poetry by his Edinburgh patrons: Revd Hugh Blair complained that 'the Whole of What is called the Cantata, the Songs of the Beggars and their Doxies, with the Grace at the end of them' are 'altogether unfit for publication. They are by much too licentious; and fall below the dignity which Mr Burns possesses in the rest of his poems and would rather degrade them' [Kin. iii. 1150].[82] When Burns was quizzed about the fate of the manuscript by Thomson in September 1793, he claimed to 'have forgotten the Cantata you allude to, as I kept no copy, and indeed did not know that it was in existence; however, I remember that none of the songs pleased myself, except the last—something about, "Courts for cowards . . . the priest" [CL ii. 244]. There's a disarming vagueness about this, which perhaps warrants Daiches's suggestion that Burns was inhibited by the potentially seditious meaning of the closing hymn to Liberty in the climate of 'Pitt's Terror'.[83]

Space forbids any detailed account of the complex publishing history of 'Love and Liberty' studied in detail by Henley and Henderson, Weston, and Kinsley. I'll argue in Chapter 9 that Currie's 1800 edition of Burns defined the poet's mainstream canon for the Romantic era and beyond; in which light his decision not to publish 'Love and Liberty' (despite having access to the manuscript) is important. Cromek followed suit in omitting it from his 1808 *Reliques*, although (censured by Walter Scott) he did include it in his *Scottish Songs* of 1810 [Henley and Henderson, ii. 305–6]. The following year most of 'Love and Liberty' (under the title of 'Jolly Beggars') appeared as a footnote to William Aiton's chapter on 'The Poor' in his *General View of the Agriculture of the County of Ayr*, an unlikely context for publication that's been overlooked by the poem's many commentators.[84] Despite his moral condemnation of the 'vagrant beggars, and sometimes with tinkers and gypsies, who sorn and thieve, and pilfer and extract alms, from the weak and the timid, to the disgrace of the police, the terror of the inhabitants,

---

[82] By describing the final song as a 'Grace', Blair picks up the eucharistic parody.

[83] Daiches, *Robert Burns*, 216.

[84] Remarkably, in his notes to 'Love and Liberty', Kinsley cites Aiton's account of Ayrshire's 'sorners', without mentioning his inclusion of 'The Jolly Beggars' [K iii. 1149–50].

and discredit of humanity' [Aiton, p. 626], Aiton's account bizarrely enough enlists Burns's poem in the service of *aestheticizing* Ayrshire's beggars. In describing the county's 'hotels des vagrantes' such as 'Poosie-Nansie's' he resorts to the language of the picturesque, evoking the 'motley group of people, from different nations' who inhabit such lodgings: 'the novelty of their oaths and curses, diversity of aspect and of dress, and degree of intoxication, etc, exhibited a picture truly hogarthian'. These 'scenes of rough festivity and low debauch' he adds, 'have been rendered classical, by the pen of the immortal Burns' [Aiton, pp. 627, 631–2].

On one level, Aiton's *enjoyment* of the spectacle of mendicancy militates against the drift of his argument to the Board of Agriculture, which diagnosed the plague of beggars afflicting Ayrshire as being the result of the parish licensing 'gaberlunzies' or badge-wearing beggars to prey on the 'ill bestowed charity' of the public. Rather than being proportionate to the real needs of the deserving poor, alms-giving to such often depends upon 'false sympathy, roused by external appearances, or to obtain a character for being charitable' [Aiton, p. 639]. The 'nobility' and 'improving' tendencies of true charity are mocked by the beggars' spectacular performance of poverty, or, just as invidiously, the insincere (because equally spectacular) bestowal of alms. As with Elizabeth Hamilton's 'improvement' of traditional Scots cottage life, Aiton's enjoyment of Burns's 'picturesque' beggars becomes, ironically, a rationale for stamping out the 'undeserving poor'. His argument that 'the dread of want and an honorable ambition to be independent are the strongest incitements to industry and frugality' [Aiton, p. 642] might draw strength from Burns's 'The Cotter', but certainly not from 'The Jolly Beggars', who are 'incited' in quite a different direction. Because genuine voluntary charity has been rendered impossible, and in the light of his bitter opposition to a statutory 'common fund' dedicated to poor relief, Aiton proposed establishing 'bridewells' or workhouses in Ayr, Irvine, and Kilmarnock in order to eliminate vagrancy and improve the morals of the inhabitants.

Ironically, 'Love and Liberty' was subsequently incorporated into the mainstream Burns canon by romantic Tory revisionists as part of a *Kulturkampf* against Whig cultural hegemony. Its exclusion by Currie and transmission in the reserved canon provided ammunition for John Gibson Lockhart in his ambitious project of discrediting the *Edinburgh Review* and the 'inauthentic' culture of enlightenment, motivated by 'a Schillerian argument for substituting aesthetics for politics as the modern discipline of national virtue'.[85] Walter Scott had attacked Currie's 'fastidious and over-delicate rejection of the bard's most spirited and happy effusions' in his 1809 *Quarterly Review* essay on Cromek's *Reliques*, citing with relish the whole of the closing song, 'A fig for those by Law protected' [*CH* pp. 197–8]. Scott's selection of this of all songs for quotation in a

---

[85] Duncan, *Scott's Shadow*, 56.

prominent Tory journal casts some doubts over Daiches's hypothesis concerning contemporary perceptions of the poem's radicalism, even allowing for ideological differences between 1793 and 1809.

In *Peter's Letters to his Kinsfolk* (1819), Scott's son-in-law took up the baton, in the chapters describing 'Peter Morris's' attendance at a Burns supper held in the Edinburgh Assembly Rooms on 22 February 1819. In a section bluntly entitled 'Whig bigotry', Morris lamented that the occasion had been hijacked by Jeffrey, Murray, Cockburn, and other prominent *Edinburgh Reviewers*. Disingenuously ignoring the recent spat between Wordsworth and Jeffrey prompted by the former's *Letter to a Friend of Robert Burns* (1816), he complained that Jeffrey had ignominiously refused to toast the English poet.[86] In the next chapter, 'Peter Morris' describes a musical performance of 'The Jolly Beggars' ('in high style') by 'Messrs Swift, Templeton, and Lees'.[87] For the benefit of his Welsh correspondent, he notes that 'this inimitable Cantata is not be found in Currie's edition, and I suspect that you are a stranger even to its name'. Lockhart/Morris proceeds to wager that if Burns had written nothing else, 'he would still have left enough to justify all the honour in which his genius is held. There does not exist, in any one piece throughout the whole range of English poetry, such a collection of true, fresh, and characteristic lyrics.'[88] Downplaying the Cantata's antinomianism and anticlericalism, Lockhart proceeds to analyse some of its lyrical offerings, pausing to admire the jingoistic sentiments of the 'Son of Mars' song.

But rather than attempting any political revision of Burns's meaning, Lockhart is more interested in interpreting the Cantata in aesthetic terms, along the lines of a Coleridgean 'poem of pure imagination'. In a masterly stroke that both highlights the reasons for its exclusion from Currie, at the same time striking a blow at the underlying principles of Whig poetics, he invites his readers to consider how the Whig poet George Crabbe would have set about representing 'the carousal of a troop of Beggars in a hedge alehouse'.[89] 'Mr Crabbe would have described the Beggars like a firm though humane Justice of the Peace—poor Robert Burns did not think himself entitled to assume such airs of superiority.' It is precisely the Cantata's *resistance* to ideological reduction, its refusal to consider the ethics of charity or the problem of poor management, that makes it a consummate

---

[86] *Peter's Letters*, i. 125. According to the account of the dinner published in *The Scotsman* for 27 Feb. 1819, Wordsworth's health was in fact proposed by 'Mr Robertson'. See William Ruddick's notes to his abridged edition of *Peter's Letters to his Kinsfolk* (Edinburgh: Scottish Academic Press, 1977), 193.

[87] Probably the version published in 1818 in George Thomson's *Select Scottish Airs*, vol. v, with some modification to the lyrics, set to music by Henry Bishop. Thomson dropped it from his collection in 1826. In 1816 Thomson had unsuccessfully attempted to persuade Beethoven to compose an opera based on 'Love and Liberty', which he entitled 'Les Gueux enjoues'. Kirsteen McCue, '*George Thomson (1757–1851): His Collections of National Airs in their Scottish Cultural Context*' (unpublished D.Phil. dissertation, Oxford University, 1993), 242–3, 305, 173.

[88] Lockhart, *Peter's Letters*, i. 137.

[89] Ibid. 139.

exemplar of Romantic poetry: 'we would have understood and pitied the one groupe [i.e. Crabbe's], but . . . we sympathise even with the joys of the other'. We might 'throwe a few shillings to Mr Crabbe's mendicants', but we're rather inclined to 'drink them ourselves along with the "orra duds" of those of Burns'.[90]

This is an inspired interpretation of 'Love and Liberty', methodizing a romantic ideology of the aesthetic that is only incipient in Burns's text; and it would provide the basis for all major readings in the century that follows. Matthew Arnold's famous comparison of 'Poosie-Nansie's Tavern' with Goethe's Auerbach's cellar apart (in an otherwise negative critique of Burns's poetry), it is interesting that Thomas Carlyle discovered the real excellence of 'Love and Liberty' to be its success as a form of pastoral, placing it close to the generic aims of 'The Cotter'; 'The subject truly is among the lowest in Nature; but it only the more shews our Poet's gift in raising it into the domain of Art' [*CH* p. 368].

---

[90] Ibid. 140.

# 8

# The Deil and the Exciseman

*A chield's amang you, taking notes,*
*And, faith, he'll prent it.*[1]

## POETRY AND THE EXCISE YEARS

Much of Burns's poetry written during and after his Edinburgh fame 1787–8 is composed in the strained poetic diction of 'Caledonia's Bard' and addressed to aristocratic or polite patrons.[2] Absent from many of these polite, Anglicized efforts is the vernacular energy of the Mossgiel period, although it still resonates in the songs Burns anonymously 'mended and polished' for Johnson's Scots *Musical Museum*, as well as of course in 'Tam o' Shanter', [K 321] written in 1790 and added to the Edinburgh edition in 1793. It is no surprise that the theme of Burns's most famous poem is illicit pleasure and the abuse of supernatural sanctions in its regulation, defiantly 'counterpoised' to the disciplinary demands of his new occupational concerns as an excise officer, i.e. a gauger and tax-collector for the British state. (Peter Murphy notes perceptively that 'Edinburgh taught him that legitimate poetic pleasures are subject to taxation'.)[3] In a sense, as I'll argue, Tam's near escape from hellish retribution anticipates the fate of the radicalized poet in the darkening political climate of the 1790s.

This final chapter on Burns's poetry and song will explore some of the ways in which the new mobility afforded by Burns's excise career, as well as his antiquarian connections during the Ellisland years (1788–91), were important factors in shaping his art as a 'national' rather than a 'local' poet and songwriter. Chapter 1 has shown the extent to which Burns's ambivalent experience as an

---

[1] 'On the Late Captain Grose's Peregrinations thro' Scotland' [K 275 ll. 5–6].

[2] Of this order are the poems concerning Excise promotion addressed to Robert Graham of Fintry, but also elegiac poems such as 'Elegy on the Death of Sir James Hunter Blair' [K 160], 'On the Death of Lord President Dundas' [K 186], and 'Lament for James, Earl of Glencairn' [K 334]. The list also includes much of the verse inspired by the Highland tour of 1787, such as 'The Humble Petition of Bruar Water, to the Noble Duke of Athole' [K 172].

[3] Peter Murphy, *Poetry as an Occupation and an Art in Britain, 1760–1830* (Cambridge: Cambridge University Press, 1993), 90.

improving tenant farmer influenced the dialectical critique of the poems in the Kilmarnock and Edinburgh volumes. But the institutional and epistemological disciplines informing Burns's career after 1788 were likewise an important matrix for the poems and songs produced in the later years of his brief life. His abandonment of farming for full-time excise employment in late 1791 (entailing a new urban lifestyle in Dumfries) cut the ligature between Burns's agricultural career and the poetic discourse of 'Scots pastoral' that has been my theme in this book. Nevertheless, in many respects the songs that he produced in these years represent Burns at his most conventionally 'pastoral': as he himself wrote in 1792, 'in the sentiment & style of our Scotish [*sic*] airs, there is a pastoral simplicity, a something that one may call, the Doric style & dialect of vocal music, to which a dash of our native tongue & manners is particularly, nay peculiarly apposite' [CL ii. 153]. Regrettably, space forbids a dedicated chapter-length study of the songs, many of them in any case written after the period with which I'm principally concerned.

## 'THE DE'IL'S AWA WI' TH' EXCISEMAN': BURNS'S SONG ART

In 1796, Coleridge, reminding Charles Lamb of the fate of his friend's favourite poet Burns, anathaemized the classical personification of patronage: 'Ghost of Maecenas! Hide thy blushing face! | They snatched him from the sickle and the plough— | To gauge ale-firkins.'[4] Like many English radical admirers of Burns, Coleridge regarded Burns's excise commission as a shameful failure of patronage on the part of the Scottish Tory establishment.[5] In fact, the truth was rather the opposite: Burns opted to join the Excise service (against the wishes of patrons such as Frances Dunlop, Sir John Whitefoord, and the Earl of Glencairn) in a quest for the financial independence guaranteed by a fixed and pensionable salary of £50 (rising to £70) per annum, in order to free himself from the credit-trap of farming, and the constant and humiliating struggle to solicit patronage. (William Donaldson rightly argues that 'a man could do more for himself by his own efforts [in the Excise] than in any other branch of the public administration', although Burns's ambition to achieve a Collectorship did in fact require a

---

[4] S. T. Coleridge, 'To a Friend who had declared his intention of writing no more poetry', *Coleridge Poetical Works*, ed. J. C. Mays, 6 vols. (Princeton, NJ: Princeton University Press, 2001), i. 271, ll. 22–4.
[5] In fact Burns's plan was to combine farming at Ellisland with a career in the Excise: the £50 p.a. starting salary would underwrite the 'improvements' necessary on the farm, at least in theory avoiding any repetition of his severely undercapitalized predicament at Mossgiel. This was all the more important considering that Ellisland was (in his own words) 'in the last stage of worn-out poverty, and will take some time before it pay the rent' [CL i. 314].

continuing quest for political patronage.)[6] In contrast to another famous excise-man of the period, Tom Paine, Burns was a conscientious employee who actively sought promotion, and, despite a scrape with his employers over his political loyalties in late 1792, with considerable success.[7]

At the same time, the poet had no illusions about the nature of his chosen profession; as we saw in Chapter 4, Burns's poem 'Scotch Drink' captured the popular mood in lambasting 'Thae curst horse-leeches o' the' Excise, | Wha mak the *Whisky stills* their prize!' [K 77 ll. 115–16]. Excise officers were especially loathed in Scotland because they enforced unpopular taxes on malt and barley which many regarded as breaching the conditions of the 1707 Act of Union, a mood that Burns captured in his song 'The De'il's awa wi' th' Exciseman' [K 386]. It is often forgotten that this song was written for performance at an Excise 'court-dinner', an instance of the concentrated camaraderie and self-laughter that united excisemen in their unpopular vocation;[8] it was dispatched in March 1792 to John Leven, Excise Supervisor at Edinburgh, as part of Burns's bid for promotion [CL ii. 139]. In a similar spirit, his 'Extemporaneous Effusion on being appointed to the Excise' [K 193] regretted that 'clarty barm should stain my laurels': at the same time, his often-repeated excuse was the responsibility of providing for 'these muvin' things ca'd wives and weans' (ll. 3, 5–6).

The Excise embodied one of the eighteenth-century 'spaces of modernity' recently theorized by Miles Ogborn, upon the efficiency of which depended the power of Britain's military-fiscal state.[9] Britain was the most highly taxed nation in Europe, and the efficacy of its Excise officers in collecting 'indirect taxation' greatly outstripped the haphazard tax-farming techniques of its main military rival, France.[10] This was based upon the precise, geometrically informed gauging of casks and firkins, as well as a rigorous bureaucratic control of national

---

[6] William Donaldson, 'The Glencairn Connection: Robert Burns and Scottish Politics, 1786–96', *Studies in Scottish Literature* 16 (1981), 71.

[7] Most unusually, after only sixteen months of full employment, Burns's name was put forward for promotion, realized in his appointment to Dumfries Port Division on 26 April 1792, with a salary of £70 p.a. Challenging allegations that Burns was passed over by his Excise employers, Graham Smith writes that his promotion was 'without precedent or parallel in both the English and Scottish Excise services'. In sixteen months Burns had achieved what took ordinary officers six or seven years. Graham Smith, *Robert Burns the Exciseman* (Ayr: Alloway Publications, 1989), 68.

[8] For the 'laughter' that gave excisemen some 'elbow room' within their disciplinary milieu, see Miles Ogborn, *Spaces of Modernity: London's Geographies, 1680–1780* (New York: Guilford, 1998), 193. 'The Deil's awa' is one of Burns's many 'occupational' songs, mainly published in Johnson's *Musical Museum*: others include 'The Ploughman' [K 205], The Dusty Miller [K 201], 'The Taylor Fell thro' the Bed' [K 286], 'The Gardener wi' his Paidle' [K 291], 'The Gallant Weaver' [K 380], 'The Sutor's o' Selkirk' [K 568], and 'The Sodger's Return' [K 406].

[9] Ogborn, *Spaces of Modernity*, 158–200.

[10] John Brewer, *The Sinews of Power: War, Money and the English State, 1688–1783* (London: Unwin Hyman, 1989), 89–91; William Ashworth, *Customs and Excise: Trade, Production and Consumption in England, 1640–1845* (Oxford: Oxford University Press, 2003), 4.

space, in the interests of efficient tax collection. Excisemen like Burns were trained in using 'decimals, square roots and cube roots as well as the geometry of cones, spheres, rhomboids and cylinders . . . [they] were also instructed in book-keeping and accounting, the use of the slide rule and the art of gauging . . . the work performed by the excise officers was technical, complex and time-consuming.'[11]

Given the decentralized nature of power in eighteenth-century Britain, excisemen were the most visible embodiment of the state's authority, in the words of John Brewer 'the symbol of a new form of government'.[12] To this end, the Scottish, like the English Excise, was deliberately 'delocalized' to the extent that its employees were 'national officers who worked locally'.[13] The unpopular 'remove' system was designed periodically to transfer officers to new stations (or 'Rides'), thereby avoiding entanglement with traders or smugglers, or else the formation of political alignments at local level. (Unusually, although he wasn't a native of Dumfriesshire, Burns was permitted to break Excise regulations by occupying Ellisland farm, situated on his own 'Ride', the result of intense lobbying on his part, as well as his poetic celebrity.)[14] Officers were exhorted to avoid alcoholic or venal 'contamination' in the taverns, breweries, and distilleries in which they plied their trade, maintaining a 'separatism' upon which their professional efficacy depended; at the same time, they owed a duty to the public in estimating duties precisely and fairly. Although they were the oath-sworn servants of the Georgian state, many held progressive political views; while there's no doubt that Burns's increasing radicalism in the 1790s was largely prompted by the French Revolution, ironically the rationalism and egalitarian *esprit de corps* of the Excise (whose officers referred to each other as 'brother') may well also have contributed.[15]

What perhaps hasn't been appreciated by Burns scholars and biographers is the role played by the Excise in the poet's creative development in the years after 1788, and not only in a negative sense. In September 1788 Burns, eager for an excise appointment, assured Graham of Fintry that 'my wanderings in the way of my business would be vastly favourable to my picking up original traits of Human nature', in accordance with his plan of composing 'something, in the rural way, of the Drama-kind', maybe along the lines of Ramsay's *Gentle Shepherd* [CL i. 314] Many of his best songs, for the most part published anonymously, were a product of the professional mobility of his life between

[11] Brewer, *Sinews of Power*, 105, 104.

[12] Ibid. 114.

[13] Ogborn, *Spaces of Modernity*, 182.

[14] Burns persuaded his Excise patron Graham of Fintry to dismiss the present encumbent Leonard Smith, in a letter of September 1788 [CL i. 314] enclosing his poem 'To Robert Graham of Fintry, Esq., With a Request for an Excise Division' [K 230].

[15] In November 1790 Burns wrote to Dr James Anderson, editor of the new reformist periodical *The Bee*, subscribing on behalf of Alexander Findlater, his Excise Supervisor at Dumfries, and five of his brother officers [CL ii. 60].

1788 and 1796. Although Burns's refusal of remuneration for his songs from his editors Johnson and Thomson was patriotically motivated ('to talk of money, wages, fee, hire, &c. would be downright Sodomy of Soul!' [CL ii. 149]) it was doubtless also linked to the fact of his secure excise salary. By April 1793 he described 'ballad-making' as 'compleatly my hobby-horse, as ever Fortification was Uncle Toby's' [CL ii. 204]. To a hard-worked Excise officer, the 'gay science' of song collecting made a pleasant contrast to the workaday world of gauging casks and assessing tax duties.

Jeff Skoblow has observed that Burns's song work 'is a kind of gauging itself... the plumbing and notation of a folk musical idiom, but a work which nevertheless repudiates the very Powers of Calculation'.[16] Maybe so, but the very 'method' of measuring and gauging in which Burns had been trained and examined may have suggested to him the 'improvement' of fragmentary or debased song sources into 'standard' lyrical form. The art of gauging had taught him to 'reduce' irregularly shaped casks into ideal cylindrical form, in order to calculate volume from diameter and depth. As Miles Ogborne writes, this involved 'conjuring an imaginary calculable space—an idealized container made of mathematical lines—that abstracted the cask and its commodities from the artisanal circuits of wood and beer within which they also existed'. This calculation demanded a nationally uniform system of gauging common to all excise 'collections'.[17] Analogously, accurately to render one particular song, it was necessary to be networked into the full range of its variants in diverse oral and printed sources (musical equivalents of Ogborn's 'artisanal circuits'). This is why Burns's correspondence with his editors reveals a constant process of 'southing' and comparison of words and airs in order to achieve the most appropriate pairing, or the best old melodic setting for a new lyric, as well as notional reconstruction of traditional song fragments in the composition of newly coherent wholes.

Like the meticulous recording and book-keeping required of the Excise officer, Burns was also assiduous in noting down information relating to the provenance of traditional songs; as he wrote to Revd John Skinner in 1787, describing his involvement with Johnson's project, 'I have been absolutely crazed about it, collecting old stanzas, and every information remaining, respecting their origin, authors, &c.' [CL i. 168]. (This is especially evident in the 'notes and anecdotes' entered in the interleaved copy of Riddell's *Musical Museum*: these reveal that Burns was formidably well read in the copious eighteenth-century scholarly literature on Scottish song.) But there was also an 'unofficial' side to Burns the collector of national songs, just as there was to Burns the exciseman. Like the smuggled brandy he presented to Frances Dunlop, or the confiscated French gloves gifted to Maria Riddell, many of Burns's bawdy and 'Cloaciniad' songs

[16] Jeffrey Skoblow, *Dooble Tongue: Scots, Burns, Contradiction* (Newark: University of Delaware Press, 2001), 198.

[17] Ogborn, *Spaces of Modernity*, 177.

were collected into a reserved canon (albeit aimed at a strictly male readership, circulating as far as London, where they were read by Lord Byron in 1813), perhaps relished all the more for being 'smuggled goods'.[18] Constructing a national canon involved huge acts of exclusion, but the fact that the gains outweigh the losses is suggested by the quality of such songs as 'Dainty Davie', 'Duncan Gray', 'Andrew and his cuttie gun', 'Comin' through the Rye', and 'John Anderson my Jo', all rendered by Burns from bawdy originals.[19]

I've mentioned that gaugers imposed a national 'standard' of weights and measures in assessing the taxable contents of casks and ale-firkins. Although the term 'standard' seems inadequate to describe the rich diversity and pathos of Burns's songs, he himself frequently used it to describe the larger patriotic aim of song collecting. In April 1793 he told Thomson that '*your Book will be the Standard of Scots Songs for the future*' [CL ii. 198], and later assured Johnson that the *Musical Museum* would be the 'text book & standard of Scotish [*sic*] Song & Music' [CL ii. 382]. Burns's song collection participated in the project of 'constructing Scotland' both *historically* (songs such as 'Caledonia' and 'The Lament of Mary Queen of Scots', battle songs such as 'Sherramuir', 'Killiecrankie', 'Johnie Cope', as well as a wide variety of other Jacobite songs) and *topographically*. 'Local' Ayrshire songs such as 'Bonny Doon' and 'The Braes o' Ballochmyle' reflected his wish (expressed in the First Commonplace Book) to remedy the poetic neglect of his native county. But Burns's Scottish tours of 1787–8, as well as his Excise 'Rides' in Dumfriesshire after 1788, afforded him the opportunity to reimagine the *whole* of Scotland as a sentimental topography, evident in the frequent allusions to 'touristic' rivers in such songs as 'The Banks of the Devon' and 'The Birks o' Aberfeldy'.

At a literal level Burns's use of the term 'standard' here of course derives from the language of aesthetics, and the problem of defining a 'standard of beauty' that had exercised philosophers such as Hume, Kames, and Smith throughout the eighteenth century. If Johnson and Thomson both represented 'standards' of Scots song collection, they did so in rather different ways, however. Although James Johnson was a humble Edinburgh engraver, he was well supported by such 'gentlemen of indubitable taste' as James Beattie, Thomas Blacklock, William Tytler (Lord Woodhouslie), and Burns's Dumfriesshire neighbour Robert Riddell of Glenriddell; tellingly, after 1803 his *Scots Musical Museum* was dedicated to the 'Society of Antiquaries of Scotland' discussed below.[20] Hamish

---

[18]  *CH* pp. 257–8. Byron was shown Burns's bawdy material by Dr John Allen who had personal acquaintance with the poet. Allen, stepson of Burns's friend Robert Cleghorn, was librarian of Holland House in London. For the best modern edition, see *The Merry Muses of Caledonia*, ed. James Barke and Sydney Goodsir Smith, with a new intro. and music by Valentina Bold (Edinburgh: Luath, 2009).

[19]  See McCue, 'George Thomson', 174–93.

[20]  Hans Hecht, *Robert Burns: The Man and his Work*, trans. Jane Lymburn (1936) (repr. Ayr: Alloway, 1981), 184–5. Riddell may have introduced Burns to his friend Johnson.

Mathison has drawn attention to Johnson's claims to 'patriotic inclusivity' in appealing for subscribers, as well as his guarantee that the songs are truly of the 'Ancient Caledonian strain'.[21] To Johnson and his coadjutator Burns (who played a major editorial role after 1788), the songs' undiluted 'Scottishness' compensates for their uneven quality, and in this respect patriotic antiquarianism gets the better of a more cosmopolitan *belletrisme*, reflected also in Stephen Clarke's simple and unadorned musical settings. As an unprecedented and nearly comprehensive collection of over 600 Scottish popular songs, this resolution served the *Musical Museum* well, and despite its limited contemporary success, it is now indeed regarded as the 'standard of Scottish song'. This is largely a tribute to Burns's huge contribution: the first volume, published before he could influence it, contained a large number of indifferent lyrics of the *Tea-Table Miscellany* variety, but this changed dramatically with his editorial involvement from the second volume on.

The contrast with George Thomson's handsome *Select Scottish Airs*, to which Burns began to contribute in 1792, is well summed up by Hans Hecht: 'in contrast to the *Museum*, where completeness was aimed at, its contents were to be carefully selected and revised, with a view to publishing only the very best, and thus illuminating only the highest peaks in the mass of literary material which the collaborators had at their disposal'.[22] The securely middle-class Thomson was principal clerk to the Board of Trustees in Edinburgh, and a talented amateur violinist and singer. Inspired by the performance of Scottish songs by celebrated Italian singers such as Tenducci and Domenico Corri at Edinburgh's St Cecilia's Hall and other venues, he contracted notable Continental composers Pleyel, Kozeluch, Haydn, Beethoven, Weber, and Hummel to provide settings and 'symphonies' for songs by Burns, 'Peter Pindar', Scott, Byron, Moore, Hogg, Campbell, and other less celebrated names.[23]

The first part of *Select Scottish Airs* appeared in 1793 and the collection rose to six handsomely engraved folio volumes over the next forty years, to which Burns contributed 114 songs in all, although only 60 were printed there for the first time.[24] Thomson's genteel musical and poetic aesthetic often jarred with

---

[21] Hamish Mathison, 'Robert Burns and National Song', in David Duff and Catherine Jones (eds.), *Scotland, Ireland, and the Romantic Aesthetic* (Lewisburg, Pa.: Bucknell University Press, 2007), 77–92 at 81. See also Donald Low (ed.), *The Scottish Musical Museum*, 2 vols. (repr. Aldershot: Scholar Press, 1991), i. 8.

[22] Hecht, *Robert Burns*, 213. Kirsteen McCue links this to rapid developments in the Scottish publishing trade in the last decades of the eighteenth century. See 'The Most Intricate Bibliographical Enigma': Understanding George Thomson and his Collection of National Airs', in Richard Turbet (ed.), *Music Librarianship in the United Kingdom* (Aldershot: Ashgate, 2003), 99–119 at 101.

[23] See David Johnson, *Music and Society in Lowland Scotland in the Eighteenth Century* (London: Oxford University Press, 1972), 142–9.

[24] Hecht, *Robert Burns*, 209.

Burns's taste, but the fruit of that discordant relationship was a voluminous correspondence lasting from September 1792 virtually until the poet's death, in which Burns gave a very full account of his theory and practice of song collecting and writing. In contrast to Johnson, Thomson sought to 'improve' and polish the lyrics of Scottish songs for an English, as well as a polite Scottish, public; he particularly had his sights on young female amateur performers and their drawing-room audiences, to which end he beseeched Burns to avoid 'wound[ing] that charming delicacy, that forms the most precious dowry of our daughters'.[25] Thomson's 'standard of taste' was perhaps just as concerned with moral propriety as with aesthetics, although his connoisseurship was equally at the service of both. 'Let me tell you, that you are too fastidious in your ideas of Songs & ballads', Burns complained in one of his first letters to Thomson in October 1792 [CL ii. 153]. Thomson often confused Burns's criterion of 'simplicity' with 'vulgarity', unsurprising given that his conventional view of pastoral poetry (articulated in a letter to Burns of 26 April 1793), comes straight out of the pages of Dr Blair's *Lectures*: 'The lowest scenes of simple nature will not please generally, if copied precisely as they are. The poet, like the painter, must select what will form an agreeable as well as a natural picture' [Currie, iv. 69].

Despite the currency of such 'English' pastorals as 'Sensibility, How Charming' [K 317] or the rather more successful 'Clarinda, Mistress of my Soul' [K 217] (both addressed to Agnes McLehose), Burns preferred a more robust idiom and what he called a 'sprinkling of our native tongue' [CL ii. 149], elsewhere expressed as 'the naiveté, a pastoral simplicity, in a slight intermixture of Scots words & phraseology' [CL ii. 181]. This wasn't just an attempt to meet Thomson halfway, because it's also a feature of many of his earlier songs, including those contributed to the more consciously 'Scottish' project of the *Musical Museum*. (Thomson in the end conceded 'you shall freely be allowed a sprinkling of your native tongue . . . one thing only I beg, which is, that however gay and sportive the muse may be, she may always be decent' [Currie, iv. 6–7]). Both Johnson and Thomson were important pioneers in transforming 'popular' into 'national' song, but the latter term has a slightly different inflection in each case. Compared to Johnson's 'patriotic inclusivity', Thomson's collection was in its very conception an 'act of union' presenting alternative Scottish and English lyrics to each of its elaborately set melodies, thus for example, 'My Patie is a lover gay' was combined with the anonymous English song 'Come, dear Amanda, quit the town', etc.

Perhaps Burns's most haunting pastoral song is 'Ca the Ewes to the Knowes' [K 185], first published in the *Scottish Musical Museum* in 1790, then rewritten for Thomson and published as 'Ca' the Yowes to the Knowes' in *Select Scottish*

---

[25] Thomson to Burns, 13 Oct. 1792 [Currie, iv. 467]. See Kirsteen McCue, '"An Individual Flowering on a Common Stem": Melody, Performance and National Song', in Philip Connell and Nigel Leask (eds.), *Romanticism and Popular Culture in Britain and Ireland* (Cambridge: Cambridge University Press, 2009), 88–106 at 95.

*Airs* in 1805 [K 456] (although it had appeared in Currie's edition five years before, without a musical setting). The two versions of the song aptly illustrate the differences between Burns's work for Johnson and Thomson, as well as (in the later version especially ) his success in infusing traditional material with poetic pathos in creating a 'lyrical ballad'.[26] The first version takes the traditional form of a *pastourelle* or love dialogue between a young woman and her 'shepherd lad'; Burns's manuscript notes describes it as a 'beautiful song . . . in the true old Scotch taste, yet I do not know that ever either air or words, were in print before' [Kin. iii. 1251–2]. Although the song is sometimes associated with the singing of Isobel Pagan, an Ayrshire tavern keeper, Burns makes no mention of the fact, claiming that he collected it (and Clarke took down the air) from a clergyman 'a Mr Clunzie, who sang it charmingly' [Kin. iii. 1252]. Kirsteen McCue is surely right in surmising that 'the lyric was a popular one',[27] so for once Burns gets the credit for having preserved a fine traditional song, even although he admitted that he'd 'added some Stanzas to the song & mended others' [CL ii. 306].

In the sung dialogue, the shepherd makes a romantic proposal to the girl to 'gang down the water-side'; the girl plays hard to get, and only when the shepherd promises her 'gowns and ribbons meet, | Cauf-leather shoon upon your feet' (ll. 17–18) does she agree to let him 'rowe me in your plaid'. Clearly the girl is determined to avoid the fate of an abandoned lover, demanding an economic guarantee of the shepherd's devotion (including an expensive pair of leather shoes for kirk attendance). But this note of pragmatism is eclipsed by the powerful evocation of enduring love in the final verse; 'While waters wimple to the sea; | While Day blinks in the lift sae hie; | Till clay-cauld Death sall blin' my e'e, | Ye sall be my Dearie' (ll. 25–8).

In his September 1794 letter to Thomson enclosing the revised text of the song, Burns sketched the history of the early version; for all his mending, he felt that 'still it will not do for *you*.—In a solitary stroll which I took today, I tried my hand on a few pastoral lines, following up the idea of the chorus, which I would preserve' [CL ii. 306]. The *Musical Museum* version exemplifies Burns's ability to conform to the Thomson 'formula': the Scots diction (despite the shift from 'ewes' to 'yowes') is lightened to a 'sprinkling' and the indeterminate topography of the first version is localized to 'Clouden's Woods'. 'Clouden' is a tributary of the river Nith and the 'silent towers' are those of the ruined Lincluden Abbey nearby, topographical details which of course identified it with Burns's Ellisland.

---

[26] Burns referred to John Aikin's taxonomy of pastoral songs [CL ii. 336] and would have been familiar with his second category of songs 'abstracted from the tale and rural landscape, and improved by a more studied observation of the internal feelings of passion and their external symptoms'; Aikin, *Essays on Song Writing: with a Collection of such English Songs as are most Eminent for Poetical Merit* (London: Joseph Johnson, 1773), 22. See also McGuirk, *Sentimental Era*, 124.

[27] 'Burns, Women, and Song', in Robert Crawford (ed.), *Robert Burns and Cultural Authority* (Edinburgh: Polygon, 1999), 46.

Although the lovers are engaged in 'faulding' sheep (as opposed to making a tour) and the chorus remains intact, their pastoral dialogue is replaced by a picturesque description of the moonlight ruins. The song dilates on the gothic frisson these might be expected to arouse, and the protection the lover offers against any 'ghaist or bogle' that might haunt such 'romantic' places:

> Yonder Clouden's silent towers
> Where at moonshine midnight hours,
> O'er the dewy bending flowers
> Fairies dance sae cheary.
>     Ca the yowes, &c.

> Ghaist nor bogle shalt thou fear;
> Thou'rt to Love and Heaven sae dear,
> Nocht of Ill may come thee near,
> My bonie Dearie.
>     Ca the yowes, &c.   [K 456 ll. 13–20]

As McGuirk writes, 'vernacular words in this song become the basis for a self-conscious pastoral diction—a synthesized language more than a dialect'.[28] Burns has effectively translated a popular song into the lyrical idiom of fashionable sensibility, albeit without losing too much of the charm and freshness of the earlier version, kept alive by the recurring chorus and 'unique modal tune'.[29]

## BURNS AND ANTIQUARIAN IRONY

Thomas Crawford writes that 'the gathering and publishing of Scottish songs was one of the most important branches of the antiquarian movement of the eighteenth century; and on this subject, so closely bound up with the contemporary national revival, Burns became the greatest expert of them all' [Crawford *BPS* p. 258].[30] We've seen that Burns's new profession as an exciseman didn't preclude him from this other kind of 'collecting', especially given his close proximity to Scottish and British antiquarian networks via his friend and Ellisland neighbour Capt. Robert Riddell of Glenriddell (1755–94). Going beyond an earlier fixation with Roman antiquities, by the end of the eighteenth century British antiquarians

---

[28] McGuirk, *Sentimental Era*, p. xvii.

[29] Cedric Thorpe Davie, 'Robert Burns, Writer of Songs', in Donald Low (ed.), *Critical Essays on Robert Burns*, 170. I'd dissent from his opinion that 'nowadays nobody would want to sing the earlier words' in preference to the Thomson version, in favour of Jo Miller's view that the *Musical Museum* version has 'a more personal voice than the later version, and engages us more closely with the thoughts and dialogue of the courting couple in working out their relationship'. 'Burns's Songs: A Singer's View', in Kenneth Simpson (ed.), *Burns Now* (Edinburgh: Canongate Academic, 1994), 199.

[30] For a rather different view, see McGuirk, *Sentimental Era*, 147.

studied, recorded, and drew 'Druidical', Celtic, Pictish, and Danish antiquities, as well as medieval castles and ecclesiastical monuments, exchanging information across national and European-wide networks linking metropolitan and provincial societies.[31] Increasingly, they also recorded the customs and superstitions of the common people as living relics of the past, an inquiry known as 'popular antiquities'.[32] There was no simple or univocal political programme underlying these researches, although as Emma Rothschild writes, antiquarianism generally represented 'a cosmopolitan idea about national identities, or the assertion of a universal stock of variety, in opposition to the uniformity of universal empires'.[33] In Scotland, as we'll see, this often translated into a patriot discourse critical of the cultural homogenization that followed the 1707 union.

In the eighteenth century, however, antiquarians were often regarded as something of a laughing stock. On the one hand, they were involved in the enlightenment project of 'knowing the past' by painstaking empirical research: travelling, describing, notating, drawing, comparing material and textual fragments alike. But the antiquarian's obsessive desire to collect seemed unmatched by an ability to organize his (they were seldom 'her') acquisitions according to any rational taxonomy other than the private pleasure of possessing the 'relics' of the past. This is famously illustrated in Sir Walter Scott's description of the random clutter of Jonathan Oldbuck's 'sanctum sanctorum' in his 1816 novel *The Antiquary*: 'a chaos of maps, engravings, scraps of parchments, bundles of papers, pieces of old armour, swords, dirks, helmets, and Highland targets.'[34] As Iain Gordon Brown puts it, 'the antiquary's dwelling . . . was the image of his mind'.[35]

In Scotland, as elsewhere in Europe, antiquarianism was considered as *marginal* to mainstream discourses of scholarship and taste, representing in Susan Manning's words 'the "other" of Enlightenment historiography, the double agent on its boundaries . . . the taxonomic and fragmented language of things offered by antiquarians lacked the connecting parts of articulated speech that made a single coherent narrative possible, and the "progression" into the anglophone homogeneity of Civil Society inevitable'.[36] Heavily invested in the

---

[31] Stuart Piggot, *Ruins in a Landscape: Essays in Antiquarianism* (Edinburgh: Edinburgh University Press, 1976), 33–53.

[32] Peter Burke, *Popular Culture in Early Modern Europe* (repr. Aldershot: Scolar Press, 1994), *passim*; Philip Connell and Nigel Leask, *Romanticism and Popular Culture in Britain and Ireland* (Oxford: Oxford University Press, 2001), 3–48.

[33] Emma Rothschild, '"The Swanlike Strains of a Slaughtered Nation": Antiquarians, Historians, Philologists, and Empires,' unpublished paper, Sept. 2003.

[34] Sir Walter Scott, *The Antiquary*, ed. David Hewitt, intro. David Punter (London: Penguin, 1998), 21.

[35] Iain Gordon Brown *The Hobby-Horsical Antiquary: A Scottish Character 1640–1830* (Edinburgh: NLS, 1980), 20.

[36] Susan Manning, 'Antiquarianism and the Scottish Science of Man', in Leith Davis, Ian Duncan, and Janet Sorensen (eds.), *Scotland and the Borders of Romanticism* (Cambridge: Cambridge University Press, 2004), 57–76 at 68, 67.

evidentiary particulars of textual glosses and footnotes, antiquarian narrative was commonly criticized for being dry and rebarbative. In reaction David Hume had deliberately omitted including any notes in the first volume of the *History of England* (for which he was attacked by the antiquarian Horace Walpole), and Adam Smith dismissed the footnote as 'a blemish or imperfection; indicating, either an idle accumulation of superfluous particulars, or a want of skill and comprehension in the general design'.[37] In this respect, it's highly significant that Burns's 'Tam o' Shanter' was first published (at least in hard covers) as a long footnote to a work of antiquarian topography.

The eccentric personality of Burns's patron, David Steuart Erskine, 11th Earl of Buchan (whom we've seen commenting on the poet's 'little Doric pieces . . . in the provincial dialect' [Chambers-Wallace, ii. 46]) was a gift for the satirists.[38] But contrary to the image of the antiquary as an unworldly enthusiast for rusty daggers and broken potsherds, Buchan's rationale was both unashamedly patriotic in its strong endorsement of Scottish national virtue, and deeply political in its Whig criticism of the corruption of the 1688 constitution. In establishing the Society of Antiquaries of Scotland in 1780 (inspired by the longer-established London society, of which he was a fellow), Buchan threw down the Whig gauntlet at the Moderate establishment of the Edinburgh enlightenment, especially the Tory alliance of Henry Dundas and the Duke of Buccleuch. Mobilizing his formidable connections as one of Scotland's senior aristocrats, Buchan defeated the Moderates' attempt to prevent the Society of Antiquaries being awarded a Royal Charter, proceeding to appoint Burns's friend and printer William Smellie as secretary and keeper of its museum.[39] Members of the Society of Antiquaries of Scotland included many of Burns's closest acquaintances, Smellie, John Syme, William Dunbar, Robert Riddell, Fergusson of Craigdarroch, and his patron the Earl of Glencairn.[40] The Society struggled to make headway in the uncongenial climate of the Dundas Despotism, to the extent that in 1790, cold-shouldered by the Edinburgh establishment, the petulant Buchan resigned his membership and retired to his Borders estate at Dryburgh Abbey.

---

[37] Rosemary Sweet, *Antiquaries: The Discovery of the Past in Eighteenth-Century Britain* (New York: Hambledon, 2004), 6; Manning 'Antiquarianism and the Scottish Science of Man', 65, quoting Dugald Stewart's *Life of Robertson.*

[38] See also Buchan to James Currie, 14 Sept. 1799, Currie/Burns Correspondence, Mitchell Library, Glasgow, MS 10/C-196 C, Envelope 18. For Buchan's life see Ronald G. Cant, 'David Steuart Erskine, 11th Earl of Buchan: Founder of the Society of Antiquities of Scotland', in A. S. Bell (ed.), *The Scottish Antiquarian Tradition* (Edinburgh: John Donald, 1981), 1–30; James Gordon Lamb, 'David Steuart Erskine, 11th Earl of Buchan: A Study of His Life and Correspondence' (unpublished Ph.D. diss., St Andrew's University, 1963).

[39] Stephen Shapin, 'Property, Patronage, and the Politics of Science: The Founding of the Royal Society of Edinburgh', *British Journal for the History of Science* 7 (1974), 1–41; Sweet, *Antiquaries*, 111–14.

[40] Burns never appears to have met the 'reform martyr' Thomas Muir of Huntershill whose name also appears on the membership list. The overlap between members of the SAS and the subscription list to Burns's 1787 Edinburgh volume remains to be investigated.

Here, under the pseudonym of 'the Hermit of the Tweed' he rode his antiquarian hobby-horses, compiling a *Biographica Scotica* commemorating the lives of eminent Scots, and establishing a 'Temple of Caledonian Fame' in the medieval Chapter House.[41]

In contrast to Buchan, Robert Riddell of Glenriddell exerted a direct and major influence on Burns's literary output after 1788. In many respects Riddell's establishment, at Friar's Carse on the banks of the Nith six miles north of Dumfries and adjacent to Burns's farm at Ellisland, was a downscaled version of Buchan's Dryburgh. (Despite his disdain for Buchan, Walter Scott's neighbouring establishment at Abbotsford was a later attempt at emulation, its name also mimicking Dryburgh's monastic history, but with a significant change of ideological bearing.) Copying Buchan's 'retired' role as 'Hermit of the Tweed' (although not his teetotalism), Riddell invented an antique persona for himself as 'the Bedesman of Nithsdale', and in 1790 published a fragmentary 'faux medieval' ballad in Middle Scots entitled *The Bedesman on Nidsyde*.[42] True to the antiquarian obsession with concretizing the past, he constructed a fake Druid circle, as well as a hermitage (or 'Bedesman's cell') in the woods by the Nith on the southern end of his estate. Shortly after being introduced to Burns, he presented the poet with the keys to the hermitage, who by 28 June 1788 had repaid the compliment by composing 'Verses written in Friar's Carse Hermitage' [K 223], written in the persona of the sage old anchorite who signs off as 'the BEADSMAN ON NID-SIDE'.

A celebrated instance of the more ludic side of Riddell's antiquarianism was a drinking contest that he organised on 16 October 1789 with his cousins Sir Robert Lowrie of Maxweltown and Alexander Fergusson of Craigdarroch, the prize being 'a little ebony Whistle' of some antiquarian curiosity. This allegedly re-enacted a similar competition (first held during the reign of James VI) between a Danish giant, owner of the whistle, and Sir Robert Lowrie, ancestor of two of the present contenders. In the event Craigdarroch won after downing five bottles of claret without losing consciousness [K 272]. Burns was present in the capacity of an (apparently sober) witness, and composed a narrative ballad entitled 'The Whistle' to commemorate the occasion, which he set to a melody of Riddell's composition [K iii. 1317]. Complete with a mythological, Ossianic genealogy that derived the whistle from the Norse deity Loda, Burns's anacreontic ballad praises the conviviality of Riddell ('so skilled in old coins', l. 23) and his friendly rivals. A similar spirit of tipsy antiquarian re-enactment seems to have inspired the unfortunate 'Rape of the Sabine Women' incident in late December 1793 which abruptly terminated Burns's friendship with Riddell, as well as with

---

[41] See Buchan Papers, Glasgow University Special Collections, Murray MSS 502/53/3 and 502/54/10.

[42] [Anon.], *The Bedesman on Nydsyde* (London, 1790). The poem is inspired by Chatterton's forged 'Rowley' Poems, or Pinkerton's continuation of the 'old' Scots ballad 'Hardyknute'.

his sister-in-law Maria; this time, unfortunately, the poet was the principal protagonist rather than merely an observer [Mackay, pp. 555–64].

But for all the hard-drinking fun and games, Riddell was far from being merely 'a loud blustering squire, a hollow and unsubstantial mind' as De Lancey Fergusson claimed [Mackay, p. 465]. Like Buchan, his strongly held Foxite Whig politics reveal that, for all its fixation with the past, antiquarianism was far from entailing a conservative reverence for the established order. A member of the London Friends of the People, in 1792 Riddell published essays on county reform, signed 'Cato', in the radical *Edinburgh Gazetteer* [CL ii. 174]. Burns's poem 'On Glenriddell's Fox Breaking his Chain, Ellisland 1791' [K 527], dilates on the irony of a good Whig such as Riddell keeping a pet fox, which couldn't help trying to break its chain after absorbing its master's faith in the 'Rights of Man' and women (and, presumably, beasts). Riddell shared Burns's sympathies for Jacobite as well as Jacobin politics, despite the fact that his father Walter had been captured by the Jacobite army in 1745.[43] This supports Marilyn Butler's contention that if in England popular antiquarianism 'epitomized . . . fringe subcultures . . . in conveying a resentment of metropolitan ascendancy', in Scotland, as in Ireland and Wales, it [often] aligned itself with cultural nationalism.[44]

Riddell's credentials as a serious antiquarian have in general been undervalued by scholars, despite the fact that by the time of his death in 1794, Richard Gough (secretary of the London Antiquarian Society) was calling him 'the first antiquary of his country', having tapped him for local information for his updated, translated edition of William Camden's *Britannia*, published in 1789.[45] Riddell had a special interest in the neglected antiquities of Dumfries and Galloway and published several essays in *Archaeologica*, the journal of the London Society of Antiquaries. An enthusiast for popular antiquarianism, especially Scottish song and music, Riddell's manuscript collection was an important source for Walter Scott in compiling *Minstrelsy of the Scottish Border*.[46] Burns was granted full access to Riddell's extensive private collection of curiosities, as well as books, manuscripts, and paintings, which inspired and informed the poems and songs written in this period, many included in the Glenriddell Manuscripts, presented by Burns to his neighbour. I've already mentioned that Riddell's interleaved copy

---

[43] See especially his marginal notes in his copy of Thomas Pennant's *Tour in Scotland, 1769*, 4th edn., (London, 1776), 57; and *Tour in Scotland and Voyage to the Hebrides, 1772*, 2nd edn. (London, 1776), 84. (University of Glasgow Special Collections, Murray Collection, Mu6-d.9-10.)

[44] Marilyn Butler, 'Antiquarianism (Popular)', in *An Oxford Companion to the Romantic Age: British Culture 1776–1832*, ed. Iain McCalman (Oxford: Oxford University Press, 1999), 329.

[45] Robert Thornton, 'Robert Riddell, Antiquary', *Burns Chronicle*, 3rd ser. 2 (1953), 444–67. This article is based on the unpublished Riddell/Paton/Gough correspondence held by the Scottish Society of Antiquaries, and corrects the unreliable information contained in J. Maxwell Wood's *Robert Burns and the Riddell Family* (Dumfries: J. Maxwell & Son, 1922).

[46] Hecht, *Robert Burns*, 170. Riddell's *Collection of Reels, Minuets, Hornpipes, Marches and Two Songs in the Old Scotch Taste* was published by James Johnson in 1785.

of Johnson's *Scottish Musical Museum* contained the poet's notes on the songs published therein; as James Mackay indicates, Riddell 'stimulated Burns into a scholarly examination of the old fragments, as distinct from his original inclinations merely to recover, mend, and add to these fragments' [Mackay, p. 468].[47]

Perhaps Riddell's most important service to Burns was to introduce him to Captain Francis Grose (1731–91) during the latter's visit to Friar's Carse in the spring and summer of 1789 (see Fig. 7). Commonly denominated 'the British Antiquarian', Grose was the son of an immigrant Swiss jeweller who had retired after a chequered military career. Building on the success of his *Antiquities of England and Wales* (1772–6), part of an ongoing project to pay off heavy debts accruing from his financial incompetence as a regimental paymaster, the corpulent topographer was touring Scotland to research and draw ancient monuments for his *Antiquities of Scotland* (1789–91).[48] Soon Burns and Grose 'were unco pack and thick thegither';[49] in July the poet wrote to Frances Dunlop how Grose's 'delight is to steal thro' the country almost unknown, both as favourable to his humour & his business' [CL i. 423]. Grose's *Antiquities of Scotland* (like the earlier *Antiquities of England and Wales*) is a collection of engraved plates of the relics of Scotland's pre-reformation monuments, accompanied by a remarkably spare letterpress. Aimed at the commercial end of the market and the new fashion for domestic tourism, it was published in parts at the price of 6*d.* a plate, undercutting its competitors.[50] Although Grose's drawings tapped the contemporary mood of Gothic melancholy, the picturesque frisson of some of the plates was seldom replicated by the dry, factual letterpress that accompanied them.

Grose was a great admirer of Burns's account of popular superstitions in 'Halloween' [K 73] as published in the Kilmarnock volume.[51] In June 1790 the poet responded to Grose's request for similar information on his Ayrshire birthplace by dispatching three prose 'Witch Stories I have heard relating to Aloway Kirk', the second of which provided the source for his 220-line verse masterpiece, submitted to Grose on 1 December 1790 [CL ii. 29-31].[52] In his covering letter, Burns wrote with characteristic modesty, 'should you think it worthy a place in your Scots Antiquities, it will lengthen not a little the altitude of

---

[47] These notes provided the basis for 'Strictures on Scottish Songs and Ballads', first published in Cromek's *Reliques*, 187–311.

[48] The unpublished manuscript of *Journal of a Tour of Scotland in 1789 by Capt Grose and Mr Riddell* is in the library of the Scottish Antiquarian Society.

[49] Gilbert Burns's expression in Chamber-Wallace, iii. 211.

[50] Sweet, *Antiquaries*, 318.

[51] See Francis Grose, *Antiquities of Scotland*, 2 vols. (London 1789–91), ii. 210.

[52] Gerry Carruthers points out that the 'folkloristic' provenance of the 'Witch stories' is more often affirmed than proven: '"Tongues turn'd inside out": The Reception of Tam o'Shanter', *Studies in Scottish Literature* 35–6 (2007), 455–63 at 457. The third story, describing a boy riding through the air on a stem of ragwort, develops an incident in ll. 49–54 in 'Address to the Deil', which suggests a common folk origin.

FIG. 7. 'Captain Grose'.

my Muse's pride'. 'Print my piece or not as you think proper', he continued, only requesting, if possible, to see a copy of the proof-sheets [CL ii. 62–3]. And print it Grose did: the long poetic footnote is an exercise in antiquarian irony, relating more closely to Grose's and Burns's shared interest in *popular* than monumental antiquities, the 'official' object of the text.

'Tam o' Shanter' reveals Burns's enthusiasm for popular culture in a spirit diametrically opposed to the regulatory appropriation of Hannah More and the Tory evangelical *Cheap Repository Tracts*, which poured from the press over the next few years. It is saturated with the playful spirit of antiquarian re-enactment to which Burns had been exposed through his friendship with Riddell and his circle at Friar's Carse, bringing it close to the irreverent, demotic celebration of popular culture characteristic of the works of such radical antiquaries as Francis Grose, Joseph Ritson, and later William Hone. Given that Grose commissioned the poem in the first place, it's surprising that his own essays in popular antiquarianism haven't been more carefully examined as sources for Burns's masterpiece. In an essay in *The Grumbler* of 1791 (its very title a travesty of Johnson's *The Rambler*) Grose boasted that 'with regard to politics, I am a staunch Opposition-man and Grumbletonian, having neither place, contract, nor pension'.[53] Marilyn Butler describes Grose's *Classical Dictionary of the Vulgar Tongue* (London 1785) and *A Provincial Glossary, With a Collection of Local Proverbs and Popular Superstitions* (1787) as 'clever, original books on the spoken language (slang and dialect) and other forms of modern communication' that between them contained over 9,000 words excluded by Dr Johnson.[54] The hegemony of metropolitan culture and historiography (affirmed by scholars such as Johnson, Warton, Blair, and Percy) was here quite literally 'challenged from the margins'.

There's no record of Burns's reading of the *Classical Dictionary*, but in the likely event that he did, the Ayrshire poet and collector of bawdry and 'old Cloaciniad songs' must have relished Grose's anti-Johnsonian lexicon of vulgar speech: choice entries such as 'BAGPIPE, TO B-PE, a lascivious practice too indecent for explanation'; 'BUD SALLOGH, an Irish appellative for a sodomite'; 'COFFEE HOUSE, a necessary house, to make a coffee house of a woman's ****, to go out and spend nothing', etc.[55] In addition to its list of proverbs, *A Provincial Glossary* contained a lengthy appendix on 'Popular Superstitions', containing a wealth of information on 'Ghosts', 'Witches', 'Second Sight', 'Charms and Ceremonies for Knowing Future Events' (several of which overlap with customs described in Burns's 'Halloween'), the 'Hand of Glory', and 'Cures and Preventatives'. There is indeed something obsessive about Grose's collecting. In *The Grumbler*, he had

---

[53] Francis Grose, *The Grumbler: Containing Sixteen Essays* (London, 1791), 2.

[54] Butler, 'Antiquarianism (Popular)', 315. See also Janet Sorensen, 'Vulgar Tongues: Canting Dictionaries and the Language of the People in Eighteenth-Century Britain', in *Eighteenth-Century Studies* 37/4 (2004), 435–54.

[55] Grose, *A Classical Dictionary of the Vulgar Tongue* (London 1785). See under individual entries.

parodied the 'Irrational Pursuits of Virtu' in the fictional person of 'John Cockle', a 'lover of rarities' who collected 'monsters and curiosities of every denomination, dried, stuffed, and floating in spirits; and as his possessions increased, his rage for collecting grew more violent'.[56] In another essay, the 'Complaint of a Wife at her Husband's Rage for Antiquities', a wife raged against her husband who had joined the 'Society of Antic-queer-ones'. Tirelessly rattling on about 'Tumbulusses and Cram-licks' she feared that his melancholy fixation with the relics of the past would drive him to suicide.[57] All of this, including the raging wife, would contribute to the witches' brew that is 'Tam o' Shanter'.

Burns responded to Grose directly with his own exercise in antiquarian irony in 'Address to the People of Scotland', later retitled 'On the Late Captain Grose's Peregrinations Thro' Scotland Collecting the Antiquities of that Kingdom' [K 275].[58] As the corpulent Grose 'steal[s] thro' the country almost unknown' [CL ii. 423], Burns warns his compatriots that 'A chield's amang you, taking notes, | And, faith, he'll prent it (ll.5–6). The proem to a Glasgow broadside version announced that it 'exhibits a just picture of the sentiments of the low peasantry in Scotland, respecting any gentleman who is professedly an Antiquarian. —He is deemed to be in colleague with SATHAN, and to be a dealer in *Magic*, and the Black Art—a vulgar prejudice, which all the light and learning of the present day have not yet been able totally to eradicate'.[59]

This glosses Burns's description of Grose's *diablerie*:

> By some auld, houlet-haunted biggin,
> Or kirk deserted by its riggin,
> It's ten to ane ye'll find him snug in
>          Some eldritch part,
> Wi' deils, they say, Lord safe's! colleaguin'
>          At some black art.—
>
> Ilk ghaist that haunts auld ha' or chamer,
> Ye gypsy-gang that deal in glamour,
> And you, deep-read in hell's black grammar,
>          Warlocks and witches;
> Ye'll quake at his conjuring hammer,
>          Ye midnight bitches.

[56] Grose, *The Grumbler*, 19.

[57] Ibid. 51.

[58] It was first printed in the *Edinburgh Evening Courant* for 11 Aug. 1789, signed 'Thomas A. Linn', referring to the bewitched protagonist of the ballad 'Tam Linn', captured by the fairies. For Burns's beautiful version of the ballad, see K 558.

[59] *Address to the People of Scotland, Respecting Capt Grose, Esq, The British Antiquarian*, by Robert Burns, the Ayrshire Poet (Glasgow, n.d.). (According to the ECCO note, this is possibly part of a Brash and Reid edn. of 1796–9, the poems of which were issued separately and subsequently collected.)

'Thomas A. Linn' comically exposes the dangerous proximity between the antiquarian's obsession and the 'pre-cultural' object of his inquiry, the danger he always runs of confusing erudition (he's 'deep-read in hell's black grammar') with a fetishism of the morbid particular. This notion of Grose's 'colleaguing with Satan' may have provided a key idea for the central episode of 'Tam o' Shanter'.

In the remainder of 'Address to the People of Scotland', Burns rehearses the satire on antiquarian collection later canonized by Scott's description of Old-buck's 'sanctum sanctorum'. He translates the antiquarian's cabinet of curiosities into a fantastical *capriccio* of biblical and secular mythology, 'a fouth o' auld nick-nackets':

> Of Eve's first fire he has a cinder;
> Auld Tubelcain's fire-shool and fender;
> That which distinguished the gender
>         O' Balaam's ass;
> A broom-stick o' the witch o' Endor,
>         Weel shod wi' brass.   (ll. 31–42)

Collecting the penis of Balaam's ass comically underlines the *morbidity* of Grose's collecting of mythic body parts, emphasized again in the next stanza's description of the 'jocteleg' (kail-knife) used by Cain to murder his brother Abel.

## 'TAM O' SHANTER' AS 'NATIONAL TAIL'

For three whole pages the text of Grose's *Antiquities of Scotland* is completely overwhelmed, squeezed into a narrow band at the top of each page, by the double column footnote, the first published version (in book form, for it had appeared twice in the newspapers) of 'Tam o' Shanter' [K 321] (see Fig. 8).[60] Even in its paratextual apparition on the page, the poem underlines and plays with the marginality of antiquarian discourse, as (quite literally) 'the "other" of Enlightenment historiography, the double agent on its boundaries'. To this extent, Grose's antiquarian irony imbues the form as well as the content of the poem that he had commissioned and redacted.

Central to what Carol McGuirk calls the poem's 'elusive meaning' [*BSP* 265–6] is the pattern of structural contrasts dividing hedonistic pleasure from self-regulation, upheld at one level by the narrator's use of English or light Scots diction, compared to the fuller Scots of the main narrative (most famously exemplified by lines 59–66, 'But pleasures are like poppies spread'), and of course Tam's ejaculation, 'Weel done, Cutty-Sark!'[61] Prudently, the narrator doesn't

[60] Grose, *Antiquities of Scotland*, ii. 199–201.
[61] Although Murray Pittock, *Scottish and Irish Romanticism*, 160, rightly indicates that the rhyme 'river/ever' (ll. 61–2) only works in Scots pronunciation.

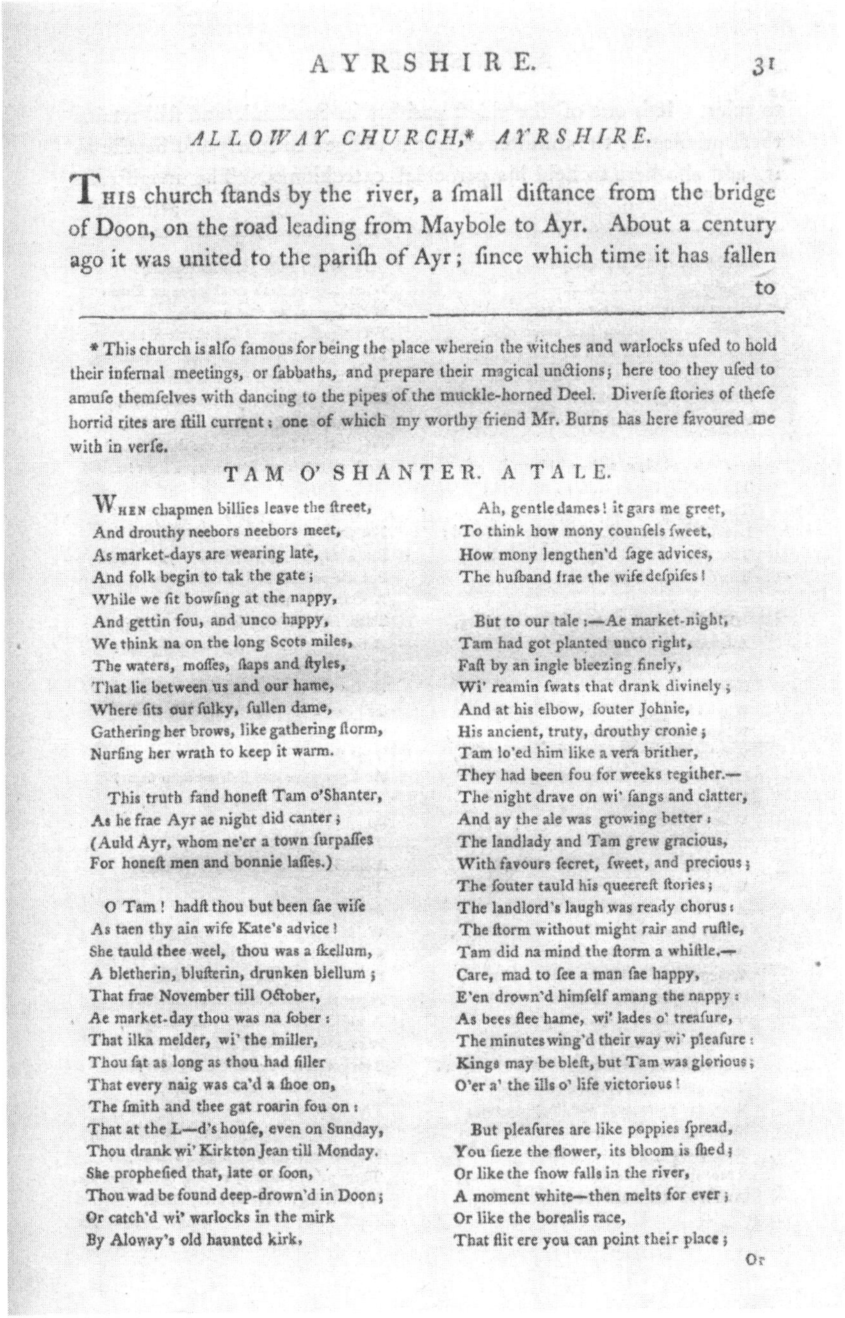

AYRSHIRE.     31

*ALLOWAY CHURCH,\* AYRSHIRE.*

This church ſtands by the river, a ſmall diſtance from the bridge of Doon, on the road leading from Maybole to Ayr. About a century ago it was united to the pariſh of Ayr; ſince which time it has fallen

to

---

\* This church is alſo famous for being the place wherein the witches and warlocks uſed to hold their infernal meetings, or ſabbaths, and prepare their magical unctions; here too they uſed to amuſe themſelves with dancing to the pipes of the muckle-horned Deel. Diverſe ſtories of theſe horrid rites are ſtill current; one of which my worthy friend Mr. Burns has here favoured me with in verſe.

### TAM O' SHANTER. A TALE.

When chapmen billies leave the ſtreet,
And drouthy neebors neebors meet,
As market-days are wearing late,
And folk begin to tak the gate;
While we ſit bowſing at the nappy,
And gettin fou, and unco happy,
We think na on the long Scots miles,
The waters, moſſes, ſlaps and ſtyles,
That lie between us and our hame,
Where ſits our ſulky, ſullen dame,
Gathering her brows, like gathering ſtorm,
Nurſing her wrath to keep it warm.

This truth fand honeſt Tam o'Shanter,
As he frae Ayr ae night did canter;
(Auld Ayr, whom ne'er a town ſurpaſſes
For honeſt men and bonnie laſſes.)

O Tam! hadſt thou but been ſae wiſe
As taen thy ain wife Kate's advice!
She tauld thee weel, thou was a ſkellum,
A bletherin, bluſterin, drunken blellum;
That frae November till October,
Ae market-day thou was na ſober;
That ilka melder, wi' the miller,
Thou ſat as long as thou had ſiller;
That every naig was ca'd a ſhoe on,
The ſmith and thee gat roarin fou on;
That at the L—d's houſe, even on Sunday,
Thou drank wi' Kirkton Jean till Monday.
She propheſied that, late or ſoon,
Thou wad be found deep-drown'd in Doon;
Or catch'd wi' warlocks in the mirk
By Aloway's old haunted kirk.

Ah, gentle dames! it gars me greet,
To think how mony counſels ſweet,
How mony lengthen'd ſage advices,
The huſband frae the wife deſpiſes!

But to our tale:—Ae market-night,
Tam had got planted unco right,
Faſt by an ingle bleezing finely,
Wi' reamin ſwats that drank divinely;
And at his elbow, ſouter Johnie,
His ancient, truſty, drouthy cronie;
Tam lo'ed him like a vera brither,
They had been fou for weeks tegither.—
The night drave on wi' ſangs and clatter,
And ay the ale was growing better;
The landlady and Tam grew gracious,
With favours ſecret, ſweet, and precious;
The ſouter tauld his queereſt ſtories;
The landlord's laugh was ready chorus;
The ſtorm without might rair and ruſtle,
Tam did na mind the ſtorm a whiſtle.—
Care, mad to ſee a man ſae happy,
E'en drown'd himſelf amang the nappy;
As bees flee hame, wi' lades o' treaſure,
The minutes wing'd their way wi' pleaſure:
Kings may be bleſt, but Tam was glorious;
O'er a' the ills o' life victorious!

But pleaſures are like poppies ſpread,
You ſieze the flower, its bloom is ſhed;
Or like the ſnow falls in the river,
A moment white—then melts for ever;
Or like the borealis race,
That flit ere you can point their place;

Or

FIG. 8. 'Tam o' Shanter, A Tale'.

underestimate the tax due upon the indulgence of pleasure; although content to join his protagonist in an after-work glass of 'nappy' in the opening lines, it's not long before he assumes a sententious tone that aligns him with the forces of moral regulation, of the sort likely to be endorsed by Tam's wife. Crucially, lacking any other sanctions to control her wayward husband, other than wifely 'flyting', Kate resorts to threats of supernatural retribution. It is a tactic fully endorsed by the narrator, even if he regrets (on behalf of Kate, and other wives in a similar predicament) that her supernatural threats are likely to fall on deaf ears:

> She prophesied that late or soon,
> Thou would be found deep-drown'd in Doon;
> Or catch'd wi' warlocks in the mirk,
> By *Alloway's* auld haunted kirk.

> Ah, gentle dames! it gars me greet,
> To think how mony counsels sweet,
> How mony lengthen'd sage advices,
> The husband frae the wife despises!   (ll. 29–36)

Space forbids any detailed consideration of Burns's masterly scene-setting in the first half of 'Tam o' Shanter': carefully modulated octosyllabic couplet, controlled variations in tempo, and deft narrative pace are the poetic expressions of the poet's new professional mobility in these years, one shared with the poem's addressee, the 'peregrinating' Capt Grose. But just as the euphoric Tam recalls those 'lang Scotch miles' dividing him from his angry wife, the poet seems to remember that he had promised Grose a horrifying 'witch-story'; accordingly, the supernatural menace of the Kirkalloway section contrasts starkly with the couthy camaraderie of the Ayr tavern 'ingle-side'.

Yet the 'unco sight' awaiting Tam in the ruined Kirk is after all a voyeuristic pleasure tinged with pain, approaching the equivocal affect of Burke's sublime of terror. Burns's initial description makes a dramatic contrast with the stark, skeletal ruin depicted on the monochrome plate in Grose's *Antiquities of Scotland*: 'When, glimmering thro' the groaning trees, | *Kirk-Alloway* seem'd in a bleeze; | Thro' ilka bore the beams were glancing; | And loud resounded mirth and dancing' (ll. 101–4). In the prose source, the witches dance is 'seen through the ribs and arches of an old gothic window', an architectural detail in the fashionable taste perhaps calculated to satisfy readers of Grose's *Antiquities.* Versified, however, the uncanny 'bleeze' and resounding din of the witches's furious dancing pulses outwards from the ruin over the midnight landscape. Appropriate to a witches' sabbath held in a ruined church, Burns here represents the inverted social order of Poosie-Nansie's (as celebrated in 'Love and Liberty') in spades, the 'liberty' of which is indeed 'a glorious feast'. A rational explanation of the supernatural spectacle that meets Tam's eyes might of course be that it's a bad case of delirium tremens, exacerbated by his subliminal memory of Kate's 'prophecy'. But rather than turning tail, the 'pot-valiant' Tam urges Maggie forward to get a better view of the 'unco sight' (l. 114) driven by a macabre curiosity, like that motivating the antiquarian Grose in Burns's 'Address to the People of Scotland': 'Wi' deils . . . colleaguin', | At some black art'. The passage is a masterpiece of Burnesian scene-painting:

> Warlocks and witches in a dance;
> Nae cotillion brent new frae *France*,
> But hornpipes, jigs, strathspeys, and reels,
> Put life and mettle in their heels.
> A winnock-bunker in the east,
> There sat auld Nick, in shape o' beast;
> A towzie tyke, black, grim and large,
> To gie them music was his charge:
> He screw'd the pipes and gart them skirl,
> Till roof and rafters a' did dirl'—     (ll. 115–24)

It has been rightly pointed out that Satan's 'place is significantly in the church, though in opposition to it', a macabre 'return of the repressed' to the holy ground of Calvinism [Crawford, *BPS* 229–30]. But in contrast to his devious agency in 'Address to the Deil' and other poems, the Devil is here 'charged' merely to provide music for the dancers; and patriotically, he plays strictly Scottish 'hornpipes, jigs, strathspeys, and reels' rather than the polite French 'cotillion'.[62] (A year or two later, dancing to French music would have a distinctly political significance, but in the autumn of 1790, Burns's poem celebrates a more indigenous variety of 'sans-culottisme'.) Trapped in the body of a 'touzie tyke' (shaggy dog), the devil 'keeps [the dancers] alive with the powers of his bagpipe' [CL ii. 30]. This demonic bagpiping introduces an element of sexual innuendo that permeates the remainder of the poem, for both the diabolic and phallic associations of the instrument are well attested in Scottish tradition, going back as far as Dunbar's 'Dance of the Sevin Deidly Sins', but more immediately in popular eighteenth-century songs such as 'Maggie Lauder'. Burns may have remembered laughing at Grose's tongue-in-cheek definition of 'to bagpipe' in the *Dictionary of the Vulgar Tongue*, as 'a lascivious practice too indecent for explanation', probably a reference to sodomy.[63]

The poem's energetic description of the dancing witches is interrupted at lines 125–44 by a tableau descriptive of the kirk interior, with open coffins arrayed around the walls, and an inventory of the satanic 'offerings' laid out on the 'haly table' (I quote here from the text published in Grose's *Antiquities*):

---

[62] Although the devil's dances are indigenous, they aren't necessarily ancient; the 'Strathspey' was an invented tradition, which only became popular with the explosion of Scottish country dancing in the 1760s. See Johnson, *Music and Society in Lowland Scotland*, 121; Kin. iii. 1359.

[63] The bagpipe is associated with sodomy in a satirical article describing a homosexual club, signed 'A Complete Macaroni-Man', in *Weekly Magazine, or Edinburgh Amusement* 27 (2 March 1775), 300–3; quoted in D. D. McElroy, 'Literary Clubs and Societies of Eighteenth-Century Scotland' (unpublished Ph.D. thesis, University of Edinburgh, 1952), 459–62.

A murderer's banes, in gibbet-airns:
Twa span-lang, wee, unchristen'd bairns;
A thief, new cutted frae a rape,
Wi' his last gasp his gab did gape;
Five tomahawks, wi' blood red-rusted;
Five scymiters, wi' murder crusted;
A garter which a babe had strangled;
A knife a father's throat had mangled,
Whom his ain son of life bereft,
The grey-hairs yet stak to the heft:
Wi' mair of horrible and awefu',
That e'en to name would be unlawfu':—
Three lawyers' tongues, turn'd inside out,
Wi' lies seam'd like a beggar's clout:
Three priests' hearts, rotten, black as muck,
Lay stinking, vile, in every neuk.[64]

Critical attention to this passage (the manuscripts show heavy revision and emendation) has usually focused on Burns's omission of the final four lines in the 1793 Edinburgh text on the advice of Alexander Fraser Tytler, on the grounds that 'though good in themselves, yet, as they derive all their merit from the satire they contain, are here rather misplaced among the circumstances of pure horror' [Kin. iii. 1362]. The Edinburgh literati were doubtless relieved by the omission of this strong satire on lawyers and priests (another rejected line included 'doctor's bottles'), although as Crawford comments, 'it strengthen[s] the Romantic impressions of the scene and suppress[es] the intention to be satirical in . . . the conventional sense' [Crawford, *BPS* 231]. As we've seen, axiomatic to Grose's subversive, anti-Johnsonian epistemology of demotic language was an attack on the regulative discourse of official culture; as Marilyn Butler notes, 'like its French model, Le Roux's *Satirical and Burlesque Dictionary* (1718), the book contains offensive words and insults directed at unpopular groups such as the higher clergy, apothecaries, soldiers, and tailors'.[65] Burns's omission of what he called 'the hit at the lawyer and priest' [CL ii. 85] from the 1793 Edinburgh text had the effect of further removing the poem from the subversive orbit of Grose's influence, taking its place as a free-standing narrative poem in its own right, rather than a 'parasitic' footnote to an antiquarian itinerary.

On one level the macabre objects represented in the tableau are 'offerings made by the witches as evidence of devotion to their master's service . . . made before the climax of the witch dance, and [representing] some of the traditional

---

[64] G. Ross Roy points out that the only major edition of Burns which retained these last four lines was the 1808 Bewick edn., but with the order changed (Carruthers, 'Tongues turn'd inside out', 462).

[65] Butler, 'Antiquarianism (Popular)', 331.

materials of witchcraft' [Kin. iii. 1360]. On another, their tabular arrangement conforms to that of 'a cabinet of curiosities', as noted by Gerry Carruthers.[66] Intertextually, they're related to Grose's antiquarian curiosities satirized in 'Address to the People of Scotland'.[67] The dismembered body parts of criminals or murder victims, and the murder instruments themselves, indicating both domestic violence and the 'tomahawks' and 'scymiters' of colonial wars in Canada and India, are here represented not so much as devotional objects in a Satanic mass (their literal function), but rather as antiquarian *collectibles*. As Susan Stewart writes 'souvenirs of the mortal body are not so much a nostalgic celebration of the past as they are an erasure of the significance of history'.[68] Yet inasmuch as such haunted objects represent a version of antiquarian collection, they 'survive their connective tissue, whose reconstruction depends on conjecture'.[69]

In this sense, for all its comical inflection, Burns's 'national tale' rejects the distancing teleology of Scottish enlightenment historiography 'based on the disavowal, the concealment of [the nation's] past wounds', insisting that these relics of violence be displayed, inventorized, and acknowledged.[70] How appropriate that 'Tam o' Shanter'—perhaps originally conceived, in the Grosian spirit, as a mock-epic satire on the grand historical narratives of the enlightenment—should have ended up as the Scottish national tale par excellence. I've suggested that antiquarianism's libidinous absorption in the particular 'relic' crosses the epistemological threshold between the observer and the curious object, the policing of which was fundamental to the project of enlightenment. The narrative grammar of progressive history is broken up into a paratactic miscellany of random objects, representing a kind of Satanic parody of 'official' knowledge; as an inversion of the law, it's aptly figured by the description of 'lawyers tongues, turn'd inside out'. In this respect it's appropriate that the narrative momentum of Burns's poem (a digressive footnote to Grose's antiquarian text) should at this point itself be interrupted by a protracted tabular description of diabolical curiosities.

As far as I'm aware, no critic has noted Burns's allusions in the poem to Grose's highly eroticized account of witchcraft in *A Provincial Glossary*. It is possible that he inserted them as a private joke aimed at his friend, who had commissioned him to supply 'witch stories' about Kirkalloway: Burns ironizes

[66] Carruthers, *Robert Burns*, 92.

[67] A cinder of Eve's first fire, the penis of Balaam's ass, the Witch of Endor's broomstick, 'the knife that cutted Abel's craig', 'the coins o' Satan's coronation', etc.

[68] Susan Stewart, *On Longing: Narratives of the Miniature, the Gigantic, the Souvenir, the Collection* (Durham, NC: Duke University Press, 1993), 140.

[69] Manning, 'Antiquarianism and the Scottish Science of Man', 72.

[70] John Barrell, 'Putting down the Rising', in Davis, Duncan, and Sorensen, *Scotland and the Borders of Romanticism*, 130–8 at 135. 'Tam o' Shanter' thus anticipates James Hogg's fascination (in *Three Perils of Women* and *Confessions of a Justified Sinner*) for 'the figure of the upright corpse' that refuses to lie still in the grave, thereby 'meditat[ing] on how modern Scotland should regard its violent history'.

his position as a 'native informant' by echoing Grose's own earlier account of popular superstitions, creating a bizarre feedback loop. In the *Glossary*'s long appendix on 'Superstitions', Grose goes into some considerable detail of the 'witches' sabbath': 'At these meetings they have feastings, music, and dancing, the Devil himself sometimes condescending to play on the pipe, or cittern; and some of them have carnal copulation with him, the produce of which is toads and serpents: sometimes the Devil, to oblige a male Witch or Wizard, of which there are some few, puts on the shape of a woman.'[71] Grose's commentary illuminates the demonic dancing of 'hornpipes, jigs, strathspeys, and reels' evoking orgiastic copulation, hinted at in the climactic effect of Burns's lines with their 'crossed alliterations and internal vowel rhymes' [Crawford, *BPS* p. 232]: 'The piper loud and louder blew; | The dancers quick and quicker flew; | They reel'd, they set, they cross'd, they cleekit, | Till ilka carlin swat and reekit, | And coost her duddies to the wark, | And linket at it in her sark.' [K 321 ll.145–50].

Murray Pittock has stressed 'Tam o' Shanter's re-inscription of a "hidden Scotland" of "music, song and dance" here;[72] ironically one that reacts to Grose's uninhibited essay on witchcraft, which itself draws heavily upon Scottish sources. Citing George Sinclair's *Satan's Invisible World Discovered* (1685), Grose associates the Devil both with gender shifting and sodomy:

[The wife of the warlock George Barton] confessed that the devil went before them to a dancing, in the shape of a dog, playing upon a pair of pipes; and by coming down the hill back again, he carried the candle in his bottom, under his tail, which played *ey wig wag, wig wag*: that, she said, was almost all the pleasure she ever had. Generally, before the assembly breaks up, they all have the honour of saluting Satan's posteriors, who, for that ceremony, usually appears under the figure of a he-goat, though in Scotland it was performed when he appeared under the human form.[73]

Although the meaning is somewhat obscure, Barton's wife here associates the devil with a bagpiping dog (Burns's 'towzie tyke') and bagpiping with sodomy (the candle inserted in the devil's rectum plays *ey wig wag, wig wag*, the sum of the witness's 'pleasure') which is the act of 'saluting Satan's posteriors'. This evokes Burns's definition of 'houghmagandie' in the glossary to the Kilmarnock volume: 'a species of gender composed of the masculine and feminine united' [Kil. p. 238], itself perhaps an allusion to Iago's 'making the beast with two backs' in *Othello*.

Tam's erotic interest in the dancing witches is of course initially limited by the fact that they're 'wither'd beldames, auld and droll, | Rigwoodie hags wad spean a foal' (ll. 159–60). Dropping his sanctimonious mask, this immediately follows the point where the narrator bizarrely enough identifies with Tam's voyeuristic

---

[71] Francis Grose, *A Provincial Glossary, with a Collection of Local Proverbs and Popular Superstitions* (London, 1787), Appendix: 'Superstitions', 19–20.
[72] *Scottish and Irish Romanticism*, 163.
[73] *Provincial Glossary*, 'A Witch', 20.

gaze, and switching into broad Scots, anticipates his imprudent outburst. He vows that, were the dancing witches 'queans, | A' plump and strapping in their teens', he'd have sacrificed 'thir breeks o' mine . . . off my hurdies, | For ae blink o' the bonie burdies!' (ll. 155–8). His wish suddenly comes true, as if by demonic fiat: 'There was ae winsome wench an wawlie, | That night enlisted in the core . . .' (ll. 164–5). Building up to Tam's sudden outburst, the narrator then proceeds to lament how 'my Muse her wing maun cour; | Sic flights are far beyond her pow'r' (ll. 179–80). He nevertheless manages to 'sing how Nannie lap and flang, | (A souple jade she was, an strang), | And how *Tam* stood, like ane bewitch'd, | And thought his very e'en enrich'd' (ll. 181–4). Were it not for the fact that Burns introduces an oddly circumstantial account of the history of Nannie's 'cutty sark', and of her subsequent supernatural depredations on the Carrick coast at lines 166–70, it would be tempting to think (especially in the light of Grose's *Provincial Glossary*) that her sudden apparition among the old witches is the effect of Satan 'putting on the shape of a [beautiful young woman]' in a bid to seduce the watching Tam into committing an indiscretion. The figure of the seductive young Nannie is certainly nowhere to be found in any of Burns's prose versions of the story, in which all the witches were 'old women of [the narrator's] acquaintance in the neighbourhood' [CL ii. 30].

Although Burns steers away from *The Glossary*'s allusion to queer practices here, the demonic ritual of 'saluting Satan's posteriors' mentioned by Grose is acknowledged by the poem's general fixation with 'bare-arsedness'. As we've seen, even the upright narrator volunteers to get his breeks off in return for a view of some nubile young witch: Nannie's 'cutty sark, o' Paisley harn' is 'in longitude . . . sorely scanty' (ll. 171–3), presumably revealing her 'tail' to the watching Tam.[74] As McGuirk notes in this connection, '['Tam o' Shanter''s] alternating homophones, its counterposed "tales" (lying narrative shared with an audience) and "tails" (exposed posteriors, also shared with an audience), are a dynamic feature of the poem's language and also mark its chief contrast' [McGuirk, *BSP* p. 265]. Moreover, in a letter to Burns dated 3 January 1791, Grose referred to the poem as 'the pleasant tale of the Grey Mare's Tail', no doubt underlining the pun.[75]

The climactic pace of the dancing, as well as the heightening atmosphere of 'comic self-exposure' in which even the Devil 'fidg'd fu' fain', leads to the climactic moment when the 'bewitched' Tam 'tint his reason a'thegither' and ejaculates 'Weel done, Cutty-Sark!' (l. 189). In an instant all is dark as the 'hellish legion' sallies out to assail the voyeur who has thus unwittingly exposed himself.

---

[74] Meaning either the female genitals or backside. In Burns's bawdy song 'Nine Inch will please a Lady' [K 252], 'tail' clearly refers to the former: 'The carlin clew her wanton tail'. But see also the song 'Tail Todle' where 'Tammie gart my tail toddle; | At my arse wi' diddle doddle' (*Merry Muses*, p. 193).

[75] MS reproduced in Peter Westwood, *Definitive Illustrated Companion to Robert Burns*, 8 vols. (Irvine: Distributed National Burns Collections Project, 2004–6), ii. 1641.

(Grose had written that during a witches' Sabbath 'any one repeating the name of GOD, instantly put the whole assembly to flight'. Here, an expression of admiration has the reverse effect.)[76] Tam's outburst is his sole locution in the whole poem, replacing the more cumbersome 'Well luppen Maggy wi the short sark!' in the prose source [Kin. iii. 1351].[77] It reveals Burns's awareness of the narrative convention of traditional balladry whereby eating or speaking are strict taboos in the enchanted world, on pain of eternal captivity.[78] 'Weel done, Cutty-Sark!' brings the poem to its climax by breaking the erotic enchantment, as well as the observer's detachment from the diabolical spectacle, but in doing so summons the vindictive powers of darkness. Surrendering his silent invisibility, the watching Tam is instantaneously 'contaminated' through his identification with the anarchic and orgiastic powers gathered within the ruined kirk. His admiration for the half-naked dancing Nannie connects him with Grose's fascination with the queer and curious, the Satanic 'other' of history, the antiquarian's libidinous desire to 'possess' (or be possessed by) the epistemological object, in contrast to the judicious distance of the enlightenment historian.

Although readings of Burns's poetry are over-saturated with biography, it's hard to resist the thought that Tam's reckless outburst at one level ventriloquizes the poet's desire to break his oathsworn silence as a loyal excise officer. Tam's cry voices a libidinous poetic sympathy with popular disorder over the regulatory gaze, 'Glenriddell's fox' breaking free of his chains, in a historical moment pregnant with revolution. But like Burns's own dangerous involvement in the singing of the revolutionary anthem 'Ça ira' in Dumfries theatre in 1792, which nearly cost him his excise post, Tam has much to lose from his heedless act of self-exposure. Kate's prophecy, the conventions of ballad narrative, and the demands of poetic justice, all require that he be punished for his transgression; as the narrator thunders in the lines that immediately follow, not without a note of comic mockery: 'Ah, *Tam*! ah, *Tam*! thou'll get thy fairin! | In hell they'll roast thee like a herrin! | In vain thy *Kate* awaits thy comin! | *Kate* soon will be a woefu' woman!' (ll. 201–4).

Despite the narrator's threats, Tam gets off Scot-free. Unfortunately his mare Maggie, who has saved him from the furious witches by leaping across the bridge, isn't so lucky; 'ere the key-stane she could make, | The fient a tail she had to shake!. . . . . The carline claught her by the rump, | And left poor Maggie scarce a

---

[76] *Provincial Glossary*, Appendix, 'Superstitions', 21.

[77] Tam's arousal chimes with a bawdy metaphor in Burns's letter to Ainslie in May 1787: 'in the words of the Highlandman when he saw the Deil on Shanter-hill in the shape of five swine—'My hair stood and my p—stood, and I swat & trembled' [CL i. 119]. The devil's power to cause an erection, and the location on 'Shanter Hill', perhaps connects this to Tam's verbal ejaculation.

[78] See e.g. the version of 'Thomas Rhymer' (no. 37 in Child, below) published in Scott's *Minstrelsy of the Scottish Border*: the Queen of Elfland warns Thomas, 'But Thomas, ye maun hold your tongue, | Whatever ye may hear or see, | For, if you speak word in Elflyn land, | Ye'll neer get back to your ain countrie' (*English and Scottish Popular Ballads*, ed. Francis James Child, 5 vols. (New York: Dover, 1965), i. 325–6, stanza 14.

stump' (ll. 209–10; 217–18). Tam's near-emasculation at the hands of the witches is suffered instead by his mare, the only 'innocent' creature in the poem; it's a misogynistic conclusion to a misogynistic poem, even if Maggie is a mare not a woman, her fate the complete reversal of the cherished 'auld Mare Maggie' in Burns's earlier poem. Robert Crawford puts it nicely in describing this as a 'kind of joke-castration visited on the female who for a moment took the dominant part and became the active protector of her supposed "master". Tam triumphs over his wife's prophecies and over Nannie's hellish pursuit.'[79]

We might even imagine Maggie's unrooted tail (like the penis of Balaam's ass in the poem to Grose) becoming a Satanic 'curiosity' displayed on the altar table alongside the hangman's halters and bloody knives; if so, then Tam can only hope that such a metonymic 'possession' by the witches won't permit their performance upon him of what Grose's *Provincial Glossary* calls 'sympathetic magic', doubtless for *un*sympathetic ends. But if Maggie's 'tail' stays on the dark side, Tam o' Shanter's 'tale' is brought into the light, working a different kind of sympathetic magic on generations of readers. To the extent that it forgoes folkloristic closure (Carlyle complained that Burns 'has not gone back . . . into that dark, earnest, wondering age, when the tradition was believed, and when it took its rise'[*CH* p. 367]), 'Tam o' Shanter' still has the power to entertain in a sceptical and post-romantic age.

Although ostensibly a cautionary tale for tavern hedonists, Burns's poem lodges a protest against the abuse of supernatural terror to enforce conventional morality, a familiar theme to readers of the Kirk satires. This is what John Gibson Lockhart meant (in a far more misogynistic construction) by complaining that the poem's 'catastrophe appears unworthy of the preparation'. Critical of Burns's failure to fulfil his regulatory obligations, he regretted that he hadn't chosen to follow the Galloway version of the legend, whereby Nannie's bloody hand is found clinging to the horse's tail the next morning, permitting the exposure of the witch (none other than 'the pretty wife of a farmer residing in the same village with himself'), who is summarily burnt at the stake [Lockhart, p. 150].[80]

But in Burns's poem, not only does Tam get away with it by a hair's breadth, he also escapes poetic justice, as does the sexy and terrifying Nannie, *pace* Lockhart. To this extent, Murray Pittock rightly describes the poem's defiance of 'the culture of its own incorporation, the forensic closure of the collector's story', with the proviso that, ironically, the act of defiance is itself made in the subversive spirit of Grose's antiquarian irony, a pre-emptive caution to Romanticism's 'discovery of the people'.[81] The feckless narrator's parting homily obtrudes

---

[79] Robert Crawford, 'Robert Fergusson's Robert Burns', in Crawford (ed.), *Robert Burns and Cultural Authority* (Edinburgh: Polygon, 1999), 19.

[80] To be fair to Lockhart, he does in the end suggest that Burns's inconclusive version, 'exhibiting a maimed and fragmentary character' is preferable to the strict execution of poetic justice [p. 151].

[81] Pittock, *Scottish and Irish Romanticism*, 164.

like an awkward 'stump' at the end of the poem, sounding more like a parody than a believable moral. It serves only to remind us (to coin a critical cliché) never to trust the teller, trust the tale:

> Whene'er to drink you are inclin'd,
> Or cutty-sarks run in your mind,
> Think, ye may buy the joy's o'er dear,
> Remember Tam o' Shanter's mare!   (ll. 221–4)

# 9

## Across the Shadow Line: Robert Burns and British Romanticism

*A slight acquaintance with the peasantry of Scotland, will serve to convince an unprejudiced observer that they possess a degree of intelligence not generally found among the same class of men in the other countries of Europe.*

(*James Currie*, 'Prefatory Remarks on the Character and Condition of the Scottish Peasantry')[1]

*'I have read several of Burn's* [sic] *Poems with great delight', said Charlotte as soon as she had time to speak, 'but I am not poetic enough to separate a Man's Poetry entirely from his Character; —& poor Burns's known Irregularities, greatly interrupt my enjoyment of his Lines.—'*

(*Jane Austen*, Sanditon, 1817)[2]

### DR JAMES CURRIE'S *LIFE OF BURNS*

Dr James Currie's anonymously published 1800 *Works of Robert Burns; with an Account of his Life, and a Criticism of his Writings, to which is Prefixed, Some Observations on the Character and Condition of the Scottish Peasantry*, particularly the 335-page critical biography of the poet which makes up the first of its four volumes, was immensely popular in its time, going through five editions and about 10,000 copies by 1805, and at least twenty editions by 1820.[3] Currie's edition was the main portal through which Burns's life and poetry reached the Romantic and nineteenth-century reader, the standard Burns edition for Romantic writers including Wordsworth, Coleridge, Lamb, Scott, Hogg, Moore,

---

[1] Currie, i. 1–31 at 3.

[2] Jane Austen, *Northanger Abbey, Lady Susan, The Watsons, and Sanditon*, ed. John Davie, intro. Terry Castle (Oxford: Oxford University Press, 1990), 352.

[3] Information on sales from the Currie/Burns Correspondence, Mitchell Library, Glasgow MS 10/C -196 C, Envelope 2, letters from Cadell and Davis to Currie. The first edition evidently sold out by Aug. 1800. (See also Mackay, p. 661.) For comparison with sales of Wordsworth's *Lyrical Ballads*, see William St Clair, *The Reading Nation in the Romantic Period* (Cambridge: Cambridge University Press, 2004), 661.

Jane Austen, Byron, Shelley, Keats, and Hazlitt. Despite the critical campaign mounted against it by its many critics, it continued to influence the reception of Burns well into the twentieth century. But for all that, Currie's *Burns* has long been vilified by Burns scholars and unjustly marginalized in Romantic studies. In this closing chapter I will revisit Currie's biography of the poet, and particularly his preliminary 'Observations on the Scottish Peasantry', in order to assess the afterlife of Burns's poetry, and the fate of 'Scots pastoral' in the Romantic era, especially beyond the Scottish border.

On one level, my chapter title alludes to the shadow line separating the poet's work and life from that posthumous reputation. But it also refers to the geopolitics of Burns's afterlife, his reputation in the rapidly changing world of nineteenth-century Scottish and British culture, which I've also touched upon in preceding chapters. The fact that Scotland within Britain, according to Tom Nairn, was a 'decapitated national state, as it were, rather than an ordinary assimilated nation-ality' suggests exactly why the Scottish border was a shadowy line, especially around 1800, when the significance of the 1707 Treaty of Union between England and Scotland came under new scrutiny in the light of the parliamentary union of Britain and Ireland that same year.[4] The staunchly unionist Currie himself referred to 'the invisible line which divides the nations of Scotland and England' [*Mem.* ii. 358]: invisible maybe, but nevertheless one that still cast a long shadow upon the development of a supposedly 'homogenized' British culture. Ironically, Currie's hugely popular Burns biography, despite seeking to promote Scotland within the Union, contributed to the growing discourse of her cultural marginality, as glossed by Cairns Craig: 'England remained the kind of culture Scotland had failed to develop: a complete, a complex, a sustained culture. It is a "national-romantic" culture corresponding to its appropriate stage of development: a plenitude against which Scotland is a vacuum'.[5]

Dr James Currie was well placed as an Anglo-Scot (like Wordsworth, Scott, and Hogg, he hailed from the Borders) to negotiate Burns's border crossing, as is clear from the first page of his edition:

Though the dialect in which many of the happiest effusions of Robert Burns are composed, be peculiar to Scotland, yet his reputation has extended itself beyond the limits of that country, and his poetry has been admired as the offspring of original genius by persons of taste in every part of the sister islands. . . . It seems proper therefore to write

---

[4] Tom Nairn, *The Break-Up of Britain: Crisis and Neo-Nationalism* (London: Verso, 1981), 140, 129. For Currie's views on Irish Union, see William Wallace Currie, *Memoir of the Life, Writing and Correspondence of James Currie, MD, FRS, of Liverpool*, 2 vols. (London: Longman, 1831), ii. 314–17. Henceforth *Mem.* in text.

[5] Cairns Craig, *Out of History: Narrative Paradigms in Scottish and British Culture* (Edinburgh: Polygon, 1996), 97. See also the editors' introduction to Leith Davis, Ian Duncan, and Janet Sorensen (eds.), *Scotland and the Borders of Romanticism* (Cambridge: Cambridge University Press, 2004), 1–19.

the memoirs of his life, not with the view of their being read by Scotchmen only, but also by natives of England, and of other countries where the English language is spoken or understood. [Currie, i. 1–2]

In most respects, Currie conforms to Christopher Harvie's Stendhalian discrimination between the 'red' and the 'black' Scot; the former 'cosmopolitan, self-avowedly enlightened, and, given a chance, authoritarian, expanding into and exploiting bigger and more bountiful fields than [his] own country could provide'; as opposed to '[his] black brethren, demotic, parochial and reactionary, but keeping the ladder of social promotion open, resisting the encroachments of the English governing classes'.[6] Born in 1756, a son of the manse from Annandale in Dumfriesshire, Currie had studied medicine at Edinburgh University after an ill-favoured sojourn as a tobacco merchant's clerk in revolutionary Virginia. He subsequently practised as a physician in Liverpool and played a prominent role in that city's rise to civic as well as commercial eminence in the latter decades of the eighteenth century.[7] Although affiliated to the liberal, Midlands intelligentsia recently studied by Jenny Uglow in *The Lunar Men*,[8] Currie's Unionist sympathies never eclipsed a fierce loyalty to the Presbyterian and Enlightenment heritage of his Scottish nationality and education.

Currie's involvement with the first posthumous Burns edition was initially philanthropic, an extension of his social activism as a concerned bourgeois liberal. He was the sort of late enlightenment intellectual who might have been invented by Michel Foucault if he hadn't actually existed: a physician in the Liverpool Dispensary for the poor, co-founder of the Liverpool Fever Hospital and Lunatic Asylum, and member of the city's Committee for Managing the Poor. He was also, honourably, a prominent campaigner for the Abolition of Slavery and for the Repeal of the Test Acts and campaigned against the mistreatment of French prisoners of war in the early 1800s. A man who justifiably claimed expertise in the management of the poor, the sick, and disadvantaged brought a particular set of (often regulative) attitudes to bear on the case of Burns, many of them fairly unpalatable to the poet's admirers early and late.

Before turning to the 'Life of Burns' itself, I'll briefly survey the rationale for the 1800 Burns edition in relation to the polemic surrounding the death of Burns

[6] Christopher Harvie, *Scotland and Nationalism: Scottish Society and Politics, 1707–1977* (London: George Allen & Unwin, 1977), 17. Currie's edition was dedicated to another 'red' Scot, Captain (later Admiral) Graham Moore, Anglo-Scottish son of the novelist Dr John Moore, and brother of General John Moore of Corunna. See my '"Their Groves o' Sweet Myrtles": Robert Burns and the Scottish Colonial Experience', forthcoming in Murray Pittock (ed.), *Robert Burns in Global Culture, 1759–2009* (Lewisburg, Pa.: Bucknell University Press, 2010).

[7] See R. D. Thornton, *James Currie: The Entire Stranger and Robert Burns* (Edinburgh: Oliver & Boyd, 1963).

[8] Jenny Uglow, *The Lunar Men: The Friends Who Made the Future* (London: Faber & Faber, 2002).

in 1796. Despite its Unionist animus, Currie's biography was motivated by what might be called 'a Scottish difference' overriding party politics, a desire to exonerate his countrymen from blame in precipitating Burns's (highly publicized) premature sickness and death, allegedly in a condition of alcoholism and debt.[9] Lurid accounts of Burns's decline into seedy inebriation in the Dumfries years flowed from the pens of George Thomson and Robert Heron shortly after the poet's death, and were broadcast in the popular press; an ineffectual defence by his friend Maria Riddell did little to redeem the situation.[10] English commentators, especially those of a radical stamp, blamed Scotland's detested 'Dundas despotism' for failing to patronize the humbly born genius in their midst: the fact that Burns's Edinburgh edition had been dedicated to the Caledonian Hunt, the flower of the Scottish gentry and nobility, made his subsequent neglect at their hands seem all the more unpardonable. As we saw in the previous chapter, most commentators seemed to agree that an Excise Commission was an utterly inadequate form of patronage, ignoring Burns's desire for independence from the trammels of farming: Coleridge even concluded his 1796 poem, 'To a Friend who had declared his intention of writing no more poetry' by imagining a garland of 'rank hensbane' and deadly nightshade twined upon the 'illustrious Brow of Scotch Nobility' (ll. 34–7).[11]

In Currie's Liverpool, the fate of Burns became something of a *cause célèbre* in liberal circles, resulting in a spate of poems by Currie's friend and collaborator William Roscoe (author of *Life of Lorenzo de' Medici*), the blind abolitionist poet Edward Rushton, and others, often adopting the habbie stanza in tribute to Burns, although employing English diction. These poems were originally published in the *Liverpool Phoenix*, but later collected in an 1800 subscription volume dedicated to Burns's family, entitled *Liverpool Testimonials to the Departed Genius of Robert Burns*.[12] Behind all these dark visions of the half-starved Scottish exciseman/poet hovered the spectres of Thomas Muir and the 'Scottish Martyrs' exiled to Botany Bay in 1794 on exaggerated charges of sedition, although ironically the Scotophobia of some of the poems echoed the cadences of Charles Churchill and the anti-Bute campaign of the 1760s.

[9] Mackay argues that 'the notion that Burns died a pauper is . . . quite ludicrous—yet it persists to this day' (p. 632).
[10] See *CH* pp. 99–101, 101–7, 117–30.
[11] *Coleridge: Poetical Works*, ed. J. C. C. Mays, i. 271 ll. 34–7.
[12] *Liverpool Testimonials to the Departed Genius of Robert Burns, The Scottish Bard* (Liverpool: Merritt & Wright [1800]). Roscoe feared that Coleridge would share the same neglect as Burns, and in a letter to Revd John Edwards of 28 August 1796 wrote, '[Burns's] example has fixed the value of High poetical attainments in Scotland; & they amount to the place of an Exciseman, with a salary of 50£ a year. Such has been the munificence of the Scotch peerage & the Scotch Gentry to a man who has done more honour to his country than all the Throat Cutters it ever bred. May they never have another opportunity of insulting genius with paltry and insidious rewards.' Quoted by Daniel Sanjiv Roberts, 'Literature, Medical Science and Politics, 1795–1800: *Lyrical Ballads* and Currie's *Works of Robert Burns*', in C. C. Barfoot, *'A Natural Delineation of the Human Passions': The Historic Moment of the Lyrical Ballads* (Amsterdam: Rodopi, 2003), 128.

Burns's friends John Syme and Alexander Cunningham had quickly established a charitable subscription to raise money for his widow Jean and their surviving children, and were understandably anxious to play down rumours concerning the poet's 'drinking excessively... amours and tom-catting as a husband and father; proclivity to offend others with abuse of mouth or pen; and democratic and Jacobin sentiments'.[13] Given the imminent expiry of Creech's copyright and the proliferation of pirate editions of Burns's poetry, the trustees decided to publish an authorized edition of his poetry and correspondence in aid of the subscription. In the light of the rumours and anecdotes about Burns circulating in and out of the press, it would be necessary to preface the poet's poems and correspondence with an officially sanctioned 'Life'. Syme wishfully assumed that the philosopher Dugald Stewart, who had been well acquainted with Burns, would accept full responsibility for both. It is quite clear, however, from surviving correspondence that Stewart, already ideologically compromised by his earlier support for the French Revolution, wanted nothing to do with such a hot chestnut as Burns; besides, he was too busy writing biographies of more 'respectable' Scottish literati, William Robertson and Thomas Reid.[14]

Currie's name first appears in connection with Burns (he had met the poet only once, briefly, in 1792) when Syme wrote asking him to publicize the subscription on Merseyside and the Midlands; he quickly raised £73 10s. from his wealthy circle in Liverpool.[15] Currie's correspondence with Syme reveals the extraordinary delicacy required in managing Burns's reputation (as well as his intellectual property, given the number of compromising letters amongst his surviving papers, to and from leading members of the Scottish establishment) in the years following his death, against a background of political recrimination and witch-hunting. No wonder, given the problems involved, that Currie wrote despairingly: 'There is no getting any Editor in Scotland, and in England no man can possibly edite [*sic*] them, for reasons I cannot go into.'[16] Yet it soon transpired that there *was* such a man in England, and (despite his heavy medical workload) Currie was himself that man. He accepted the role of biographer with some reluctance, initially on the grounds that Maria Riddell had put her name forward; quite apart from the chauvinistic consideration that as a young Englishwoman she seemed an inappropriate biographer of Scotland's national poet, Currie feared that as a disciple of Rousseau, Wollstonecraft, and Godwin, Maria

[13]  Thornton, *Entire Stranger*, 315.

[14]  Stewart/Currie Correspondence, Mitchell Library, Glasgow, Envelope 15, MS 10/C-196 C. See also my essay 'Robert Burns and Scottish Common Sense Philosophy', in Gavin Budge (ed.), *Romantic Empiricism: Poetics and the Philosophy of Common Sense, 1780–1830* (Lewisburg, Pa.: Bucknell University Press, 2007), 64–87 at 689.

[15]  Thornton, *James Currie*, 320.

[16]  Currie to Graham Moore, 2 Feb. 1797, Mitchell Library, Glasgow; MS 10/C, -196 C, Envelope 3.

would be a dangerous hostage to fortune in the current political climate.[17] But tellingly, Currie chose to preserve his own authorial and editorial anonymity by withholding his name from the titlepage.

Sensing that the tone adopted by his liberal English friends would do little service to the project of raising a subscription for Burns's family (Roscoe had provocatively hailed Burns as 'Thy Country's glory, and her Shame'),[18] Currie wrote in a letter of 8 February 1797, when his biography was already underway: 'To speak my mind [ . . . ] fully, it appears to me that [Burns's] misfortunes arose chiefly from his errors. This it is unnecessary and, indeed, improper to say; but his biographer must keep it in mind, to prevent him from running into those bitter invectives against Scotland, &c., which the extraordinary attractions and melancholy fate of the poet naturally provoke' [*Mem.* i. 281]. Currie needed to blame Burns in order to exonerate Scotland; and the rhetoric of moral blame that subsequently attached itself to the narrative of the poet's life is without doubt the most regrettable, and most enduring, legacy of his biography.

It is also regrettable, however, that Currie has been unfairly cast in the role of sole scapegoat. As is evident from the Currie archive held in Glasgow's Mitchell Library, the reluctant biographer received extensive assistance from the more forthcoming Scottish literati, many of whom had known Burns personally, who were happy to collaborate from the wings as long as they didn't have to enter the limelight. The antiquarians Ramsay of Ochtertyre and the Earl of Buchan, legal theorists Baron David Hume (nephew of the philosopher) and Alexander Fraser Tytler (Lord Woodhouselee), philosophers and literati such as Dugald Stewart, Henry Mackenzie, Walter Scott, and George Thomson, all contributed copious materials and were fulsome in their praise for the finished product. To this extent the 'Life of Burns' might be regarded as a composite production of the late Scottish Enlightenment rather than the work of a single author, providing a full cultural, biographical, and literary context for Burns's poetry and song, rendering it more intelligible to non-Scottish readers.

Currie modelled his biography on James Boswell's recent *Life of Dr Johnson* (1790), which rather than 'melting down [its] materials into one mass, and constantly speaking in my own person', preferred to 'produce . . . his own minutes, letters or conversation . . . an accumulation of intelligence from various points, by which his character is more fully understood and illustrated'.[19] This 'documentary' method also provided the model for subsequent nineteenth-century biographies of Burns, even when they sought to supplement or superannuate Currie's work, namely those of John Gibson Lockhart (1828), Allan Cunningham (1834), James Hogg and William Motherwell (1834–6), and

[17] Thornton, *James Currie*, 341–2.
[18] *Liverpool Testimonials*, 15.
[19] James Boswell, *Life of Johnson*, ed. R. W.Chapman, rev. J. D. Fleeman, new intro. Pat Rogers (Oxford: Worlds Classics, 1980), 22.

Scott Douglas (1877). Robert Chambers's influential edition of the *Life and Works* (1856–7) was extensively revised by William Wallace in 1896 (and subsequently known as the 'Chambers–Wallace' edition); in both, Burns's poetry and correspondence were 'enfolded' within a developmental biographical narrative, the consummate triumph of 'life' over 'work'.[20]

Compositionally, and despite the organicist tendency of all literary biographies, the documentary approach of all these works in the wake of Currie's *Works of Burns* relates to the fragmentary condition of Scottish letters as analysed by Susan Manning in her study *Fragments of Union*; that's to say, their principle of organization was associative and 'federative' rather than 'incorporative' and unifying. In this respect they resembled the structure of David Hume's prose, which, Manning argues, exerted an enduring (although often unwanted) influence upon Scottish romantic literature: '[its] syntax is paratactical not hypotactic; there is no 'core' of identity other than the sum of the parts, which may, philosophically if not experientially speaking, be regarded separately'.[21] The Coleridgean organic principle cherished by English Romantic theory seemed signally inappropriate in narrating the life of Burns, although both Wordsworth and Carlyle attacked the tradition of Burns biography from the wings on the grounds of its failure to locate the transcendental unity of the poet's life and work.

Although intellectually a creature of the Scottish enlightenment, and especially of its medical pedagogy, it would be a mistake to regard Currie as a materialist or sceptic in the Humean mould. Notwithstanding his strong links with English 'Rational Dissent', his understanding of Burns and the Lowland peasantry was largely influenced by the Scottish Common Sense philosophy of Thomas Reid and his disciple Dugald Stewart, which he polemically opposed to the English necessitarian ethics of David Hartley and Joseph Priestley.[22] In his long review of Thomas Reid's *Essays on the Active Powers of Man*, Currie championed Reid's voluntaristic Common Sense philosophy against the determinists of nearby Warrington Academy.[23] To a necessitarian, an act of free will was an impossibility to the extent that it was an effect without a cause. Against this mechanistic doctrine Reid urged that motives (effectively habits, desires, or subliminal determinants to action) were subordinate to acts of conscious will, and were therefore *not* causally determined; as Currie glossed the matter, 'a free action is not an effect without a cause, since it is caused by a being who had power and will

---

[20] See G. Ross Roy, 'Editing Burns in the Nineteenth Century', in Kenneth Simpson (ed.), *Burns Now* (Edinburgh: Canongate Academic, 1994), 129–49. Ross Roy documents Currie's tampering with some of Burns's papers in an attempt to 'whitewash' him (p. 138).

[21] See Susan Manning, *Fragments of Union: Making Connections in Scottish and American Writing* (Basingstoke: Palgrave, 2002), 32–64 at 39.

[22] For Currie's political liberalism, see his pseudonymous pamphlet *A Letter, Commercial and Political, Addressed to the Rt Hon William Pitt by Jasper Wilson, Esq.* (London: Robinson, 1793).

[23] *Analytical Review* 1 (1788), 145–53, 521–9; 2 (1788), 265–70, 549–58.

to produce it'.[24] Currie's intervention represents an important aspect of Scottish intellectual influence on the English Romantic scene that has been overlooked by scholars, too ready to accept Coleridgean or Peacockian caricatures of 'Scotch feelosophers' as merely grim harbingers of steam intellect and the 'dismal science' of political economy.

Charles Lamb's complaint in 1800 that Currie's 'Life of Burns' was 'very confusedly and badly written, and interspersed with dull pathological and *medical* discussions' accurately registered the fact that Currie was just as concerned to air his theory of the psychopathology of genius as to write a sympathetic biography of the poet.[25] Currie's account of Burns's 'symptomology' drew heavily on Reid's critique of Hume's materialist ethics, but there's also a sense that this was endemic to Burns's vocation as a poet: 'The fatal defect in [Burns's] character', wrote Currie,

lay in the comparative weakness of his volition, that superior faculty of the mind, which governing the conduct according to the dictates of the understanding, alone entitles it to be denominated rational; which is the parent of fortitude, patience and self-denial . . . The occupations of a poet are not calculated to strengthen the governing power of the mind, or to weaken that sensibility which requires perpetual controul, since it gives birth to the vehemence of passion as well as to the higher powers of imagination.   [Currie, i. 236–7]

Although Burns confessed that he had resorted to dissipation in fleeing from constitutional 'hypochondriasis', after his abandonment of farming and move into Dumfries, Currie regretted that 'temptations to *the sin that so easily beset him*, continually presented themselves; and his irregularities grew by degrees into habits' [Currie, i. 205]. Without any real evidence to support his allegations except the textual evidence of such poems as 'Scotch Drink' and 'Tam o' Shanter', Currie uncritically accepted Robert Heron's 1797 account of Burns's alcohol-fuelled downward spiral in the Dumfries period; as James Mackay has shown, the respectable Currie's endorsement of this version of events meant that it was accepted by most of the poet's subsequent biographers [Mackay, 660–74].[26] Currie described how, stimulated by his initial hopes for the success of the French Revolution, and deeply depressed by its failure, Burns compromised his Excise career by imprudent statements of his radical views. Currie

---

[24] *Analytical Review* 2 (1788), 266, 269.

[25] Lamb to Coleridge, 28 July 1800 [*CH* p. 112]. Space has forbidden discussion of Burns's self-diagnosis of his own 'hypochondriac complaint' [CL i. 142] or his satire on medical pretensions in 'Death and Dr Hornbook' [K 55]. On the medical theory underlying Currie's biography, see my essay 'Robert Burns and the Stimulant Regime', in Johnny Rodger and Gerard Carruthers (eds.), *The Fickle Man: Robert Burns in the Twenty-First Century* (Dingwall: Sandstone, 2009), 135–62.

[26] Mackay rightly criticizes Thornton for allowing the myth of Burns's alcoholism to go unchallenged as a result of his avid—and laudable—desire to defend Currie from his modern detractors [p. 661].

(whose preface assured readers that the 'Life' would omit all topics with a tendency 'to awaken the animosity of party' [Currie, i. p. xxii]) timidly hinted that the 'measures of persecution' introduced by Pitt's government had damaged Burns's 'hopes of independence' and 'aggravated those excesses which were soon to conduct him to an untimely grave' [Currie, i. 217].

But, Currie insisted, it was mainly the poet's own fault, to the extent that, fleeing from disappointment into the arms of 'fictitious gaiety' [Currie, i. 249] he became 'perpetually stimulated by alkohol [sic] . . . the inordinate actions of the circulating system became at length habitual; the process of nutrition was unable to supply the waste, and the powers of life began to fail' [ibid. 220] Even worse, Currie hinted darkly that 'he who suffers the pollution of inebriation, how shall he escape other pollution?' [ibid. 221]. Generalizing from the specific case of Burns, Currie suggested that the pathology of genius was an 'interesting subject' that 'deserves a particular investigation' [ibid. 248]: one offshoot of which was an ongoing debate on the 'irritability of genius' involving Coleridge, Isaac Disraeli, De Quincey, and others of the Romantic generation.[27]

As well as exonerating the Scottish establishment by placing the blame for Burns's depressing decline and premature death squarely upon the poet's own shoulders, Currie also sought to exorcize a particularly Scottish pathology of mind that he associated with the philosophical associationism and mental *impotence* of Hume's metaphysics. Currie's 'Life of Burns' recasts Scottish genius in a new, voluntaristic form, sacrificing the weakness of the poet to the demotic energy of his poetry, which he hoped might have the power to stimulate the jaded taste of a polite but deracinated reading public. (As an instance of this, Currie cited the effect on Mrs Dunlop—Burns's first patron—of her first encounter with 'The Cotter's Saturday Night' after recent bereavement and family misfortune; the poem 'operated on her mind like the charm of a powerful exorcist, expelling the demon *ennui*, and restoring her to her wonted inward harmony' [Currie, i. 133–4].) According to Currie, similar effects were to be expected from English, as well as Scots readers, thereby suturing the still-fragmentary Union between the two nations. As Leith Davis puts it in her suggestive essay on Currie, 'if Burns is the undertaker of an independent Scotland, Currie is the doctor of a united Britain, offering a cure for the kind of 'National Enmity' that continues to erupt'.[28] Currie thus sacrifices the 'genius of Burns' on the altar of Scottish *amour propre*, 'the Scottish difference', to ensure a more successful integration on her own terms, into the British Union.

---

[27] See David Higgins, *Romantic Genius and the Literary Magazines: Biography, Celebrity, and Politics* (London: Routledge, 2005).

[28] Leith Davis, 'James Currie's *Works of Robert Burns*: The Politics of Hypochondriasis', *Studies in Romanticism* 36 (Spring 1997), 43–60, 57–8.

## OBSERVATIONS ON THE SCOTTISH PEASANTRY

If Burns' psychopathology of genius was one critical element of Currie's 'Life', his analysis of the poet's humble social background was also delivered with something like missionary zeal. After proclaiming the charitable motivation for his edition, Currie reminded his readers that 'Robert Burns was in reality what he has been represented to be, a Scottish peasant' [Currie, i. 2]. While this acknowledged Mackenzie's description of Burns as a 'Heaven-taught Ploughman', Currie proceeded to dismantle the cult of natural genius which sustained it, apparently without grasping the significance of Burns's pastoral persona as diagnosed by Logan and Anderson.[29] Currie's 'philosophical' approach to Burns' genius, *contra* Mackenzie, offered a rational, socialized explanation of the poet's achievements in order to dispel his reputation as a vulgar, nine days' wonder, at the same time obscuring his real social background in the 'middling' tenant class, as discussed in Chapter 1. There was nothing 'heaven-taught' about Burns, Currie insisted, because the Scottish peasantry 'possess a degree of intelligence not generally found among the same class of men in the other countries of Europe' and in this respect Burns was utterly representative of his class [ibid. 3].[30] Currie's prefatory 'Observations on the Scottish peasantry' provides a historical analysis of Scotland's 'popular enlightenment'—the matrix of Burns's genius—in the history of Scotland before and after the Union, particularly the excellence of Scottish parochial education, and the 'self-help' mentality (uncontaminated by Poor Laws or statutory welfare provision) that had nurtured the domestic affections of the Lowland peasantry. To the extent that he had developed an 'independent intellect', Burns was an exemplary avatar of the Scottish ideology of 'improvement', but at the same time, Currie hinted, an object lesson concerning its possible dangers.

Space prohibits any detailed account here of the philosophical basis of Currie's social thought, in the Scottish Enlightenment discourse described by John Robertson and J. G. A. Pocock as 'civil jurisprudence', a *commercial*, as opposed to civic, humanism.[31] Currie believed that government should be 'chiefly negative

---

[29] See my discussion in the Introduction.

[30] Jeffrey reiterated Currie's argument in his 1809 review of Cromek's *Reliques of Burns* in the *Edinburgh Review* 13 (Jan. 1809), 249–76. '[Burns] will never be correctly estimated as a poet, till that vulgar wonder be entirely repressed which was raised on his having been born a ploughman' (p. 249). But whereas for Currie this plebeian filiation raised the Scottish peasantry to the level of genius, for Jeffrey it sank the poet, helping to explain his 'undisciplined harshness . . . of invective', 'want of polish', and lack of 'chivalrous gallantry' (p. 232).

[31] John Robertson, 'The Scottish Enlightenment at the Limits of the Civic Tradition', and J. G. A. Pocock, 'Cambridge Paradigms and Scotch Philosophers: a Study of the Relations between the Civic Humanist and the Civil Jurisprudential Interpretation of Eighteenth-Century Social Thought', in Istvan Hont and Michael Ignatieff (eds.), *Wealth and Virtue: The Shaping of Political Economy in the Scottish Enlightenment*, (Cambridge: Cambridge University Press, 1983).

or preventative, so to speak, extending to as small an abridgement of liberty as possible, but absolute on the points on which it interferes' [*Mem.* ii. 177]. He cited the main inspiration for his political principles as Dugald Stewart's chapter on the 'Use and Abuse of General Principles in Politics' in his 1793 *Elements of the Philosophy of the Human Mind*, hailed as the most incisive attack on Burkean prescription to have emerged from the whole revolution controversy [ibid. 150].

Donald Winch has proposed that Stewart differed from his teachers David Hume and Adam Smith in his optimism regarding the future of commercial society, sustained and promoted by public opinion and the diffusion of knowledge in the shape of the printing press.[32] If Adam Fergusson and Smith (perhaps to a lesser degree Hume) worried about the deleterious effects of modern society on public spirit, it was Stewart's faith that enlightened public opinion would more than substitute for virtue; it 'cannot fail to operate in undermining local and national prejudices, and in imparting to the whole species the intellectual acquisitions of each particular community'.[33] Echoing his teacher Thomas Reid, Stewart pinned his hopes on what would come to be called 'the spirit of the age', rather than the unassisted 'efforts of original genius' in improving society: 'not merely the force of a single mind, but the intellectual power of the age in which he lives'.[34] Stewart looked to a cosmopolitan futurity in conceiving the present (in the words of James Chandler) as 'the age of the spirit of the age'.[35] Stewart and Currie's social thought was premised upon the broad diffusion of what George Davie has called Scottish 'democratic intellect', popular education, and print culture, distinct from the regulative ideas of progressive English social theorists such as Bentham, Malthus, or Paley, as well, of course, as Coleridge's reactionary disdain for 'the reading public'.[36]

To this end Currie extolled the effects of Scottish parochial education on a relatively impoverished society blessed with few other benefits or endowments. This section of 'Observations' was clearly intended to explain the extraordinary extent of Burns's education, as described in the poet's letter of 2 August 1787 to Dr Moore (quoted in full by Currie in the opening section of the 'Life'). Currie attributed the intellectual 'curiosity' and 'information' of Scottish peasants to the legal provision made by the Scottish Parliament in 1646 (i.e. *before* the Union with England) 'for the establishment of a school in every parish throughout the kingdom, for the

---

[32] Donald Winch, 'The System of the North: Dugald Stewart and his Pupils', in *That Noble Science of Politics: A Study in Nineteenth-Century Intellectual History*, ed. Stefan Collini, Donald Winch, and John Burrow (Cambridge: Cambridge University Press, 1983), 40–3.

[33] Dugald Stewart, *Elements of the Philosophy of the Human Mind*, 2 vols., 6th edn. (London, 1818), i. 265. See Winch, 'System of the North', 43.

[34] Stewart, *Elements*, 271.

[35] James Chandler, *England in 181: The Politics of Literary Culture and the Case of Romantic Historicism* (Chicago: Chicago University Press, 1998), 105–13.

[36] See George Davie, *The Democratic Intellect: Scotland and Her Universities in the Nineteenth Century* (Edinburgh: Edinburgh University Press, 1961).

express purpose of educating the poor' [Currie, i. 4].[37] Added to the excellence of parochial education was the 'collision of opinion' [ibid. 118] stimulated by the more recent institution of plebeian conversation clubs, such as Burns's 'Tarbolton Bachelors Club'. But Currie doubted that literary, as opposed to technical, education was in the end serviceable to peasants and artisans, arguing that the point of such clubs was that '[their members] should be made happy in their original condition, [rather] than furnished with the means or with the desire of rising above it' [ibid. 115]. Burns, the reader might infer from this, was therefore an *exceptional*, rather than exemplary, case of the extraordinary achievements and upward mobility facilitated by popular enlightenment; and to the extent that he had failed to regulate his passions by strengthening his will, he served as a warning rather than an example to others of his class with similar ambitions.

In the wake of 1707, Currie wrote, 'as the minds of the poor received instruction, the union opened new channels of industry, and new fields of action to their view' [ibid. 352]. One unintended effect of Scottish popular education was to engender a desire to emigrate across the 'shadow line' to England and the colonies. By a Smithian law of 'all things finding their level', a well-educated peasantry in 'a country comparatively poor, in the neighbourhood of other countries rich in natural and acquired advantages', is bound to flow from the former to the latter [ibid. 7]. Overlooking the real historical cause for the depopulation of rural Scotland in improvement and the 'cotter clearances', Currie both acknowledged and challenged a commonplace metaphor of English Scotophobia: 'by the articles of the Union, the barrier was broken down which divided the two British nations, and knowledge and poverty poured the adventurous natives of the north, over the fertile plains of England, and more especially, over the colonies which she had settled in the east and north' [ibid]. The Scottish patriotism underpinning the ideology of agricultural improvement that I've discussed in Chapter 1 is here subordinated to a view of rural Scotland as a kind of *officina gentium* spawning a well-educated, sober, and Protestant workforce for export, offered up as the present and future manpower of the British empire.

Currie's panegyric on the export value of Scottish agricultural 'improvement', as subsequently refined by the Whig ideologues and political economists of the *Edinburgh Review*, was just the sort of thing targeted by William Cobbett's memorable satire in his *Tour of Scotland* (1832). Travelling on the eve of the Reform Bill, Cobbett described 'improved' Lothian farmyards as 'factories for making corn and meat', 'the labourers are their slaves, and the farmers their slave-drivers'.[38] And, he continued, parodying the Scots pronunciation of a word

---

[37] Currie's claim was commonplace in this period; for a sceptical assessment of its accuracy, see R. A. Houston, *Scottish Literacy and the Scottish Identity: Illiteracy and Society in Scotland and Northern England, 1600–1800* (Cambridge: Cambridge University Press, 1985).

[38] William Cobbett, *Tour in Scotland*, ed. and intro. Daniel Green (Aberdeen: Aberdeen University Press, 1984), 27.

cherished by Currie, 'as to the '*antalluct*... the Scotch labourers would not be a bit less intellectual, if they were to sit down to dinner every day, to wheaten bread and meat, with knives and forks and plates ... as they do in a considerable part of the farm-houses in the southern counties of England'.[39] In his impassioned tirade addressed to the 'chopsticks' of the Southern English counties, Cobbett protested against the importation by English farmers of 'SCOTCH BAILIFFS who are so justly detested by you', because they seek to level English agricultural labourers 'to the shed and to the brose'.[40] 'Our precious government', he warned in a reversal of Currie's argument, 'seems to wish to reduce England to the state of Scotland; and you are reproached and abused and called ignorant, because you will not reside in a '*boothie*', and live upon the food which we give to horses and to hogs!'[41] But for all his distrust of Scottish '*feelosophers*', Cobbett was a profuse admirer of Robert Burns, 'one single page of whose writings is worth more than a whole cart load that has been written by Walter Scott'.[42] Ironically, after dismantling the Currie-style promotion of Scottish '*antalluct*' at home and abroad, Cobbett (who opposed dram drinking) wholeheartedly subscribed to his cautionary narrative of Burns's alcoholism, suggesting the real reason for the poet's downfall: 'sobriety! How manifold are they blessings!...how complete the protection thou givest to talent; and how feeble is talent unless it has that protection!'[43]

If Currie's account of Scottish parochial education offered a clue to the intellectual precocity of Burns's social class, he next considered the effect of a *negative* ordinance on the moral character of the Scottish peasantry, another wing of 'the Scottish difference'. He praised Scotland for the absence of a Poor Law like that of England, whereby the parish or local government raised money from the propertied classes to offer support for the old, the infirm, the mendicant, or the unemployed. Like many liberal social thinkers of his day, including Wordsworth, it was a provision to which he was implacably opposed. As a member of the Committee for Managing the Poor, Currie actively campaigned against increasing the Poor Rate in Liverpool; although somewhat to his credit, he didn't entirely abandon the poor to the 'invisible hand' or Malthusian 'natural checks', sketching a plan to institute workers' savings banks modelled on David Dale's New Lanark scheme. Philip Connell notes that 'Rational dissenting attitudes to charity placed a particular stress upon the importance of private philanthropy, partly because of their hostility to state interference in matters of conscience.'[44] I've argued in previous chapters that Burns's attitude to the ethics of charity and

---

[39] Ibid. 30.        [40] Ibid. 44.        [41] Ibid. 27.

[42] Ibid. 120. Like Coleridge and the English radicals of 1796, Cobbett regretted that Burns 'died in this town, an *exciseman*, after having written so well against that species of taxation, and that particular sort of office' (ibid.).

[43] Ibid.

[44] Philip Connell, *Romanticism, Economics and the Question of 'Culture'* (Oxford: Oxford University Press, 2001), 23.

welfare are more difficult to gauge than Wordsworth's, who proposed that the beggar's suffering stimulated charitable affections, in stark contrast to the statutory management of poor relief, or the establishment of workhouses.

Currie argues that the English 'Speenhamland' system discouraged thrift and moral self-governance among the poor, and that its absence in Scotland explained the superior domestic affections of the Scottish peasantry, so well illustrated in Burns's 'Cotter's Saturday Night'. Poor Relief, he argued 'take[s] away from vice and indolence the prospect of their most dreadful consequences, and from virtue and industry their peculiar sanctions' [Currie, i. 10–11]. (No wonder he didn't include 'Love and Liberty' in his 1800 edition, however much the denizens of Poosie-Nansie's exemplify a raucous and hedonistic kind of self-sufficiency.) But as we've seen, what is remarkable about Currie's argument is that it's based on a narrowly ideological understanding of Scottish welfare provision. He completely ignored the 1672 Act of the Scottish Parliament that entrusted the implementation of the Poor Law jointly to the Kirk session and local landowners, who had the legal power to raise assessments in support of the local poor in the event of a shortfall in parish funds, however inefficacious the system was in the new urban centres.[45] Tom Devine argues that the low level of social unrest in Lowland Scotland accompanying the 'lowland clearances' may have been partly linked to the flexibility of the Scottish Poor Law in cushioning the effects of poverty and dispossession.[46] Although Cobbett uncritically accepted Whig claims about the absence of poor relief in Scotland, he drew quite a different moral from them, exhorting English labourers to fight for the preservation of their welfare system against the laissez-faire '*feelosophy*' of the *Edinburgh Review*.[47]

The whole question was of course extremely pertinent, as well as delicate, in the context of a 'Life of Robert Burns' introducing a publication intended to raise charitable relief for the poet's family, left virtually destitute by his alleged fecklessness and imprudence. Currie implied that although Burns's genius was the fruit of the marvellous system of Scottish parochial education, neither he nor his family could expect any support from parish relief when both patronage and moral self-government had failed. The poet's family must therefore depend upon the charitable exertions of a subscription fund, and the selling power of the poetry itself, for their future sustenance. Indeed, Currie's 1800 Burns edition was itself intended to demonstrate the triumph of private charity over public patronage, the absence of which Burns's English supporters such as Coleridge had decried in the Scottish establishment. This became an important article in the

---

[45] See above, Chs. 4 and 5. Currie's (widely held) view was probably based on the Scottish Poor Law's failure to 'set up a clear right in a claimant to relief, or even a clearly defined standard of living which it would protect' (Rosalind Mitchison, 'The Poor Law', in T. M. Devine and R. Mitchison [eds.], *People and Society in Scotland*, i. *1760–1830*, 254).

[46] T. M. Devine, *The Scottish Nation*, 102.

[47] Cobbett, *Tour*, 23, 28, 91.

Victorian Burns cult, memorably expressed in Carlyle's remark, already quoted in an earlier chapter, that the poet 'preferred self-help, on the humblest scale, to dependence and inaction, though with hope of far more splendid possibilities' [*CH* p. 380].

Currie's 'Observations' portrays a Scotland that, in the century since the Union of 1707, was only just beginning to cross the shadow line dividing political youth from maturity. He regretted that Scottish agriculture was well behind that of England, and that its system of land-tenure was locked in by penurious entails, just as the 'improvement of the people' was hindered by the 'detestable practice' of dram drinking, a weakness that he believed was 'fostered by their national songs and music' [Currie, i. 25]. (This last must have been an uncomfortable prejudice for a professed admirer of Burns's poetry.) Nonetheless, Currie insisted that it was a matter of hope rather than regret that post-Union Scots, 'enjoying a great part of the blessings of Englishmen, and retaining several of their own happy institutions, might be considered, if confidence could be placed in human foresight, to be as yet only in an early stage of their progress' [ibid. 24].

This version of 'the Scottish difference' appealed to the discourse of 'uneven development' in the ideological service of Scotland within the Union. For Currie, the 'anachronistic' education and independence of her peasantry, symbolized by the vernacular vigour and intellectual energy of Burns's poetry, offers a developmental potential within the Union superior to that of an 'overdeveloped' and enervated England. But post-Union Scots have to learn, not just 'to see oursels as others see us!', but as 'Others' (with a capital 'O') see us. Or perhaps rather a capital 'E', for Currie continued: 'since the Union, the manners and language of the people of Scotland have no longer a standard among themselves, but are tried by the standard of the nation to which they are united' [ibid. 25–6].

Currie concluded his prefatory essay with a celebration of the 'strength of the domestic affections of the Scottish peasantry . . . which it is hoped will not be lost' [ibid. 26]. The *gemeineschaft* of Scottish rural society (as portrayed in poems like 'Scotch Drink', 'Halloween', 'The Holy Fair', and 'The Cotter's Saturday Night') is here proposed as a regulative idea for Scotland within the Union, rather than as a discourse of nationalism, which, as Tom Nairn suggests, was the goal of similar mobilizations of 'ethnic and historical differentiae' in nearly all other small European countries.[48] Currie would go on to promote the moral community figured in such poems as 'The Cotter's Saturday Night' as a form of naturalized civil society operating harmoniously with minimum state intervention. What's curious, though, in this final section of the 'Observations', is the extent to which Currie draws upon the very different discourse of civic

---

[48] Nairn, *Break-Up of Britain*, 145.

humanism and (what Murray Pittock terms) the 'taxonomy of glory', in praising the patriotism and 'national spirit' of the Scottish peasantry.[49]

Currie insisted that patriotic attachment flourishes in the stoic economic conditions of mountain communities, an argument (apparently at odds with his 'commercial humanism') deriving from the classical republicanism of Rousseau's encomia on Swiss liberty, or Macpherson's idealization of the sentimental savagery of the Ossianic past. The embodiment of martial achievements and the Scottish independence struggle in 'national songs, and united to national music' (Burns's stirring anthem 'Scots wha hae' was the obvious example) underpins the affective power of Scottish patriotism, as defined in the intellectual tradition of George Buchanan and Andrew Fletcher of Saltoun. But whereas Burns's poetry and song radicalized this antiquarian discourse, Currie now recast it as an infantile memory-trace in the more mature modern era of Union and Empire: 'The images of infancy, strongly associated with the generous affections, resist the influence of time, and of new impressions; they often survive in countries far distant, and amidst far different scenes, to the latest periods of life, to soothe the heart with the pleasures of memory, when those of hope die away' [Currie, i. 30–1].

The patriotism evoked here is that of the expatriate 'red Scot', an ingrained Scottishness of the mind, but one physically removed from any *actual* Scottish life-world, a removal that gestures towards the Kailyard nostalgia of the coming century. Ironically, given the strength of the Burns cult in Scotland over the subsequent century and beyond, Currie held that Burns's poetry might actually be better appreciated outwith Scotland's borders. Whereas his vernacular diction might 'disgust' Scottish readers (especially members of 'the superior ranks' who has 'sought to approximate in their speech to the pure English standard'), an Englishman might on the contrary be 'pleased with the rustic dialect, as he may be with the Dorick Greek of Theocritus' [ibid. 331]. On the other hand, members of Scotland's diaspora in the colonies (and United States) were likely to be emotionally captivated by Burns's sentimental evocation of 'the interesting scenes of infancy and youth'; for which reason, 'literary men, residing at Edinburgh or Aberdeen, cannot judge on this point for one hundred and fifty thousand of their expatriated countrymen' [ibid. 333]. Currie here accurately predicted the power of a globalized Burns in consolidating an expatriate Scottish identity, a possibility that I suggested was already encoded in the Kilmarnock volume's 'Meliboean' subtext of exile and dispossesion.[50]

The Scottish patriot tradition survives here only as a fading memory of the martial and cultural achievements that safeguarded national independence, memories well served by Burns's poems and songs. Developing Ramsay of Ochtertyre's argument about Scottish pastoral, Currie believed that 'the peace and security

---

[49] Murray Pittock, *Scottish and Irish Romanticism* (Oxford: Oxford University Press, 2008), 27 *et passim*.

[50] See Ch. 2.

derived from the [1688] Revolution and the Union, produced a favourable change on the rustic poetry of Scotland', especially in the 'Arcadian vales' of the formerly war-torn Borders, where love now replaced 'glory and ambition' as the principle theme of poetry and song [ibid. 281]. In his account of Burns's precursors Ramsay and Fergusson [ibid. 281–9] Currie misrecognizes 'Scots pastoral' as essentially a 'peasant poetry', and like the class which produced it, symptomatic of an early stage on the road to cultural maturity, and Scotland's ongoing integration into the British polity. Currie's Scottish pastoral peasants *reculent pour mieux sauter*, looking back the better to march forward, in the service of a British and imperial futurity.

Despite the exemplary nationalist appeal 'to the people' contained in Burns's poetry, Currie's anomalous concern was to *exorcize* the spectre of an 'independence' (personal or national) which he believed had proved fatal to the poet himself.[51] Enshrining a cultural memory at once infantile, and *posthumous*, Burns' poetry 'displays, and as it were *embalms*, the peculiar manners of his country; and it may be considered as a *monument* not to his name only, but to the expiring genius of an ancient and once independent nation' [ibid. 31, my italics]. Evident here is a bid to remove Burns's pastoral poetry from 'the valley of its saying', its critical, dialectical purchase on Scotland's traumatic era of improvement, and its uninhibited attempt to breathe modernity into an attenuated, localized idiom, while maintaining the traits of a distinctively Scottish mindset. Despite his desire to connect Burns to the values of enlightenment, Currie initiated the habit of interpreting him as 'ultimus Scotorum', discussed in my Introduction. Although proudly proclaiming the national virtues of thrift, piety, and the dignity of labour, Burns's poetry is nevertheless 'embalmed' and monumentalized, its author (another 'expiring genius') personifying the vigour, but also the fatal debility, of the old Scotland.

## BURNS, WORDSWORTH, AND ROMANTIC PASTORAL

Conceived as an act of charitable recuperation, the enormous influence of Currie's 'embalming' of Burns—which undoubtedly shaped the manner of the poet's appeal in the Victorian era of Union and Empire—might help to explain the depressing fact of its diminished reputation in our present post-colonial and devolutionist era. (The current situation is aptly characterized by Murray Pittock as 'a confined realm of celebratory anaphora in Scotland and neglect abroad'.[52])

---

[51] Echoed by Jeffrey in his complaint about 'that perpetual boast of his independence, which is obtruded upon the reader of Burns in almost every page of his writings' [*Edinburgh Review* 26 (Jan. 1809), 254.

[52] Murray Pittock, 'Robert Burns and British Poetry', *Proceedings of the British Academy* 121 (London: British Academy, 2003), 191.

In tracing the booms and busts of Burns's reputation, however, and his over-whelming influence on nineteenth-century Scottish letters from Hogg to Ste-venson, it's easy to miss Burns's immediate effect on English Romantic pastoral, the subject of this brief concluding section.[53]

Part of the problem, even in the case of Wordsworth, lies in the depth at which Burns's poetry and exemplary life were assimilated (after Currie, the two were inseparable). Wordsworth generously acknowledged the extent of Burns's influ-ence in his poem 'At the Grave of Burns', written in the habbie stanza; 'whose light I hailed when first it shone, | And showed my youth | How verse may build a princely throne | On humble truth'.[54] Daniel Sanjiv Roberts has shown that Wordsworth and Coleridge were reading Currie's edition of Burns in September 1800, the very month in which they were composing the Preface to *Lyrical Ballads*.[55] (In contrast to his friend Lamb, in July 1800 Coleridge described Currie's 'Life' as 'a masterly specimen of philosophical Biography' [*CH* p. 108]). Whereas the Advertisement to the 1798 edition of *Lyrical Ballads* declares the linguistic model for its poetic 'experiments' to be 'the language of conversation in the middle and lower classes of society', the 1800 Preface (composed *after* reading Currie's 'Observations on the Scottish Peasantry') specifies 'low and rustic life' as the pastoral locus of 'the real language of men in a state of vivid sensation'.[56] Burns was far from being the only 'peasant poet' enjoying huge popularity in 1800; nonetheless, in this respect the Preface appears to respond quite specifically to Currie's 'philosophical' attribution of Burns's genius to the manners of the Scottish peasantry as a class.

In contrast to Currie's 'sociological history' and dense contexualization of Burns's life, society, and poetry, the Preface's bid to recover an authentic poetic language is stated in baldly theoretical terms. This abstract idiom makes more sense if we read Wordsworth's 'real language of men in a state of vivid sensation' as a response to Currie's 'Observations', an attempt to deterritorialize Burns's exemplary genius, a species that could hardly flourish on English soil. Judging from verbal echoes alone, Wordsworth (long an admirer of Burns's poetry) appears to have been particularly attracted to Currie's account of the *amor patriae* of the Scottish peasantry, a transference from nature to man brought forward by 'objects capable, or supposed capable, of feeling our sentiments, and of returning

---

[53] This is clearly the subject for another book. But for a recent overview that gives Currie his due, see Fiona Stafford, 'Burns and Romantic Writing' in Gerard Carruthers (ed.), *Edinburgh Companion to Robert Burns* (Edinburgh: Edinburgh University Press, 2009), 97–109.

[54] *Wordsworth: The Poems*, ed. John O. Hayden, 3 vols. (Harmondsworth: Penguin, 1977), i. 588, ll.33–6.

[55] 'Literature, Medical Science and Politics, 1795–1800: *Lyrical Ballads* and Currie's *Works of Robert Burns*', 115–28.

[56] Wordsworth and Coleridge, *Lyrical Ballads*, ed. R. L. Brett and A. R. Jones, 2nd edn. (London: Routledge 1991), 7, 245, 241.

them' [Currie, i. 27]. This resonates with Wordsworth's celebrated account of the superiority of rustic language due to 'hourly communicat[ion] with the best objects from which the best part of language is originally derived'.[57] But Wordsworth was also responsible for a more covert act of ideological assimilation: for as Leith Davis puts it, 'Scotland and Burns symbolize a difference within Britain, which Wordsworth both acknowledges and attempts to deny by incorporating it into a universal scheme.'[58]

'Universal scheme' may only be partly right, however; for if the Preface 'universalizes' Currie's Burns by an act of theoretical deterritorialization, Wordsworth's 1801 'Letter to Charles James Fox' seeks on the contrary to *re-territorialize* ideals associated with the Scottish poet on the *English* side of the border. I've argued elsewhere that in pursuing this critical goal, Wordsworth needed to devise an alternative language for pastoral poetry (impossibly) based on a rural lower-class vernacular imitating neither Scots, nor any English regional dialect.[59] In many respects the 'Letter to Fox' is the missing link which reveals the interplay between the 1800 Preface and Currie's 'Life of Burns'. Wordsworth's letter, accompanying a gift of the new edition of *Lyrical Ballads*, bewails the 'rapid decay of the domestic affections among the lower orders of society',[60] largely blamed upon the rise of manufacturing, and the increasingly centralized management of English poor relief. Wordsworth echoes Currie's linkage of domestic affections among the poor with the necessity of self-reliance or 'resolution and independence' (a favourite theme of many of his poems early and late), without of course making any allusion to the supposedly superior arrangement in Scotland.

Wordsworth's jeremiad is intended, however, to usher in the more optimistic and patriotic claim that 'the spirit of independence is, even yet, rooted in some parts of the country', meaning of course, the English Lakes.[61] This is supported by the 'Cumberland Pastorals' 'Michael' and 'The Brothers' added to the 1800 volume, which, although illustrating Currie's 'Burnesian' claims for the exemplary domestic affections of the peasantry, explicitly deny his assumption that they are exclusive to Scotland.[62] Unlike Burns's tenants and cotters, Wordsworth's rustics are 'small independent *proprietors* of land here called statesmen, men of respectable education who daily labour on their own little properties'.[63]

---

[57] Ibid. 243.

[58] *Acts of Union: Scotland and the Literary Negotiation of the British Nation, 1707–1830* (Stanford: Stanford University Press, 1998), 129.

[59] See my essay 'Burns, Wordsworth, and the Politics of Vernacular Poetry', in Peter de Bolla, Nigel Leask, and David Simpson (eds.), *Land, Nation, Culture, 740–1840: Thinking the Republic of Taste* (Basingstoke: Palgrave Macmillan, 2005), 202–22.

[60] 'Letter to Charles James Fox', in *William Wordsworth: Selected Prose*, ed. John O. Hayden (Harmondsworth: Penguin 1988), 162.

[61] Ibid. 163.

[62] See my brief discussion of 'Michael' in Ch. 7.

[63] 'Letter to Charles James Fox', 164.

And in contrast to Currie, the 'Letter to Fox' makes no mention of popular education on the Scottish model, focusing instead on the possession of 'their little tracts of land', which renders Lakeland 'statesmen' morally superior to mill workers and farm labourers. Ironically (as David Simpson has argued) there was as little historical warrant for locating such a 'perfect republic of Shepherds and Agriculturalists' in Wordsworth's Lakes, as there was for Currie's idealized view of a 'self-help Scotland' in which poor relief was replaced by domestic thrift and private charity.[64]

Francis Jeffrey's distaste for Wordsworth's *Lyrical Ballads* was famously expressed in the first number of the *Edinburgh Review*, but it wasn't until his 1809 review of Cromek's *Reliques of Burns* that the leading reviewer of the age had an opportunity to express his views on Burns, or the Wordsworthian 'appropriation' of Burns, to which his ear was evidently highly sensitive. As I've already indicated, the review was in many ways indebted to Currie's 'Life' in its Whiggish demystification of the 'wonder' of Burns's genius, which it viewed as an encouraging symptom of Scottish popular enlightenment and the 'spirit of the age'. In Jeffrey's hands, however, Currie's 'psychopathological' diagnosis of Burns' s character was coarsened into a moralizing rant that regretted the poet's 'contempt . . . for prudence, decency and regularity; and his admiration of thoughtlessness, oddity, and vehement sensibility . . . [that] communicated to a great part of his productions a character of immorality, at once contemptible and hateful'.[65]

In this strangely inconsistent essay, Jeffrey decried Burns's plebeian independence and insubordinate spirit, while at the same time extolling his use of the Scots language. As much of an anglicizer as any of the Edinburgh literati, Jeffrey nevertheless

beg[ged] leave . . . to observe, that the Scotch is not to be considered as a provincial dialect,—the vehicle only of rustic vulgarity and rude local humour. It is the language of a whole country,—long an independent kingdom, and still separate in laws, character, and manners . . . Scotch is, in reality, a highly poetical language . . . it is an ignorant, as well as an illiberal prejudice, which would seek to confound it with the barbarous dialects of Yorkshire or Devon.[66]

In the final paragraph he set up a comparison between the 'authentic rustics of Burns' 'Cottar's Saturday Night', and Wordsworth's 'fantastical personages of hysterical schoolmasters and sententious leech-gatherers': 'these gentlemen are outrageous for simplicity; and we beg leave to recommend to them the simplicity of Burns'.[67] Seen through the partisan lens of the *Edinburgh Review*, Burns was

---

[64] Simpson shows that Wordsworth glossed over the fact that land tenure in late eighteenth-century Westmoreland and Cumberland bore many resemblances to the Scottish system, *Wordsworth's Historical Imagination: The Poetry of Displacement* (New York: Methuen, 1987), 84.

[65] *Edinburgh Review* 26 (Jan. 1809), 249–76, 253.

[66] Ibid. 259.

[67] Ibid. 276.

the national poet, Wordsworth the provincial, a judgement which had the unfortunate effect of making Burns (and Scottish writing generally) a hostage to fortune in the subsequent Romantic offensive against the literary values of Jeffrey and his ilk.

Wordsworth was justifiably infuriated by Jeffrey's review, and (as Leith Davis has pointed out) his subsequent hatred of the Scottish literati such as Jeffrey further complicated his relationship with Burns.[68] Wordsworth's 1816 *Letter to a Friend of Burns* was inspired by (and boldly endorsed) Alexander Peterkin's well-meaning bid to contest the charges of alcoholism and dissipation levelled against Burns by Currie, Jeffrey, Scott, and others.[69] Wordsworth made the valuable objection that these critics would never have used the sort of patronizing language that they applied to Burns if he had been their social equal [*CH* p. 282]. Above all, he argued that literary biography had its limits and that, regarding poets, 'our business is with their books,—to understand and to enjoy them ... if their works be good, they contain within themselves all that is necessary to their being comprehended and relished' [*CH* p. 284]. Given the nature of the charges against Burns, this was an evasion rather than a rebuttal, however, and in consequence, as James Mackay suggests, Wordsworth 'unwittingly left the reader with the impression that the charges were essentially correct' [Mackay, p. 669]. And, unfortunately, Wordsworth further weakened his defence of Burns by employing him as a stalking horse for a savage retaliatory attack on Jeffrey. As John Wilson noted in a *Blackwood's* article the following year, 'all the while he is exclaiming against the Reviewer's injustice to Burns, he writes under the lash which that consummate satirist has inflicted upon himself'.[70] Ironically, both Peterkin's *Review* and Gilbert Burns's timid exoneration of his brother's character appeared (respectively) as prefaces to the 1815 and 1820 republications of Currie's four-volume *Works*, in which the introductory 'Life' remained intact.

If Currie's strictures on Burns's irregularities became a cautionary paradigm of the romantic discourse of genius, then, his attempt to rationalize Burns's genius as a healthy symptom of Scotland's popular enlightenment was soon dispelled by the romantic backlash against 'Scotch feelosofy' and the 'democratic intellect'.

---

[68]  *Acts of Union*, 135–41.

[69]  Alexander Peterkin, *A Review of the Life of Robert Burns, and of Various Criticisms on his Character and Writing* (Edinburgh, 1815). Scott's criticism of Burns appeared in an anonymous review in the *Quarterly* in Feb. 1809 [*CH* pp. 196–209]. James Gray, a mutual friend of Burns and Wordsworth, sent a copy of Peterkin to Wordsworth, 'passing on a query from Gilbert Burns about how his brother's name could be vindicated': Gilbert had been approached by Currie's publishers with an invitation to produce a new edition of the *Works* of Burns [Mackay, p. 668].

[70]  *Blackwood's Magazine*, July 1817 [*CH* pp. 296–7]. In his 1818 lecture on 'Burns and the Old English Ballads' William Hazlitt suggested that Wordsworth 'sought to get him out of the unhallowed clutches of the Edinburgh Reviewers ... only to bring him before a graver and higher tribunal, which is his own' [*CH* p. 298].

In Chapter 7 I've discussed Lockhart's complaint in *Peter's Letters* that Burns's poetry had been exclusively appropriated by Scots Whigs and *Edinburgh Reviewers*, examining his attempt to win him back into the fold of a more authentic national culture, based on the principles of romantic organicism derived from Wordsworth and Coleridge.[71] Indeed, Wordsworth's increased focus on the exemplary figure of the poet (rather than the rustic) in the 1802 'Preface' already represented a swerve away from Currie's influence, anticipating Coleridge's account of poetic language in his 1817 *Biographia Literaria*. Coleridge substituted his own canonical notion of 'lingua communis' in place of the 'Preface''s 'real language of men in a state of vivid sensation', as well as returning to a conventional poetics of pastoral.[72]

Tellingly, Coleridge explicitly raised the spectre of Burns in objecting to the mistaken theory of Wordsworth's 1800 Preface, a rite of exorcism designed to restore Wordsworth to the English poetic mainstream, despite his delusions about imitating 'the real language of men'. Recovering the rubric of Mackenzie's 'Heaven-taught ploughman' (while reversing the priority of Currie's argument), Coleridge insinuated that Wordsworth has erred in mistaking Burns, an *exceptional*, for an *exemplary*, denizen of rural life: '[We] find even in situations the most favourable, according to Mr Wordsworth, for the formation of a pure and poetic language; in situations which ensure familiarity with the grandest objects of the imagination; but *one* BURNS, among the shepherds of *Scotland*, and not a single poet of humble life among those of the *English* lakes and mountains; I conclude, that POETIC GENIUS is not only a very delicate but a very rare plant'.[73]

Coleridge here foreshadowed the Romantic Burns (safely shorn of the taint of Scottish popular enlightenment or Jacobinical sympathies) proclaimed by John Gibson Lockhart's anodyne biography of 1828,[74] or, with more vigour, by the young Thomas Carlyle in his infinitely more memorable *Edinburgh Review* article on Lockhart's book. While arguing that Burns's total poetic achievement was 'no more than a poor mutilated fraction of what was in him' [*CH* p. 355],

---

[71] See also Ian Duncan, *Scott's Shadow*, 46–69.

[72] See my *The Politics of Imagination in Coleridge's Critical Thought* (London: Macmillan, 1988), 68–74.

[73] S. T. Coleridge, *Biographia Literaria*, ed. Nigel Leask (London: Everyman, 1996), 269–70. Coleridge's catachrestic description of Burns as a 'shepherd' suggests a return to the traditional discourse of pastoral in relation to which even Mackenzie's 'ploughman' represented a critical innovation.

[74] Despite incorporating new material, largely furnished by Allan Cunningham, James Hogg was correct in designating Lockhart's *Life of Burns* as being 'rather a supplement to [Currie] than a concise history of the poet's life from beginning to end'. *Works of Robert Burns*, ed. The Ettrick Shepherd and William Motherwell, Esq., 5 vols. (Glasgow, 1834–6), i. 3. *Mutatis mutandis*, exactly the same might be said of Hogg and Motherwell. Disappointingly, Hogg's prefatory essay 'Of the Peasantry of Scotland' lapses into sentimental religiosity before reprinting much of Wilson's 'Observations on the Poetry of the Agricultural and that of the Pastoral District of Scotland' originally published in *Blackwood's* in Feb. 1819 [*CH* pp. 309–21].

Carlyle nonetheless praised him as a harbinger of Romanticism who had created a distinctly Scottish poetry (albeit as a subset of 'British literature') in reaction to the bloodless cosmopolitanism of Kames, Robertson, and Smith. After Burns and Scott, 'our chief literary men...no longer live among us like a French Colony, or some knot of Propaganda Missionaries; but like natural-born subjects of the soil, partaking and sympathising in all our attachments, humours, and habits' [*CH* p. 372]. Like Currie's, Carlyle's Burns is certainly a peasant, but one individually imbued with all the self-sufficiency and independence, the pride of a 'king in exile', that Currie had feebly generalized in his social class. But beyond that pastoral role, he is also (like his Anglo-Scottish admirer Lord Byron) a 'missionary to his generation' whose vocation is 'to teach it a higher Doctrine, a purer Truth' [*CH* p. 391]. For Carlyle, Burns's tragedy (symptomatic of modern Scottish literature in general) was that he fell foul of the shallow materialism of the age of enlightenment into which he was born, and therefore delivered only a fragment of that truth.[75]

Carlyle's own background was that of a humble stone-cutter's son from Ecclefechan, who (like Burns) had benefited from the unique educational opportunities vaunted by Currie and Jeffrey. Accordingly, his pronouncements concerning the realities of a Scottish peasant's life carried more weight than those of an Anglo-Scottish Liverpool physician, or an Edinburgh Whig literatus, in cutting the ligatures connecting Burns to the spirit of popular enlightenment: 'Is not every genius an impossibility till he appear? Why do we call him new and original, if we saw where his marble was lying, and what fabric he could rear from it? . . . A Scottish peasant's life was the meanest and rudest of all lives, till Burns became a poet in it, and a poet of it; found it a man's life, and therefore significant to men...Our *Halloween* had passed and repassed, in rude awe and laughter, since the era of the Druids; but no Theocritus, till Burns, discerned in it the materials of a Scottish Idyl' [*CH* p. 360]. In this passage Carlyle squarely connects Burns's poetry with the pastoral tradition discussed in previous chapters. Unfortunately though, he is less concerned to credit its spirited engagement with its historical age, than to celebrate the transcendental genius of the 'Heaven-taught Ploughman'. In rethinking the relationship between pastoral poetry and improvement in late eighteenth-century Scotland, it has been the goal of this book to challenge that influential and still-abiding image of Robert Burns.

---

[75] Andrew Elfenbein argues that the strain of romantic biography inaugurated by Currie and exemplified by Lockhart's *Life of Burns* and Tom Moore's *Life of Byron* engendered its own powerful riposte in the shape of Carlyle's *Sartor Resartus. Byron and the Victorians* (Cambridge: Cambridge University Press, 1995), p 106. See also my 'His Hero's Story': Currie's Burns, Moore's Byron, and the Problem of Romantic Biography', *The Byron Foundation Lecture, 2006* (Nottingham: Centre for the Study of Byron and Romanticism, 2007).

# Glossary

Burns's own glosses from the 1786 and 1787 volumes are given in inverted commas.

| | |
|---|---|
| Aboon | 'above, up' |
| Abread | 'abroad, in sight' |
| Aiblins | 'perhaps' |
| Aits, aiten | oats, oaten |
| Aith | 'an oath' |
| Aiver | 'an old horse' |
| Aft | often |
| Agley | 'wide of the aim' |
| Ance | 'once' |
| Ane | one |
| Army | having many arms or branches |
| Asklent | askew, on the side (*see* **Sklent**) |
| Auld Hornie | the Devil |
| Auld Lichts | Old Lights, the orthodox party of the Church of Scotland |
| Auld Reikie | Edinburgh |
| Aumous dish | alms-dish |
| Auldfarran | 'sagacious, cunning, prudent' |
| Awnie | 'bearded' (of barley, oats) |
| Ayont | 'beyond' |
| | |
| Bairn | 'a child' |
| Bairntime | 'a family of children, a brood' |
| Ballats | ballads |
| Bane | bone |
| Bang | 'an effort' |
| Bardie | n. 'diminutive of bard'; adj. bold, impudent of speech, rude, uncivil, forward, quarrelsome |
| Barm | balm |
| bauks o corn | rigs of corn |
| Bauld | bold |
| Bear | barley |
| Beet | 'to add fuel to fire' |
| Bield | 'shelter' |
| Bien | 'wealthy, plentiful' |
| Big | 'to build' |
| Biggan | 'a house' |
| Birkie | 'a clever fellow' (ironic) |

| | |
|---|---|
| Blastet | 'blasted' |
| Blate | 'bashful, sheepish' |
| Blather | bladder |
| Bleeze | blaze |
| Blink | 'a glance, an amorous leer, a short space of time' |
| Blinkan | 'smirking' |
| Bogle | ghost, spectre, or goblin |
| Boost | 'behoved, must needs' |
| Bore | crevice, crack |
| Boss | hollow, empty |
| Brae | 'a declivity, a precipice, the slope of a hill' |
| Braid | broad |
| Brash | 'a sudden illness' |
| Brattle | loud clattering noise |
| Braw | 'fine, handsome' |
| Brent | brand (new) |
| Brig | bridge |
| Brock | badger |
| Brogue | 'a hum, a trick' |
| Broose | 'race at a country wedding, who shall first reach the bridegroom's house on returning from church' |
| Brulzie | 'a broil, a combustion' |
| Brunstane | brimstone |
| Burdies | girls |
| Burn, burnie | 'water, a rivulet' |
| Busk, buskit | to dress, dressed up |
| But and ben | 'the country kitchen and parlour'. Coll. for a rural dwelling |
| | |
| Caff | 'chaff' |
| Caintrip | 'a charm, a spell' |
| Caird | 'a tinker' |
| Cauldrife | cold, chilly |
| Caller | 'fresh, sound' |
| Callet | wench |
| Cannie | 'gentle, mild, dextrous' |
| Canty | merry |
| Carlin | 'a stout old woman' |
| Causey | street |
| Cavie | hen-coop |
| Chanler-chaftit | lantern-jawed |
| Chaumer | chamber |
| Chiel, chield | 'a young fellow' |
| Chimla lug | 'the fireside' |
| Chirming | chirping |
| Chow | chew |
| Chuck | hen, sweetheart |

| | |
|---|---|
| Clachan | 'a small village about a church, a hamlet' |
| Claes | clothes |
| Clarket | to maintain a bank account |
| Clarty | dirty |
| Claught | clutched |
| Clautet | 'scraped' |
| Cleek | link arms while dancing |
| Clismashclaver | 'idle conversation' |
| Clooted | patched |
| Clootie | the Devil |
| Cod | pillow |
| Cog, coggie | 'a wooden dish' |
| Coof | fool, lout |
| Coost | 'did cast', discarded |
| Core | a merry company |
| Corn't | 'fed with oats' |
| Cosh | snug, cosy |
| Cotter | 'the inhabitant of a cot house or cottage' |
| Cotillion | cotillion, eighteenth-century French dance. |
| Cot-toun | a hamlet |
| Coulter | vertical cutting blade fixed in a ploughshare |
| Cour | cower |
| Couthy | 'kind, loving' |
| Cowe | 'to terrify, to keep under, to lop' |
| Cowran | cowering |
| Cowte | 'a colt' |
| Crabbit | 'crabbed, fretful' |
| Crack | 'conversation, to converse' |
| Craft, croft | 'a field near a house, *in old husbandry*' |
| Cramb o-clink or -jingle | 'rhymes, doggerel verses' |
| Cranreuch | 'the hoar frost' |
| Croft land | *see* **Craft** |
| Crowlan | 'crawling' |
| Cruizy | oil-lamp |
| Crunt | 'a blow on the head with a cudgel' |
| Cut-luggit | crop-eared |
| Cuttie | short |
| Cutty-stool | stool of repentance (in kirk) |
| | |
| 'Daft days' | the holidays at Christmas and New Year |
| Daimen-icker in a thrave | 'an ear of corn now and then' |
| Daur | dare |
| Daurk, durk | dirk |
| Deil | devil |
| Deil-haet | 'damn all', nothing |
| Ding | to beat or strike |
| Dirl | 'slight tremulous stroke or pain' |

| | |
|---|---|
| Doited | 'stupefied, hebetated' |
| Douce | 'sober, wise, prudent' |
| Dought | 'was or were able' |
| Dowie | melancholy, 'worn with grief, fatigue' |
| Doylt | 'stupefied, crazed' |
| Dribble | 'drizzling, slaver' |
| Droddum | backside |
| Drone | bagpipe drone |
| Droop-rumpl't | 'that droops at the crupper' |
| Druken | drunk |
| Drumly | 'muddy' |
| Duan | 'a term of Ossian's for the different divisions of a digressive poem' |
| Duark | a day's labour |
| Dub | puddle |
| Duddies | ragged clothes |
| Dwyne | to waste or pine away |
| | |
| E'e, ein | eye, eyes |
| Eistacks | rarities |
| Eithly | easily |
| Eldritch | 'ghastly, frightful' |
| Eleckit | elected, chosen |
| Eneugh | enough |
| Ether-stane | adder stone, used as amulet |
| | |
| Fairin | reward, present from the fair |
| Fash | 'trouble, care' |
| Fatt'rels | 'ribbon ends' |
| Fauld | 'a fold, to fold' |
| Fause | false |
| Fause-house | makeshift structure for drying corn |
| Fawsont | 'decent, seemly' |
| Ferlie | a wonder |
| Ferm toun | a hamlet |
| 'Fidge fu' fain' | fidget with excitement |
| Fient ('the fient o' pride') | strong negative, 'the devil a . . .' |
| Fire-shool | fire-shovel |
| Fit | foot, feet |
| Fittie-lan | 'the near horse of the hindmost pair in the [four-horse] plough [team]' |
| Fow | bushel |
| Flainen toy | woman's flannel cap (*see* **Toy**) |
| Fley'd | 'frightened, feared' |
| Flichter | 'to flutter *as young nestlings when their dam approaches*' |
| Flyting | scolding, railing |
| Foggage | rank grass |

| | |
|---|---|
| Forfairn | 'distresed, worn out, jaded' |
| Fother | fodder |
| Fou | 'full, drunk' |
| Fouth | plenty, abundance |
| Fowks | folk |
| Fulmart | pine-marten |
| Furrs | furrows |
| flingin-tree | 'a flail' |
| | |
| Gab | 'the mouth' |
| Gaet or gate | 'way, manner, road' |
| Gang | to go, to walk |
| Gangrel | vagrant, tramp |
| Gar | 'to make, to force to' |
| Gart | 'forc'd to' |
| Gaudsman | boy who 'goads' the plough team |
| Gaun | going |
| Gawsie | ample, jolly |
| Gibbet-airns | gibbet irons |
| Gin | 'if, against' |
| Glaive | sword |
| Glaizie | 'glittering, smooth' |
| Glamour | enchantment, magic |
| Gleyb | a portion of land |
| Gleyde | a squint |
| Glib-gabbet | 'that speaks smoothly and readily' |
| Gloamin shot | a twilight interval taken before using lights indoors |
| Gnaps | bites |
| Gooms | gums |
| Gowan | daisy |
| Gowff | golf, to strike |
| Graith | 'accoutrements, furniture, dress' |
| Graunie | grannie |
| Gree ('bear the gree') | to triumph, 'to be decidedly victor' |
| Greet | to weep |
| Grozet | 'gooseberry' |
| Grumphie | 'a sow' |
| Grun | ground |
| Gudeman | 'master of the household' |
| Guid | good |
| | |
| Ha' folk | servants |
| Haffet | lock of hair growing on temples |
| Hafflins-wise | in half-measure |
| Hairst | harvest |
| Half-sarket | half-clothed |
| Hallan | partition between living quarters and byre in a cottage |

| | |
|---|---|
| Hameil | native to one's home or country |
| Hansel | a new-year or good-luck gift |
| Harn | coarse linen |
| Hash | waster or ne'er do well |
| Haughs | 'low-lying rich lands, valleys' |
| Hawkie | 'a cow *properly one with a white face*' |
| Heapit | heaped |
| Heeze | to elevate, raise' |
| Heft | handle (of a knife) |
| Hellim | helm |
| Heritor | a landed proprietor |
| Herryment | 'plundering, devastation' |
| Hing | hang |
| Hizzie | wench |
| Horn | comb |
| Hornie | the Devil |
| Houghmagandie | copulation, 'a species of gender composed of the masculine and feminine united' |
| Houlet | owl |
| Howm | water-meadow |
| Hum | mumble |
| Hurchin | urchin |
| Hurdies | buttocks, 'the loins, the crupper' |
| Hyvie | well-to-do |
| | |
| Icker | an ear of corn |
| Ilk, ilka | each |
| Incog | incognito |
| Ingine | 'genius, ingenuity' |
| Ingle | 'fire, fire-place' |
| | |
| Jad | jade, 'familiar term among country folks for a giddy young girl' |
| Jauk | 'to dally, to trifle' |
| Jinkin | 'dodging' |
| Jocteleg | 'a kind of knife', often used to cut cabbage stalks |
| | |
| Kailyard | cabbage patch |
| Kebbuck | cheese |
| Kelpies | 'a sort of mischievous spirits, said to haunt fords and ferries at night, especially in storms' |
| Ken | to know |
| Ket | 'a matted, hairy fleecy of wool' |
| Kiaugh | 'carking anxiety' |
| Kirn | 'the harvest supper, a churn' |
| Kist | 'a chest, shop counter' |
| Kittle | 'to tickle', excite; adj. difficult, tricky |

| | |
|---|---|
| Kittle up | tune up, play |
| Kiutlin | 'cuddling' |
| Knowes | 'small round hillocks' |
| | |
| Laggen | 'the angle between the side and bottom of a wooden dish' |
| Laigh | low |
| Laimpet | limpet |
| Laith | 'loath' |
| Laithfu | 'bashful, sheepish' |
| Lallan | 'Lowland' |
| Lallands | 'Scotch dialect' |
| Lave | 'the rest, the remainder, the others' |
| Laverock | skylark |
| Leal | 'loyal, true, faithfu' |
| Lear | 'learning' |
| Leather | vagina |
| Leed | language |
| 'Leeze me [on]' | 'a phrase of congratulatory endearment' |
| Link | 'to trip along' |
| Lintie | linnet |
| Loup | to leap, jump, dance |
| Lug | ear |
| Luggie | 'a small wooden dish with a handle' |
| Luppen | danced |
| | |
| Mailin | arable land held on lease, a smallholding |
| Maingie | mangy |
| Manse | dwelling of the minister adjacent to the Kirk |
| Maukin | a hare |
| Maun | must |
| Meere | mare |
| Messan | lap-dog, cur |
| Mim-mou'd | reserved, affected |
| Mixtie-maxtie | 'confusedly mixed' |
| Moistify | 'to moisten' |
| 'Moop an mell' | nibble and mingle with others (of sheep) |
| Mottie | 'full of motes', dusty |
| Mowe | copulate (vulg.) |
| Muckle house | House of Commons |
| Muckle | 'great, big, much' |
| Muir | moor |
| | |
| Naig | horse, nag |
| Nappy | foaming strong ale |
| Neebor | neighbour |
| New Lichts | New Lights, the Moderate party of the Church of Scotland |

| | |
|---|---|
| Newk | Corner |
| Nickie-ben | the Devil |
| Nick-nakets | knick-knacks |
| Nieve | the fist |
| Nocht | nothing |
| Nowt(e) | 'black cattle' |
| | |
| O'ercome | profit, surplus |
| Orra | odd, spare, extra |
| | |
| Pack | 'intimate, familiar' |
| Painch-lippit | blubber lipped |
| Paitrick | partridge |
| Pattle | a plough staff |
| Pego | penis (vulg.) |
| Pet | 'a domesticated sheep, &c.' |
| Pit | to put |
| Placad | 'a public proclamation' |
| Plack | 'an old Scotch coin' |
| Plaiden | a tartan cloak |
| Plainstanes | pavement |
| Pleugh | plough |
| Plough-gang | a long piece of ground, ploughed into a ridge, equivalent to the English 'furlong' |
| Poind | distrain, seize goods and sell them under a warrant |
| Poortith | poverty |
| Pou | pull |
| Poutch | pouch |
| Pow | 'the head, the skull' |
| Prent | print |
| Prine | to pin, pierce |
| Pussy | 'a hare or cat' |
| Pyle | a grain: '*a pyle o' caff* = a single grain of chaff' |
| | |
| Quat | to quit |
| Quean | a young, sturdy girl |
| | |
| Raible | 'to rattle nonsense' |
| Raize | 'to madden, to enflame' |
| Ram-stam | 'forward, thoughtless' |
| Randie | rude, course-tongued, riotous |
| Rape | rope |
| Rash-buss | 'a bush of rushes' |
| Rattons | rats |
| Raucle | 'rash, stout, fearless' |
| Raw | 'a row' |
| Reave | to plunder |

| | |
|---|---|
| Red(e) | to counsel, advise |
| Red-wud | 'stark-mad' |
| Reek | smoke |
| Reft | 'torn, ragged' |
| Remead | remedy |
| Riggin | roof |
| Rigwoodie | withered, course, yellow |
| Ringbane | a disease of horses |
| Rip(p) | 'a handful of unthreshed corn' |
| Road o' airn | iron rod |
| Rockin | spinning party |
| Roon | 'round, in the circle of neighbourhood' |
| Roose | 'to praise, to commend' |
| Rozet | rosin |
| Rug | to take a cut or a rake-off |
| Rung | a cudgel |
| Runrig | Agrarian system widely practised in Scotland prior to improvement. *See* Chapter 1. |
| | |
| Sark | 'a shirt' |
| Saunt | saint |
| Saut | salt |
| Sax rood | an acre and a half |
| Scauld | scold |
| Scowry | scruffy, unprepossessing |
| Scrievin | 'gleesomely, swiftly' |
| Scrimp | 'to scant' |
| Scrog | scrub, bushland |
| Shangan | 'a stick cleft at one end for putting the tail of a dog, &c. into, by way of mischief, or to frighten him' ('clap a shangan') |
| Shavie | a trick |
| Shaw | 'to show; a small wood in a hollow place' |
| Shog | 'a shock' |
| Shoon | shoes |
| Shure | sheared |
| Sic | such |
| Simmer | summer |
| Skaith | 'to damge, to injure; injury' |
| Skinklin | showy |
| Skirl | 'to shriek, to cry shrilly' |
| Sklent | 'slant; to run aslant, to deviate from truth' |
| Slae | sloe |
| Slap | 'a gate, a breach in a fence' |
| Slee | sly |
| Sleeket | sleek, smooth |
| Smeddum | 'dust, powder; mettle, sense' |

| | |
|---|---|
| Snash | abusive language |
| Snaw-tapit | snow-topped |
| Sned | 'to lop, cut off' |
| Snell | 'bitter, biting' |
| Snick-drawing | 'trick contriving' |
| Snodit | bound up |
| Sock and couter | old form of ploughshare |
| Sole (window sole) | lower part of window |
| Sootyman | chimney sweep |
| Sorn | to behave as a layabout |
| Soudland | the Southern country |
| Souple | 'flexible, swift' |
| Sowth, south | 'to try over a tune with a low whistle' |
| Spavies | lameness, especially of horses |
| Spaw | Spa |
| Spean | to wean |
| Spence | 'the country parlour' |
| Sprattle | 'to scramble'. |
| Sprittie | rushy |
| Spunk | a spark, light |
| Spunkie | will o' the wisp |
| Squatter | 'to flutter in water *as a wild duck* &c.' |
| Squattle | 'to sprawl' |
| Stacher | stagger |
| Staincher-fittit | iron-footed |
| Stang | to goad, sting |
| Staumrel | stammering, half-witted |
| Staw | stole |
| Steel-waimet | steel-bellied |
| Steer | 'to molest, to stir' |
| Stell | whisky still |
| Stent | impost, duty |
| Stimpart | measure of grain |
| Stoor | dust |
| Straik | 'to stroke' |
| Stroan't | pissed |
| Strunt | liquor |
| Sugh | 'the continued running noise of wind or water' |
| Suthron | 'an old name for the English nation' |
| Sutor (souter) | shoemaker |
| Swat | sweated |
| Swatch | 'a sample' |
| Synd | washed down |
| | |
| Tacksman | a leaseholding farmer, a tenant |
| Taets | tufts |
| Tail | vagina, or woman's backside (vulg.) |

| | |
|---|---|
| Tak tent | beware |
| Tap | top |
| Tap-pickle | grain at the top of a stalk of barley or oats |
| Tarrow | 'to murmur at one's allowance' |
| Tawted | matted, shaggy |
| Tester | sixpence |
| Thole | suffer |
| Thrang | 'throng, crowd' |
| Thraw | 'to sprain, to twist, to contradict' |
| Thristed | thirsted |
| Thristle | thistle |
| Throwe-gang | passage way in a house |
| Thummert | polecat |
| Tight | neat, shapely |
| Timmer | rim |
| Tint | lost |
| Tod | fox |
| Toy | 'a very old fashion of female head-dress' |
| Toddlan | staggering |
| Toom | empty |
| Toop | a tup, ram |
| Towzie tyke | shaggy dog |
| Trams | upright posts of the gallows |
| Trashtrie | trash |
| Trow | pledge |
| Tulzie | 'a quarrel, to quarrel, to fight' |
| Twa | two |
| Tyne | lose |
| | |
| Unco | 'strange, uncouth, very, very great, prodigious' |
| | |
| Virls | 'a ring around a column' |
| | |
| Wad | would; n. a bet or pledge |
| Wae | woe |
| Wal'd | chose, chosen |
| Walie | 'ample, large, jolly; also an interjection of distress' |
| Wanrestfu | 'restless' |
| Warklum | 'a tool to work with', penis |
| Warly | 'wordly, eager on amassing wealth' |
| Warp | weave |
| Warran | 'a warrant, to warrant' |
| Wastrie | 'prodigality' |
| Wauk | wake |
| Waur | worse |
| Waur them | defeat them |
| Wawlie | *see* Walie |

| | |
|---|---|
| Wean | child |
| Web | woven cloth |
| Wecht | a quantity or weight |
| Weel-hain'd | well-matured |
| Westlin | westerly |
| Whang | 'a leathern string, a piece of cheese, bread, &c.; to give the strappado' |
| Whirligigums | 'useless ornaments, trifling appendages' |
| Whitter | 'a hearty draught of liquor' |
| Whittle | a dagger |
| Whyles | sometimes |
| Wiel | eddy |
| Wight | a man |
| Wil'cat | wildcat |
| Wimple | 'to meander' |
| Winna | will not |
| Winnock | window |
| Winnock-bunker | window recess |
| Wintle | 'a staggering motion; to stagger; to reel' |
| Winze | 'an oath' |
| Wonner | wonder |
| Woo | wool |
| Wylecoat | 'a flannel vest' |
| | |
| Yett | gate |
| Youngker | youngster |
| yowe, yowie | ewe |

# *Bibliography*

PRIMARY TEXTS

[Anon.], 'Letter from a Blacksmith to the Ministers and Elders of the Church of Scotland', (1759).

—— 'Observations on the Gentle Shepherd and Strictures on Pastoral Poetry', *Edinburgh Magazine* (June 1802), 417.

Aikin, John, *Essays on Song Writing: with a Collection of such English Songs as are most Eminent for Poetical Merit* (London: Joseph Johnson, 1773).

Aiton, William, *General View of the County of Ayr: with Observations on the Means of its Improvement; drawn up for the Consideration of the Board of Agriculture* (Glasgow, 1811).

Austen, Jane, *Northanger Abbey, Lady Susan, The Watsons, and Sanditon*, ed. John Davie, intro. Terry Castle (Oxford: Oxford University Press, 1990).

Barbauld, Anna, *Poems* (London, 1773).

Bartlett, Thomas (ed.), *Life of Theobald Wolfe Tone, compiled and arranged by William Wolfe Tone (1826)*, 2 vols. (Dublin: Lilliput, 1998).

Beattie, James, *Original Poems and Translations* (London, 1760).

—— *Poetical Works*, new intro. Roger J. Robinson (London: Routledge; Thoemmes, 1996).

—— *The Minstrel, in Two Books* (London, 1784).

Blair, Hugh, *Lectures on Rhetoric and Belles Lettres*, 3 vols. (Dublin, 1783).

Boswell, James, *London Journal, 1762–1763*, ed. Frederick Albert Pottle (New York: McGraw-Hill, 1950).

—— *Life of Johnson*, ed. R. W. Chapman, rev. J. D. Fleeman, new intro. Pat Rogers (Oxford: World's Classics, 1980).

Buchan Papers, Glasgow University Special Collections, Murray MSS 502/53/3 and 502/54/10.

Burns, Robert, *Poems, chiefly in the Scottish Dialect* (Kilmarnock: John Wilson, 1786).

—— *Poems chiefly in the Scottish Dialect*, (Edinburgh, 1787).

—— *Poems, chiefly in the Scottish Dialect*, 2 vols. (Edinburgh, 1793).

—— *Address to the People of Scotland, Respecting Capt Grose, Esq, The British Antiquarian, by Robert Burns, the Ayrshire Poet* (Glasgow, n.d.).

—— *The Cottagers' Saturday Night: A Poem Containing a very pleasing and affecting Description of a Cottager and his Family* (London: Printed by A. Applegarth, Stamford St: J. Davis, J. Nisbet, J. and C. Evans, n.d.).

—— *The Twa Herds: An Unco Mourfu' Tale* (Glasgow: Stewart and Meikle, 1796).

—— *The Jolly Beggars; or, Tatterdemallions. A Cantata* (Glasgow: Stewart and Meikle, 1799).

—— *The Works of Robert Burns; with an Account of his Life, and a Criticism of his Writings. To which are prefixed, Some Observations on the Character and Condition of the Scottish Peasantry*, ed. James Currie, 4 vols. (Liverpool, London, Edinburgh, 1800).

—— *Reliques of Robert Burns*, ed. R. H. Cromek (London, 1808).

Burns, Robert, *Poems and Songs of Robert Burns*, ed. Rev. Hamilton Paul (Ayr: Wilson, M'Cormick & Carnie, 1819).

—— *Prophecies of Thomas the Rhymer . . . An Account of the Battle of Bannockburn . . . 'The Cottagers' Saturday Night'* (Stirling: W. Macnie, 1828).

—— *Works of Robert Burns*, ed. the Ettrick Shepherd and William Motherwell, Esq., 5 vols. (Glasgow, 1834–6).

—— *The Life and Works of Robert Burns*, ed. Robert Chambers, rev. William Wallace, 4 vols. (Edinburgh: William Chambers, 1896).

—— *The Poetry of Robert Burns*, ed. W. E. Henley and T. F. Henderson, 4 vols. (London: Blackwood, 1896).

—— *Robert Burns. The Jolly Beggars: A Cantata*, ed. John C. Weston (Northampton, Mass.: Gehenna, 1963).

—— *The Poems and Songs of Robert Burns*, ed. James Kinsley, 3 vols. (Oxford: Clarendon, 1968).

—— *Robert Burns' Common Place Book 1783–5*, ed. Raymond Lamont Brown (Wakefield: S.R. Publishers, 1969).

—— *Robert Burns's Tour of the Borders*, ed. Raymond Lamont Brown (Ipswich: *Boydel*, 1972).

—— *The Glenriddell Manuscripts*, facsimile; intro. and notes Desmond Donaldson (Wakefield: EP Publishing, 1973).

—— *Robert Burns's Tour of the Highlands and Stirlingshire*, ed. Raymond Lamont Brown (Ipswich: Boydell, 1973).

—— *The Letters of Robert Burns*, i. *1780–1789*; ii. *1790–1796*, ed. J. De Lancey Ferguson; 2nd edn. G. Ross Roy (Oxford: Clarendon, 1985).

—— *Robert Burns: Selected Poems*, ed. Carol McGuirk (Harmondsworth: Penguin, 1993).

—— *The Canongate Burns: The Complete Poems and Songs of Robert Burns*, intro. Andrew Noble, ed. Andrew Noble and Patrick Scott Hogg (Edinburgh: Canongate, 2001).

—— *The Merry Muses of Caledonia*, ed. James Barke, Sydney Goodsir Smith, new intro. and music Valentina Bold (Edinburgh: Luath, 2009).

Cervantes, Miguel De, *A Dialogue between Scipio and Berganza, Two Dogs belonging to the City of Toledo. Giving an Account of their Lives and Adventures, with their Reflections on the Lives, Humours, and Employments of the Masters they lived with*, anon. trans. (London, 1766).

Child, Francis James (ed.), *English and Scottish Popular Ballads*, 5 vols. (New York: Dover, 1965).

Churchill, Charles, *Poetical Works of Charles Churchill, with memoir, critical dissertation, and explanatory notes*, ed. Revd George Gilfillan (Edinburgh: James Nichol, 1855).

*John Clare: The Oxford Authors*, ed. Eric Robinson and David Powell (Oxford: Oxford University Press, 1984).

Cobbett, William, *Tour in Scotland*, ed. Daniel Green (Aberdeen: Aberdeen University Press, 1984).

Coleridge, Samuel Taylor, *Coleridge's Writings on Politics and Society*, ed. John Morrow (Princeton: Princeton University Press, 1991).

—— *Biographia Literaria*, ed. Nigel Leask (London: Everyman, 1996).

—— *Coleridge Poetical Works*, ed. J. C. Mays, 6 vols. (Princeton: Princeton University Press, 2001).

Cowan, Edward J. and Paterson, Michael, *Folk in Print: Scotland's Chapbook Heritage, 1750–1850* (Edinburgh: John Donald, 2007).

Cowper, William, *William Cowper, Verse and Letters*, selected by Brian Spiller (Cambridge, Mass.: Harvard University Press, 1968).

Cromek, R. H., *Reliques of Robert Burns; Consisting Chiefly of Original Letters, Poems, and Critical Observations on Scottish Songs* (London, 1808).

Cunningham, John, *Poems, Chiefly Pastoral* (Dublin, 1766).

Currie, James, *Works of Robert Burns: with an Account of his Life, and a Criticism of his Writings. To which is prefixed, Some Observations on the Character and Condition of the Scottish Peasantry*, 4 vols., (Liverpool, London, Edinburgh, 1800).

——Articles in *Analytical Review* 1 (1788), 145–53, 521–9; 2 (1788), 265–70, 549–58.

——Currie/Burns Correspondence, Mitchell Library, Glasgow MS 10/C -196 C.

——*A Letter, Commercial and Political, Addressed to the Rt Hon William Pitt by Jasper Wilson, Esq.* (London: Robinson, 1793).

Currie, William Wallace, *Memoir of the Life, Writing and Correspondence of James Currie, MD, FRS, of Liverpool*, 2 vols. (London: Longman, 1831).

Dent, William, *The Jovial Crew or Merry Beggars. A comic opera as performed at Brighton by the Carleton Company* (British Museum Satires, 1786).

Duck, Stephen, *Poems on Several Occasions* (London, 1738).

Fergusson, Alexander, *The Rt Hon. Henry Erskine, Lord Advocate of Scotland* (Edinburgh: Blackwood, 1882).

Fergusson, Robert, *The Poems of Robert Fergusson* (*1954–6*), ed. Matthew P.McDiarmid, 2 vols. (repr. Eastbourne: Scottish Text Society, n.d.).

Fullarton, Col. William, *A General View of the Agriculture of the County of Ayr, with Observations on the Means of Improvement. Drawn up for the consideration of the Board of Agriculture and Internal Improvement* (Edinburgh: John Paterson, 1793).

Galt, John, *George the Third, His Court, and Family*, 2 vols. (London, 1824).

Geddes, William, 'Three Scottish Poems, with a Previous Dissertation on the Scoto-Saxon Dialect', *Transactions of the Society of the Antiquaries of Scotland* 1 (Edinburgh, 1792).

Goldie, John, *Essays on Various Important Subjects Moral and Divine* (Glasgow, 1779).

Goldsmith, Oliver, *History of the Earth*, 2nd edn., 8 vols. (London, 1779).

Grant, Archibald, *The Farmer's New-Year Gift to his Countrymen, Heritors and Farmers* (Aberdeen, 1757).

Gregory, John, *A Comparative View of the State and Faculties of Man with those of the Animal World (1765)*, 6th edn. (Edinburgh, 1774).

Grose, Francis, *A Classical Dictionary of the Vulgar Tongue* (London, 1785).

——*A Provincial Glossary, with a Collection of Local Proverbs and Popular Superstitions* (London, 1787).

——*Antiquities of Scotland*, 2 vols. (London, 1789–91).

—— *The Grumbler: Containing Sixteen Essays* (London, 1791).

Herd, David (ed.), *Ancient and Modern Scottish Songs* (Edinburgh, 1776).

Home, Henry, Lord Kames, *The Gentleman Farmer. Being an attempt to Improve Agriculture, by subjecting it to the test of rational principles* (Edinburgh, 1776).

Heron, Robert, *Observations made in a Journey through the Western Counties of Scotland, in the Autumn of 1792*, 2nd edn. (Perth, 1799).

Hutcheson, Frances, *A System of Moral Philosophy*, 2 vols. (London, 1755).

Jeffrey, Francis, 'Review of Cromek's *Reliques*', *Edinburgh Review* 26 (Jan. 1809), 249–76.

Johnson, Samuel, *The Rambler* 36 and 37, 21 and 24 July 1750.

Langhorne, John, *Genius and Virtue: a Scotch Pastoral* (London, 1763).

Lapraik, John, *Poems on Several Occasions* (Kilmarnock: John Wilson, 1788).

*Liverpool Testimonials to the Departed Genius of Robert Burns, The Scottish Bard* (Liverpool: Merritt & Wright, 1800).

Locke, John, *Essay Concerning Human Understanding*, ed. P. H. Nidditch (Oxford: Clarendon, 1975).

Lockhart, J. G., *Peter's Letters to his Kinsfolk*, 3rd edn., 3 vols. (Edinburgh: W. Blackwood, 1819).

—— *Life of Robert Burns (1828)*, ed. James Kinsley (London: Dent & Sons, 1959).

—— *Peter's Letters to his Kinsfolk*, ed. William Ruddick (Edinburgh: Scottish Academic Press, 1977).

Lonsdale, Roger (ed.), *Eighteenth-Century Women Poets* (Oxford: Oxford University Press, 1990).

—— (ed.), *New Oxford Book of Eighteenth Century Verse* (Oxford: Oxford University Press, 1984).

Low, Donald A. (ed.), *Robert Burns: The Critical Heritage* (London: Routledge & Kegan Paul, 1974).

—— (ed.), *The Scots Musical Museum*, 2 vols. (repr. Aldershot: Scolar Press, 1991).

McGill, Rev. William, *Practical Essay on the Death of Jesus Christ* (1786).

Mackay, Charles, *Extraordinary Popular Delusions, and the Madness of Crowds* (London, 1841).

Mackenzie, Sir George, *Moral History of Frugality, with its Opposite Vices* (1691).

Mackintosh, William of Borlum, *An Essay on the Ways and Means for Inclosing, Fallowing, Planting, etc. Scotland . . . By a Lover of his Country* (Edinburgh: The Society of Improvers, 1729).

Maclachlan, Christopher (ed.), *Before Burns: Eighteenth-Century Scottish Poetry* (Edinburgh: Canongate, 2002).

Macneill, Hector, *Scotland's Skaith; or the History of Will and Jean* (Edinburgh, 1795).

—— *The Pastoral, or Lyric Muse of Scotland* (Edinburgh, 1808).

Maxwell, James, *Animadversions on Some Poets and Poetasters of the Present Age* (Paisley, 1788).

Nichol, John, *Robert Burns: A Summary of his Career and Genius* (Edinburgh, 1882).

Paine, Thomas, *Common Sense: Addressed to the Inhabitants of America* (Edinburgh: Stirling, 1776).

—— *The Tom Paine Reader*, ed. Michael Foot and Isaac Kramnick (London: Penguin, 1987).

Paley, William, *Reasons for Contentment; Addressed to the Labouring Part of the British Public* (Carlisle, 1792).

Pennant, Thomas, *Tour in Scotland and Voyage to the Hebrides, 1772*, 2nd edn. (London, 1776).

——*A Tour in Scotland; MDCCLXIX*, 4th edn. (London, 1776).

Pennecuik, Alexander, *Streams from Helicon; or, poems on various subjects. In three parts*, 2nd edn. (London, 1720).

Peterkin, Alexander, *A Review of the Life of Robert Burns, and of Various Criticisms on his Character and Writing* (Edinburgh, 1815).

Pinkerton, John, *Antient Scottish Poems* (London, 1786).

Pope, Alexander, *Pope: Poetical Works*, ed. Herbert Davis, intro. Pat Rogers (Oxford: Oxford University Press, 1978).

Ramsay, Allan, *The Works of Allan Ramsay*, 6 vols., i–ii ed. Burns Martin and John W. Oliver; iii–vi ed. Alexander M. Kinghorn and Alexander Law, Scottish Text Society (Edinburgh: William Blackwood, 1953–74).

——*The Poems of Allan Ramsey* (Edinburgh, 1721).

——*Collection of Scots Proverbs* (Edinburgh, 1737).

——*The Tea-Table Miscellany*, 18th edn. (Glasgow, 1782).

——*The Gentle Shepherd* (Glasgow, 1788).

——*Poems of Allan Ramsay, a new edition, to which are prefixed a life of the author [by George Chalmers] and remarks on his poems [by Alexander Tytler, Lord Woodhouselee]*, 2 vols. (London: Cadell & Davies, 1800).

Ramsay of Ochtertyre, John, 'On Scottish Songs', *The Bee* (13 April 1791), 201–10.

Riddell, Robert, *Collection of Reels, Minuets, Hornpipes, Marches and Two Songs in the Old Scotch Taste* (James Johnson, 1785).

——*The Bedesman on Nydsyde* (London, 1790).

Ritson, Joseph, 'An Historical Essay on Scotish Song', *Scotish Songs, in two volumes* (London: Joseph Johnson, 1794).

Roscoe, William, *The Life of Lorenzo De' Medici, Called The Magnificent*, 2nd edn., 2 vols. (London: Cadell & Davies, 1796).

Ross, Alexander, *Helenore, or the Fortunate Shepherdess*, ed. John Longmuir (Edinburgh: William Nimmo, 1866).

*Scots Musical Museum*, published by James Johnson, 6 vols. (Edinburgh, 1787–1818), repr. ed. Donald Low, 2 vols. (Aldershot: Scholar Press, 1991).

Scott, Sir Walter, *The Heart of Midlothian*, ed. Tony Inglis (London: Penguin, 1994).

——*The Antiquary*, ed. David Hewitt, intro. David Punter (London: Penguin, 1998).

Shairp, John Campbell, *Robert Burns* (London: Macmillan, 1887).

Sillar, David, *Poems* (Kilmarnock: John Wilson, 1789).

Simson, William, 'Provincial Terms and Glossary', in William Aiton (ed.), *General View of the Agriculture of Ayrshire* (Glasgow, 1811), 681–93.

Sinclair, Sir John, *Specimens of Statistical Reports, Exhibiting the Progress of Political Society from the Pastoral State, to that of Luxury and Refinement* (London, 1793).

——(ed.), *The Statistical Account of Scotland, 1791–99*, with a new introduction by John Strawhorn, 20 vols. (Wakefield: EP Publishing, 1982).

Smith, Adam, *Lectures on Rhetoric and Belles Lettres*, ed. J. C. Bryce, *Glasgow Edition of the Works and Correspondence of Adam Smith* (Indianapolis: Liberty Fund, 1985).

——*The Wealth of Nations*, 2 vols., ed. with intro. Andrew Skinner; i. *Books I–III*, ii. *Books IV–V* (London: Penguin, 1999).

——*Theory of Moral Sentiments*, 5th edn. (London, 1781).

Smith, Adam, *Theory of Moral Sentiments*, ed. Knut Haakonssen (Cambridge: Cambridge University Press, 2002).

Stewart, Dugald, *Elements of the Philosophy of the Human Mind*, 6th edn., 2 vols. (London, 1818).

Tannahill, Robert, *Works of Robert Tannahill, with a Life of the Author*, ed. Philip A. Ramsey (London: Fullarton, n.d.).

Taylor, Dr John, *The Scripture Doctrine of Original Sin* (1741).

Thomson, George, ed. *Select Collection & Scottish Airs*, 5 vols, (Edinburgh and London, 1793–1818).

Virgil, *Virgil's Pastorals translated into English Prose; as also his Georgicks*, trans. James Hamilton (Edinburgh, 1742).

—— *Virgils' Works, Containing his Pastorals, Georgics and Aeneis*, trans. John Dryden, 3 vols. (London, 1763).

—— *The Works of Virgil, in English Verse, The Aeneid*, trans. Revd Christopher Pitt; the *Eclogues* and *Georgics*, with notes on the whole, trans. Revd Joseph Warton, 4 vols. (London: Dodsley, 1763).

—— 'The Pastorals of Virgil Translated', in James Beattie, *Original Poems and Translations* (London, 1760).

—— *The Eclogues and The Georgics*, trans. C. Day Lewis, intro. and notes R. O. A. M. Lyne (Oxford: Oxford University Press, 1983).

Wallace, William (ed.), *Robert Burns and Mrs Dunlop* (London, 1898).

Warton, Thomas, *Poems on Various Subjects* (London, 1791).

Watson, James, *Choice Collection of Comic and Serious Scots Poems* (Edinburgh: James Watson, 1706–11).

Westwood, Peter (ed.), *Definitive Illustrated Companion to Robert Burns*, 8 vols. (Irvine: Distributed National Burns Collections Project, 2004–6).

Wight, Andrew, *Present State of Husbandry in Scotland, Extracted from Reports made to the Commissioners of the Annexed Estates and Published by their Authority*, 2 vols. (Edinburgh, 1778).

Willison, John, *A Sacramental Directory, Or a Treatise Concerning the Sanctification of a Communion Sabbath* (Edinburgh, 1716).

Wilson, John, 'The Radical's Saturday Night', *Blackwood's Magazine* 6 (Dec. 1819), 257–62.

Wolcot, John ('Peter Pindar'), *The Lousiad: An Heroi-Comic Poem* (London, 1785).

—— 'Instructions to a Celebrated Laureate: alias the Progress of Curiosity; alias a Birth-Day Ode' (1787).

Wordsworth, William, *Wordsworth: The Poems*, ed. John O. Hayden, 3 vols. (Harmondsworth: Penguin, 1977).

—— *The Ruined Cottage, The Brothers, Michael*, ed. Jonathan Wordsworth (Cambridge: Cambridge University Press, 1985).

—— *William Wordsworth: Selected Prose*, ed. John O. Hayden (Harmondsworth: Penguin, 1988).

Wordsworth, William, *The Fenwick Notes of William Wordsworth*, ed. Jared Curtis (London, England: Bristol Classical, 1993).

—— and Coleridge, Samuel Taylor, *Lyrical Ballads*, ed. R. L. Brett and A. R. Jones, 2nd edn. (London: Routledge, 1991).

## SECONDARY TEXTS

Adams, I. H., *The Mapping of a Scottish Estate* (Edinburgh: Dept. of Education Studies, 1971).

Agamben, Giorgio, *The Open: Man and Animal*, trans. Kevin Attell (Stanford, Calif.: Stanford University Press, 2004).

Andrews, Corey, *Literary Nationalism in Eighteenth-Century Scottish Club Poetry* (Lampeter: Edwin Mellen, 2004).

Aravamudan, Srinivas, *Tropicopolitans: Colonialism and Agency, 1688–1804* (Durham, NC: Duke University Press, 1999), 29–70.

Ashworth, William, *Customs and Excise: Trade, Production and Consumption in England, 1640–1845* (Oxford: Oxford University Press, 2003).

Barrell, John, *The Idea of Landscape and the Sense of Place, 1730–1840: An Approach to the Poetry of John Clare* (Cambridge: Cambridge University Press, 1972).

—— *The Dark Side of the Landscape: The Rural Poor in English Painting, 1730–1840* (Cambridge: Cambridge University Press, 1980).

——*English Literature and History, 1730–1780: An Equal, Wide Survey* (London: Hutchinson, 1983).

——*Poetry, Language, Politics* (Manchester: Manchester University Press, 1988).

——'Putting down the Rising', in Leith Davis, Ian Duncan, and Janet Sorensen (eds.), *Scotland and the Borders of Romanticism* (Cambridge: Cambridge University Press, 2004), 130–8.

—— *The Spirit of Despotism: Invasions of Privacy in the 1790's* (Oxford: Oxford University Press, 2006).

——'Rus in Urbe', in Philip Connell and Nigel Leask (eds.), *Romanticism and Popular Culture* (Cambridge: Cambridge University Press, 2009), 109–27.

Bayly, C. A., *Imperial Meridian: The British Empire and the World, 1780–1830* (Harlow: Longman, 1989).

Bentman, Raymond, 'Robert Burns's Use of Scottish Diction', in Frederick Hilles and Harold Bloom (eds.), *From Sensibility to Romanticism* (Oxford: Oxford University Press, 1965), 239–58.

——'Robert Burns's Declining Fame', *Studies in Romanticism*, 11/3 (1972), 206–24.

Bermingham, Ann, 'The Simple Life: Cottages and Gainsborough's Cottage Doors' in Peter de Bolla, Nigel Leask, and David Simpson (eds.), *Land, Nation and Culture: Thinking the Republic of Taste* (Basingstoke: Palgrave Macmillan, 2005), 37–62.

Bourdieu, Pierre, 'The Field of Cultural Production: or: The Economic World Reversed', in Randal Johnson (ed.), *The Field of Cultural Production* (Cambridge: Polity, 1993), 29–73.

Boyd, William, *Education in Ayrshire Through Seven Centuries* (London: University of London Press, 1961).

Brewer, John, 'Commercialisation and Politics', in Neil McKendrick, John Brewer, and J. H. Plumb (eds.), *The Birth of a Consumer Society* (London: Europa, 1982).

—— *The Sinews of Power: War, Money and the English State, 1688–1783* (London: Unwin Hyman, 1989).

Broadie, Alexander, *The Scottish Enlightenment: The Historical Age of the Historical Nation* (Edinburgh: Birlinn, 2007).

Brown, Callum G., 'Protest in the Pews: Interpreting Presbyterianism and Society in Fracture during the Scottish Economic Revolution', in T. M. Devine (ed.), *Conflict and Stability in Scottish Society, 1700–1850* (Edinburgh: John Donald, 1990), 83–105.

—— *Religion and Society in Scotland since 1707* (Edinburgh: Edinburgh University Press, 1997).

Brown, Iain Gordon, *The Hobby-Horsical Antiquary: A Scottish Character 1640–1830* (Edinburgh: NLS, 1980).

Burke, Peter, 'The Virgin of the Carmine and the Revolt of Masaniello', *Past and Present* 99 (1983), 3–21.

—— *Popular Culture in Early Modern Europe* (repr. Aldershot: Scolar Press, 1994).

Burke, Tim, 'Robert Burns', in John Goodridge (ed.), *Eighteenth-Century Labouring-Class Poets* (London: Pickering Chatto, 2002), 103–15.

—— 'Labour, Education and Genius: Burns and the Plebeian Poetic Tradition', in Johnny Rodger and Gerard Carruthers (eds.), *The Fickle Man: Robert Burns in the Twenty-First Century* (Dingwall: Sandstone, 2009), 13–24.

Butler, Marilyn, 'Antiquarianism (Popular)', in Iain McCalman (ed.), *An Oxford Companion to the Romantic Age: British Culture 1776–1832* (Oxford: Oxford University Press, 1999), 328–38.

—— 'Burns and Politics', in Robert Crawford (ed.), *Burns and Cultural Authority* (Edinburgh: Polygon, 1999), 86–112.

Butt, John, 'The Revival of Vernacular Scottish Poetry', in Frederick W. Hilles and Harold Bloom (eds.), *From Sensibility to Romanticism: Essays presented to Frederick A. Pottle* (Oxford: Oxford University Press, 1965), 219–37.

Cage, R. A., *The Scottish Poor Law 1745–1845* (Edinburgh: Scottish Academic Press, 1981).

Cant, Ronald G., 'David Steuart Erskine, 11th Earl of Buchan: Founder of the Society of Antiquities of Scotland', in A. S. Bell (ed.), *The Scottish Antiquarian Tradition* (Edinburgh: John Donald, 1981), 1–30.

Carruthers, Gerard, 'Alexander Geddes and the Burns "Lost Poems" Controversy', *Studies in Scottish Literature*, 31 (1999), 81–5.

—— 'James Thomson and 18th Century Scottish Literary Identity', in Richard Terry (ed.), *James Thomson: Essays for the Tercentenary* (Liverpool: Liverpool University Press, 2000), 165–90.

—— 'The New Bardolatry', *Burns Chronicle*, (Winter, 2002), 9–15.

—— *Robert Burns* (Tavistock: Northcote House, 2006).

—— '"Tongues turn'd inside out": The Reception of Tam o' Shanter', *Studies in Scottish Literature*, 35–6 (2007), 455–63.

Chandler, James, *England in 1819: The Politics of Literary Culture and the Case of Romantic Historicism* (Chicago: Chicago University Press, 1998).

Christmas, William, *The Lab'ring Muses: Work, Writing, and the Social Order in English Plebeian Poetry, 1730–1830* (Newark: Associated University Presses, 2001).

Clare, John Robinson Eric, and Powell, David, *John Clare* (Oxford: Oxford University Press, 1984).

Clive, John, 'The Social Background of the Scottish Renaissance', in N. T. Phillipson and Rosalind Mitchison (eds.), *Scotland in the Age of Improvement* (Edinburgh: Edinburgh University Press, 1970), 225–44.

Cohen, Ralph, 'History and Genre', *New Literary History* 17/2 (1986), 203–18.

Colley, Linda, *Britons: Forging the Nation, 1707–1837* (London: Pimlico, 1994).

Congleton, J. E., *Theories of Pastoral Poetry in England, 1684–1798* (Gainesville: University of Florida Press, 1968).

Connell, Philip, *Romanticism, Economics, and the Question of 'Culture'* (Oxford: Oxford University Press, 2001).

——'British Identities and the Politics of Ancient Poetry in Later Eighteenth-Century England', *Historical Journal* 49/1 (2006), 161–92.

——and Leask, Nigel (eds.), *Romanticism and Popular Culture in Britain and Ireland* (Cambridge: Cambridge University Press, 2009).

Corbett, John, *Written in the Language of the Scottish Nation: A History of Literary Translation into Scots* (Clevedon: Multilingual Matters, 1999).

Cowan, Edward J., 'Burns and Superstition', in Kenneth Simpson (ed.), *Love and Liberty: Robert Burns, A Bicentenary Celebration* (East Linton: Tuckwell, 1997), 229–38.

Craig, Cairns, *Out of History: Narrative Paradigms in Scottish and English Culture* (Edinburgh: Polygon, 1996).

Craig, David, *Scottish Literature and the Scottish People, 1680–1830* (London: Chatto & Windus, 1961).

——'The Radical Literary Tradition', in Gordon Brown (ed.), *The Red Paper on Scotland* (Edinburgh: EUSPB, 1975), 289–303.

Crawford, Rachel, *Poetry, Enclosure, and the Vernacular Landscape, 1700–1830* (Cambridge: Cambridge University Press, 2002).

Crawford, Robert (ed.), *Robert Burns and Cultural Authority* (Edinburgh: Edinburgh University Press, 1997).

——(ed.), *The Scottish Invention of English Literature* (Cambridge: Cambridge University Press, 1998).

——'Robert Fergusson's Robert Burns', in id. (ed.), *Robert Burns and Cultural Authority* (Edinburgh: Polygon, 1999), 1–22.

——*Devolving English Literature*, 2nd edn. (Edinburgh: Edinburgh University Press, 2000).

——*The Bard: Robert Burns, a Biography* (London: Jonathan Cape, 2009).

——'Burns and the Heart of Europe', paper given at Glasgow Burns Conference, Glasgow, 17 Jan. 2009.

Crawford, Thomas, *Society and the Lyric* (Edinburgh: Scottish Academic Press, 1979).

——*Burns: A Study of the Poems and Songs, (1960)* (repr. Edinburgh: Canongate Academic, 1994).

Curran, Stuart, *Poetic Form and British Romanticism* (Oxford: Oxford University Press, 1986).

Daiches, David, *Robert Burns* (London: G. Bell & Sons, 1952).

——*The Paradox of Scottish Culture: The Eighteenth-Century Experience* (London: Oxford University Press, 1964).

Darnton, Robert, *Mesmerisim and the End of Enlightenment in France* (Cambridge, Mass.: Harvard University Press, 1968).

Davie, George, *The Democratic Intellect: Scotland and Her Universities in the Nineteenth Century* (Edinburgh: Edinburgh University Press, 1961).

Davie, Cedric Thorpe, 'Robert Burns, Writer of Songs', in Donald Low (ed.), *Critical Essays on Robert Burns* (London: Routledge Kegan Paul, 1975), 157–84.

Davis, Leith, 'James Currie's *Works of Robert Burns*: The Politics of Hypochondriasis', *Studies in Romanticism* 36 (Spring 1997), 43–60.

——*Acts of Union: Scotland and the Literary Negotiation of the British Nation, 1707–1830* (Stanford, Calif.: Stanford University Press, 1998).

——Duncan, Ian, and Sorensen, Janet (eds.), *Scotland and the Borders of Romanticism* (Cambridge: Cambridge University Press, 2004).

Devine, T. M., *The Transformation of Rural Scotland: Social Change and the Agrarian Economy, 1660–1815* (Edinburgh: Edinburgh University Press, 1994).

—— *The Scottish Nation: 1700–2000* (London: Penguin, 2000).

——*Scotland's Empire, 1600–1815* (London: Allen Lane, 2003).

Donaldson, William, 'The Glencairn Connection: Robert Burns and Scottish Politics, 1786–96', *Studies in Scottish Literature* 16 (1981), 61–79.

Doody, Margaret Anne, *The Daring Muse: Augustan Poetry Reconsidered* (Cambridge: Cambridge University Press, 1985).

Douglas, Mary, *Purity and Danger: An Analysis of the Concepts of Pollution and Taboo* (London: Routledge, 1991).

Drayton, Richard, *Nature's Government: Science, Imperial Britain, and the 'Improvement' of the World* (New Haven: Yale University Press, 2000).

Drummond, Andrew, and Bulloch, James, *The Scottish Church, 1688–1843* (Edinburgh: St Andrew's, 1973).

Duncan, Ian, 'Fergusson's Edinburgh', in Robert Crawford (ed.), *'Heaven-taught Fergusson': Robert Burns's Favourite Poet* (Phantassie: Tuckwell, 2003), 65–84.

—— *In Scott's Shadow: The Novel in Romantic Edinburgh* (Princeton: Princeton University Press, 2007).

Dunn, Douglas, '"A Very Scottish Kind of Dash": Burns's Native Metric', in Robert Crawford (ed.), *Robert Burns and Cultural Authority* (Edinburgh: Polygon, 1999), 58–85.

Dwyer, John, 'Virtue and Improvement: The Civic World of Adam Smith', in Peter Jones and Andrew S. Skinner (eds.), *Adam Smith Reviewed* (Edinburgh: Edinburgh University Press, 1992), 190–216.

Elfenbein, Andrew, *Byron and the Victorians* (Cambridge: Cambridge University Press, 1995).

Empson, William, *Some Versions of Pastoral* (London: Chatto & Windus, 1935).

Fairer, David, *English Poetry of the Eighteenth Century, 1700–1789* (Harlow: Pearson Education, 2003).

Fechner, Roger J., 'Burns and American Liberty', in Kenneth Simpson (ed.), *Love and Liberty: Robert Burns: A Bicentenary Celebration* (East Lothian: Tuckwell, 1997), 274–88.

Fergusson, James, *Lowland Lairds* (London: Faber & Faber, 1959).

Fielding, Penny, *Scotland and the Fictions of Geography: North Britain, 1760–1830* (Cambridge: Cambridge University Press, 2008).

Findlay, Richard, 'The Burns Cult and Scottish Identity in the Nineteenth and Twentieth Centuries', in Kenneth Simpson (ed.), *Love and Liberty. Robert Burns: A Bicentenary Celebration* (East Linton: Tuckwell, 1997), 69–78.

Folkenflik, Robert, 'Patronage and the Poet Hero', *Huntingdon Library Quarterly* 48/4 (Autumn, 1985), 363–79.

Fowler, Richard Hindle, *Robert Burns* (London: Routledge, 1988).

Freeman, F. W., 'Robert Fergusson: Pastoral and Politics at Mid-Century', in Andrew Hook (ed.), *The History of Scottish Literature*, ii. *1660–1800* (Aberdeen: Aberdeen University Press, 1987), 141–55.

Fry, Michael, *The Dundas Despotism* (Edinburgh: Edinburgh University Press, 1992).

Garrett, Aaron, 'Anthropology: the "Original" of Human Nature', in Alexander Broadie (ed.), *Cambridge Companion to the Scottish Enlightenment* (Cambridge: Cambridge University Press, 2003), 79–93.

Gilmartin, Kevin, *Writing Against Revolution: Literary Conservatism in Britain, 1790–1832* (Cambridge: Cambridge University Press, 2006).

Goodman, Kevis, *Georgic Modernity and British Romanticism: Poetry and the Mediation of History* (Cambridge: Cambridge University Press, 2004).

Griffin, Dustin, *Literary Patronage in England, 1650–1800* (Cambridge: Cambridge University Press, 1996).

Guest, Harriet, ' "These Neuter Somethings": Gender Difference and Commercial Culture in Mid-Eighteenth-Century England', in Kevin Sharpe and Steven N. Zwicker (eds.), *Refiguring Revolutions: Aesthetics and Politics from the English Revolution to the Romantic Revolution* (Berkeley and Los Angeles: University of California Press, 1998), 173–6.

Guillory, John, *Cultural Capital: The Problem of Literary Canon Formation* (Chicago: University of Chicago Press, 1993).

Hamilton, Henry, *Selections from the Monymusk Papers, 1713–1755* (Edinburgh: Scottish History Society, 1945).

——*An Economic History of Scotland in the Eighteenth Century* (Oxford: Clarendon, 1963).

Handley, James, *The Agricultural Revolution in Scotland* (Glasgow: John S. Burns & Sons, 1963).

Harris, Bob, *The Scottish People and the French Revolution* (London: Pickering & Chatto, 2008).

Harris, Tim (ed.), *Popular Culture in England, c.1500–1850* (New York: St Martin's, 1995).

Harvie, Christopher, *Scotland and Nationalism: Scottish Society and Politics, 1707–1977* (London: George Allen & Unwin, 1977).

Hecht, Hans, *Robert Burns: the Man and his Work (1936)*, trans. Jane Lymburn (Ayr: Alloway, 1981).

Heinzelman, Kurt, 'The Last Georgic: *Wealth of Nations* and the Scene of Writing', in Stephen Copley and Kathryn Sutherland (eds.), *Adam Smith's* Wealth of Nations: *New Interdisciplinary Essays* (Manchester: University of Manchester Press, 1995), 171–94.

Higgins, David, *Romantic Genius and the Literary Magazines: Biography, Celebrity, and Politics* (London: Routledge, 2005).

Hobsbawm, Eric, 'Capitalisme et Agriculture: Les Réformateurs Ecossais au XVIIIè Siècle', *Annales* 33 (1978), 580–601.

Hook, Andrew, *Scotland and America* (London: Blackie, 1975).

Houston, R. A., *Scottish Literacy and the Scottish Identity: Illiteracy and Society in Scotland and Northern England, 1600–1800* (Cambridge: Cambridge University Press, 1985).

Jack, R. D. S., *The Italian Influence on Scottish Literature* (Edinburgh: Edinburgh University Press, 1972).

Johnson, David, *Music and Society in Lowland Scotland in the Eighteenth Century* (London: Oxford University Press, 1972).

Jones, Charles, *A Language Suppressed: The Pronunciation of Scots in the Eighteenth Century* (Edinburgh: John Donald, 1995).

Jones, Gareth Stedman, *An End to Poverty? A Historical Debate* (London: Profile Books, 2004).

Jones, Jean, 'James Hutton's Agricultural Research and his Life as a Farmer', *Annals of Science* 42 (1985), 573–601.

Kenyon-Jones, Christine, *Kindred Brutes: Animals in Romantic-Period Writing* (Aldershot: Ashgate, 2001).

Kerrigan, John, *Archipelagic English: Literature, History, Politics, 1603–1707* (Oxford: Oxford University Press, 2008).

Kidd, Colin, *Subverting Scotland's Past: Scottish Whig Historians and the Creation of an Anglo-British Identity, 1689–c.1830* (Cambridge: Cambridge University Press, 1993).

——'Scotland's Invisible Enlightenment: Subscription and Heterodoxy in the Eighteenth-Century Kirk', *Records of the Scottish Church History Society* 30 (2000), 28–59.

—— *Union and Unionism: Political Thought in Scotland, 150–2000* (Cambridge: Cambridge University Press, 2008).

——'Burns and Politics', in Gerard Carruthers (ed.), *The Edinburgh Companion to Robert Burns* (Edinburgh: Edinburgh University Press, 2009), 61–73.

Korshin, Robert, 'Types of Eighteenth-Century Patronage', *Eighteenth-Century Studies* 7/4 (Summer, 1974), 453–73.

Kristeva, Julia, *The Powers of Horror: An Essay on Abjection*, trans. Leon S. Roudiex (New York: Columbia University Press, 1982).

Lamb, James Gordon, 'David Steuart Erskine, 11th Earl of Buchan: A Study of his Life and Correspondence' (unpublished Ph.D. diss., St Andrew's University, 1963).

Lamb, Jonathan, *Preserving the Self in the South Seas, 1680–1840* (Chicago: Chicago University Press, 2001).

Lamont, Claire, 'Burns's Saturday Night: Work and Time in Agricultural Poems of his Era', paper given at Robert Burns 1759–2009 Anniversary Conference, University of Glasgow, 16 January 2009.

Landry, Donna, *The Muses of Resistance: Labouring-Class Women's Poetry in Britain, 1739–1796* (Cambridge: Cambridge University Press, 1990).

Langan, Celeste, *Romantic Vagrancy: Wordsworth and the Simulation of Freedom* (Cambridge: Cambridge University Press, 1995).

Leask, Nigel, *The Politics of Imagination in Coleridge's Critical Thought* (London: Macmillan, 1988).

——'Burns, Wordsworth, and the Politics of Vernacular Poetry', in Peter de Bolla, Nigel Leask, and David Simpson (eds.), *Land, Nation and Culture, 1740–1840: Thinking the Republic of Taste* (Basingstoke: Palgrave Macmillan, 2005), 202–22.

——'His Hero's Story': Currie's Burns, Moore's Byron, and the Problem of Romantic Biography', *The Byron Foundation Lecture, 2006* (Nottingham: Centre for the Study of Byron and Romanticism, 2007).

——'Robert Burns and Scottish Common Sense Philosophy', in Gavin Budge (ed.), *Romantic Empiricism: Poetics and the Philosophy of Common Sense, 1780–1830* (Lewisburg, Pa.: Bucknell University Press, 2007), 64–87.

——'Burns and the Politics of Abolition', in Gerard Carruthers (ed.), *The Edinburgh Companion to Robert Burns* (Edinburgh: Edinburgh University Press, 2009), 47–60.

——'Robert Burns and the Stimulant Regime', in Johnny Rodger and Gerard Carruthers (eds.), *The Fickle Man: Robert Burns in the Twenty-First Century* (Dingwall: Sandstone, 2009).

Lindsay, Maurice (ed.), *The Burns Encyclopedia* (London: Robert Hale, 1995).

Low, Anthony, *The Georgic Revolution* (Princeton: Princeton University Press, 1985).

Low, Donald, (ed.), *Critical Essays on Robert Burns* (London: Routledge Kegan Paul, 1975).

Lutz, Alfred, '"The Deserted Village" and the Politics of Genre', *Modern Language Quarterly* 55/2 (June 1994), 149–69.

McCue, Kirsteen, 'George Thomson (1757–1851): His Collections of National Airs in their Scottish Cultural Context (unpublished D.Phil. diss., University of Oxford, 1993).

——'Burns, Women, and Song', in Robert Crawford (ed.), *Robert Burns and Cultural Authority* (Edinburgh: Polygon, 1999), 40–57.

——'"The Most Intricate Bibliographical Enigma": Understanding George Thomson and his Collection of National Airs', in Richard Turbet (ed.), *Music Librarianship in the United Kingdom* (Aldershot: Ashgate, 2003), 99–119.

——'"An Individual Flowering on a Common Stem": Melody, Performance and National Song', in Philip Connell and Nigel Leask (eds.), *Romanticism and Popular Culture in Britain and Ireland* (Cambridge: Cambridge University Press, 2009), 88–106.

MacDiarmid, Hugh, *Burns Today and Tomorrow* (Edinburgh: Castle Wynd, 1954).

——*Selected Poems*, ed. Alan Riach and Michael Grieve (Harmondsworth: Penguin, 1994).

McElroy, David D., 'The Literary Clubs and Societies of Eighteenth-Century Scotland, and their Influence on the Literary Productions of the Period from 1700 to 1800' (unpublished Ph.D. thesis, University of Edinburgh, 1952).

——*Scotland's Age of Improvement: A Survey of Eighteenth-Century Literary Clubs and Societies* (Washington: Washington State University Press, 1969).

McGinty, Walter, *Robert Burns and Religion* (Aldershot: Ashgate, 2003).

McGuirk, Carol, *Robert Burns and the Sentimental Era* (Athens, Ga.: University of Georgia Press, 1985).

——(ed.), *Critical Essays on Robert Burns* (New York: G. K. Hall, 1998).

——'"The Rhyming Trade": Fergusson, Burns, and the Marketplace', in Robert Crawford (ed.), *'Heaven-Taught Fergusson': Robert Burns's Favourite Scottish Poet* (Phantassie: Tuckwell, 2003), 135–59.

McIlvanney, Liam, *Burns the Radical: Poetry and Politics in Late Eighteenth-century Scotland* (East Lothian: Tuckwell, 2002).

McIlvanney, Liam, 'Hugh Blair, Robert Burns, and the Invention of Scottish Literature', *Eighteenth-Century Life* 29/2 (Spring 2005), 25–46.

Mackay, James, *Burns: A Biography of Robert Burns* (Edinburgh: Mainstream, 1992).

McKenna, Steven R., 'Burns and Virgil', in Gerard Carruthers (ed.), *The Edinburgh Companion to Robert Burns* (Edinburgh: Edinburgh University Press, 2009), 137–49.

McKeon, Michael, 'The Pastoral Revolution', in Kevin Sharpe and Steven Zwicker (eds.), *Refiguring Revolutions: Aesthetics and Politics from the English Revolution to the Romantic Revolution* (Berkeley and Los Angeles: University of California Press, 1998), 267–90.

MacLaine, Allan H., *Scots Poems of Festivity: The Christis Kirk Tradition* (Glasgow: ASLS, 1996).

MacMillan, Duncan, *Painting in Scotland: The Golden Age* (Oxford: Phaidon, 1986).

McVie, John, *Burns and Stair* (Kilmarnock: 'Standard', 1927).

Magnusson, Paul, *Reading Public Romanticism* (Princeton: Princeton University Press, 1998).

Manning, Susan, 'Burns and God', in Robert Crawford (ed.), *Robert Burns and Cultural Authority* (Edinburgh: Polygon, 1999), 113–35.

——*Fragments of Union: Making Connections in Scottish and American Writing* (Basingstoke: Palgrave, 2002).

——'Robert Fergusson and Eighteenth-Century Poetry', in Robert Crawford (ed.), *'Heaven-Taught Fergusson': Robert Burns's Favourite Scottish Poet* (Phantassie: Tuckwell, 2003), 87–112.

——'Antiquarianism and the Scottish Science of Man', in Leith Davis, Ian Duncan, and Janet Sorensen (eds.), *Scotland and the Borders of Romanticism* (Cambridge: Cambridge University Press, 2004), 57–76.

Mathison, Hamish, '"Gude Black Prent": How the Edinburgh Book Trade Dealt with Burns's Poems', *Bibliotheck* 20 (1995), 70–87.

——'Robert Burns and National Song', in David Duff and Catherine Jones (eds.), *Scotland, Ireland, and the Romantic Aesthetic* (Lewisburg, Pa.: Bucknell University Press, 2007), 77–92.

Meek, Ronald, *Social Science and the Ignoble Savage* (Cambridge: Cambridge University Press, 1976).

Millar, Robert McColl, '"Blind Attachment to Inveterate Custom": Language Use, Language Attitude and the Rhetoric of Improvement in the first Statistical Account', in Marina Dossena and Charles Jones (eds.), *Insights into Late Modern English* (Berne: Peter Lang, 2003), 311–30.

Miller, Jo, 'Burns's Songs: A Singer's View', in Kenneth Simpson (ed.), *Burns Now* (Edinburgh: Canongate, 1994), 193–207.

Mitchison, Rosalind, *Agricultural Sir John: The Life of Sir John Sinclair of Ulbster, 1754–1835* (London: Geoffrey Bles, 1962).

——'The Poor Law', in T. M. Devine and Rosalind Mitchison (eds.), *People and Society in Scotland*, i. *1760–1830* (Edinburgh: John Donald, 1988), 252–67.

Moir, D.G. *Early Maps of Scotland to 1850*, 2 vols. (Edinburgh: Royal Scotland Geographical Society, 1973).

Muir, Edwin, *Scott and Scotland: the Predicament of the Scottish Writer* (Edinburgh: Polygon, 1982).

Murison, David, 'The Speech of Ayrshire in the Time of Burns', in John Strawhorn (ed.), *Ayrshire at the Time of Burns* (Kilmarnock: Ayrshire Archaeological and Natural History Society, 1959), 222–31.

—— 'The Language of Burns', in Donald Low (ed.), *Critical Essays on Robert Burns* (London: Routledge Kegan Paul, 1975), 54–69.

Murphy, Peter, *Poetry as an Occupation and an Art in Britain, 1760–1830* (Cambridge: Cambridge University Press, 1993).

Nairn, Tom, *The Break-up of Britain: Crisis and Neo-Nationalism* (London: Verso, 1981).

Newman, Steve, 'The Scots Songs of Allan Ramsay: "Lyrick" Transformation, Popular Culture, and the Boundaries of the Scottish Enlightenment', *Modern Language Quarterly* 63/3 (Sept. 2002), 277–314.

Noyes, Russel, 'Wordsworth and Burns', *PMLA* 59 (1944), 813–32.

O'Donoghue, Yolande, *William Roy 1726–1790: Pioneer of the Ordnance Survey* (London: British Museums Publications, 1977).

Ogborn, Miles, *Spaces of Modernity: London's Geographies, 1680–1780* (New York: Guilford, 1998).

Overton, Bill, *The Eighteenth-Century Verse Epistle* (Houndmills: Palgrave Macmillan, 2007).

Patterson, Annabel, *Pastoral and Ideology: Virgil to Valery* (Oxford: Clarendon, 1988).

Perkins, David, *Romanticism and Animal Rights* (Cambridge: Cambridge University Press, 2003).

Pfau, Thomas, *Wordsworth's Profession: Form, Class, and the Logic of Early Romantic Cultural Production* (Stanford, Calif.: Stanford University Press, 1997).

Piggot, Stuart *Ruins in a Landscape: Essays in Antiquarianism* (Edinburgh: Edinburgh University Press, 1976).

Pittock, Murray, 'Robert Burns and British Poetry', Chatterton Lecture on British Poetry, *Proceedings of the British Academy* 121 (London: British Academy, 2003).

—— 'Historiography', *The Cambridge Companion to the Scottish Enlightenment* (Cambridge: Cambridge University Press, 2003), 258–79.

—— *Scottish and Irish Romanticism* (Oxford: Oxford University Press, 2008).

—— 'Nibbling at Adam Smith', in Johnny Rodger and Gerard Carruthers (eds.), *The Fickle Man: Robert Burns in the Twenty-First Century* (Dingwall: Sandstone, 2009), 118–31.

Pocock, J. G. A., 'Cambridge Paradigms and Scotch Philosophers: A Study of the Relations between the Civic Humanist and the Civil Jurisprudential Interpretation of Eighteenth-Century Social Thought', in Istvan Hont and Michael Ignatieff (eds.), *Wealth and Virtue: The Shaping of Political Economy in the Scottish Enlightenment* (Cambridge: Cambridge University Press, 1983), 235–45.

—— *The Discovery of Islands: Essays in British History* (Cambridge: Cambridge University Press, 2005).

Purser, John, ' "The Wee Apollo"—Burns and Oswald', in Kenneth Simpson (ed.), *Love and Liberty: Robert Burns, A Bicentenary Celebration* (East Lothian: Tuckwell, 1997), 326–33.

Radcliffe, David Hill, 'Imitation, Popular Literacy, and "The Cotter's Saturday Night"', in Carol McGuirk (ed.), *Critical Essays on Robert Burns* (New York: G. K. Hall, 1998), 251–62.

Riach, Alan, 'MacDiarmid's Burns', in Robert Crawford (ed.), *Robert Burns and Cultural Authority* (Edinburgh: Polygon, 1999), 198–215.

Ricks, Christopher, *Allusion to the Poets* (Oxford: Oxford University Press, 2002).

Rilke, Rainer Maria, *Duino Elegies*, trans. David Young (New York: Norton, 1978).

Ritvo, Harriet, *The Animal Estate* (Cambridge, Mass.: Harvard University Press, 1987).

Roberts, Daniel Sanjiv, 'Literature, Medical Science and Politics, 1795–1800: Lyrical Ballads and Currie's Works of Robert Burns', in C. C. Barfoot (ed.), *"A Natural Delineation of the Human Passions": The Historic Moment of the Lyrical Ballads* (Amsterdam: Rodopi, 2003), 115–28.

Robertson, John, 'The Scottish Enlightenment at the Limits of the Civic Tradition', in Istvan Hont and Michael Ignatieff (eds.), *Wealth and Virtue: The Shaping of Political Economy in the Scottish Enlightenment* (Cambridge: Cambridge University Press, 1983), 137–78.

—— *The Scottish Enlightenment and the Militia Issue* (Edinburgh: John Donald, 1985).

Robinson, Mairi (ed.), *Concise Scots Dictionary* (Aberdeen: Aberdeen University Press, 1985).

Rothschild, Emma, *Economic Sentiments: Adam Smith, Condorcet, and the Enlightenment* (Cambridge, Mass.: Harvard University Press, 2001).

—— 'The Swanlike Strains of a Slaughtered Nation': Antiquarians, Historians, Philologists, and Empires' (unpublished paper, 2003).

Rowbotham, John, 'Burns's Reading', *Bulletin of the New York Public Library* 74 (Nov. 1970), 561–76.

Roe, Nicholas, 'Authenticating Robert Burns', in Robert Crawford (ed.), *Robert Burns and Cultural Authority* (Edinburgh: Polygon, 1999), 159–79.

Roy, G. Ross, 'Editing Burns in the Nineteenth Century', in Kenneth Simpson (ed.), *Burns Now* (Edinburgh: Canongate, 1994), 129–49.

St Clair, William, *The Reading Nation in the Romantic Period* (Cambridge: Cambridge University Press, 2004).

Sales, Roger, *English Literature in History 1780–1830* (London: Hutchinson, 1983).

Schaffer, Simon, 'The Earth's Fertility as a Social Fact in Early Modern Britain', in Mikulas Teich, Roy Porter, and Bo Gustafsson (eds.), *Nature and Society in Historical Context* (Cambridge: Cambridge University Press, 1997), 124–47.

Schmidt, Leigh Eric, *Holy Fairs: Scotland and the Making of American Revivalism* (Princeton, NJ: Princeton University Press, 1989).

Shapin, Stephen, 'Property, Patronage, and the Politics of Science: The Founding of the Royal Society of Edinburgh', *British Journal for the History of Science* 7 (1974), 1–41.

Sher, Richard, *Church and University in the Scottish Enlightenment: The Moderate Literati of Edinburgh* (Edinburgh: Edinburgh University Press, 1985).

—— *The Enlightenment and the Book: Scottish Authors and their Publishers in Eighteenth-Century Britain, Ireland, and America* (Chicago: University of Chicago Press, 2006).

Simpson, David, *Wordsworth's Historical Imagination: The Poetry of Displacement* (New York: Methuen, 1987).

—— *Wordsworth, Commodification and Social Concern: The Poetics of Modernity* (Cambridge: Cambridge University Press, 2008).

Simpson, Kenneth, *The Protean Scot: The Crisis of Identity in Eighteenth-Century Scottish Literature* (Aberdeen: Aberdeen University Press, 1988).

—— 'Robert Burns: "Heaven-Taught Ploughman"?' in Kenneth Simpson (ed.), *Burns Now* (Edinburgh: Canongate Academic, 1994), 70–91.

——(ed.), *Love and Liberty. Robert Burns: A Bicentenary Celebration* (East Lothian: Tuckwell, 1997).

Simpson, Matthew, '"Hame Content": Globalization and a Scottish Poet of the Eighteenth Century', *Eighteenth-Century Life* 27/1 (2003), 107–29.

Siskin, Clifford, *The Work of Writing: Literature and Social Change in Britain, 1700–1830* (Baltimore; London: John Hopkins Press, 1998).

Skoblow, Jeffrey, '*Dooble tongue*': Scots, Burns, Contradiction (Newark: University of Delaware Press, 2001).

Smith, Graham, *Robert Burns and the Excise* (Ayr: Alloway, 1989).

Smith, Jeremy, 'Copia Verborum: Linguistic Choices in Robert Burns', *Review of English Studies* ns 58/233 (2007), 73–88.

Smith, J. V., 'Manners, Morals and Mentalities: Reflections on the Popular Enlightenment of Early-19th Century Scotland', in Walter Humes and Hamish Paterson (eds.), *Scottish Culture and Scottish Education, 1800–1980* (Edinburgh: John Donald, 1983), 25–54.

Smith, Olivia, *The Politics of Language, 1791–1819* (Oxford: Clarendon, 1984).

Smout, T. C., *A History of the Scottish People 1560–1830* (London: Fontana, 1998).

Sorensen, Janet, *The Grammar of Empire in Eighteenth-Century British Writing* (Cambridge: Cambridge University Press, 2000).

——'Vulgar Tongues: Canting Dictionaries and the Language of the People in Eighteenth-Century Britain', *Eighteenth-Century Studies* 37/4 (2004), 435–54.

Sprott, Gavin, *Robert Burns, Farmer* (Edinburgh: National Museums of Scotland, 1990).

Stafford, Fiona, *The Sublime Savage: A Study of James Macpherson and the Poetry of Ossian* (Edinburgh: Edinburgh University Press, 1988).

——'Burns and Romantic Writing', in Gerard Carruthers (ed.), *Edinburgh Companion to Robert Burns* (Edinburgh: Edinburgh University Press, 2009), 97–109.

Stewart, Susan, *On Longing: Narratives of the Miniature, the Gigantic, the Souvenir, the Collection* (Durham, NC: Duke University Press, 1993).

Strawhorn, John (ed.), *Ayrshire at the Time of Burns* (Newmilns: Ayrshire Archaeological and Natural History Society, 1959).

——'An Introduction to Armstrong's Maps', in John Strawhorn (ed.), *Ayrshire at the Time of Burns* (Newmilns: Ayrshire Archaeological and Natural History Society, 1959), 232–55.

——*Ayrshire: The Story of a County* (Newmilns: Ayrshire Archaeological and Natural History Society, 1975).

——'Ayrshire and the Enlightenment', in Graham Cruikshank (ed.), *A Sense of Place: Studies in Scottish Local History* (Edinburgh: Scotland's Cultural Heritage, 1988), 188–201.

Sunter, R. M., *Patronage and Politics in Scotland, 1707–1832* (Edinburgh: Donald, 1986).

Sweet, Rosemary, *Antiquaries: The Discovery of the Past in Eighteenth-Century Britain* (New York: Hambledon, 2004).

Thomas, Keith, *Man and the Natural World: Changing Attitudes in England, 1500–1800* (Harmondsworth: Penguin, 1983).

Thompson, E. P., 'Patrician Society, Plebeian Culture', *Journal of Social History* 7 (1974), 382–405.

Thompson, E. P., 'Eighteenth-Century English Society: Class Struggle without Class?' *Social History* 3/2 (1978), 133–65.

—— *Customs in Common* (London: Merlin, 1991).

Thornton, Robert, 'Robert Riddell, Antiquary', *Burns Chronicle*, 3rd ser. 2 (1953), 444–67.

—— *James Currie: The Entire Stranger and Robert Burns* (Edinburgh; London: Oliver & Boyd, 1963).

Tribe, Keith, *Land, Labour and Economic Discourse* (London: Routledge Kegan Paul, 1978).

Trumpener, Katie, *Bardic Nationalism: The Romantic Novel and the British Empire* (Princeton, NJ: Princeton University Press, 1997).

Uglow, Jenny, *The Lunar Men: The Friends Who Made the Future* (London: Faber & Faber, 2003).

Voges, Freidhelm, 'Moderate and Evangelical Thinking in the Later Eighteenth Century: Differences and Shared Attitudes', *Records of the Church History Society* 22 (1986), 141–57.

Wahrman, Dror, *Imagining the Middle Class: The Political Representation of Class in Britain, c.1780–1840* (Cambridge: Cambridge University Press, 1995).

Werkmeister, Lucylle, 'Robert Burns and the London Newspapers', *Bulletin of the New York Public Library* 65/8 (Oct. 1961), 483–504.

Weston, John C., *Robert Burns. The Jolly Beggars: A Cantata* (Northampton, Mass.: Gehenna, 1963).

—— 'Burns's Use of the Scots Verse-Epistle Form', *Philological Quarterly* 49/2 (Apr. 1970), 188–210.

Whatley, Christopher, 'How Tame Were the Scottish Lowlanders During the Eighteenth Century?' in T. M. Devine (ed.), *Conflict and Stability in Scottish Society 1700–1850* (Edinburgh: John Donald, 1990), 1–30.

—— 'Burns: Work, Kirk and Community', in Kenneth Simpson (ed.), *Burns Now* (Edinburgh: Canongate, 1994), 92–116.

—— *Scottish Society, 1707–1830: Beyond Jacobitism, Towards Industrialisation* (Manchester: Manchester University Press, 2000).

Williams, Raymond, *The Country and the City* (London: Hogarth, 1993).

Wilson, Penny, 'Classical Greek and Latin Literature', in Stuart Gillespie and Peter France (eds.), *The Oxford History of Literary Translation in English* (Oxford: Oxford University Press, 2005), iii.

Winch, Donald, 'The System of the North: Dugald Stewart and his Pupils', in Stefan Collini, Donald Winch, and John Burrow (eds.), *That Noble Science of Politics: A Study in Nineteenth-Century Intellectual History* (Cambridge: Cambridge University Press, 1983), 40–3.

Withers, Charles W. J., 'How Scotland Came to Know Itself: Geography, National Identity and the Making of a Nation, 1680–1790', *Journal of Historical Geography* 21/4 (Oct. 1995), 371–98.

Wood, J. Maxwell, *Robert Burns and the Riddell Family* (Dumfries: Dinwiddie, 1922).

Wood, Harriet Harvey, 'Burns and Watson's *Choice Collection*', *Studies in Scottish Literature* 30 (1998), 19–30.

Zenziger, Peter, 'Low Life, Primitivism and Honest Poverty in Ramsay and Burns', *Studies in Scottish Literature* 30 (1998), 43–58.

# Index

Notes and figures are indexed in bold.

Printed and bound by CPI Group (UK) Ltd, Croydon, CR0 4YY